Special Edition
Using
Enterprise
JavaBeans™ 2.0

Chuck Cavaness

Brian Keeton

201 W. 103rd Street
Indianapolis, Indiana 46290

SPECIAL EDITION USING ENTERPRISE JAVABEANS™ 2.0

International Standard Book Number: 0-7897-2567-3

Library of Congress Catalog Card Number: 2001087886

Printed in the United States of America

First Printing: September 2001

04   03   02   01   4   3   2   1

Associate Publisher
Dean Miller

Acquisitions Editor
Todd Green

Development Editor
Sean Dixon

Managing Editor
Thomas F. Hayes

Project Editor
Tonya Simpson

Copy Editor
Sossity Smith

Indexer
Bill Myers

Proofreaders
Kaylene Riemen
Harvey Stanbrough
Plan-It Publishing

Technical Editors
Alan Moffet
Tim Drury
Steven Haines
Jon Hassell
Grant Holland
Alex Kachur

Team Coordinator
Cindy Teeters

Media Developer
Michael Hunter

Interior Designer
Ruth Harvey

Cover Designers
Dan Armstrong
Ruth Harvey

Page Layout
Mark Walchle

TABLE OF CONTENTS

About the Authors

Chuck Cavaness is a Java Architect at NetVendor Inc, a B2B Supplier Enablement Company specializing in the Electronics, Aerospace, and Automotive industries located in Atlanta, Georgia. His area of expertise spans server-side Java, distributed object computing, and application servers. Currently, he moderates the "Java in the Enterprise" discussion forum at JavaWorld. He has also taught object-oriented courses at the Georgia Institute of Technology and spent several years writing Smalltalk and CORBA software. Chuck earned his degree in Computer Science from the Georgia Institute of Technology. Chuck is co-author of *Special Edition Using Java 2 Standard Edition*.

Brian Keeton is a Java Architect at NetVendor Inc. where he develops components to support B2B trading using EJB. He is a Sun Certified Java Developer with over ten years of professional software development experience. He spent five years developing object-oriented applications in C++ for the defense industry before transitioning to distributed application development using CORBA and EJB. Brian earned his Master of Science in Electrical Engineering from Georgia Tech and is co-author of *Special Edition Using Java 2 Standard Edition*.

DEDICATION

From Chuck

To my mom, who gave me everything that a child needs to grow. To my wife Tracy and my two boys, Joshua and Zachary, thanks for all the poking, prodding, and nagging to keep writing when it was hard to find the energy. Also a big thanks to my co-author, Brian, for being a great person to write a book with and such a good friend.

From Brian

To my wife Rebeccah and daughter Emily for your love and patience, my parents for your unconditional support, and my sister Donna who calls me a geek only occasionally.

ACKNOWLEDGMENTS

We would like to give thanks to the many individuals who helped make this book possible. Writing a book is a team effort and we were fortunate to have a great team that was sincerely interested in making the material in this book as informative and accurate as possible.

First and foremost, we would like to thank all the editors who painstakingly read through every chapter, page, paragraph, and sentence to help mold our thoughts and ramblings into what you will hopefully find a very enjoyable and worthwhile journey. We especially want to recognize the technical editors, whose job it was to pour through more than a few voluminous specifications and documents to ensure that we never strayed too far from reality: Grant Holland, Steven Haines, Jon Hassell, Alex Kachur, Alan Moffet, and Tim Drury. We are also greatly appreciative of the work done by our project editor Tonya Simpson and copy editor Sossity Smith and for Michael Hunter's work in securing the software for the CD. The quality and polish of this book are to their credit (and any mistakes are ours alone).

We would like to in particular thank Todd Green and Sean Dixon for giving us enough rope to hang ourselves and for trusting that we knew what we were doing from the beginning. Your patience was dearly appreciated.

Finally, we would like to collectively thank our families and friends for the understanding and support throughout the entire process. It wouldn't have been possible without your undying support.

TELL US WHAT YOU THINK!

As the reader of this book, *you* are our most important critic and commentator. We value your opinion and want to know what we're doing right, what we could do better, what areas you'd like to see us publish in, and any other words of wisdom you're willing to pass our way.

As an associate publisher for Que, I welcome your comments. You can fax, e-mail, or write me directly to let me know what you did or didn't like about this book—as well as what we can do to make our books stronger.

Please note that I cannot help you with technical problems related to the topic of this book, and that due to the high volume of mail I receive, I might not be able to reply to every message.

When you write, please be sure to include this book's title and author as well as your name and phone or fax number. I will carefully review your comments and share them with the authors and editors who worked on the book.

Fax: 317-581-4666

E-mail: feedback@quepublishing.com

Mail: Dean Miller
           Que Publishing
           201 West 103rd Street
           Indianapolis, IN 46290 USA

INTRODUCTION

In this chapter

Welcome to Enterprise JavaBeans 2.0! As part of the Java 2 Enterprise Edition (J2EE), the Enterprise JavaBeans architecture has become the accepted standard for the development of distributed, mission-critical business applications. The Enterprise JavaBeans (EJB) specification turns J2EE application servers into a foundation for building applications that are secure, transactional, scalable, and portable. If you develop large-scale business systems and you've never used EJB, now is the time to join the momentum that's thriving on an ever-growing number of success stories. If you already use EJB, the 2.0 Specification offers you even more in the way of productivity and component portability.

What is EJB? EJB is a specification for a server-side component architecture. Not to be confused with regular JavaBeans, EJBs are industrial-strength components that encapsulate reusable business logic and access to external resources such as relational databases for an enterprise. Foremost among the goals for EJB is that it makes it possible for developers to focus on business logic without having to worry about the low-level details of the life cycle, transactional, security, and persistence needs of their applications. These requirements are handled for you in a way that enables you to create components that are portable across application servers—thus meeting another goal of the architecture. On top of everything else, EJB takes stock in the fact that the value of a component often is measured in terms of its reusability. EJB takes a declarative approach for deploying applications that supports extensive customization of components without requiring changes to the code.

The EJB specification was first introduced by Sun Microsystems alone, but it has now matured to its current form through the Java Community Process (JCP). Benefiting from the participation of the leading application server and software vendors, EJB 2.0 will almost certainly continue the success of the architecture.

THIS BOOK IS FOR YOU

This book is targeted foremost toward programmers who know Java but are new to EJB. EJB is a complex topic, but the chapters that follow are organized to build your knowledge of the underlying technologies as a way to get you started. When you have a foundation, detailed discussions and examples introduce you to what you need to build your skills as an EJB developer before moving on to more advanced topics.

Although programmers without experience in EJB should feel at home with this book, this is more than a beginner's introduction. If you already know EJB, you're likely aware that the EJB 2.0 Specification has introduced significant changes in several key areas of the architecture (check out Appendix B, "Changes from EJB 1.1," if you want a summary). For those of you who are familiar with EJB, this book will teach you how to take advantage of what's new. It also will expose you to several proven EJB design practices that are taking shape within the industry. If you already use EJB 1.1 and are considering moving to the EJB 2.0 Specification, this book points out some important issues you should consider before moving your architecture. If you've already decided to stay with EJB 1.1 for now and are just wanting to get up to speed on what's coming with 2.0, this book can also help guide your transition from 1.1 to 2.0 when you're ready.

How This Book Is Organized

This book is organized into five parts that walk you through the concepts behind EJB and the process of designing and implementing your own enterprise beans. Related topics have been organized to build your knowledge of EJB programming as you progress through the book.

Part I, "Developing Enterprise JavaBeans," teaches you the mechanics of building EJB classes and their interfaces. This part begins with an overview of component-based development and describes the role of EJB within a multitier architecture. The chapters that follow introduce each of the enterprise bean types with detailed examples that teach you what you need to know to begin building and deploying your own EJBs. To be sure you understand the other J2EE technologies that EJB relies on directly, separate chapters provide in-depth coverage of the Java Naming and Directory Interface (JNDI) and the Java Message Service (JMS). This part also defines the role of transactions within EJB applications and describes exception handling and security management.

Part II, "Design and Performance," goes beyond the basics of building EJBs and introduces you to a set of design and performance strategies to apply to your enterprise development efforts. Although EJB is a relatively new technology, there are already standard practices emerging that you must be aware of as a designer. This part also includes a discussion of several approaches you can take to stress test your applications.

Part III, "Building the Web Tier," crosses the boundary of what you might expect to see in an EJB book. The chapter included here looks at several patterns you can apply to building a servlet- and JSP-based presentation tier that interacts with an application tier built using EJB.

Part IV, "Advanced Concepts," gets you up to speed on the concerns of experienced EJB developers. Here you'll get information on a new requirement introduced with EJB 2.0 that makes it possible for an EJB to communicate with CORBA objects or EJBs running in another vendor's container. You'll also be introduced to some recommended practices for building a foundational service layer for your applications. To build on the performance chapter in Part II, you'll also learn about clustering of EJB components and services here. The final chapter in Part IV will especially interest you if you're the type of person who always wants to know why when someone tells you not to do something. This chapter looks in particular at the things you're not supposed to do within the EJB container and why.

Part V, "Appendixes," offers some quick-reference material that includes a summary of the EJB 2.0 API and a description of what's changed since EJB 1.1.

Conventions Used in This Book

This book uses various stylistic and typographic conventions to make it easier to use.

Note

When you see a note in this book, it indicates additional information that can help you better understand a topic or avoid problems related to the subject at hand.

Tip

Tips introduce techniques applied by experienced developers to simplify a task or to produce a better design. The goal of a tip is to help you apply standard practices that lead to robust and maintainable applications.

Caution

Cautions warn you of hazardous procedures (for example, actions that have the potential to compromise the security of a system).

Cross-references are used throughout the book to help you quickly access related information in other chapters.

→ For an introduction to the terminology associated with transactions, **see** "Understanding Transactions," **p. 332**.

Many of the chapters in this book conclude with a "Troubleshooting" section that provides solutions to some of the common problems that you might encounter regarding a particular topic. Throughout the main chapter text, cross-references such as these are included to direct you to the appropriate heading within the "Troubleshooting" section to address these problems.

DEVELOPING ENTERPRISE JAVABEANS

INTRODUCTION TO ENTERPRISE APPLICATIONS

In this chapter

THE ENTERPRISE JAVABEANS ARCHITECTURE

The EJB 2.0 Specification defines Enterprise JavaBeans (EJB) as an architecture for component-based distributed computing. Although this definition works well if you are already familiar with terms such as component-based and distributed computing, the definition doesn't help much if you are brand-new to Enterprise JavaBeans or enterprise application development. It might even be helpful to define what is meant by an enterprise application. Before we do that, however, let's get a picture of what the EJB architecture looks like. This way, you'll have an image in your head as we go through this discussion. Figure 1.1 illustrates the EJB architecture from a high level.

Figure 1.1
A high-level view of the EJB architecture.

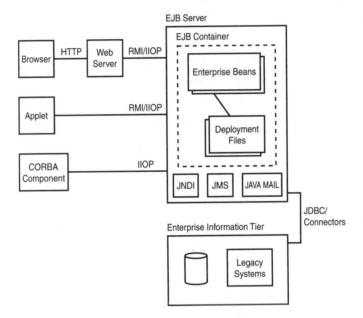

If you were to ask 100 software developers or architects what an enterprise application is, you probably would get 101 different definitions. It's not because software developers can't count, it's because the definition of an enterprise application can be somewhat ambiguous. Each development or business organization might have its own definition of what an enterprise application is. However, it would be nice if we could get a single definition that the majority of software developers could agree on.

Enterprise development did not begin with the advent of EJB, or Java for that matter. In fact, it has been around for many years and was a term that was used often when mainframe development was all the rage. However, it might be a new concept for some of you, who might have been involved only with applications that performed a relatively small business task and that were usually contained within a single address space.

Although companies have been using the Common Object Request Broker Architecture (CORBA) since the early '90s, due to the boom of the Internet and the decentralization of the Information Technology (IT) departments within organizations, more and more applications are being developed that cross the network boundaries and encompass more of the business's day-to-day functionality. At the same time, these applications are being spread out further and further from other components or applications that exist in the enterprise. By *enterprise*, we are referring to all the software applications or services that an organization has built, bought, and acquired that provide service to an organization. These services might be dealing with inventory management, pricing, or anything else that organizations must manage on a regular basis. Enterprise applications are not bound by the four walls of the data center like they used to be. Now, components and services are being decentralized throughout the organization.

Riding right on the back of this decentralization is an entire posse of new technical challenges and complexities that must be dealt with by the development organization. These new technical challenges must be considered during design and development because of this spreading out of the services over the network. It's no longer true that an organization's data or business processes are located in a single physical location. Most companies must now be global and can no longer assume that customers will be within the same geographical location. Therefore, the applications must be flexible and extensible to accommodate customers and other business partners from around the world and at any time of the day or night. Add to this that, hopefully, new customers and partners are being added every day, and this can have a tremendous effect on the scalability and performance of the application.

As you can start to see, enterprise developers must deal with many complex technological issues that just are not present in many smaller applications. Enterprise applications must support multiple sites that can be geographically separated, deal with customers and partners that can usually access an application at all hours of the day and night, support multiple languages and concurrent user access, and take into account the complex issues that go hand in hand with this wide separation. Other issues, such as interfacing with existing applications in the enterprise, are also very common and must be supported. It's also true that the physical hardware and software applications within the enterprise are very heterogeneous. For example, some enterprise applications might require a Unix operating system to function, while others run only on a Windows platform. This diverse set of constraints only adds to the complexity for the enterprise developers.

Going back to the EJB definition that was provided from the specification and considering a different definition of what enterprise application development is, let's try to come up with our own EJB definition. We need a definition that we can intuitively grasp and understand without a great deal of confusion and be able to communicate it to others. So here is an attempt at a definition that you should be able to understand with a little bit of thought:

> "Enterprise JavaBeans are Java components that a Java developer writes and installs into an application server, which provides naming, security, transactional, and other enterprise services for the components.
>
> These installed components can be utilized over a network in a distributed manner."

Although the previous definition contains a few terms that might be new to you, it should take you a little closer to understanding how the EJB architecture helps you build enterprise applications.

Note

The application server that was mentioned in the definition is typically built by a third party and installed into your environment.

There are other characteristics that you will need to understand when building enterprise applications using EJBs. These include such things as scalability, multi-user, load balancing, fault-tolerance, and many more. The problem is that there is so much to learn that you will have an easier time grasping all these concepts if you are exposed to them at the right pace and at the right time. That's one of the main goals of this book: to introduce concepts gradually and when it makes sense to introduce them. Learning Enterprise JavaBeans can sometimes seem overwhelming because of the supporting concepts and technologies that accompany it. Hopefully, you will learn by the time you are finished with this book that one of the greatest benefits from using EJB and its supporting technologies is that much of the infrastructure is provided for you.

COMPONENT-BASED DISTRIBUTED COMPUTING

What is component-based distributed computing and why is it so important? This is an excellent question to answer before going much further. The first question to answer is *"What is a component and what value do components offer to enterprise application developers?"*

QUICK SOFTWARE COMPONENT REFRESHER

When we talk about a component, what are we referring to? We could say that an EJB is a component. We could also call a Java class a component. Trying to come up with a single definition of a component that everyone in the software community would agree on would be pretty tough. For years, software developers and architects all over the world have attempted to describe what a component is. In 1996, the European Workshop on Component-Oriented Programming (ECOOP) came up with this definition:

"A software component is a unit of composition with contractually specified interfaces and explicit context dependencies only. A software component can be deployed independently and is subject to composition by third parties."

Notice there was no mention of Java or EJB in the definition. That's because the concept of a component has been around longer than Java. Although Java supports the idea of components, it sure didn't invent them. There are really three important features to take away from the previous component definition:

- Specified interfaces
- Explicit dependencies
- Deployment capabilities

A component generally provides one or more business services to its clients. A client could be a GUI interface (Web-based or otherwise) or in many cases, another component. The services that a component can offer could be as simple as returning the e-mail address for a customer to as complicated as calculating the shipping charges for an order being shipped to Berchtesgaden. No matter what services the component provides, it provides them through a publicly specified interface. This means that a client who interacts with a component is not shown the internals of the component, but only the result of the request that the client made on the component. This is sometimes also referred to as *encapsulation*.

A component usually has operations (methods), properties (state), and some type of events (possibly asynchronous notifications) that it generates. A good component will hide the details of how it maintains its internal state from the client. This helps to decouple the client from the component. For example, if the logic of how a component calculated the shipping charges changed, the client would not care as long as it still provided the same interface and charged the correct amount. Whether the amount was calculated by the Shipping component or the Shipping component communicated across the network to a legacy system to get the amount, the client shouldn't care.

You can think of the public interfaces that the component provides to a client as a contract between the client and the component. The component is saying, "I'll calculate the amount to ship the order, if you'll give me the order ID so I can look at the weight of what you are shipping." The set of interfaces a component exposes to a client is what makes up the contract between the client and the component. This is sometimes referred to as the *component interface*.

The next concept that is important from the definition is that a component may have dependencies on another component to complete its business services. These dependencies should be explicit and documented. In our example, the Shipping component that calls on the mainframe system to calculate the amount to ship the order depends on the mainframe application. It has a dependency on it. Without that mainframe system being able to provide the amount, the Shipping component would have to inform the customer that it can't complete the order at this time, and that can mean loss of revenue to the business. There's nothing incorrect or wrong about having these dependencies between components as long as everyone understands them. Having components depend on other components is very normal in an enterprise application. They just need to be comprehensible and cohesive. By understanding the dependencies, you are able to quickly determine which other components are affected when one of the public interfaces needs to change or be removed.

The last concept to take from the definition is the one of deployment. This is a little ambiguous because the definition of deployment has not been given and probably means many different things to different people. Java classes must be deployed. They must be in the correct package and in the system classpath. CORBA classes are deployed, but in an entirely different manner. Nonetheless, a component has some type of deployment that must be performed before its services are made available to clients. With some technologies or architectures, a distinction is made regarding who is responsible for deployment. The original developer is usually the one responsible for deploying a standard Java class, although it sometimes can be part of a much larger deployment. As you'll see in the section "EJB Roles and Their Responsibilities" in Chapter 3, EJB defines the roles and responsibilities for the component provider, deployer, and other necessary roles with the application.

→ For more on EJB roles and their responsibilities, **see** "EJB Roles and Their Responsibilities," **p. 37**.

Figure 1.2 shows an example of a component that supports all three features that we described.

Figure 1.2
A component has public interfaces and dependencies and can be deployed.

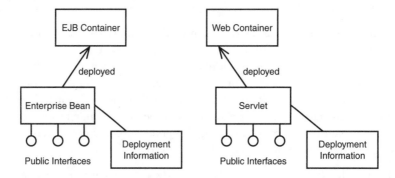

ASSEMBLING COMPONENTS INTO AN ARCHITECTURE

After you have begun to create individual components, the next step is to assemble them into a larger set of components. This larger set is known as a component architecture. A *component architecture* usually consists of a set of components and services for building applications and can utilize one or more frameworks. A *framework* is a library of other components that can be reused throughout multiple applications and save development time by providing proven and tested services and functionality. You might have heard the saying, "Don't reinvent the wheel." That's the purpose of a framework. Many companies are in the business of providing frameworks, but often they are built by the organization building the application.

There are many different styles and classifications of architectures. You can have system architectures, application architectures, network architectures, database architectures, and the list could go on.

If you do a search on the Internet for "What is an architecture?" you will see results ranging from space defense contract information to a hundred different thesis papers describing what the authors' ideas of an architecture are. For our purposes, an *architecture* is just a set of related components and frameworks that help describe what dependencies exist between the components and how they should react to events during the lifecycle of the application. This is in a sense what the EJB specification describes.

N-TIERED ARCHITECTURES

Another classification that architectures fall into is the number of different layers, or tiers, the architecture has. A *tier* is a grouping of software and possibly hardware, components, and services. This grouping can be both logical and physical. The purpose of using tiers is to enable the software components and services to be distributed across multiple computers for scalability and security. For example, as you'll see in Chapter 19, "Building a Presentation Tier for EJB," the Web server components and services are sometimes distributed in a different tier than the application services. This adds security to the application because more of the application can be located deeper in a protected network. The three most common architectures that you will hear about are

- Two-tier
- Three-tier
- The ubiquitous n-tier

> **Note**
>
> The n-tier name is referred to here as ubiquitous because this term is used to describe many different types of enterprise application architectures.

The n refers to how many tiers the architecture has, from 1 to some number (n). In most cases, n is usually 3, 4, or more. Most often, developers use the term "n-tiered" to refer to a three-tiered architecture. Let's take a quick look at a few of the typical architectures and how they are used today.

TWO-TIER COMPONENT ARCHITECTURES

No technical book would be worth its weight in salt if it didn't at least mention the two-tiered client/server architecture. It's often said, "Those who forget the mistakes of the past are doomed to repeat them." The two-tier or client/server application-programming model was very big up through the early 1990s. In fact, it's still a very popular architecture for certain types of applications. The problem is that it just doesn't scale when many users are using the system at the same time. I'm sure there are many of you screaming right now because you found a way to make it scale, but generally speaking it doesn't scale very well when the number of concurrent users starts to climb. This typically is due to the inability of the database to handle large numbers of client connections.

The two-tier architecture had other problems as well. To distribute a new version of the software, all clients had to be updated with the new client software, which contained all the business logic, database logic, and everything else. This also meant that very complex code, such as security and database interaction, was done in every client. This added overhead to the client application and increased the network traffic. The process of distribution became easier with Java applets, but the applet still contained some logic that could be better located elsewhere. With some of the security restrictions that were placed on the applet, this particular technology still does not work for all applications.

This architecture is usually referred to in a negative way as a *fat client* because it contains virtually all the components within this one tier. The second tier was usually a database of some type, most often a relational database. Figure 1.3 illustrates a typical two-tiered client/server architecture.

Figure 1.3
An example of a typical client/server architecture.

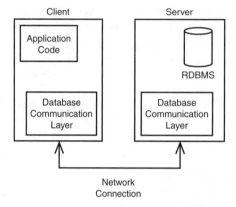

During the late '80s and early '90s, many development organizations started to replace the two-tier model with a three-tier model. Basically what the developers and architects did was to add a new tier between the previous two, and some of the software components were installed or deployed into this tier rather than the client tier. Most of the components and services that were moved to this new tier were the ones responsible for the business logic of the application.

N-TIER COMPONENT ARCHITECTURES

This new middle tier could be installed somewhere on the network and it could be shared with many different clients, rather than belonging on the client machine. It also helped because the size and complexity of the client application was reduced, which was good because, compared to the typical middle-tier server, the client machines were usually smaller in processing power and less capable of handling the application.

So with all these benefits, surely there are some negatives with an n-tiered architecture. The answer is, yes, there are. The negatives are associated with the distributed nature of the application. When the middle tier was created, it added complexity because the application now needed to handle things such as security, concurrent access, multi-threading issues, how the client locates the middle tier and other things that the client/server model didn't necessarily have to deal with. Of course, the 2-tier model had to deal with things such as security, but because each client was self-contained, these things were easier to deal with. One of the most obvious complexities that must be dealt with for the multi-tier architectures is the necessity for network computing between the first and middle tiers. Figure 1.4 illustrates a typical multi-tier architecture.

Figure 1.4
An example of a multi-tier architecture.

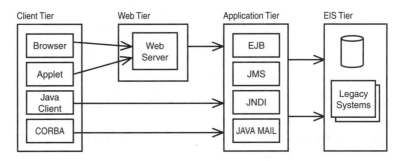

You must be asking yourself whether using a distributed component architecture is really so great. With all the pieces and technologies to learn, do you really get a return on your investment? In short, the answer is absolutely yes. And hopefully, the rest of the book will show that, by separating a system into pieces where each piece has a single or small set of responsibilities, each piece is able to concentrate on the work it was designed to do. This also enables developers or vendors to optimize a component for exactly what it should do best. Other justifications, such as having thinner clients and the ability to swap out the UI without worry about porting business logic, are beneficial as well. Not to mention that by having a physically distributed application, you are better able to take advantage of clustering techniques. We'll discuss clustering concepts in Chapter 22, "EJB Clustering Concepts."

By isolating the tiers, organizations are able to buy and install third-party complex software components into their architecture and spend more of their time solving the core business problem.

WHY USE EJB?

By now, hopefully you understand the importance and value of components, but we have not made a case yet for using EJB over any other distributed component-based technology.

The reasons for using Enterprise JavaBeans build on the same reasons for using Java as your development language. Those reasons are

- Write once, run anywhere philosophy
- Specification separate from implementation
- Interoperability
- Ability of developers to focus on business logic
- Compatibility with CORBA/IIOP protocols

WRITE ONCE, RUN ANYWHERE PHILOSOPHY

Even from the beginning, Java was intended to be platform-neutral. This means that developers could use the Java language to develop applications without regard to the underlying operating system that would be hosting the application. It allows this because Java runs inside a virtual machine that works between the application and the operating system. The virtual machine is dependent on the operating system, but the application code isn't. This offers a tremendous amount of flexibility and portability for Java applications. This behavior is not true of most other languages. Smalltalk works this way, but not languages like C++ or Visual Basic.

Because Enterprise JavaBeans are based on the Java language, you may also take advantage of this portability. Enterprise JavaBeans that are developed on one particular operating system can be ported to another. This sometimes happens when you have a customer that refuses to use a particular operating system and you must port your application to a different one. It's nice to have the flexibility to move your components to a different virtual machine without modifying your code.

SPECIFICATION SEPARATE FROM IMPLEMENTATION

Another facet about the Java language that has been around from the beginning is the idea of separating the interfaces for a service from the implementation. With the introduction of new Java features such as the extension mechanism, it has become easier to achieve this separation. The idea of separating the interface from the implementation is also used in the CORBA world. With CORBA, you specify your interfaces by using the Interface Definition Language (IDL). IDL is language- and platform-neutral. You then generate your implementation based on the IDL. This gives you the freedom to generate the implementation for almost any language and platform.

You surely are familiar with the various application programming interfaces (APIs) for Java, such as JDBC. You probably are aware that the APIs are just that: interfaces. This means that many components in the `java.sql` and `javax.sql` packages are just Java interfaces. Little or no implementation is provided within the APIs. You must install a JDBC driver provided by one of many different vendors, who provide implementations for the JDBC APIs. This separation or *decoupling* of the real implementation from the client APIs provides developers with the opportunity to select the best vendor out there and use their implementation. Other languages don't take this approach, and you can find yourself stuck with a slow, awkward implementation without any recourse. EJB is similar in this respect. An industry committee of system vendors defines the EJB specification, which is primarily a set of Java APIs. Any software company or open source community is then free to build products (EJB servers) that implement the EJB specification. This leaves developers free to select the brand that meets their requirements.

PROVIDES INTEROPERABILITY

Many languages and architectures provide a means by which an application can communicate with other languages. With Microsoft technologies, you can use DCOM. Applications written in CORBA use the Internet Interoperability Protocol (IIOP) to allow distributed components to communicate with one another over TCP/IP.

EJB is no exception and provides several different ways to achieve interoperability with applications written in other languages and on other platforms. Similar to CORBA, EJB interoperability is based on standards and committees. This has the effect of bringing more vendors and technologies into the fold, which increases the chance that you can communicate with other applications. EJB interoperability is covered in Chapter 20.

DEVELOPERS CAN FOCUS ON BUSINESS LOGIC

Any time you start building an enterprise application, you must answer many questions. How are you going to handle the distributed communication, security, persistence, messaging, and many more complicated services? You can see how easy it might be to spend most of your time building these infrastructure services, when you really should be solving the business problem.

EJB and the other technologies that make up the Java 2 Enterprise Edition (J2EE) provide most of these services for you. Again, what Sun and its committee members provide are the specifications or APIs. It's up to different technology vendors to provide the implementations. In a typical EJB server you'll find services for security, logging, persistence, and the other necessary services. You are able to spend more of your time building the business logic required by the application. Also, because there are specifications for the services, you can plug in services from different vendors to optimize the performance. In this way, the best-of-breed approach can be used.

COMPATIBLE WITH CORBA/IIOP PROTOCOLS

Many enterprise applications are written based on the CORBA specification. One of the reasons that there are so many is because CORBA enables you to develop applications in several different languages, including C++, Visual Basic, Cobol, Java, and others. Because there are so many already written using this technology, it would be nice to leverage what's already done when designing new enterprise applications or components. Fortunately, the EJB specification is designed especially for interoperability with CORBA and the IIOP wire protocol, which is at the heart of the CORBA specification.

This again opens the door for EJB applications to be easily integrated with existing enterprise applications and brings many more vendors into the EJB market. All this helps support portability and flexibility in designing and developing new applications.

CHAPTER 2

SETTING THE STAGE—AN EXAMPLE AUCTION SITE

In this chapter

THE AUCTION EXAMPLE

With a subject as complex as EJB, it's not always easy to illustrate the concepts using a short example that can be covered within a single chapter. With this in mind, we decided to introduce a central example early on and build on it throughout the book. Other examples will still be used where they're helpful (for variety if nothing else), but having a core example to fall back on minimizes the background explanation needed whenever a new example is introduced. This approach should help you stay more focused on the details of EJB and make it easier to cover them without distraction. Of course, the background for any example must go somewhere, so the thought here is to get it out of the way early so that the remaining chapters can focus on the technical details that are being introduced.

There are, of course, tradeoffs tied to any decision. The downside to building a large example in a book like this is that it's impossible to pick an application that's relevant to everyone. However, the intent has been to choose a problem domain that's addressed fairly often in both B2C and B2B Web applications and, even more important, easy to understand. With these goals in mind, the majority of the code developed throughout the book will be that needed to support an online auction site. Such a site can be fairly simple or quite complex depending on the requirements it must satisfy. To make the example worthwhile without risking being spread too thin, we'll emphasize depth of implementation and not necessarily breadth. In other words, you won't see every aspect of an auction addressed, but the characteristics that are included in the example will hopefully be somewhat realistic. Of course, the areas of the application where J2EE and especially EJB offer unique advantages will be looked at in the most detail.

In the sections that follow, you'll get a quick introduction to the various types of auctions that an online site might support and the business rules that go along with them. The goal is to scope the requirements for the example well enough to produce a set of class diagrams that will serve as the foundation for the code developed in later chapters.

Reading this chapter before diving into the technical details of EJB that follow is optional. You might want to skip this material at first and then refer to it when the requirements for the auction site start to matter. The idea is that whenever you do need to be familiar with the requirements of the auction site as part of understanding an example, it's better to have them all in one place—and that place is here.

OVERVIEW OF AN ENGLISH AUCTION

There are many types of auctions—English, Japanese, Dutch, and sealed-bid to name a few. Each type has its own rules, but the goal of most auctions is simply to sell an item for the highest price someone is willing to pay. The terminology you must know to understand auctions is quite simple as well and is probably already familiar to you. To start with, a price offered for an item in an auction is called a *bid* and the people submitting the bids are called the *bidders*—nothing difficult so far. The other terms and business rules that are involved get a little more complicated than this, but not much.

The different auction formats are, for the most part, defined by how the bidding process is handled. English auctions start at a low price and the participants submit higher bids until no one wants to bid higher than the current leader. The auction then is closed and the bidder who placed the leading bid is named the winner. Japanese auctions start at a low price as well, but there's a twist in how the bidding takes place. In this format, everyone willing to pay at least the starting price enters the auction as a bidder. The price then is raised in steps with the bidders each given the option to stay in or drop out at each step. The auction ends when only a single bidder remains and is named the winner. Dutch auctions offer another option by taking an opposite approach. Here, an auction starts with a high price that is decreased in steps until it reaches an amount someone is willing to pay. The first bidder to jump in and agree to a price gets the item.

Even with their differences, English, Japanese, and Dutch auctions are the same in that the bidding is public to all the participants. Basically, as a bidder you know what all the other bidders are doing. You won't necessarily know how high a price someone is ultimately willing to pay, but you will know what everyone does at each step along the way. Sealed-bid auctions offer an alternative by soliciting bids without publicly announcing the prices that have been offered. You might have seen this done as a fundraiser at a charitable event where the attendees drop written bids for various items into sealed boxes. Once the time limit for bidding has been reached, each set of bids is opened and the winners are determined. It's not as exciting to watch as the other formats, but it's easy to manage and it adds a twist by forcing the bidders to try to guess what the other participants might bid. The seller won't benefit from a heated bidding war that drives the price up, but might get lucky and have someone go way over the top of the other bidders to ensure a win.

Even if these four formats were the only auction types that existed, sellers would have a fairly adequate set from which to choose. However, this list is far from complete. The number of auction types basically doubles if the seller allows more than one winner to split multiple quantities of an item instead of holding to a "single winner takes all" approach. This option falls more in line with B2B needs where a company might need to, for example, auction off an inventory of surplus parts.

Still more auction formats are possible when the tables are turned on the buyer and seller. In a reverse auction, sellers are asked to compete for a buyer's business by naming the lowest price they will accept for an item they supply. This take on purchasing has gathered more interest as the option to trade with multiple sellers over the Internet has begun to be capitalized on by companies looking to cut procurement costs.

That's a whirlwind description of some of the more common auction types. It's not enough detail to make you an expert, but hopefully it's enough for you to appreciate that merely saying that you want to build an online auction site doesn't narrow your requirements down very much. That's an important point because the goal for the example site is to make it easier to spend more time discussing EJB, not to teach you more than necessary about the business of auctions. With that said, it's important to set some boundaries right away. The quickest and cleanest way to do this is to pick a single auction format to implement. A production site would likely need to support several auction formats, but the example here will be limited to supporting English auctions to keep it manageable. With that decided, the rest of this section can cover the business rules the example site will need to satisfy.

BUSINESS RULES

When you first think of an auction, you probably picture a room full of people filled with the sound of a fast-talking auctioneer wielding a gavel. The auctioneer quickly describes an item up for sale, and then works to propel the bidding as high as possible. The bidders signal their intent to bid by raising a numbered paddle (or scratching their noses at the wrong time if they're not careful) and the price grows until the gavel falls and a single winner is named. This is an English auction (sometimes called a *Standard* auction) and it is quite common in both the live version described here and in online auction sites.

An English auction isn't overly complicated, but you do need to understand a little more about one to make the requirements for the example site clear. As with any business application, the requirements for the auction site depend on the business rules and the entities needed to model the problem domain. Auctions are run by *auction houses*. A seller contracts with an auction house to sell an item at auction in exchange for a fee (usually a percentage of the eventual selling price). The auction house maintains a staff of auctioneers and holds the knowledge needed to manage the entire process of planning and running the auction.

As part of laying the groundwork for a particular auction, the auction house prepares a description of the item up for sale and assigns a minimum bid that defines the starting point for the first bidder. To keep the bidders from drawing the process out unnecessarily, the auction house also establishes a minimum bid increment that determines how much each bid must exceed the preceding one (you wouldn't want to get into a bidding war like \$4,000.01, \$4,000.02, \$4,000.03, and so on). For a live auction, the auctioneer can obviously handle this situation, but such details must be spelled out in advance for the electronic equivalent.

After the auctioneer starts an auction, the competition for a winner is on as successively higher bids are submitted. The auctioneer accepts bids until no one is willing to outbid the current leader or a pre-established time limit is reached. In either case, the gavel comes down and the auction is closed. The item is then sold to the leading bidder at the offered price—with one possible exception. In addition to setting a minimum starting bid, a seller might also set a reserve amount (higher than the required starting bid) that defines the actual minimum price that will be accepted. If the leading bid for a closed auction meets the reserve amount, the item is awarded to the winner. However, if the reserve amount is not met, the auction is closed without a winner and no sale is made.

CHOOSING THE USE CASES TO IMPLEMENT

With the basics of an English auction defined, the remaining task is to come up with a set of software requirements for the example. There's no need to be too rigid or formal here, but it's worth the effort to set your expectations of what the site will be built to do. The fact that you're reading an EJB book makes it relatively safe to assume that you've had some experience with object-oriented (OO) analysis and design. This chapter won't attempt to cover the details of a formal requirements gathering or analysis and design methodology, but it will hit the highlights and use some standard notation to lay the foundation for the auction site.

Software must satisfy both functional and nonfunctional requirements. The distinction between the two is that functional requirements relate directly to the business needs a system must address. As an example, being able to accept and record a bid from a participant is a functional requirement for an auction site because it relates directly to the business at hand. Nonfunctional requirements are equally important but not as directly related. This category often includes needs such as security and system maintenance.

The nonfunctional requirements for the auction site can be left somewhat vague for now while attention is focused on the functional ones. To set a foundation for using J2EE though, several nonfunctional requirements can be assumed for the example. First, the primary reason for building an online auction system is to make it easily accessible as compared to attending a live auction. With this in mind, the site should use standard Web browsers for all its user interfaces so that virtually anyone can access it. Of course, making the site easy to access brings up other issues. The system will be of value only if the winning bids are placed by legitimate participants intent on following through with their purchases. This makes it necessary to provide some level of user authentication and authorization to control access to both the maintenance and bidding functions that are eventually implemented. You should also assume that many bidders are expected and that the scalability and reliability demands placed on the system are enough to require the use of a distributed, multi-tiered architecture.

The operations the auction site will support can be defined by a set of functional requirements. There are different ways to go about capturing these requirements and documenting them, but there are similarities in how most developers do this. When documenting the functional requirements for an OO application, it's accepted practice to start with a set of use cases that define the operations needed from a system. The purpose of a use case is to describe the interaction of a user with a system to perform some tangible operation that satisfies a goal of the user. Use cases are best defined by the eventual users of the system or application developers working with domain experts to capture what is required.

Use cases can vary widely in format and in the level of detail provided, but the idea is to define what a system has to do without any mention of how it might do it. They are not intended to be technical, but should instead be easily understandable to the users. The key criteria are that they avoid implementation details and include only tasks of true benefit to the user. For an auction site, the most obvious use case is that a bidder (one of the eventual user types) must be able to submit a bid for an active auction. Although it's also a requirement, including the capability for the system to prompt the user for a username and password as a use case would likely be inappropriate because that function does nothing to help the user accomplish a business goal.

Two developers looking at the same system would almost certainly come up with two different use-case breakdowns. That might sound discouraging, but all that really matters is that the required functionality is captured by the set as a whole. Crafting a good set of use cases is as much art as it is science. Given that, we'll be careful not to let the possible nuances get in the way of progress. The use cases presented here need to be broken out and defined only to the extent that you understand the scope of the problem to be addressed.

Working from a use-case perspective fits well with our need to limit the scope of the example. Considering a wide range of use cases is important when designing flexibility into a system, but carefully selecting a subset of those to implement initially is an easy way to place limits on what has to be built. Obviously, an auction site will be useful only if bidders can place bids on an auction, so that sets the bar for the minimum amount of functionality to require. To keep the example from being trivial, we'll also include requirements for some of the auction house functionality needed to create and administer an auction. Figures 2.1 and 2.2 illustrate the use cases the auction site will support.

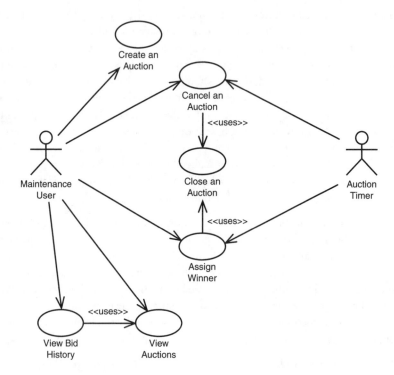

Figure 2.1
Maintenance use cases define the requirements for administering auctions.

The notation defined by the Unified Modeling Language (UML) developed by Grady Booch, Ivar Jacobson, and James Rumbaugh is used throughout this chapter. UML is not a design methodology, but a modeling language used to communicate a design. Before its introduction, each design methodology tended to use its own notation, forcing developers to learn the differences. The standard provided by UML allows developers to focus on the software they're developing and not on the syntax used to communicate the ideas. You might already be familiar with this notation, but to make sure, quick overviews of the diagram types are included as they're introduced.

Figure 2.2
Bidder use cases define how the end user will interact with the site.

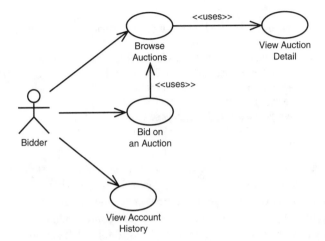

Use-case notation is quite simple and consists of only a few elements. The stick figures in Figures 2.1 and 2.2 depict external interfaces to a system and are referred to as *actors*. An actor usually represents a human user, but it can also depict another system or process that relies on a use case being presented. You should think of an actor as a role and not an individual person; every user that takes on a particular role when accessing a system is represented by the one actor that defines that role.

An actor initiates a use case, and the operations contained within that use case define the system's response. An actor is usually tied to multiple use cases, and a use case can interact with multiple actors as well. For the auction example, Maintenance User and Bidder represent the two user roles defined for the auction site. Any user will either be creating and administering auctions as part of a maintenance role or participating in an auction as a bidder. Figure 2.1 also includes an Auction Timer actor, which represents a process that must be able to end an auction in the same way the human Maintenance User can. This supports the need to automatically close an auction when its time limit has been reached.

The labeled ovals in Figures 2.1 and 2.2 are the use cases themselves. An arrow from an actor to a use case identifies the actor as the stimulus that starts the use case or the recipient of information produced by the use case. You can also see that several of the use-case ovals are connected to other use cases by arrows and the text <<uses>>. A *uses* relationship allows you to indicate reuse of certain operations. You might also see this referred to as an *includes* relationship. For example, Figure 2.1 indicates that the "Close an Auction" use case defines operations that are needed by both "Cancel an Auction" and "Assign a Winner." Similarly, Figure 2.2 shows that "Browse Auctions" is an activity directly requested by the Bidder actor and also a required part of the "Bid on an Auction" use case. Also notice that "View Auction Detail" is separated out from "Browse Auctions." This isn't strictly necessary because this functionality isn't reused, but sometimes splitting out part of a task this way makes the requirements more clear.

Note

Although not needed in the use cases shown in this chapter, UML also supports the concept of an *extends* relationship between two use cases. This relationship allows you to show that a variation exists for a use case that is performed when a certain condition occurs. For example, an online ordering site might have a "Submit Order" use case that is extended by a "Submit Order for New Customer" use case. The second use case would likely perform all the operations done by the first, but might also add the processing of a first-time customer survey or a credit check.

A use-case diagram identifies the use cases to be supported by a system and the actors that interact with them, but it doesn't provide any explanation of what the actual operations are. A narrative description of a use case is where you get the actual meat. The rest of this section describes the details of each of the use cases to be implemented by the auction example. Again, the intent is only to give you enough detail to follow the example as it is built throughout the book. With that as a guideline, the use cases are presented using a simple narrative that cuts right to the chase.

CREATE AN AUCTION

A Maintenance User must be able to define an auction to be held on the site. This includes assigning the item to be sold and defining the parameters that determine how the auction is to be run. In particular, the user must define the starting bid, minimum bid increment, reserve amount (optional), start time, and scheduled end time for an auction. The system must provide the user with an interface for defining this information and must store it so that the site can execute the auction.

CANCEL AN AUCTION

A Maintenance User must be able to cancel an auction that either has not started or has started but has not had a winner assigned. The Auction Timer must be able to cancel an auction whose time limit has expired without a winner being declared. No winner should be assigned if either no bids were submitted or no bid that exceeded the auction's reserve amount was submitted.

ASSIGN A WINNER

A Maintenance User must be able to select a bid submitted for an active auction and assign the corresponding bidder as the auction winner. The Auction Timer must be able to assign the leading bidder as an auction winner when an auction expires and the leading bid exceeds the reserve amount (if one is defined). When an auction winner is assigned, the system must update the auction status and notify the winner.

CLOSE AN AUCTION

This use case defines functionality shared by "Cancel an Auction" and "Assign Winner." When an auction is closed, the system shall no longer accept bid submissions. If the closed auction had already started, the system shall set the actual end time of the auction to the time at which it was closed.

View Auctions

A Maintenance User must be able to view a list of auctions defined within the system. The system shall display each auction by name, status, starting bid amount, reserve amount, current leading bid, and time remaining. The user shall have the option to sort the auctions by name, status, or time remaining.

View Bid History

A Maintenance User must be able to view the bids submitted for a particular auction. When the user selects this option for an auction, the system shall display each bid for the auction sorted in descending order of the submission time. The information for each bid shall include the bidder's name, the bid amount, and the submission date and time.

Browse Auctions

A bidder must be able to browse a list of auctions that are currently active or have been started and subsequently closed. This list shall include an entry for each auction that consists of the auction name, status, current leading bid, minimum next bid, and time remaining.

View Auction Detail

A bidder must be able to view the detailed information for an auction. When the user selects an auction from the auction list provided by the "Browse Auctions" use case, the system shall display the auction detail. The detail display shall include the information shown in the auction list plus the auction description and the name, description, and image of the item being auctioned.

Bid on an Auction

A bidder must be able to submit a bid for an active auction. The system shall allow the user to enter and submit a bid price from either the auction list or auction detail display. The system shall only accept bids for auctions that have started but not yet expired. The system shall only accept bids that are greater than or equal to the required next bid amount. The required next bid shall be the starting bid amount until the first bid has been submitted. After the first bid has been submitted, the required next bid shall be the amount of the current leading bid plus the minimum bid increment for the auction.

View Account History

A bidder must be able to view an account history that shows all auctions bid on by the Bidder. The system shall display a list of auctions that includes the auction name, status, current leading bid, time remaining, and the user's bid status. The user's bid status shall be indicated as one of Leader, Trailer, Winner, or Non-Winner (to be polite).

DEFINING THE OBJECT MODEL

The code for the auction site's application tier will evolve as new concepts are introduced, but an initial object model can still be defined as a foundation. A good bit of analysis and design work is needed to go from use cases to an object model, but most of that detail will be skipped for now so that the interesting design decisions can be looked at relative to EJB in later chapters. Even though it's too early to talk about where EJB fits into the design, some basic architectural goals can still be covered to start firming up what needs to be built.

First of all, the subject of this book makes it a given that the auction site will be built on a multi-tiered J2EE architecture. In a nutshell, this means that all HTML generation for the user interface will be performed using servlets and JSPs in a Web tier that is decoupled from the business logic. All business logic will be contained in EJBs running within an application tier that is responsible for all communication to the enterprise information systems tier (a single relational database in this case). These decisions alone short-circuit a lot of potential design issues that would normally have to be considered.

To stay focused on EJB, the detail in the remainder of the chapter will focus on defining a set of initial class and sequence diagrams for the application tier.

IDENTIFY THE BUSINESS OBJECTS

In addition to using a multi-tiered architecture, the auction site should also reflect a layered architecture. This is especially true in the application tier where both business objects and application logic are found. Business objects represent the key concepts of a problem domain and are typically the persistent objects associated with an application. These objects need to encapsulate the details of the entities they represent, but they should be isolated from the application logic that knows how to use to them collectively to perform application-specific tasks. For example, the items offered for auction by the site might be represented by an Item business object that holds the attributes that define an item and the methods that manipulate them. However, an item can be used in applications other than an auction, so the Item business object shouldn't hold any auction-specific processing. The code that knows how to use an item in an auction should instead be captured in an application controller layer. Maintaining this type of separation makes it easier to reuse business objects across applications.

This section comes up with an initial list of business objects needed by the auction site, and the following one looks at a set of application controllers. You'll see in later chapters how the EJBs known as entity beans play a role in business object implementation and those known as session beans do the same for application controllers.

In the case of an auction site, a designer would quickly conclude that entities such as the individual auctions, the items available for auction, the participating bidders, and the bids submitted are the primary business objects to be represented in the system. Again, detailing a design process is outside the intent of this chapter, so we'll cover only what you need to get to the results needed to build the example. Many designs are possible, so the one presented here is simply one that was selected to meet the requirements laid out and make for an interesting example. All that's needed at this point is a basic understanding of the classes involved and how they're associated. Figure 2.3 illustrates this using a class diagram.

Figure 2.3
Business objects represent the persistent entities needed by the auction site.

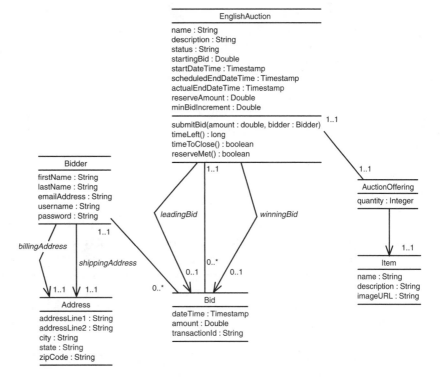

A class diagram identifies a set of classes in a system and the relationships among them. These relationships include both inheritance relationships and associations between classes. Using UML, a class is represented by a box that contains the name of the class and a list of its attributes and methods. As an example, Figure 2.3 shows an auction business object represented as an EnglishAuction class. This class has several attributes that include a name for the auction and a startingBid. For this particular example, the methods listed in the diagram are limited to the true business methods; so simple get/set methods for the fields aren't shown even though they would likely be needed. The methods that are included identify the business functionality required from the class. For example, an EnglishAuction must be able to accept a bid through a submitBid method that expects an amount and a reference to a Bidder as parameters.

Figure 2.3 shows the associations between the business object classes as well. An association is shown in UML using a line drawn between two classes that indicates the cardinality of the association as being one-to-one, one-to-many, or many-to-many. The numbers placed adjacent to this line specify the cardinality using either a single value or a range of values for each side of the association. An asterisk can be used to indicate some number greater than or equal to zero (or the lower bound if the asterisk is used as an upper bound in a range).

For example, the association between `Bidder` and `Bid` is identified using `1..1` and `0..*`. These values mean that a given bid belongs to one and only one auction (`1..1`) and a bidder can submit any number of bids (`0..*`). This is a typical one-to-many association.

Two classes are not limited to having a single association between them. As shown in Figure 2.3, three associations exist between `EnglishAuction` and `Bid`. These associations represent all the bids submitted for an auction (one-to-many), an auction's leading bid (one-to-one), and an auction's winning bid (one-to-one). The leading and winning bid associations are shown using a slightly different notation that includes an arrow on one end of the line. This notation indicates navigability of an association. In this example, an auction knows its leading and winning bids (that is, it can navigate to them), but a bid does not know if it is the leading or winning bid for an auction. When the arrows are omitted, the association is navigable by either class.

IDENTIFY THE APPLICATION CONTROLLERS

Defining the business objects is a big step toward reaching the goal of this chapter, but the application controllers that interact with these objects also need to be identified. The controller classes are ultimately responsible for implementing the use cases.

There are different ways to allocate controller functionality to specific classes, but the approach taken here is to develop a set of classes that represent the real-world individuals or organizations that do the same functions. Specifically, the auction site will be built using controller classes such as `AuctionHouse` and `AuctionManager`. `AuctionHouse` represents the functionality presented to a bidder for obtaining information about the auctions defined by the system and submitting bids. `AuctionManager` covers the specific functions within an auction house needed to administer auctions. This separation provides the functionality needed by a maintenance user. This type of mapping to controller classes helps a developer intuitively understand where responsibilities lie.

It's not necessary to break the controllers down into supporting classes at this point, so there's little need to build additional class diagrams here. However, what is useful is to develop a few sequence diagrams to understand how the controllers are expected to interact with the business objects. A sequence diagram depicts interactions between class instances as messages being passed between the objects. The messages in turn correspond to methods that need to be supported by the associated classes. As an example, Figure 2.4 shows a sequence diagram defining the interactions necessary to support a bid submission.

A sequence diagram focuses on how objects interact to perform a requested operation. This type of diagram illustrates how associations between objects are created and used to perform the work required by a use case. These diagrams provide a dynamic view of a system to complement the static view provided by class diagrams. Each box along the top of a sequence diagram represents an object (not a class, but a single instance). Each object is identified by its class name preceded by a colon that might optionally be preceded by an object name. Typically, you include object names only if more than one object of a particular class type participates in the sequence. The order of the objects across the top of the diagram is unimportant; you should, however, select an order that places the objects with the most interaction near each other to reduce clutter in the diagram.

Figure 2.4
A sequence diagram illustrates how application controllers interact with business objects.

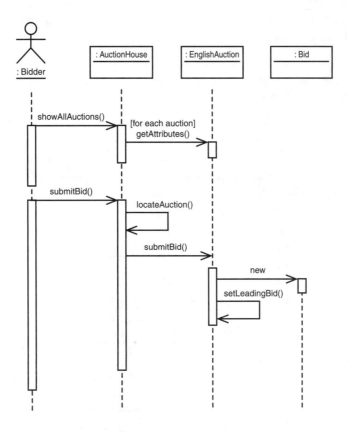

The vertical line that extends beneath each object in a sequence diagram is a *lifeline*. A lifeline begins when an object is created and ends when it is destroyed. If a lifeline begins at the top of the diagram (just beneath an object box), the associated object exists before the task described by the diagram starts. Similarly, if a lifeline extends to the bottom of a diagram, the associated object still exists when the task is completed. The horizontal arrows between lifelines indicate messages being passed to objects as execution control is transferred. The rectangles drawn along the lifelines are known as *activations*. An activation indicates that the associated object is either performing work at that time or waiting for another object to return control to it after being sent a message. Activation rectangles are often omitted from sequence diagrams that do not include any concurrent processing by the objects involved. In those cases, the transitions of object activity coincide with the message arrow locations.

The sequence in Figure 2.4 begins when the `Bidder` actor requests the option to view the available auctions. This request is represented by a `showAllAuctions` message sent to an `AuctionHouse` instance. This `AuctionHouse` controller satisfies the request by interacting with each instance of `EnglishAuction` to obtain the attribute values needed to build the auction list. The user bids on an auction by selecting one from the list and sending a `submitBid` message to the `AuctionHouse`. The controller passes the request to the desired `EnglishAuction`.

This auction object creates a new `Bid` based on the bid amount and the bidder's identity and assigns the new `Bid` to be the current leading bid.

Figure 2.5 shows a similar sequence diagram that illustrates how the Maintenance User uses the `AuctionManager` controller to create a new auction, define its attributes, and assign an item to be auctioned to it.

Figure 2.5
Maintenance Users access the `AuctionManager` controller to create auctions.

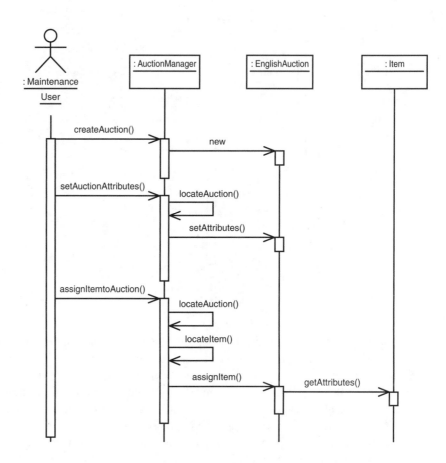

WHAT'S NEXT?

With this background behind you, it's time to move on to what you've been waiting for. The chapters that follow first introduce you to some of the underlying technologies and concepts associated with EJB before covering what you need to know to build and deploy your own enterprise beans. Hopefully, this overview of auctions will make the examples that follow more interesting as you see how EJB can be applied to a practical business problem.

CHAPTER 3

EJB CONCEPTS

In this chapter

GRASPING THE CONCEPTS EARLY

There is quite a bit of work ahead for you to learn and understand Enterprise JavaBeans. It will make the task much easier if you come to understand the concepts of the EJB architecture before you attempt to dive into the nuts and bolts of building enterprise applications using it.

You must solidify these ideas and concepts in your mind before you start soaking up the rest of the topics in this book. Everything else after this chapter is predicated on your understanding the concepts and ideas presented in this chapter. In reality, this might be a better approach anyway. Other EJB books attempt to introduce these ideas either immediately before or during the process of building your first enterprise beans. This doesn't give you a great deal of time to understand what's going on behind the scenes before you are exposed to what you need to do to build an EJB application. Take enough time to read this chapter thoroughly.

If you spend any time on the EJB-related newsgroups and discussion lists, you probably know that many of the questions that are being asked are related to the conceptual ideas about the EJB architecture, what the roles and responsibilities are for the many parties involved, and why things are done in a particular way. To ensure a consistent understanding for the rest of the book and to hopefully clear up some of these questions, we present the concepts of the EJB architecture here in this chapter, well ahead of the time that you will need to apply them.

→ If you feel that you already have a solid understanding of the basic concepts, feel free to jump ahead to Chapter 4, "Java Naming and Directory Interface," but do so at your own peril.

WHAT IS AN ENTERPRISE BEAN?

As it was mentioned in Chapter 1, "Introduction to Enterprise Applications," Enterprise JavaBeans is an architecture for component-based distributed computing. Enterprise beans are arguably the most important aspect of that architecture. They are the bread and butter, so to speak, of the architecture. Although other components work alongside the enterprise beans to make all the magic happen, the enterprise beans are the mainstay of what you need to understand.

Enterprise beans are components that are part of a distributed transaction-oriented enterprise application. They typically have the following characteristics:

- They depend on a container environment to supply life-cycle services for them.
- They contain business logic that operates on the enterprise's data.
- EJB instances are created and maintained by the container.
- They can be customized at deployment time by editing an XML-based deployment descriptor.
- System-level services, such as transaction management and security, are described separately from the enterprise bean.

- A client never accesses an enterprise bean directly; the container environment mediates access for the client.
- The enterprise bean is designed to be portable across EJB servers provided by different vendors.

Starting with the EJB 2.0 Specification, there are three types of enterprise beans:

- Entity bean
- Session bean
- Message-driven bean

Each type of enterprise bean is used for a different purpose in your enterprise application. Although you will get a very detailed explanation of each bean type later in this book, the following sections briefly describe the purposes of each.

ENTITY BEAN

An entity bean typically represents a row in a relational database. Although this is not the only purpose it can be used for, it's generally the most common. Just as there is a row in a database table for each record, there is possibly a single entity bean instance created for each row. For example, if you have an Order table that represents all the orders placed by customers, you would have one entity bean instance for each Order, although there is some flexibility for how the vendors implement this exactly.

> **Note**
>
> Mapping an entity bean to a single row in a relational database might be too simplified and might lead to a poor design. Whether an entity bean maps to a single table or across multiple tables really depends on your specific application needs and requirements.

This doesn't mean that a container creates an entity bean instance in memory for every database row when the server starts up. That obviously wouldn't scale very well and would be wasteful. There is, however, a different instance used for each row when a client needs it. All clients accessing the same row in the database would be doing so through the same entity bean instance. As you'll see, the EJB architecture provides for concurrent user access to the same EJB instance through proper synchronization. Due to limited resources on the server, however, it might be necessary for less-often used instances to be put back into a pool of beans so that other clients can use them. You'll see more about object pools later in this chapter.

An entity bean is considered to be long-lived because it will survive a server crash. When the server is restarted, the entity bean is still there because the state that the entity bean represents is persisted in the database. Not every table in your persistence schema has to

PART
I

CH
3

map to a single entity bean. You might have entity beans that are composed of several tables. As you'll see in Chapter 5, "Entity Beans," not every persistent object must be an entity bean. There are other factors to consider when deciding whether something is an entity bean or not.

SESSION BEAN

A session bean typically represents business-level logic that an application needs to execute. It usually combines several processing steps that must be completed as an atomic unit. *Atomic* means that all the operations should be completed or none of them should. For example, if you had a method called completeOrder that needed to confirm and charge a customer's credit card, submit the order to the system, and then generate an e-mail message to the shipping department to start pulling the order, these operations may be combined and put into a session bean method. If the order could not be submitted, the customer should not be charged. All these operations can be combined into a single session bean method call.

There are two variations of session beans, stateful and stateless. A *stateful* session bean is designed to be used by one client at a time and can maintain conversational state between method invocations. *Conversational state* is a state that is maintained for a specific client/ session pair. This means that a stateful session bean maintains instance variable state for a specific client. Although a *stateless* session bean can also have instance variables, it shares this state among various clients. This is one of the most commonly misunderstood things about session beans. A stateless session bean can hold state—it just can't be counted on to hold client-specific state because a client is not guaranteed to use the same session bean instance for different method invocations. The container has the freedom to swap stateless instances back and forth between clients. This helps increase scalability because a smaller number of session bean instances can service a larger number of clients.

All instances of stateless session beans are considered identical from the client viewpoint, which is why most EJB developers try to use stateless session beans whenever possible. Stateful session beans are not identical to each other because they maintain conversational state. One client's ShoppingCart will probably contain different items from another client's ShoppingCart. In this way, the session bean has knowledge about a specific client and can't be shared with other clients.

MESSAGE-DRIVEN BEAN

The message-driven bean is new to the EJB architecture starting with version 2.0. The new bean type is used to handle Java Message Service (JMS) messages asynchronously. It is very different from the other types of enterprise beans in two key ways. For one, the message-driven bean is not exposed directly to clients. A message-driven bean listens for messages that are sent using JMS and processes those messages anonymously. For more information on JMS, see Chapter 10, "Java Message Service."

The container delegates a received message either to an existing method-ready instance or to a new instance allocated to handle the message. Message-driven beans are stateless; therefore, any instance may service a message equally. Likewise, similar to stateless session beans, message-driven beans are anonymous, having no identity to a client. The second key difference is that message-driven beans are managed completely by the container, rather than allowing a client to possibly manage the life cycle by creating and removing them. You'll see more about message-driven beans in Chapter 11, "Message-Driven Beans."

EJB ROLES AND THEIR RESPONSIBILITIES

As you probably are aware or will most definitely learn by the time you finish this book, there are many pieces to the enterprise application puzzle. Fitting all of them together is sometimes very much like putting together a jigsaw puzzle blindfolded. From building the infrastructure that handles database access to ensuring security of the application, the amount of knowledge that one must posses to build an entire enterprise application is mind-boggling and sometimes can be overwhelming. In fact, just trying to learn how much there is to learn can be tiring and frustrating.

PART
I

CH
3

The first thing you need to learn is what pieces make up an EJB application. The second and much harder task is learning how to build each individual piece of the EJB puzzle. Back in Chapter 1, you were introduced to some of the large-grained components of an enterprise application. In Chapter 2, "Setting the Stage—An Example Auction Site," you were introduced to the fictitious auction site that we will be using and building upon throughout the book to illustrate the different components of an enterprise application built using EJB technology. In this chapter, we start the education process on what pieces make up an application that uses enterprise beans. The rest of the book covers how to build an enterprise application using the EJB architecture. Before we get into details of building an EJB application, you need to know who is responsible for which pieces in the process.

No single software developer can be an expert at all facets of building enterprise applications. Of course, some might believe that they are experts at all things enterprise, but in reality this is typically not the case. For example, building an Object to Relational Mapping architecture framework (ORM) is a very complicated task for any serious production-level implementation. For this, you need to be an expert at database technologies; an expert in the Java Database Connectivity API; and understand issues of caching, pooling, transactions, and many other complicated tasks. One could, and many often do, spend their entire careers learning these technologies alone. Similarly, building an architecture or framework to handle distributed communications is also very complicated, but in different subject areas and technologies. The point here is that you can have a solid understanding and be very proficient at many things, but it's quite a different matter to be an expert at everything related to enterprise application development.

If you are evaluating a particular technology implementation by a vendor, you want to believe that the very best people built that implementation. You hope that the people whose product your company is about to spend big bucks on are complete experts in that area.

Because not many are experts in all areas, the EJB specification has separated the development, deployment, and management of an enterprise application into six distinct roles. Each EJB role plays a different part in the overall life cycle of the application development and deployment process. Some of these roles might be merely logical with smaller projects or organizations and might be performed by the same vendor or developer. Nonetheless, it's valuable to understand the distinction that's being made between the roles and responsibilities within the EJB architecture. The six distinct roles are

- Enterprise bean provider
- Application assembler
- EJB deployer
- EJB server provider
- EJB container provider
- System administrator

BEAN PROVIDER

The enterprise bean provider is the Java developer that is responsible for creating the EJB components that help solve the business problem. The bean provider may build all three types of enterprise beans. A bean provider is usually a Java developer who understands the domain in which he is operating. It's someone who understands what business logic or functionality should be in an `Order` component or a `ShoppingCart` component, for example.

The bean provider generally creates one or more enterprise beans, the required Java interfaces that must accompany the enterprise beans, other Java classes that are used by these enterprise beans, and an XML file that will be used to describe how the beans should be assembled and deployed. The XML file describes certain aspects of the enterprise beans that the bean provider has created. The aspects in the deployment file can include things like the name of the bean or beans, external dependencies the beans have, and other things that you will see later in this book when we talk about deploying EJBs.

The bean provider will normally deliver the beans in an `ejb-jar` file that typically contains the necessary items to assemble and deploy the enterprise beans with the rest of the application. An `ejb-jar` file is a standard JAR file that is used by vendor tools to package one or more enterprise beans along with their assembly instructions so that assembly and deployment tools can process the enterprise beans. This JAR file is delivered to an application assembler who takes the responsibility for the next step in the process. Figure 3.1 shows the role of the enterprise bean provider.

→ For more information on how the various EJB roles interact with the `ejb-jar` file, **see** "Deployment Descriptors and EJB Roles," **p. 422**.

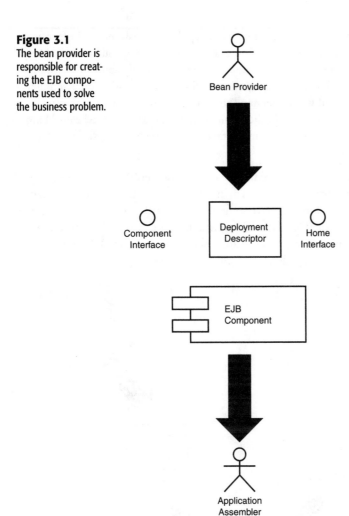

Figure 3.1
The bean provider is responsible for creating the EJB components used to solve the business problem.

APPLICATION ASSEMBLER

An application assembler receives enterprise beans in the form of ejb-jar files from one or more bean providers and assembles these beans into larger units of deployment. For example, bean provider A might build and hand over a ShoppingCart component while bean provider B creates and delivers an OrderFulfillment component. Both of these components may be in separate ejb-jar files. The application assembler can choose to leave the beans in separate ejb-jar files or create a single ejb-jar that contains all the enterprise beans being assembled. The decision to put the bean components in a single ejb-jar or into separate ejb-jar files is really up to the assembler and how the application needs to be deployed.

The assembler also will insert assembly instructions into the deployment descriptor files that were created and provided by the bean provider. The type and nature of the assembly instructions depend on the type of enterprise bean being included. With smaller projects or organizations, the bean provider can also function as the application assembler. In fact, if you are including multiple enterprise beans within a single ejb-jar file, you are most likely performing the role of the assembler anyway. The assembler is typically someone with technical knowledge within the development organization. Although the application assembler might also be a domain expert and will understand the interfaces to the bean components, there's no requirement that they understand the implementation details of the beans being assembled. It's sufficient for the assembler to understand the interfaces and external requirements for the enterprise beans.

Generally, application assembly occurs before deployment. However, the specification does not prevent assembly from occurring after deployment. The specification committee members did this primarily so that vendors will have some flexibility with tools that are used for assembly and deployment. It is possible to modify some application assembly instructions after the beans are deployed, but generally this is done beforehand. Figure 3.2 shows the responsibilities of the application assembler.

Figure 3.2
The application assembler is responsible for assembling one or more enterprise beans into a larger set for a specific application.

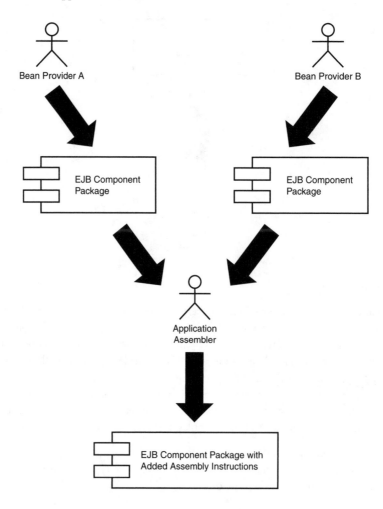

Other than the ejb-jar file that can contain enterprise beans and Java classes, there are two other types of deployment files you may use when building enterprise applications. One is called web application archive (WAR) and the other is called enterprise application archive (EAR). A WAR file contains the Web components for your application, including server-side utility classes, static Web resources such as HTML files and images, and client-side classes needed to communicate with the server application. The EAR file is a J2EE application deployment file that contains everything needed for deploying an application into a J2EE container. Because this book deals exclusively with EJB, the WAR and EAR deployment files will not be covered. Instead, we will focus exclusively on the enterprise bean deployment information in Chapter 15.

EJB DEPLOYER

The EJB deployer takes one or more of the ejb-jar files produced by the bean provider or application assembler and deploys the bean components into an EJB operational environment. The operational environment consists of the container and server. The deployer must use the specific deployment tools that are provided by the container vendor. The deployer must also understand the external dependencies that are required by each enterprise bean. Among these external dependencies are things such as database connections and JMS administration components. The deployer must also pay attention to the application assembly instructions provided in the deployment descriptor files.

The EJB deployer should be an expert with the particular operational environment and is usually responsible for mapping the security roles defined in the assembly instructions to actual groups and accounts that exist in the environment.

Usually, there are two major steps to deploying beans into an environment. The first is to use the container-specific tools to generate the necessary helper classes that are used by the container to manage the life cycle of the beans. The output of these tools varies somewhat with each vendor, but generally it's another JAR file similar to the ejb-jar file that the deployer started with. The new JAR file contains everything that the container needs to manage the bean life cycle. In smaller development shops, the bean provider might perform this step instead of the deployer.

The second step is to install the entire set of application components into the environment. You do this by placing the appropriate JAR files and classes in a vendor-specific location where the container can locate them. Each vendor is somewhat different, so check the EJB vendor's documentation for exact details on where the files need to go. Figure 3.3 shows the responsibilities for the EJB deployer.

In a typical development group, it's not uncommon to have a single developer perform the roles of the bean provider, assembler, and deployer. In fact, as you work through the examples of your own and the ones in this book, you are actually performing all three of these roles.

Figure 3.3
The EJB deployer is responsible for installing the bean components into the operational environment.

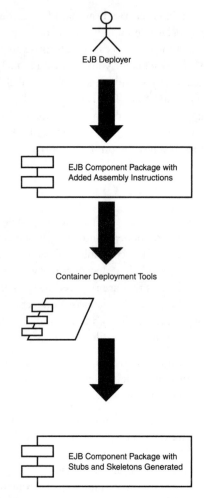

EJB Deployer

EJB Component Package with Added Assembly Instructions

Container Deployment Tools

EJB Component Package with Stubs and Skeletons Generated

EJB SERVER PROVIDER

Currently, the EJB specification does not define any specific requirements for the server provider. The specification assumes that the same vendor provides the server and the container. In the future, this might not always be the case. The server provider is responsible for low-level services such as transaction management, thread management, and middleware. It's usually more infrastructure services than bean life-cycle services. Figure 3.4 shows the relationship between the server and container.

Figure 3.4
The EJB server provider provides the server component, which handles the low-level services and management capabilities.

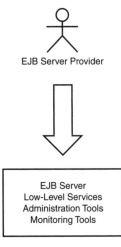

EJB Server Provider

EJB Server
Low-Level Services
Administration Tools
Monitoring Tools

EJB CONTAINER PROVIDER

The container provider is the vendor or organization that provides the necessary operational environment for your enterprise beans to function. This includes the deployment tools that were mentioned in the previous sections. In the current EJB 2.0 Specification, there really is no clear separation of server versus container responsibilities. The specification leaves it up to the EJB server and container vendors to figure out which services are managed in the server and which ones the container performs. This is not that difficult right now because vendors generally implement both as a combined set of services, and the distinction is more of a logical one than physical. However, the separation seems to be heading in the direction of the server managing the necessary infrastructure services and the container managing bean life cycle services and the component contract, as well as providing the deployment tools.

Examples of some services that the server might be responsible for are thread management, network management, and other low-level system services. Examples of services handled by the container are bean instance pools, transaction management for beans, and deployment tools. Another responsibility that the container provider might be responsible for is to provide the tools to monitor the set of installed beans and, in some cases, allow for reinstalling existing beans without stopping the server. This is often referred to as a *hot-swap* or *hot-deploy*. These examples might not hold for all vendors.

For some vendors, no real distinction is made between the server and container. Usually, the container is more of an abstraction than a physical component. Throughout this book, we will refer to the *server* and *container* as the same component and will not draw any further distinction. We will use the terms interchangeably from this point on. In the future, you might be able to buy a container separate from the server. Before that can happen, the specification will need to decide which component will implement which set of services and what the contracts between the two will be. For now, it's safe to treat the server and container as a single component that provides all the necessary EJB contract services, such as transaction and security management, distributed component support, resource management, and other system services.

As was mentioned in the beginning of this chapter, not many developers are experts at all things enterprise. The server and container providers usually are experts with system-level services. It's their job to provide a scalable, secure, transaction-aware environment and to make these low-level services readily available in a set of easy-to-use interfaces. The enterprise beans that are deployed should be insulated from any of the low-level services, and the bean provider should not have to worry about the underlying infrastructure unless it's a unique situation. Figure 3.5 shows the relationship between the EJB components and the server/container.

Figure 3.5
The EJB container provider provides the life cycle services for the enterprise components.

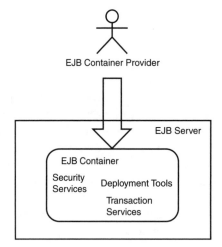

SYSTEM ADMINISTRATOR

The responsibilities of the system administrator include such things as ensuring that the EJB server is available to other network services and applications and that the EJB servers are configured correctly to handle the current and expected user loads. The administrator will typically use the monitoring tools that are provided by the server and container vendors to ensure that the EJB servers are healthy and running appropriately. The EJB specification does not specify any contracts or specific responsibilities; each organization must establish its own processes for this role. Figure 3.6 shows a typical relationship between the system administrator and the EJB environment.

Figure 3.6
The system administrator is responsible for monitoring the EJB application.

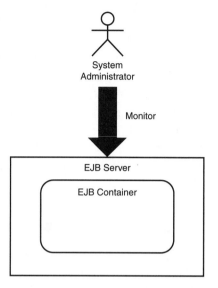

LOCAL VERSUS REMOTE EJB CLIENTS

An EJB *client* is an object that needs to interact with an enterprise bean in order for the bean to perform some service on behalf of the client. This interaction is in the form of the client invoking operations on the bean's component interface. The *component interface* of an enterprise bean defines the methods that are available for clients to invoke.

With earlier versions of the EJB specification, only invocations on a remote interface were defined. However, with the release of version 2.0, there are two types of EJB component interfaces, local and remote. Depending on your applications needs and requirements; you may choose to expose your enterprise beans to local clients, remote clients, or, in some cases, both.

LOCAL EJB CLIENTS

Local clients are always located within the same Java Virtual Machine (JVM) as the enterprise bean. The client can invoke methods on the bean, just as it would on any other Java object using normal Java method call semantics. However, exposing an enterprise bean to a local client does have a few drawbacks in terms of losing location transparency. This is due to the fact that a local client and the enterprise bean that it accesses must always be collocated. *Collocated* means that an enterprise bean and its local client must be deployed within the same JVM. However, using local clients can have positive impacts on the performance of your application. The arguments and results of method calls for local clients are passed by reference, rather than by value. This reduces the amount of network latency and overhead required to copy the arguments and results for the method's invocations. Generally, a local client of an enterprise bean will be another enterprise bean.

REMOTE EJB CLIENTS

A remote client to an enterprise bean does not have to be located within the same JVM to access the methods of the bean. It can, and usually does, reside in a different JVM on another physical machine. The remote client does not care about the physical location of the bean that it accesses. This is sometimes referred to as *location transparency*.

The remote client can be another enterprise bean residing in the same or different location, or it also can be a Web application, applet, or Java console program. The remote client can even be a non-Java program, such as a CORBA application written in C++. The client uses a special remote protocol to access the enterprise bean that is much different than the normal semantics that a local client uses. The next section describes this remote protocol in detail.

USING RMI TO COMMUNICATE WITH ENTERPRISE JAVABEANS

One of the key aspects of the EJB architecture is its distributed nature. By distributed, we mean that all the objects might not be located within the same JVM. So the question becomes, how can you invoke methods from a Java object in JVM A on a Java object in JVM B? The EJB answer is through Remote Method Invocation (RMI). RMI predates EJB and Java. In fact, it has been used by other distributed technologies, such as CORBA and DCOM. For Java, there is a specific version called Java RMI. Java RMI is a distributed object protocol that is specifically designed to allow Java objects to communicate with other Java objects residing in different Java virtual machines. Java RMI is specifically Java-to-Java remote communication. Figure 3.7 shows how a client and server use RMI to communicate.

Figure 3.7
A remote Java client communicates with a Java RMI server.

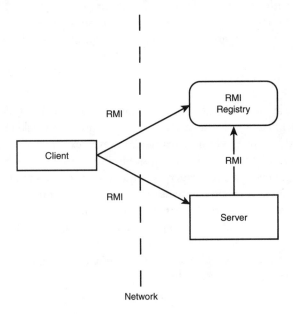

Java RMI provides transparency to the client objects making calls on remote objects so that it appears that the remote object is located within the same JVM as the client. The Java RMI protocol provides this transparency through two components, the *stub* and *skeleton*.

What Are Stubs and Skeletons?

Invoking a method call on a Java object that resides in a different JVM has much more overhead than one located within the same JVM. The client object must first be able to locate the remote object over the network and then invoke a particular method and pass along any parameters to the remote object over the network. On the server side, the object that is receiving the call must be listening for incoming requests and somehow provide for things like security and synchronous message handling so that data returned from the method or exceptions thrown by the remote object can be returned to the client. Care also has to be taken to make sure that responses to requests are returned to the correct client.

If you had to implement this functionality for your Java classes that needed to talk to remote objects, it would make for some tedious work. This would also be a waste of your time because no real business logic is happening in the remote calls. It's all code to handle the fact that you are invoking an operation on a remote object. The only thing that is really different from one remote Java class to another is the specific Java methods that are being invoked, the parameters that are passed, and the return values or exceptions thrown. Fortunately, tools can be used to inspect your classes and generate all the necessary code to handle the remote calls. This helps reduce the complexity of your classes and also decouples the business domain from the infrastructure of communicating with the remote objects. This is exactly the purpose of the stub and skeleton classes. The *stub* object is a remote proxy that is responsible for processing the remote method invocation. A *remote proxy* is an object that hides the fact that the client is communicating with a remote object and usually implements the method signatures of the remote object exactly. The stub serves as a proxy for the RMI client in the following manner:

1. Initiates a connection with the object in the remote JVM.
2. Marshals (writes and transmits) the parameters to the remote JVM.
3. Waits for the result of the method invocation.
4. Unmarshals (reads) the return value or exception returned.
5. Returns the value or exception to the caller.

The stub object exposes the same business methods and signatures as the actual remote instances. In the remote JVM, each remote object might have a corresponding skeleton object associated with it. The *skeleton* object is responsible for dispatching a client invocation to the correct remote instance. Normally there is one skeleton for every remote object. However, since the Java 2 platform was released, a skeleton is no longer necessary. This is because there can be generic code that handles the dispatching of client requests to the remote instance. However, it still helps to think of skeleton objects being used, even if the implementation can be different.

When a skeleton receives an incoming method invocation, it does the following:

1. Unmarshals (reads) the parameters for the remote method.

2. Invokes the method on the actual remote object implementation.

3. Marshals (writes and transmits) the result (return value or exception) to the caller.

For every enterprise bean that is made available to remote clients, a stub and possibly a skeleton object are created. The stub and skeleton are normally created at the time that a bean is deployed into the container and must be done with the tools provided by the vendor. How the container uses the stub and skeleton to handle the remote method invocation or whether there is a skeleton object created at all, depends on the vendor. As a bean provider or assembler, you should not have to worry about how it works, unless you are the curious type. If you are the curious type, we'll give a brief example of what takes place during a remote method invocation. To keep things simple for now, we'll show an example using Java RMI over Java Remote Method Protocol (JRMP). As we'll see later in this chapter, Java RMI can also use the Object Management Group's (OMG) Internet Inter-Orb Protocol (IIOP) as the communication protocol. This small example should be enough to give you the idea of how RMI is generally done. You'll see examples of using RMI/IIOP throughout the book.

We are going to create a remote object that implements an interface with just one method. Listing 3.1 shows the Java interface for which our remote object will provide an implementation.

LISTING 3.1 A REMOTE INTERFACE THAT THE REMOTE OBJECT WILL IMPLEMENT

```
import java.rmi.Remote;
import java.rmi.RemoteException;

public interface RMIExample extends Remote {
  public String getMessage() throws RemoteException;
}
```

The only method that is declared by our RMI interface is the getMessage method. Notice that the interface extends the java.rmi.Remote interface. Also, because calling remote methods can fail in ways that are not possible with local method calls due to network issues, all methods defined in a Remote interface must include java.rmi.RemoteException in their throws clause.

Next, we need to provide a class that implements the remote interface. This is our remote object that eventually will receive the remote method invocation from the client. Listing 3.2 shows the remote object.

LISTING 3.2 THE REMOTE OBJECT FOR OUR EXAMPLE

```
Import java.rmi.*;
import java.rmi.RemoteException;
import java.rmi.server.UnicastRemoteObject;

public class RMIExampleImpl extends UnicastRemoteObject
  implements RMIExample {

    public RMIExampleImpl() throws RemoteException  {
      super();
    }

    public String getMessage() {
      return "Hello from the RMI Server";
    }
}
```

Listing 3.2 is fairly straightforward. It extends `java.rmi.server.UnicastRemoteObject`, which is a class that takes care of many of the complex network issues for you.

> **Note**
>
> Remember for this example, we are showing Java RMI using JRMP as the communication protocol. *JRMP* is the default communications or "wire" protocol for allowing remote Java objects to communicate. Later in this chapter, you'll see an example of Java RMI using the IIOP protocol. This is the protocol that EJB uses by default.

The `RMIExampleImpl` class also implements the `RMIExample` interface and provides the required `getMessage` method by just returning a Hello World kind of string. Notice that the implementation does not throw the `RemoteException`. The network and marshalling aspects of the remote call are handled by the stub or skeleton object. In Java, you can't add any new exceptions to an interface method, but you can take them away as this example did.

Now, it's time to take a look at what the stub and skeleton classes would look like for this example. Be warned, it will not be pretty, but that's acceptable because you rarely have to look at or be concerned about them. If you run the `rmic` tool that comes with the Java SDK (it's located in the `bin` directory of the base Java home directory), the stub and skeleton classes will be generated. The `rmic` compiler generates stub and skeleton class files for remote objects from the names of compiled Java classes that contain remote object implementations. A remote object is one that implements the interface `java.rmi.Remote`. The classes named in the `rmic` command must be classes that have been compiled successfully with the `javac` command and must be fully qualified. Be sure to use the `-keep` option if you want the `rmic` tool to provide you with the source files as well as the class files.

Listing 3.3 shows the stub that gets generated, and Listing 3.4 shows the skeleton class. We have modified the format to make it fit a little cleaner on the written page.

Listing 3.3   Stub Class for `RMIExampleImpl` Class

```
// Stub class generated by rmic, do not edit.
// Contents subject to change without notice.
import java.rmi.*;

public final class RMIExampleImpl_Stub
    extends java.rmi.server.RemoteStub
    implements RMIExample, java.rmi.Remote
{
    private static final java.rmi.server.Operation[] operations = {
    new java.rmi.server.Operation("java.lang.String getMessage()")
    };

    private static final long interfaceHash = 6819080097909274298L;

    private static final long serialVersionUID = 2;

    private static boolean useNewInvoke;
    private static java.lang.reflect.Method $method_getMessage_0;

    static {
    try {
        java.rmi.server.RemoteRef.class.getMethod("invoke",
        new java.lang.Class[] {
            java.rmi.Remote.class,
            java.lang.reflect.Method.class,
            java.lang.Object[].class,
            long.class
        });
        useNewInvoke = true;
        $method_getMessage_0 =
            RMIExample.class.getMethod("getMessage", new java.lang.Class[] {});
    } catch (java.lang.NoSuchMethodException e) {
        useNewInvoke = false;
    }
    }

    // constructors
    public RMIExampleImpl_Stub() {
    super();
    }
    public RMIExampleImpl_Stub(java.rmi.server.RemoteRef ref) {
    super(ref);
    }

    // methods from remote interfaces

    // implementation of getMessage()
    public java.lang.String getMessage()
    throws java.rmi.RemoteException
```

Listing 3.3   Continued

```
    {
    try {
        if (useNewInvoke) {
        Object $result =
          ref.invoke(this, $method_getMessage_0, null, 5353407034680111516L);
        return ((java.lang.String) $result);
        } else {
        java.rmi.server.RemoteCall call =
          ref.newCall((java.rmi.server.RemoteObject) this,
                      operations, 0, interfaceHash);

        ref.invoke(call);
        java.lang.String $result;
        try {
            java.io.ObjectInput in = call.getInputStream();
            $result = (java.lang.String) in.readObject();
        } catch (java.io.IOException e) {
            throw new UnmarshalException("error unmarshalling return", e);
        } catch (java.lang.ClassNotFoundException e) {
            throw new UnmarshalException("error unmarshalling return", e);
        } finally {
            ref.done(call);
        }
        return $result;
        }
    } catch (java.lang.RuntimeException e) {
        throw e;
    } catch (java.rmi.RemoteException e) {
        throw e;
    } catch (java.lang.Exception e) {
        throw new UnexpectedException("undeclared checked exception", e);
    }
    }
}
```

Listing 3.4   Skeleton Class for RMIExampleImpl Class

```
// Skeleton class generated by rmic, do not edit.
// Contents subject to change without notice.
import java.rmi.server.*;

public final class RMIExampleImpl_Skel
    implements java.rmi.server.Skeleton
{
    private static final java.rmi.server.Operation[] operations = {
    new java.rmi.server.Operation("java.lang.String getMessage()")
    };

    private static final long interfaceHash = 6819080097909274298L;

    public java.rmi.server.Operation[] getOperations() {
    return (java.rmi.server.Operation[]) operations.clone();
    }
```

LISTING 3.4   CONTINUED

```java
public void dispatch(java.rmi.Remote obj,
        java.rmi.server.RemoteCall call, int opnum, long hash)
throws java.lang.Exception
{
if (opnum < 0) {
    if (hash == 5353407034680111516L) {
    opnum = 0;
    } else {
    throw new java.rmi.UnmarshalException("invalid method hash");
    }
} else {
    if (hash != interfaceHash)
    throw new SkeletonMismatchException("interface hash mismatch");
}

RMIExampleImpl server = (RMIExampleImpl) obj;
switch (opnum) {
case 0: // getMessage()
{
    call.releaseInputStream();
    java.lang.String $result = server.getMessage();
    try {
    java.io.ObjectOutput out = call.getResultStream(true);
    out.writeObject($result);
    } catch (java.io.IOException e) {
    throw new java.rmi.MarshalException("error marshalling return", e);
    }
    break;
}

default:
    throw new java.rmi.UnmarshalException("invalid method number");
}
}
}
```

We warned you that it wasn't going to be pretty. There's quite a bit going on in these two classes. We are not going to go through them, but take a look at the stub class and see if you can see how it's invoking the method on the remote object. Then take a look at the skeleton and see if you see how it determines which method to call and how it returns the results from the method call back to the remote client. Again, the details are not as important as the fact that you realize that something is going on behind the scenes when a client invokes a method on a remote object. It's enough that you understand that a stub object, and in some cases, a skeleton, are working on your behalf to help complete the remote method invocation. Again, since Java 2, skeletons are not always implemented. However, there's still code on the server side to handle the dispatching of client requests.

Even though each EJB vendor may implement RMI for EJB slightly different from other vendors, and even though the container is in the middle of all this, the concepts are still the same. The client makes a call-by-reference onto a remote interface, which is implemented by a stub object, which is located in the same JVM as the client. The stub class determines which method needs to be invoked on the remote object and packages all the parameter data up so that it can be marshaled across the network. A skeleton object, or some alternative to a skeleton object, receives the call and gets it routed to an appropriate remote object. As you'll see in the next sections, there's a little more to RMI with EJB, but it's pretty much the same idea.

When doing Java RMI, you must create an interface that describes all the business methods that will be called on the remote object. This is what we called the component interface from the previous section. In the case of RMI, the component interface is a remote interface. This interface serves as a contract between the remote calling client and the server object that is receiving the message and servicing the request. The container also uses this component interface to build the stub and skeleton objects for your bean. This interface describes the client/server contract in terms of what methods might be invoked by a client. The stub is a Java class that implements the remote interface and is typically generated by the vendor tools during deployment. The remote interface and the stub object that implements it serve as a remote proxy for the client. All calls that the client makes on the remote interface are really handled by the stub class and are sent across the network to the server implementation.

The most important aspect to take away from this section is that when you invoke a method call on an EJB object from a remote client, you are not invoking a call on the real bean instance directly. The manner in which the vendor implements stubs and skeletons has much to do with this. This allows the vendor to do optimizations for better performance and scalability. Figure 3.8 shows how a typical EJB application uses RMI.

Figure 3.8
An EJB client uses RMI to communicate with enterprise beans.

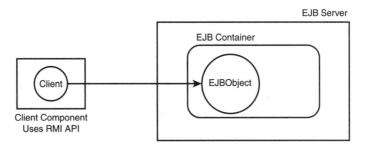

For more information on Java RMI, check the Sun documentation at

`http://java.sun.com/j2se/1.3/docs/guide/rmi`

There is also a good tutorial on Java RMI at the same location.

PART

I

CH

3

USING RMI OVER IIOP

One of the main issues with Java's version of RMI is that a JVM must be running on both the client and the server. It's dependent on Java being the language for the application on the client and the server. With the amount of so-called *legacy* systems that are written in other languages like C++, Java needs a way to communicate with these systems. As you read earlier in this chapter, Java RMI uses JRMP by default. It would be nice if a different communication protocol could be used to allow for more flexibility and interoperability.

Enter RMI over IIOP (RMI/IIOP). By using this protocol rather than JRMP, developers can write remote interfaces between clients and servers of different languages and vendors and implement them using only Java technology and the Java RMI APIs. The developer uses the RMI API and then takes advantage of the IIOP protocol to communicate with remote objects. It uses the best features of Java RMI and the Common Object Request Broker Architecture (CORBA) and helps speed application development by allowing the Java developer to work completely with the Java language.

Unlike CORBA, there is no Interface Definition Language (IDL) or mapping to learn for RMI over IIOP, so it's easier and faster to start developing than CORBA. Like Java RMI, RMI over IIOP allows developers to pass any serializable object to distributed components through pass-by-value methods. With RMI over IIOP, developers create Java interfaces and provide an implementation in other languages that support the OMG mapping and provide an Object Request Broker (ORB). Objects can be passed by value or by reference using RMI over IIOP. Figure 3.9 shows how RMI is used over the IIOP protocol.

Figure 3.9
You can use RMI
on top of the IIOP
protocol for better
interoperability.

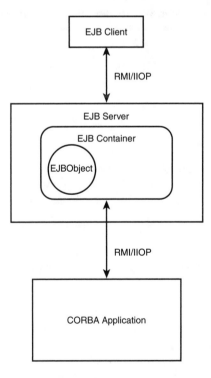

To round out our discussion of RMI, we'll provide a very basic example of using RMI over IIOP. We'll use the same example remote interface from Listing 3.1. Our new remote object will have to make some changes to accommodate the IIOP way of doing things. For our RMI implementation class, this means that instead of extending `UnicastRemoteObject`, it must extend `javax.rmi.PortableRemoteObject`. Listing 3.5 shows the small changes necessary to the implementation class.

LISTING 3.5   THE RMI IMPLEMENTATION CLASS FOR RMI/IIOP

```
import java.rmi.RemoteException;

public class RMIUsingIIOPExampleImpl extends javax.rmi.PortableRemoteObject
  implements RMIExample {

    public RMIUsingIIOPExampleImpl() throws RemoteException  {
      super();
    }

    public String getMessage() {
      return "Hello from the RMI Server";
    }
}
```

PART

I

CH

3

The other required changes must be made in the server startup class that first creates an instance of the remote server object from Listing 3.5. The main difference there is that instead of using RMI's `rebind` method to bind an instance of the remote object to the RMI registry, you should use something like Java Naming and Directory Interface (JNDI) to bind an instance of the remote object to the JNDI tree. The last minor changes are required to the client that is looking up and invoking operations on the remote object. The following code fragment illustrates the code inside the client application:

```
// Create a hashtable to store the jndi properties
Hashtable env = new Hashtable();
env.put("java.naming.factory.initial",
        "com.sun.jndi.cosnaming.CNCtxFactory");
env.put("java.naming.provider.url", "iiop://<hostname>:900");
// Create an initial context
Context ic = new InitialContext(env);

RMIExample obj = (RMIExample)PortableRemoteObject.narrow(
                 initialNamingContext.lookup("RemoteObject"),
                 RMIExample.class);

// invoke the remote operation
String msg = obj.getMessage();
```

The main difference to pick up on between a RMI client that uses JRMP and one that uses IIOP is that you must use the static `narrow` method on the `PortableRemoteObject` before you attempt to cast the object returned to the remote interface type. The reason for this is that, with JRMP, you are assured that both the client and server are written in Java and you can simply use a Java cast. However, with IIOP the server might be a CORBA C++ component and you will need to narrow the object type to one of the proper class before you use Java's cast operator. With EJB applications where the client and server are both written in Java and the remote interface object is already an instance of the correct type, the narrow method might just return the object directly. However, you should always use the narrow method before using the Java cast operator.

> **Tip**
>
> Local EJB clients don't have to use the narrow method on the PortableRemoteObject. They are free to use the normal Java cast operator because the local client and the enterprise bean must be collocated within the same JVM.

This code fragment exposes some new information that is not covered until Chapter 4, "Java Naming and Directory Interface," so don't worry too much about trying to understand it. There will be plenty of time for that in Chapter 4.

You can get more information on RMI over IIOP at Sun's Web site at

http://java.sun.com/products/rmi-iiop

ACCESSING AN EJB THROUGH ITS COMPONENT INTERFACE

As you saw earlier in this chapter, when accessing an enterprise bean, a client always uses the component interface to invoke operations on the bean. The type of interface depends on whether you are using local or remote clients to access the bean.

If local clients will be accessing your enterprise bean, you must create an interface that extends the javax.ejb.EJBLocalObject interface. This interface provides the local client view of the EJB object and defines the business methods that are available to the local client. Table 3.1 displays the methods defined in the EJBLocalObject interface.

TABLE 3.1   THE METHODS DEFINED IN THE EJBLocalObject INTERFACE

Return	Method	Description
EJBLocalHome	getEJBLocalHome	Obtain the enterprise bean's local home interface.
Object	getPrimaryKey	Obtain the primary key of the EJB local object.
boolean	isIdentical	Test whether a given EJB local object is identical to the invoked EJB local object.
void	remove	Remove the EJB local object.

On the other hand, if your enterprise bean will be accessed by remote clients, the component interface for the bean must extend the `javax.ejb.EJBObject` interface.

Table 3.2 displays the methods defined in the `EJBObject` interface.

TABLE 3.2   THE METHODS DEFINED IN THE `EJBObject` INTERFACE

Return Type	Method	Description
`EJBHome`	`getEJBHome`	Obtain the enterprise bean's remote home interface.
`Handle`	`getHandle`	Obtain a `Handle` for the EJB object.
`Object`	`getPrimaryKey`	Obtain the primary key of the EJB object.
`boolean`	`isIdentical`	Test whether a given EJB object is identical to the invoked EJB object.
`void`	`remove`	Remove the EJB remote object.

Note

Some of the methods in Table 3.2 have different behaviors depending on which type of enterprise bean it's invoked on. For example, session beans do not have a primary key, so the `getPrimaryKey` method would not be valid to call on it. Also, the `remove` method acts differently whether you are calling it on a session bean or an entity bean. Don't worry if this doesn't makes sense yet, it will shortly. It's enough to realize for now that methods called on enterprise beans can act differently depending on the type of enterprise bean.

The enterprise bean class does not actually implement its own component interface, but it must contain the same business methods that the component interface defines. You probably are wondering why this is. There are two key reasons for this behavior.

The first reason is that the component interface either extends the `EJBLocalObject` interface or `EJBOjbect` interface, depending on the type of client. Both of these interfaces contain method signatures that should be handled by the container and not the bean instance itself. Take another look at the method signatures in Tables 3.1 and 3.2. If an enterprise bean implemented the component interface directly, it would have to define these methods in the bean class. The container will never invoke these methods if they're implemented by the instance.

The second reason why a bean should not implement its component interface has to do with letting the compiler help you detect when you are incorrectly passing references to the bean instances in method calls or as return values. As it was mentioned at the top of this section, EJB clients should never access the enterprise bean instance directly. Instead, clients should always perform method calls on the component interface. This ensures that the container performs all system-level services, such as transactions, concurrency, and security, before the bean instance is called. If a client, whether local or remote client, made a call directly to the bean instance, these services would be bypassed. To prevent this from happening, your bean class should not implement the component interface. This way, if you were to pass your bean instance, rather than the object that implements the component interface to another object, the compiler will catch it because it would be the incorrect type.

To get the object that implements your component interface, you can get it from either the `javax.ejb.SessionContext` or the `javax.ejb.EntityContext`, depending on your enterprise bean type. Both interfaces have the methods `getEJBLocalObject` and `getEJBObject`, which return an instance of the local or remote interface respectively.

→ It sounds confusing that a bean should not implement its own component interface, but it will be explained further in Chapter 16, "Patterns and Strategies in EJB Design." If you just can't wait, **see** "Using a Business Method Interface," **p. 448**.

With all this talk of the local and remote component interfaces, maybe it would help to see a small example of each. Listings 3.6 and 3.7 show examples of using a local and remote interface, respectively, for an enterprise bean called `OrderFulfillmentProcessorBean`.

Both interfaces declare a single method called `completeOrder`. This is the only method available to the client for this basic example.

LISTING 3.6   THE LOCAL INTERFACE FOR AN `OrderFulfillmentProcessorBean`

```
import javax.ejb.EJBLocalObject;

public interface OrderFulfillmentProcessorLocal extends EJBLocalObject {
  /**
    * Completes an order and prepares it for shipping.
    *
    * @param orderId      String Order identifier
    * @return             void
    */
public void completeOrder (String orderId);
}
```

Notice how the component interface for the local client extends the `EJBLocalObject` interface in Listing 3.6. On the other hand, the remote interface for the same enterprise bean extends the `EJBObject` interface. You can see this in Listing 3.7.

LISTING 3.7   THE REMOTE INTERFACE FOR AN `OrderFulfillmentProcessorBean`

```
import java.rmi.RemoteException;
import javax.ejb.EJBObject;

public interface OrderFulfillmentProcessor extends EJBObject {
  /**
    * Completes an order and prepares it for shipping.
    *
    * @param orderId      String Order identifier
```

LISTING 3.7   CONTINUED

```
 * @return              void
 * @exception           RemoteException if there is
 *                      a communications or systems failure
 */
public void completeOrder (String orderId) throws RemoteException;
}
```

The EJB specification describes the EJBLocalObject and EJBObject interfaces and indicates that the container generates an object that implements one of these interfaces for every bean instance, depending on the type of client accessing the bean instance. The container performs the prerequisite services, such as checking security, possibly starting a transaction, getting an instance of the bean from the pool, and so on. The vendors have some flexibility in how they implement this functionality. A question that comes up very often is, does the container create an EJBLocalObject or EJBObject for every bean instance? If it does, how will an EJB application scale? Well, the answer to this question is the one that EJB developers hear all the time, it depends on the vendor's implementation.

For example, the EJB servers from JBoss and Sybase don't create EJBObjects at all. The container intercepts the call from the stub using a type of dispatch design (like the dispatcher from OMG's portable object adapter [POA] specification) and handles the call without using an EJBObject for the bean. If there are 10,000 clients, there will not be 10,000 EJBObjects. In fact, there might be no EBObjects at all with certain vendors. Of course these are details that a typical EJB developer should not be concerned with, other than evaluating performance results for the vendor. The point to get clear is that certain concepts that seem concrete in the EJB specification are meant to be abstract, and the vendors have wiggle room to optimize as they see fit.

LOCATING ENTERPRISE BEANS USING THE HOME INTERFACE

Before a client can invoke a method on the enterprise bean's component interface, it must first obtain a reference to the object that implements this interface. The component that is responsible for creating instances of the component interface for an enterprise bean is the bean's home interface. This is the other Java interface that must be created for every enterprise bean you deploy.

Every enterprise bean that is exposed to a client has a home interface. As you'll see in Chapter 11, the message-driven bean is not exposed to a client directly and has no component interface. It therefore does not need a home interface. An enterprise bean's home interface defines the methods that allow clients to create, find, and remove EJB objects. Depending on whether the client will be a local client or a remote client, the home interface must extend one of two interfaces.

If you are building a home interface for local clients, you must create an interface that extends the `javax.ejb.EJBLocalHome` interface. There is only one method defined by the `EJBLocalHome` interface, which is the `remove method`. The remove method for the `EJBLocalHome` interface is used only for entity beans however, because this version takes a primary key. Calling this method on a home interface for a session bean will result in a `javax.ejb.RemoveException` being thrown. The `remove` method on the `EJBLocalHome` interface is a convenience method so that a client can remove an entity bean without acquiring a reference to its component interface.

Tip

> As shown in Tables 3.1 and 3.2, the `EJBLocalObject` and `EJBObject` interfaces also contain a remove method that can be called, regardless of the type of EJB.

If the enterprise bean is intended for a remote client, the home interface should extend the `javax.ejb.EJBHome` interface. Table 3.3 describes the method signatures in the `EJBHome` interface.

TABLE 3.3   THE METHODS DEFINED IN THE `javax.ejb.EJBHome` INTERFACE

Return	Method	Description
EJBMetaData	getEJBMetaData	Obtain the `EJBMetaData` interface for the enterprise bean.
HomeHandle	getHomeHandle	Get the `HomeHandle` for the home object.
void	remove(Handle handle)	Remove the EJB object identified by its `Handle`.
void	remove(Object key)	Remove the EJB object identified by the primary key. This will work only for entity beans.

Note

> If you're wondering why you don't see methods such as `create` or `find` in either the local or remote home interfaces, there's a very good reason for this. It's because each `create` or `find` method can take different parameters in its method signature. There's no way to standardize on a set of `create` or `find` methods that will work in all situations. EJB developers need the flexibility to pass whatever arguments they need into the `create` or `find` methods to create or locate a bean instance.

Continuing with our `OrderFulfillment` example from earlier in the chapter, Listings 3.8 and 3.9 illustrate examples of a local and a remote interface, respectively.

LISTING 3.8   THE LOCAL HOME INTERFACE FOR `OrderFulfillmentProcessorBean`

```
import javax.ejb.CreateException;
import javax.ejb.EJBLocalHome;

public interface OrderFulfillmentProcessorHomeLocal extends EJBLocalHome {
  /**
   * This method corresponds to the ejbCreate method in the bean
   * "OrderFulfillmentProcessorBean.java".
   * The parameter sets of the two methods are identical. When the client calls
   * <code>OrderFulfillmentProcessorHome.create()</code>, the container
   * allocates an instance of the EJBean and calls <code>ejbCreate()</code>.
   *
   * @return              OrderFulfillmentProcessor
   * @exception           CreateException
   *                      if there is a problem creating the bean
   */
  OrderFulfillmentProcessor create() throws CreateException;
}
```

PART

I

CH

3

LISTING 3.9   THE REMOTE HOME INTERFACE FOR `OrderFulfillmentProcessorBean`

```
import javax.ejb.CreateException;
import javax.ejb.EJBHome;

public interface OrderFulfillmentProcessorHome extends EJBHome {
  /**
   * This method corresponds to the ejbCreate method in the bean
   * "OrderFulfillmentProcessor.java".
   * The parameter sets of the two methods are identical. When the client calls
   * <code>OrderFulfillmentProcessorHome.create()</code>, the container
   * allocates an instance of the EJBean and calls <code>ejbCreate()</code>.
   *
   * @return              OrderFulfillmentProcessor
   * @exception           CreateException
   *                      if there is a problem creating the bean
   */
  OrderFulfillmentProcessor create() throws CreateException;
}
```

Notice that the main difference between the two types of home interfaces is that the local home extends `EJBLocalHome` and the remote home extends `EJBHome`.

The home interface for an enterprise can declare zero or more `create` methods, one for each way an instance of the bean can be initialized. The arguments of the create methods typically are used to initialize the state of the created object.

The session bean home interface must define at least one `create` method, whereas the entity bean is not required to.

Just as with the component interface for an enterprise bean, the container will create an implementation object that implements the home interface of the enterprise bean.

The purpose of the home object is to provide a factory for creating objects that implement the component interface. There is typically only a single home object for a particular bean class. Because it's a factory, all clients can go through this factory to acquire a reference to a bean that the `home factory` is for. The container generates an object that implements your home interface and which provides a concrete implementation for clients to use. The home interface manages the life cycle of all instances of a particular bean. When client A needs to get a reference to an instance of the `OrderFulfillmentProcessorBean`, it asks the home object for that bean to do so. When client B asks for a different instance, the same home object does the work. Different home factories are used for local and remote client views, however.

DECIDING WHETHER TO USE A LOCAL OR REMOTE CLIENT

Because the local component interface is new to the EJB 2.0 Specification, we can't really say that there's years of practical experience that you can leverage when determining whether an enterprise bean should be exposed to a local client view or a remote. It really depends on many different factors, all of which are specific to your particular application.

However, there are some truths about each type of component interface that might help provide some guidelines when trying to decide. The following sections describe some of the more important characteristics about each type of component interface.

THE LOCAL MODEL NORMALLY WILL PROVIDE BETTER PERFORMANCE

Remote method calls typically are very expensive and usually are performed with *coarse-grained access*. Course-grained access is where objects attempt to expose a larger set of data with a smaller number of method invocations. This is done when the cost of invoking the method is very expensive, normally due to network-related issues.

Because local calls are within the same JVM, they can take advantage of pass-by-reference and not suffer the performance disadvantages of pass-by-value semantics.

Remote calls also can suffer network latency, overhead of the client and server software stacks, argument copying, and other RMI issues. Local clients don't have to deal with any of these problems and, therefore, typically perform better.

FINE-GRAINED ACCESS IS BETTER WITH THE LOCAL MODEL

As mentioned previously, remote method access can be very expensive. Therefore, a remote client typically will want to get all the data it needs from the remote object with one call. Because local clients don't have the same performance disadvantage when invoking operations, they can afford to use more of a fine-grained access and not worry about making more than a single call on the enterprise bean.

THE REMOTE MODEL PROVIDES BETTER LOCATION TRANSPARENCY

With the remote programming model, no assumption is made about the location of the enterprise bean, with respect to the client. Local clients must be located within the same JVM as the enterprise bean, but this is not true of remote clients. Therefore, the deployment considerations for enterprise beans that are accessed by remote clients are much simpler. Local clients must be deployed within the same container as the enterprise beans they access. This is not true of remote clients.

REMOTE CLIENTS MUST DEAL WITH REMOTE EXCEPTIONS

Because many things can go wrong when accessing a remote object, a remote client must be prepared to handle these exceptions. Things such as communication loss due to network errors are unexpected, but can happen nevertheless with the remote model. Local clients don't have to handle remote exceptions and, therefore, are a little less complicated from an error-handling standpoint.

CREATION AND REMOVAL OF EJBS

Creating instances of enterprise beans is much different that creating regular Java objects where all the objects reside in the same JVM. The container steps in and performs many system services when a bean is instantiated. In fact, the container might not need to even create a new bean, but rather pull an existing one from a bean pool or possibly from another user if resources are limited. To create a new bean, or really to obtain a local or remote reference to a new bean, you must go through the home interface. After a client has located an enterprise bean's home interface, the client can get a reference to an instance of the enterprise bean by using one of the `create` methods on the home interface. For example, assuming that the home interface for the `OrderFulfillmentProcessorBean` has already been located, the following code fragment shows how you can create a remote reference:

```
// Other code here to lookup the home interface
OrderFulfillmentProcessor remoteProcessor = null;
remoteProcessor = orderFulfillmentProcessorHome.create();
```

The `create` method on the `OrderFulfillmentProcessorHome` returns a remote interface reference to the new enterprise bean instance. Remember that the enterprise bean that the remote reference points to might have come from an object pool. It's entirely up to the container whether it creates a new object or pulls one from somewhere else. There's no requirement that the container create a new instance of the bean when a client calls one of the create methods, just as long as the client gets a valid reference. In fact, some containers might not even prepare a bean for the client when a create method is called. In some vendor's products, an instance of the bean might not even be prepared for the client until the client makes the first remote method call.

→   In the previous example, the details of how to locate a home interface for an enterprise bean were not shown. For information on how to obtain a home interface for an enterprise bean, **see** "Locating EJB Objects," **p. 97**.

To remove instances of your enterprise beans, you should use one of the several remove methods available through the home or component interfaces. Which version of the remove method you use depends on which type of enterprise bean you are using and also whether you have a reference to the home or remote component interface. Both the entity bean and session bean interfaces support a no-argument remove method from the component interface. You can also call one of several remove methods on the home interface for your enterprise bean. You can pass the handle in the remove method for either the session bean or the entity bean. Also for the entity bean, you can pass in the primary key for the bean that you want to remove. For both types of enterprise beans, the remove method might not actually remove the object and free the memory for the object because the enterprise bean might just be put back into the bean pool. Whether or not the removed bean is truly removed or just put back into the pool is entirely up to the container implementation.

Caution

A javax.ejb.RemoveException will be thrown if you call the remove method that takes a primary key for a session bean. The reason that it's even there is because both the entity bean and session bean home interfaces share javax.ejb.EJBHome as the interface for their homes, and this method is defined there.

PASSIVATION AND ACTIVATION

Because resources for the container are finite, it might become necessary for the container to temporarily remove enterprise bean objects to a secondary storage so that the resources the enterprise bean were using can be reclaimed and used for something else. This process of removing EJBs from the container is known as *passivation* and when the server brings the EJB back into memory from secondary storage, this is known as *activation*.

Passivation and activation can happen as part of the container's normal resource management policy. The container doesn't have to be out of resources for passivation to occur for a bean. In fact, to prevent ever getting close to being out of resources, the container can initiate this action on one or more idle enterprise beans. When and under what circumstances this will occur is totally up to the container and vendor implementation. However, the container is not permitted to passivate a bean that is within a current transaction or when a bean is servicing a client. If the container were allowed to passivate beans that were in the middle of a transaction or in a business method for a client, this would most likely cause the database or application to be put into an unpredictable state, so this is prevented by the specification.

Although vendors have flexibility on how they persist the state of an EJB object during passivation, the passivation mechanism by an EJB server must follow the rules of Java serialization. This is in case serialization is used to passivate the objects. This will help ensure portability across EJB vendors. The rules also include ones that normally apply to transient fields on a serializable object. Bean providers should assume that transient fields would not be saved during passivation and activation.

All entity and session beans are required to implement the `ejbPassivate` and `ejbActivate` methods. These methods are declared in the `javax.ejb.EntityBean` and `javax.ejb.SessionBean` interfaces. The method `ejbPassivate` is called right before the container removes the bean instance from memory or returns it back to a pool. You'll see more on what pools are used for in the next section. The method `ejbActivate` is called after the EJB object is re-created and before any client invocations occur on it.

When the `ejbPassivate` method is complete, the bean provider must ensure that the bean is ready to be stored by the container. This means that all external resources held by the bean (like JDBC connections or client sockets) must be released and cleaned up.

Note

For references that hold on to JDBC connections and other external resources, you should also set the instance fields storing these references to `null`.

Also, all instance fields must be ready for serialization. Objects that are held by the bean that is going to be passivated must be one of the following for passivation to work:

- A serializable object
- Null
- A reference to an enterprise bean's component interface
- A reference to an enterprise bean's home interface
- A reference to the `SessionContext` object
- A reference to the environment-naming context
- A reference to the `UserTransaction` interface
- A reference to a resource manager connection factory
- An object that is not initially serializable but acquires the ability to be serializable based on the home and component references serialization process

> We have not discussed what a SessionContext or UserTransaction is yet, but
> don't worry if these terms don't make sense. We formally introduce SessionContext
> in Chapter 9 and UserTransaction in Chapter 12.

Because the ejbPassivate and ejbActive methods reside in interfaces that your bean must
implement, these methods must be implemented in every bean. In cases where you're not
holding onto resources within your bean instance that must be maintained during passivation and activation, you won't need to do anything during these methods. However, you are
still required to have the callback methods in your beans. In the cases where you don't need
to do anything, you can just provide empty methods. The class in Listing 3.10 provides
empty implementations for the passivation and activation methods.

LISTING 3.10   EXAMPLE BEAN IMPLEMENTING ejbPassivate AND ejbActive METHODS

```java
import javax.ejb.CreateException;
import javax.ejb.SessionBean;
import javax.ejb.SessionContext;
import javax.ejb.*;

public class OrderFulfillmentProcessorBean implements SessionBean {

  private SessionContext ctx;
  /**
   * This method is required by the EJB Specification,
   * but is not used by this example.
   *
   */
  public void ejbActivate() {
  }
  /**
   * This method is required by the EJB Specification,
   * but is not used by this example.
   *
   */
  public void ejbRemove() {
  }
  /**
   * This method is required by the EJB Specification,
   * but is not used by this example.
   *
   */
  public void ejbPassivate() {
  }

  /**
   * Sets the session context.
   *
   * @param ctx   SessionContext Context for session
   */
```

LISTING 3.10   CONTINUED

```
public void setSessionContext(SessionContext ctx) {
  this.ctx = ctx;
}
/**
 * Complete the customer's order and prepare for shipping
 *
 * @param orderId      Unqiue Order identified
 * @return             void
 *
 */
public  void completeOrder (String orderId) {
  // Do something in this method to complete the order
}

}
```

Note

> You should also be aware that there are other callback methods required by the container in your enterprise beans. A session bean must also implement the `ejbRemove` and `setSessionContext` methods, for example. You can provide an empty implementation for the `ejbRemove` method if you don't need to do anything special, but you should set the `SessionContext` reference passed to your bean to an instance variable in your bean. The `SessionContext` provides access to the container's environment.

PART

I

CH

3

OBJECT POOLING

As it has been mentioned several times in the previous sections, EJB containers can use object pools to keep from having to create new enterprise bean instances when a client asks for one. The container has the flexibility to create instances ahead of time and put them into a pool of ready objects. When a client invokes a `create` method on a home interface, the container may pull an instance from the pool and call a few service methods on the instance to prepare it and then allow the instance to be used by the client. The service methods depend on the type of enterprise bean, but usually include giving the enterprise bean an `EJBContext` object, which gives the enterprise bean access to the container's runtime environment. When a client calls one of the `remove` methods, the instance may be placed back into the pool so it can be reused for another client.

This is a very common pattern for optimizing performance of regularly used resources. By using an object pool, the container does not continue to create new instances of objects and then have to garbage collect them later. It maintains the life cycle of these beans to save performance and cleanup. You as a bean provider do not need to be concerned with this behavior, except to understand there is really no connection between when a `create` method is called and when the container performs a `newInstance` call on an enterprise bean.

HANDLES

Handles in EJB provide a mechanism to store a reference to a remote home or a remote interface to a long-term persistent store and later re-acquire that reference back to the same home or remote object. Because handles only relate to remote objects, local clients are not exposed to handles and have no need for them.

Two types of handles are defined in the EJB 2.0 Specification. One is the `javax.ejb.Handle` interface and the other is `javax.ejb.HomeHandle` interface. You might wonder if the `HomeHandle` interface extends the `Handle` interface, but it doesn't. In the same way that there is no direct relationship between a home and remote interface, a `HomeHandle` and a `Handle` are not directly related. Here is the single method signature for the `Handle` interface:

```
public EJBObject getEJBObject() throws java.rmi.RemoteException;
```

and here is the method signature for the `HomeHandle` interface:

```
public EJBHome getEJBHome() throws java.rmi.RemoteException;
```

Although you might be tempted to share a handle for one client with another client, you must be careful. If for example, you shared a handle to a session bean between two clients and the clients attempted to invoke operations on the same instance at the same time, an exception will occur. The safest thing to do is to only use handles to save access for a specific client so that the same client can access the instance at a later time. `Handle` and `HomeHandle` references can be serialized and deserialized, and therefore are valid RMI types.

Handles really will work this way only if the object that they are referencing in the container is still available when a client attempts to use the reference later. A server crash or timeout might have removed the object and made it unavailable.

The following code fragment illustrates how you can use a Handle to obtain a remote reference:

```
public void loadShoppingCart( Handle handle ) {
    // The handle is a javax.ejb.Handle that has been created
    // by another client and passed in.

    ShoppingCart otherCart = null;
    // Get a remote interface reference to the shopping cart
    otherCart = (ShoppingCart)javax.rmi.PortableRemoteObject.narrow(
                                              handle.getEJBObject(),
                                              ShoppingCart.class );

    // Invoke a method call on the remote reference
    List shoppingCartContents = cart.getContents();

    // Call a method to load this clients shopping cart from
    // the contents of the other shopping cart
    loadMyShoppingCart( shoppingCartContents );
}
```

When another client invokes a method call on a remote interface obtained from a Handle as above, the normal security checks are performed to ensure that the client can invoke the methods on the bean.

THE EJBMetaData CLASS

Another class that is generated by the tools provided by the container provider is a class that implements the javax.ejb.EJBMetaData interface. This interface, or rather the class that implements this interface, is used to discover, sort of dynamically, meta-information about the EJB object for which it is obtained. This interface and resulting container class that is created are used for two primary purposes:

- Can be used by development tools that need to discover information about deployed EJB objects.
- Can be used by clients using a scripting language to access EJB objects.

The interface contains the methods listed in Table 3.4.

TABLE 3.4 THE METHODS FOR javax.ejb.EJBMetaData INTERFACE

Return	Method	Description
EJBHome	getEJBHome	Obtain the home object.
Class	getHomeInterfaceClass	Obtain the class for the EJB home interface.
Class	getPrimaryKeyClass	Obtain the class for the EJB primary key.
Class	getRemoteInterfaceClass	Obtain the class for the EJB remote interface.
boolean	isSession	Test whether the EJB is a session bean.
boolean	isStatelessSession	Test whether the EJB is a stateless session bean.

Caution

Some of the methods on the EJBMetaData class are specific to certain bean types and will cause exceptions if sent to the wrong bean. For example, if you call getPrimaryKeyClass on a session bean, a java.lang.RuntimeException will be thrown. You should first use the isSession method to determine the bean type before calling the getPrimaryKeyClass method.

PART

I

CH

3

You can obtain an instance of the EJBMetaData class by calling the getEJBMetaData method on a remote home interface of an enterprise bean.

Note

Because the EJBMetaData class is designed for remote clients specifically, it is not available to local clients.

The following code fragment gives a small example of how to do this:

```
// For this code fragment, we assume that the remote home
// Interface has been acquired correctly

// Get the meta data for the bean
EJBMetaData metData = orderFulfillmentProcessorHome.getEJBMetaData();
```

The EJBMetaData object returned to a client is not a remote interface. It's a value object that is a valid RMI/IIOP value type because it's serialized to the client. In fact, the container can use the same EJBMetaData object for all enterprise beans of the same type because the metadata for all instances of the same class should be the same. However, the specification does not mandate this behavior.

EJB SERVER AND CONTAINER IMPLEMENTATIONS

Throughout this section, we tried to introduce the EJB concepts that you will need to be familiar with as you go through this book. The concepts can be difficult to grasp and, in some cases, it just takes repeated exposure to the material. So, if you feel that your mind is not clearly focused and these concepts are not quite clear, take a few minutes and quickly scan through this chapter again. It will help you tremendously through the book if you don't have to stop and think about *"What is a home object used for again."* This is a great time to get these ideas and concepts solidified in your mind, before we really get into the details of EJB.

The other thing that we want to point out in this wrap-up of the EJB concepts is something like a disclaimer for many things that were discussed in this chapter and that will be discussed later. One of the best things—or maybe the worst, depending on which side of the enterprise bean you're standing on—is that the specification is just that, a specification. It provides a framework for vendors to build the necessary and required infrastructure components that help us as bean providers hopefully sleep better at night. This is both good and bad. It's good because vendors have the flexibility to develop the EJB server and container in ways that they think optimize the execution environment. It's also bad because they can develop the EJB server and container in ways they think optimize the execution environment.

Do you get the drift? Not all server/containers are created equal. Some are open-source projects and good free products to develop and maybe even deploy production applications on. Others are not really ready for prime time, but are good learning environments that don't cost anything to try and sales people won't bother you after downloading it.

The point here is that you must evaluate an EJB server/container based on your set of requirements. Not every project is the same and most have a different set of functional requirements, as well as financial ones. Do the legwork up front and select a vendor that meets your particular requirements. In fact, it's probably wise to select a primary and a secondary vendor, because you most certainly will encounter a customer that refuses to use your primary vendor, regardless of the one that you choose. If you've already selected a secondary EJB vendor, you will look like you really know what you're doing.

PART

I

CH

3

4

JAVA NAMING AND DIRECTORY INTERFACE

In this chapter

WHY APPLICATIONS NEED NAMING AND DIRECTORY SERVICES

A fundamental facility of any enterprise application is the capability to locate components and services. A client wishing to locate a component or service in an enterprise typically will know the name of the component or service, but probably will be unaware of the physical location of that component. The name of the component usually is an alias or user-friendly substitution for the real name, which might be more of a computer-friendly name. This is similar to how the Internet Domain Name Service (DNS) maps machine names, such as www.apache.org, to Internet Protocol (IP) addresses such as 64.208.42.41.

Building software applications where components and services are decentralized throughout the enterprise increases the need for a naming service when compared to a more traditional two-tier client/server application. In a multi-tier enterprise application, you typically have the Client tier (browser), Web tier (Web server), Application tier (application server), and the Enterprise Information System tier (RDBMS and ERP systems). All these tiers can be located on different machines.

So now that components are spread throughout the network, how do they find each other when they need to request services from one another? The whole idea of separating services into components is to assign responsibilities and to allow for components to invoke requests on other components. They need a way to locate each other that is transparent. By *transparent*, we mean that the client component does not know the exact physical location of the server component. For example, if we had an OrderFulfillment component that was called by the Web tier, and the OrderFulfillment component moved to a different physical server, it should not negatively affect the other components that use its services. The reason why enterprise applications need some type of naming and/or directory service is to help locate each other in this vast expanse we call the enterprise. Remember, for an enterprise application, a component might be a client in one request and then a server in another.

For enterprise applications, a naming and directory service provides a means by which your application can locate a reference to needed services. The service might be a JDBC data-source, a JMS connection factory, a reference to a home interface for an enterprise bean, or any other object or data that is needed by the enterprise.

Naming and directory services each provide a distinct purpose for use in enterprise applications. Although we'll describe each service briefly in the next section, our aim is to understand the naming service. We'll not spend any considerable amount of time on directory services other than to describe what they are. For the purpose of this book, it's the naming service that we need to understand.

NAMING SERVICE

A naming service is an application that holds on to a collection of objects or references to objects and associates a user-friendly name with each one. This association is known as a *binding*. Figure 4.1 shows an example of a binding.

Figure 4.1
An example of a naming service binding.

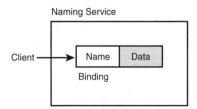

A resource bound to a name can be an object or possibly a reference to an object that resides somewhere else on the reachable network. For example, you could build a Hashtable with data in it and store this object into a naming service and associate it with a name. You could also build a Hashtable and create an RMI server to access that Hashtable and associate the RMI stub with a name. In either case, clients who wanted to get the information from the Hashtable could connect to the naming service and find it by using the name that it was associated with.

Note

How you go about connecting to a naming service and locating objects in it are covered later in this chapter.

This is similar to a phone book, if you use your imagination a bit. In a phone book, let's say the name "Fred's Plumbing Service" points to an advertisement for a plumbing service. I use the name of the service to locate the telephone number, which is just a reference to the actual service. If I wanted to make a request on the service, I would have to follow the reference, in this case make a phone call. If we were referring to an actual naming service instead of a phone number, we might locate an RMI proxy object. In that case, we could follow the reference and invoke methods on the remote object.

This also is analogous with how a DNS works. When you look up a Web site address such as java.sun.com, the DNS doesn't store the sun.com domain; it stores a reference to the IP address that has been associated with this domain. Using the IP address, a client can get in touch with the Web site by using the address 204.160.241.48.

Figure 4.2 shows how references can be stored as well as objects in a naming service.

Figure 4.2
Naming services can store references as well as the object data.

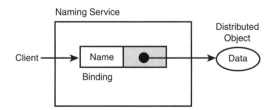

A collection of interconnected bindings make up something called a *namespace*. All telephone numbers in a phone book, for example, could be considered a namespace, just as the sun.com domain is essentially a namespace. The naming service is responsible for managing the bindings within the namespace. For enterprise applications, you can locate a resource within a namespace by using the user-friendly name and getting the resource that is associated with that name. Figure 4.3 shows how bindings and namespaces are related.

Figure 4.3
Namespaces are
made up of a set of
bindings.

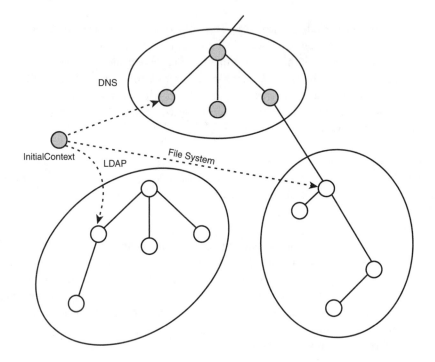

DIRECTORY SERVICES

A Directory service is just an extension of the features provided by a naming service. Directory services allow attributes to be associated with a binding. Clients can use a directory service to search for a specific binding with specific attribute values.

We'll use one of the most common examples to describe how you might use a directory service. Let's say an organization has several printers and each one of these printers is accessible through a naming and directory service. Each printer in the directory service could have an attribute that says whether or not it can print in duplex mode (this means on both sides). A client could find a printer in the directory service by filtering bindings where the duplex mode is true.

The following is a list of some common directory service implementations:

- Lightweight Directory Access Protocol (LDAP)
- Network Directory Service (NDS)
- Network Information Service Plus (NIS+)
- X.500

OVERVIEW OF THE JNDI ARCHITECTURE

The *Java Naming and Directory Interface* (JNDI) enables Java clients to have access to various naming and directory services. Like other things in the J2EE Specification, JNDI provides a set of APIs that contain Java interfaces and classes.

JNDI is divided into five core packages:

- `javax.naming`
- `java.naming.directory`
- `javax.naming.event`
- `javax.naming.ldap`
- `javax.naming.spi`

For most EJB applications, the naming service features are used more than the directory service features. The directory service features are very important but are a little out of scope for this book. We will cover the naming service only as it relates to EJB. If you are interested in more information on the directory service features offered through JNDI, see the Sun JNDI site:

`http://java.sun.com/products/jndi`

Because we are focusing strictly on the naming service features, we will look exclusively at the `javax.naming` package.

You must have a vendor-provided implementation to take advantage of JNDI services. This is similar to the Java Database Connectivity (JDBC) API where you must have a JDBC driver to use the JDBC APIs to connect to a database. With JNDI, the vendor-provided implementation is known as a Service Provider Interface (SPI), and it allows the JNDI methods to be called on a particular naming service. Figure 4.4 shows how an SPI provides the implementation behind the APIs.

Figure 4.4
Java clients use the JNDI APIs and a Service Provider Interface to take advantage of naming and directory services.

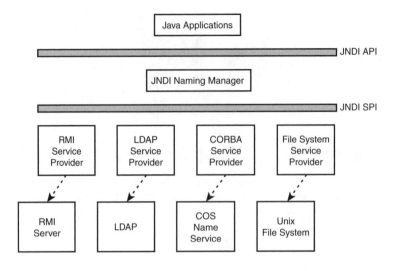

The SPI enables JNDI to connect to a particular naming service implementation and it wraps the proprietary naming service APIs with the ones defined by JNDI. The SPI maps the JNDI calls to ones that a particular naming service can understand. This allows the client to use the JNDI APIs only and to switch between different naming services without negatively affecting the client application. In fact, a client can navigate from one type of naming service to another using JNDI without knowing it. For example, a binding from an LDAP server might have a reference to an object that exists in an RMI Registry naming service. As long as the client uses the JNDI API, the transition from one naming service to another will be transparent. All the proprietary code for the particular naming service is encapsulated within the SPI.

THE AVAILABLE JNDI SERVICE PROVIDERS

There are several different types of naming services. There is a JNDI implementation for most of the different types. There also might be different providers for a particular type. For example, both Iona and Inprise have a Common Object Services (COS) name service within their CORBA products. You can use JNDI to access both of them. The following is a list of the JNDI implementations available:

- Lightweight Directory Access Protocol (LDAP)
- CORBA Common Object Services (COS) Name Service
- RMI Registry
- NIS (Sun's version for Network Information Service)
- DSML (Sun's version for Directory Services Markup Language)
- DNS (Domain Name System)
- File System (the file system can be used as a naming service)

Some of these are still beta releases. The list is being added to frequently. To get a current list of implementations that are available, see the list maintained on the Sun site at

`http://java.sun.com/products/jndi/serviceproviders.html`

Looking at the different types of naming services, you might be able to imagine that not all naming services are created equal. The way in which they store binding information or allow clients to locate certain bindings can be very different. Each naming service might store the information in a slightly different format than another. Because some names in a binding might point to another name in a different binding, most naming services store the bindings in a hierarchical fashion. However, the manner in which a client sees this hierarchy and navigates through it can be completely different from one naming service to another. For example, the DNS uses dots (".") to separate the bindings, as in `www.sun.com`. LDAP, on the other hand, uses a completely different format. Because naming services can be so different, there must be a Java way of hiding the naming service-specific details and allowing for a single API. This is the purpose of JNDI. JNDI allows a client to see all these different naming services in the same way.

SELECTING AND CONFIGURING A JNDI PROVIDER

As with virtually every other Java technology, JNDI must be properly configured before you can begin to use it. This is mainly due to the separation of interfaces and implementation. The naming service must be properly configured so that an installed provider will handle the work when a client uses the JNDI APIs. Also, any client application that wants to use the naming service must also be properly configured so that it can locate the naming service and then look up resources within it.

PART

I

CH

4

Configuring JNDI sometimes can cause great frustration unless you really understand what you are trying to set up and why. When using an EJB server, JNDI is usually already configured for the server and starts up when the EJB server starts up. The only part that you typically need to configure is the client application that is looking for home or remote references. The EJB server typically has an implementation that handles the JNDI service, and you just need to know how to find and connect to it.

To provide you with a little more depth about JNDI and how it is used, we will take you through the steps of setting up your own JNDI naming service and not using the one provided with the EJB server. This should give you a little more insight on what's going on within the EJB server for JNDI and how an SPI really handles the service, not just the JNDI APIs.

Note

To reiterate, if you are using an EJB server, you will typically not have to set up your own JNDI service. The JNDI server configuration is taken care of by most EJB servers. However, you still will need to set up the client applications that need to use JNDI.

The Java SDK 1.3 comes with three different naming service providers already included. The three are

- LDAP
- COS Naming
- RMI Registry

We could select one of these SPIs for our example, but each one is somewhat complicated to set up and understand. We would spend too much time talking about a separate technology that really doesn't have much to do with EJB and JNDI. There are a few extra naming service providers that we can download. You can download the extra SPIs from the following URL:

http://java.sun.com/products/jndi

If you get the JNDI 1.2.1 download, which is separate from the main JNDI download, it provides the following extra SPIs:

- LDAP v3
- NIS
- File System

These extra SPIs are in beta right now, but fine for what we need to do. We are going to be using the file system service provider for our examples. This will allow your file system to act as a JNDI naming service. This works out well for our example, because you already know how to use your computer's file system. You can download the File System (FS Context) naming service provider separately from the rest and install it on your computer. It comes with installation instructions, but the installation mainly involves putting the fscontext.jar and providerutil.jar JAR files from the download into your <JAVA_HOME>/lib directory. The other nice thing about using this SPI is that there's really no naming service to start. Because your file system is the service, it's already started for you. The other setup procedure that you will need to do is to create a directory on your file system that will act as the root of the naming service. If you are using the Windows platform, it could be something like

C:\JNDI_ROOT

For Unix, you might create a directory under your user account like

/home/chuck/jndi_root

If you would like to use a different JNDI provider, such as LDAP or WebLogic's naming service, check with the vendor on how to set up and start the service. The examples that will be used in this chapter are designed for the file system service provider, but with little modifications it can work with other providers.

Note

Java SDK 1.3 includes the `jndi.jar` file, which contains the necessary JNDI APIs. This JAR file must be in your classpath for your JNDI client applications to work. If you have an earlier version of Java, you will need to download the JNDI APIs separately and follow the installation instructions for the particular version of Java that you're using. You can download JNDI from `http://java.sun.com/products/jndi`.

It should also be said that if you're planning to use a different naming service provider other than the file system provider, you will also need to include the JAR files for that provider in your client classpath or you will get compiler or runtime errors. The client applications that will be accessing JNDI will need to import the necessary JNDI packages. For our discussion of EJB 2.0, the only JNDI package that you will need to import into your client applications is the `javax.naming` package.

THE EXAMPLE FILE SYSTEM NAMESPACE

The nice thing about using the file system SPI for JNDI is that nothing needs to be started for the JNDI naming service. All you need to do is set up a directory to represent the JNDI namespace. For our examples, we will use the directory structure shown in Figure 4.5.

Figure 4.5
The JNDI namespace that will be used for the file system example.

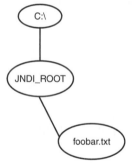

If you would like to use a different drive, or if you are using Linux or Unix as your operating system, then change the names and drive accordingly wherever the namespace is referenced in the examples.

THE JNDI ENVIRONMENT PROPERTIES

Before the client can use the services offered by JNDI, it must first locate the service on the network and get a connection. It's sort of a paradox if you think about it. A client uses JNDI to locate remote services, but the JNDI service is possibly a remote service itself. So how is a naming service located if you don't have a naming service to start with? The JNDI answer is by using environment properties.

Environment properties are the way that a JNDI client application communicates various preferences and properties that are used to establish a connection with the JNDI environment. Not only properties about where to find the JNDI naming service, but many more types of properties can be specified. For example, you might need to specify security credentials, such as a username and password, to connect to the naming service. A client can specify these by adding them to the JNDI environment properties. The properties are specific to a client. Each JNDI vendor implementation might have some common environment properties (such as where the JNDI service is), but also might contain specific properties (such as username and password of the client).

Each JNDI service provider can use the properties in different ways. In fact, each provider might have provider-specific properties that are used only by it. The specific environment properties that must be defined for a client to connect to the naming service are provider-dependent. For example, for BEA's WebLogic EJB server, you must tell the client application that you will be using the WebLogic-provided JNDI service and where it can be found on the network. With the file system service provider, you will also need to set these environment properties, but the format and type of properties are somewhat different.

Note

Check with your JNDI provider documentation to see which properties are important and which ones are not for that specific provider. You might be wondering how a client can be portable if the properties are different across JNDI providers. As you'll see later in this chapter, you can specify these properties outside your code in properties files. This enables the client application to switch the properties without negatively affecting the application source code.

Other information might be required depending on the SPI and naming service implementation. Typically, you will create a set of key/value pairs, where the keys are strings, which define a specific property. An example of one of these keys is

```
java.naming.provider.url
```

You must associate a value with this key. It might be something like this:

```
ldap://ldap.wiz.com:389
```

The entire environment property might look like this:

```
java.naming.provider.url=ldap://ldap.wiz.com:389
```

As you can see, the format is *key=value*.

Table 4.1 describes all the standard environment properties that are available to a JNDI application and what each environment property is used for.

TABLE 4.1   STANDARD ENVIRONMENT PROPERTIES THAT CAN BE USED BY JNDI

Property Value	Description
java.naming.applet	When using applets, this value is the java.applet.Applet instance that is being executed.
java.naming.authoritative	This is a normally a true or false value. If true, it bypasses any cache or replicas that are being used by JNDI. The default value is false.
java.naming.batchsize	Used to specify the batch size to use when returning data via the service's protocol. It must be a string representation of an integer. It is only a hint to the service provider and may be ignored.
java.naming.dns.url	Used to specify the DNS host and domain names to use for the JNDI URL context. Not used by all service providers.
java.naming.factory.initial	Used to specify which factory class will create the initial context objects. It must be the fully qualified class name.
java.naming.language	Specifies the preferred language to use. If not specified, the language will be determined by the provider.
java.naming.factory.object	A list of fully qualified class names that will be used as factories for creating JNDI objects. If a list is used, a colon is used to separate the items.
java.naming.provider.url	Used to specify configuration information for the provider to use. This should be a URL string such as ldap://ldap.wiz.com:38.
java.naming.referral	Used to specify how referrals encountered by the provider should be handled. It can be "follow," "ignore," or "throw."
java.naming.security.authentication	Used to specify the security level to use. It can be "none," "simple," or "strong."
java.naming.security.credentials	Specifies the credentials (password) of the principal. Depends on the authentication scheme used. If the value is not specified, the behavior depends on the provider.
java.naming.security.principal	Used to specify the identity (username) of the principal for authenticating the caller to the service. Depends on the authentication scheme specified.
java.naming.security.protocol	Used to specify the security protocol to use. Its value depends on the service provider. An example is "SSL."
java.naming.factory.state	This property should be a colon-separated list of the fully qualified factory class names that will be used to get an object's state given the object itself.
java.naming.factory.url.pkgs	This property should be a colon-separated list of package prefixes for the class name of the factory class that will create a URL context factory.

PART

I

CH

4

Note

Notice that the property names specified in Table 4.1 have a prefix of `java.naming` and not `javax.naming`. You would think that because the APIs are defined in the `javax.naming` package, this would be the prefix, but it's not. Don't get the two confused. If you are including the JNDI packages in your applications, you will need to import `javax.naming`, but if you are using the environment property values, they begin with `java.naming`.

For each environment property in Table 4.1, the `javax.naming.Context` interface also defines a static `String` constant that can be used programmatically. So, if you needed to specify the `java.naming.initial.context` property in your code, you could instead use the constant

`Context.INITIAL_CONTEXT_FACTORY`

It's recommended that you use these constants in your source code. Of course, you can't use them in the resource files or system properties, but using them in your source code will help with readability.

Two environment properties are very important, no matter which service provider you are using. These two JNDI environment properties are

- `java.naming.factory.initial`
- `java.naming.provider.url`

A client sets these two JNDI properties so that the naming service can be located. Most of the other environment properties are optional, but these two are generally required. The next two sections cover each of these two properties in detail.

java.naming.factory.initial

This value is a string that holds the name specifying the initial context factory that should be used to create new `InitialContext` references.

Note

We have not covered what the `Context` or `InitialContext` objects are yet. For now, you can think of the `Context` as a reference to a binding within the naming service and the `InitialContext` as a reference to the root level of that naming service. If you imagine a tree hierarchy, the `InitialContext` reference is a reference to the top of the tree and a `Context` reference is a reference to a branch in the tree. The `Context` and `InitialContext` are covered in detail later in this chapter.

The value of this property should be the fully qualified class name of the factory class to use. Here's an example using a BEA WebLogic JNDI factory:

`java.naming.factory.initial=weblogic.jndi.WLInitialContextFactory`

If you don't specify the initial context factory property or if you specify it incorrectly, you will get a `NoInitialContextException` or possibly a `NamingException` thrown when attempting to connect to the naming service.

⚠ *If you are getting a `NoInitialContextException` while trying to create the `InitialContext`, see the "Troubleshooting" section at the end of the chapter.*

java.naming.provider.url

This property value is also a string. This property holds the name of the environment value for specifying configuration information for the SPI to use. Although its syntax is somewhat dependent on the provider, the property typically follows the following format:

```
protocol://host:port
```

Here's an example using WebLogic:

```
java.naming.provider.url=t3://localhost:7001
```

The protocol `t3` you see here is a BEA-specific protocol. A few other protocols that you might see are `iiop` and `ldap`. This URL informs the SPI where the JNDI naming service is located so that objects can be found during a lookup.

SETTING THE JNDI ENVIRONMENT PROPERTIES

PART
I
CH
4

There are three main ways to set the environment properties for JNDI:

- Use an environment object in the `InitialContext` constructor
- Use system properties
- Use resource files

Resource files allow you to externally define environment properties using files that follow the `java.util.Properties` format. This prevents you from having to change your source code when environment properties are changed. This usually is the best approach, but not all situations are the same, so you might need to use one of the alternative methods. The following sections describe each of the approaches.

USING A Hashtable TO SET ENVIRONMENT PROPERTIES

The first method allows the environment properties to be set inside your JNDI client application by passing a `java.util.Hashtable` into the constructor of the `InitialContext`. The following code fragment shows an example of setting the environment properties for locating the JNDI service:

```
Hashtable env = new Hashtable();
env.put(Context.INITIAL_CONTEXT_FACTORY, "com.sun.jndi.ldap.LdapCtxFactory");
env.put(Context.PROVIDER_URL, "ldap://localhost:389/o=JNDITutorial");
Context ctx = new InitialContext(env);
```

This approach has the down side of being explicitly implemented within the client application code. If you wanted to change where the JNDI service was located or which initial context factory you were using, you would have to modify and recompile your source code. That's why this approach is the least desirable.

USING SYSTEM PROPERTIES

Another way to specify JNDI environment properties is to provide them through the system properties when starting a Java application. Java allows you to specify system properties on the command line with a -D option. You specify properties on the command line using a key=value syntax. JNDI will only look for the following environment properties from the command line:

- `java.naming.factory.initial`
- `java.naming.factory.object`
- `java.naming.factory.state`
- `java.naming.factory.control`
- `java.naming.factory.url.pkgs`
- `java.naming.provider.url`
- `java.naming.dns.url`

You can set the JNDI environment properties using the command line like this:

```
# java -Djava.naming.factory.initial=com.sun.jndi.ldap.LdapCtxFactory
     -Djava.naming.provider.url=ldap://localhost:389/o=JNDITutorial
```

Using system properties to configure your JNDI applications provides a way to set the environment properties outside your source code. However, you must worry about typing all the properties in on the command line. Although you could create startup scripts to do this for you, you would need to add the system properties for all your JNDI client applications. You would also need to change each script when the JNDI configuration changed. Setting JNDI environment properties with the command line is somewhat better than putting them in your source code, but we can still do better. The next section talks about using resource files.

Tip

If you are using JNDI from an applet, it's best to specify the environment properties in the applet using normal applet parameters. Here's an example:

```
<param
name=java.naming.factory.initial
value=com.sun.jndi.ldap.LdapCtxFactory>

<param
name=java.naming.provider.url
value= ldap://localhost:389/o=JNDITutorial >
```

This is because applets generally are not allowed to read system properties or system files because of the tight security restrictions that are placed on them.

USING RESOURCE FILES

The third way of setting JNDI environment properties is to use a resource file. Resource files are probably the best approach to setting the properties, because they completely decouple the application from the JNDI properties. A resource file is a file in the `java.util.Properties` format that contains a list of key=value pairs. Here is an example of a JNDI resource file:

```
java.naming.factory.initial=com.sun.jndi.ldap.LdapCtxFactory
java.naming.provider.url=ldap://localhost:389/o=JNDITutorial
```

The key is the name of the environment property and the value is a string in the format defined for that property. The format of the value may be provider-dependent, so be sure to check the documentation for your JNDI provider. There are two types of resource files:

- Provider resource files
- Application resource files

The service provider and JNDI class libraries locate and read the resource files automatically, and the environment properties that are contained within these files become available to the environment without having to load them programmatically. This is why this method is the most flexible and gives you the most portability. How this is done will be covered later in this chapter.

PROVIDER RESOURCE FILES

Each JNDI service provider might have an optional resource file that lists properties specific to that provider. The name of this resource is typically

```
[prefix/]jndiprovider.properties
```

where *prefix* is the package name of the provider's context implementation.

For example, suppose a service provider defines a context implementation with class name `com.sun.jndi.ldap.LdapCtx`. The provider resource file for this provider would be named `com/sun/jndi/ldap/jndiprovider.properties`. If the class is not in a package, the resource's name is simply `jndiprovider.properties`.

A provider can put properties that are specific to its service within the provider resource file, but it can also override the standard environment properties. The following standard JNDI environment properties can be set in the provider resource file and override any value already set for the property:

- `java.naming.factory.object`
- `java.naming.factory.url.pkgs`
- `java.naming.factory.state`
- `java.naming.factory.control`

PART

I

CH

4

The JNDI library will consult the provider resource file when determining the values of these properties. The provider might not allow you to set certain properties here. Check the provider's documentation to determine which properties can be set in the provider specific resource file.

APPLICATION RESOURCE FILES

Application resource files are text files that are in the `java.util.Properties` format that can specify additional key=value pairs that are loaded and made available to the environment of the `InitialContext`. These files can be located within the application classpath and will be automatically picked up. The JNDI class libraries will locate these files using one of the `getResources` methods defined in the `java.lang.ClassLoader` class.

Listing 4.1 shows a sample `jndi.properties` resource file.

LISTING 4.1   A SAMPLE `jndi.properties` FILE

```
java.naming.factory.initial=com.sun.jndi.ldap.LdapCtxFactory
java.naming.provider.url=ldap://localhost:389/o=JNDITutorial
```

JNDI will automatically read the `jndi.properties` resource files from the system classpath and `<JAVA_HOME>/lib`, where *JAVA_HOME* is the directory that contains your JRE (Java Runtime Environment).

Note

If you are using Java 1.1 or earlier, JNDI will not search the system classpath for the `jndi.properties` resource file. However, you can put the application resource file in the `<JAVA_HOME>/lib` directory and have JNDI find the properties.

You can have multiple `jndi.properties` files defined in several locations, and JNDI will just use the first value for a property that it finds or concatenate them together, if the property can have multiple values. JNDI then makes these properties from the application resource files available to the service providers and other components that need to use them.

Caution

Because the system will load the files automatically, application resource files should be considered *world-readable* and should not contain sensitive information, such as clear-text passwords.

When the `jndi.properties` file is located correctly based on the version of Java that you are using, you can create an `InitialContext` object without supplying the environment properties in the constructor. You can now replace the code that used a `Hashtable` of environment properties and passed them to the constructor of the `InitialContext` with just the call to the default no-argument constructor of the `InitialContext`. The following line shows what this would look like:

```
Context ctx = new InitialContext();
```

Notice that we didn't have to provide any environment properties to the `InitialContext`. They would be picked up from the `jndi.properties` resource file. This makes your code much more portable. The use of application resource files to specify any JNDI environment properties allows the JNDI to be configured with minimal programmatic setup. You don't have to change any source code when any of the environment properties need to be modified. You can also configure the JNDI for all applications and applets that use the same Java interpreter and keep the properties in one place. That way, you have to make changes in only a single location.

If you use application resource files with applets, you must remember to grant your applet permission to read all the application resource files.

SEARCH ALGORITHM FOR FINDING RESOURCE FILES

When a client application attempts to connect to a JNDI naming service, there is a particular algorithm that the JNDI libraries will use to locate environment properties. First, if any environment properties are passed in the constructor of the `InitialContext`, they will be used to initialize the context's environment. Second, system properties will be added to the JNDI environment. If an applet is being used, any applet parameters will be added next. Finally, the environment properties from any resource files that have been included will be added.

PART
I
CH
4

Note

If a JNDI environment property is listed in both an application and a provider resource file, the property that will be used is the one from the application resource file. That is, unless it is one of the `java.naming.factory` properties mentioned previously in the provider resource section that overrides ones from the application resource file.

THE Context AND InitialContext OBJECTS

We have mentioned the term *binding* several times in this chapter. Although there is a `Binding` class in the JNDI API, you deal most often with something called a `Context`. A `Context` plays a central role in JNDI. It is used to bind, unbind, and locate objects that have been associated with a name in JNDI. The `Context` is represented by the `javax.naming.Context` interface. This interface has the necessary methods to put objects into the naming service and also to locate them. Table 4.2 lists the most commonly used methods from the `Context` interface when dealing with EJB.

TABLE 4.2 MOST OFTEN USED METHODS IN THE Context INTERFACE FOR EJB

Return Type	Method	Description
Object	lookup(String name)	Returns the object associated with the name.
NamingEnumeration	listBindings(String name)	Returns a list of bindings that are under the context at this name.
Hashtable	getEnvironment()	Retrieves the environment for this context.
void	close()	Closes the context.

Many other methods are defined in the Context interface, but the ones in Table 4.2 are the ones that you will be using the most with EJB.

All naming services have a root entry point. Think of this as the beginning of the namespace. All clients need to start from somewhere in the namespace and this starting point is called an InitialContext. Typically, the first step for any client that wants to use a naming service is to create an instance of the InitialContext. The javax.naming.InitialContext class represents the starting point for a client using a JNDI naming service. The InitialContext class implements the Context interface; it has all the methods in Table 4.2 and more at its disposal.

To create an InitialContext, you just need to call the constructor for it. The InitialContext must be able to find the environment properties that we discussed earlier. The particular environment properties that are required depend on the naming service SPI that you are using. For our file system example, we need to specify the following two properties:

- java.naming.factory.initial
- java.naming.provider.url

In fact, these two properties are typically always needed by the InitialContext to find and acquire a connection to the naming service.

There are really just three steps in obtaining an InitialContext.

1. Select the service provider of the corresponding service you want to access.
2. Specify any configuration that the InitialContext needs.
3. Call the InitialContext constructor, either by supplying the environment properties or by allowing them to be found either by a resource file or the system properties.

Caution

> A single instance of an `InitialContext` is not guaranteed to be thread-safe. If you have multiple threads that need to access the instance of the `InitialContext`, they should synchronize themselves or use separate instances of the `InitialContext`. You can pass null into the `lookup` method and get back a new reference to the same `Context`, which may have its environment modified without affecting the original `Context`. You can also access this new `Context` concurrently with the original.

Listing 4.2 shows an example of creating an `InitialContext` to our file system naming service.

There are two environment properties that we must specify when using the file system as a JNDI naming service. The first one is to tell which initial context factory we will be using. For the file system, the value of this property is

```
Context.INITIAL_CONTEXT_FACTORY=com.sun.jndi.fscontext.RefFSContextFactory
```

The second environment property is the provider URL. In the case of the file system, this will be the directory that we want to be the root context. As mentioned previously in this chapter, the format of this value is dependent on the service provider that's being used. For the file system, it should look like this:

```
Context.PROVIDER_URL=file:///c:/jndi_root/
```

This file system service provider requires the prefix `file:///` to be added to the root directory.

For this example, we are going to pass the environment properties into the constructor of the `InitialContext`. The provider URL for this example comes from the command line because everyone might be using a different directory for the root context. As we said earlier, there are times when putting everything into the `jndi.properties` isn't the best approach.

PART

I

CH

4

LISTING 4.2   AN EXAMPLE OF OBTAINING AN `InitialContext`

```java
import javax.naming.*;
import java.util.Hashtable;
import java.util.Properties;

public class JNDIClient {

  // Default Constructor
  public JNDIClient(){
    super();
  }

  // Create an InitialContext using the environment properties passed in
  public Context getInitialContext( Hashtable env ) throws NamingException{
    // Create the InitialContext using a Hashtable of properties
    return new InitialContext( env );
  }
```

LISTING 4.2 CONTINUED

```java
public static void main( String[] args ){
  // Reference for the InitialContext
  Context initCtx = null;

  // Ensure that the providerURL is passed in on the command line
  if ( args.length == 0 ){
    System.out.println( "Usage: JNDIClient <providerURL>" );
    System.exit( 0 );
  }

  // Create an instance of the JNDIClient
  JNDIClient client = new JNDIClient();

  // Create the environment variables for the InitialContext
  Hashtable env = new Hashtable();
  env.put( Context.INITIAL_CONTEXT_FACTORY,
           "com.sun.jndi.fscontext.RefFSContextFactory" );
  env.put( Context.PROVIDER_URL, args[0] );

  try{
    // try to get the InitialContext
    initCtx = client.getInitialContext( env );

    if ( initCtx != null ) {
      System.out.println ("InitialContext was created successfully");
    }else{
      System.out.println ("InitialContext was not created successfully");
    }
  }catch( NoInitialContextException ex ){
    ex.printStackTrace();
  }catch( NamingException ex ){
    ex.printStackTrace();
  }finally{
    try{
      System.out.println( "Closing the InitialContext" );
      // Only call close on a non-null InitialContext reference
      if ( initCtx != null )
        initCtx.close();
    }catch( Exception ex ){
      System.out.println( "Could not close the InitialContext" );
    }
  }
}
}
```

It's probably a good idea to walk through the example in Listing 4.2 and figure out what's really going on. The JNDIClient program takes a single argument, which is the providerURL. This argument will be passed into the environment properties. We could have also set the value in the jndi.properties resource file, but this way is easier for you to change and see what different results are obtained based on different values. For the file system SPI, this value represents the root directory.

After a Hashtable is created with the correct values, the getInitialContext method is called and the environment properties are passed in. Remember, we could have also specified the values in a resource file or the system properties. We did it this way to provide a little more insight and to make it easier to change the providerURL value on the command line. You'll see an example later in this chapter on using a resource file.

After the InitialContext object is created, the program immediately closes it because for this example, we are only trying to show how to create one.

Assuming you are using the directory c:\jndi_root, if you run the preceding program from the command line and pass in the root directory like this:

```
java JNDIClient file:///c:/jndi_root/
```

you should see the following output:

```
C:\>java JNDIClient file:c://jndi_root
InitialContext was created successfully
Closing the InitialContext

C:\>
```

 Be sure that you have fscontext.jar and providerutil.jar in your system classpath to run the examples. If you still are having trouble running the JNDIClient example, check the "Troubleshooting" section at the end of this chapter for help.

PART

I

CH

4

CLOSING AN InitialContext

You should always close the InitialContext object when you are finished with it. This is similar to closing any other finite resource such as a JDBC connection. You should also ensure that you close the InitialContext even when an exception is thrown. The best way to do this is by putting the close method in a finally block. You also should put a try/catch around the close method. Listing 4.3 illustrates how you can ensure that the InitialContext is always closed when your application is finished with it.

LISTING 4.3 THE PROPER METHOD FOR CLOSING AN InitialContext

```
try{
  // some jndi work being performed
}catch( Exception ex ){
  // handle the exception
}finally{
  try{
    if ( initCtx != null )
      initCtx.close();
  }catch( Exception ex ){
    System.out.println( "Could not close the InitialContext" );
  }
}
```

GETTING THE ENVIRONMENT FOR A Context OBJECT

The method getEnvironment in the Context interface will return a Hashtable with all the environment properties that are in effect for the Context. To modify the environment properties for a Context, you must use the addToEnvironment and removeFromEnvironment methods.

Let's look at an example of getting the environment for a Context. For this example, we are going to create a jndi.properties resource file and let the InitialContext discover the environment properties through this method, instead of specifying them in a Hashtable as Listing 4.2 did. Listing 4.4 shows the jndi.properties file that we will be using.

LISTING 4.4   THE jndi.properties FILE FOR LISTING 4.5

```
java.naming.factory.initial=com.sun.jndi.fscontext.RefFSContextFactory
java.naming.provider.url=file:///c:/jndi_root/
```

The jndi.properties can be anywhere in your system classpath if you are using Java 2. Refer to the "Setting the JNDI Environment Properties" section earlier in this chapter for more help on where to put this file based on your version of the SDK.

Listing 4.5 shows an example of how to get the environment properties programmatically and print them out.

LISTING 4.5   AN EXAMPLE SHOWING HOW TO GET ALL THE ENVIRONMENT PROPERTIES FOR A Context

```java
import javax.naming.*;
import java.util.Hashtable;
import java.util.Iterator;
import java.util.Properties;
import java.util.Set;

public class ListJNDIEnvironment {

  // Default Constructor
  public ListJNDIEnvironment(){
    super();
  }

  public void listEnvironmentProperties(){
    Context initCtx = null;
    try {
      // Create the InitialContext. The jndi.properties resource file
      // will be used for the environment properties
      initCtx = new InitialContext();

      // List all of the environment properties for this Context
      Hashtable env = initCtx.getEnvironment();
```

LISTING 4.5   CONTINUED

```
      Set keys = env.keySet();
      Iterator iter = keys.iterator();
      while( iter.hasNext() ) {
        String key = (String)iter.next();
        String value = (String)env.get( key );
        System.out.println( key + "=" + value );
      }
    }catch( NoInitialContextException ex ){
      System.out.println( "You did not specify an InitialContext Factory" );
      System.out.println( "Check the jndi.properties resource file" );
    }catch( NamingException ex ){
      ex.printStackTrace();
    }finally{
      // Close up the open resources
      closeInitialContext( initCtx );
    }
  }

  // Always close your InitialContext when you are done with it
  public void closeInitialContext( Context ctx ){
    try {
      if ( ctx != null )
        System.out.println( "Closing the InitialContext" );
        ctx.close();
    }catch( NamingException ex ) {
      ex.printStackTrace();
    }
  }

  public static void main( String[] args ){
    ListJNDIEnvironment client = new ListJNDIEnvironment();
    // List the environment properties
    client.listEnvironmentProperties();
  }
}
```

The output should look similar to this:

```
C:\ejb20book\ejb20book\classes>java ListJNDIEnvironment
java.naming.factory.initial=com.sun.jndi.fscontext.RefFSContextFactory
java.naming.provider.url=file:///c:/jndi_root/
Closing the InitialContext

C:\ejb20book\ejb20book\classes>
```

The output might be different if you are using a different service provider or URL to run the example.

⚠ *If you are having trouble getting the ListJNDIEnvironment program to find your jndi.properties resource file, check the "Troubleshooting" section at the end of this chapter.*

PART

I

CH

4

USING THE lookup METHOD TO LOCATE JNDI RESOURCES

Now that you've learned how to get the InitialContext, it's time to do something with it. That something is to look up objects and references to objects. Because we are using the file system service provider, the object that we will be using to look up will be a text file.

Create a text file called foobar.txt and save the file into your jndi_root directory. You can add some text to the file if you want; it doesn't matter for our example. Now, let's use JNDI to look up this file and print out some information about it. Listing 4.6 shows a program that creates an InitialContext on our JNDI root directory and then performs a lookup on a name. The name is the name of the file foobar.txt.

LISTING 4.6   A SAMPLE PROGRAM USING THE lookup METHOD

```java
import java.io.File;
import javax.naming.*;
import java.sql.Timestamp;
import java.util.Hashtable;
import java.util.Properties;

public class JNDILookupExample {

  // Default Constructor
  public JNDILookupExample(){
    super();
  }

  public void runExample( String fileName ){
    Context initCtx = null;
    try {
      // Create an InitialContext using properties from resource files
      initCtx = new InitialContext();

      // Perform the lookup
      File file = (File)initCtx.lookup( fileName );

      // Print out something about the file
      long fileSize = file.length();
      Timestamp ts = new Timestamp( file.lastModified() );
      System.out.println( "File name: " + fileName );
      System.out.println( "File size: " + fileSize + " bytes" );
      System.out.println( "Last Modified: " + ts );

    }catch (Exception ex ) {
      ex.printStackTrace();
    }finally{
      try{
        System.out.println( "Closing the InitialContext" );
        if ( initCtx != null )
          initCtx.close();
      }catch( Exception ex ){
        System.out.println( "Could not close the InitialContext" );
```

LISTING 4.6 CONTINUED

```
      }
    }
  }

  // Main used to get things going
  public static void main( String[] args ){
    // Make sure the user passes in the filename
    if ( args.length != 1 ){
      System.out.println( "Usage: JNDILookupExample <filename>" );
      System.exit( 0 );
    }

    String fileName = args[0];
    JNDILookupExample example = new JNDILookupExample();
    // Run the example
    example.runExample( fileName );
  }
}
```

The example in Listing 4.6 doesn't do much except locate the file and print out the name, file size, and last time the file was modified. You can pass in different files on the command line to see what happens when a lookup fails. You should get a NameNotFoundException if you do. If you put the file foobar.txt into a directory under your jndi_root, you'll need to add the directory path to the argument on the command line. For example, if the file foobar.txt is in a directory called test under the jndi_root, you would need to run the program like this:

```
java JNDILookupExample test/foobar.txt
```

This example also uses the jndi.properties resource file. Make sure that you have the correct properties specified or it will not work. Your jndi.properties file should look like this for this example:

```
java.naming.factory.initial=com.sun.jndi.fscontext.RefFSContextFactory
java.naming.provider.url=file:///c:/jndi_root
```

LOCATING EJB OBJECTS

Up to this point, we have stayed away from talking specifically about how JNDI and EJB are used together. This was done intentionally so that you can have time to understand the JNDI concepts without being clouded by the EJB aspects of it. However, it's now appropriate to introduce how a client uses JNDI to locate enterprise beans. Even though we haven't fully discussed the details of enterprise beans, the procedure is pretty much the same regardless of whether it's an entity or session bean.

Note

> Remember, the message-driven bean is not exposed to the client. So, you will not be able to perform a lookup and obtain a reference to a message-driven bean.

PART

I

CH

4

You learned in Chapter 3, "EJB Concepts," that each enterprise bean that is exposed to a client has a home interface. If you remember, the home interface, or actually the object that implements the home interface, acts as a factory for the enterprise bean that it is associated with. A client locates the factory object through JNDI just as it would locate any other object in the JNDI namespace.

The EJB container is responsible for making the home factories for the enterprise beans that are deployed in the container available to clients through JNDI. This is normally done when the EJB container starts up. The client must get an InitialContext to the JNDI service and then locate the home interface reference for an enterprise bean. Once a client has the home interface, it can invoke methods on the home and obtain remote references to the enterprise bean.

The Context interface defines two different lookup methods that can be used to look up objects within the JNDI service. One of the methods takes a javax.naming.Name reference and the other takes a string. Typically, you'll see the string version in EJB applications just because it's easier to use. The string argument to the lookup method is the name of the binding that you want a reference to. If there is no binding with that name, a javax.naming.NameNotFoundException is thrown.

NARROWING THE HOME INTERFACE

Because the lookup method on the Context interface returns an Object, client applications must *narrow* and then cast the instance to the correct type. In earlier versions of EJB, only a Java cast operation had to be performed. However, starting with EJB 1.1, a client should use the static narrow method located on the javax.rmi.PortableRemoteObject class. This helps to ensure portability with other containers that are using RMI-IIOP as the underlying communication transport. The following code fragment illustrates how to narrow the Object returned from a lookup:

```
Context initCtx = new InitialContext();
Object obj = initCtx.lookup( "java:comp/env/EnglishAuctionHome" );
EnglishAuctionHome home =
  (EnglishAuctionHome)javax.rmi.PortableRemoteObject.narrow( obj,
                                        EnglishAuctionHome.class );
```

All objects returned from a lookup should be narrowed before using the Java cast operator.

ACCESSING AN EJB'S ENVIRONMENT

One of the questions that new EJB developers are always asking is how to provide configuration properties and values to an enterprise bean. Because enterprise beans are not supposed to access the file system, how does an enterprise bean get access to general configuration properties?

When we say configuration properties, we're talking about properties that help enforce business rules. An example might be the maximum number of auctions a user can participate in. There are many different ways to give this data to the enterprise that needs it. We could hard-code it inside the bean, but that's not a very flexible solution. We could store it into a database, but in some cases that's overkill and too much trouble. Another way is to put it into the enterprise bean's deployment descriptor so that it can be modified without recompiling. When we add it to the deployment descriptor, it becomes available to the enterprise bean through the environment for the bean.

To add it to the deployment descriptor, we add an env-entry tag like this:

```
<env-entry>
  <description>Max number of auctions a user can bid on.</description>
  <env-entry-name>maxAuctionsParticipation</env-entry-name>
  <env-entry-type>java.lang.Integer</env-entry-type>
  <env-entry-value>10</env-entry-value>
</env-entry>
```

An enterprise bean that declared this environment entry in its deployment descriptor could use this value to limit the number of auctions in which a user could participate. This tag would be placed under a specific enterprise bean in the deployment descriptor. An enterprise bean gets access to its declared environment properties by using an InitialContext object and looking up the environment property by its name.

Note

This environment entry is available only to the enterprise bean for which it's defined. It's not available to other enterprise beans. The same entry name can be defined in other deployment descriptors without causing a conflict.

The following code fragment illustrates how an enterprise bean method might locate and use the environment entry:

```
public void submitBid( User user, EnglishAuction auction, Bid aBid ) {
  // Get the bean's environment naming context
  Context initCtx = new InitialContext();
  Context myCtx = (Context)initCtx.lookup( "java:comp/env" );

  // Get the environment property for the max number of auctions
  Integer maxAuctionParticipate =
      (Integer)myCtx.lookup("maxAuctionsParticipation")

  if ( user.auctionsAlreadyIn < maxAuctionsParticipate.intValue() ) {
    // Allow the bid to go through
  }else{
    // Inform the user that they are already in too many auctions
  }
}
```

Using the enterprise bean's environment entries is a great way to provide customizable business rules when the rules can be expressed in a set of properties. The entry types can be one of the following Java types:

- String
- Integer
- Boolean
- Double
- Byte
- Short
- Long
- Float
- Character

ESTABLISHING SECURITY THROUGH THE `InitialContext`

Some naming service providers like LDAP might require a username and password for a client to connect to it and look up objects within the namespace. The manner in which you can do this is by setting the environment properties for an `InitialContext`.

Three primary environment properties are defined in the `Context` interface and help establish the level of security you want to use when interacting with JNDI. The three security-related environment properties are

- `java.naming.security.authentication`
- `java.naming.security.principal`
- `java.naming.security.credentials`

The first property defines the level of security that you will use when creating the `InitialContext`. There are three basic types of security authentication that you can do through JNDI. The authentication environment property must be set before an `InitialContext` is created. The three types of authentication are

- None
- Simple
- Strong

You set the authentication environment property just as you set any of the other environment properties. You can set the property in a resource file like other properties in a `jndi.properties` file like this:

```
java.naming.security.authentication=simple
```

or you can set it in your source code if you are passing in environment properties to the `InitialContext` constructor. To set the authentication property programmatically, you can do something like the following:

```
properties.put( Context.SECURITY_AUTHENTICATION, "simple" );
```

This tells the JNDI service that you want to use the simple authentication protocol. With the simple and strong authentication, you must provide values for the `java.naming.security.principal` and `java.naming.security.credentials` properties. The principal is typically the username or login for the user and the credentials property normally represents the password for the user.

Note

If you don't provide an authentication property, the behavior is up to the JNDI service. Some will default the authentication to none and provide a login and password of "guest." Others will just ignore these values completely.

When using the strong authentication, you will normally have to provide a digital certificate to the JNDI service for a stronger form of authentication. Depending on the JNDI provider, you also might have to set the `java.naming.security.protocol` environment property when using the strong authentication. Some providers will automatically determine this value. An example of a security protocol is `SSL`. In most cases, `simple` will suffice and `strong` will not be necessary. However, it's up to your specific application requirements to determine what type of client authentication is needed.

JNDI AND CLUSTERING

To achieve better scalability and high availability, J2EE services, including EJB servers and naming services, can be clustered. Clustering is when a set of identical services or components is started so that the system can be more fault-tolerant and also balance the load across the redundant services. We will only briefly mention clustering of JNDI services in this section.

→ For more of a general discussion on clustering concepts and EJB, **see** Chapter 22, "EJB Clustering Concepts."

Because JNDI can also be considered a limited resource and is a point of failure for an enterprise application, the JNDI service can also be clustered.

Clustering is very dependent on the vendor implementation. Each EJB server might have different features and might implement support for JNDI clustering differently. EJB servers are not required to support clustering, but most have some type of support for it. Even when a vendor supports clustering, the level of support can be limited. Therefore, you will need to read the vendor documentation for your EJB server to determine the level of clustering support available.

An example of a vendor that has a broad range of support for clustering is BEA's WebLogic 6.1. WebLogic has different options for supporting clustering, but the premise is that each EJB server can contain objects that get attached to a JNDI tree. The JNDI might be replicated across the clustered nodes. If one of these clustered nodes fails, another node would be able to pick up the workload. However, unless the component itself was clustered, a client would not be able to access it even though the object might still be registered in the JNDI tree.

An alternative to this cluster design might be to replicate all the objects for one EJB server across to all the other nodes in the enterprise. Obviously, this would have a negative effect on performance due to the necessary copying of objects to all JNDI trees. However, you can gain failover support of the JNDI service with this method.

Whether you need to cluster the JNDI services or not depends on your particular application requirements and constraints. Make sure to check with your EJB server vendor to verify that it supports clustering for JNDI services and that it is a requirement for your application.

TROUBLESHOOTING

`ClassNotFoundException` WAS THROWN

I get a `ClassNotFoundException` when I try to run my JNDI application.

Be sure that you have the `jndi.jar` and the JAR files required by your JNDI service provider in your system classpath. If you are using a SDK version prior to 1.3, check the JNDI documentation for where these go so that they can be found.

INCOMPATIBLE JAVA PLATFORM VERSIONS

I get an exception complaining about missing Java files.

Be sure you are using a version of Java higher than 1.2.2. If possible, you should download and use Java 2 SDK 1.3. You can download it from `http://java.sun.com/products/jdk`.

`NoClassDefFoundError`

I get a `NoClassDefFoundError` when I run my JNDI application.

This is a runtime error that happens because one or more of the necessary classes were not found in the classpath. Check to make sure that you have the `jndi.jar` and the JAR files required by your service provider in the system classpath.

NO INITIAL CONTEXT

I get a `NoInitialContextException` when I try to run my JNDI application.

You either did not specify the `java.naming.initial.context` environment property or it could not be found. This property is required to create the `InitialContext`.

CommunicationException WAS THROWN

I get a CommunicationException when I run my JNDI application.

This can happen for several reasons, but commonly it's because you specified incorrect configuration information about where the JNDI service is running. Check that the host and post that you've specified are correct.

jndi.properties RESOURCE FILE WASN'T FOUND

My JNDI client is unable to locate the jndi.properties file.

The location of the jndi.properties file is very important because the JNDI libraries must be able to find it. Typically, as long as the file is located somewhere within the system classpath, it will be found. If that doesn't work, try the <JAVA_HOME>/lib directory. You must be careful if you have more than one copy of the jndi.properties file on your machine. The first one that JNDI finds will be used.

NameNotFoundException WAS THROWN

I get a NameNotFoundException when I run my JNDI application.

Usually this happens because you specified a name in the lookup method that doesn't exist in the JNDI service or you didn't specify the name correctly as you need to. Some JNDI services force you to use java:/comp/env prefixed to the name of an enterprise when using the lookup method, while others allow you to just specify the name.

## CHAPTER 5

ENTITY BEANS

In this chapter

WHAT IS AN ENTITY BEAN?

As you saw in Chapter 3, "EJB Concepts," the EJB specification defines three types of enterprise beans: entity, session, and message-driven beans. As was pointed out there, the specification assigns distinct roles to each of these bean types. This chapter and the three that follow introduce you to the purpose behind entity beans and teach you how to implement and deploy them. Later chapters do the same for session and message-driven beans. The fact that four chapters are dedicated to entity beans should be your first indication that there's plenty to learn about this first type of enterprise bean.

An entity bean represents a persistent object that usually corresponds to a row in a relational database table (or several related rows in multiple tables). Having long-term persistence is what distinguishes entity beans from the other types of EJBs more than anything else. As you'll see in Chapter 9, "Session Beans," a session bean can be stateful but that state is maintained for a relatively short time. Because the data that defines an entity object is stored in a database or provided by some other enterprise system, entity beans have state that persists beyond the lifetime of the processes in which they execute. Short of a catastrophic database failure, entity objects have long-term persistence that is intended to survive even a server crash.

Virtually any enterprise application you develop must interact with information stored in a database. Whether a system supports order entry, access to patients' medical records, or wireless stock trading from a PDA, persistent data is typically critical to what a business application does. Given this, defining a category of EJB for working with persistent data makes sense. A lot of processing can take place related to retrieving and updating the contents of a database, so the EJB architecture provides a foundation to support it.

It's true that the need for persistent data goes along with using entity beans, but that isn't the sole intent. Multitudes of enterprise applications have been built without the use of entity beans, so there must be more to them than just persistence. What you should be thinking when you design entity beans is that the goal is to create reusable business objects that manage persistent data as part of their responsibilities. Entity beans should represent key business entities that can be reused across an enterprise's applications. Examples of business entities can include objects that represent customers, orders, invoices, medical records, stock trades, and so on.

The responsibilities of the EJB container include the management of concurrent access and transactions so that entity beans can fulfill their role when faced with the demands of multiple clients. When multiple clients access a particular business object that's been implemented using an entity bean, the container enforces serialized access to that object. This means that two clients can't modify the state of such an object at the same time. For example, if you and your business partner maintain a joint bank account, an application that uses an entity bean to represent an account could correctly handle simultaneous requests from both of you to withdraw funds without any special effort by the application programmer. If your request reached the entity instance first (in the form of a method call on the enterprise bean), it would be processed completely before the container would allow any other calls to be made on the bean instance that is representing your account. The concurrency management provided for entity beans supports this type of scenario even without the use of transactions (you'll see much more about the role of transactions in EJB in Chapter 12, "Transactions"). Entity beans aren't always the preferred approach for read-only access to a database, but their support for concurrent access makes them well suited for modifying persistent data.

Another advantage of entity beans relates to instance pooling and scalability. As you'll learn more about later in this chapter, the container maintains a pool of entity instances that are used to support the specific business entities accessed by an application. This pooling provides for efficient sharing of memory while ensuring the integrity of the data associated with your business entities. This built-in scalability is something you wouldn't get if you were to use session beans or regular Java classes to manage entity state.

The rest of this section looks more at the characteristics of an entity bean. One of the first things you need to learn is how to decide whether a particular type of object warrants an entity bean representation. You then need to learn what you have to do as a bean provider to develop an entity bean and the interfaces, classes, and deployment descriptors that support it.

BUSINESS LOGIC

If you've worked with regular JavaBeans, you know that they typically implement GUI widgets or simple data structures. Those that serve as data structures are usually more concerned with exposing properties to the classes that use them than they are with implementing any significant application logic. JavaBeans are primarily client-side and Web tier components, so you wouldn't want them to do any more than this in most cases.

EJBs have some similarity to JavaBeans in that they share the idea of component-based development. That's about as far as the similarity goes, however. EJBs live on the server and are given far more responsibility than their distant cousin, JavaBeans. EJBs are heavyweight components, so they need to offer more than access to a simple set of properties to make their use worthwhile. Primarily, an EJB justifies its existence and the overhead incurred when accessing it through the container by providing business logic to an application.

An entity bean class is usually expected to contain more than its persistent attributes and a list of get and set methods to go with them. Otherwise, it would be hard to justify its reuse across applications. An entity bean typically is expected to do more by providing the business logic related to the data it represents. At a minimum, this can include the validation rules that control how an entity's state can be modified. It's also reasonable to expect an entity bean to define the methods that manipulate its data and aid in its interpretation by the applications that use it. As a developer, it's business logic like this that you want to reuse. As with any good object-oriented design, putting business logic into components that are reused means that the logic is written only once and it can be maintained in one place. As part of this, you must be conscious of the type of business logic that's appropriate for an entity bean. The logic implemented within an entity bean class should, in general, apply

PART

I

CH

5

only to the data for which the entity is responsible and the relationships it maintains. As you'll see in later chapters, more elaborate workflow or controller logic usually is more appropriately placed in a session bean.

Although most entity beans contain non-trivial business logic, this isn't as strict a guideline as it might seem at first. Because of the persistence mechanisms associated with entity beans and the concurrent access control provided by the container, it sometimes makes sense to implement an entity bean that is significant from a data standpoint but not from a business logic one. The services offered by the EJB container provide a relatively simple way to support manipulation of shared data by multiple users of a system. If this is important to a system you're building, it might be all the justification you need to use entity beans.

COARSE-GRAINED OBJECTS

Even though entity beans represent persistent objects and provide a number of benefits, you shouldn't automatically implement every persistent class in your application as an entity bean. The services that the EJB container provides to an entity bean are great when you need them, but they don't come for free. Every call to a method exposed through an EJB's remote interface has the potential of being a remote call. Even if an EJB is called by a local client or a remote client EJB running in the same JVM, the container must still intercede and enforce security and manage the transactional needs of the method. The use of an entity bean requires a certain amount of overhead, and that overhead should be justified.

In general, you should limit entity beans to representing the coarse-grained persistent objects in your system. This means that concepts such as a Customer or an Order might be good candidates for entity beans but those such as an Address or an OrderLineItem likely aren't. Objects such as Address and OrderLineItem are better handled by allowing an entity bean to manage them behind a higher-level interface that is presented to clients. This way, a client accessing the details of an order can rely on an Order entity bean to manage its OrderLineItems instead of the client being expected to have the knowledge necessary to do it directly. Using this approach, the business logic stays inside the entity bean where it belongs, and the entity provides significant behavior that's worthy of reuse.

The overhead of accessing an entity bean is the greatest for remote clients because of the marshalling of arguments and the potential network traffic involved. If you're using EJB 1.1, remote clients are your only option, so limiting entity beans to coarse-grained objects has significant performance advantages. EJB 2.0, however, has changed the playing field somewhat with its support for local clients. If an entity bean supports only local clients, the overhead of remote calls can be avoided. In fact, as will be pointed out as the examples are developed, local client access is the recommended approach for using entity beans. Even with the advantages brought about by local clients, it's still a better idea in most cases to limit your entity beans to coarse-grained objects. This encourages the encapsulation of related business logic. The use of local clients makes it reasonable to perform many fine-grained calls on a coarse-grained entity without suffering a severe performance penalty.

→   The need to limit remote calls to entity beans in EJB 1.1 led to patterns based on accessing and setting multiple fields of an entity bean in a single call. To learn more about this approach, **see** "Minimizing Remote Calls," **p. 465**.

You can often identify candidate entity beans by looking for the independent objects in your problem domain. These are the objects that exist regardless of the state of any other objects with which they're associated. A Customer object has a unique identity and would likely exist in a system until you decided to remove it directly. On the other hand, an address associated with a customer has no identity of its own and would be of no use if the customer were deleted.

By itself, the independence test might not be enough to justify using an entity bean for a particular type of object. You also must consider whether a class needs the services the container provides to an entity bean. The need for persistence is a minimum requirement for a potential entity bean, but if a class doesn't need any of the concurrency, security, transactional, or other services offered by the container, it's likely that an entity bean isn't a good choice. If you're using EJB 1.1, you especially need to be conscious of the distributed nature of EJB. If a candidate class doesn't need remote exposure to distributed clients, an entity bean implementation isn't appropriate unless you're using EJB 2.0 and plan to limit yourself to local clients.

REPRESENTING DEPENDENT OBJECTS

Given that you won't often implement all your persistent classes as entity beans, you have to do something else with the ones that don't make the cut. The objects that you don't implement as entity beans are known as dependent objects.

> **Note**
>
> If you followed the draft versions of the EJB 2.0 Specification, you know that, for a time, formal support for dependent objects and the management of their persistence was proposed. This idea later was dropped in favor of support for local client access to entity beans. The use of "dependent objects" in this book simply refers to persistent objects that aren't represented by entity beans. This term was used in much of the literature on entity beans before the EJB 2.0 Specification was written, and it continues to be used in the same way.

A dependent object is often, but not always, an object that's owned by one of your entity objects. Going back to the customer example, a Customer entity bean in an order entry system would likely have several associated Address objects (maybe one for billing and another for shipping). These addresses are dependents of the Customer and are owned by it. Access to them should be done through the Customer so that they aren't made directly accessible to clients (especially remote ones). This encapsulates the functionality related to these objects and allows them to be accessed and manipulated without incurring the overhead of working through the container. In this example, the Customer should have sole responsibility for creating and deleting its addresses. If a Customer is deleted, its Address objects should be deleted along with it. A dependent object is often one whose life cycle is controlled by some other object. You can think of this as an example of composition. A customer entity can be composed of a Customer object and its Address objects plus any other objects that are necessary to define its persistent state.

There's nothing overly complicated about declaring a class to represent a dependent object. In general, you simply implement a dependent object as a regular Java class (or possibly multiple classes if it's complex enough).

Dependent objects can be relatively simple but that's not always the case. A dependent object can be just as complex as some entity beans. The decision to implement an object using a dependent object instead of an entity bean is based on the life-cycle management for the object and how it needs to be accessed. Nothing requires a dependent object to be free of business logic. You'll even find examples of dependent objects having their own dependent objects that they're responsible for managing.

Each dependent object class can be associated with one or more tables in your database. This build-up of classes and tables is where the coarse-grained aspect of an entity bean is evident. When you consider an entity bean, you must take its dependent objects and everything that they do into account as well. The interface an entity bean presents to its clients can be a facade for a very complex set of associated objects and business logic.

As with anything, tradeoffs are attached to encapsulating functionality within an entity bean using dependent objects. If the idea of making an entity bean coarse-grained gets taken too far, the entity can become so tied to a specific application that it ends up being difficult, if not impossible, to reuse. One way to avoid this problem is to keep the concepts of association and aggregation in mind. If an entity is simply associated with some object, a dependent object representation might be inappropriate. This is true even if it appears that this associated object will be accessed only through the entity. For example, in an order entry system, it might seem like a good idea at first to encapsulate a customer's orders within a Customer entity. The orders are definitely owned by the customer, but to a reporting application that looks at all orders taken by the system, it might be much more efficient to access each order directly. An entity bean is better suited for representing an aggregation of objects than it is for encapsulating associations.

IDENTIFYING THE AUCTION ENTITY BEANS

The guidelines covered so far in this section make it possible to take the first step toward mapping the example auction application to an EJB design. Back in Chapter 2, "Setting the Stage—An Example Auction Site," you saw several persistent business objects presented as an initial class design for the example. In particular, EnglishAuction, AuctionOffering, Item, Bid, Bidder, and Address were identified to support the given set of requirements. At that point, no distinction was made as to which of the objects would be implemented as entity beans. Based on the guidelines covered in this section, it's now possible to look at the role of each of these classes and choose an appropriate representation.

EnglishAuction represents the primary object responsible for maintaining the data associated with an auction. This class is the core of the application tier for the auction site, and its implementation will surely include many of the business rules to be enforced within the system. Given all this, it's a straightforward decision to choose an entity bean representation for EnglishAuction. It's also straightforward to conclude that an AuctionOffering associated with an auction is not a coarse-grained, independent business object. The only purpose of this class is to hold a quantity value and link an auction to the item it offers.

The Bid class isn't quite so easy to categorize as some of the others. It does have an identity to some extent, but it's owned by an auction (or possibly a bidder depending on how you choose to look at it) and it's closely tied to the auction business logic. An EnglishAuction should be responsible for accepting bid submissions and creating corresponding Bid objects, so a dependent object representation is the better choice for this class.

Items can be assigned to auctions, but their life cycle isn't determined by an auction. If an EnglishAuction is cancelled and deleted from the system, there's no reason for the Item it was offering for sale to go away with it. The same is obviously true for the auction bidders. An auction is associated with items and bidders, but it's not an aggregation of them. For the auction application, Item and Bidder are independent objects but they don't require much business logic. You could argue that they don't need to be entity beans, but that thought could be shortsighted. If the system were to expand and offer functionality other than auctions, items and bidders (or customers in a more general sense) could quickly take on new requirements.

Table 5.1 summarizes the representation chosen for each of the persistent auction classes.

TABLE 5.1 CHOOSING THE AUCTION ENTITY BEANS

Class	Representation
EnglishAuction	Entity bean
AuctionOffering	Dependent object
Bid	Dependent object
Item	Entity bean
Bidder	Entity bean
Address	Dependent object

BEAN PROVIDER RESPONSIBILITIES

As you've seen so far in this chapter, it's important for you to understand the issues to consider when choosing to implement a business object class as an entity bean. After that decision is made, you need to know what to do to actually implement and deploy your entity beans. That's the purpose of the rest of this chapter and the three chapters that follow.

As a bean provider, you're responsible for defining an entity bean class and its dependent objects (if it has any). To make your bean accessible to a client, you also must define its home and component interfaces. Entity beans are unique among EJBs in that they must have an associated primary key class that you're responsible for specifying. This can be as simple as identifying a standard Java class to use, or it can mean declaring a new class to serve that purpose (which isn't that difficult either). The final step in the process is to specify the initial deployment information for your bean.

The biggest choices you have to make as a bean provider for an entity bean relate to the types of clients you support and how the bean's persistence is managed. Under EJB 2.0, an entity bean can support both local and remote clients. However, EJB designers are in rare agreement that entity beans serve their purpose best when they serve other enterprise beans as their only clients. As you'll learn in Chapter 9, session beans function as extensions of their client applications. This bean type is well suited for coordinating the work of one or more entity beans and grouping several calls under a single method exposed to the client. Entity beans, on the other hand, are not intended to function as extensions of the client. An entity bean should encapsulate a set of functionality that is independent of its clients and suitable for reuse across applications. For this reason, entity beans shouldn't be directly exposed to clients outside the application tier. Using EJB 2.0 and session beans deployed in the same container allows you to limit your entity beans to local client use only.

As far as persistence management, you have the option to either write the database access code for an entity bean yourself or define mappings to the database declaratively and let the container interact with the database for you. Each of these approaches has its advantages. Each approach is also complex enough to warrant its own chapter, so you'll learn how to implement your entity bean and dependent object classes in Chapter 6, "Bean-Managed Persistence," and Chapter 7, "Container-Managed Persistence." Container-managed persistence also supports a standard query language for retrieving entity objects that is covered in Chapter 8, "EJB Query Language."

The two persistence approaches for entity beans differ in many ways, but there are plenty of common issues to address regardless of which one you choose. Those issues are what you'll see covered in the rest of this chapter. No matter how you choose to implement an entity bean, you must understand the concepts behind how they're intended to be used. From the practical side, you also need to know how to declare home and component interfaces, specify primary key classes, and define deployment descriptors.

DECLARING THE COMPONENT INTERFACE

As you saw earlier in Chapter 3, the client's view of an entity or session bean is defined by the bean's component interface, which consists of a local interface, a remote interface, or both. Clients don't access your EJB classes directly, so any functionality you want to make available has to be exposed through the component interface. The methods you declare in a local or remote interface are commonly referred to as a bean's business methods.

When you declare a remote interface, you must declare it to extend `javax.ejb.EJBObject`. Similarly, a local interface must extend `javax.ejb.EJBLocalObject`. As a bean provider, this requirement doesn't affect you that much (unless you forget to do it) because you don't have to provide a direct implementation of the component interface yourself. Although your bean class must implement the business methods that you declare in its component interface, the class doesn't have to implement the entire interface. It's up to the container to implement the component interface and delegate calls to the business methods to an instance of your bean class. This means that you don't have to worry about coding `EJBObject` and

EJBLocalObject methods, such as getPrimaryKey or remove, when you implement an entity bean. Be sure you understand this point because it might seem strange at first. An enterprise bean supports its component interface, but it doesn't literally implement it in the way you're accustomed to seeing interfaces used in Java.

You can declare an entity bean class to implement its local or remote interface by including the interface in the bean declaration's implements clause. If so, you should provide empty implementations of the EJBObject or EJBLocalObject methods because the container will never invoke them on your bean (it uses its own implementations). However, declaring a bean to implement its component interface isn't an accepted approach among EJB developers. Chapter 16, "Patterns and Strategies in EJB Design," covers the reasons why in more detail.

→ For cautions against directly implementing the component interface, **see** "Using a Business Method Interface," **p. 448**.

The Client View of an Entity Bean

Entity beans support a variety of clients. Most often an entity's clients are session beans but they can also be message-driven beans or other entity beans. If an entity bean is remotely accessible, a Java application, applet, JSP, or servlet could also be a client. If you need to access an entity bean from a non-Java client, CORBA offers that possibility for remote clients as well.

A remote client's view of an entity bean is the same regardless of the client type or location. The client view is always defined by the bean's remote interface, and this view is location independent. A JSP running in the Web tier accesses an entity bean using the same API as a remote client session bean running in the same container as the entity. This characteristic is key to a distributed architecture.

Unlike a remote client, a local client must be an enterprise bean located in the same JVM as the entity bean it's accessing. This type of client accesses the bean through the local interface, but its view of the entity isn't location independent. The biggest difference compared to a remote interface is that method arguments passed through the local interface are passed by reference instead of by value. For example, suppose a Customer entity bean provided both a local and a remote interface that each included a getAddress method that returned an Address object comprised of several strings. If a remote client called this method and modified the values held in the returned Address, the Customer entity would be unaffected. The only way to update the Address would be for the entity to provide another method for that purpose. However, any changes made to the Address by a local client would be seen by the Customer entity because they would both be referencing the same local object. This might sound like a pure advantage, but it can be a little dangerous. When an entity exposes an object is this manner, it's potentially giving up control of how that object is modified.

Although an entity bean is allowed to support both local and remote clients, this isn't typical. As a bean provider, you'll more often select a single type of access to support (usually local in the case of an entity bean). Because of the differences in pass-by-value and pass-by-reference behavior, the choice of client type affects the bean implementation and the granularity of methods exposed through the component interface. The choice of client type should be made early in the design because simply converting a local interface to a remote or vice versa would be an oversimplification of an entity's behavior. For example, more would have to be done to make an entity that exposed fine-grained method access to local clients suitable for remote access. Changing the interface type would make the entity remotely accessible, but the overhead associated with many fine-grained remote calls would likely make it a performance nightmare.

Whether you choose to support local or remote clients, the component interface provides the methods they need to work with an entity bean. After a client obtains a reference to an entity's local or remote interface, it can manipulate the entity object in several ways. In particular, a client can

- Call the entity object's business methods, which is normally what you're most interested in doing
- Call remove to remove the instance from the container and delete the entity from the database
- Obtain the entity object's primary key (using getPrimaryKey)
- Obtain the entity object's handle (only done by remote clients using getHandle)
- Obtain a reference to the entity's home interface (using getEJBLocalHome or getEJBHome)
- Pass the reference as a parameter or return value of a method call (limited to local methods when using the local interface)

EXPOSING BUSINESS METHODS

You don't have to expose every method you plan to implement within your entity bean through its component interface, but you do have to include any methods you want to be accessible from outside the class. At a minimum, you should include get and set methods for the entity's fields that you want clients to be able to access. This is especially true for local interfaces. Remote interfaces work best using methods that group multiple fields into simple data structures. This is a straightforward way to reduce the number of remote calls needed to obtain or set an entity's state. If clients aren't allowed to modify an entity's fields, you can limit the methods in the component interface to get methods. You should also include the business methods that the bean exposes to perform its work in the component interface. Simply put, you should include declarations in the component interface for the methods that make up the public interface you want to expose for your bean.

Because of how a component interface is used, some restrictions are placed on how you declare your methods within it. You can include any type of method that you want—you just have to live with a few rules. In particular, you must declare your methods such that

- No method name starts with ejb (as you'll see later, the container uses methods that have names starting with ejb for special purposes).

- All methods are declared as `public` (remember that you're in effect declaring the public interface for your bean implementation).

- No method can be declared as `static` or `final` (this is true for any Java interface).

- All method arguments and return types for methods in a remote interface must be legal RMI-IIOP types.

- All methods in a remote interface include `java.rmi.RemoteException` in their `throws` clauses (these are remote calls that could fail because of an underlying system or communications problem). Local interface methods use `javax.ejb.EJBException` to report system-level problems instead of `RemoteException`. This unchecked exception doesn't have to be included in the declarations.

Note

The requirements for legal RMI-IIOP types span five pages in OMG's *Java Language to IDL Mapping* document. However, in general, the legal RMI-IIOP types include the Java primitives, remote interfaces, `Serializable` classes, arrays that hold objects of a legal type, and checked exceptions. You can download this document from OMG at `http://www.omg.org/cgi-bin/doc?ptc/00-01-06` if you want a more precise description.

NAMING CONVENTIONS

Because the capability to expose local interfaces is so new to EJB, accepted practices related to them are still in their infancy. One area that comes to the forefront immediately is that of naming conventions. Prior to EJB 2.0, every enterprise bean you created had to have a remote interface, a home interface, and an implementation class. Based on Sun's guidelines in the early EJB specifications, developers quickly standardized how to assign names to each of these elements. To start with, `EnglishAuction` would be a suitable remote interface name for the central entity bean in the auction example. Because clients use the remote interface to interact with a bean, it's always been given the logical name that represents the bean. Based on this name choice, `EnglishAuctionHome` would be the name of the corresponding home interface. The implementation class typically would be named `EnglishAuctionBean`, although some developers prefer a form such as `EnglishAuctionEJB` instead. Situations in which you need more than one implementation of a particular bean are application-specific, so no standard convention exists for that case.

PART

I

CH

5

The fact that a bean can expose both local and remote interfaces complicates your use of the naming convention adopted before EJB 2.0. If you still wanted to name a bean's remote interface `EnglishAuction`, what would you name the local interface if it needed one? Solutions such as the following are possible:

- Name the remote interface `EnglishAuction` (because that's what's always been done) and name the local interface `EnglishAuctionLocal` to distinguish the two.

- Name the remote interface `EnglishAuctionRemote` and the local interface `EnglishAuctionLocal` to be consistent.

- Name the local interface EnglishAuction (because that's typically the only interface exposed by an entity bean) and use EnglishAuctionRemote for the less common remote interface. For a session bean, remote interfaces are more common, so reverse the rule and use AuctionHouse and AuctionHouseLocal for examples of remote and local interface names.

You could come up with arguments both for and against each of these proposals, so it will likely take some time before a clear winner emerges. For the examples presented throughout the remainder of the book, the last option in the list was selected. Applying this same convention to the home interface, the auction entity bean will expose its local home as EnglishAuctionHome. Similarly, session beans will use remote home interfaces with names such as AuctionHouseHome.

THE AUCTION COMPONENT INTERFACES

You saw a simple example of component interfaces back in Chapter 3 when the topic was first introduced. This section goes beyond that to present a set of interfaces applicable to the auction example. To start with, Listing 5.1 declares a local interface for the auction entity bean.

LISTING 5.1 EnglishAuction.java—A LOCAL INTERFACE FOR AN AUCTION ENTITY BEAN

```
package com.que.ejb20.auction.model;
/**
 * Title:       EnglishAuction<p>
 * Description: Local interface for the EnglishAuction entity bean<p>
 */
import java.sql.Timestamp;
import javax.ejb.EJBLocalObject;
import com.que.ejb20.auction.exceptions.InvalidAuctionStatusException;
import com.que.ejb20.auction.exceptions.InvalidBidException;
import com.que.ejb20.auction.view.AuctionDetailView;
import com.que.ejb20.auction.view.BidView;
import com.que.ejb20.item.model.Item;

public interface EnglishAuction extends EJBLocalObject {
  public Integer getId();

  public void setName(String newName);
  public String getName();

  public void setDescription(String newDescription);
  public String getDescription();

  public void setStatus(String newStatus) throws InvalidAuctionStatusException;
  public String getStatus();

  public void setStartingBid(Double newStartingBid)
    throws InvalidAuctionStatusException;
  public Double getStartingBid();

  public void setMinBidIncrement(Double newMinBidIncrement)
    throws InvalidAuctionStatusException;
  public Double getMinBidIncrement();
```

```
public void setReserveAmount(Double newReserveAmount)
  throws InvalidAuctionStatusException;
public Double getReserveAmount();

public void setStartDateTime(Timestamp newStartDateTime)
  throws InvalidAuctionStatusException;
public Timestamp getStartDateTime();

public void setScheduledEndDateTime(Timestamp newScheduledEndDateTime)
  throws InvalidAuctionStatusException;
public Timestamp getScheduledEndDateTime();

public void setActualEndDateTime(Timestamp newActualEndDateTime);
public Timestamp getActualEndDateTime();

public void assignItem(Item newItem, int newQuantity)
  throws InvalidAuctionStatusException;
public Item getItem();
public Integer getQuantity();
public void removeItem() throws InvalidAuctionStatusException;

/**
 * Submit a bid to an open auction
 *
 * @param bidAmount the amount of the bid
 * @param bidder the participant submitting the bid
 * @return the automatically assigned bid transaction ID
 * @throws InvalidBidException if the bid does not meet the criteria for
 *    the next acceptable bid
 * @throws InvalidAuctionStatusException if the auction is not open
 */
public String submitBid(double bidAmount, Bidder bidder)
  throws InvalidBidException, InvalidAuctionStatusException;

/**
 * Determine the next required bid for an auction
 *
 * @return the next acceptable bid amount
 */
public double computeNextBidAmount()
  throws InvalidAuctionStatusException;

public BidView getLeadingBidView();

public BidView getWinningBidView();

public AuctionDetailView getAuctionDetail();

/**
 * Get the time remaining before the auction closes
 *
 * @return the time remaining in msec
 */
public long getTimeLeft();

/**
 * Report whether or not the current leading bid satisfies the reserve
 *
```

LISTING 5.1   CONTINUED

```
    * @return true if the reserve has been met or there is no reserve and
    *    at least one bid has been submitted
    */
  public boolean reserveMet();

  /**
   * Assign the current leading bid as the auction winner
   *
   * @throws InvalidAuctionStatusException if the auction is not Open
   */
  public void assignWinner() throws InvalidAuctionStatusException;
}
```

Listing 5.1 shows that EnglishAuction exposes a number of get and set methods and an equal number of business methods related to auction management and bid submission. The declared methods are a subset of what we would be needed in a fully functioning system, but they're adequate for the purposes here. One of the first things to notice about this interface is that it hides the implementation details of the Bid and AuctionOffering dependent objects that were specified as part of the design. Because AuctionOffering contains only a quantity value, it can be managed using business methods that work with an Item reference and an integer value. Bid is slightly more complex and is handled using a different approach. The Bid dependent object isn't exposed by EnglishAuction, but a BidView class is used to report information about leading and winning bids to clients. This allows an auction to report information about its bids without giving up any control of the persistent objects that represent them.

EnglishAuction makes several references to Item, which is the local interface for the entity bean that will be used to represent the items up for auction. The Item local interface appears in Listing 5.2. It consists solely of get methods for the item properties needed by an auction. The simplifying assumption made for the example is that the items available for auction already exist in the system and don't need to be created or modified.

LISTING 5.2   Item.java—A LOCAL INTERFACE FOR AN ITEM ENTITY BEAN

```
package com.que.ejb20.item.model;
/**
 * Title:        Item<p>
 * Description:  Local interface for the Item entity bean<p>
 */
import javax.ejb.EJBLocalObject;

public interface Item extends EJBLocalObject {

  public Integer getId();

  public String getName();

  public String getDescription();

  public String getImageURL();
}
```

Note

Ignoring the appropriateness of the method granularity found in `EnglishAuction` and `Item`, you could convert these two interfaces to remote interfaces simply by changing their `extends` clauses to reference `EJBObject` and adding `throws RemoteException` to each method declaration. Because `EnglishAuction` exposes `Item` in its component interface (and a remote interface cannot expose a local interface type), changing `EnglishAuction` to a remote interface would require changing `Item` as well.

`EnglishAuction` also references the `Bidder` local interface to associate a bidder with each submitted bid. This interface appears in Listing 5.3. Similar to `Item`, it consists of get methods. It includes methods to report a bidder's shipping and billing addresses using an `AddressView` object in the same way `EnglishAuction` uses `BidView`.

LISTING 5.3   `Bidder.java`—A LOCAL INTERFACE FOR A BIDDER ENTITY BEAN

```java
package com.que.ejb20.auction.model;
/**
 * Title:       Bidder<p>
 * Description: Local interface for the Bidder entity bean<p>
 */
import java.util.List;
import javax.ejb.EJBLocalObject;
import com.que.ejb20.auction.view.AddressView;

public interface Bidder extends EJBLocalObject {

  public Integer getId();

  public String getFirstName();

  public String getLastName();

  public String getEmailAddress();

  public String getUsername();

  public String getPassword();

  public AddressView getShippingAddressView();

  public AddressView getBillingAddressView();

  /**
   * Retrieve all bids submitted by this bidder
   *
   * @return a List of BidView objects
   */
  public List getBids();
}
```

Listing 5.4 and Listing 5.5 show the source for `BidView` and `AddressView`. These classes provide simple data structures that the entity beans can use to report information from their dependent objects. The classes are designated as views to emphasize the fact that manipulating their values has no impact on the underlying persistent data managed by the entity beans. Updates to this type of data are typically done by creating a new instance of one of the view classes with the desired values and passing that to an update method exposed by the associated entity bean. A `Bid` is immutable (you wouldn't want to change a bid amount or any of the other attributes after it's been submitted), so adding the option to perform updates would only apply to `Address` objects in this case.

LISTING 5.4   `BidView.java`—VIEW OF A BID

```
package com.que.ejb20.auction.view;
/**
 * Title:        BidView<p>
 * Description:  Value object for an auction bid<p>
 */
import java.io.Serializable;
import java.sql.Timestamp;

public class BidView implements Serializable {

  private Integer auctionId;
  private Integer bidderId;
  private Timestamp dateTimeSubmitted;
  private String transactionId;
  private Double amount;

  public BidView(Integer newAuctionId, Integer newBidderId,
   Timestamp newDateTimeSubmitted, Double newAmount, String newTransactionId) {

    setAuctionId(newAuctionId);
    setBidderId(newBidderId);
    setDateTimeSubmitted(newDateTimeSubmitted);
    setAmount(newAmount);
    setTransactionId(newTransactionId);
  }

  public Integer getAuctionId() {
    return auctionId;
  }

  public void setAuctionId(Integer newAuctionId) {
    auctionId = newAuctionId;
  }

  public Integer getBidderId() {
    return bidderId;
  }

  public void setBidderId(Integer newBidderId) {
    bidderId = newBidderId;
  }
```

LISTING 5.4   CONTINUED

```
  public Timestamp getDateTimeSubmitted() {
    return dateTimeSubmitted;
  }

  public void setDateTimeSubmitted(Timestamp newDateTimeSubmitted) {
    dateTimeSubmitted = newDateTimeSubmitted;
  }

  public Double getAmount() {
    return amount;
  }

  public void setAmount(Double newAmount) {
    amount = newAmount;
  }

  public String getTransactionId() {
    return transactionId;
  }

  public void setTransactionId(String newTransactionId) {
    transactionId = newTransactionId;
  }
}
```

LISTING 5.5   AddressView.java—VIEW OF AN ADDRESS

```
package com.que.ejb20.auction.view;
/**
 * Title:         AddressView<p>
 * Description:   Value object for an address<p>
 */
import java.io.Serializable;

public class AddressView implements Serializable {

  private String addressLine1;
  private String addressLine2;
  private String city;
  private String state;
  private String zipCode;

  public AddressView(String newAddressLine1, String newAddressLine2,
   String newCity, String newState, String newZipCode) {

    setAddressLine1(newAddressLine1);
    setAddressLine2(newAddressLine2);
    setCity(newCity);
    setState(newState);
    setZipCode(newZipCode);
  }

  public String getAddressLine1() {
    return addressLine1;
  }
```

LISTING 5.5 CONTINUED

```java
  public void setAddressLine1(String newAddressLine1) {
    addressLine1 = newAddressLine1;
  }

  public String getAddressLine2() {
    return addressLine2;
  }

  public void setAddressLine2(String newAddressLine2) {
    addressLine2 = newAddressLine2;
  }

  public String getCity() {
    return city;
  }

  public void setCity(String newCity) {
    city = newCity;
  }

  public String getState() {
    return state;
  }

  public void setState(String newState) {
    state = newState;
  }

  public String getZipCode() {
    return zipCode;
  }

  public void setZipCode(String newZipCode) {
    zipCode = newZipCode;
  }
}
```

View objects aren't restricted to dependent objects. `EnglishAuction` also exposes a method that returns a view of the current state of the auction itself. This option, which is even more important when working with remote clients, provides a convenient way to obtain the state of an entity with a single call. Listing 5.6 defines the object type returned by `getAuctionDetail`.

LISTING 5.6 `AuctionDetailView.java`—**VIEW OF AN AUCTION**

```java
package com.que.ejb20.auction.view;
/**
 * Title:        AuctionDetailView<p>
 * Description:  Detailed view class for an English Auction that presents a
 *               complete description of an auction<p>
 */
import java.io.Serializable;
import java.sql.Timestamp;
```

LISTING 5.6   CONTINUED

```java
public class AuctionDetailView implements Serializable {
  private Integer id;
  private String name;
  private String description;
  private String status;
  private Double startingBid;
  private Double minBidIncrement;
  private Double reserveAmount;
  private Timestamp startDateTime;
  private Timestamp scheduledEndDateTime;
  private Timestamp actualEndDateTime;
  private Double leadingBidAmount;
  private Double winningBidAmount;
  private String itemName;
  private String itemDescription;
  private Integer quantity;
  private String imageURL;

  public AuctionDetailView() {
  }

  public AuctionDetailView(Integer newId, String newName, String newDescription,
    String newStatus, Double newStartingBid, Double newMinBidIncrement,
    Double newReserveAmount, Timestamp newStartDateTime,
    Timestamp newScheduledEndDateTime, Timestamp newActualEndDateTime,
    Double newLeadingBidAmount, Double newWinningBidAmount, String newItemName,
    String newItemDescription, Integer newQuantity, String newImageURL) {

    setId(newId);
    setName(newName);
    setDescription(newDescription);
    setStatus(newStatus);
    setStartingBid(newStartingBid);
    setMinBidIncrement(newMinBidIncrement);
    setReserveAmount(newReserveAmount);
    setStartDateTime(newStartDateTime);
    setScheduledEndDateTime(newScheduledEndDateTime);
    setActualEndDateTime(newActualEndDateTime);
    setLeadingBidAmount(newLeadingBidAmount);
    setWinningBidAmount(newWinningBidAmount);
    setItemName(newItemName);
    setItemDescription(newItemDescription);
    setQuantity(newQuantity);
    setImageURL(newImageURL);
  }

  public Integer getId() {
    return id;
  }

  public void setId(Integer newId) {
    id = newId;
  }
```

PART

I

CH

5

LISTING 5.6   CONTINUED

```java
public void setName(String newName) {
  name = newName;
}

public String getName() {
  return name;
}

public void setDescription(String newDescription) {
  description = newDescription;
}

public String getDescription() {
  return description;
}

public void setStatus(String newStatus) {
  status = newStatus;
}

public String getStatus() {
  return status;
}

public void setStartingBid(Double newStartingBid) {
  startingBid = newStartingBid;
}

public Double getStartingBid() {
  return startingBid;
}

public void setMinBidIncrement(Double newMinBidIncrement) {
  minBidIncrement = newMinBidIncrement;
}

public Double getMinBidIncrement() {
  return minBidIncrement;
}

public void setReserveAmount(Double newReserveAmount) {
  reserveAmount = newReserveAmount;
}

public Double getReserveAmount() {
  return reserveAmount;
}

public void setStartDateTime(Timestamp newStartDateTime) {
  startDateTime = newStartDateTime;
}

public Timestamp getStartDateTime() {
  return startDateTime;
}
```

LISTING 5.6 CONTINUED

```
public void setScheduledEndDateTime(Timestamp newScheduledEndDateTime) {
  scheduledEndDateTime = newScheduledEndDateTime;
}

public Timestamp getScheduledEndDateTime() {
  return scheduledEndDateTime;
}

public void setActualEndDateTime(Timestamp newActualEndDateTime) {
  actualEndDateTime = newActualEndDateTime;
}

public Timestamp getActualEndDateTime() {
  return actualEndDateTime;
}

public void setLeadingBidAmount(Double newLeadingBidAmount) {
  leadingBidAmount = newLeadingBidAmount;
}

public Double getLeadingBidAmount() {
  return leadingBidAmount;
}

public void setWinningBidAmount(Double newWinningBidAmount) {
  winningBidAmount = newWinningBidAmount;
}

public Double getWinningBidAmount() {
  return winningBidAmount;
}

public void setItemName(String newItemName) {
  itemName = newItemName;
}

public String getItemName() {
  return itemName;
}

public void setItemDescription(String newItemDescription) {
  itemDescription = newItemDescription;
}

public String getItemDescription() {
  return itemDescription;
}

public void setQuantity(Integer newQuantity) {
  quantity = newQuantity;
}

public Integer getQuantity() {
  return quantity;
}
```

PART

I

CH

5

LISTING 5.6   CONTINUED

```
public void setImageURL(String newImageURL) {
  imageURL = newImageURL;
}

public String getImageURL() {
  return imageURL;
}
}
```

You should include exceptions in your method declarations as appropriate to report application errors that might occur. Chapter 13, "Exception Handling," covers the details of exceptions and EJBs, but for now, just note that exception handling is an important part of designing your entity beans and their component interfaces. Listing 5.7 and Listing 5.8 show the two application exceptions referenced by EnglishAuction.

→ For more information on reporting application errors, **see** "Application Exceptions," **p. 364**.

LISTING 5.7   InvalidBidException.java—APPLICATION EXCEPTION USED TO RESPOND TO AN UNACCEPTABLE BID

```
package com.que.ejb20.auction.exceptions;
/**
 * Title:        InvalidBidException
 * Description:  Application exception used to report an attempt to submit
 *               a bid that does not meet the required bid amount
 */
import java.text.NumberFormat;

public class InvalidBidException extends Exception {

  /**
   * Construct with the relevant bid amounts
   *
   * @param submittedBid the bid amount that was rejected
   * @param requiredBid the minimum acceptable bid
   */
  public InvalidBidException(double submittedBid, double requiredBid) {
    // format using the currency of the default locale to produce a message like
    // Submitted bid of $50.00 does not satisfy required bid amount of $75.00
    super( "Submitted bid of " +
      NumberFormat.getCurrencyInstance().format(submittedBid) +
      " does not satisfy required bid amount of " +
      NumberFormat.getCurrencyInstance().format(requiredBid) );
  }

  /**
   * Construct with a string to display
   *
   * @param msg the error message to display
   */
  public InvalidBidException(String msg) {
    super(msg);
  }
}
```

> **LISTING 5.8**   `InvalidAuctionStatusException.java`—APPLICATION EXCEPTION USED TO RESPOND TO INVALID BUSINESS METHOD CALLS

```
package com.que.ejb20.auction.exceptions;
/**
 * Title:       InvalidAuctionStatusException
 * Description: Application exception used to report attempts to perform
 *              actions that are inconsistent with the current auction status
 */
public class InvalidAuctionStatusException extends Exception {

  public InvalidAuctionStatusException(String msg) {
    super(msg);
  }
}
```

DEFINING THE PRIMARY KEY CLASS

An entity object must have an associated primary key object. This isn't surprising given that an entity bean instance typically corresponds to a row in a relational database table. Even if you're using an entity bean to represent some other type of data, you still have to associate a primary key with each unique element of that data so the container can keep track of everything. Part of your job as a bean provider is to identify the primary key class for an entity bean within its deployment descriptor. This is true no matter which persistence management approach you choose.

> **Note**
>
> This section isn't intended to imply that all the data associated with an entity bean comes from a single table in a database. More often, an entity bean provides a coarse-grained representation of data from multiple associated tables. However, it's usually the case that a single table is central to the entity so that the association of a primary key is straightforward.

PART

I

CH

5

Just like the database tables to which they map, entity beans need to support primary keys that are defined either by a single field or by a combination of multiple fields. The difference isn't significant, but when you need to use a multiple-field key, you must do a little more work. The rest of this section looks at both approaches.

USING A SINGLE-FIELD KEY

It's common for a table's primary key to be a single field. Usually this field holds an integer value or a string that uniquely defines each row. When this is the case, defining the primary key for a corresponding entity bean is simple. You simply need to define the class that is used to store the primary key as part of the bean's deployment descriptor. You'll see more details about deployment descriptors in Chapter 6 and Chapter 7, but for now, here's how an integer primary key would be identified:

```
<?xml version="1.0"?>

<!DOCTYPE ejb-jar PUBLIC
   '-//Sun Microsystems, Inc.//DTD Enterprise JavaBeans 2.0//EN'
   'http://java.sun.com/dtd/ejb-jar_2_0.dtd'>

<ejb-jar>
  <enterprise-beans>
    ...
    <entity>
      <ejb-name>EnglishAuction</ejb-name>
      <local-home>com.que.ejb20.auction.model.EnglishAuctionHome</local-home>
      <local>com.que.ejb20.auction.model.EnglishAuction</local>
      <ejb-class>com.que.ejb20.auction.model.EnglishAuctionBean</ejb-class>
      <persistence-type>Bean</persistence-type>
      <prim-key-class>java.lang.Integer</prim-key-class>
      <reentrant>False</reentrant>
      ...
    </entity>
    ...
  </enterprise-beans>
  ...
</ejb-jar>
```

As you can see, the `prim-key-class` element is used to identify an entity bean's primary key class by specifying its fully qualified name. The primary key class can be any legal RMI-IIOP value type, which mostly means that it must implement `Serializable` and it must not implement `java.rmi.Remote`. For example, you can use standard Java types, such as `String`, `Integer`, and `Long`, as a primary key.

If you're using container-managed persistence (CMP) with a single-field key, you also must identify the entity bean field that maps to the primary key using the `primkey-field` element:

```
...
<prim-key-class>java.lang.Integer</prim-key-class>
<primkey-field>id</primkey-field>
...
```

The field you identify with `primkey-field` must be a container-managed field and it must be of the type specified by `prim-key-class`. Don't include `primkey-field` in your deployment descriptor if you're using bean-managed persistence (BMP) or you're using CMP with a multiple-field key.

USING A MULTIPLE-FIELD KEY

If you map an entity bean to a table whose primary key is composed or more than one field, you must declare a primary key class to represent the key in the entity bean. The class must follow the rules for RMI-IIOP value types, so you must declare it to implement `Serializable` and it can't implement `java.rmi.Remote`. The class must also provide appropriate implementations of the `hashCode` and `equals` methods. There are a few other rules to adhere to if you're using CMP (you should follow the first three for BMP as well):

- A primary key class must be declared `public`.

- A primary key class must declare a `public`, no-argument constructor.

- All fields that make up the key in a primary key class must be declared `public`.

- Each field name in a primary key class must exactly match one of the container-managed field names.

When you create a primary key class, you'll often be doing it to support a specific entity bean. You're also allowed to use the same primary key class for multiple beans if you want—this is no different than using `String` or `Integer` for multiple classes.

Listing 5.9 shows an example of a primary key class that defines a two-field key. `CarModelPK` represents a key that could be used to uniquely identify a car model by its make and model.

LISTING 5.9 `CarModelPK.java`—AN EXAMPLE OF A PRIMARY KEY CLASS

```java
public final class CarModelPK implements java.io.Serializable {
  public String make;
  public String model;
  private Integer myHashCode;

  public CarModelPK() {
  }

  public CarModelPK(String make, String model) {
    this.make = make;
    this.model = model;
  }

  public String toString() {
    return make + " " + model;
  }

  public int hashCode() {

    if (myHashCode == null) {
      // the components of a primary key are immutable
      // so this only needs to be computed once
      myHashCode = new Integer(make.hashCode() ^ model.hashCode());
    }
    return myHashCode.intValue();
  }

  public boolean equals(Object other) {
    // always check for the same object in an equals method
    if (this == other) return true;

    // declaring the class as final makes this a fast comparison
    if (!(other instanceof CarModelPK)) return false;

    CarModelPK otherPK = (CarModelPK)other;
    if (!make.equals(otherPK.make)) return false;
    if (!model.equals(otherPK.model)) return false;
```

LISTING 5.9   CONTINUED

```
    return true;
  }
}
```

SPECIFYING THE PRIMARY KEY AT DEPLOYMENT

Sometimes an entity bean has a natural primary key, but not always. For example, identifying a car by its make and model is intuitive, and so is identifying an employee by an employee number assigned by an HR department. However, many times a primary key is nothing but a unique number or string. Even though it's consistent with common practices, there's nothing natural about assigning an integer value to be the primary key for an auction. It gives you a unique way to identify an auction, but there's no real-world business meaning to it. When this is the case, it's possible to defer the choice of a primary key class to the deployer if you're using CMP.

Even if you assign a somewhat arbitrary primary key class to an entity bean, you should go ahead and specify it in the deployment descriptor if you know the type of key that will be stored in the database. That is, if you're using a sequence number as a primary key, you should go ahead and specify that the primary key class is Integer (or whatever integer type you decide on). The only time you might want to defer this choice is if you're not sure how the key will ultimately be implemented in the database or if you have to support multiple database types that use different keys. For example, if you have to support native sequencing with one database but unique strings with another, you can't specify a single key class that works in both situations. The solution here is to define the prim-key-class as Object and defer the final choice until deployment.

This approach is not without its drawbacks. When you defer the choice of your primary key class, you can't write code in your beans that depend on any specific primary key class behavior. This is also true for the clients that access your bean because the primary key exposed to them will be declared as Object as well. The actual subclass type isn't known until deployment, so no code can assume a particular choice.

DECLARING THE HOME INTERFACE

Every entity or session bean must have a home interface that extends javax.ejb.EJBHome, or a local home interface that extends javax.ejb.EJBLocalHome, or both. The home interface provides factory operations that allow clients to create and remove EJB instances. In the case of entity beans, this interface also allows clients to obtain references to existing entity beans and to execute business methods that aren't specific to a particular entity object. The methods for removing an entity object are included for you in the declarations of EJBHome and EJBLocalHome, but you're responsible for declaring your own methods to create and find entities and execute business logic.

Note

The EJB 2.0 Specification uses the term *component interface* when referring to the local and remote interfaces collectively. However, there isn't an equivalent name used when referring to both the home and the local home interfaces. This book follows the same convention used by the specification and identifies these interfaces generically as the *home interface*. When a point specific to a local client is being made, the interface is referred to as the *local home interface*. Similarly, *remote home interface* is used when necessary for clarity.

CREATING AN ENTITY BEAN

You might define entity beans that represent read-only data in a system. You might also define entity beans whose attributes can be modified by a client with changes written to the underlying data store. Both of these situations can be supported without a client ever needing to create a new entity object. However, if you do want a client to be able to create a new entity, you must define at least one `create` method in the bean's home interface.

You should declare a `create` method for each way you want a client to be able to create an entity. This is similar to declaring multiple constructors in a class that accept different types of initialization parameters. To allow a client to create an entity without proving any initialization data, you might define a method like the following:

```
public EnglishAuction create() throws CreateException;
```

To support initialization data, you might use the following:

```
public EnglishAuction createWithData(String name, String description)
  throws CreateException;
```

As you can see from these examples, which are valid for a local home interface, `create` methods follow a prescribed form. In particular, each of your `create` methods in a local home must

- Have a name that starts with `create`
- Be declared to return the local interface type
- Include `javax.ejb.CreateException` in its `throws` clause

The requirements for a remote home interface are similar in that each `create` method declared here must

- Have a name that starts with `create`
- Be declared to return the remote interface type
- Include `java.rmi.RemoteException` and `javax.ejb.CreateException` in its `throws` clause

As you'll see later, each `create` method you declare must have corresponding `ejbCreate` and `ejbPostCreate` methods in the bean implementation class. If these methods declare additional exceptions, those exceptions must be included in the `throws` clause of the `create` method as well. Home interface methods provided for remote clients represent remote calls,

PART

I

CH

5

so declaring that they might throw a RemoteException is necessary just as it is for remote interface methods. CreateException is a standard exception used to report an error during creation from which a client might be able to recover. This exception is covered more in Chapter 13.

→ To learn more about reporting a problem during entity creation, **see** "CreateException," **p. 367.**

FINDING AN ENTITY BEAN

Often, more important than creating an entity object is locating one that already exists. To support this, you declare methods known as *finder methods* in the home interface. A finder method is responsible for locating all objects that match some particular criteria. At a minimum, every home interface supports finding an entity by primary key using a method declaration such as

```
public EnglishAuction findByPrimaryKey(Integer primaryKey)
    throws FinderException;
```

The findByPrimaryKey method is required to have this exact name, to return the local (or remote) interface type, and to accept a single parameter of the primary key type. As with create methods, there are certain rules to follow when you declare your own finder methods. Each of your finder methods declared in the local home interface must

- Have a name that starts with find
- Be declared to return the local interface type or a collection of objects that implement the local interface
- Include javax.ejb.FinderException (see Chapter 13) in its throws clause

The requirements for a remote home interface are similar in that each of these finder methods must

- Have a name that starts with find
- Be declared to return the remote interface type or a collection of objects that implement the remote interface
- Include java.rmi.RemoteException and javax.ejb.FinderException in its throws clause

As an example, you might declare additional finders used by local clients to locate auctions based on their current state:

```
public Collection findAllAuctions() throws FinderException;
public Collection findNonPendingAuctions() throws FinderException;
public EnglishAuction findAuctionForItem(Integer itemId)
    throws FinderException;
```

REMOVING AN ENTITY BEAN

EJBHome declares two methods that you can use to remove enterprise bean instances:

```
void remove(Handle handle) throws RemoteException, RemoveException;
void remove(Object primaryKey) throws RemoteException, RemoveException;
```

Local clients don't need to work with handles to enterprise beans, so `EJBLocalHome` declares only a single `remove` method:

```
void remove(Object primaryKey) throws EJBException, RemoveException;
```

The container implements these methods for you, so you don't have to worry about defining them. You should remember that the component interface also includes a `remove` method. The difference with the methods defined here is that you don't have to go to the effort to obtain a local or remote reference to an entity object to delete it if you know its handle or primary key value. The important point to make about the `remove` methods in both the component and home interfaces is that they result in the referenced entity being deleted from the underlying data store. After an entity has been removed, any call made to it by a client that still holds a remote interface reference to it results in a `java.rmi.NoSuchObjectException`. A local client call on an invalid local interface reference results in a `javax.ejb.NoSuchObjectLocalException`.

DECLARING HOME INTERFACE BUSINESS METHODS

Prior to the EJB 2.0 Specification, all entity bean business methods had to be accessed through the component interface. This meant that an invocation of a business method was always associated with a particular entity object even if the logic of the method didn't require access to that entity's state. If you needed to perform some processing related to a certain entity class but independent of an instance, you either declared the method as part of the component interface anyway or implemented it in a session bean. You can't declare EJB business methods as `static`, so there was no way to indicate the intent of these methods when they were declared within the entity bean class.

EJB 2.0 introduced the concept of the *home method*. As the name implies, a home method is a business method declared in the home interface instead of in the remote. Home methods are intended to support business logic that is closely tied to an entity bean class but not to a single instance. Because the home interface is a factory that is never associated with a single instance, home methods can't access any instance data when executing. The following rules govern home methods:

- A home method can be named anything in general, but its name can't start with `create`, `find`, or `remove`.

- The parameters and return type of a home method declared in a remote home interface must be legal RMI-IIOP types.

- The `throws` clause of a home method may include application exceptions as appropriate. When declared in a remote home interface, the `throws` clause must include `java.rmi.RemoteException`.

A use of a home method for the auction entity bean might be to report all the items that are currently up for auction:

```
public Collection getItemsBeingAuctioned();
```

PART

I

CH

5

THE EnglishAuctionHome INTERFACE

Listing 5.10 puts all the possibilities together to present a possible local home interface for the auction entity bean. This listing includes several create and finder methods and an example of a home method declaration.

LISTING 5.10   EnglishAuctionHome.java—A LOCAL HOME INTERFACE FOR AN AUCTION ENTITY BEAN

```java
package com.que.ejb20.auction.model;
/**
 * Title:        EnglishAuctionHome<p>
 * Description:  Home interface for the EnglishAuction entity bean<p>
 */
import java.util.Collection;
import javax.ejb.EJBLocalHome;
import javax.ejb.CreateException;
import javax.ejb.FinderException;

public interface EnglishAuctionHome extends EJBLocalHome {

  /**
   * Create an auction without initializing it
   */
  public EnglishAuction create() throws CreateException;

  /**
   * Create an auction and perform some limited initialization
   */
  public EnglishAuction createWithData(String name, String description)
    throws CreateException;

  /**
   * Retrieve an auction using its primary key
   */
  public EnglishAuction findByPrimaryKey(Integer primaryKey)
    throws FinderException;

  /**
   * Retrieve all the auctions
   */
  public Collection findAllAuctions() throws FinderException;

  /**
   * Retrieve all the auctions that are open, cancelled, or closed
   */
  public Collection findNonPendingAuctions() throws FinderException;

  /**
   * Home method for reporting all auction items
   */
  public Collection getItemsBeingAuctioned();
}
```

IMPLEMENTING AN ENTITY BEAN

A goal of this chapter has been to cover how to declare the interfaces for an entity bean that are exposed to clients, but not to get into the implementation details (that's saved for the two chapters that follow). However, some implementation topics relate to both BMP and CMP, so it's better to get to them now. No matter which persistence mechanism you choose, you need to understand the interfaces specific to an entity bean implementation class, and you need to know how to implement a bean's business and home methods. It's also important to cover how the container interacts with your bean classes.

THE EntityBean INTERFACE

Your bean classes must always either directly or indirectly implement the javax.ejb.EntityBean interface. This interface is an extension of the EnterpriseBean marker interface and it defines several of the callback methods used by the container to interact with your bean classes. The interface consists of the following declarations:

```
public interface EntityBean extends EnterpriseBean {
    public void ejbActivate() throws EJBException, RemoteException;
    public void ejbPassivate() throws EJBException, RemoteException;
    public void ejbLoad() throws EJBException, RemoteException;
    public void ejbStore() throws EJBException, RemoteException;
    public void ejbRemove() throws RemoveException, EJBException,
        RemoteException;
    public void setEntityContext(EntityContext ctx) throws EJBException,
        RemoteException;
    public void unsetEntityContext() throws EJBException, RemoteException;
}
```

Note

A *marker interface* such as EnterpriseBean doesn't declare any methods or fields. Its purpose is simply to identify a class as belonging to a particular category. In this case, you identify an entity bean as being an enterprise bean by (indirectly) implementing the EnterpriseBean interface.

You'll see the use of the ejb callback methods declared by EntityBean discussed later in this section. Two of the EntityBean methods, setEntityContext and getEntityContext, are used to associate a runtime context with an entity instance. This context is an object that implements the EntityContext interface. It is through this interface that an entity bean instance is able to make calls to the container.

An important point to note about the declarations found in EntityBean relates to the references to RemoteException. This exception is used by methods declared in a remote interface or remote home interface to report system errors. RemoteException cannot be used in local interface or local home declarations, which should makes its use here seem out of place to you. The only reason RemoteException is included in these declarations is for backward compatibility with EJB 1.0. When using EJB 2.0, you must throw EJBException instead of

RemoteException to report system errors. So, your implementations of the EntityBean methods will never actually include RemoteException in their throws clauses. This is fine because a method implementation can always throw fewer exceptions than what its declaration in an interface indicates. You should take this same approach when using EJB 1.1, but the container will let you get away with throwing RemoteException if you don't.

→ To learn more about EJBException and RemoteException, **see** "System Exceptions," **p. 372**.

THE EntityContext INTERFACE

EntityContext extends EJBContext to define an interface to an entity bean's runtime context that is provided by the container. EJBContext allows a bean instance to obtain a reference to its home, obtain security information about its caller (see Chapter 14, "Security Management"), or work with the current transaction (see Chapter 12). Table 5.2 summarizes the purposes of the methods declared by EJBContext. You'll see more on these methods in later chapters.

TABLE 5.2 METHODS OF THE EJBContext INTERFACE

Return Type	Method Name	Description
Principal	getCallerPrincipal()	Get the security Principal that identifies the caller.
boolean	getRollbackOnly()	Test whether the current transaction has been marked for rollback.
void	setRollbackOnly()	Mark the current transaction for rollback.
EJBHome	getEJBHome()	Get the bean's remote home interface.
EJBLocalHome	getEJBLocalHome()	Get the bean's local home interface.
UserTransaction	getUserTransaction()	Get the transaction demarcation interface.
boolean	isCallerInRole (String role)	Test to see whether the caller has a given security role.

EntityContext adds the following three methods to those declared by EJBContext:

```
public EJBObject getEJBObject() throws IllegalStateException;
public EJBLocalObject getEJBLocalObject() throws IllegalStateException;
public Object getPrimaryKey() throws IllegalStateException;
```

These methods can be called by an instance from within a business method or certain callback methods. Some callback methods, such as ejbCreate, are invoked at a point where the EntityContext methods aren't accessible. You'll learn more about ejbCreate shortly, but in this case, there isn't an EJB object identity associated with the instance when the method is called. If you try to call getEJBObject, getEJBLocalObject, or getPrimaryKey in this situation, an IllegalStateException is thrown.

The purpose of the `getPrimaryKey` method should be fairly obvious. You can call this method to get a reference to the primary key associated with an entity bean instance. The meaning of the `getEJBObject` and `getEJBLocalObject` methods might not be quite so apparent to you at first glance. Remember that `EJBObject` is the interface that must be extended by any enterprise bean's remote interface, and `EJBLocalObject` must be extended by any local interface. The `getEJBObject` and `getEJBLocalObject` methods allow you to obtain a reference to the component interface associated with an instance. This is useful if an entity needs to pass a reference to itself as a method parameter or return value. You'll see more about this in Chapter 16.

> **Caution**
>
> Because an entity bean isn't required to have both a local and a remote interface, calls to `getEJBLocalObject` and `getEJBObject` aren't always valid. If you call a method for which a corresponding interface doesn't exist, an `IllegalStateException` is thrown. The same is true for invalid calls to `getEJBHome` or `getEJBLocalHome`.

BUSINESS METHODS

Every business method you define in a bean's component interface must have a corresponding implementation in your bean class. Just as with any interface method implementation, a method in the bean class must have the same name, parameter list, and return type as the declaration in the interface. If the method implementation is declared to throw any exceptions, you must include those exceptions in the interface declaration as well. This is typically the case when you define application-specific exceptions to report business logic errors. Even though your remote interface declarations must always include `RemoteException` in their throws clauses, your bean class implementations should never list this exception. If an entity bean method calls a remote method that might throw a `RemoteException`, it needs to catch that exception and throw `EJBException` to its client instead.

You'll see examples of business method implementations in the next two chapters. These implementations are independent of your choice of BMP or CMP. This is because your business methods access the persistent fields within an entity bean instead of accessing the database directly. All database access for an entity bean is encapsulated in methods such as `ejbLoad` and `ejbStore`.

HOME METHODS

You must provide an implementation for every home method declared in an entity bean's home interface. The requirements for these method implementations are, for the most part, the same as those for component interface business methods. A home method implementation must be declared with the same parameter list and return type as its declaration in the interface, but there's a difference when it comes to the method name. Instead of naming a home method implementation to match the home interface, you must name it using that name (with its first character uppercased) with `ejbHome` in front of it. For example, `ejbHomeGetItemsBeingAuctioned` would correspond to a home interface declaration for `getItemsBeingAuctioned`.

The same rules for declaring exceptions that apply to component interface methods apply to home methods as well. Any exceptions that you include in the `throws` clause of a home method declaration must appear in the home interface declaration too.

An interesting aspect of home methods relates to how the container executes one. While reading the description that's been provided of them so far, you've likely considered them to be similar to `static` methods in regular Java classes. They do share the fact that both of these method types are used by a class to do work that doesn't depend on the instance variables of the class. You never even have to create an instance of a class to execute one of its `static` methods. In this respect, home methods are handled differently than `static` methods. The good news is that the mechanism for executing home methods, which makes use of the bean pool, is handled transparently by the container.

You were introduced to the concept of bean pooling back in Chapter 3. There you saw that the container optimizes resources by maintaining a pool of objects that can be associated with a particular bean instance as needed. When a client calls a home method, the container pulls an object from the pool without associating it with a particular entity object. It then invokes the home method that was called on that object and returns the result to the client. A home method isn't allowed to access the attributes of a particular entity instance, so there's no need for the object to be associated with one. When the method call completes, the object is returned to the pool.

Callback Methods and an Entity Bean's Life Cycle

The container manages an entity bean's existence using a set of callback methods that it invokes on a bean instance. These methods include those defined by the `EntityBean` interface and the methods that are required to support the operations declared by the home interface. You're responsible as a bean provider for implementing these methods, so it's important to understand when they're called and what they're expected to do. This chapter is mostly concerned with when they're called by the container because what you do within them is determined by whether you're using BMP or CMP.

Callback methods are invoked based on where an entity bean is within its life cycle. The EJB specification defines three states that an entity bean instance can be in: *does not exist*, *pooled state*, and *ready state*. Transitions between these states are, for the most part, associated with a call to one or more callback methods.

The existence of an entity bean instance begins when the container creates an instance of the bean implementation class using the `Class.newInstance` method. The container then calls `setEntityContext` to assign a runtime context to the instance. It's important to understand that the instance isn't yet associated with any particular entity object identity. Its attributes hold nothing but their default values because no data has been retrieved from the database and assigned to the instance. The instance has only moved into the pooled state where it can eventually be associated with a particular entity when needed. The container places a number of instances into the pooled state to help with resource management and to satisfy client requests that don't depend on a particular entity's state. Instances in the pooled state are all equivalent, and any one of them can be used by the container to execute a finder or home method without ever having to have an entity object identity assigned to it. Remember from the preceding discussion of home methods, that ejbHome methods are the callbacks used by the container to execute them.

> **Note**
>
> All instances of an enterprise bean are created by the container using Class.newInstance, which requires a no-argument constructor to be available for each bean class. You'll never use a bean's constructor yourself, so the simplest way to support this requirement is to never declare any constructors for your bean classes. This way, the default constructor will always be present for the container's use.

An entity bean instance moves into the ready state when it's assigned an entity object identity. This happens either when a new entity is created or an existing entity is activated. The container creates an entity in response to a client call of a create method. You don't implement the create method in your bean class—you implement corresponding ejbCreate and ejbPostCreate methods instead. As an example, the earlier createWithData method defined in EnglishAuctionHome would have a corresponding declaration of

```
public Integer ejbCreateWithData(String name, String description)
  throws CreateException {

  // do the required work and return the primary key if doing BMP
  // or null if doing CMP
}
```

After the container creates an entity object, it selects an instance from the pool and calls its ejbCreate method. This method must have the same parameter list as the create method and it must be declared to throw CreateException. Instead of returning a component interface reference, an ejbCreate method must be declared to return the primary key type. After completion of the ejbCreate method, the instance has a primary key value that corresponds to its entity object identity. Its ejbPostCreate method is then called. This method is declared like the following:

```
public void ejbPostCreateWithData(String name, String description) {
  // do any initialization required after creation
}
```

After the ejbPostCreate method completes, the entity instance moves into the ready state and the container returns a corresponding local or remote interface reference to the client, as appropriate.

An entity instance can also move into the ready state in response to a call to its ejbActivate method. This is a result of the object pooling used by the container to manage its resources.

PART

I

CH

5

Entity objects referenced by a client can be passivated and returned to the pool if the resources used by the instance need to be applied elsewhere. In this case, an entity object identity exists but it's not currently assigned to a bean instance. The same is true when a finder method is executed. For each finder method you declare, either you (BMP) or the container (CMP) must supply a corresponding `ejbFind` method like the following:

```
public Collection ejbFindAllAuctions() throws FinderException {
   // determine the primary keys of all the existing auctions
   // and return a collection of them
}
```

An `ejbFind` method must accept the same parameter list as its corresponding finder declaration and it must be declared to throw `FinderException`. Instead of returning one or more component interface references, an `ejbFind` method must return primary key values. The object identities are known for the results of a finder method, but no operations have yet been performed on them that require knowledge of their state from the database. This means that these entity objects are in effect in a passivated state. The same is true after the invocation of CMP select methods that you'll learn about in Chapter 7.

No matter how an entity object enters a passivated state, it becomes active only when the container selects an entity instance to associate with it and invokes the `ejbActivate` method of that instance to move it into the ready state. An instance in the ready state has an assigned object identity, but it doesn't necessarily know the attribute values for that object yet. At the point a business method is first executed on an instance that hasn't loaded its object's state, that state must be loaded from the database. If you're using BMP, the container calls the `ejbLoad` method you're responsible for implementing to retrieve the object's state. For CMP, the container loads the object's state and then calls `ejbLoad` in case there's anything you need to do after the object's state has been synchronized. While in the ready state, updates to the entity are transferred to the database by calls to your `ejbStore` method (BMP) or by the container. It is within the ready state that an entity instance services business method calls from clients.

An instance is returned to the pooled state if it's passivated or removed. If the container decides to passivate an instance, it calls its `ejbStore` method to make certain that the object's state is correctly synchronized with the database, and then it calls `ejbPassivate`. The purpose of `ejbPassivate` isn't to write an object's state to the database, it's just to give you the chance to do anything that might be necessary (such as releasing some resource being used by the instance) before the instance is returned to the pool.

When a client invokes a `remove` method on either the home or component interface, the container calls `ejbRemove` on the corresponding bean instance. If you're using BMP, `ejbRemove` is where you delete the object from the database and release any resources associated with it. For CMP, the container calls your `ejbRemove` method to allow you to release its resources (if necessary) before the object is deleted. After a call to `ejbRemove`, the container returns the instance to the pooled state.

The container might allow an instance in the pooled state to be garbage collected. If so, the instance's `unsetEntityContext` method is called and it is removed from the pool. As you'll see later in Chapter 13, an instance throwing a system exception is one reason the container will discard it in this manner.

Figure 5.1 summarizes the method calls and state transitions that define an entity bean's life cycle.

Figure 5.1
An entity bean instance can be described by one of three states during its life cycle.

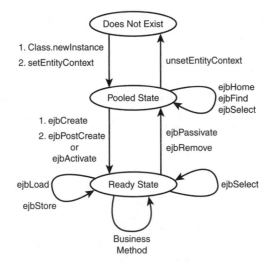

ACCESSING THE ENVIRONMENT

Entity bean instances are obviously highly configurable because most of their attribute values are read from a database. It's also possible that some of your bean method implementations could benefit from configuration information that applies to all instances of an entity bean. As you saw back in Chapter 4, "Java Naming and Directory Interface," the correct way to do this is to use entries in the bean's environment. For example, you might use a JNDI lookup from a create method to set the default minimum bid increment for an auction:

```
InitialContext ctx = new InitialContext();
Double minIncrement = (Double)ctx.lookup("java:comp/env/DefaultBidIncrement");
```

→ To learn more about environment entries, **see** "Accessing an EJB's Environment," **p. 98**.

INHERITANCE AND ENTITY BEANS

Inheritance is central in object-oriented design, but it's a topic that, for the most part, is sidestepped by the EJB specification. It's not that you're prevented from using inheritance with your EJBs, but there are a few issues to consider when you do. The central question relates to the type of inheritance that you implement.

In an ideal world, you could seamlessly define a hierarchy of entity bean classes and corresponding home and component interface hierarchies. Here an entity bean and all its constituent parts could be declared to extend some other entity bean without any special consideration on your part. This resulting component inheritance would reflect what you typically do with regular Java classes by allowing you to treat any subclass like the common superclass. This concept carries over quite well to entity bean classes and component interfaces. Inheritance in this case is handled as the normal addition of method implementations and any accompanying overrides. Home interfaces are not quite as simple, though.

When you declare `create` and single-object finder methods in a home interface, you declare their return type to be the corresponding component interface type. The corresponding `ejbCreate` and `ejbFind` methods in the implementation class must be declared to return the primary key type, though. It's important to remember here that it's illegal for two methods in a class hierarchy to have signatures that differ only in return type. This creates a problem if the primary key class in a hierarchy of EJB classes isn't the same for every class. This issue is the primary reason mentioned by the EJB 2.0 Specification for not supporting transparent component inheritance. A possible solution is to declare the primary key to be `Object`, but that limits the knowledge of the key class that bean methods and clients can use. The home interface and parts of the bean implementation must operate in a generic manner for this to work. This is basically the same as deferring the primary key choice until deployment that was discussed earlier in the chapter.

Finder methods bring up a limitation of home interface inheritance as well. Intuitively, calling a finder method on the home interface of an entity bean with subclasses should produce results that include references to any subclass instances that fit the criteria used by the finder. It might be possible to achieve this using BMP by applying some knowledge of the subclasses, but it won't be the case for CMP. Instead, you'd have to implement a home method or a session bean method that called the individual finders and consolidated the results for return to the client.

DECLARING AN ENTITY BEAN CLASS HIERARCHY

Although it's true that you should avoid inheritance of home interfaces in general, you shouldn't avoid inheritance altogether. Inheritance within bean class implementations and component interfaces allows you to build a certain amount of layering into a design, just as you would if you weren't using EJBs. What you typically do to avoid any issues with home interfaces, though, is to stop subclassing when you reach the first concrete entity bean along a branch in the inheritance tree. The first step in this approach is to create an abstract implementation of `EntityBean`, as shown in Listing 5.11.

LISTING 5.11 `AbstractEntity.java`—AN ABSTRACT IMPLEMENTATION OF `EntityBean`

```
package com.que.ejb20.common.ejb;
/**
 * Title:       AbstractEntity<p>
 * Description:  Abstract class for entity beans. This class implements
 *    setEntityContext and unsetEntityContext and provides do-nothing
 *    implementations for the other methods declared by EntityBean.<p>
 */
import javax.ejb.EntityBean;
import javax.ejb.EntityContext;
import javax.ejb.RemoveException;
```

LISTING 5.11 CONTINUED

```java
public abstract class AbstractEntity implements EntityBean {

  protected EntityContext ctx;

  public void ejbActivate() {}

  public void ejbLoad() {}

  public void ejbPassivate() {}

  public void ejbRemove() throws RemoveException {}

  public void ejbStore() {}

  public void setEntityContext(EntityContext newCtx) {
    ctx = newCtx;
  }

  public void unsetEntityContext() {
    ctx = null;
  }
}
```

The implementation of AbstractEntity does little more than manage the assignment of the EntityContext, but even that reduces what you have to implement in a concrete entity class. This class also provides do-nothing implementations of the container callback methods, which, as you'll see in Chapter 7, is often all you need when you're using CMP. If your design called for any other behavior common to all entity beans, a class like AbstractEntity would provide a place to implement that also.

> **Note**
>
> Declaring a base class that implements an interface by providing do-nothing implementations of its methods is a well-established pattern in object-oriented design. This approach is documented as the Adapter pattern in *Design Patterns: Elements of Reusable Object-Oriented Software* by Erich Gamma, Richard Helm, Ralph Johnson, and John Vlissides. If you only need to implement behavior for a subset of an interface's methods, you can extend an Adapter for the interface and override the methods you care about. This frees your classes from being cluttered with methods that don't do anything.

You can next build on AbstractEntity to define application-specific behavior. This can mean extending AbstractEntity to declare your concrete entity beans or it might mean having one or more other layers in between them. Suppose, for example, that the requirements for the auction site included supporting both English and reverse auctions. You might want to extend AbstractEntity to define the behavior common to both auction types in a class called AbstractAuction. You could then extend AbstractAuction to define

PART

I

CH

5

`EnglishAuctionBean` and `ReverseAuctionBean` classes. The business methods implemented by the auction classes could be defined by a parallel set of interfaces. Each bean's component interface would be declared to extend its corresponding business method interface in addition to `EJBObject` or `EJBLocalObject`. You'll see this topic discussed more in Chapter 16.

What this approach doesn't address is any inheritance of the home interfaces. The `EnglishAuctionHome` and `ReverseAuctionHome` interfaces would be independent. Because there aren't any concrete entity beans that are superclasses of other beans, this isn't too much of a limitation. Figure 5.2 shows the resulting relationship between the classes and interfaces.

Figure 5.2
Creating a hierarchy of component interfaces and bean classes allows you to layer a design.

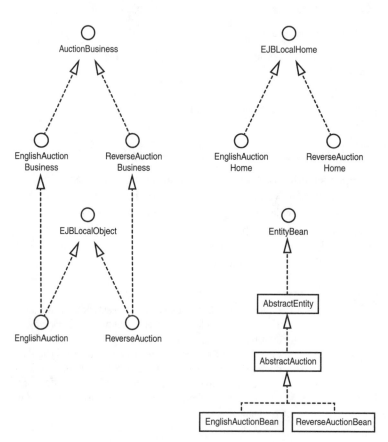

ARE ENTITY BEANS WORTH IT?

You might find this section title to be a strange one given that this is the entity bean chapter of an EJB book. Many developers are successfully using entity beans to build complex enterprise applications while others are debating whether the benefits entity beans offer outweigh their overhead. As with most technology issues, the answer to this question depends on what you're trying to do. EJB is a heavyweight architecture that's designed to support distributed transactions and concurrent access to shared data by multiple users. There are obviously many applications that don't need the horsepower offered by EJB, and its use for them isn't appropriate. Even when EJB is appropriate for an application, some developers question whether entity beans are a good choice.

Entity beans are singled out in discussions about EJB performance and overhead in part because other alternatives exist for managing persistent data. Most of the description of entity beans focuses on persistence because that's their unique role within EJB. If all you're doing with an entity bean is simple persistence of a set of attributes, it's probably true that the overhead involved isn't justified. The first point to remember here is that entity beans are intended to do more than read and write database entries. It's true that an entity bean does this, but it should also provide the business logic associated with these attributes so that coarse-grained objects can be built up and reused across an enterprise. These reusable components can then be composed as needed to do the transactional work of a system.

Session beans are sometimes proposed as an alternative to working with the database in an EJB system. As you'll see in later chapters, this can be appropriate in certain situations. Session beans provide the same transactional support as entity beans do without some of the additional overhead. They don't, however, offer the same support for relationships between persistent objects, so you would likely use them in a limited fashion when working with the database. Perhaps more significant is that session beans don't offer the support for concurrency provided by entity beans. Access to an entity bean instance by multiple clients is managed so that use of the entity is automatically serialized. If you use a session bean to write to the database, you have to manage the possibility of simultaneous attempts to read and write the same data yourself. Session beans can be highly beneficial for read-only access to data, though. This is true even in the case of data that's mapped to an entity bean for creation and editing.

The new CMP features offered by the EJB 2.0 Specification have helped to calm some of the criticism of entity beans. As you'll see in Chapter 7 and Chapter 8, CMP now requires vendor support for managing relationships between entity beans. A common syntax also has been defined to support the implementation of finder methods. Although there are still plenty of features that would be nice to have, the latest CMP specification is definitely a step in the right direction. The increased standards should result in more sophisticated tools for implementing CMP beans and simplify the task of developing entity beans for use in multiple vendor's containers.

JAVA DATA OBJECTS

While EJB continues to mature in its own right, other parallel efforts are taking place that have the potential to offer some interesting solutions for enterprise development. Of particular interest when discussing entity beans is the Java Data Objects (JDO) Specification. A goal of JDO is to provide a transparent mechanism that allows application developers to build persistent classes without writing any of the persistence code themselves. This responsibility is transferred to a pluggable JDO implementation that can provide the required interaction between a persistent class and an underlying data store.

PART

I

CH

5

It's beyond the scope of this book to go into the details of JDO, but it's a technology you should be watching. At the time of this writing, the JDO Specification 1.0 is in proposed final draft form under the Java Community Process. The specification spells out explicit requirements for the integration of JDO with EJB. In particular, this technology is targeted toward the management of dependent objects by session beans and the persistence of BMP entity beans and their dependent objects. The potential of JDO to be a standard mechanism for managing lightweight persistent objects has caught the attention of many EJB developers looking for alternatives to entity beans.

CHAPTER  6

BEAN-MANAGED PERSISTENCE

In this chapter

CHOOSING TO MANAGE PERSISTENCE YOURSELF

For every entity bean you develop, you have the option to write the database access code to manage its persistence yourself. The other choice is to define mappings between your bean's fields and the database and put the responsibility on the container to keep your bean and the database in synch. This chapter looks at what you have to do to manage a bean's persistence yourself. The two chapters that follow look at what you do to let the container do more of the work for you.

Most of this chapter is focused on the mechanics of implementing a bean using bean-managed persistence (BMP). You'll learn what you're expected to do within each of the callback methods that were introduced in the preceding chapter. Before doing that, though, it's important to consider what the implications of using BMP are and how to determine when it's an appropriate choice. EJB 2.0 in particular places a strong emphasis on container-managed persistence (CMP), so before starting down a path of using BMP, you should have a solid reason for doing it.

When you use BMP to implement an entity bean mapped to a relational database, you either write JDBC code or use a framework, such as WebGain's TOPLink for Java or CocoBase Enterprise O/R from THOUGHT Inc., to implement the required database access code. Your code and that in any framework you might use have precise control over the SQL that is generated to maintain your persistent objects. This trait points out both the good and the bad about BMP. Because this approach gives you complete control over the SQL that's generated, BMP is most useful when you need to do something that the CMP implementations available to you don't support. You have full flexibility in persisting an entity in any way you see fit. The obvious disadvantage is that you're responsible for writing and maintaining more code when you do this. You have to rely more on the code within a bean than on the declarative mappings used with CMP that can be modified at deployment without changing code.

In general, BMP has the potential to be more error-prone than CMP. It's never easy to admit that you write defective code at times, but everyone does it. It's also true that it isn't easy to uncover the most reliable and efficient solution to a problem when you're working in areas in which you don't have extensive experience. This is why much of the evolution in software development has been based on raising the bar on what you have to write yourself. Often the best way to reduce errors is to write less code. The Java API provides classes that keep you from having to reinvent the wheel when you need to do a lot of the common tasks of developing an application. When you use these classes, you have a tested foundation to build on and you can focus more on the parts of the application you understand in depth. EJB takes this same concept further by providing a foundation for building distributed applications. CMP goes one step more to reduce the coding tasks you have to do to persist your data. BMP requires you to write more of the code yourself so it increases the risk of coding errors.

When you use BMP, it's more difficult to code beans that are independent of a particular database or application server. Even though JDBC protects you from most of the differences between database platforms, you'll still run into some issues if you have to use unique features such as automatic primary key generation. You also must be careful about managing table and column names so that simple schema changes don't ripple throughout your code. It's natural that having more of your persistence details show up in your bean code makes your beans less adaptable.

Even with its faults, you shouldn't view BMP as a bad approach to take. In fact, many EJB developers would argue that the benefits of BMP make up for any shortcomings it might have. This is especially true as CMP implementations are still trying to evolve to the point of being robust and portable. Many of the drawbacks of BMP can be addressed if you use an object-to-relational mapping (ORM) framework instead of directly coding JDBC calls within your beans. For example, TOPLink can maintain the mappings between class fields and database columns external to your code for BMP as well as CMP. This means that you're isolated from simple schema name changes. A framework such as this also manages differences between database platforms for you. You might have to lock yourself into a particular ORM framework to some extent, but the resulting portability across databases might be worth it. A BMP approach like this can often give you more portability than CMP. EJB 2.0 is looking to change this by adding container-managed relationships between entity beans and common finder method definitions to the standard features offered by vendors.

The debate between BMP and CMP has experienced developers on both sides. If the CMP implementations available to you for your particular application server just won't do what you need, then it's a somewhat easy choice to use BMP. Before doing this, be sure you've considered any third-party CMP implementations that support your application server.

ORM FRAMEWORKS AND BMP

If you implement an entity bean using BMP, you can take the approach of using an ORM framework or you can use JDBC directly. ORM products, such as TOPLink and CocoBase, provide a Java API that allows you to persist objects using method calls on Java objects. You define mappings between your persistent classes and the database tables using a tool provided by the vendor. These mappings are then used at runtime to translate from the object world to the relational database world. Under the hood, Java ORM frameworks are still using JDBC to talk to the database, but they hide the details of the SQL from you unless you need to define a custom query.

PART

I

CH

6

Every ORM vendor that supports BMP has its own API for doing it. This is one of the few drawbacks to using one of these tools. The uniqueness of APIs also makes it impracticable to cover the details of using an ORM framework for BMP in this book. If you do choose to use one, your vendor's documentation will cover what you need to know to use it for BMP. This chapter focuses on how to use JDBC to implement a BMP solution, but you'll find that a lot of the issues apply even if you're using an ORM product.

JDBC PRIMER

If you're not using an ORM framework to do BMP, then you must understand at least the basics of JDBC to implement your entity beans. Of course, you ought to understand JDBC even if you're not interfacing with it directly. No matter which BMP approach you take, it's always JDBC that allows the required database access to take place in the end.

This section describes the fundamental interfaces and a key exception that you need to understand to follow the explanation of BMP given in this chapter. These interfaces and classes are all defined in the java.sql package. If you've worked with JDBC before, this will simply be a refresher because EJB doesn't place any new requirements on JDBC. If you're new to JDBC but you've worked with relational databases before, don't get anxious, because it's not an overwhelming topic by any means. If you're new to writing programs that access a database, there are entire books dedicated to the subject of JDBC. However, the coverage offered by most introductory Java books is adequate for what you need to understand for BMP. Many of the complicated aspects of working with a database, such as connection pooling, are handled for you by the container even when you use BMP.

THE Connection INTERFACE

A Connection object provides the interface you need to execute SQL statements using JDBC and retrieve the result sets that are returned. Obtaining a Connection is the first step in accessing the database from within a callback method. This is also the step that's the most different when you compare EJB to other applications that use JDBC. In a typical Java application, you call a static method on the DriverManager class and pass a database URL and login information to get a connection. As you'll see a little later, you use a different procedure to do this from an EJB.

For a simple BMP implementation, you really only need to be concerned with the following two methods of Connection:

```
public PreparedStatement prepareStatement(String sql) throws SQLException;
public void close() throws SQLException;
```

The prepareStatement method creates and precompiles a SQL statement based on a string you supply. You can include question marks in the string to serve as placeholders for any parameters required by the statement. The close method simply releases the resources associated with the Connection when you're finished with it.

THE PreparedStatement INTERFACE

The PreparedStatement interface allows you to supply values for a statement's parameters and then execute it. Parameter values are accessed using a number of setXXXX methods that accept an integer parameter index and a value. Some of the more common methods consist of

```
public void setBigDecimal(int paramIndex, BigDecimal x) throws SQLException;
public void setBoolean(int paramIndex, boolean x) throws SQLException;
public void setDouble(int paramIndex, double x) throws SQLException;
```

```
public void setFloat(int paramIndex, float x) throws SQLException;
public void setInt(int paramIndex, int x) throws SQLException;
public void setLong(int paramIndex, long x) throws SQLException;
public void setNull(int paramIndex, int sqlType) throws SQLException;
public void setObject(int paramIndex, Object x) throws SQLException;
public void setString(int paramIndex, String x) throws SQLException;
public void setTimestamp(int paramIndex, Timestamp x) throws SQLException;
```

Note

Unlike what you normally see with Java, the parameter indexes for a `PreparedStatement` start with 1 and not 0.

The setXXXX method you use to assign a parameter value determines the SQL type that the value is converted to before being sent to the database. Notice that the signature for setNull requires you to specify the SQL type of the column to which you're writing a null value. These types are defined as constants by the java.sql.Types class. To write non-null values, you must make sure you call the correct set method. Table 6.1 defines the mappings between the Java and SQL types. You can use this to determine which set method to call based on the type of column you're accessing.

TABLE 6.1   MAPPING JAVA TYPES TO SQL TYPES

Java Type	SQL Type
BigDecimal	NUMERIC
boolean	BIT
byte	TINYINT
Date	DATE
double	DOUBLE
float	FLOAT
int	INTEGER
long	BIGINT
short	SMALLINT
String	VARCHAR (or LONGVARCHAR if necessary)
Time	TIME
TimeStamp	TIMESTAMP

After you've created a `PreparedStatement` and assigned its parameter values, it's ready to be executed. You can do this using one of the following methods:

```
public boolean execute() throws SQLException;
public ResultSet executeQuery() throws SQLException;
public int executeUpdate() throws SQLException;
```

PART

I

CH

6

You use executeQuery to execute a select statement and retrieve its results. The executeUpdate method executes an insert, update, or delete statement and returns the number of rows that were affected by the statement. You can use the execute method in place of either of the other two, but it's intended to support statements that return multiple result sets or row counts. If you don't need this behavior, it's easier to work with executeQuery and executeUpdate.

THE ResultSet INTERFACE

The ResultSet interface gives you access to the data returned by a select statement. This interface includes a number of methods used to navigate through a result set and extract values for a particular column of a selected row. For simple forward navigation, the next method can be used to move through the ResultSet one row at a time until it's exhausted. A ResultSet cursor is initially positioned before the first row when it's returned, so you must call next before attempting to access any data. After the cursor is positioned on a valid row, you can call a getXXXX method and pass it either a column index or a column name to access the value for that field. The following declarations are examples of these methods:

```
public int getInt(int columnIndex) throws SQLException;
public int getInt(String columnName) throws SQLException;
```

THE SQLException CLASS

Virtually every JDBC method is declared to throw a SQLException in case any failure occurs. If a SQLException is thrown, you can access a text description of the error and a vendor-specific error code. It's also possible for this type of exception to include other exceptions chained to it to provide more information about the underlying error.

CONFIGURING A DATA SOURCE

A benefit of EJB is that the container manages database connection pooling for you. It also enlists the resource manager to manage transactions automatically. You'll learn more about resource managers and transaction enlistment in Chapter 12, "Transactions," so don't worry about what that part means yet if it's unfamiliar to you. In short, a resource manager provides access to a data store of some type. In this chapter, a relational database management system is the resource manager of the most interest.

Most of the JDBC coding you do in a bean class that uses BMP is no different than what you'd do in a non-EJB application. The only significant difference is in how you configure a data source and obtain a connection to it. For a container to do its work for you, you must obtain a connection to a database a certain way so that the container can manage it. The way you do this is to obtain your connections through a resource manager connection factory. In the case of databases, this factory is an object that implements the javax.sql.DataSource interface. This might sound more difficult than what you're accustomed to with JDBC, but once you have a data source configured, it's easier than working with the methods of DriverManager to obtain connections.

Note

This section focuses only on database resources because that's what matters to BMP, but other types of resources are managed by the container in the same way described here. In particular, JMS and JavaMail resources are managed using resource manager connection factories.

DEFINING A CONNECTION POOL

A J2EE application server makes the pooling of database connections transparent to you as an application developer. Managing this type of resource is difficult to do yourself but it's critical to scalability in an enterprise system. Having it done for you behind the scenes is a significant benefit of EJB.

For an application server to manage connections for you, it needs to know about the data stores you're using. More than one application can use the same database, so you provide this information separate from any details about your applications. There's no standard way to do this, so it's up to each vendor to provide the necessary tools to define data sources and connection pools. The following configuration information illustrates the data you supply to WebLogic 6.1 to do this:

```
<Domain
  Name="mydomain"
>
  ...
  <JDBCDataSource
    JNDIName="auctionSource"
    Name="auctionSource"
    PoolName="auctionPool"
    Targets="myserver"
  />
  <JDBCConnectionPool
    CapacityIncrement="1"
    DriverName="weblogic.jdbc.mssqlserver4.Driver"
    InitialCapacity="1"
    MaxCapacity="3"
    Name="auctionPool"
    Properties="user=ejb20;password=ejb20;server=localhost;port=4073"
    Targets="myserver"
    URL="jdbc:weblogic:mssqlserver4:ejb20"
  />
  ...
</Domain>
```

PART

I

CH

6

This particular example defines a connection pool named auctionPool associated with a SQL Server database running on the same machine as the application server at the specified port. This pool is associated with a data source named auctionSource. It's actually the data source and not the pool that's referenced by the deployer of an EJB application to associate the application with a particular database. Other application servers have a similar mechanism for defining data sources.

DEFINING A RESOURCE MANAGER CONNECTION FACTORY REFERENCE

For a bean class to access a connection factory, it must have a reference to it defined within its environment. The first step in doing this is to define a `resource-ref` entry in the `ejb-jar.xml` deployment descriptor for the bean, as shown in the following:

```
<ejb-jar>
  <enterprise-beans>
    <entity>
      <ejb-name>EnglishAuction</ejb-name>
      ...
      <reentrant>False</reentrant>

      <resource-ref>
        <description>Define a reference to a resource manager connection
          factory for the auction database
        </description>
        <res-ref-name>jdbc/auctionSource</res-ref-name>
        <res-type>javax.sql.DataSource</res-type>
        <res-auth>Container</res-auth>
      </resource-ref>
      ...
    </entity>
    ...
  </enterprise-beans>
  ...
</ejb-jar>
```

The complete deployment descriptor for the auction entity bean is provided at the end of this chapter, but you'll see it built up along the way. A `resource-ref` element in the deployment descriptor lets the deployer know of an EJB's dependence on a particular data source. The `res-ref-name` defines the name used for the entry in the bean's environment. As shown in this example, you should use the `jdbc` subcontext for all JDBC resources that you define. The `res-type` of `javax.sql.DataSource` designates this reference as being one to a `Connection` object factory. The `res-auth` element can be assigned a value of either `Application` or `Container`. If you specify `Application`, your bean code must programmatically log in to the resource manager. If you specify `Container`, as was done here, the container logs in for you using the information supplied by the deployer to define the connection pool. This is the recommended approach.

The `resource-ref` entry in `ejb-jar.xml` defines an entry in the bean's environment for a connection factory but it doesn't map that entry to an actual data source. You must do that using whatever method your application server vendor provides. In the case of WebLogic, that means including an entry in the `weblogic-ejb-jar.xml` deployment descriptor as shown in the following:

```
<weblogic-ejb-jar>
  <weblogic-enterprise-bean>
    <ejb-name>EnglishAuction</ejb-name>
    ...
    <reference-descriptor>
      <resource-description>
        <res-ref-name>jdbc/auctionSource</res-ref-name>
```

```
          <jndi-name>auctionSource</jndi-name>
        </resource-description>
        ...
      </reference-descriptor>
    ...
    </weblogic-enterprise-bean>
  ...
</weblogic-ejb-jar>
```

This deployment descriptor associates the res-ref-name for the auction data source given in the ejb-jar.xml file with a data source known by the application server. The jndi-name given here for the data source has to match a data source name recognized by the server.

GETTING A CONNECTION FROM WITHIN AN EJB

After you've configured a data source and defined a reference to a connection factory for it, getting a connection to a database is easy. Listing 6.1 shows an example method you can use for doing this. You could implement this within an entity bean class, but it's shown here as a static helper method that can be used by multiple bean classes. The name you use in the lookup must match the res-ref-name in the deployment descriptor. For the auction data source, you would call this method and pass the string "auctionSource" as the argument.

LISTING 6.1   getConnection—A METHOD FOR OBTAINING A JDBC DATABASE CONNECTION USING JNDI

```
package com.que.ejb20.common.ejb;
...
public class BMPHelper {
  ...
  public static Connection getConnection(String dataSourceJNDIName) {
    InitialContext initCtx = null;
    try {
      initCtx = new InitialContext();
      // look up the reference in the jdbc subcontext
      DataSource source =
       (DataSource)initCtx.lookup("java:comp/env/jdbc/" + dataSourceJNDIName);
      // get a connection from the pool
      return source.getConnection();
    }
    // wrap any JNDI or SQL exception with a system exception
    catch (NamingException ne) {
      throw new EJBException(ne);
    }
    catch (SQLException se) {
      throw new EJBException(se);
    }
    finally {
      // close the InitialContext
      try {
        if (initCtx != null) {
          initCtx.close();
        }
      }
      catch (Exception ex) {
```

PART

I

CH

6

LISTING 6.1 CONTINUED

```
        throw new EJBException(ex);
      }
    }
  }
  ...
}
```

Note

Listing 6.1 and the other examples in this chapter use the approach described in Chapter 4, "Java Naming and Directory Interface," of calling the no-argument construc-tor of `InitialContext`. This assumes that a `jndi.properties` file containing the necessary environment entries exists in the classpath.

THE AUCTION SCHEMA

The intent of this chapter isn't to build up all the code needed to implement the auction site, but it does use parts of the `EnglishAuctionBean` implementation to illustrate BMP method implementations. These methods make more sense if you understand the under-lying database schema, so the SQL needed to create a database for the auction code appears in Listing 6.2.

LISTING 6.2 DDL FOR CREATING THE AUCTION SCHEMA

```
CREATE TABLE address (
  id int NOT NULL ,
  AddressLine1 varchar (50) NOT NULL ,
  AddressLine2 varchar (50) NULL ,
  City varchar (25) NOT NULL ,
  State varchar (2) NOT NULL ,
  ZipCode varchar (10) NOT NULL
);

CREATE TABLE auction (
  id int NOT NULL ,
  Name varchar (30) NOT NULL ,
  Description varchar (100) NULL ,
  Status varchar (15) NULL ,
  StartingBid numeric (19,4) NULL ,
  MinBidIncrement numeric (19,4) NULL ,
  ReserveAmount numeric (19,4) NULL ,
  StartDate datetime NULL ,
  ScheduledEndDate datetime NULL ,
  ActualEndDate datetime NULL ,
  ItemId int NULL ,
  Quantity int NULL ,
  LeadingBidId int NULL ,
  WinningBidId int NULL
);

CREATE TABLE bid (
  id int NOT NULL ,
```

LISTING 6.2 CONTINUED

```
  TransactionId varchar (15) NOT NULL ,
  BidDateTime datetime NOT NULL ,
  Amount numeric (19,4) NOT NULL ,
  AuctionId int NOT NULL ,
  BidderId int NOT NULL
);

CREATE TABLE bidder (
  id int NOT NULL ,
  FirstName varchar (20) NOT NULL ,
  LastName varchar (40) NOT NULL ,
  EmailAddress varchar (50) NULL ,
  UserName varchar (15) NOT NULL ,
  Password varchar (15) NOT NULL ,
  BillingAddressId int NULL ,
  ShippingAddressId int NULL
);

CREATE TABLE item (
  id int NOT NULL ,
  Name varchar (50) NOT NULL ,
  Description varchar (100) NULL ,
  ImageURL varchar (100) NULL
);

ALTER TABLE address ADD CONSTRAINT PK_address PRIMARY KEY (id);

ALTER TABLE auction ADD CONSTRAINT PK_auction PRIMARY KEY (id);

ALTER TABLE bid ADD CONSTRAINT PK_bid PRIMARY KEY (id);

ALTER TABLE bidder ADD CONSTRAINT PK_bidder PRIMARY KEY (id);

ALTER TABLE item ADD CONSTRAINT PK_item PRIMARY KEY (id);

ALTER TABLE auction ADD CONSTRAINT FK_auction_item FOREIGN KEY (ItemId)
  REFERENCES item (id);

ALTER TABLE auction ADD CONSTRAINT FK_auction_leadbid FOREIGN KEY
  (LeadingBidId)
  REFERENCES bid (id);

ALTER TABLE auction ADD CONSTRAINT FK_auction_winbid FOREIGN KEY (WinningBidId)
  REFERENCES bid (id);

ALTER TABLE bid ADD CONSTRAINT FK_bid_auction FOREIGN KEY (AuctionId)
  REFERENCES auction (id);

ALTER TABLE bid ADD CONSTRAINT FK_bid_bidder FOREIGN KEY (BidderId)
  REFERENCES bidder (id);

ALTER TABLE bidder ADD CONSTRAINT FK_bidder_billaddress
  FOREIGN KEY (BillingAddressId) REFERENCES address (id);

ALTER TABLE bidder ADD CONSTRAINT FK_bidder_shipaddress
  FOREIGN KEY (ShippingAddressId) REFERENCES address (id);
```

PART

I

CH

6

Note The DDL in Listing 6.2 was developed for Microsoft SQL Server 2000. If you're using a different database, you'll need to adapt this to the syntax and types supported by your vendor.

This database schema is for the most part a direct mapping of the object model given back in Chapter 2, "Setting the Stage—An Example Auction Site." The most notable difference is that the AuctionOffering class has been collapsed down and implemented as two attributes of EnglishAuctionBean stored in the ItemId and Quantity fields in the auction table.

CREATING AN ENTITY BEAN

To implement BMP, you must code the callback methods within the bean class to perform the required database access. When a client calls a create method on the home interface, the container calls the corresponding ejbCreate on an instance of your bean class. The instance on which the method is called is the instance the container has selected from the pool to associate with the new entity object that's being created. Your ejbCreate method is responsible for initializing the attributes of the entity, inserting it into the database, and returning its primary key value. Remember from Chapter 5 that the signature of an ejbCreate method must have the same parameter list as the corresponding create method in the home interface, and its return type must be the primary key class. Listing 6.3 shows an example of the method you could implement for the createWithData method declared in EnglishAuctionHome. As shown here, the bean class is declared to extend the AbstractEntity class introduced in Chapter 5. This class is an adapter for the EntityBean interface. Because EnglishAuctionBean extends AbstractEntity, it isn't necessary to declare this class to implement EntityBean. However, some development tools won't recognize a class as an enterprise bean if it doesn't explicitly extend the corresponding interface.

LISTING 6.3 ejbCreateWithData—A BMP ejbCreate METHOD INSERTS AN ENTITY INTO THE DATABASE

```
package com.que.ejb20.auction.model;
...
public class EnglishAuctionBean extends AbstractEntity implements EntityBean {
  ...
  public Integer ejbCreateWithData(String name, String description)
    throws CreateException {

    // throw an application exception if the name isn't valid
    if ((name == null) || (name.trim().length() == 0)) {
      throw new CreateException("Cannot create an auction without a name");
    }

    Connection con = null;
    PreparedStatement stmt = null;
    try {
```

LISTING 6.3   CONTINUED

```
      // assign the primary key and the initialization parameters
      setId(computeNextPK("auctionseq"));
      setName(name);
      setDescription(description);
      // default to Pending status
      status = IAuctionStatus.AUCTION_PENDING;

      con = BMPHelper.getConnection("auctionSource");
      // build a prepared statement and insert the new entity into the
      // database (let the other attributes default to null)
      stmt = con.prepareStatement(
       "INSERT INTO auction (id, Name, Description, Status) VALUES (?,?,?,?)");
      stmt.setInt(1, id.intValue());
      stmt.setString(2, name);
      stmt.setString(3, description);
      stmt.setString(4, status);

      // perform the insert and throw an exception if it fails
      int rowsInserted = stmt.executeUpdate();
      if (rowsInserted != 1) {
        throw new EJBException(
          "Could not insert the auction into the database");
      }

      // everything worked, return the primary key
      return getId();
    }
    catch (SQLException e) {
      // throw a system exception if a database access error occurs
      throw new EJBException;
    }
    finally {
      // close the connection
      BMPHelper.cleanup(stmt, con);
    }
  }
  ...
}
```

The `ejbCreateWithData` method starts by performing any data validation that's required and then assigning its parameter values to the bean instance. You should report errors related to initialization data using a `CreateException`. You'll see more about exceptions such as `CreateException` in Chapter 13, "Exception Handling."

The `getConnection` method of `BMPHelper` from Listing 6.1 provides a `Connection` object to `ejbCreateWithData` that's used to build an insert statement. After the insert statement is executed, the method returns the primary key assigned to the entity object. The `cleanup` method of `BMPHelper` called from the `finally` block is a simple utility method used to encapsulate the checks and exception handling needed by all the callback methods to close a statement and database connection before returning. This method appears in Listing 6.4. Because the application server is managing the pooling of connections for you, you're not really closing the connection by calling the `close` method. Calling this method lets the container know that you're finished with the connection so that it can be returned to the pool. It's important to release a limited resource such as this, so the call to the `close` method (or the `cleanup` method in this example) should always be placed in a `finally` block.

LISTING 6.4   `cleanup`—COMMON BEHAVIOR FOR CLOSING A `Statement` AND A `Connection`

```
package com.que.ejb20.common.ejb;
...
public class BMPHelper {
  ...
  public static void cleanup(Statement stmt, Connection con) {
    try {
      if (stmt != null) {
        stmt.close();
      }
      if (con != null) {
        con.close();
      }
    }
    catch (SQLException e) {
      throw new EJBException;
    }
  }
  ...
}
```

Managing Connection References

All code examples in this chapter use the approach shown in Listing 6.3 for working with `Connection` objects. When a method that needs to access the database is called, the method obtains a connection from the pool, performs its work, and then releases the connection back to the pool. This is a commonly used approach, but it's not your only option. One advantage of obtaining and releasing the connection within each method is that it's simple to implement. It does require some repetitive code as part of each method call, but you can take care of that using methods like the `getConnection` and `cleanup` examples used here. Besides its simplicity, this approach also has the advantage of only tying up a connection while it's being actively used.

Another option you have is based on keeping a connection for a longer period of time. Previously in Chapter 5, you saw how the container manages the life cycle of an entity bean instance. Part of this management consists of invoking callback methods on an entity as life cycle events occur. This includes calling `setEntityContext` after an instance is first created and calling `unsetEntityContext` immediately before it's destroyed. Instead of obtaining a connection each time you need one, you could instead obtain one in `setEntityContext` and release it in `unsetEntityContext`. The obvious advantage here is that you can avoid the overhead of obtaining a connection on each call. The drawback is that you're holding a connection from the pool even when it's not being used.

The main point to be made here is that there's more than one way to deal with connections when you're using BMP. The approach shown in the examples in this chapter is adequate for what you'll typically need. If you're wondering about the performance penalty of obtaining a connection within each method, remember that these method calls don't actually require a connection to be opened and closed. Because of the automatic pooling provided to you, connections are simply pulled from the connection pool and then returned when you're finished with them. However, you might improve performance when an application's clients access only a relatively small number of entity objects by holding onto the connection during the lifetime of each instance. This advantage diminishes when the number of entities being accessed increases. Here, the number of connections required from the pool goes up even if they are not all being used simultaneously. In this situation, you're better off releasing connections and reacquiring them when you need them.

Notice that `ejbCreateWithData` calls a `computeNextPK` method to assign its primary key value. Each table in the auction database uses an integer primary key. Using a unique number or string that has nothing to do with the data for a primary key value is a common approach. Just as common is the accompanying problem of deciding how to generate these unique values when rows are inserted. Most databases provide the capability to automatically generate a unique sequence number when a row is inserted. Using these native sequence numbers removes the problem of key generation but it can lead to portability problems. Even though most databases support this feature, not all of them do, and the implementations differ in how an application retrieves a newly generated key from the database.

Another approach is to use a routine that merges information, such as the IP address or some other unique property of the server, with the current time and date to produce a unique string. This approach is reliable but it has poor performance compared to approaches that don't depend on string manipulation. A fairly simple alternative to the two mentioned so far is to implement your own sequence table in the database for each table that requires an integer primary key. A sequence table needs to hold only a single value to represent the last primary key value assigned to the table with which it's associated. This approach was selected for the auction example. Listing 6.5 shows how you can generate sequence numbers using a simple sequence table.

LISTING 6.5 computeNextPK—A METHOD FOR GENERATING A PRIMARY KEY VALUE USING A SEQUENCE TABLE

```
package com.que.ejb20.auction.model;
...
public class EnglishAuctionBean extends AbstractEntity implements EntityBean {
  ...
  protected Integer computeNextPK(String tableName) throws SQLException {
    Connection con = null;
    PreparedStatement stmt = null;
    ResultSet rs = null;
    try {
      con = BMPHelper.getConnection("auctionSource");
      // update the sequence value in the database
      stmt = con.prepareStatement("UPDATE " + tableName +
        " set next_id = next_id + 1");
      if (stmt.executeUpdate() != 1) {
        throw new SQLException("Error generating primary key");
      }
      stmt.close();

      // retrieve the sequence value and use it as the primary key
      stmt = con.prepareStatement("SELECT next_id from " + tableName);
      rs = stmt.executeQuery();
      boolean found = rs.next();
      if (found) {
```

LISTING 6.5   CONTINUED

```
      return new Integer(rs.getInt("next_id"));
    }
    else {
      throw new SQLException("Error generating primary key");
    }
  }
  finally {
    // close the connection
    BMPHelper.cleanup(stmt, con);
  }
}
...
}
```

The sequence tables accessed by computeNextPK can be created using the following SQL:

```
CREATE TABLE auctionseq (
  next_id int NOT NULL
);
insert into auctionseq (next_id) values (1);

CREATE TABLE bidseq (
  next_id int NOT NULL
);
insert into bidseq (next_id) values (1);
```

Besides the source shown so far, ejbCreateWithData also references the IAuctionStatus interface. This interface, which appears in Listing 6.6, simply defines the strings used in the database to represent the auction state.

LISTING 6.6   IAuctionStatus.java—A DECLARATION OF THE STRINGS USED TO REPORT AUCTION STATE

```
package com.que.ejb20.auction.model;
/**
 * Title:        IAuctionStatus<p>
 * Description:  Constants that define the allowed auction states<p>
 */
public interface IAuctionStatus {
  public static final String AUCTION_PENDING   = "Pending";
  public static final String AUCTION_OPEN      = "Open";
  public static final String AUCTION_CANCELLED = "Cancelled";
  public static final String AUCTION_CLOSED    = "Closed";
}
```

Each ejbCreate method must have a matching ejbPostCreate method that is declared with the same parameter list but with a return type of void. The container calls this method after the ejbCreate method completes. Unlike ejbCreate, your instance is associated with an entity object identity within an ejbPostCreate method. This means that you can access the methods of the instance's EntityContext to get the primary key or the EJBObject. What this offers you is the capability to define associations between the entity and other objects. If, as part of creating an entity object, you need to insert a row into another table that has a foreign key back to your entity, `ejbPostCreate` is the place to do it. In the case of the auction entity, its associations to its bids and the item it offers aren't established at creation, so there's nothing to do at this point. `EnglishAuctionBean` only needs a do-nothing implementation of this method as shown in the following:

```
public void ejbPostCreateWithData(String name, String description)
 throws CreateException {
  // nothing to do
}
```

LOADING AND STORING AN ENTITY

Other than executing business methods, most of the work done by your entity bean involves keeping its state in synch with its corresponding data in the database. This work is done by your `ejbLoad` and `ejbStore` methods.

IMPLEMENTING `ejbLoad`

The container calls `ejbLoad` when an entity is activated and needs to guarantee that its state in memory matches what's in the database. Listing 6.7 shows the `ejbLoad` method for `EnglishAuctionBean`.

LISTING 6.7 `ejbLoad`—A BMP `ejbLoad` METHOD RETRIEVES DATA FROM THE DATABASE

```
package com.que.ejb20.auction.model;
...
public class EnglishAuctionBean extends AbstractEntity implements EntityBean {
  ...
  public void ejbLoad() {
    Connection con = null;
    PreparedStatement stmt = null;
    ResultSet rs = null;
    try {
      con = BMPHelper.getConnection("auctionSource");
      // build a select statement for the auction fields
      stmt = con.prepareStatement("SELECT Name, Description, Status, " +
        "StartingBid, MinBidIncrement, ReserveAmount, StartDate, " +
        "ScheduledEndDate, ActualEndDate, LeadingBidId, WinningBidId, " +
        "ItemId, Quantity FROM auction WHERE id = ?");
      Integer primaryKey = (Integer)ctx.getPrimaryKey();
      stmt.setInt(1, primaryKey.intValue());

      // execute the select
      rs = stmt.executeQuery();
      boolean found = rs.next();
      if (found) {
        // transfer the result set values into the instance fields
        id = primaryKey;
        name = rs.getString("Name");
        description = rs.getString("Description");
        status = rs.getString("Status");
        // the SQL numeric type is returned as a BigDecimal
```

PART

I

CH

6

LISTING 6.7   CONTINUED

```
        BigDecimal bd = rs.getBigDecimal("StartingBid");
        startingBid = bd != null ? new Double(bd.doubleValue()) : null;
        bd = rs.getBigDecimal("MinBidIncrement");
        minBidIncrement = bd != null ? new Double(bd.doubleValue()) : null;
        bd = rs.getBigDecimal("ReserveAmount");
        reserveAmount = bd != null ? new Double(bd.doubleValue()) : null;
        startDateTime = rs.getTimestamp("StartDate");
        scheduledEndDateTime = rs.getTimestamp("ScheduledEndDate");
        actualEndDateTime = rs.getTimestamp("ActualEndDate");
        leadingBidId = (Integer)rs.getObject("LeadingBidId");
        winningBidId = (Integer)rs.getObject("WinningBidId");
        itemId = (Integer)rs.getObject("ItemId");
        quantity = (Integer)rs.getObject("Quantity");

        // will load the item when requested
        item = null;

        // will load the bids when requested
        setBids(null);
        leadingBid = null;
        winningBid = null;
      }
      else {
        throw new EJBException("Error loading data for auction id " +
          primaryKey);
      }
    }
    catch (SQLException e) {
      // throw a system exception if a database access error occurs
      throw new EJBException;
    }
    finally {
      // close the connection
      BMPHelper.cleanup(stmt, con);
    }
  }
  ...
}
```

Within ejbLoad, you can use an instance's EntityContext to get the primary key assigned to it. You can then build a select statement that retrieves the entity's attribute values from the database. An entity also needs to retrieve its associated objects or at least load the key values it can use to access them when they're needed. Chapter 17, "Addressing Performance," covers some options you can employ with BMP but for now, the ejbLoad method for the auction defers any reading of its list of bids until they're needed. The leading and winning bids and the auction's item assignment are simply held as primary key values at this point as well. This is the nice thing about BMP: You can decide what you want to load at this point quite easily.

IMPLEMENTING ejbStore

The counterpart to ejbLoad is the ejbStore method. The container calls ejbStore when a transaction that includes an entity object commits or when the entity is about to be passivated. You have to provide an implementation of ejbStore that writes an entity's persistent state to the database. Listing 6.8 shows this method for EnglishAuctionBean.

LISTING 6.8 ejbStore—A BMP ejbStore METHOD WRITES AN ENTITY'S STATE TO THE DATABASE

```
package com.que.ejb20.auction.model;
...
public class EnglishAuctionBean extends AbstractEntity implements EntityBean {
  ...
  private Collection bidsToStore = new ArrayList();
  ...
  public void ejbStore() {
    Connection con = null;
    PreparedStatement stmt = null;
    try {
      con = BMPHelper.getConnection("auctionSource");

      if (!bidsToStore.isEmpty()) {
        // store bids added during this transaction
        stmt = con.prepareStatement(
          "INSERT INTO bid (id, AuctionId, BidderId, BidDateTime, Amount, " +
          "TransactionId) VALUES (?,?,?,?,?,?)");
        Iterator iter = bidsToStore.iterator();
        while (iter.hasNext()) {
          Bid newBid = (Bid)iter.next();
          stmt.setInt(1, newBid.getId().intValue());
          stmt.setInt(2, newBid.getAuctionId().intValue());
          stmt.setInt(3, newBid.getBidderId().intValue());
          stmt.setTimestamp(4, newBid.getDateTimeSubmitted());
          stmt.setDouble(5, newBid.getAmount().doubleValue());
          stmt.setString(6, newBid.getTransactionId());

          int rowsInserted = stmt.executeUpdate();
          if (rowsInserted != 1) {
            throw new EJBException(
              "Could not insert bid into the database");
          }
        }
        bidsToStore.clear();
        stmt.close();
      }

      // build an update statement to write the auction state to the database
      stmt = con.prepareStatement("UPDATE auction SET Name = ?, " +
        "Description = ?, Status = ?, StartingBid = ?, MinBidIncrement = ?, " +
        "ReserveAmount = ?, StartDate = ?, ScheduledEndDate = ?, " +
        "ActualEndDate = ?, LeadingBidId = ?, WinningBidId = ?, ItemId = ?, " +
        "Quantity = ? FROM auction WHERE id = ?");
      stmt.setString(1, getName());
      stmt.setString(2, getDescription());
```

LISTING 6.8 CONTINUED

```java
        stmt.setString(3, getStatus());
        if (getStartingBid() != null) {
          stmt.setDouble(4, getStartingBid().doubleValue());
        }
        else {
          stmt.setNull(4, java.sql.Types.DOUBLE);
        }
        if (getMinBidIncrement() != null) {
          stmt.setDouble(5, getMinBidIncrement().doubleValue());
        }
        else {
          stmt.setNull(5, java.sql.Types.DOUBLE);
        }
        if (getReserveAmount() != null) {
          stmt.setDouble(6, getReserveAmount().doubleValue());
        }
        else {
          stmt.setNull(6, java.sql.Types.DOUBLE);
        }
        stmt.setTimestamp(7, getStartDateTime());
        stmt.setTimestamp(8, getScheduledEndDateTime());
        stmt.setTimestamp(9, getActualEndDateTime());
        if (getLeadingBid() != null) {
          stmt.setInt(10, getLeadingBid().getId().intValue());
        }
        else {
          stmt.setNull(10, java.sql.Types.INTEGER);
        }
        if (getWinningBid() != null) {
          stmt.setInt(11, getWinningBid().getId().intValue());
        }
        else {
          stmt.setNull(11, java.sql.Types.INTEGER);
        }
        if (getItemId() != null) {
          stmt.setInt(12, getItemId().intValue());
        }
        else {
          stmt.setNull(12, java.sql.Types.INTEGER);
        }
        if (getQuantity() != null) {
          stmt.setInt(13, getQuantity().intValue());
        }
        else {
          stmt.setNull(13, java.sql.Types.INTEGER);
        }
        // set the primary key for the WHERE clause
        stmt.setInt(14, getId().intValue());

        // execute the update and throw an exception if it fails
        int rowsUpdated = stmt.executeUpdate();
        if (rowsUpdated != 1) {
          throw new EJBException("Error storing data for auction id " + id);
        }
    }
```

LISTING 6.8 CONTINUED

```
    catch (SQLException e) {
      // throw a system exception if a database access error occurs
      throw new EJBException;
    }
    finally {
      // close the connection
      BMPHelper.cleanup(stmt, con);
    }
  }
  ...
}
```

Besides updating the state of the auction, ejbStore also inserts any new Bid objects created for the auction into the database. The complete listing for EnglishAuctionBean included on the CD shows how bidsToStore is used by the submitBid method. Listing 6.9 shows the implementation of Bid.

LISTING 6.9 Bid.java—DEPENDENT OBJECT IMPLEMENTATION

```
package com.que.ejb20.auction.model;
/**
 * Title:         Bid<p>
 * Description:   An auction bid<p>
 */
import java.sql.Timestamp;
import com.que.ejb20.auction.view.BidView;

public class Bid {

  private Integer id;
  private Integer auctionId;
  private Integer bidderId;
  private Timestamp dateTimeSubmitted;
  private Double amount;
  private String transactionId;

  public Bid() {
  }

  public Bid(Integer newId, Integer newAuctionId, Integer newBidderId,
   Timestamp newDateTimeSubmitted, Double newAmount, String newTransactionId) {

    setId(newId);
    setAuctionId(newAuctionId);
    setBidderId(newBidderId);
    setDateTimeSubmitted(newDateTimeSubmitted);
    setAmount(newAmount);
    setTransactionId(newTransactionId);
  }
```

PART

I

CH

6

LISTING 6.9 CONTINUED

```java
public Integer getId() {
  return id;
}

protected void setId(Integer newId) {
  if (newId != null) {
    id = newId;
  }
  else {
    throw new IllegalArgumentException("Bid id must be non-null");
  }
}

public Integer getAuctionId() {
  return auctionId;
}

public void setAuctionId(Integer newAuctionId) {
  if (newAuctionId != null) {
    auctionId = newAuctionId;
  }
  else {
    throw new IllegalArgumentException("Bid auction id must be non-null");
  }
}

public Integer getBidderId() {
  return bidderId;
}

public void setBidderId(Integer newBidderId) {
  if (newBidderId != null) {
    bidderId = newBidderId;
  }
  else {
    throw new IllegalArgumentException("Bid bidder id must be non-null");
  }
}

public Timestamp getDateTimeSubmitted() {
  return dateTimeSubmitted;
}

public void setDateTimeSubmitted(Timestamp newDateTimeSubmitted) {
  if (newDateTimeSubmitted != null) {
    dateTimeSubmitted = newDateTimeSubmitted;
  }
  else {
    throw new IllegalArgumentException("Bid time must be non-null");
  }
}

public Double getAmount() {
  return amount;
}
```

LISTING 6.9   CONTINUED

```java
  public void setAmount(Double newAmount) {
    if ((newAmount != null) && (newAmount.doubleValue() >= 0.0)) {
      amount = newAmount;
    }
    else {
      throw new IllegalArgumentException(
        "Bid amount cannot be null or negative");
    }
  }

  public String getTransactionId() {
    return transactionId;
  }

  public void setTransactionId(String newTransactionId) {
    if (newTransactionId != null) {
      transactionId = newTransactionId;
    }
    else {
     throw new IllegalArgumentException("Bid transaction id must be non-null");
    }
  }

  public BidView getView() {
    BidView view = new BidView(getAuctionId(), getBidderId(),
      getDateTimeSubmitted(), getAmount(), getTransactionId());
    return view;
  }
}
```

As you can see, the most complicated part of ejbStore for the auction entity is checking for potential null values for its attributes and then calling the appropriate methods of PreparedStatement. Besides inserting new bids, an auction's associations are taken care of as long as you write all the foreign key values out to the database.

The problem with this simple implementation of ejbStore is that it isn't very efficient. It always writes to the database when it's called, and it always writes every attribute even if all of them haven't changed. You'll see alternatives to this discussed in Chapter 17.

PART

I

CH

6

ACCESSING OTHER ENTITY BEANS

The implementation of ejbLoad shown previously in Listing 6.7 loaded the primary key value for its associated item but it didn't load the item. This is a good approach as long as a component interface reference to the item can be obtained when it's needed. Just like any other client, the way an entity bean gets a reference to another entity is by calling a finder method on that entity's home interface. This means that the first step is to get a reference to the home interface. An EJB gets a reference to another EJB's home using an EJB reference defined in its environment. The following fragment from the auction entity's ejb-jar.xml deployment descriptor shows how you define an EJB reference to another bean's local home interface:

```
<ejb-jar>
  <enterprise-beans>
    <entity>
      <ejb-name>EnglishAuction</ejb-name>
      ...
      <ejb-local-ref>
        <description>This EJB reference is used to locate an auction's item
        </description>
        <ejb-ref-name>ejb/Item</ejb-ref-name>
        <ejb-ref-type>Entity</ejb-ref-type>
        <local-home>com.que.ejb20.item.model.ItemHome</local-home>
        <local>com.que.ejb20.item.model.Item</local>
      </ejb-local-ref>
      ...
    </entity>
    ...
  </enterprise-beans>
  ...
</ejb-jar>
```

You place EJB references within the `ejb` subcontext of a bean's environment. The preceding declaration allows an auction entity to reference the local home for the item entity using the `ejb-ref-name` that's defined. The following deployment information shows how you then map this `ejb-ref-name` to the JNDI name defined for the entity if you're using WebLogic:

```
<weblogic-ejb-jar>

  <weblogic-enterprise-bean>
    <ejb-name>EnglishAuction</ejb-name>

    <reference-descriptor>
      ...
      <ejb-local-reference-description>
        <ejb-ref-name>ejb/Item</ejb-ref-name>
        <jndi-name>Item</jndi-name>
      </ejb-local-reference-description>
    </reference-descriptor>
    ...
  </weblogic-enterprise-bean>
  ...
</weblogic-ejb-jar>
```

With the EJB reference fully defined, an `Item` can be located from within `EnglishAuctionBean` using its primary key value. Listing 6.10 illustrates how this is done.

LISTING 6.10 `getItem`—RETRIEVING A REFERENCED ENTITY BEAN

```
package com.que.ejb20.auction.model;
...
public class EnglishAuctionBean extends AbstractEntity implements EntityBean {
  ...
  public Item getItem() {
    if (getItemId() != null) {
      if (item == null) {
        // use lazy loading for the item reference
        try {
```

LISTING 6.10   CONTINUED

```
            // get a local interface reference to the item
            item = getItemHome().findByPrimaryKey(itemId);
          }
          catch (FinderException e) {
            throw new EJBException;
          }
        }
      }
    }
    return item;
  }
  ...
  private ItemHome getItemHome() {
    InitialContext initCtx = null;
    try {
      // Obtain the default initial JNDI context
      initCtx = new InitialContext();

      // Lookup the home interface for Item that is defined as a EJB reference
      // in the deployment descriptor
      Object obj = initCtx.lookup( "java:comp/env/ejb/Item" );
      return (ItemHome)obj;
    }
    catch (NamingException ex) {
      throw new EJBException(ex);
    }
    finally {
      // close the InitialContext
      try {
        if (initCtx != null) {
          initCtx.close();
        }
      }
      catch (Exception ex) {
        throw new EJBException(ex);
      }
    }
  }
  ...
}
```

When an EJB reference is looked up, the result is a reference to a home interface. You then can execute a finder method on the home and obtain a component interface reference for an associated entity bean.

The preceding example illustrated how to use an EJB reference to look up a local home interface. The process for obtaining a remote home interface is almost the same. Instead of declaring an `ejb-local-ref` element in the deployment descriptor, you use an `ejb-ref` instead. An `ejb-ref` identifies the remote interface and remote home for a bean using the following syntax:

```
<ejb-jar>
  <enterprise-beans>
    <entity>
```

```
    <ejb-name>EnglishAuction</ejb-name>
    ...
    <ejb-ref>
      <description>This EJB reference is for a remote bean
      </description>
      <ejb-ref-name>ejb/SomeRemoteBean</ejb-ref-name>
      <ejb-ref-type>Entity</ejb-ref-type>
      <home>com.que.ejb20.somepackage.SomeRemoteBeanHome</home>
      <remote>com.que.ejb20.somepackage.SomeRemoteBean</remote>
    </ejb-ref>
    ...
  </entity>
  ...
 </enterprise-beans>
 ...
</ejb-jar>
```

IMPLEMENTING FINDER METHODS

When a client calls a finder method, the container calls your corresponding `ejbFind` method. The most important concept here is that you're only responsible for returning the primary key values that match the criteria of a finder from an `ejbFind` method. The container responds by returning component interface references to the client, but it doesn't have to activate any entity object located by the finder until the client calls a business method on its component interface. This means that simply invoking a finder method that applies to a particular entity object doesn't cause `ejbLoad` to be called for that object.

The simplest finder method is `findByPrimaryKey`. Given the preceding discussion, the only responsibility you really have in an `ejbFindByPrimaryKey` method is to make sure that the primary key that's passed in corresponds to an entry in the database. Listing 6.11 shows this method for `EnglishAuctionBean`.

LISTING 6.11   `ejbFindByPrimaryKey`—A FINDER METHOD BY PRIMARY KEY

```
package com.que.ejb20.auction.model;
...
public class EnglishAuctionBean extends AbstractEntity implements EntityBean {
  ...
  public Integer ejbFindByPrimaryKey(Integer primaryKey)
   throws FinderException {

    // throw an application exception if the primary key isn't passed
    if (primaryKey == null) {
      throw new FinderException("Must specify a non-null primary key");
    }

    Connection con = null;
    PreparedStatement stmt = null;
    ResultSet rs = null;
    try {
      con = BMPHelper.getConnection("auctionSource");
      // perform a query to see if the primary key is valid
```

LISTING 6.11 CONTINUED

```
      stmt = con.prepareStatement("SELECT id FROM auction WHERE id = ?");
      stmt.setInt(1, primaryKey.intValue());
      rs = stmt.executeQuery();
      boolean found = rs.next();
      if (!found) {
        // the requested object doesn't exist
        throw new ObjectNotFoundException("Cannot find auction " + primaryKey);
      }
    }
    catch (SQLException e) {
      // throw a system exception if a database access error occurs
      throw new EJBException;
    }
    finally {
      // close the connection
      BMPHelper.cleanup(stmt, con);
    }

    // the requested auction was found so return the primary key
    return primaryKey;
  }
  ...
}
```

Listing 6.12 shows a slightly more complex finder method implementation that retrieves the primary keys for all the auctions defined in the database and returns them as a collection of Integer objects. Finder method implementations are basically the same with the significant difference being in the select statement they execute.

LISTING 6.12 ejbFindAllAuctions—A FINDER METHOD FOR RETRIEVING ALL AUCTIONS

```
package com.que.ejb20.auction.model;
...
public class EnglishAuctionBean extends AbstractEntity implements EntityBean {
  ...
  public Collection ejbFindAllAuctions() throws FinderException {

    Connection con = null;
    PreparedStatement stmt = null;
    ResultSet rs = null;
    Collection keys = new ArrayList();
    try {
      con = BMPHelper.getConnection("auctionSource");
      // perform a query to select all the primary key values
      stmt = con.prepareStatement("SELECT id FROM auction");
      rs = stmt.executeQuery();
      while (rs.next()) {
        Integer pk = (Integer)rs.getObject("id");
        keys.add(pk);
      }
    }
    catch (SQLException e) {
```

LISTING 6.12   CONTINUED

```
      // throw a system exception if a database access error occurs
      throw new EJBException;
    }
    finally {
      // close the connection
      BMPHelper.cleanup(stmt, con);
    }

    // return the primary keys
    return keys;
  }
  ...
}
```

DELETING AN ENTITY

A client can call either of the two remove methods of the home interface or the component interface's remove to delete an entity object. The container responds to this request by calling your ejbRemove method for the instance that needs to be deleted. You're responsible for doing whatever is necessary to remove the entity from the database within this method. Listing 6.13 shows the ejbRemove method for EnglishAuctionBean.

LISTING 6.13   ejbRemove—A BMP ejbRemove METHOD DELETES AN ENTITY FROM THE DATABASE

```
package com.que.ejb20.auction.model;
...
public class EnglishAuctionBean extends AbstractEntity implements EntityBean {
  ...
  public void ejbRemove() throws RemoveException {
    // an open auction has to be closed or cancelled
    // before it's allowed to be deleted
    if (IAuctionStatus.AUCTION_OPEN.equals(getStatus())) {
      throw new RemoveException("Cannot delete an open auction");
    }

    Connection con = null;
    PreparedStatement stmt = null;
    try {
      con = BMPHelper.getConnection("auctionSource");
      // do all deletes based on the primary key
      Integer primaryKey = (Integer)ctx.getPrimaryKey();

      // delete the auction's bids first
      if (!getBids().isEmpty()) {
        int numBids = getBids().size();
        // build a prepared statement and delete the dependent bid objects
        stmt = con.prepareStatement("DELETE FROM bid WHERE auction_id = ?");
        stmt.setInt(1, primaryKey.intValue());
```

LISTING 6.13   CONTINUED

```
      // perform the delete and throw an exception if it fails
      int rowsDeleted = stmt.executeUpdate();
      if (rowsDeleted != numBids) {
        throw new EJBException("Error deleting bids for auction " + id);
      }
    }

    // now build a prepared statement to delete the auction
    stmt = con.prepareStatement("DELETE FROM auction WHERE id = ?");
    stmt.setInt(1, primaryKey.intValue());

    // perform the delete and throw an exception if it fails
    int rowsDeleted = stmt.executeUpdate();
    if (rowsDeleted != 1) {
      throw new EJBException("Error deleting auction " + id);
    }
  }
  catch (SQLException e) {
    // throw a system exception if a database access error occurs
    throw new EJBException;
  }
  finally {
    // close the connection
    BMPHelper.cleanup(stmt, con);
  }
}
...
}
```

You'll learn more about exception handling in Chapter 13, but Listing 6.13 demonstrates that you're allowed to throw an application exception from an ejbRemove method to, in effect, veto a client request to delete an entity. Here, ejbRemove is implemented to enforce a business rule that requires an active auction to be closed or cancelled instead of being deleted while it's still in progress. If the auction is in a valid state for removal, its bids are deleted and then the auction itself is deleted.

DEPLOYING AN ENTITY BEAN USING BMP

After you've defined a bean's home and component interfaces and developed a bean implementation class, the last step is to provide the deployment information for it. As you've seen throughout the chapter, this information controls a number of characteristics of a bean. Listing 6.14 shows a complete ejb-jar.xml deployment descriptor for the auction, item, and bidder entity beans.

LISTING 6.14   ejb-jar.xml—XML DEPLOYMENT DESCRIPTOR

```
<?xml version="1.0"?>

<!DOCTYPE ejb-jar PUBLIC
  '-//Sun Microsystems, Inc.//DTD Enterprise JavaBeans 2.0//EN'
  'http://java.sun.com/dtd/ejb-jar_2_0.dtd'>
```

PART

I

CH

6

LISTING 6.14   CONTINUED

```
<ejb-jar>
  <enterprise-beans>
    <entity>
      <ejb-name>EnglishAuction</ejb-name>
      <local-home>com.que.ejb20.auction.model.EnglishAuctionHome</local-home>
      <local>com.que.ejb20.auction.model.EnglishAuction</local>
      <ejb-class>com.que.ejb20.auction.model.EnglishAuctionBean</ejb-class>
      <persistence-type>Bean</persistence-type>
      <prim-key-class>java.lang.Integer</prim-key-class>
      <reentrant>False</reentrant>

      <ejb-local-ref>
        <description>This EJB reference is used to locate an auction's item
        </description>
        <ejb-ref-name>ejb/Item</ejb-ref-name>
        <ejb-ref-type>Entity</ejb-ref-type>
        <local-home>com.que.ejb20.item.model.ItemHome</local-home>
        <local>com.que.ejb20.item.model.Item</local>
      </ejb-local-ref>

      <resource-ref>
        <description>Define a reference to a resource manager connection
          factory for the auction database
        </description>
        <res-ref-name>jdbc/auctionSource</res-ref-name>
        <res-type>javax.sql.DataSource</res-type>
        <res-auth>Container</res-auth>
      </resource-ref>
    </entity>

    <entity>
      <ejb-name>Bidder</ejb-name>
      <local-home>com.que.ejb20.auction.model.BidderHome</local-home>
      <local>com.que.ejb20.auction.model.Bidder</local>
      <ejb-class>com.que.ejb20.auction.model.BidderBean</ejb-class>
      <persistence-type>Bean</persistence-type>
      <prim-key-class>java.lang.Integer</prim-key-class>
      <reentrant>False</reentrant>

      <resource-ref>
        <description>Define a reference to a resource manager connection
          factory for the auction database
        </description>
        <res-ref-name>jdbc/auctionSource</res-ref-name>
        <res-type>javax.sql.DataSource</res-type>
        <res-auth>Container</res-auth>
      </resource-ref>
    </entity>

    <entity>
      <ejb-name>Item</ejb-name>
      <local-home>com.que.ejb20.item.model.ItemHome</local-home>
      <local>com.que.ejb20.item.model.Item</local>
      <ejb-class>com.que.ejb20.item.model.ItemBean</ejb-class>
      <persistence-type>Bean</persistence-type>
```

LISTING 6.14 CONTINUED

```
      <prim-key-class>java.lang.Integer</prim-key-class>
      <reentrant>False</reentrant>

      <resource-ref>
        <description>Define a reference to a resource manager connection
          factory for the auction database
        </description>
        <res-ref-name>jdbc/auctionSource</res-ref-name>
        <res-type>javax.sql.DataSource</res-type>
        <res-auth>Container</res-auth>
      </resource-ref>
    </entity>
  </enterprise-beans>

  <assembly-descriptor>
    <container-transaction>
      <method>
        <ejb-name>EnglishAuction</ejb-name>
        <method-name>*</method-name>
      </method>
      <trans-attribute>Required</trans-attribute>
    </container-transaction>

    <container-transaction>
      <method>
        <ejb-name>Bidder</ejb-name>
        <method-name>*</method-name>
      </method>
      <trans-attribute>Required</trans-attribute>
    </container-transaction>

    <container-transaction>
      <method>
        <ejb-name>Item</ejb-name>
        <method-name>*</method-name>
      </method>
      <trans-attribute>Required</trans-attribute>
    </container-transaction>
  </assembly-descriptor>

</ejb-jar>
```

You can refer to Chapter 15, "Deployment," for information on all the deployment descriptor options available to you. Basically, the descriptor in Listing 6.14 specifies that the auction entity uses BMP, supports only local clients, has an Integer primary key, needs a local reference to the item entity, uses the auction data source, and should have a transaction associated with all its method calls. Refer to Chapter 12 for a discussion of transaction attributes and their assignment.

Listing 6.15 contains the complete WebLogic deployment descriptor for the auction entity. As seen earlier in the chapter, it completes the definitions of the data source and EJB reference. It also defines the JNDI name for the entity bean.

LISTING 6.15 `weblogic-ejb-jar.xml`—WEBLOGIC DEPLOYMENT DESCRIPTOR

```xml
<?xml version="1.0"?>

<!DOCTYPE weblogic-ejb-jar PUBLIC
  '-//BEA Systems, Inc.//DTD WebLogic 6.0.0 EJB//EN'
  'http://www.bea.com/servers/wls600/dtd/weblogic-ejb-jar.dtd'>

<weblogic-ejb-jar>

  <weblogic-enterprise-bean>
    <ejb-name>EnglishAuction</ejb-name>

    <entity-descriptor>
      <entity-cache>
        <max-beans-in-cache>100</max-beans-in-cache>
      </entity-cache>
    </entity-descriptor>

    <reference-descriptor>
      <resource-description>
        <res-ref-name>jdbc/auctionSource</res-ref-name>
        <jndi-name>auctionSource</jndi-name>
      </resource-description>

      <ejb-local-reference-description>
        <ejb-ref-name>ejb/Item</ejb-ref-name>
        <jndi-name>Item</jndi-name>
      </ejb-local-reference-description>
    </reference-descriptor>

    <local-jndi-name>EnglishAuction</local-jndi-name>
  </weblogic-enterprise-bean>

  <weblogic-enterprise-bean>
    <ejb-name>Bidder</ejb-name>

    <entity-descriptor>
      <entity-cache>
        <max-beans-in-cache>100</max-beans-in-cache>
      </entity-cache>
    </entity-descriptor>

    <reference-descriptor>
      <resource-description>
        <res-ref-name>jdbc/auctionSource</res-ref-name>
        <jndi-name>auctionSource</jndi-name>
      </resource-description>
    </reference-descriptor>

    <local-jndi-name>Bidder</local-jndi-name>
  </weblogic-enterprise-bean>

  <weblogic-enterprise-bean>
    <ejb-name>Item</ejb-name>
```

LISTING 6.15   CONTINUED

```
    <entity-descriptor>
      <entity-cache>
        <max-beans-in-cache>100</max-beans-in-cache>
      </entity-cache>
    </entity-descriptor>

    <reference-descriptor>
      <resource-description>
        <res-ref-name>jdbc/auctionSource</res-ref-name>
        <jndi-name>auctionSource</jndi-name>
      </resource-description>
    </reference-descriptor>

    <local-jndi-name>Item</local-jndi-name>
  </weblogic-enterprise-bean>

</weblogic-ejb-jar>
```

TESTING THE EnglishAuction ENTITY BEAN

Typically, the simplest way to test an entity bean is to write a Java application that accesses the bean and exercises its business methods. The problem with applying this approach to the auction entity bean is that a Java application can't serve as a local client. A quick workaround for this problem is to declare a remote interface and remote home for testing purposes. These interfaces appear in Listing 6.16 and Listing 6.17. They include a subset of the methods declared in their local counterparts.

```
package com.que.ejb20.auction.model;
/**
 * Title:          EnglishAuctionRemote<p>
 * Description: Remote interface used to test the EnglishAuction entity bean<p>
 */
import javax.ejb.EJBObject;
import java.rmi.RemoteException;
import java.sql.Timestamp;
import com.que.ejb20.auction.exceptions.InvalidAuctionStatusException;

public interface EnglishAuctionRemote extends EJBObject {
  public Integer getId() throws RemoteException;

  public void setName(String newName) throws RemoteException;
  public String getName() throws RemoteException;

  public void setDescription(String newDescription) throws RemoteException;
  public String getDescription() throws RemoteException;

  public void setStartingBid(Double newStartingBid)
    throws InvalidAuctionStatusException, RemoteException;
  public Double getStartingBid() throws RemoteException;
```

PART

I

CH

6

LISTING 6.16   CONTINUED

```
public void setMinBidIncrement(Double newMinBidIncrement)
  throws InvalidAuctionStatusException, RemoteException;
public Double getMinBidIncrement() throws RemoteException;

public void setReserveAmount(Double newReserveAmount)
  throws InvalidAuctionStatusException, RemoteException;
public Double getReserveAmount() throws RemoteException;

public void setStartDateTime(Timestamp newStartDateTime)
  throws InvalidAuctionStatusException, RemoteException;
public Timestamp getStartDateTime() throws RemoteException;

public void setScheduledEndDateTime(Timestamp newScheduledEndDateTime)
  throws InvalidAuctionStatusException, RemoteException;
public Timestamp getScheduledEndDateTime() throws RemoteException;
}
```

LISTING 6.17   EnglishAuctionRemoteHome.java—A REMOTE HOME INTERFACE FOR THE AUCTION ENTITY BEAN

```
package com.que.ejb20.auction.model;
/**
 * Title:        EnglishAuctionRemoteHome<p>
 * Description:  Remote home interface for testing the EnglishAuction entity
 *               bean<p>
 */
import java.rmi.RemoteException;
import java.util.Collection;
import javax.ejb.EJBHome;
import javax.ejb.CreateException;
import javax.ejb.FinderException;

public interface EnglishAuctionRemoteHome extends EJBHome {

  public EnglishAuctionRemote create() throws CreateException, RemoteException;

  public EnglishAuctionRemote createWithData(String name, String description)
    throws CreateException, RemoteException;

  public EnglishAuctionRemote findByPrimaryKey(Integer primaryKey)
    throws FinderException, RemoteException;

  public Collection getItemsBeingAuctioned() throws RemoteException;
}
```

With these interfaces added, the deployment descriptors need to reflect them. The ejb-jar.xml file can be updated as follows to identify these new interfaces for the bean:

```
<entity>
  <ejb-name>EnglishAuction</ejb-name>
  <home>com.que.ejb20.auction.model.EnglishAuctionRemoteHome</home>
  <remote>com.que.ejb20.auction.model.EnglishAuctionRemote</remote>
  <local-home>com.que.ejb20.auction.model.EnglishAuctionHome</local-home>
```

```
    <local>com.que.ejb20.auction.model.EnglishAuction</local>
    <ejb-class>com.que.ejb20.auction.model.EnglishAuctionBean</ejb-class>
    <persistence-type>Bean</persistence-type>
    <prim-key-class>java.lang.Integer</prim-key-class>
    <reentrant>False</reentrant>
</entity>
```

The corresponding change to the WebLogic deployment descriptor is simply the addition
of a jndi-name:

```
<weblogic-enterprise-bean>
  <ejb-name>EnglishAuction</ejb-name>
  ...
  <jndi-name>EnglishAuctionRemote</jndi-name>
  <local-jndi-name>EnglishAuction</local-jndi-name>
</weblogic-enterprise-bean>
```

Deploying an enterprise bean requires creating an ejb-jar JAR file that includes the class
files for the bean implementation and its home and component interfaces, along with the
XML deployment descriptors. The deployment descriptors must be included in a META-INF
subdirectory within the JAR. Refer to Chapter 15 and the documentation for your application server for more information on completing the deployment process.

Listing 6.18 illustrates a simple client application that could be used to create an auction and
modify one of its attributes.

LISTING 6.18 EntityBeanClient.java—A SAMPLE REMOTE CLIENT APPLICATION FOR THE
AUCTION ENTITY BEAN

```
package com.que.ejb20;

import javax.naming.Context;
import javax.naming.InitialContext;
import javax.naming.NamingException;
import javax.rmi.PortableRemoteObject;
import com.que.ejb20.auction.model.EnglishAuctionRemote;
import com.que.ejb20.auction.model.EnglishAuctionRemoteHome;

public class EntityBeanClient {

  public void createAuction() {
    try {
      // pull initial context factory and provider info from jndi.properties
      Context ctx = new InitialContext();
      // obtain a reference to the auction remote home interface
      Object home = ctx.lookup("EnglishAuctionRemote");
      EnglishAuctionRemoteHome auctionHome = (EnglishAuctionRemoteHome)
        PortableRemoteObject.narrow(home, EnglishAuctionRemoteHome.class);

      // create a new auction
      EnglishAuctionRemote auction = auctionHome.createWithData("My Auction",
        "This is a test auction");
      // call a business method on the remote interface
      auction.setStartingBid(new Double(100.00));
```

PART

I

CH

6

LISTING 6.18   CONTINUED

```
      System.out.println("Created auction: " + auction.getName() +
        " with starting bid " + auction.getStartingBid());

      ctx.close();
    }
    catch (NamingException ne) {
      System.out.println(ne.getMessage());
    }
    catch (Exception e) {
      e.printStackTrace();
    }
  }


  public static void main(String[] args) {
    EntityBeanClient auctionClient = new EntityBeanClient();
    auctionClient.createAuction();
  }
}
```

TROUBLESHOOTING

INCORRECT DATABASE ACCESSED WHEN USING SQL SERVER

I get an error telling me that a table or column name doesn't exist in my database but I know that the name is valid.

You have to take an extra step when setting up a SQL Server database for use by WebLogic if you're using BEA's SQL Server JDBC driver. Even though the database name is specified as part of the database URL in the connection pool definition, it's ignored when the database server is accessed. The database that is accessed is always the default database for the login you specify. You have to create a login that has the database you want to use selected as its default.

CONNECTION FACTORY OR EJB REFERENCE NOT FOUND

I defined a connection factory or EJB reference in the `ejb-jar.xml` *deployment descriptor for my bean, but the reference isn't found when I try to access it.*

The entries you include in the `ejb-jar.xml` for a connection factory or EJB reference define part of what you need to do to put the reference in the bean's environment but not everything. You still have to do whatever your particular application server requires to complete the environment entry. If you're using WebLogic, this means adding entries to the `weblogic-ejb-jar.xml` file for the bean. For a connection factory reference, you have to associate the reference entry with a data source registered with the application server. For an EJB reference, you have to associate the reference entry with the JNDI name of the EJB you want to access.

`ejbCreate` OR `ejbPostCreate` NOT IMPLEMENTED

I get an error compiling my EJB JAR file that tells me that I haven't implemented a particular `ejbCreate` *or* `ejbPostCreate` *method.*

You must provide a corresponding `ejbCreate` and `ejbPostCreate` method for every `create` method declared in the home interface of your bean. These methods must have the same parameter list as the `create` method and they can only throw application exceptions that are declared in `throws` clause of the `create` method (or subclasses of those exceptions). You must declare your `ejbCreate` methods to return the primary key class and your `ejbPostCreate` methods to return `void`. Missing or invalid implementations of these methods aren't detected by the Java compiler but by the validations steps performed by your vendor's deployment tools before it builds the container classes for your beans.

`ejbFind` NOT IMPLEMENTED

I get an error compiling my EJB JAR file that tells me that I haven't implemented a particular `ejbFind` *method.*

You must provide a corresponding `ejbFind` method for every finder method declared in the home interface of your bean. An `ejbFind` method must have the same parameter list as the finder method and it can only throw application exceptions that are declared in `throws` clause of the finder (or subclasses of those exceptions). You must declare your `ejbFind` methods to return either the remote interface type or a collection. A missing or invalid implementation of a finder isn't detected by the Java compiler but by the validations steps performed by your vendor's deployment tools before it builds the container classes for your beans.

## CHAPTER 7

CONTAINER-MANAGED PERSISTENCE

In this chapter

BUILDING PORTABLE ENTITY BEANS

You saw in the preceding chapter that using BMP means that you're responsible for coding the database calls needed to persist an entity bean. You do this using JDBC or an ORM framework that manages the mapping of object attributes to database tables. Whichever API you choose, a BMP bean class has to load and save its assigned entity object and that entity's dependent objects as directed by the container. The container makes synchronization requests to an entity instance by invoking its callback methods (ejbLoad and ejbStore, among others). This approach gives you a great deal of control over how an entity bean is persisted and retrieved. The drawback is that you have to write and maintain the persistence code for an entity instead of being able to focus only on its business logic.

This chapter explains the alternative to BMP. Instead of coding the database access needed to manage an entity's persistent state, you can provide a set of declarative mappings and let the container generate the necessary JDBC calls for you. You give up some of the flexibility of BMP, but, with container-managed persistence (CMP), you also give up some of the coding needed to implement an entity bean. Using CMP, you're responsible for identifying the persistent attributes of an entity bean and defining its relationships with other entities, but you don't have to write any database access code.

The EJB 1.1 Specification defined CMP and required all container implementations to support it, but it left most of the details up to the individual vendors. This resulted in a wide range of functionality across implementations. It also made it difficult to port between implementations. Even though mappings between entity fields and database columns were done declaratively, there was no standard syntax. Porting to another application server usually meant using another CMP implementation, which would almost certainly require redoing the database mappings. There were a few exceptions offered by third party products, but developers who required application server portability often looked toward BMP as the only attractive choice.

A major goal of EJB 2.0 is to alleviate the portability problems of CMP. The requirements for CMP are now specified in such a way that an entity bean implemented using CMP is much more portable to another compliant container. When you implement a CMP bean, you can reuse the same bean class and the deployment information that defines its persistent fields, relationships, and finder method queries with another container. The only part of the deployment that's still vendor-specific is the pairing of persistent fields and database columns. Because these mappings are defined in a deployment descriptor, it's possible to change databases without changing (or recompiling) your entity bean classes.

CMP AND DEPENDENT OBJECTS

As you've seen through the auction example, managing dependent objects isn't too difficult when you use BMP. It takes some work, but writing your own persistence code gives you the flexibility you need to manage whatever relationships your application requires. CMP presents a more complicated problem because the container must have a predetermined way to persist objects and manage the relationships between them. Early drafts of the EJB 2.0

Specification included support for managing dependent objects using CMP. This would have allowed you to provide declarative descriptions of your dependent objects so that the container could implement the operations required to persist them. Even better, the container would have been required to maintain the relationships between them and your entity beans. However, the idea of standardizing support for dependent objects went away with the introduction of local clients. Even though this might seem like a setback, local clients have more to offer when you consider both options.

The entity beans exposed to your session bean clients are expected to be coarse-grained objects that provide something significant in terms of data or business logic. You'll often hear entity beans described as being "heavyweight" because of the overhead incurred from the container's security and transaction management when they're accessed remotely. Because dependent objects typically are maintained behind a facade provided by an entity bean, they are instead viewed as lightweight objects that don't require the overhead that comes with remote access. This viewpoint drives the idea of implementing lightweight dependent objects as something other than entity beans. The criticism directed toward using entity beans for lightweight objects has been based primarily on the performance cost of remote calls.

Some EJB 1.1 vendors optimized calls among beans in the same container to minimize the performance penalty of remote calls. Local interfaces and local homes make this type of optimization standard in EJB 2.0. If the container were to support dependent objects as part of CMP, this definitely would offer a way to reduce the overhead of accessing your lightweight persistent objects. With this approach, the calls between an entity and its dependents could be executed efficiently by avoiding the additional work required when exposing a persistent object to a remote client. However, this would be only a partial solution because it wouldn't do anything to help the calls made to the coarse-grained objects you did choose to implement as entity beans.

By supporting local interfaces, EJB 2.0 CMP improves the efficiency of interactions between persistent objects while also providing a similar benefit to session and message-driven beans that access entity beans deployed in the same container. Beyond the technical advantages of local interfaces, using entity beans for all your persistent classes also offers you the practical bonus of having to learn only a single implementation approach. Instead of having to choose between an entity bean and a regular Java class, you only have to worry about whether or not to expose a remote interface when you're creating a persistent class. Local interfaces easily have the potential to be more far-reaching than formalized dependent objects in their positive impact on your applications.

Even though you must implement what you would normally code as a regular Java class if you were using BMP as an entity bean when using CMP, you still can design and deploy your applications so that these classes are accessed only by the coarse-grained entity beans that maintain them. Just as the EnglishAuction bean hid its interaction with instances of Bid when using BMP, you can build an application where the auction entity interacts with an equivalent entity bean version of Bid that is never directly accessed by the session bean

PART

I

CH

7

clients. If you use remote clients for your session beans, you can control which entity beans are exposed simply by limiting which beans support a remote interface.

Note

> Even though the specification doesn't address dependent objects for CMP, this doesn't mean that you won't find implementations that do. Even prior to EJB 2.0, CMP implementations existed that went well beyond the specification. For example, WebGain's TOPLink for WebLogic and TOPLink for WebSphere products provide CMP solutions for EJB 1.1 that allow you to manage the persistence of both entity beans and their dependent objects. At the time of this writing, no EJB 2.0 version of a product such as these was available, but that won't be true for long.

TRANSITIONING THE AUCTION EXAMPLE TO CMP

This chapter describes the steps needed to implement the auction example using CMP. Portions of the resulting source code are included in the text of the chapter as topics are introduced. The complete source listings are included on the accompanying CD. The example is developed in such a way that the CMP entity beans can coexist in the same source tree with their BMP counterparts. To make this possible, some care has to be taken in how the new classes are named. For example, the auction bean CMP implementation class is named EnglishAuctionCMPBean to distinguish it from EnglishAuctionBean. The same approach is used for ItemCMPBean and BidderCMPBean. This wouldn't be necessary in typical circumstances because you would have only a single implementation of each bean. Changes to the dependent object names are also necessary when rewriting them as entity beans. For example, the Bid dependent object is implemented as AuctionBidBean to avoid the name collision that would result from naming its local interface Bid. Address is implemented as StreetAddressBean for the same reason. Because these objects are hidden behind the auction and bidder beans and exposed only through their corresponding view classes, clients of the entities are unaffected by these changes. As far as the clients are concerned, the auction and bidder entities are still coarse-grained objects that encapsulate their supporting classes.

DECLARING A CMP ENTITY BEAN

The basic responsibilities of the bean provider don't change that much based on whether BMP or CMP is being used. In either case, you still have to define the bean class, its home and component interfaces, its primary key class (if it's a multiple-field key), and the initial entries in its deployment descriptor. The good news is that the home and component interfaces and the primary key class are independent of the implementation choice you make. This is key because requiring any differences here would expose your implementation choice to the client. The deployment descriptor identifies persistent fields and relationships for CMP, so it's definitely affected by the persistence choice you make. The contents of the deployment descriptor will be covered in detail a little later, so that leaves the bean implementation class as the place to start.

Compared to BMP (and earlier versions of CMP), the most striking difference in declaring an EJB 2.0 CMP entity bean class is that you have to declare it to be an abstract class. This is where the nature of CMP shows itself. You're letting the container do part of the persistence work for you and the way it does that is by providing the concrete class that actually implements your bean. Your responsibility as a bean provider is to implement your business logic and supply enough information to identify the fields and relationships that need to be persisted for a particular entity, but that's where it stops. It's up to the container to determine how to implement a class that provides the persistence your entity bean needs. You can think of this as an extension to the work an application server does when it prepares an EJB for deployment. Just like the container tools are able to create the stubs and skeletons needed to deploy an EJB, they can also create classes that extend your abstract entity classes to provide implementations for their abstract methods.

Besides being declared as `abstract`, your CMP bean implementation classes must also

- Be declared as `public`.
- Implement the `EntityBean` interface.
- Provide a `public`, no-argument constructor (which is best done by not explicitly declaring any constructors at all).
- Not implement `finalize()`.

Before going on, it's important to talk about why CMP has taken the direction that it has. It all comes down to minimizing the dependencies of the classes you write on other classes and the low-level mechanisms that support them. First of all, EJB as a whole takes advantage of Java interfaces to decouple the public interfaces exposed to a client from the classes that implement them. As with any other use of interfaces, this allows you to change how a set of methods is implemented without impacting the clients that depend on the interface defined by the methods. EJB 2.0 carries this concept further to separate the persistence details of an entity bean from the rest of its implementation. Using CMP, your implementation class defines the business logic that it's responsible for but it has no knowledge of how its persistent fields are maintained. By pulling these details out of the bean class, an entity bean can be ported to another EJB container or data store without changing or recompiling any of its code. The porting process is limited to modifying the deployment information that defines the database mappings and executing the container tools to generate a new concrete bean class.

DEFINING CMP FIELDS

The reason you have to declare a CMP bean class as `abstract` is that you identify its persistent fields and relationships using `abstract` methods. You're not responsible for declaring any instance variables to represent these fields or hold references to other objects because those are implementation details left to the container. This is a big change from BMP, so it's a good idea to go ahead and look at an example. The following code shows a segment of the local interface declared for the auction example back in Chapter 5, "Entity Beans":

```
public interface EnglishAuction extends EJBLocalObject {
  ...
  public void setName(String newName);
  public String getName();

  public void setDescription(String newDescription);
  public String getDescription();
  ...
}
```

In Chapter 6, "Bean-Managed Persistence," the implementation presented for
EnglishAuctionBean supported these business methods using a set of instance fields declared
for the class:

```
public class EnglishAuctionBean extends AbstractEntity implements EntityBean {
  ...
  protected String name;
  protected String description;
  ...
}
```

These field declarations made it possible to provide implementations like the following for
the business methods in the component interface:

```
public void setName(String newName) {
  name = newName;
}

public String getName() {
  return name;
}
```

The approach for declaring a CMP field is quite different. For example, a CMP implementation of the EnglishAuctionBean class would declare a name field using the following
abstract method declarations:

```
public abstract class EnglishAuctionCMPBean extends AbstractEntity
 implements EntityBean {
  ...
  public abstract void setName(String newName);
  public abstract String getName();
  ...
}
```

Here, name is a virtual field accessible only through its JavaBean-like get and set methods. It
would be illegal for you to declare an instance variable with the identifier name in conjunction with these methods. This is because it's up to the container to provide the implementation details that support virtual fields, which are known as *CMP fields*. The container uses
reflection and entries in the deployment descriptor to identify the CMP fields of a bean
class. The get and set methods are all you provide in your bean class to represent a CMP
field (declaring an instance variable for one the way you do for BMP would result in an
error). By requiring a bean class to access its persistent fields using these methods and not
the internal representation used for the fields, the class has no dependencies on how its persistence is handled.

CMP fields are how you manage the persistent attributes of an entity bean. Each CMP field you declare must hold either a Java primitive or a serializable type. For the auction example, you would use CMP fields to represent such values as the auction name, description, and starting bid amount. A CMP field can't be used to hold a reference to a related entity bean. You'll see how relationships between entity beans are handled shortly.

Even though the get and set methods for a bean's CMP fields must be declared as `public`, you're actually only exposing them to the container because clients don't access bean instances directly. You can allow a client to access a bean's CMP fields by including their get and set methods in the component interface. The one restriction is that you can't expose any set methods that operate on fields that make up a bean's primary key. This is because the container won't allow a CMP entity's primary key to be changed after it's been assigned.

Although you're allowed to expose CMP set methods that aren't associated with the primary key, you won't typically do this. The problem with directly exposing these methods is that you can't enforce any business logic when they're called. When the container implements one of your abstract methods, all it provides is the code required to persist the field. If you need to apply any validation logic or perform any other processing when a field is updated, you must "intercept" the relevant method calls to do so. The EJB specification doesn't address this issue, so you need to choose your own approach for the applications you build. A simple solution is to expose update methods other than the CMP set methods in your component interfaces. These methods can perform any logic that's needed in addition to calling the methods that update the fields.

The get and set methods exposed by the `EnglishAuction` local interface would correspond to a convenient set of virtual field names for the auction class. As pointed out earlier, `getName` and `setName` would support a virtual `name` field. The problem with this is that using these methods to declare the CMP fields would rule out executing any business logic during a client's update to a field. An easy solution to this is to keep the interface method names but use alternative virtual field names. For example, appending `Field` to the end of each name would allow updates to be intercepted without affecting the local interface. The following code fragment shows how this can be applied to an auction's starting bid:

```
public abstract class EnglishAuctionCMPBean extends AbstractEntity
 implements EntityBean {
  ...
  public abstract void setStartingBidField(Double newStartingBid);
  public abstract Double getStartingBidField();

  public void setStartingBid(Double newStartingBid)
   throws InvalidAuctionStatusException {
    if ((getStatusField() == null) ||
     IAuctionStatus.AUCTION_PENDING.equals(getStatusField())) {
      setStartingBidField(newStartingBid);
    }
    else {
      throw new InvalidAuctionStatusException(
        "Can only set the starting bid for a pending auction");
    }
  }
}
```

```
public Double getStartingBid() {
  return getStartingBidField();
}
...
}
```

As shown in this listing, the auction virtual fields have names such as startingBidField. The get and set methods exposed in the local interface are intercepted to prevent the client from directly interacting with the abstract methods declared to support the CMP fields. You can adopt other method naming conventions to achieve the same result. For example, some developers prefer to use names such as updateStartingBid for methods in a component interface. This would allow you to use startingBid as a virtual field name if you wanted. What matters in the end is that you're able to implement business logic that is executed whenever a client accesses a field.

DEFINING CMR FIELDS

Under CMP, the container can maintain relationships between entity beans for you. The major constraints are that you can only define relationships between beans implemented using EJB 2.0 CMP, and the related beans must be declared in the same deployment descriptor. These relationships can be one-to-one, one-to-many, or many-to-many and they can be either bidirectional or unidirectional. In a bidirectional relationship, either entity can navigate to the related entity (or entities). A unidirectional relationship supports navigation from only one side. All relationships are defined in terms of local interfaces, so a bean must expose a local interface if you want to use it as the target of a navigable relationship. A bean without a local interface can be used in a unidirectional relationship only where it's the source of the navigation. From a logical standpoint, a unidirectional relationship makes sense when only one side needs to know about the other. For example, an auction needs to know about the item it's offering for sale but the item doesn't necessarily need to know that it's been assigned to an auction.

The following method declarations illustrate how you declare a relationship to another entity bean:

```
public abstract class EnglishAuctionCMPBean extends AbstractEntity
  implements EntityBean {
  ...
  public abstract void setItem(Item newItem);
  public abstract Item getItem();
  ...
}
```

This declaration defines a container-managed relationship (CMR) field that associates an item with an auction. A CMR field is declared in much the same way as a CMP field using abstract get and set methods. A related entity bean is referenced using its local interface type in a one-to-one relationship. A one-to-many or many-to-many relationship is defined using a Collection or Set where the members have to be of the related bean's local interface type (it's expected that List and Map eventually will be allowed as well). The container is free to select any implementation of these collection interfaces to support a managed relationship.

You never reference a specific implementation in your method declarations. For example, a one-to-many relationship between a customer and that customer's orders can be declared using the following methods:

```
public abstract void setOrders(Collection newOrders);
public abstract Collection getOrders();
```

> **Note**
>
> The deployment descriptor is used to identify the CMP and CMR fields associated with a bean and not simply the presence of get and set methods. This means that you can define other business methods that start with `get` and `set` without them being confused with a bean's CMP and CMR fields.

As with CMP fields, you can expose the get and set methods associated with a CMR field in the local interface of a bean. If you need to execute your own business logic when a relationship is modified, you should expose an assignment method in the local interface other than the set method for the CMR field. You can't expose the accessor methods for a CMR field in a remote interface because they're always defined using the related bean's local interface. Remember that it's always illegal to reference a local interface or local home type in a remote interface. It's just as illegal to declare a method that returns or accepts a collection of local interface references in a remote interface.

In addition to a field's set method, you can use the methods of the `Collection` interface, such as `add` and `remove`, to define the one-to-many or many-to-many relationship represented by a CMR field. Unlike what you're accustomed to with a collection declared as an instance variable in a regular class, you're not responsible for initializing a collection associated with a CMR field. If there are no related objects assigned to a particular CMR field, the container is required to return an empty collection (as opposed to `null`) as the result for the associated get method. This means that in the preceding example, you can call `getOrders` and then execute the `add` method on the collection that's returned without ever instantiating a new collection and assigning it to the field yourself. Just like the container isn't allowed to return a `null` from the get method, you can't assign a `null` to a one-to-many or many-to-many CMR field or the container will throw an `IllegalArgumentException`. This same exception is thrown if a collection is passed to a set method that holds an object that isn't of the local interface type for the related entity.

You can access an entity object related to a bean simply by calling the get method that defines the relationship. The work required to locate that entity object is performed behind the scenes by the container. It's the equivalent of looking up the local home for the related entity and executing a finder method to obtain a local interface reference to the desired entity (or collection of them). Because the work of the container is hidden from the abstract bean class, it's possible for the container to use lazy loading and only obtain a reference to a related entity object if it's accessed by the bean instance or one of its clients.

Besides maintaining the references that define a relationship between entities, the container also can cascade the deletion of an entity down to any related entities that you specify. For example, you can specify that when an auction is deleted, all of its bids should be deleted as well. You do this with a simple entry in the deployment descriptor. You'll see how to do this later in "Deploying an Entity Bean using CMP."

Cascade deletion is supported for both one-to-one and one-to-many relationships. It doesn't apply to many-to-many because a single entity doesn't "own" another in this situation.

DEPENDENT VALUE CLASSES

Typically, you'll use CMP fields to maintain values corresponding to the Java primitive types and standard classes such as String and Integer. You also can associate your own classes with CMP fields as long as they're serializable and meet a few other restrictions. These classes are referred to as *dependent value classes*.

For the container to manage the data held in a dependent value class, it must be a concrete, serializable class. As with other CMP fields, you can expose dependent value classes in the local or remote interface of an entity bean if you choose. As indicated by their name, instances of dependent value classes are fully dependent on the associated entity when it comes to life-cycle management. If an entity object is removed, any dependent value instances it owns are destroyed as well.

Unlike an entity referenced through a CMR field, you don't provide a declarative mapping of the individual elements of a dependent value class to persist it. Instead, the container treats it as a single chunk of data that can be managed using serialization for persistence purposes. When you call the get method associated with a dependent value class, the container returns a copy of the object held by the field. Similarly, a call to the set method causes the container to copy the values you supply to the field.

It's not likely that you'll need dependent value classes in a typical application, but the support is there if you do. If you're developing a new persistent class that is related to an entity in your system, you can implement the new class as an entity bean and use a CMR field to manage the relationship. Using a dependent value class with a CMP field is more useful if you have to work with an existing regular Java class that needs to be persisted.

IMPLEMENTING THE CONTAINER CALLBACK METHODS

No matter which persistence method an entity bean uses, it has to implement the EntityBean interface. This means that you're still required to implement the same callback methods when you use CMP as you do for BMP. The difference is in what you're responsible for doing within these methods. An exception to this comment applies to finder methods, which aren't implemented at all within a CMP bean class. This is because the container is completely responsible for their implementation. You'll see later in the "Deploying an Entity Bean Using CMP" section how queries are defined for finder methods.

A common restriction to remember as the various callback methods are discussed is that you can't declare your implementations for any of them as static or final. This is because the container must be able to extend your bean class and override these methods.

Tip

As you'll see throughout this section, many of the callback methods can be declared with do-nothing or common implementations when you're using CMP. It's a good idea to implement an abstract class that provides default implementations for these methods. You can then extend all your CMP entity bean classes from it. The AbstractEntity class introduced previously in Chapter 5 is an example of how this can be done.

ASSIGNING AN EntityContext

The container assigns an EntityContext object to an entity instance when it's first created. Just like in BMP, you're responsible for implementing the following two methods to accept that assignment from the container:

```
public void setEntityContext(EntityContext ctx) throws EJBException,
  RemoteException;
public void unsetEntityContext() throws EJBException, RemoteException;
```

Because of the point within a bean instance's life cycle that these methods are called, you can use them to allocate and deallocate resources that are used by all instances of the bean class. You can't allocate resources that are specific to a single entity object identity here because an instance can be reused without setEntityContext ever being called again by the container. Most of the time you won't need to do anything special in these methods and you can provide simple implementations like those shown in the following code:

```
public abstract class EnglishAuctionCMPBean implements EntityBean {
  ...
  EntityContext ctx;
  ...

  public void setEntityContext(EntityContext ctx) {
    this.ctx = ctx;
  }

  public void unsetEntityContext() {
    ctx = null;
  }
  ...
}
```

CREATION AND REMOVAL

For any entity bean you declare, you have to implement an ejbCreate method for each create method declared in the bean's home interface. Your ejbCreate method has to perform the database insert for a new entity for BMP, but that's not the case with CMP. The container performs the database insert for you, but it calls your ejbCreate method first to give you the chance to initialize the instance. Listing 7.1 shows an example CMP implementation of an `ejbCreate` method.

LISTING 7.1 `ejbCreateWithData`—A CMP `ejbCreate` METHOD INITIALIZES AN ENTITY BEFORE IT'S INSERTED

```
public Integer ejbCreateWithData(String name, String description)
 throws CreateException {

  // throw an application exception if the name isn't valid
  if ((name == null) || (name.trim().length() == 0)) {
    throw new CreateException("Cannot create an auction without a name");
  }

  // initialize the entity object before it's inserted by the container
  setNameField(name);
  setDescriptionField(description);

   // always return null from ejbCreate for CMP
  return null;
}
```

Notice that this implementation of `ejbCreateWithData` returns a `null`. BMP `ejbCreate` methods have to return the primary key value assigned to a new entity object, but CMP implementations always return `null` and leave the primary key assignment to the container. After the container calls your `ejbCreate` method, the container saves the entity (or at least assigns its primary key) and your `ejbPostCreate` method is called. As with BMP, this method is where you perform any initialization that depends on the primary key of the entity object being assigned. This is also the only point during the creation process that you can assign objects to a CMR field relationship. Unless you establish relationships when an entity object is first created, an implementation of this method that does nothing is all you usually need:

```
public void ejbPostCreateWithData(String name, String description)
 throws CreateException {
}
```

In the case of `AuctionBidBean`, it needs to define relationships to the owning auction and bidder when it's created:

```
public void ejbPostCreate(EnglishAuction newAuction, Bidder newBidder,
 Timestamp newDateTimeSubmitted, Double newAmount, String newTransactionId) {
  // CMR fields can only be set in ejbPostCreate
  setAuction(newAuction);
  setBidder(newBidder);
}
```

The life cycle for an entity includes a callback method for removal as well as creation. When a client calls a `remove` method on an entity, the container calls your `ejbRemove` method before deleting the corresponding data from the database. You can throw a `RemoveException` to veto a deletion, but you're not responsible for making the delete call on the database. The purpose of calling `ejbRemove` is to allow you to free up any resources held by the instance. After `ejbRemove` returns, the container removes the referenced entity object from any managed relationships and deletes it from the data store. The container might wait until the end of the current transaction to perform this delete, but the entity is removed immediately as far as the application can tell.

Before returning to the client that invoked the remove operation, the container deletes any related entities that you've identified as requiring a cascade deletion. Just like the initial entity object being removed, any related entities that are deleted this way are removed from any relationships after their ejbRemove method has been executed. This process continues recursively until the cascade deletion is complete.

In the simple implementation of the auction example, no processing needs to be done in ejbRemove, and the version inherited from AbstractEntity is all that's needed. A more robust bean class might want to reject deletion depending on the current state of the auction. For example, you might want to throw an exception if an attempt is made to delete an open auction without first canceling it.

PRIMARY KEY GENERATION

Several options for generating primary key values were introduced in Chapter 6. These included using native sequencing provided by the database or generating a globally unique string each time a key value is needed. For the BMP auction classes, a simple approach of accessing a sequence table in the database during a call to ejbCreate was used. No matter which approach you use to generate a key for a BMP entity, you're responsible for returning it from ejbCreate. All this changes when you move to CMP. An ejbCreate method for a CMP entity does any required initialization of its fields (other than those related to the primary key) and returns null. The container then is responsible for assigning the primary key before calling the corresponding ejbPostCreate. This is why you have to wait until ejbPostCreate to assign related objects to a new entity.

Because you don't directly assign the primary key and you don't interact with the data store yourself, you're limited in your choices for primary key generation with CMP. In short, you're dependent on the options offered to you by the CMP implementation you use. These options typically include using a particular database vendor's native sequencing capability or using a sequence table that the container interacts with directly. For the auction example, this is demonstrated using WebLogic's sequence table option. As you'll see when the deployment descriptors for the example are covered, the only change required to the BMP sequence tables is to the column name used in the table. WebLogic requires the column in a sequence table to be named SEQUENCE.

LOADING AND STORING

Whenever the container retrieves an entity object's state from the database, it follows that operation with a call to ejbLoad on the instance. This method is the appropriate place to update any transient instance fields declared by the class that depend on an entity's persistent fields. After ejbLoad, an entity's instance fields are expected to be in a consistent state.

Before writing an entity's state to the database, the container calls `ejbStore` on the instance. This method should transfer any transient data that's used to determine the value of persistent fields to those fields. This would be necessary if you were to work with an entity within an application using fields that aren't the ones actually persisted. The persistent fields might be optimized for storage and not as easy to work with as an alternate version you hold in one or more transient fields.

The uses of `ejbLoad` and `ejbStore` described here are not needed very often. In most entity bean classes that you develop, you'll only need do-nothing implementations of these methods.

PASSIVATION AND ACTIVATION

When the container is preparing to move an entity instance into the ready state, it calls its `ejbActivate` method before calling `ejbLoad`. The purpose of the `ejbActivate` method is to allow you to obtain any resources that are needed by the instance. Whenever the container decides it needs to passivate an entity object, it calls the instance's `ejbStore` method and then `ejbPassivate`. You should release any resource references obtained in `ejbActivate` when `ejbPassivate` is called. An entity bean instance isn't associated with an entity object's state when activation and passivation are taking place. Because of this, you're not allowed to call any of the instance's CMP or CMR get or set methods within either `ejbActivate` or `ejbPassivate`.

IMPLEMENTING HOME METHODS

You're restricted in what you can do within a home method because it isn't associated with a particular entity object identity when it's executed. This means that you can't access any instance fields or methods of the class within a home method. For a CMP bean, this means that you can't call a CMP or CMR get or set method as part of a home method.

The `EnglishAuctionHome` interface includes a declaration for a single home method:

```
public Collection getItemsBeingAuctioned();
```

You can implement this method with the following:

```
public Collection ejbHomeGetItemsBeingAuctioned() {
  try {
    return ejbSelectAuctionedItems();
  }
  catch (FinderException e) {
    return null;
  }
}
```

Here, the home method returns a collection of `Item` local interface references that correspond to all the items currently assigned to auctions. The implementation details are delegated to a select method. Select methods are a feature unique to CMP beans that you'll see defined in the next section.

→ To remind yourself of the rules associated with implementing these methods, **see** "Home Methods," **p. 137**.

DECLARING SELECT METHODS

A select method allows you to query the database for information about an entity or any of its related entity objects within the framework provided by the container. For example, a customer entity bean could make use of a select method to locate the orders associated with a customer that are above a certain price. Select methods are similar to finder methods in that they are implemented by the container and not the bean provider. Where they differ is that you can't expose a select method in a bean's home or component interface—these methods are only for a bean class to use internally. The only code that you write for a select method is an abstract method declaration in the bean class. Using the same pattern applied to the other bean implementation methods, select methods must be declared with a name that begins with `ejbSelect`. For example, the following is a valid select method declaration:

```
public abstract Collection ejbSelectHighPriceOrders(double minOrderAmount)
  throws FinderException;
```

As shown in this example, a select method must be declared as `public` and `abstract` and it must include `FinderException` in its throws clause, along with any other application exceptions you want to throw. A select method can return values corresponding to any CMP or CMR field declared for the bean. You can declare a select method to return a single value, but you have to be certain that only a single value will ever be returned if you do. Usually, you'll declare a select method to return either `Collection` or `Set`. If you're returning entity bean references from a select method, you need to declare the select method to return the local reference type of the entity or a collection of them.

The select method that was referenced by the implementation of the `ejbHomeGetItemsBeingAuctioned` home method is declared as

```
public abstract Collection ejbSelectAuctionedItems() throws FinderException;
```

The abstract declaration for a select method allows you to use it within the bean class. This declaration is all you need to provide in your code. The next section describes how you define the actual query for a select.

DEPLOYING AN ENTITY BEAN USING CMP

After you've implemented a bean class, the next step is to define its deployment descriptor. This section covers what you have to specify to deploy a CMP entity bean. The examples given here are representative of a typical deployment. Refer to Chapter 15, "Deployment," for a more complete discussion of the deployment descriptor contents.

THE ABSTRACT PERSISTENCE SCHEMA

The deployment descriptor for a CMP entity bean contains a description of its persistent fields and relationships known as its *abstract persistence schema*. The information provided in the `ejb-jar.xml` deployment descriptor defines a logical view of an entity and its associations but it doesn't define a physical mapping to the underlying data store. It's up to the deployer to provide that mapping using tools specific to the CMP implementation. As far as what the container needs, the schema identifies the methods that are intended to provide

PART

I

CH

7

access to the persistent fields and relationships managed by the container. This is accomplished using a set of cmp-field and cmr-field entries in the deployment descriptor.

Every virtual field that appears in your entity bean class (based on your abstract method declarations) must be identified in the abstract persistence schema as a cmp-field. You do this using entries like those shown in the following example:

```
<entity>
  <ejb-name>EnglishAuction</ejb-name>
  <local-home>com.que.ejb20.auction.model.EnglishAuctionHome</local-home>
  <local>com.que.ejb20.auction.model.EnglishAuction</local>
  <ejb-class>com.que.ejb20.auction.model.EnglishAuctionCMPBean</ejb-class>
  <persistence-type>Container</persistence-type>
  <prim-key-class>java.lang.Integer</prim-key-class>
  <reentrant>False</reentrant>
  <cmp-version>2.x</cmp-version>
  <abstract-schema-name>EnglishAuction</abstract-schema-name>
  <cmp-field>
    <description>The primary key field</description>
    <field-name>idField</field-name>
  </cmp-field>
  <cmp-field>
    <field-name>nameField</field-name>
  </cmp-field>
  <cmp-field>
    <field-name>descriptionField</field-name>
  </cmp-field>
  ...
  <primkey-field>idField</primkey-field>
  ...
</entity>
```

The abstract-schema-name can be any valid Java identifier you want to assign, but it must be unique among those declared within a deployment descriptor. As shown in this example, the name of each CMP field always must begin with a lowercase letter. Standard JavaBean naming conventions are followed when matching deployment descriptor entries to your abstract methods. For example, a CMP field named descriptionField must have corresponding setDescriptionField and getDescriptionField methods declared in the bean class. Notice in this deployment descriptor example that there is nothing specified about how these fields are mapped to the database. The ejb-jar deployment descriptor is only used to identify the persistent fields. The deployer tools and container-specific deployment descriptors define the mapping of each abstract persistence schema to the corresponding data store.

Note

Besides being unique within a deployment descriptor, the ejb-name and abstract-schema-name entries you define must not be the same as any of the EJB Query Language (EJB QL) identifiers. You're pretty safe on this because these reserved identifiers are strings such as WHERE and EMPTY. EJB QL and its uses are described in Chapter 8, "EJB Query Language."

The `primkey-field` element in the deployment descriptor was first introduced in Chapter 5. This entry only applies to CMP, and you need to use it only when you have a single-field primary key. If so, you must include this entry and define its value to be the name of the CMP field that represents the primary key for the bean.

Relationships between entity beans are defined using `ejb-relation` entries within the `relationships` section of `ejb-jar`. Listing 7.2 illustrates how this is done.

LISTING 7.2   THE `relationships` ELEMENT DEFINES CONTAINER-MANAGED RELATIONSHIPS

```
<ejb-jar>
  <enterprise-beans>
    <entity>
      <ejb-name>EnglishAuction</ejb-name>
      ...
    </entity>
    <entity>
      <ejb-name>AuctionBid</ejb-name>
      ...
    </entity>
    <entity>
      <ejb-name>Item</ejb-name>
      ...
    </entity>
    ...
  </enterprise-beans>
  ...
  <relationships>
    <ejb-relation>
      <ejb-relation-name>EnglishAuction-AuctionBid</ejb-relation-name>

      <ejb-relationship-role>
        <ejb-relationship-role-name>auction-has-bids
        </ejb-relationship-role-name>
        <multiplicity>one</multiplicity>
        <relationship-role-source>
          <ejb-name>EnglishAuction</ejb-name>
        </relationship-role-source>
        <cmr-field>
          <cmr-field-name>bids</cmr-field-name>
          <cmr-field-type>java.util.Collection</cmr-field-type>
        </cmr-field>
      </ejb-relationship-role>

      <ejb-relationship-role>
        <ejb-relationship-role-name>bid-belongs-to-auction
        </ejb-relationship-role-name>
        <multiplicity>many</multiplicity>
        <cascade-delete/>
        <relationship-role-source>
          <ejb-name>AuctionBid</ejb-name>
        </relationship-role-source>
        <cmr-field>
          <cmr-field-name>auction</cmr-field-name>
        </cmr-field>
```

LISTING 7.2   CONTINUED

```xml
      </ejb-relationship-role>
    </ejb-relation>
    ...
    <ejb-relation>
      <ejb-relation-name>EnglishAuction-Item</ejb-relation-name>

      <ejb-relationship-role>
        <ejb-relationship-role-name>auction-offers-item
        </ejb-relationship-role-name>
        <multiplicity>one</multiplicity>
        <relationship-role-source>
          <ejb-name>EnglishAuction</ejb-name>
        </relationship-role-source>
        <cmr-field>
          <cmr-field-name>item</cmr-field-name>
        </cmr-field>
      </ejb-relationship-role>

      <ejb-relationship-role>
        <ejb-relationship-role-name>item-is-offered-by-auction
        </ejb-relationship-role-name>
        <multiplicity>one</multiplicity>
        <relationship-role-source>
          <ejb-name>Item</ejb-name>
        </relationship-role-source>
      </ejb-relationship-role>
    </ejb-relation>
    ...
  </relationships>
  ...
  <assembly-descriptor>
  ...
  </assembly-descriptor>
  ...
</ejb-jar>
```

The example in Listing 7.2 illustrates a one-to-many relationship between an auction and all its bids and a one-to-one relationship between an auction and the item it offers. For each ejb-relation, you can define any unique ejb-relation-name you wish. You're then required to define an ejb-relationship-role for each side of the relationship. Here, you also can use any identifier you wish for the ejb-relationship-role-name as long as it's unique within the file. The multiplicity element defines the number of objects of the source entity that appear in the relationship. In this example, the one-to-many relationship between an auction and its bids is indicated by specifying one as the value for the EnglishAuction multiplicity and many for AuctionBid. Notice that a cascade-delete entry appears in the relationship between an auction and its bids. This instructs the container to delete associated AuctionBid objects whenever an auction is removed. You don't have to include a value for this entry in the deployment descriptor; you just include the tag if it applies. An item isn't owned by an auction, so cascade-delete isn't specified for that relationship.

The `relationship-role-source` identifies an entity involved in a relationship using its `ejb-name`. The presence of a `cmr-field` after the `relationship-role-source` element determines the navigability of a relationship. In the mapping between `EnglishAuction` and `Item`, a `cmr-field` is defined to allow the auction to navigate to the item. Because an item cannot navigate to an associated auction, no `cmr-field` is defined for the item's side of the relationship. This allows an auction to offer an item without the item implementation knowing anything about auctions. In contrast, the `cmr-field` entries for an auction and its bids result in a bidirectional relationship between these entities. Just like a CMP field, a `cmr-field-name` that appears in the deployment descriptor must be a valid Java identifier that begins with a lowercase letter and corresponds to a pair of abstract get and set methods in the bean class. For one-to-many and many-to-many relationships, you also need to indicate whether the CMR field is declared to use a `Collection` or a `Set` using a `cmr-field-type` entry.

→ For more information on deploying associated entity beans, **see** "The `relationships` Element," **p. 432**.

IMPLEMENTING FINDER AND SELECT METHODS

The finder methods declared by a bean's home interface are defined by entries in the deployment descriptor. You don't provide any implementation for finder methods in a CMP bean class (not even an abstract method declaration). Finder methods are specified using a SQL-like syntax defined in Chapter 8 as EJB QL. Two examples of finder method query definitions are shown in Listing 7.3.

LISTING 7.3   THE query ELEMENT DEFINES A QUERY FOR A FINDER OR SELECT METHOD

```
<ejb-jar>
  <enterprise-beans>
    <entity>
      <ejb-name>EnglishAuction</ejb-name>
      ...
      <query>
        <query-method>
          <method-name>findAllAuctions</method-name>
          <method-params/>
        </query-method>
        <ejb-ql>
          <![CDATA[ SELECT OBJECT(a) FROM EnglishAuction AS a]]>
        </ejb-ql>
      </query>
      <query>
        <query-method>
          <method-name>findNonPendingAuctions</method-name>
          <method-params/>
        </query-method>
        <ejb-ql>
          <![CDATA[ SELECT OBJECT(a) FROM EnglishAuction AS a
            WHERE a.statusField <> 'Pending']]>
        </ejb-ql>
      </query>
      <query>
        <query-method>
```

PART

I

CH

7

LISTING 7.3   CONTINUED

```
          <method-name>ejbSelectAuctionedItems</method-name>
          <method-params/>
        </query-method>
        <ejb-ql>
          <![CDATA[ SELECT OBJECT(i) FROM EnglishAuction AS a, IN(a.item) i]]>
        </ejb-ql>
      </query>
      ...
    </entity>
    ...
  </enterprise-beans>
  ...
</ejb-jar>
```

As shown here, a query-method element is used to identify a finder method declared in the bean's home interface. If you have a finder method declared in both the remote home and local home with the same name and parameter list, the container can implement both methods from a single query declaration. The method-name included for a query-method must match the declaration in the home interface and not the bean class. This just means that the entries in the deployment descriptor must start with find and not ejbFind. The ejb-ql entry then defines a corresponding query to be executed whenever the finder is called. You'll learn the syntax for these queries in Chapter 8. In this example, the first two queries correspond to finder methods that locate all auctions and locate all nonpending auctions, respectively.

> **Note**
>
> You're not required to declare the findByPrimaryKey method in the deployment descriptor because the container automatically provides an implementation for that finder when you're using CMP.

You define select method queries in the deployment descriptor using the same syntax used for finder methods. The only difference is that you use the query-method element to identify a select method declared in the bean class (as an abstract method) instead of a finder method declared in the home interface. The naming restrictions imposed on these two method types make it obvious to the container which type of query method you're defining. Unlike finder methods, the method-name given for a select method must exactly match the method name in your bean class. Every method-name specified for a select method must begin with ejbSelect. In the preceding example, the query entry for ejbSelectAuctionedItems defines the statement used to satisfy the select method of the same name declared in EnglishAuctionCMPBean.

MAPPING THE ABSTRACT PERSISTENCE SCHEMA TO A DATABASE

When it's time to map an entity bean's abstract persistence schema to a database (or other data store), the deployer becomes dependent on the tools specific to the container. These tools usually produce vendor-specific deployment descriptors that are used along with the ejb-jar deployment descriptor to deploy an entity. For example, Listing 7.4 and Listing 7.5 show excerpts from the two descriptors used by WebLogic to deploy CMP entity beans.

LISTING 7.4 `weblogic-ejb-jar.xml`—A VENDOR-SPECIFIC DEPLOYMENT DESCRIPTOR
IDENTIFIES THE CMP IMPLEMENTATION

```xml
<?xml version="1.0"?>

<!DOCTYPE weblogic-ejb-jar PUBLIC
  '-//BEA Systems, Inc.//DTD WebLogic 6.0.0 EJB//EN'
  'http://www.bea.com/servers/wls600/dtd/weblogic-ejb-jar.dtd'>

<weblogic-ejb-jar>
  <weblogic-enterprise-bean>
    <ejb-name>EnglishAuction</ejb-name>

    <entity-descriptor>
      <entity-cache>
        <max-beans-in-cache>100</max-beans-in-cache>
      </entity-cache>
      <persistence>
        <persistence-type>
          <type-identifier>WebLogic_CMP_RDBMS</type-identifier>
          <type-version>6.0</type-version>
          <type-storage>META-INF/weblogic-cmp-rdbms-jar.xml</type-storage>
        </persistence-type>
        <persistence-use>
          <type-identifier>WebLogic_CMP_RDBMS</type-identifier>
          <type-version>6.0</type-version>
        </persistence-use>
      </persistence>
    </entity-descriptor>

    <reference-descriptor>
      <ejb-local-reference-description>
        <ejb-ref-name>ejb/AuctionBid</ejb-ref-name>
        <jndi-name>AuctionBid</jndi-name>
      </ejb-local-reference-description>
    </reference-descriptor>

    <jndi-name>EnglishAuctionRemote</jndi-name>
    <local-jndi-name>EnglishAuction</local-jndi-name>
  </weblogic-enterprise-bean>

  ...

</weblogic-ejb-jar>
```

LISTING 7.5 `weblogic-cmp-rdbms-jar.xml`—A VENDOR-SPECIFIC DEPLOYMENT
DESCRIPTOR MAPS AN ENTITY BEAN TO A DATABASE

```xml
<?xml version="1.0"?>

<!DOCTYPE weblogic-rdbms-jar PUBLIC
  '-//BEA Systems, Inc.//DTD WebLogic 6.0.0 EJB RDBMS Persistence//EN'
  'http://www.bea.com/servers/wls600/dtd/weblogic-rdbms20-persistence-600.dtd'>
```

PART

I

CH

7

LISTING 7.5 CONTINUED

```
<weblogic-rdbms-jar>
  <weblogic-rdbms-bean>
    <ejb-name>EnglishAuction</ejb-name>
    <data-source-name>auctionSource</data-source-name>
    <table-name>auction</table-name>

    <field-map>
      <cmp-field>idField</cmp-field>
      <dbms-column>id</dbms-column>
    </field-map>
    <field-map>
      <cmp-field>nameField</cmp-field>
      <dbms-column>Name</dbms-column>
    </field-map>
    ...
    <field-map>
      <cmp-field>quantityField</cmp-field>
      <dbms-column>Quantity</dbms-column>
    </field-map>

    <automatic-key-generation>
      <generator-type>NAMED_SEQUENCE_TABLE</generator-type>
      <generator-name>auctionseq</generator-name>
      <key-cache-size>10</key-cache-size>
    </automatic-key-generation>
  </weblogic-rdbms-bean>

  <weblogic-rdbms-bean>
    <ejb-name>AuctionBid</ejb-name>
    <data-source-name>auctionSource</data-source-name>
    <table-name>Bid</table-name>

    <field-map>
      <cmp-field>idField</cmp-field>
      <dbms-column>id</dbms-column>
    </field-map>
    ...
    <field-map>
      <cmp-field>transactionIdField</cmp-field>
      <dbms-column>TransactionId</dbms-column>
    </field-map>

    <automatic-key-generation>
      <generator-type>NAMED_SEQUENCE_TABLE</generator-type>
      <generator-name>bidseq</generator-name>
      <key-cache-size>10</key-cache-size>
    </automatic-key-generation>
  </weblogic-rdbms-bean>

  <weblogic-rdbms-bean>
    <ejb-name>Bidder</ejb-name>
    ...
  </weblogic-rdbms-bean>
```

LISTING 7.5   CONTINUED

```
<weblogic-rdbms-bean>
  <ejb-name>StreetAddress</ejb-name>
  ...
</weblogic-rdbms-bean>

<weblogic-rdbms-bean>
  <ejb-name>Item</ejb-name>
  ...
</weblogic-rdbms-bean>

<weblogic-rdbms-relation>
  <relation-name>EnglishAuction-LeadingBid</relation-name>
  <weblogic-relationship-role>
    <relationship-role-name>auction-has-a-leading-bid
    ➥</relationship-role-name>
    <column-map>
      <foreign-key-column>LeadingBidId</foreign-key-column>
      <key-column>id</key-column>
    </column-map>
  </weblogic-relationship-role>
</weblogic-rdbms-relation>

<weblogic-rdbms-relation>
  <relation-name>EnglishAuction-WinningBid</relation-name>
  ...
</weblogic-rdbms-relation>

<weblogic-rdbms-relation>
  <relation-name>EnglishAuction-Item</relation-name>
  <weblogic-relationship-role>
    <relationship-role-name>auction-offers-item</relationship-role-name>
    <column-map>
      <foreign-key-column>ItemId</foreign-key-column>
      <key-column>id</key-column>
    </column-map>
  </weblogic-relationship-role>
</weblogic-rdbms-relation>

<weblogic-rdbms-relation>
  <relation-name>EnglishAuction-AuctionBid</relation-name>
  <weblogic-relationship-role>
    <relationship-role-name>bid-belongs-to-auction</relationship-role-name>
    <column-map>
      <foreign-key-column>AuctionId</foreign-key-column>
      <key-column>id</key-column>
    </column-map>
  </weblogic-relationship-role>
</weblogic-rdbms-relation>

<weblogic-rdbms-relation>
  <relation-name>Bidder-BillingAddress</relation-name>
  <weblogic-relationship-role>
    <relationship-role-name>
        bidder-has-a-billing-address
    </relationship-role-name>
```

LISTING 7.5 CONTINUED

```
      <column-map>
        <foreign-key-column>BillingAddressId</foreign-key-column>
        <key-column>id</key-column>
      </column-map>
    </weblogic-relationship-role>
  </weblogic-rdbms-relation>

  <weblogic-rdbms-relation>
    <relation-name>Bidder-ShippingAddress</relation-name>
    ...
  </weblogic-rdbms-relation>

  <weblogic-rdbms-relation>
    <relation-name>Bidder-AuctionBid</relation-name>
    <weblogic-relationship-role>
      <relationship-role-name>bid-submitted-by-bidder</relationship-role-name>
      <column-map>
        <foreign-key-column>BidderId</foreign-key-column>
        <key-column>id</key-column>
      </column-map>
    </weblogic-relationship-role>
  </weblogic-rdbms-relation>

</weblogic-rdbms-jar>
```

Beyond what you've seen in earlier BMP examples, the descriptor in Listing 7.4 does nothing more than identify the CMP implementation being used by the application. The file in Listing 7.5 associates the auction example entity beans with a particular data source and maps each CMP field to a particular table and column found within that data source. Each relationship also is qualified with entries that identify the foreign key and primary key column pairs. In defining the relationships, each `relation-name` must match an `ejb-relation-name` in the `ejb-jar.xml` file and each `relationship-role-name` must match an `ejb-relationship-role-name`.

Listing 7.5 also shows an example of selecting a primary key generation option. The `automatic-key-generation` entries for `EnglishAuction` and `AuctionBid` identify the sequence tables to be used by the container. To use the same sequence tables used for the BMP version, you need to change the name of the `next_id` column to `SEQUENCE`. Other vendors offer the same type of options for primary keys, so check your documentation to see what you have available.

CONTAINER IMPLEMENTATION OF A CMP BEAN

When you run your container vendor's tools to prepare a CMP bean for deployment, a concrete implementation class for the bean is created. A vendor is free to choose how to do this, but the deployment tools must create a subclass of your bean that provides concrete implementations of your abstract methods. Based on the vendor-specific deployment descriptor entries you provide, this class is dynamically created with the knowledge it needs to perform all the required interactions with the data store. A large part of this consists of providing implementations for the callback methods and any finder and select methods that you've declared.

Given that vendors have unique approaches for implementing a CMP bean, there's not a lot of general discussion that applies to these classes. However, if you're the curious type, you might be interested in seeing what the source code for one looks like. Listing 7.6 shows parts of the implementation class generated for the EnglishAuctionCMPBean class by WebLogic's ejbc tool.

LISTING 7.6   WEBLOGIC IMPLEMENTATION CLASS FOR A CMP ENTITY BEAN

```
/**
 * This code was automatically generated at 6:34:13 PM on Jul 16, 2001
 * by weblogic.ejb20.cmp.rdbms.codegen.RDBMSCodeGenerator -- do not edit.
 *
 * @version unknown
 * @author Copyright  2001 by BEA Systems, Inc. All Rights Reserved.
 */
package com.que.ejb20.auction.model;
...
public class EnglishAuction_WebLogic_CMP_RDBMS
  extends com.que.ejb20.auction.model.EnglishAuctionCMPBean
  implements CMPBean
{
  ...
  // Instance variable(s)
  ...
  public java.lang.Integer idField;
  public java.lang.String nameField;
  public java.lang.String descriptionField;
  public java.lang.String statusField;
  public java.lang.Double startingBidField;
  public java.lang.Double minBidIncrementField;
  public java.lang.Double reserveAmountField;
  public java.sql.Timestamp startDateTimeField;
  public java.sql.Timestamp scheduledEndDateTimeField;
  public java.sql.Timestamp actualEndDateTimeField;
  public java.lang.Integer quantityField;
  ...
  // Getter and Setter methods.
  ...
  public java.lang.String getNameField()
  {
    ...
      return nameField;
    ...
  }

  public void setNameField(java.lang.String nameField)
  {
    this.nameField = nameField;
    ...
  }
  ...
```

PART

I

CH

7

LISTING 7.6 CONTINUED

```
public com.que.ejb20.auction.model.AuctionBid getLeadingBid() {
  try {
    if (!__WL_isLoaded[11]) {
      __WL_loadGroup0();
    }
    if (__WL_leadingBid_field_==null) {
      if (!(__WL_leadingBid_idField==null))
        __WL_leadingBid_field_ = (com.que.ejb20.auction.model.AuctionBid)
          __WL_leadingBid_bm.localFindByPrimaryKey(__WL_leadingBid_finder_,
            this.__WL_leadingBid_idField);
    }
    return __WL_leadingBid_field_;
  } catch (RuntimeException re) {
    ...
  } catch (Exception ex) {
    ...
  }
}

public void setLeadingBid(com.que.ejb20.auction.model.AuctionBid
➥leadingBid) {
  if (__WL_method_state==STATE_EJB_CREATE) {
    throw new IllegalStateException("The setXXX method for a cmr-field may
    ➥  not be called during ejbCreate.
    ➥  The setXXX method should be called during ejbPostCreate
    ➥  instead.");
  }
  try {
    ...
    __WL_setNullLeadingBid(false);
    __WL_doSetLeadingBid(leadingBid);
    __WL_postSetLeadingBid();
  } catch (RuntimeException re) {
    ...
  } catch (Exception ex) {
    ...
  }
}
...
//Finder methods.
...
public java.util.Collection ejbFindNonPendingAuctions()
  throws javax.ejb.FinderException
{
  ...
  java.sql.Connection __WL_con = null;
  java.sql.PreparedStatement __WL_stmt = null;
  java.sql.ResultSet __WL_rs = null;

  try {
    __WL_con = __WL_pm.getConnection();
  } catch (java.lang.Exception e) {
    ...
  }
```

LISTING 7.6   CONTINUED

```
    try {
      java.lang.String __WL_query = "SELECT WL0.ActualEndDate, WL0.Description,
      ➡ WL0.id, WL0.MinBidIncrement, WL0.Name, WL0.Quantity,
      ➡WL0.ReserveAmount, WL0.ScheduledEndDate, WL0.StartDate,
      ➡WL0.StartingBid, WL0.Status, WL0.ItemId, WL0.LeadingBidId,
      ➡WL0.WinningBidId  FROM auction WL0
      ➡ WHERE (WL0.Status <> 'Pending')"  + __WL_pm.selectForUpdate();
      ...
      __WL_stmt = __WL_con.prepareStatement(__WL_query);
      ...
      __WL_rs = __WL_stmt.executeQuery();
    } catch (java.lang.Exception e) {
      ...
    }

    try {
      java.util.Collection __WL_collection = new java.util.ArrayList();
      ...
      return __WL_collection;

    } catch (java.sql.SQLException sqle) {
      ...
    } catch (java.lang.Exception e) {
      ...
    } finally {
      ...
    }
  }
  ...
  //Home methods.
  public java.util.Collection ejbHomeGetItemsBeingAuctioned()
  {
    ...
      result =  super.ejbHomeGetItemsBeingAuctioned();
      return result;
    ...
  }
  ...
}
```

The first point to notice about Listing 7.6 is that the generated class is declared to extend `EnglishAuctionCMPBean`. You then can see that, based on the abstract methods in the auction class and the CMP fields defined in the deployment descriptor, instance variables are declared for each field that needs to be persisted. Each of these fields is accessed using concrete implementations of the corresponding get and set methods. The get and set methods for managing the CMR fields are each implemented as well. The final portion of the source included in the listing shows an example finder method implementation. In this case, a SQL statement was generated based on the EJB QL query declaration in the deployment descriptor and the corresponding table and column information. Listing 7.6 includes only a fraction of the generated code for this bean, but it should give you a feel for what the container has to provide.

TESTING THE AUCTION EXAMPLE

The source code included on the CD-ROM includes the CMP implementation for the auction classes and the complete deployment descriptors. You can use the same EntityBeanClient class introduced in Chapter 6 to test the auction entity bean. Because the interfaces to the bean stayed the same, the example works the same under CMP as it did for BMP. The only difference is that the deployment descriptors swap the implementation classes and include the necessary CMP declarations.

MANAGING RELATIONSHIPS

There are some interesting semantics concerning how relationships between entity beans are maintained. First of all, it should be clear by now that the only ways to update a relationship defined by a CMR field are to use the associated set method or operate on the collection returned by the get method. What's interesting to look at is that the behavior of a CMR field set method is different depending on the multiplicity of the relationship.

In the case of a one-to-many relationship, an entity object that is one of the targets of the relationship can, by definition, only be associated with a single source entity. For example, a one-to-many relationship between a CustomerBean and an OrderBean implies that an order is related to one and only one customer. If an order needed to be reassigned to another customer for some reason, its relationship to the initial customer should be removed. Consider the following code segment:

```
Customer purchasingAgent = ...
Customer recipient = ...

// transfer the orders placed by a purchasing
// agent to the recipient of the orders
Collection orders = recipient.getOrders();
orders.add(purchasingAgent.getOrders());
recipient.setOrders(orders);
```

You might think that the preceding code needs to include a statement that removes the orders from the purchasingAgent, but the container does that part for you. Because this is a one-to-many relationship, assigning a collection of Order objects to one Customer implies that those Order objects must be removed from any other Customer to which they might be assigned. This is the only way referential integrity can be preserved. Also important here is that the collection object that holds the Order objects associated with a Customer isn't being reassigned—the Order objects are instead being cleared from one collection and added to the other.

A one-to-one relationship is similar to a one-to-many in that a target object in the relationship can only belong to a single entity. Whenever a set method is called to assign the target of a one-to-one relationship, the object being assigned is removed from any other object it's assigned to under the same relationship. A many-to-many relationship is handled similarly to a one-to-many in that the collection associated with an entity isn't changed when a set method is called, only the contents of the collection are. What's different here is that the entity objects aren't removed from any existing relationships when a new assignment is made.

The way collections are used with managed relationships might seem somewhat strange at first. Normally, you would expect a set method that accepts a Collection parameter to assign the argument it receives to the corresponding Collection reference. With CMP, the container always creates the collections associated with CMR fields, and they aren't replaced when you call set methods that manipulate them. The container's implementation of such a set method transfers the contents of the Collection argument, but doesn't assign it directly. The collection objects you instantiate are never used by the container to maintain a relationship. However, if you pass a null or a collection that doesn't include objects of the expected type to a CMR set method, you'll get an IllegalArgumentException.

The behavior of one-to-many CMR fields when an object is reassigned can cause a problem when you're iterating a collection if you're not careful. The only correct way to remove an element while iterating a collection that's part of a container-managed relationship is to use the remove method of Iterator. If a statement is executed that transfers an object out of the collection without first calling remove, an IllegalStateException is thrown. The following code segment uses the purchasing agent example again to show the correct way to transfer an object out of a collection that's being iterated:

```
Customer purchasingAgent = ...
Customer recipient = ...

// transfer the orders placed by a purchasing
// agent to the recipient of the orders
Iterator iter = purchasingAgent.getOrders().iterator();
while (iter.hasNext()) {
  Order o = (Order)iter.next();
  // have to include the following line to make this safe
  iter.remove();
  recipient.add(o);
}
```

Note

The interfaces in the Java collection framework include some methods that are designated as optional. A class can implement such an interface and simply throw an UnsupportedOperationException for methods it chooses to not allow. The remove method of Iterator is one of these optional methods. Because of the requirement for transferring objects out of a managed relationship collection, the container must use collection classes whose iterators support remove.

Whenever an entity object is deleted as the result of a call to remove (or a cascade deletion that follows), the container does whatever is necessary to remove the entity from any relationships. If an entity that is the target of a one-to-one or one-to-many relationship is deleted, the get method for that relationship will return null. Similarly, the collection returned for a one-to-many or many-to-many relationship that once held the entity will no longer include it.

An important subject to you when you consider how the container manages relationships is that of referential integrity. As long as you manipulate assignments using the methods of `Collection` and `Set` and follow the rule of using `remove` for an `Iterator`, you don't have to worry about maintaining the referential integrity of your data. If you declare all your relationships in the deployment descriptor and apply `cascade-delete` wherever it's appropriate, the container is responsible for maintaining referential integrity for you.

USING EJB 1.1 CMP

CMP as defined by EJB 2.0 offers many improvements over earlier versions so it's not expected that developers will continue developing new applications based on the EJB 1.1 model. However, it's also not expected that developers of existing systems will immediately rewrite their CMP entity beans to use the new specification. To handle this situation, the EJB 2.0 Specification requires that a container be backward compatible and continue to support EJB 1.1 CMP.

EJB 1.1 CMP classes differ the most from EJB 2.0 in that they're concrete classes that must define all the fields that are to be persisted. In this way, they're a lot like BMP classes. Their implementations of the container callback methods are much more in line with EJB 2.0 CMP classes, however. Just as with EJB 2.0, EJB 1.1 CMP classes don't perform database access but instead leave it to the container. The callback methods serve the same purpose in both CMP versions. For example, `ejbCreate` and `ejbPostCreate` are intended for initializing a new entity object no matter which version you're using.

Once you get past the abstract versus concrete class distinction, the differences between EJB 1.1 and 2.0 beans show up the most in their deployment information. The following example shows deployment information for an EJB 1.1 CMP bean:

```
<ejb-jar>
  <enterprise-beans>
    <entity>
      <ejb-name>EnglishAuction</ejb-name>
      ...
      <reentrant>False</reentrant>
      <cmp-version>1.1</cmp-version>
      <cmp-field>
        <field-name>id</field-name>
      </cmp-field>
      <cmp-field>
        <field-name>name</field-name>
      </cmp-field>
      <cmp-field>
        <field-name>description</field-name>
      </cmp-field>
      ...
    </entity>
    ...
  </enterprise-beans>
</ejb-jar>
```

The standard deployment descriptor information for an EJB 1.1 CMP bean is nearly the same as that for EJB 2.0. You change the value for the cmp-version and you omit the abstract-schema-name element, but you're still specifying cmp-field entries in either case. What's different is that the CMP fields, which must correspond to public fields in the bean class in this case, are all you can define here if you're using EJB 1.1. There's no standard support for relationships between entities or for the syntax of defining finder methods. As far as select methods, they didn't exist at all in EJB 1.1. Any information beyond the identification of the CMP fields is vendor specific, so it appears in vendor-specific deployment files (assuming anything else is supported by a particular implementation). For many EJB 1.1 developers, the most effective persistence choice has been to use BMP or CMP using an ORM product such as TOPLink.

TROUBLESHOOTING

EntityBean INTERFACE NOT IMPLEMENTED

I get an error when I'm attempting to deploy an entity bean stating that a method from the EntityBean interface isn't implemented.

Even though the container tools are responsible for creating a concrete class that extends your bean class, you're still responsible for implementing the methods declared by the EntityBean interface. You have to pay careful attention to this because a side effect of declaring your entity bean classes as abstract is that the compiler won't consider the fact that you haven't implemented a particular interface method as an error.

INCORRECT VALUE FOR multiplicity ELEMENT

I get an error stating that the multiplicity element must be assigned a value of one or many.

The EJB 2.0 Specification defines the allowed values of the multiplicity element to be One and Many. However, some implementations expect the lowercase versions of these strings. If you encounter this error, simply change the entries in your ejb-jar.xml deployment descriptor to use lowercase.

CMP FIELD ABSTRACT METHODS NOT FOUND

I get an error when I'm attempting to deploy an entity bean using EJB 1.1 CMP that tells me that it can't find the abstract methods corresponding to my CMP fields.

An EJB 2.0 application server is required to support EJB 1.1 CMP, but it assumes you're using 2.0 by default. To deploy an EJB 1.1 CMP bean, you have to include the cmp-version element that was added to entity as part of EJB 2.0 and assign it a value of 1.1.

CHAPTER

EJB QUERY LANGUAGE

In this chapter

WHAT IS THE EJB QUERY LANGUAGE?

The EJB Query Language (EJB QL) is a SQL-like language defined for use with EJB 2.0 CMP. EJB QL is what you use to define the queries that determine the results of finder and select methods. Select methods didn't exist prior to EJB 2.0, and every vendor had a different syntax for defining finder methods. EJB QL offers portability across vendors using a syntax based on a subset of SQL92. Because it's based on SQL, the language is easy to learn if you're comfortable with relational databases. More importantly, once you learn it, you won't have to learn a new query language if you later switch CMP implementations. The introduction of the EJB QL is central to the goal of portability across CMP implementations touted by EJB 2.0, and it's a major factor in distinguishing EJB 2.0 from 1.1.

When your entity beans are mapped to a relational database, the queries you define using EJB QL are compiled to SQL. You saw examples of this in the preceding chapter. The two finder methods and the select method needed for the auction entity bean were declared in the `ejb-jar.xml` file using EJB QL. When the container tools were executed to create the concrete bean class, SQL statements were generated to implement each query. Compiling an EJB QL statement to the target language of the data store moves the responsibility of query execution to the native facilities of the database. This is a more portable approach than requiring the container to execute queries based on its representation of entity objects. When you define a query in EJB QL, it's independent of how your entities are eventually mapped to the data store used by an application. Whenever a set of related entities needs to be deployed in a new environment, you execute the corresponding vendor tools to map your logical model to the persistent store and create the concrete classes. Tying the implementation of a query to the selected deployment environment allows for performance optimization that wouldn't be possible otherwise. Even though you define your queries generically, the container provider's tools generate code to execute them that uses knowledge of the data store it's accessing.

> **Note**
>
> Although EJB QL queries used with a relational database are implemented using SQL statements, the results you see in your applications are always returned as objects and not data rows. As you'll see throughout this chapter, these objects typically are entity objects, but they also can include any type associated with a CMP field.

EJB QL is used only with finder and select methods, which you've been introduced to in earlier chapters. Given that you have an initial understanding of how those methods are used, what you need to know about EJB QL revolves around learning the syntax for a query. You should be somewhat comfortable with finder methods at this point because you've seen examples of them using both BMP and CMP. They're also fairly straightforward in purpose because all they ever do is return component interface references for the entity bean class for which they're defined. Select methods aren't quite as straightforward. First of all, they apply only to CMP and they're limited to internal use by the bean class that defines them. As far as learning EJB QL goes, an even bigger difference is that they can return references to other entity bean types or values other than component interface references altogether. By learning the EJB QL syntax for select methods, you should gain a better understanding of how you might use them in your applications.

Whether it's used for a finder or a select method, an EJB QL query is defined by a string in a deployment descriptor that includes a SELECT, a FROM, and an optional WHERE clause. You'll learn how to define each of these clauses as the chapter progresses.

DEPENDENCE ON THE ABSTRACT PERSISTENCE SCHEMA

The first concept to get accustomed to is that EJB QL refers to an entity bean using the name defined in its abstract persistence schema. In fact, the only reason you assign a name to an abstract persistence schema is to provide a way to reference the corresponding entity bean in a query. The only names you can use when you declare an EJB QL query are the abstract schema names of the beans in the same deployment descriptor and the names of their CMP and CMR fields. You never reference the names of any implementation classes or interfaces when you're using EJB QL, although it's accepted practice for the abstract schema name of an entity bean to be the same as the name of its local interface.

If you think back to the contents of the ejb-jar deployment descriptor related to CMP covered in Chapter 7, "Container-Managed Persistence," you'll remember that the abstract persistence schema for a bean defines only the schema name and the names of the bean's CMP fields. Table and column names don't enter the picture until the vendor-specific files generated by the deployer come into play. Any relationships between beans in an ejb-jar deployment descriptor are defined by identifying the CMR fields involved and the multiplicity of each role. Again, foreign and primary keys aren't identified at this point. Because the EJB QL queries for a bean also are declared in the ejb-jar.xml file, the schema names and the CMP and CMR field names are all you have available when defining a query. The result is that your queries never include references to the particular data store used when deploying the application. You can implement and deliver your bean classes and their query declarations without having any knowledge of the physical mapping used to persist them.

DEFINING A FROM CLAUSE

The SELECT and FROM clauses of a query are always required. A WHERE clause is part of most queries, but if the results don't need to be restricted based on a conditional expression, one isn't required. The FROM clause determines to which entities a query applies, so it's the part you need to understand first.

From the basics of SQL, you know that a FROM clause identifies the tables from which a query pulls its results. Carrying this concept over to the object world defines what a FROM clause does in EJB QL. It defines the classes associated with a query. To be technical, a FROM clause defines the domain of objects to which a query applies.

The simplest type of query is one that retrieves all the objects of a given type. For example, you saw a declaration equivalent to the following for the findAllAuctions finder method in Chapter 7:

```
SELECT OBJECT(auction) FROM EnglishAuction AS auction
```

Here, FROM EnglishAuction uses an abstract schema name to specify that the domain for the query consists of all the auction entity objects. The AS auction part of the query provides a way to reference an auction entity using what's known as an identification variable. The identification variable is given the arbitrary name auction in this case. Finally, SELECT OBJECT(auction) defines the result of the query using this variable. When all the pieces are combined, this query instructs the container to return all objects auction where auction is an EnglishAuction.

IDENTIFICATION VARIABLES

The character strings that appear in a query are known as identifiers. To support the various operators that make up the query language, EJB QL defines SELECT, FROM, WHERE, DISTINCT, OBJECT, NULL, TRUE, FALSE, NOT, AND, OR, BETWEEN, LIKE, IN, AS, UNKNOWN, EMPTY, MEMBER, OF, and IS as reserved identifiers. The question mark (?) is also a reserved character within EJB QL used for query parameters. Unlike Java identifiers, the EJB QL identifiers are case insensitive. This is true for the identifiers you define as well. This chapter always uses the upper-case form of the reserved identifiers, but select is the same as SELECT in EJB QL. Other than this behavior, you follow the same rules for naming identifiers in EJB QL that you do in your Java code. Your identifiers must start with a letter, an underscore, or a currency symbol. The remainder of an identifier can include any of these characters, digits, and certain types of control characters that you'll likely never use.

Caution

Even though not specifically prohibited, it's best to avoid using any other SQL reserved words as identifier names in your queries. As EJB QL capabilities expand in later releases, the list of reserved identifiers is likely to grow.

Identification variables are identifiers declared in a FROM clause using the AS or IN operator. You can name an identification variable anything other than a reserved identifier name or the value of an ejb-name, or abstract-schema-name element in the same deployment descriptor. In the preceding example, auction was declared as an identification variable using the AS operator. This type of declaration is called a *range variable declaration* because it ranges over the abstract schema of a particular entity bean without being constrained by any relationships to other entities. This type of declaration is always done by referencing an abstract schema name. The AS operator is optional and is assumed if you omit it. The same findAllAuctions query could be written as

```
SELECT OBJECT(auction) FROM EnglishAuction auction
```

A FROM clause can include multiple identification variable declarations separated by commas. The following example declares both auction and aBid as identification variables:

```
SELECT OBJECT(auction) FROM EnglishAuction auction, IN(auction.bids) aBid
```

Here a query is being performed that retrieves all auctions that have at least one associated bid. The identification variable auction is declared using the implicit AS operator as before. After you declare an identification variable for an entity, you can navigate to any of its CMR fields. The IN operator allows you to declare an identification variable that represents an entity that's reached by navigating a CMR field in a one-to-many or many-to-many relationship. In the example, aBid represents any bid in the collection of bids associated with a particular auction. You refer to the auction's bids using the name of the CMR field. You can't classify aBid as a range variable because it doesn't refer to all the AuctionBid objects in the system. A declaration that uses IN is referred to as a *collection member declaration* instead. Within the query, auction.bids represents a collection of objects of the abstract schema type AuctionBid. Identification variables are evaluated left to right, so it's legal for auction to be referenced in the declaration of aBid but not the other way around. The IN operator uses an implicit AS if you omit it, so the query also could be written as

```
SELECT OBJECT(auction) FROM EnglishAuction AS auction, IN(auction.bids) AS aBid
```

You might be confused by the intent of this query because it's not immediately clear. If you remove the part of the FROM clause that uses the IN operator, this query reverts back to the findAllAuctions declaration. By specifying that the bids CMR field should be navigated for each retrieved auction, the query effectively filters out all auctions that have an empty collection of bids. This is an important side effect to be aware of when declaring identification variables. You'll see a more intuitive version of this query when the WHERE clause is covered.

Identification variables always represent entity beans (as opposed to a CMP field or any other value). You can declare them only using AS and IN, which can appear only in the FROM clause of a query.

PATH EXPRESSIONS

The expression auction.bids in the preceding example is known as a path expression. A *path expression* consists of an identification variable and a CMR or CMP field separated by the dot navigation operator (.). You use path expressions to further narrow the domain of a query. The type of field that a path expression navigates to defines the type of the path expression itself. This means that the result of the navigation defines the result of a path expression. The expression auction.bids evaluates to a collection of AuctionBid objects. An expression such as this that navigates to a collection-valued CMR field is called a *collection-valued path expression*. This is the only type of path expression you can use with the IN operator. When you use IN, you're declaring a variable to represent an object of a particular abstract schema type in a collection that was reached by navigating a CMR field. A path expression that navigates a CMP field or a one-to-one or many-to-one CMR field is called a *single-valued path expression*.

If a path expression navigates to a CMR field, you can continue navigating to that entity's CMP fields or its other relationships. As an example, the following path expression navigates to the bidder who placed the winning bid for an auction:

```
auction.winningBid.bidder
```

Here, `auction.winningBid` is a single-valued expression that evaluates to a CMR field that holds an `AuctionBid`. Because this is a single-valued CMR field, it can be further navigated. In this case, the dot operator is applied to navigate to the `Bidder` that is associated with the winning bid. You can navigate to CMP fields as well. The navigation here could continue as in the following:

```
auction.winningBid.bidder.emailAddressField
```

This path expression gets the e-mail address of the winning bidder. Applying the dot operator to the result of `auction.winningBid` allows you to navigate to the bidder and produce a result of the bidder's abstract schema type. This result is then navigated to one of its CMP fields. In this example, the result of the entire expression is the CMP field (a `String`) that defines the bidder's e-mail address.

Because `auction.bids` produces a collection-valued result, it can't be navigated. You must use the `IN` operator to further access the results of a collection-valued path expression.

DEFINING A WHERE CLAUSE

As with SQL, an EJB QL `WHERE` clause defines a conditional expression that is used to filter the results of a query. A simple example of a `WHERE` clause is

```
SELECT OBJECT(auction) FROM EnglishAuction auction,
  IN(auction.bids) aBid WHERE aBid.amountField > 500.0
```

This modified query now limits the auctions it returns to those that have received a bid for an amount greater than $500. Identification variables, such as `aBid` in this case, can be referenced in a `WHERE` clause but they cannot be declared there.

A `WHERE` clause supports a number of literal types, such as the floating-point value 500.0 used in this example. You can use string, integer, floating-point, and Boolean literals in a `WHERE` clause. String literals must be enclosed in single quotes (you can use a double quote to represent a single quote within a literal). An integer literal can be any value legal for the Java `long` primitive. A floating-point literal can be any legal `double` value and can be expressed in either standard or scientific notation (for example, 123.45 or 1.2345e2). The Boolean literals are `TRUE` and `FALSE` (case doesn't matter).

INPUT PARAMETERS

Many finder and select methods accept parameters that define the criteria for their results. A finder or select method parameter can be referenced in the `WHERE` clause of an EJB QL query using a `?` followed by an integer number. For example, the bid threshold in the example could be replaced by an input parameter using

```
SELECT OBJECT(auction) FROM EnglishAuction auction,
  IN(auction.bids) aBid WHERE aBid.amountField > ?1
```

The number that follows the ? indicates the parameter number. Unlike typical Java indexing, parameter numbers in EJB QL start with 1. A query doesn't have to use all the input parameters that are available to it, but it's definitely an error to reference a parameter number that's higher than the number of parameters declared by the finder or select method.

The type of a parameter in a query is determined by the corresponding finder or select method declaration. You're not limited to simple numeric types for parameters. Finder and select methods can accept more complex parameters, such as component interface references, that you can use within your queries as well. The one restriction on using input parameters is that you can reference them only in conditional expressions that involve single-valued path expressions.

EXPRESSIONS AND OPERATORS

The expression associated with a WHERE clause is known as its conditional expression. Complex conditional expressions can be built using the operators defined by the language. Expressions can include logical operators, relational operators, arithmetic operators, Boolean literals, and path expressions that evaluate to Boolean results. One of the few restrictions is that you can't compare instances of dependent value classes as part of a conditional expression. Operators are evaluated based on the order of precedence shown in Table 8.1 (starting with the highest precedence).

TABLE 8.1   PRECEDENCE OF CONDITIONAL EXPRESSION OPERATORS

Operator	Description
.	Navigation operator
+, -	Unary sign operators
*, /	Multiplication and division
+, -	Addition and subtraction
=, >, >=, <, <=, <>	Relational operators
NOT	Logical NOT
AND	Logical AND
OR	Logical OR

You can use parentheses within a query to group operators when the precedence rules won't produce the intended results. Of the relational operators shown, only = and <> apply to String or Boolean operands.

BETWEEN

You can use the BETWEEN comparison operator within an arithmetic expression. This operator compares an expression result to a lower and an upper limit using the following syntax:

expression [NOT] BETWEEN *lowerLimit* AND *upperLimit*

As an example, you could look for auctions with a starting bid within a certain range using

```
SELECT OBJECT(auction) FROM EnglishAuction auction
  WHERE auction.startingBidField BETWEEN 100 AND 500
```

The lower and upper limits in a BETWEEN expression don't have to be literals. The limits can be parameters or any arithmetic expression that evaluates to a result of the same type as the expression being tested. If an expression used with a BETWEEN operator evaluates to null, the value of the expression is unknown. You'll see more about what this means a little later.

IN

When used in a WHERE clause, the IN operator serves a purpose other than what you use if for in the FROM clause. The IN comparison operator allows you to form a conditional expression that is evaluated based on whether a string is found within a specified set of string literals. This operator is used only with single-valued path expressions that evaluate to the String value of a CMP field. This operator can also be used as NOT IN to return a negated result. As an example, the following conditional looks for bidders located in a certain region of the United States:

```
SELECT OBJECT(b) FROM Bidder b WHERE b.shippingAddress.stateField
  IN ('GA', 'FL', 'AL', 'TN')
```

When using the IN operator, you must include at least one string literal in the list being used for the comparison. If the single-valued path expression evaluates to null, the result of an expression using IN is unknown.

LIKE

The LIKE operator allows you to build a conditional that looks for strings that either match or don't match a pattern you specify. The syntax for the LIKE operator is

```
single_valued_path_expression [NOT] LIKE pattern [ESCAPE escape-character]
```

The pattern used with the LIKE operator must be a string literal, so the operator can be used only with a single-valued path expression that evaluates to a String. The pattern can include an underscore (_) to represent any single character in a given position or a percent sign (%) to represent any sequence of characters starting in a certain position. If you need to search for underscores or percent signs, you must precede them with an escape character within the pattern and then include the ESCAPE identifier to identify the escape character you're using. The following examples illustrate the uses of LIKE:

- WHERE auction.statusField LIKE 'C%' is true for all auctions that are either Closed or Cancelled.

- WHERE auction.statusField NOT LIKE 'C%' is true for all auctions that are either Pending or Open.

- `WHERE bidder.shippingAddress.stateField LIKE 'A_'` is true for all bidders who live in Alabama, Alaska, Arkansas, or Arizona.
- `WHERE auction.nameField LIKE '\_%' ESCAPE '\'` is true for all auctions with a name that starts with an underscore.

If the single-valued expression evaluates to `null`, the result of a `LIKE` expression is unknown.

MEMBER OF

You can use `MEMBER OF` to test whether an identification variable, an input parameter, or the object returned by a single-valued navigation is contained in the collection returned by a collection-valued path expression. A *single-valued navigation* is defined by navigating an identification variable to a single-valued CMR field. For example, the following query returns all bidders who have submitted a winning bid using `MEMBER OF` with the single-valued navigation `auction.winningBid`:

```
SELECT OBJECT(b) FROM EnglishAuction auction, Bidder b
  WHERE auction.winningBid MEMBER OF b.myBids
```

`MEMBER OF` always returns a Boolean result. If the collection-valued path expression with which it's used is empty, `FALSE` is returned. You also can use `NOT MEMBER OF` to build conditional expressions. The `OF` part of the operator is optional and is assumed if you leave it out of an expression.

NULL VALUES AND EMPTY COLLECTIONS

As you've seen from a few of the cautions about undefined query results, you must be careful about `null` results from path expressions. If a path expression encounters a `null` value anywhere along its navigation, the expression evaluates to `null`. EJB QL provides a way to test for `null` results from a single-valued path expression using the `IS NULL` and `IS NOT NULL` comparison operators. You can apply these operators to a CMP field or single-valued CMR field to get a Boolean `TRUE` or `FALSE` result based on whether the field is `null`. For example, you could locate only the auctions with a valid winning bid using

```
SELECT OBJECT(auction) FROM EnglishAuction auction
  WHERE auction.winningBid IS NOT NULL
```

The preceding operator descriptions pointed out that applying certain operators to a `null` value (which can include `null` input parameter values) produces an unknown result. This is true for any arithmetic or comparison operator. For example, the sum of a number and an unknown value is unknown. Asking if an unknown value is less than some number can't produce a known result either. Unlike arithmetic and comparison operators, the Boolean operators are defined to produce known results when working with unknown values in some cases. The `AND` operator produces an unknown result when applied to two unknown values or an unknown value and a `TRUE`, but it produces a `FALSE` if applied to an unknown value and a `FALSE`. This is because a `FALSE` and anything produces a `FALSE` with the `AND` operator. Similarly, applying `OR` to a `TRUE` and an unknown value produces a `TRUE`, but any other use of `OR` with an unknown produces an unknown result. Applying the unary `NOT` operator to an unknown value produces an unknown result as well. If you apply an equality test to an unknown value, the result of the conditional is always FALSE. This is because unknown isn't TRUE and it isn't FALSE. So a test for either will report FALSE as its result.

Caution

> EJB QL considers an empty string and a null string to be two different things. However, not all data stores do the same. You can't rely on consistent results when you define queries that could involve the comparison of an empty string to null.

Besides checking for null values, you also must be able to recognize empty collections. The IS EMPTY and IS NOT EMPTY comparison operators allow you to test for empty collection results when you're working with a collection-values path expression. For example, you might want to look for auctions that have at least one bid using

```
SELECT OBJECT(auction) FROM EnglishAuction auction
  WHERE auction.bids IS NOT EMPTY
```

This query is much more straightforward than the following one that was presented earlier to find the same set of auctions:

```
SELECT OBJECT(auction) FROM EnglishAuction auction, IN(auction.bids) aBid
```

Adding a WHERE clause to this original query to test auction.bids for an empty collection would be invalid. This is because the FROM clause filters out empty collections automatically as written. You can't make an empty collection comparison using a collection-valued path expression that is used to declare an identification variable in the FROM clause.

Note

> You've now seen the only three places you can use a collection-valued path expression: an identification variable declaration using IN, an empty collection comparison expression using IS [NOT] EMPTY, and a collection member expression using [NOT] MEMBER [OF].

DEFINING A SELECT CLAUSE

A SELECT clause is always required when you define an EJB QL query. It is the SELECT clause that determines the type of values returned by a query, so it must be consistent with the declaration of the select or finder method that it's supporting. For a finder method, this means that the SELECT clause must always return the abstract schema type of the entity bean for which the method is defined. The container takes care of returning local or remote interface references as necessary. You've seen examples of SELECT clauses such as the following throughout this chapter:

```
SELECT OBJECT(auction) FROM EnglishAuction auction
```

The SELECT clause in this example references a range variable associated with the EnglishAuction abstract schema type. This approach allows you to start with all objects of a given abstract schema type and filter them using a conditional expression in a WHERE clause.

When you use a standalone identification variable such as `auction` as the return value in a `SELECT` clause, you have to apply the `OBJECT` operator to it.

In addition to range variables, you can declare a `SELECT` clause for a finder method using a single-valued path expression. The result of this expression must be a CMR field that evaluates to the abstract schema type required by the finder. For example, you could declare a `findAllWinningBids` method for `AuctionBid` using

```
SELECT auction.winningBid FROM EnglishAuction auction
```

This query returns a collection of all the winning bids assigned to auctions in the system. Because a path expression is used in this `SELECT` clause, you don't use the `OBJECT` operator with it. The syntax changes when you encounter a collection-valued path expression. As an example, you could retrieve all bids for a particular bidder using

```
SELECT OBJECT(bids) FROM Bidder b, IN(b.myBids) bids
  WHERE b.usernameField = 'jsmith'
```

Notice in this example that the identification variable `bids` is used in the `SELECT` clause instead of `b.myBids`. The `SELECT` clause allows only single-valued path expressions, and `b.myBids` is a collection value. You must use `IN` to obtain a corresponding identification variable to return in this situation.

The return value of a select method isn't as constrained as that for a finder. A select method can return entities of any abstract schema type or the value of a CMP field (including those declared using Java primitive types). If a select method returns entity references, you specify whether local or remote interfaces are returned using the `result-type-mapping` element in the deployment descriptor as shown in the following:

```
<query>
  <query-method>
    <method-name>ejbSelectAuctionedItems</method-name>
    <method-params/>
  </query-method>
  <result-type-mapping>Local</result-type-mapping>
  <ejb-ql>
    <![CDATA[ SELECT OBJECT(i) FROM EnglishAuction AS a, IN(a.item) i]]>
  </ejb-ql>
</query>
```

If you omit the `result-type-mapping`, `Local` is assumed. You also could express the query shown in the deployment descriptor using `SELECT a.item` instead of declaring the second identification variable. As another example of a select method, you could obtain all the auction names using

```
SELECT auction.nameField FROM EnglishAuction auction
```

Because `nameField` is a `String`-valued CMP field, this select method query would return either a `Collection` or a `Set` of `String` objects. The choice of `Collection` or `Set` is made based on the declaration of the select method in the bean implementation class. When you implement a query for a method that is declared to return a `Set`, the container takes care of removing any duplicate values in the query results for you. If the method returns a

Collection, you can use the DISTINCT qualifier in the SELECT clause to prevent duplicates. This can be used both with range variables and path expressions. The following query would return a list of home states for all auction winners:

```
SELECT DISTINCT b.stateField FROM EnglishAuction auction,
  IN(auction.winningBid.bidder) b
```

SELF JOINS

If you're familiar with SQL statements that compare rows of the same table to each other, you know that you have to reference the table twice in the FROM clause of the statement. The same is true for EJB QL. For example, you could use the following query to be sure that no two auctions are offering the same item:

```
SELECT OBJECT(a1) FROM EnglishAuction a1, EnglishAuction a2
  WHERE (a1.item IS NOT NULL) AND
  (a1.id <> a2.id) AND
  (a1.item.id = a2.item.id)
```

Notice that the only test for a null value is the one used to make sure that only auctions with an item assigned are considered. In the other path expressions, a null is returned if a null is encountered anywhere in the navigation, so you don't have to worry about any intermediate tests yourself.

USING THE BUILT-IN FUNCTIONS

EJB QL provides a few built-in functions for performing some common string and arithmetic manipulations to build your queries. The functions that are supported are standard SQL operations that all JDBC 2.0 and higher drivers are required to support.

STRING FUNCTIONS

EJB QL supports the following string manipulation functions:

- CONCAT(String first, String second) concatenates its two arguments and returns the resulting String.

- SUBSTRING(String source, int start, int length) returns a String that is a substring of its argument based on the specified starting index and requested string length.

- LOCATE(String source, String pattern) returns an int value that defines the starting index within the source string that a pattern string is found.

- LOCATE(String source, String pattern, int start) is an overloaded version of LOCATE that only looks at the portion of the source string starting with a specified index.

- LENGTH(String source) returns an int value that reports the number of characters found in its string argument.

ARITHMETIC FUNCTIONS

EJB QL supports the following arithmetic functions:

- `ABS(int number)` returns the absolute value of an `int` argument as an `int`.
- `ABS(float number)` returns the absolute value of a `float` argument as a `float`.
- `ABS(double number)` returns the absolute value of a `double` argument as a `double`.
- SQRT(`double number`) returns the square root of its argument as a `double`.

Currently, there's no support for aggregate functions, such as `MIN` and `MAX`, in EJB QL. That likely will be added in later versions of the specification. Until then, you're somewhat limited in what you can do in a select method.

EJB QL Syntax in BNF Notation

The Backus Naur Form (BNF) developed by John Backus and Peter Naur (circa 1960) is the mechanism most often used to define the syntax of a programming language. Using a few meta-symbols, BNF allows the elements of a language to be defined recursively. There are alternate forms of these symbols, which can lead to some confusion if you're not familiar with how to interpret them. To keep things simple, the notation presented in this section follows that used in the EJB 2.0 Specification for the most part. These symbols are defined in Table 8.2.

TABLE 8.2 BNF SYMBOLS

Symbol	Description
::=	Read as "is defined as."
<>	Angle brackets surround elements that describe portions of the language but aren't part of the actual syntax. Elements without these brackets are written as they actually appear in the language.
[]	Square brackets enclose optional elements.
{}	Braces group elements for clarity.
*	Elements followed by an asterisk can be repeated one or more times.
|	A logical OR.

EJB QL BNF

This section presents the BNF used to describe EJB QL in the EJB 2.0 Specification. You might be tempted to skip over this because BNF can be confusing at first. However, if you can follow this description of EJB QL, you'll have little difficulty declaring your queries. Just as a DTD governs how you construct a valid deployment descriptor, this BNF is the ultimate guide to correct EJB QL syntax.

```
<EJB QL> ::= <select_clause> <from_clause> [<where_clause>]

<from_clause> ::= FROM <identification_variable_declaration>
    [, <identification_variable_declaration>]*

<identification_variable_declaration> ::= <collection_member_declaration> |
    <range_variable_declaration>

<collection_member_declaration> ::= IN (<collection_valued_path_expression>)
    [AS] <identifier>

<range_variable_declaration> ::= <abstract_schema_name> [AS] <identifier>

<single_valued_path_expression> ::=
    {<single_valued_navigation> | <identification_variable>}.<cmp_field> |
    <single_valued_navigation>

<single_valued_navigation> ::= <identification_variable>.
    [<single_valued_cmr_field>.]*<single_valued_cmr_field>

<collection_valued_path_expression> ::= <identification_variable>.
    [<single_valued_cmr_field>.]*<collection_valued_cmr_field>

<select_clause> ::= SELECT [DISTINCT] {<single_valued_path_expression> |
    OBJECT (<identification_variable>)}

<where_clause> ::= WHERE <conditional_expression>

<conditional_expression> ::= <conditional_term> | <conditional_expression>
    OR <conditional_term>

<conditional_term> ::= <conditional_factor> | <conditional_term>
    AND <conditional_factor>

<conditional_factor> ::= [NOT] <conditional_test>

<conditional_test> ::= <conditional_primary>

<conditional_primary> ::= <simple_cond_expression> | (<conditional_expression>)

<simple_cond_expression> ::= <comparison_expression> | <between_expression> |
    <like_expression> | <in_expression> | <null_comparison_expression> |
    <empty_collection_comparison_expression> | <collection_member_expression>

<between_expression> ::= <arithmetic_expression> [NOT] BETWEEN
    <arithmetic_expression> AND <arithmetic_expression>

<in_expression> ::= <single_valued_path_expression>
    [NOT] IN (<string_literal> [, <string_literal>]*)

<like_expression> ::= <single_valued_path_expression>
    [NOT] LIKE <pattern_value> [ESCAPE <escape-character>]

<null_comparison_expression> ::= <single_valued_path_expression> IS [NOT] NULL

<empty_collection_comparison_expression> ::=
    <collection_valued_path_expression> IS [NOT] EMPTY
```

```
<collection_member_expression> ::=
{<single_valued_navigation> | <identification_variable> |
    <input_parameter>} [NOT] MEMBER [OF]
    <collection_valued_path_expression>

<comparison_expression> ::=
    <string_value> { = | <>} <string_expression> |
    <boolean_value> { = | <>} <boolean_expression>} |
    <datetime_value> { = | <> | > | < } <datetime_expression> |
    <entity_bean_value> { = | <> } <entity_bean_expression> |
    <arithmetic_value> <comparison_operator> <single_value_designator>

<arithmetic_value> ::= <single_valued_path_expression> |
    <functions_returning_numerics>

<single_value_designator> ::= <scalar_expression>

<comparison_operator> ::=
    = | > | >= | < | <= | <>

<scalar_expression> ::= <arithmetic_expression>

<arithmetic_expression> ::= <arithmetic_term> | <arithmetic_expression>
    { + | - } <arithmetic_term>

<arithmetic_term> ::= <arithmetic_factor> | <arithmetic_term>
    { * | / } <arithmetic_factor>

<arithmetic_factor> ::= { + | - } <arithmetic_primary>

<arithmetic_primary> ::= <single_valued_path_expression> | <literal> |
    (<arithmetic_expression>) | <input_parameter> |
    <functions_returning_numerics>

<string_value> ::= <single_valued_path_expression> |
    <functions_returning_strings>

<string_expression> ::= <string_primary> | <input_expression>

<string_primary> ::= <single_valued_path_expression> | <literal> |
    (<string_expression>) | <functions_returning_strings>

<datetime_value> ::= <single_valued_path_expression>

<datetime_expression> ::= <datetime_value> | <input_parameter>

<boolean_value> ::= <single_valued_path_expression>

<boolean_expression> ::= <single_valued_path_expression> | <literal> |
    <input_parameter>

<entity_bean_value> ::= <single_valued_navigation> |
    <identification_variable>

<entity_bean_expression> ::= <entity_bean_value> | <input_parameter>

<functions_returning_strings> ::=
    CONCAT (<string_expression>, <string_expression>) |
```

```
      SUBSTRING (<string_expression>, <arithmetic_expression>,
          <arithmetic_expression>)

<functions_returning_numerics> ::=
    LENGTH (<string_expression>) |
    LOCATE (<string_expression>, <string_expression>
        [,<arithmetic_expression>]) |
    ABS (<arithmetic_expression>) |
    SQRT (<arithmetic_expression>)
```

TROUBLESHOOTING

ENTITY BEAN NAMES

I'm confused about how to refer to an entity bean within a query.

EJB QL does not care about the name of your bean implementation classes or the home and component interfaces. When you're defining a finder or select method for an entity, you refer to that bean using its abstract-schema-name as specified in the deployment descriptor.

EMPTY STRINGS AND null

My conditional expression that checks for a null string is returning true for empty strings.

EJB QL considers an empty string to be non-null. However, you're at the mercy of how your data store interprets empty strings when your queries are executed. Remember that your EJB QL queries are converted in the target language of the data store when your beans are deployed. If the data store treats empty strings as nulls, so will your queries that were specified using EJB QL.

DATES

I don't know how to use a date in an EJB QL query.

EJB QL only knows how to work with dates using a long value expressed in milliseconds since January 1, 1970, 00:00:00 GMT. Use the facilities of java.util.Calendar to generate the millisecond equivalent of any dates you need to use as literals in your queries .

CHAPTER 9

SESSION BEANS

In this chapter

WHAT IS A SESSION BEAN?

In Chapter 5, "Entity Beans," you were introduced to the first type of enterprise bean. This chapter introduces you to the second type, the session bean. Just as entity beans have a purpose in manipulating persistent data, session beans have a purpose in executing business logic on behalf of a client. In fact, you can think of a session bean as an extension of a client. The EJB architecture provides to session beans the same transactional, security, and concurrency support given entity beans. This allows clients to execute reusable business logic running in an application server to do transactional work. The container takes care of the low-level details, so the session bean and client application developers can focus on the application logic they need to implement without worrying about the infrastructure.

A client for a session bean can be a remote client, such as a servlet, a CORBA client, or another enterprise bean deployed in a different container. Just like an entity bean, a session bean can also support an enterprise bean deployed in the same container as a local client.

Typically, you'll design your applications so that entity beans only have other EJBs for clients (session beans mostly). It's your session beans that you'll most often expose to the non-EJB clients of your application. As an example, a banking application might use entity beans to represent customers and their accounts and session beans to perform any work related to them. A request to transfer funds between a customer's savings and checking accounts could be handled by a session bean method that makes the necessary updates to the two entity objects representing the accounts. All the logic related to account transfers would be executed within the application server where the corresponding security and transactional concerns could be managed transparently to the client. Session beans are a good place to implement an application's workflow logic.

Because entity beans typically are accessed only by other enterprise beans, their clients are most often local clients. The nature of session beans makes it more likely for them to be used by remote clients. This is because their behavior is often an extension of the client applications that access them.

Just like an entity bean, a remote client interacts with a session bean through the bean's remote interface. Conceptually, a session bean object that serves a remote client is implemented in the container by an EJBObject, which implements the session bean's remote interface. When a client invokes a method on a session bean, the EJBObject executes on behalf of the client and delegates the method call to an instance of your session bean class. In the case of a local client, an EJBLocalObject that implements the bean's local interface delegates calls to a bean instance. Because calls to a session bean instance are always intercepted by the container, the container is able to handle security, transactions, concurrency, and other life-cycle services for the bean.

DESCRIBING A SESSION BEAN

A session bean exhibits the following characteristics:

- It supports transactions.
- It executes on behalf of a single client.

- It's relatively short-lived compared to an entity bean.
- It doesn't represent data in a database, although it can access shared data on behalf of a client.

All enterprise bean types support transactions, but the other characteristics just listed for session beans set them apart from entity beans. When multiple clients want to access the same entity bean object, the container uses a single instance of the bean class to service their requests. The requests are serialized so that each client call waits in line to be serviced. A session bean, on the other hand, is activated by the container for the purpose of serving a single client. You'll see more of how the container manages this behavior when the two types of session beans are described in the next section.

An entity bean represents long-lived persistent data and the container can regenerate a particular entity object in the event of a system restart (either an intentional one or after a crash). A session bean instance is instead intended to serve the needs of its client and then go away. What this really means is that any state associated with that client goes away and the instance is placed back into the object pool ready to be used for a different client.

The final point to address here describes the relationship between session beans and the database. Unlike entity beans, the state held by a session bean doesn't correspond to data held in a database or other persistent data store. However, it's common for a session bean to indirectly modify persistent data by calling methods on entity beans. You'll also find it useful to perform read-only database access directly from session beans. With this as an option, you don't have to limit yourself to using entity beans for all your database access.

DIFFERENCES BETWEEN STATELESS AND STATEFUL SESSION BEANS

Unlike the other EJB types, session beans are divided into two categories. A session bean can either be *stateful* or *stateless*. A stateful session bean is said to "maintain conversational state" with its client. *Conversational state* means that the bean maintains knowledge of actions performed by a specific client across multiple method calls made by that client. The EJB specification states that this is the normal behavior for a session bean. A form of session bean that maintains no conversational state (stateless) is also defined by the specification. The primary tradeoff between the two is efficient use of resources versus client application complexity. Even though stateful is described as being the normal type of session bean, you'll actually find that stateless session beans are more common in typical EJB applications.

With stateless session beans, once a method invocation is completed, the container may use this instance to service a different client. Because stateless session beans don't maintain conversational state, each instance of a particular session bean class is identical to any other as far as the container is concerned. The identity of a session object isn't exposed, so a client of a stateless session bean never knows whether the method calls it makes on a component interface reference are serviced by the same session object each time or not. This and the fact that a client usually does some processing of its own in between calls to a session bean give the container some flexibility. In particular, the container can swap instances back and forth between clients so that it can service many more clients than its number of activated session bean instances. This is an obvious boost to scalability because the number of stateless session beans doesn't have to increase with every increase in the number of clients.

The anonymity of stateless session beans brings up a major difference between the two types of session beans. All instances of a single stateless session bean class are identical, but this isn't true for stateful session beans. After a stateful session bean instance has been activated and associated with a client, it's uniquely identified with that client and it stays with the client until the client is finished with it or the instance is passivated or times out. You'll see how passivation is handled when the session bean life cycle is discussed a little later.

Just as some EJB developers question the relative worth of entity beans, session beans don't come without a small debate of their own. Stateless session beans are accepted without opposition, but some developers believe the nature of stateful session beans makes them a performance bottleneck that should be avoided. It's true that stateful session beans don't scale as well as stateless ones do, but they're being asked to serve a different purpose. First, it's important to recognize that the leading EJB containers are designed to support a large number of concurrent session bean instances executing at one time. If an application serves many concurrent users, it can exceed this number and have to passivate and activate its stateful session bean instances—but not necessarily any more than it will its entity bean objects. The passivation mechanism is built into the EJB architecture to support scalability, so it doesn't have to be interpreted as a performance barrier. You should keep in mind that there are definite situations where it makes sense to use stateful session beans. If you're implementing workflow functionality that requires the client to perform multiple steps, avoiding stateful session beans forces you to either require more sophisticated clients (capable of maintaining their own state and sending it to the methods of a stateless bean) or store intermediate results somewhere. For approaches that use a database, you might even want to consider an entity bean implementation. You shouldn't use stateful session beans when you don't need to maintain specific client information between method invocations, but you shouldn't avoid them when you do. As long as you recognize the intent of this bean type, you can use it effectively.

Note

A stateless session bean doesn't maintain conversational state with a client, but that doesn't mean that it can't have state. A stateless session bean can have instance variables that hold state just like any other class. The distinction is that a client can't assume that the state held by a stateless session bean is specific to it. If a client sets the value of a stateless bean instance field, there's no guarantee that the field will have that value when the client calls another method. This is because another bean instance might be used to service subsequent calls. You should use instance fields in a stateless session bean only to maintain state that's common to all its clients. For example, a stateless session bean could hold a reference to a data source connection factory that can be used no matter which client calls it.

IDENTIFYING THE AUCTION SESSION BEANS

Chapter 5 identified a set of entity beans and dependent objects capable of managing the persistent data for a simple auction site. These entity beans are responsible for business logic specific to the concepts they represent, but a layer of session beans is needed between them and the client to isolate them and implement the workflow business logic. To start with, an `AuctionHouse` session bean can be used to implement the functionality needed to supply bidders with information about the available auctions and to receive bid submissions and pass them on to the corresponding `EnglishAuction` entity object. Separating the operations needed to create and maintain auctions into an `AuctionManager` session bean supports a clear division of responsibility. It also simplifies the management of security roles by isolating end-user bidding functionality from the needs of internal data maintenance users. Both `AuctionHouse` and `AuctionManager` represent fairly discrete tasks (for example, generating a list of the open auctions, submitting a bid, creating a new auction, and so on) so stateless session beans can satisfy the requirements for these beans.

PART
I
CH
9

As an example of a stateful session bean, a conversational state might be useful when an auction winner is being led through the steps needed to complete the purchase of an item that's been won. You'll often see an online shopping cart concept such as this used as an example of a stateful session bean. This representation can be used for an `AuctionCheckout` bean to handle the purchasing workflow.

Table 9.1 summarizes the representation chosen for the auction controller classes.

TABLE 9.1   THE AUCTION SESSION BEANS

Object	Representation
AuctionHouse	Stateless session bean
AuctionManager	Stateless session bean
AuctionCheckout	Stateful session bean

BEAN PROVIDER RESPONSIBILITIES

Many of the responsibilities of a session bean provider are the same as the ones that apply to entity beans. A bean provider that develops a session bean must define its home and component interfaces, implement the bean class, and provide the initial version of its deployment descriptor. This is nothing beyond what's required to develop an entity bean. Session beans don't have primary keys, so you don't have to be concerned about declaring a primary key class. You also don't have to consider BMP versus CMP type issues. The most significant choice you make right away for a session bean is whether to design it as stateful or stateless. Along with this goes the question of whether the bean will support local or remote clients (or both). You'll also see later in Chapter 12, "Transactions," that you must choose between two methods of managing transactions when you implement a session bean. This chapter will stick with the assumption that the container is managing the transactions, which is the more common approach.

→ For more information on implementing transactional bean methods, **see** "Using Container-Managed Transactions," **p. 344**.

By the end of this chapter, you'll be able to declare the interfaces for a session bean, implement the bean class, and specify its deployment information.

DECLARING THE COMPONENT INTERFACE

As with entity beans, a client's view of a session bean is defined by the bean's component interface. Remember that a remote interface must always be declared to extend EJBObject and a local interface must extend EJBLocalObject. As illustrated previously with entity beans, the remote and local interfaces are where you define the business methods you want to expose to clients of your beans. Again, these methods must be declared such that

- No method name starts with ejb
- All methods are declared as public
- No method is declared as static or final
- All remote interface methods include java.rmi.RemoteException in their throws clauses
- All remote interface method arguments and return types must be legal RMI-IIOP types

Note

The requirements for legal RMI-IIOP types span five pages in OMG's "Java Language to IDL Mapping" document. However, in general, the legal RMI-IIOP types include the Java primitives, remote interfaces, serializable classes, arrays that hold objects of a legal type, and checked exceptions. You can download this document from OMG at http://www.omg.org/cgi-bin/doc?ptc/00-01-06 if you want a more precise description.

Work can be done through a session object after a client obtains a reference to its component interface. A client with a reference to a session object's component interface can

- Call the session object's business methods
- Call remove to remove a stateful session object
- Obtain the session object's handle (only done by remote clients using getHandle)
- Obtain a reference to the session object's home interface (using getEJBLocalHome or using getEJBHome)
- Pass the reference as a parameter or return value of a method call (limited to local methods when using the local interface)

Caution

> Even though a session bean's remote interface must extend EJBObject, a client should never call the getPrimaryKey method for a session bean. Calling this method will result in a RemoteException. Similarly, calling getPrimaryKey on EJBLocalObject for a session bean results in a javax.ejb.EJBException.

COMPARING OBJECT IDENTITY

The component interface, and its isIdentical method in particular, offers some insight into how the container views session bean instances. Unlike entity beans, session beans are intended to be anonymous to the client. This is why they don't have an identity that's exposed to the client through a primary key. However, each session object is in fact assigned an identity by the container when it's created. The meaning and behavior of this identity differ depending on what type of session bean you're talking about. Because each stateful session bean instance is different due to the state it holds for its client, each instance is assigned a unique identity by the container when the instance is created. The behavior is somewhat different for stateless session beans. Each stateless session bean object created from the same home factory has the exact same identity. This is because stateless session bean instances should be interchangeable as far as both the client and the container are concerned.

Note

> It's not common, but you're allowed to deploy the same session bean into the container more than once under a distinct home factory. When you do this, the container assigns a different unique identity to each home deployment. Otherwise, all instances of a particular stateless session bean in a given container will have the same identity assigned to them when they're created.

Testing whether one session object is identical to another is done the same way regardless of whether it's a stateful or stateless session bean. To test whether session beans are identical, you should use the isIdentical method defined by the EJBObject and EJBLocalObject interfaces. The isIdentical method takes a single argument, which is the corresponding remote or local interface of the object to which you're making the comparison. Although the same method is used for both stateful and stateless session beans, its result depends on which one you're using.

USING isIdentical WITH STATEFUL SESSION BEANS

Because each stateful session bean instance is created for a specific client, references to session objects of this type are identical only if they point to the object that was created in response to the same client request. Remember that the container assigns a unique identity to each stateful session bean instance. It's this identity that's being used for the comparison. To illustrate this behavior with an example, the following code fragment declares references to two unique stateful session objects:

```
// Obtain a reference to a stateful session bean's home interface
AuctionCheckoutHome checkoutHome = ...;

// Create two different stateful session objects
AuctionCheckout checkout1 = checkoutHome.create();
AuctionCheckout checkout2 = checkoutHome.create();
```

If you then execute the following test using the checkout1 and checkout1 remote interface references the if statement returns false because each stateful session bean instance has a unique identity so that no two are identical:

```
// This test would return false
if ( checkout1.isIdentical( checkout2 ) ) {
  ...
}
```

If you instead execute this test, it returns true because the stateful session bean instance and itself have the same identity, by definition:

```
// This test would return true
if ( checkout1.isIdentical( checkout1 ) ) {
  ...
}
```

USING isIdentical WITH STATELESS SESSION BEANS

The behavior of isIdentical for stateless session beans is the same as that for stateful when a reference is compared to itself. However, the results change when two different instances from the same home are compared. If the preceding example is repeated for two stateless session using the following code fragment:

```
// Obtain a reference to a stateless session bean's home interface
AuctionHouseHome auctionHouseHome = ...;

// Create two different stateful session beans
AuctionHouse auctionHouse1 = auctionHouseHome.create();
AuctionHouse auctionHouse2 = auctionHouseHome.create();
```

and you execute the following test:

```
// This test would return true
if ( auctionHouse1.isIdentical( auctionHouse2 ) ) {
  ...
}
```

it returns true because all instances of a stateless session bean from the same home factory have the same unique identity and are considered to be identical.

THE AUCTION COMPONENT INTERFACES

For the auction example, the session beans identified in Table 9.1 provide the interface to the Web tier. This means that they must be written and deployed to support remote clients. Listing 9.1 shows a remote interface declaration that could be used for the auction house stateless session bean.

LISTING 9.1 AuctionHouse.java—A REMOTE INTERFACE FOR AN AUCTION HOUSE SESSION
BEAN

```java
package com.que.ejb20.auction.controller;
/**
 * Title:       AuctionHouse<p>
 * Description: The EJB remote interface for the AuctionHouse bean<p>
 */
import java.util.List;
import java.rmi.RemoteException;
import javax.ejb.EJBObject;
import javax.ejb.FinderException;
import com.que.ejb20.auction.exceptions.InvalidAuctionStatusException;
import com.que.ejb20.auction.exceptions.InvalidBidException;
import com.que.ejb20.auction.view.AuctionDetailView;

public interface AuctionHouse extends EJBObject {

  /**
   * Return a list of all open, closed, or cancelled auctions
   *
   * @return a List of AuctionSummaryView objects
   */
  public List getNonPendingAuctions() throws RemoteException;

  /**
   * Return a detailed description of a specific auction
   *
   * @param auctionId the primary key for the selected auction
   * @return a description of the auction and its offered item
   */
  public AuctionDetailView getAuctionDetail(int auctionId)
    throws FinderException, RemoteException;

  /**
   * Submit a bid to an open auction
   *
   * @param bidAmount the amount bid
   * @param auctionId the primary key for the selected auction
   * @param bidderId the primary key for the bidder
   *
   */
  public String submitBid(double bidAmount, int auctionId, int bidderId)
    throws InvalidBidException, InvalidAuctionStatusException, RemoteException;

  /**
   * Return a list of BidView objects describing all bids submitted by a bidder
   */
  public List getBids(int bidderId) throws FinderException, RemoteException;
}
```

This example of a remote interface shows the minimum set of business methods that the
auction house session bean would need to provide. As defined here, the AuctionHouse interface allows a client to get a list of auctions, get detailed information about a single auction,
submit a bid, and get a list of bids submitted by a particular user. The application exceptions

referenced by the methods, InvalidAuctionStatusException and InvalidBidException, and
AuctionDetailView were declared previously in Chapter 5. For an actual site, you would
likely supply other functionality such as displaying information to a bidder about all the auctions that had been participated in or displaying a summary of all the bids submitted on a
particular auction.

The getNonPendingAuctions method of the AuctionHouse interface uses a view class to
return information about particular auctions using a simple data structure. Listing 9.2 shows
this class, which is appropriate for summarizing an auction's state.

LISTING 9.2   AuctionSummaryView.java—A SUMMARY DESCRIPTION OF AN AUCTION

```
package com.que.ejb20.auction.view;
/**
 * Title:        AuctionSummaryView<p>
 * Description:  Summary view class for an English Auction suitable for
 *               building a list of defined auctions<p>
 */
import java.io.Serializable;
import java.sql.Timestamp;

public class AuctionSummaryView implements Serializable {
  private Integer id;
  private String name;
  private String status;
  private Double leadingBidAmount;
  private Timestamp scheduledEndDateTime;

  public AuctionSummaryView() {
  }

  public AuctionSummaryView(Integer newId, String newName, String newStatus,
    Timestamp newScheduledEndDateTime, Double newLeadingBidAmount) {

    setId(newId);
    setName(newName);
    setStatus(newStatus);
    setScheduledEndDateTime(newScheduledEndDateTime);
    setLeadingBidAmount(newLeadingBidAmount);
  }

  public Integer getId() {
    return id;
  }

  public void setId(Integer newId) {
    id = newId;
  }

  public void setName(String newName) {
    name = newName;
  }

  public String getName() {
    return name;
  }
```

LISTING 9.2   CONTINUED

```
  public void setStatus(String newStatus) {
    status = newStatus;
  }

  public String getStatus() {
    return status;
  }

  public void setLeadingBidAmount(Double newLeadingBidAmount) {
    leadingBidAmount = newLeadingBidAmount;
  }

  public Double getLeadingBidAmount() {
    return leadingBidAmount;
  }

  public void setScheduledEndDateTime(Timestamp newScheduledEndDateTime) {
    scheduledEndDateTime = newScheduledEndDateTime;
  }

  public Timestamp getScheduledEndDateTime() {
    return scheduledEndDateTime;
  }
}
```

Returning objects, such as `AuctionSummaryView` and `AuctionDetailView`, instances from the methods of `AuctionHouse` provides a separation between the clients of this data and the objects that maintain it. As discussed in the beginning of this chapter, a client rarely interacts directly with an entity bean. The preferred approach is for clients to go through session bean methods and work with entity beans indirectly. This tends to make a client's use of an entity more coarse-grained. A client often needs to perform multiple fine-grained operations on an entity object.

Think about how you update the state of an object or retrieve it for display. It's likely that you want to update or retrieve multiple attributes as part of a single action, which could lead to multiple calls on an entity from a client. Encapsulating a related set of entity bean calls in a session bean method simplifies the transaction management of an entity update, and it also can reduce the network traffic required to set or retrieve multiple attributes. If your clients don't call your entities directly, you need a means of passing the associated data between a client and a session bean. View classes provide a way for session beans to expose the data associated with an entity without directly exposing the entity to a client.

You can declare view classes to support the various ways clients of your application need to interact with an entity's data without having any impact on the interface supported by the entity bean. As long as the entity exposes all the information that's important to its clients, its implementation doesn't need any knowledge of how its data is pieced together for use by the applications that are built using it. This use of view classes also lends itself to entity reuse as well. If an entity provides all the data and business logic that are appropriate for the business object it's modeling, you can reuse it by defining additional view classes that can be supported by your session beans to build new applications. Remember that session beans can be thought of as extensions to your application clients. This means that it's acceptable for session beans to have application-specific knowledge.

You have several options when defining view classes like AuctionSummaryView and AuctionDetailView. The approach selected here was to use a JavaBean with accessor and mutator methods for each attribute. This makes them easy to use in a variety of clients, such as JSP pages. Another option is to use a simple data structure that declares all its attributes as public without providing any methods at all. This approach emphasizes the fact that classes like these are for passing data and not implementing business logic. Yet another option is to declare a view class as immutable by providing get methods and a constructor that accepts values for all the attributes but no set methods. You just need to consider the types of clients you're trying to support when you design the interface presented by your session beans.

You might remember from Chapter 5 that the auction entity bean declares a getAuctionDetail method in the EnglishAuction local interface that returns an AuctionDetailView. This view is somewhat generic in that it contains a complete copy of an auction's attributes. AuctionSummaryView is quite different in that it includes a subset of data that reflects a particular client need. Because AuctionSummaryView is client-specific, it isn't appropriate for the entity bean to have any knowledge of this view class or be able to generate an instance of it. Client-specific views are better generated by session beans or their helper classes. This helps keep your entity beans immune to changing client requirements.

The administrative functions for auction maintenance belong in the AuctionManager interface. Listing 9.3 shows a simple version of this interface with a representative set of methods.

LISTING 9.3   AuctionManager.java—A REMOTE INTERFACE FOR AN AUCTION MANAGER SESSION BEAN

```java
package com.que.ejb20.auction.controller;
/**
 * Title:        AuctionManager<p>
 * Description:  The EJB remote interface for the AuctionManager bean<p>
 */
import java.rmi.RemoteException;
import java.util.List;
import javax.ejb.CreateException;
import javax.ejb.EJBObject;
import javax.ejb.FinderException;
import com.que.ejb20.auction.exceptions.InvalidAuctionStatusException;
import com.que.ejb20.auction.view.AuctionDetailView;

public interface AuctionManager extends EJBObject {
  /**
   * Create a new auction and return it's primary key
   */
  public Integer createAuction(AuctionDetailView view) throws CreateException,
    RemoteException;
```

LISTING 9.3   CONTINUED

```
/**
 * Assign an item to be auctioned
 */
public void assignItemToAuction(Integer auctionId, Integer itemId,
  int quantity) throws InvalidAuctionStatusException, FinderException,
  RemoteException;

/**
 * Get a view of the auction's state
 */
public AuctionDetailView getAuctionDetail(int auctionId)
  throws FinderException, RemoteException;
}
```

Listing 9.4 shows a remote interface for a stateful session bean that might be used to manage the order entry process for an auction win. What you should notice here is that there's nothing about a session bean's component interface that indicates whether the bean is stateful or stateless.

LISTING 9.4   AuctionCheckout.java—A REMOTE INTERFACE FOR A STATEFUL SESSION BEAN USED TO COMPLETE AN AUCTION ORDER

```
package com.que.ejb20.auction.controller;
/**
 * Title:        AuctionCheckout<p>
 * Description:  Remote interface for the Auction Checkout
 *               stateful session bean<p>
 */
import java.rmi.RemoteException;
import javax.ejb.EJBObject;
import com.que.ejb20.auction.view.AddressView;

public interface AuctionCheckout extends EJBObject {

  public void setBidder(int bidderId) throws RemoteException;

  /**
   * Attach the item from an auction to an order
   *
   * @param auctionId the primary key for the selected auction
   */
  public void addAuctionWinToOrder(int auctionId) throws RemoteException;

  /**
   * Supply a shipping address for the order
   *
   * @param shippingAddress the address to use for this order
   */
  public void updateShippingAddress(AddressView shippingAddress)
    throws RemoteException;
```

LISTING 9.4 CONTINUED

```
/**
 * Select a shipping carrier and method
 *
 * @param carrierId an identifier for the shipping carrier
 * @param priorityId an identifier for the shipping method
 */
public void selectShippingMethod(int carrierCode, int priorityCode)
  throws RemoteException;

/**
 * Submit the order
 */
public void completeOrder() throws RemoteException;
}
```

DECLARING THE HOME INTERFACE

The home interface for a session bean declares the methods for creating and removing session objects. You can also use a remote home interface to get a reference to the bean's EJBMetaData or the home handle. Both the EJBMetaData and the HomeHandle interfaces were described previously in Chapter 3, "EJB Concepts." One restriction related to a session bean's EJBMetaData is that you can't call the getPrimaryKeyClass method or a RuntimeException will be thrown.

Unlike entity beans, you can't declare finder methods or home methods for a session bean. Finder methods wouldn't make sense for a session bean because a session object's identity is hidden from the client. When a client needs to obtain a reference to a session object, any instance pulled from the pool and made available by the container in response to a call to a create method is just as good as any other. As for home methods, session bean business methods already have the flexibility to manipulate multiple entities stored in a database (usually by accessing multiple entity objects). In fact, the functionality provided by a home method in an entity bean is something you would have most likely implemented in a session bean method prior to EJB 2.0.

CREATING A SESSION BEAN

A client obtains a component interface reference to a session object by calling a create method on a reference to the bean's home interface. Unlike entity beans, you must declare at least one create method for a session bean. Because session beans don't support the concept of a finder method, a session object always must be "created" for a client to have one with which to work.

You're allowed to define multiple create methods if you want to give clients more than one way to initialize a session object. However, this is useful only for stateful session beans because they're the only ones capable of maintaining state supplied by a client across method calls. For a stateless session bean, you're only allowed to declare a single `create` method like the following example:

```
public AuctionHouse create() throws CreateException, RemoteException;
```

This or any other `create` method you declare must

- Have a name that starts with `create` (for a stateless session bean, the name must be exactly `create` and the method must not accept any arguments)
- Be declared to return the remote interface type if found in a remote home interface, or the local interface type if found in a local home interface
- Include `javax.ejb.CreateException` in its `throws` clause and `java.rmi.RemoteException` (if found in a remote home interface)

PART

I

CH

9

As with entity beans, you must implement a corresponding `ejbCreate` for each `create` method you declare, but there's no concept of an `ejbPostCreate` for session beans. Other than the rules already given, the declaration of your `create` methods must include any application exceptions declared in the `throws` clause of the corresponding `ejbCreate` method. The required `CreateException` is the standard application exception you can use to report problems with initialization parameters passed to the `create` method.

→ For more information on reporting initialization problems when creating an enterprise bean instance, **see** "CreateException," **p. 367**.

REMOVING A SESSION BEAN

When a remote client has finished with a session object, it should call the `remove()` method declared by `EJBObject` or `remove(Handle handle)` declared by `EJBHome`. A local client only has the option of calling the `remove()` method declared by `EJBLocalObject`. For either client type, calling the `remove(Object primaryKey)` method declared by `EJBHome` or `EJBLocalHome` results in a `RemoveException` because a session bean doesn't have a primary key.

Typically, a client calls a `create` method to get a reference to a session object component interface, calls business methods on the reference to do some work, and then calls `remove` on the reference to free up the bean instance. It's also possible for a remote client to obtain the handle to the object from the home interface and serialize it for later use. In particular, this can be done for a stateful session bean to reconnect to a session object holding the conversational state established for a client. Regardless of whether the handle is used to access a particular client's session object again, it can be used to remove the object from the container using the `remove` method declared by the home interface. Once a session object has been removed, any calls to its remote interface result in a `java.rmi.NoSuchObjectException`, and any calls to its local interface cause a `javax.ejb.NoSuchObjectLocalException`.

THE `AuctionCheckoutHome` INTERFACE

Listing 9.5 contains a home interface declaration for the auction checkout stateful session bean. This interface illustrates the use of multiple `create` methods. Unlike a component interface, a session bean home interface with multiple `create` methods gives away the fact that it belongs to a stateful bean.

LISTING 9.5 `AuctionCheckoutHome.java`—A HOME INTERFACE FOR A STATEFUL SESSION BEAN

```
package com.que.ejb20.auction.controller;
/**
 * Title:        AuctionCheckoutHome<p>
 * Description:  Home interface for the Auction Checkout stateful
 *               session bean<p>
 */
import java.rmi.RemoteException;
import javax.ejb.CreateException;
import javax.ejb.EJBHome;

public interface AuctionCheckoutHome extends EJBHome {

  /**
   * Create a session object using default initialization
   */
  public AuctionCheckout create() throws CreateException, RemoteException;

  /**
   * Create a session object by supplying the auction and bidder primary keys
   */
  public AuctionCheckout create(int auctionId, int bidderId)
    throws CreateException, RemoteException;
}
```

The `AuctionManagerHome` and `AuctionHouseHome` interfaces are less interesting than the one shown in Listing 9.5. All you need to do in the home interface for a stateless session bean is declare a single `create` method that accepts no arguments.

IMPLEMENTING A SESSION BEAN

Now that you've seen how to declare the component and home interfaces for a session bean, the next step is to look at implementing the bean class itself. What's important here is to understand the methods you're required to implement, how the container manages the life cycle of a session bean, and how to access other EJBs and resources, such as a database, from a session bean's methods.

THE `SessionBean` INTERFACE

All session beans must implement the `SessionBean` interface, which extends `EnterpriseBean` just like the `EntityBean` interface does. Remember that `EnterpriseBean` is simply a marker interface, so it doesn't add any methods to the set that your session beans have to implement. The container uses the methods declared by `SessionBean` to notify a bean instance of life-cycle events. Table 9.2 describes the methods of the `SessionBean` interface. The `ejb` callback methods declared by this interface should look very familiar to you from the discussion of entity beans back in Chapter 5.

TABLE 9.2   METHODS OF THE SessionBean INTERFACE

Return Type	Method Name	Description
void	ejbActivate()	Called by the container just after an instance is activated from its "passive" state.
void	ejbPassivate()	Called by the container just before an instance is passivated.
void	ejbRemove()	Called by the container just before an instance is removed.
void	setSessionContext (SessionContext ctx)	Called by the container to associate a runtime session context with an instance.

You'll see more about how these methods fit into a session bean's life cycle a little later.

THE SessionContext INTERFACE

The SessionContext passed to a session bean instance in the setSessionContext method provides the bean with access to the runtime session context that the container manages for the life cycle of the bean instance. The session bean will normally store the SessionContext object in an instance variable within the session bean to hold it as part of its conversational state. As shown in Table 9.3, the SessionContext interface only declares the methods needed to obtain a reference to the component interface.

TABLE 9.3   THE SessionContext INTERFACE

Return Type	Method Name	Description
void	getEJBObject()	Get the EJBObject (the remote interface) currently associated with this instance.
void	getEJBLocalObject()	Get the EJBLocalObject (the local interface) currently associated with this instance.

The SessionContext interface extends the EJBContext interfaces and therefore has access to the methods defined there. Table 9.4 summarizes the methods of EJBContext.

TABLE 9.4   METHODS OF THE EJBContext INTERFACE

Return Type	Method Name	Description
Principal	getCallerPrincipal()	Get the security Principal that identifies the caller.
boolean	getRollbackOnly()	Test whether the current transaction has been marked for rollback.
void	setRollbackOnly()	Mark the current transaction for rollback.

TABLE 9.4 CONTINUED

Return Type	Method Name	Description
EJBHome	getEJBHome()	Get the bean's remote home interface.
EJBLocalHome	getEJBLocalHome()	Get the bean's local home interface.
UserTransaction	getUserTransaction()	Get the transaction demarcation interface.
boolean	isCallerInRole (String role)	Test to see whether the caller has a given security role.

Other than providing access to the home interface, EJBContext is concerned with security and transaction management. Principals and roles and how the getCallerPrincipal and isCallerInRole methods are used are covered in Chapter 14, "Security Design and Management." The getRollbackOnly and setRollbackOnly methods of EJBContext are valid only if you're using container-managed transaction demarcation. You can call getUserTransaction only if you're using bean-managed demarcation. You'll learn more about what these methods do in Chapter 12.

> **Caution**
>
> Because a session bean isn't required to have both a local and a remote interface, calls to getEJBLocalObject and getEJBObject are not always valid. If you call a method for which a corresponding interface doesn't exist, an IllegalState Exception is thrown. The same is true for invalid calls to getEJBHome or getEJBLocalHome.

SESSION BEAN'S LIFE CYCLE

The container manages a pool of session bean instances to efficiently serve its clients. Based on the pooling configuration and the requests received from clients, the container determines when an instance is created, assigned to a client, passivated, activated, and destroyed. Part of this control consists of invoking methods on the instance that include the methods declared by SessionBean and the ejbCreate method (or methods) you implement. The container also delegates the execution of business method requests to your bean implementation. The stages in the life cycle of a session bean are different for stateless and stateful beans. As you might expect, the life cycle for a stateless session bean is much simpler than that for a stateful one, so it's best to start there.

The EJB specification defines two states for a stateless session bean instance: it either *does not exist* or it's in a *method-ready* state. A session object comes into existence when the container calls newInstance on the associated Class object that represents your bean implementation class. This could be done in response to a client calling a create method, but usually the container works independently from its clients in this case and creates instances only when it populates its object pool. After an instance is created, the container calls the object's setSessionContext and ejbCreate methods. You can declare only a single create method for a stateless bean, so the only `ejbCreate` method you declare should look something like the following:

```
public void ejbCreate() throws CreateException {
  // do any required initialization that's common to all clients
}
```

Just like entity beans, an `ejbCreate` method for a session bean must be `public`, have a name that begins with `ejbCreate`, and it can't be declared as `static` or `final`. It can throw any application exceptions, such as `CreateException`, to report a problem, but it doesn't have to be declared to throw any. Unlike entity beans, an `ejbCreate` method must be declared to return `void` (because there's no primary key). For a stateless session bean, the one `ejbCreate` method you implement must be named `ejbCreate` exactly and it must not take any arguments. Remember that you don't need any arguments because an instance can't be used to hold state specific to a client. Most stateless session beans you implement will have an `ejbCreate` method that does nothing. The exception is when you want to hold a reference to a common resource, such as a connection factory object.

PART

I

CH

9

When the `ejbCreate` method has completed, the instance moves into the method-ready state. It's within this state that a stateless session object services client requests by executing its business methods. When a client calls a business method on a reference to the bean's component interface, the container selects an instance from the pool of those in the method-ready state and delegates the call to it. When the call completes, the instance is returned to the pool and no longer is associated with a particular client. Subsequent calls are handled the same way, so there is little chance of a client being assigned the same instance again.

Just like a `create` call by a client doesn't necessarily cause an instance of a session bean to be created, a call to `remove` doesn't cause an instance to be destroyed. After a client calls a business method on a stateless session object, the instance is returned to the method-ready state for use by any client. A client can call `remove`, but the container doesn't need to do anything in response. Only when the container is shutting down or reducing the number of instances in the method ready pool does it remove any session objects. Just before an object is removed, the container calls the `ejbRemove` method on the instance. This is where you should release any resources that you obtained references to in `ejbCreate`.

Figure 9.1 illustrates the life cycle of a stateless session bean instance.

Figure 9.1
A stateless session bean has a relatively simple life cycle.

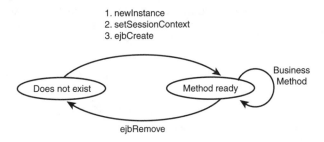

1. newInstance
2. setSessionContext
3. ejbCreate

Does not exist — Method ready — Business Method

ejbRemove

Like a stateless session bean, a stateful bean can be described using the states *does not exist* and *method ready*. A stateful session bean can also be classified as being in a *passive* or a *method-ready in transaction* state. The life cycle for a stateful bean is more complex because stateless beans are never passivated and a stateful bean instance must ensure that it's involved in only a single transaction at a time.

Unlike stateless beans, the client exercises some control over the life cycle of a stateful bean. To start with, instead of being pulled from a pool, an instance of a stateful session bean is created when a client calls a create method on the bean's home interface. The container then invokes the newInstance method on the class and calls setSessionContext and ejbCreate. Remember that you can have multiple create methods (and corresponding ejbCreate methods) for a stateful bean based on how you want to initialize an instance. When the appropriate ejbCreate method completes, the instance moves into the method-ready state. The client then receives a component interface reference back from the create method.

When a client calls a business method on a stateful session bean, the container always delegates the call to the instance created specifically for the client. If there isn't a transaction context associated with the call, the session object simply executes the method and remains in the method-ready state. The interaction of the container with a stateful session bean in the method-ready state changes if a business method is called within the context of a transaction. You'll see a more complete description of transactions in Chapter 12, but it's important to cover enough now for you to see all the states in a stateful bean's life cycle.

A stateful session bean can optionally implement the SessionSynchronization interface. The bean can use this interface to be notified when it first becomes involved in a transaction and when that transaction completes. A session bean doesn't have to implement this interface, so you should do so only if a bean needs to be notified about transaction events.

Caution

This will become more relevant when you get to Chapter 12, but it's important to note that, although session beans participate in transactions, their instance variables aren't controlled by them. If a session bean instance variable is modified during a transaction, it isn't automatically reset to its previous value if the transaction rolls back. This is true for both stateful and stateless session beans. You'll see later how the SessionSynchronization interface allows you to handle this for stateful session beans. For stateless beans, this point emphasizes the fact that instance variables in stateless session beans are really appropriate only for holding resource references that can be established and held throughout the lifetime of a bean instance.

→ For more information on the SessionSynchronization interface, **see** "Transaction Synchronization," **p. 352**.

Table 9.5 describes the method of the SessionSynchronization interface so that you can see where they fit into a session object's life cycle.

TABLE 9.5   METHODS OF THE `SessionSynchronization` INTERFACE

Return Type	Method Name	Description
void	afterBegin()	Notifies the bean instance that a new transaction has started.
void	afterCompletion (boolean committed)	Notifies the bean instance whether a transaction was successful or rolled back.
void	beforeCompletion()	Notifies the bean instance that a transaction is about to be committed.

When a stateful session bean that implements `SessionSynchronization` is included in a transaction, the container calls its `afterBegin` method when the client makes its first call on a business method after the transaction has started. The instance then enters the method ready in transaction state and executes the business method. The instance remains in this state while business methods are invoked within the transaction. When the transaction is about to commit, the `beforeCompletion` method is invoked. After the transaction has completed, the `afterCompletion` method is invoked with an argument that informs the instance of the transaction's outcome. The instance then returns to the method-ready state where it can execute non-transactional methods or be enlisted in another transaction.

While a session object is in the method ready in transaction state, it's an error for it to be called with another transaction context. The container is also prohibited from passivating the object while it's in this state. If the container chooses to passivate an instance in the method-ready state, it calls the `ejbPassivate` method on the instance and moves it into the passive state. An instance should release any resources it holds within `ejbPassivate`. An instance leaves the passive state either by being activated or removed. If a passivated instance is activated, the container calls its `ejbActivate` method and returns it to the method-ready state. If a timeout occurs (based on a time limit determined by the deployer), the container can remove a passivated instance. A timeout can apply to an instance in either the passive or the method-ready state. The client can also cause an instance in the method-ready state to be destroyed by calling a `remove` method on it. Before an instance is removed, its `ejbRemove` method is called. This method should release its resources just like in `ejbPassivate`. After a client has called `remove` on either the component reference or the home interface for a session bean, the client can no longer reference the instance. If the client does attempt to reference the instance after the `remove` operation, a `NoSuchObjectException` or `NoSuchObjectLocalException` will be thrown.

Figure 9.2 summarizes the life cycle of a stateful session bean instance.

Figure 9.2
A stateful session bean moves between four states during its life cycle.

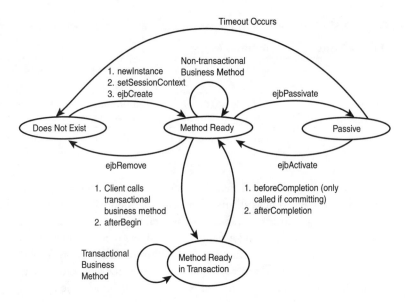

MAINTAINING CONVERSATIONAL STATE

In general, the conversational state of a stateful session bean is made up of all the bean's instance variables and the objects that can be reached by following the references held by its instance fields. Other conversational state might include open resources such as sockets or database connections. Because the container can passivate a stateful session bean, it's the responsibility of the bean provider to ensure that the conversational state is ready to be passivated at the proper time. The container gives you the chance to do this by invoking `ejbPassivate` right before a bean instance is passivated. The container must be able to serialize a session object after `ejbPassivate` is called. This means that after `ejbPassivate` completes, all non-transient fields must be one of the following:

- `null`.
- A serializable object.
- A component interface reference to an enterprise bean.
- A home interface reference to an enterprise bean.
- A reference to a `SessionContext` object.
- A reference to a resource manager connection factory.
- A reference to a `UserTransaction` interface.
- A reference to an environment naming context or any of its subcontexts.
- An object that is not immediately serializable but becomes serializable during the serialization process. For example, storing a collection of remote interfaces in the conversational state.

Any reference held by a session bean that doesn't correspond to one of the choices just listed needs to be replaced so that it does. What this means in practical terms is that some references held by a stateful session bean need to be released within `ejbPassivate`. For example, an open database connection held in an instance field must be closed in `ejbPassivate` and the reference set to `null`. The connection can then be reopened in `ejbActivate`.

> **Caution**
>
> You should never count on the values of transient fields to be maintained when an instance is passivated and subsequently activated. You must assume that a container might use Java serialization to perform passivation, which doesn't save transient fields. You also can't assume that transient fields are reset to their default values when an instance is activated. Because of these issues, the EJB specification discourages the declaration of transient fields in session beans.

Even though a stateful session bean can be included in a transaction, the container doesn't roll its conversational state back to its initial state if the transaction rolls back. If you need to reset the conversational state back to what it was prior to the start of the transaction, you must use the `afterCompletion` method of `SessionSynchronization`. If this method is called with an indication of a rollback, you can reset the conversational state back to its original state.

ACCESSING THE ENVIRONMENT

Session beans have the same capability as entity beans to access their environment. You can use a JNDI lookup within a session bean method to obtain the value of an environment entry or a reference to a connection factory. If you need to access the database directly from a session bean, you can obtain a connection using the same approach defined for a BMP entity bean in Chapter 6, "Bean-Managed Persistence."

→ For more information on obtaining a connection to a database, **see** "Configuring a Data Source," **p. 152**.

ACCESSING OTHER EJBS

Many of the session beans you write will need to access one or more entity objects to do their work. The way to do this is to declare an EJB reference in the session bean's deployment descriptor for each entity bean it uses. You can then use this reference to look up the home interface for the entity. For example, the auction house session bean needs to pass a submit bid request on to the appropriate auction entity. This session bean's descriptor must include a reference like the following:

```
<ejb-jar>
  <enterprise-beans>
    <session>
      <ejb-name>AuctionHouse</ejb-name>
      ...
      <ejb-local-ref>
        <description>This EJB reference is used to locate an auction
```

```
        </description>
        <ejb-ref-name>ejb/EnglishAuction</ejb-ref-name>
        <ejb-ref-type>Entity</ejb-ref-type>
        <local-home>com.que.ejb20.auction.model.EnglishAuctionHome</local-home>
        <local>com.que.ejb20.auction.model.EnglishAuction</local>
      </ejb-local-ref>
      ...
    </session>
    ...
  </enterprise-beans>
  ...
</ejb-jar>
```

The deployment information would need to include a similar entry for the bidder entity
bean. With these two references available, the submitBid method of AuctionHouseBean could
be implemented as shown in Listing 9.6.

LISTING 9.6   submitBid—USING EJB REFERENCES IN A SESSION BEAN

```
package com.que.ejb20.auction.controller;
...
public class AuctionHouseBean implements SessionBean {
  ...
  public String submitBid(double bidAmount, int auctionId, int bidderId)
    throws InvalidBidException, InvalidAuctionStatusException {

    try {
      // Get the home interface for the english auction bean
      EnglishAuctionHome auctionHome = getEnglishAuctionHome();

      // Get the home interface for the bidder bean
      BidderHome bidderHome = getBidderHome();

      // locate the specified auction
      EnglishAuction auction = auctionHome.findByPrimaryKey(
        new Integer(auctionId) );

      // locate the specified bidder
      Bidder bidder = bidderHome.findByPrimaryKey( new Integer(bidderId) );

      // submit the bid to the auction
      return auction.submitBid(bidAmount, bidder);
    }
    catch (FinderException fe) {
      throw new InvalidBidException("Auction/Bidder ID is invalid");
    }
  }
  ...
  private EnglishAuctionHome getEnglishAuctionHome() {
    InitialContext initCtx = null;
    try {
      // Obtain the default initial JNDI context
      initCtx = new InitialContext();

      // Look up the home interface for the English Auction
      // that is defined as an EJB reference in the deployment
```

LISTING 9.6   CONTINUED

```java
      // descriptor
      Object obj = initCtx.lookup( "java:comp/env/ejb/EnglishAuction" );
      return (EnglishAuctionHome)obj;
    }
    catch (NamingException ex) {
      throw new EJBException(ex);
    }
    finally {
      // close the InitialContext
      try {
        if (initCtx != null) {
          initCtx.close();
        }
      }
      catch (Exception ex) {
        throw new EJBException(ex);
      }
    }
  }

  private BidderHome getBidderHome() {
    InitialContext initCtx = null;
    try {
      // Obtain the default initial JNDI context
      initCtx = new InitialContext();

      // Look up the home interface for the Bidder
      // that is defined as an EJB reference in the deployment
      // descriptor
      Object obj = initCtx.lookup( "java:comp/env/ejb/Bidder" );
      return (BidderHome)obj;
    }
    catch (NamingException ex) {
      throw new EJBException(ex);
    }
    finally {
      // close the InitialContext
      try {
        if (initCtx != null) {
          initCtx.close();
        }
      }
      catch (Exception ex) {
        throw new EJBException(ex);
      }
    }
  }
  ...
}
```

DEPLOYING A SESSION BEAN

The deployment information for a session bean must identify the associated interfaces and classes, specify a session bean type, and select the transaction management option. It also must declare any EJB reference, environment entries, and transaction attributes. You'll see more about these entries in Chapter 12 and Chapter 15, "Deployment." For now, the relevant portions of a deployment descriptor for the auction house stateless session bean are shown in the following:

```
<ejb-jar>
  <enterprise-beans>
    ...
    <session>
      <ejb-name>AuctionHouse</ejb-name>
      <home>com.que.ejb20.auction.controller.AuctionHouseHome</home>
      <remote>com.que.ejb20.auction.controller.AuctionHouse</remote>
      <ejb-class>com.que.ejb20.auction.controller.AuctionHouseBean</ejb-class>
      <session-type>Stateless</session-type>
      <transaction-type>Container</transaction-type>

      <ejb-local-ref>
        <description>This EJB reference is used to locate an auction
        </description>
        <ejb-ref-name>ejb/EnglishAuction</ejb-ref-name>
        <ejb-ref-type>Entity</ejb-ref-type>
        <local-home>com.que.ejb20.auction.model.EnglishAuctionHome</local-home>
        <local>com.que.ejb20.auction.model.EnglishAuction</local>
      </ejb-local-ref>

      <ejb-local-ref>
        <description>This EJB reference is used to locate a bidder
        </description>
        <ejb-ref-name>ejb/Bidder</ejb-ref-name>
        <ejb-ref-type>Entity</ejb-ref-type>
        <local-home>com.que.ejb20.auction.model.BidderHome</local-home>
        <local>com.que.ejb20.auction.model.Bidder</local>
      </ejb-local-ref>
    </session>
    ...
  </enterprise-beans>
  <assembly-descriptor>
    ...
    <container-transaction>
      <method>
        <ejb-name>AuctionHouse</ejb-name>
        <method-name>*</method-name>
      </method>
      <trans-attribute>Required</trans-attribute>
    </container-transaction>
    ...
  </assembly-descriptor>
</ejb-jar>
```

→ For more information on assigning transaction attributes, **see** " Using Container-Managed Transactions," **p. 344**.

Deploying a session bean also requires you to specify any vendor-specific deployment parameters. The following fragment shows an example for WebLogic:

```xml
<?xml version="1.0"?>

<!DOCTYPE weblogic-ejb-jar PUBLIC
  '-//BEA Systems, Inc.//DTD WebLogic 6.0.0 EJB//EN'
  'http://www.bea.com/servers/wls600/dtd/weblogic-ejb-jar.dtd'>

<weblogic-ejb-jar>
  ...
  <weblogic-enterprise-bean>
    <ejb-name>AuctionHouse</ejb-name>

    <reference-descriptor>
      <ejb-local-reference-description>
        <ejb-ref-name>ejb/EnglishAuction</ejb-ref-name>
        <jndi-name>EnglishAuction</jndi-name>
      </ejb-local-reference-description>

      <ejb-local-reference-description>
        <ejb-ref-name>ejb/Bidder</ejb-ref-name>
        <jndi-name>Bidder</jndi-name>
      </ejb-local-reference-description>
    </reference-descriptor>

    <jndi-name>AuctionHouse</jndi-name>
  </weblogic-enterprise-bean>
  ...
</weblogic-ejb-jar>
```

TESTING THE AUCTION SESSION BEANS

The complete source for the classes and interfaces referenced by this chapter are included on the CD. Using these source files, you can test the entity and session beans developed for the example. Unlike previous chapters, you no longer need to deploy the entity beans with remote interfaces for testing purposes. Now that the session beans are defined, you can use a Java application as a remote client to them. These session beans then can act as local clients to the entity beans. The first step is to create some sample bidder and item data. Possible SQL statements for this appear in Listing 9.7.

LISTING 9.7   SAMPLE DATA DDL

```sql
INSERT INTO address (id, AddressLine1, AddressLine2, City, State, ZipCode)
  VALUES (1, '123 Main Street', null, 'AnyTown', 'NY', '10101');
INSERT INTO address (id, AddressLine1, AddressLine2, City, State, ZipCode)
  VALUES (2, '333 Warehouse Row', null, 'AnyTown', 'NY', '10101');
INSERT INTO address (id, AddressLine1, AddressLine2, City, State, ZipCode)
  VALUES (3, '225 North Avenue', null, 'Atlanta', 'GA', '30332');

INSERT INTO bidder (id, FirstName, LastName, EmailAddress, UserName, Password,
  BillingAddressId, ShippingAddressId) VALUES (1, 'John', 'Smith',
  'jsmith@mydomain.com', 'jsmith', 'smitty', 1, 2);
```

LISTING 9.7 CONTINUED

```
INSERT INTO bidder (id, FirstName, LastName, EmailAddress, UserName, Password,
  BillingAddressId, ShippingAddressId) VALUES (2, 'G', 'Burdell',
  'gburdell@mydomain.com', 'gburdell', 'ramblin', 3, 3);

INSERT INTO item (id, Name, Description, ImageURL)
  VALUES (1, 'DVD Player', 'A-100 DVD player. New, in the original box.',
  'images\items\dvd_a100.jpg');
```

It's now possible to access the AuctionManager bean and create an auction. Listing 9.8 shows a client application that locates the home interface for this session bean, creates an instance of the bean, creates an auction, and assigns the existing item to it.

LISTING 9.8 AuctionManagerClient.java—A TEST CLIENT FOR THE AuctionManager

```java
package com.que.ejb20;

import java.sql.Timestamp;
import javax.naming.Context;
import javax.naming.InitialContext;
import javax.naming.NamingException;
import javax.rmi.PortableRemoteObject;
import com.que.ejb20.auction.controller.AuctionManager;
import com.que.ejb20.auction.controller.AuctionManagerHome;
import com.que.ejb20.auction.view.AuctionDetailView;

public class AuctionManagerClient {

  public void createAuction() {
    try {
      // pull initial context factory and provider info from jndi.properties
      Context ctx = new InitialContext();
      // obtain a reference to the auction manager remote home interface
      Object home = ctx.lookup("AuctionManager");
      AuctionManagerHome managerHome = (AuctionManagerHome)
        PortableRemoteObject.narrow(home, AuctionManagerHome.class);

      // define the desired auction information
      AuctionDetailView view = new AuctionDetailView();
      view.setName("DVD Player Auction");
      view.setDescription(
        "This auction is a 3 day auction for a new DVD player");
      long currentTime = System.currentTimeMillis();
      view.setStartDateTime(new Timestamp(currentTime));
      view.setScheduledEndDateTime(new Timestamp(currentTime +
          3*24*60*60*1000));
      view.setStartingBid(new Double(75.00));
      view.setMinBidIncrement(new Double(5.00));
      view.setReserveAmount(new Double(120.00));

      // create the auction
      AuctionManager manager = managerHome.create();
      Integer auctionId = manager.createAuction(view);
      System.out.println("Created auction id: " + auctionId);
```

LISTING 9.8   CONTINUED

```java
      // assign the item
      Integer itemId = new Integer(1);   // the key used by the sample data
      manager.assignItemToAuction(auctionId, itemId, 1);

      view = manager.getAuctionDetail(auctionId.intValue());
      System.out.println(view);
      ctx.close();
    }
    catch (NamingException ne) {
      System.out.println(ne.getMessage());
    }
    catch (Exception e) {
      e.printStackTrace();
    }
  }


  public static void main(String[] args) {
    AuctionManagerClient auctionClient = new AuctionManagerClient();
    auctionClient.createAuction();
  }
}
```

With an auction defined, the client defined in Listing 9.9 can be used to submit a bid from each of the two bidders found in the sample data.

LISTING 9.9   `AuctionHouseClient.java`—A TEST CLIENT FOR THE `AuctionHouse`

```java
package com.que.ejb20;

import java.sql.Timestamp;
import java.util.Iterator;
import java.util.List;
import javax.naming.Context;
import javax.naming.InitialContext;
import javax.naming.NamingException;
import javax.rmi.PortableRemoteObject;
import com.que.ejb20.auction.controller.AuctionHouse;
import com.que.ejb20.auction.controller.AuctionHouseHome;
import com.que.ejb20.auction.view.AuctionDetailView;

public class AuctionHouseClient {

  public void submitBids(int auctionId) {
    try {
      // pull initial context factory and provider info from jndi.properties
      Context ctx = new InitialContext();
      // obtain a reference to the auction house remote home interface
      Object home = ctx.lookup("AuctionHouse");
      AuctionHouseHome auctionHouseHome = (AuctionHouseHome)
        PortableRemoteObject.narrow(home, AuctionHouseHome.class);
      AuctionHouse auctionHouse = auctionHouseHome.create();
```

LISTING 9.9 CONTINUED

```
      // submit a bid from each bidder
      auctionHouse.submitBid(110.00, auctionId, 1);
      auctionHouse.submitBid(130.00, auctionId, 2);

      AuctionDetailView view = auctionHouse.getAuctionDetail(auctionId);
      System.out.println(view);

      List bids = auctionHouse.getBids(1);
      Iterator iter = bids.iterator();
      while (iter.hasNext()) {
        System.out.println(iter.next());
      }
      ctx.close();
    }
    catch (NamingException ne) {
      System.out.println(ne.getMessage());
    }
    catch (Exception e) {
      e.printStackTrace();
    }
  }

  public static void main(String[] args) {
    AuctionHouseClient auctionClient = new AuctionHouseClient();
    // pass whatever auction id the bids are for
    auctionClient.submitBids(9);
  }
}
```

REENTRANT ISSUES

Session beans do not support concurrent access by multiple clients. Stateful session bean instances uniquely belong to a single client and stateless beans belong to a single client while a business method is being executed. The container enforces that only a single thread will be executing inside a session bean instance at a time. It's the responsibility of the container to serialize the requests, not the bean provider. This frees you from having to worry about concurrency issues related to your beans.

This behavior agrees with the overall purpose of session beans. That is that they are in theory just extensions of a client. Even though session beans are typically used as a service-oriented interface that hides or encapsulates a layer of entity beans, it doesn't make sense that multiple clients should be invoking methods on the same instance. Unlike entity beans, the EJB specification also does not allow a single client to make reentrant (loopback) calls to a session bean. If a remote client request arrives at an instance that is already in the middle of servicing a request, a RemoteException will be thrown to the second request. A local client would receive an EJBException in this situation.

TROUBLESHOOTING

INSTANCE FIELD VALUES LOST

I set the value of an instance field in a session bean but the value gets lost.

Only stateful session beans maintain the values of their instance fields for a particular client. The container doesn't stop you from declaring instance fields in a stateless session bean because they're useful in managing resources used by all clients. However, manipulating the instance fields with client-specific data in the business methods can lead to unpredictable results. Subsequent calls by a client to a component interface reference for a stateless session bean can be serviced by a different bean instance, so there's no guarantee that the instance field values will be available. If you need to maintain client-specific data in a bean across method calls, use a stateful session bean. If you're having this problem with a stateful bean, make sure you aren't using transient fields for this instance field. The values of a transient field are lost if the instance is ever passivated.

create METHOD DECLARATION ERRORS

I get errors related to the declaration of stateless session bean create methods.

A stateless session bean can declare only a single create method and that method must not accept any arguments. This is because you can't pass any client-specific initialization data to a stateless bean. The option to declare multiple create methods is valid only for stateful session beans.

CHAPTER **10**

JAVA MESSAGE SERVICE

In this chapter

INTRODUCTION TO MESSAGING

Messaging applications, or as they are sometimes called, *Message Oriented Middleware* (MOM) products, have been used for quite some time. These messaging products help applications that normally are not connected to one another structurally communicate with each other. In applications that aren't using a messaging product, this communication might be performed using sockets, RMI, or in various other ways. A few problems are associated with communicating between applications using one of these approaches.

One of the problems is that each side involved in the communication might have direct knowledge about one another. Each side is aware of the other with respect to the transport protocol and other low-level details. This knowledge is known as a *tight coupling*. It would be more flexible if the two sides weren't so tightly coupled. This way, if something changed on either side, the other side might not be affected. Another problem is that it's hard to perform asynchronous messaging with sockets or RMI. *Asynchronous* communication is where a response is not immediately expected or returned. The alternative approaches just mentioned, such as sockets or RMI, are types of *synchronous* communication.

Message-oriented middleware can help reduce the coupling and complexity of allowing applications or components to communicate with one another asynchronously. It's also designed to help interoperability between applications, which is very important when building enterprise applications.

WHAT IS MESSAGE-ORIENTED MIDDLEWARE?

Message-oriented middleware was designed to decouple the applications or components and allow them to communicate with one another by exchanging messages asynchronously. These messages can be things such as event notifications, application data, request for services, or even objects. Any type of information that needs to be communicated from one application to another is done by passing a message to the receiving system. As you'll see later in this chapter, various types of messages can be passed from one application to another.

Although messages generally can be sent in either direction, certain names are given to the application or component that is sending or receiving a message. The component that creates or produces a message is referred to as a *producer*. The application or component that receives a message is called a *consumer*. It's possible for an application to be both a producer and a consumer of messages, but for a given transfer of information, one side must produce the message and another side must consume it. A benefit of separating the producing and the consuming of messages is that the producer and consumer only really need to agree on the format of the message. Each side doesn't need to worry about how the message is transported. To make this possible, a message is not sent directly from a producer to the consumer. As we'll see later in this chapter, how it makes its way to the consumer depends on which type of messaging model you choose for your application. Figure 10.1 illustrates a generic messaging scenario.

Figure 10.1
An application com-
municating through
messaging contains a
producer and a con-
sumer.

JAVA MESSAGE SERVICE AS A MESSAGE-ORIENTED MIDDLEWARE

Although the EJB 2.0 Specification does not cover messaging, it is part of the Java Message
Service (JMS) specification and is so fundamental to the Enterprise JavaBeans API that it
would be deficient not to cover it in any serious discussion on the subject. Because many
enterprise applications will use some level of messaging, it's a good idea to understand the
concepts. You also will need to be familiar with the Java Message Service (JMS) APIs before
understanding the new message-driven bean that has been added to the EJB 2.0
Specification.

→ **See** "Message-Driven Beans," **p. 315** for more information on the new enterprise bean added to
EJB 2.0.

DIFFERENCES AMONG JMS IMPLEMENTATIONS

Another important fact should be pointed out. JMS is not an implementation of a message-
oriented middleware. In fact, it's really nothing more than a specification for describing how
messages should be produced and consumed in a Java enterprise application. By itself, it
provides no functionality. As with other APIs that we have already discussed, the API or
interfaces are separate from the implementation. This gives the benefit of describing in
detail what the user view should be, while at the same time allowing vendors to implement
the details however they want. As long as the vendor adheres to the JMS specification, a user
shouldn't have to worry too much about how the implementation is constructed. The point
of hiding the implementation from the client and exposing only the JMS APIs is to hide the
details from the users that want a higher-level API and also to ensure portability among
implementations.

If a vendor implements the JMS specification and adheres to it completely, there is typically
no problem developing portable JMS applications and switching between vendors. As with
the rest of the specifications in the Java 2 Enterprise Edition (J2EE), JMS has a version
number that identifies that current release of the specification. The current JMS specification is 1.0.2. If you write an application based on this or any newer specification, you must
ensure that the vendor whose JMS implementation you are using adheres to this level of the
specification. You can download the latest JMS specification at the following URL:

```
http://java.sun.com/products/jms
```

Many vendors provide an implementation for the JMS specification. Some are included along
with a complete or partial implementation of the entire J2EE suite of technologies. Table 10.1
is a list of vendors who provide a commercial implementation of the JMS specification.

PART

I

Cн

10

TABLE 10.1   VENDORS WHO PROVIDE A COMMERCIAL JMS IMPLEMENTATION

Name	URL
JRUN Server	http://www.allaire.com
BEA Systems, Inc.	http://www.beasys.com
Fiorano Software	http://www.fiorano.com
GemStone	http://www.gemstone.com
IBM	http://www-4.ibm.com
Nirvana	http://www.pcbsys.com
Oracle	http://www.oracle.com
Orion	http://www.orionserver.com
Progress Software	http://www.progress.com
SAGA Software, Inc.	http://www.sagasoftware.com
SoftWired Inc.	http://www.softwired-inc.com
Sun (Java Message Queue)	http://www.sun.com
SpiritSoft, Inc.	http://www.spirit-soft.com
Sunopsis	http://www.sunopsis.com
SwiftMQ	http://www.swiftmq.com
Venue Software	http://www.venuesoftware.com

There are also several open-source JMS projects. Table 10.2 lists a few of them.

TABLE 10.2   PARTIAL LIST OF OPEN-SOURCE JMS PROJECTS

Name	URL
ObjectCube, Inc.	http://www.objectcube.com
OpenJMS	http://openjms.exolab.org
ObjectWeb	http://www.objectweb.org

Many other vendors endorse the JMS API. The following URL provides a more exhaustive listing:

http://java.sun.com/products/jms/vendors.html

COMPONENTS OF THE JMS ARCHITECTURE

The typical JMS architecture is made up of several components. Each component plays a pivotal role in allowing producers and consumers to communicate with one another. The following components are the ones that most often are used in a JMS component architecture:

- Message producers
- Message consumers
- JMS messages
- Administered JMS objects
- JNDI naming service

Figure 10.2 shows how these components are structured in a typical JMS architecture.

Figure 10.2
A typical JMS architecture uses several components to produce and consume messages.

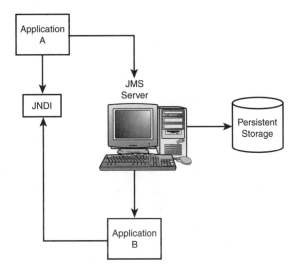

You must understand each major component in the architecture. The next sections describe how each component is used in the JMS architecture.

MESSAGE PRODUCERS

A *message producer* is a component in the application that is responsible for creating a message that needs to be delivered to a destination. As you learned from the previous section, "What Is Message-Oriented Middleware?," a message can be a notification that a system error has occurred, an e-mail message, or some other type of application event. The message content is entirely up to the application. An application can have several message producers. Each producer might be responsible for creating different types of messages and sending them to different destinations. The destination for each producer might be the same or different.

MESSAGE CONSUMERS

A *message consumer* is a component that resides on the receiving end of a messaging application. Its responsibility is to listen for messages and process the message when it arrives. Just as with producers, a JMS application can have more than one consumer processing or consuming messages. A message may have information contained within it that a consumer can use to determine whether the consumer is interested in the message. You'll see more on message selection in the section "Message Selection and Filtering," later in this chapter.

THE JMS MESSAGE

The *message* is the component that contains the information that must be communicated to another application or component. It could be raw data, state about the system, or a Java object. The data is wrapped by a JMS Message object, which serves as sort of a container for the data that is being transferred from one component to another.

ADMINISTERED JMS OBJECTS

When a producer is ready to send a message off to a consumer, the message doesn't go directly to the consumer. The producer will deliver the message to a particular destination. This destination normally is set up during application deployment or configuration and is initialized when the application is started. You'll learn more about how to set up the administered objects later in this chapter and in the examples.

NAMING SERVICE

For a producer and consumer to be able to use the administered objects to send and receive messages, they must know how to locate things such as the destination. Location of a destination and other administrative components is done through a naming service. In the case of J2EE, this is done through JNDI. For a producer or consumer to locate a JMS administrative component, they must perform a lookup on the name of the component it wants to locate.

→ For more information on locating components through JNDI, **see** Chapter 4, "Java Naming and Directory Interface."

THE TWO JMS MESSAGE MODELS

JMS supports two different ways of using messaging between a producer and consumer. The two messaging models are known as

- PTP (Point-to-Point)—Message delivered to one recipient.
- Pub/Sub (Publish/Subscribe)—Message delivered to multiple recipients.

JMS supports these two models by using distinct interfaces within the API for each messaging model. The javax.jms.Queue interface handles the PTP messaging model, while the Pub/Sub model is handled by the javax.jms.Topic interface. Other interfaces work closely with one or the other or both of these primary interfaces to help implement the messaging model. Both the Queue and Topic interfaces extend the javax.jms.Destination interface. The JMS interfaces are covered in detail in "The JMS Interfaces," later in this chapter. For now, let's describe how each messaging model is unique.

POINT-TO-POINT (PTP)

The PTP model is used to enable an application to send a message and have the message received by a single consumer. The PTP model is supported in JMS by a *queue*. A queue allows messages to come in and be consumed by a single receiver. After a particular consumer takes the message off the Queue, the message is no longer available for other consumers. Figure 10.3 illustrates the PTP messaging model.

Figure 10.3
A single consumer receives the message when a Point-to-Point (PTP) messaging model is used.

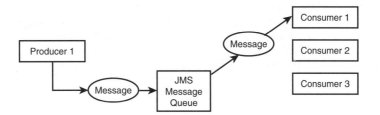

PART
I
CH
10

With the PTP model, a message producer is referred to as a QueueSender and a message consumer is referred to as a QueueReceiver. A messaging application can have multiple senders and receivers, but a message from a sender will only be delivered to a single receiver in the PTP model. You'll see that this is not the case with the Pub/Sub model described next.

PUBLISH/SUBSCRIBE (PUB/SUB)

The Pub/Sub message model in JMS is provided by a Topic. In the JMS Pub/Sub model, producers and consumers connect to a topic and send and receive messages respectively. A message producer in the Pub/Sub model is called a TopicPublisher and a message consumer is referred to as a TopicSubscriber. Figure 10.4 illustrates the Pub/Sub message model.

Figure 10.4
Multiple consumers can receive a copy of the message using a Publish/Subscribe messaging model.

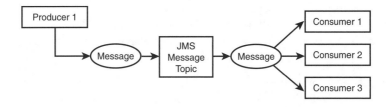

Unlike the PTP message model, the Pub/Sub message model allows multiple recipients to receive the same message. The subscribers that are interested in a particular topic can subscribe to that topic and receive a copy of the message when one arrives at the destination.

THE JMS INTERFACES

The JMS API is provided through the main package `javax.jms`. This API allows an application to create the necessary objects for both the PTP and Pub/Sub models. Different classes and interfaces are required depending on which message model your application needs to implement. The following sections describe the necessary classes and interfaces and provide more detail for each.

Note

Remember that the JMS APIs define the set of interfaces. The vendor that provides the implementation must provide concrete classes for these interfaces. For example, when you create a `Topic`, the vendor is providing a `Topic` concrete class that implements the JMS `Topic` interface. As long as you have the vendor's classes in your classpath, most of this is transparent to the developer.

ConnectionFactory

A `javax.jms.ConnectionFactory` is a factory that provides connections for clients in a JMS application. It's usually configured by an administrator and is given a name and then registered with the naming service. The `QueueConnectionFactory` and the `TopicConnectionFactory` interfaces extend the `ConnectionFactory` interface to provide a unique factory for `Queue` and `Topic` messaging models, respectively. When a client needs to get a connection to send or receive a JMS message, the first step is to locate the `ConnectionFactory` and acquire a `javax.jms.Connection`.

Connection

A `javax.jms.Connection` represents an open channel to the messaging service. This connection is then used to create a `javax.jms.Session` that can be used for this client. In some cases, a vendor may use a single instance of the connection and multiplex all JMS communication from the client to the messaging system over this single connection. This is done because creating and maintaining many connections is very resource intensive. The underlying implementation will take care of the details of multiplexing the requests. Connections normally are thread-safe and support multiple clients accessing the connection at the same time.

By default, a connection is created in what is known as the *stopped* mode. The client must call the `start` method before delivering or receiving messages. Messages can be created while the connection is stopped, but they will not be delivered and/or received until the connection is started.

To create a connection for a `Queue`, you can use either of these two methods on the `QueueConnectionFactory` class:

```
QueueConnection createQueueConnection() throws JMSException;
QueueConnection createQueueConnection(String username,
                 String password) throws JMSException;
```

The second method creates a connection with a specific user identity.

To create a connection for a topic, you can use either of these two methods on the `TopicConnectionFactory` class:

```
public TopicConnection createTopicConnection() throws JMSException;

public TopicConnection createTopicConnection(String username, String password)
  throws JMSException;
```

Session

A `javax.jms.Session` defines a serial order for producing and consuming messages. A JMS session, along with its producers and consumers, should be accessed by only one thread at a time. Although a JMS session can be used to create producers and consumers, if the same application needs to do both, you should use separate sessions for each. The `Session` interface is extended by the `javax.jms.QueueSession` and the `javax.jms.TopicSession` interfaces to provide different functionality depending on the messaging model.

PART

I

CH

10

The following method signatures can be used to create a `QueueSession` and a `TopicSession` from its respective connection:

```
public QueueSession createQueueSession(boolean transacted, int acknowledgeMode)
  throws JMSException;

public TopicSession createTopicSession(boolean transacted, int acknowledgeMode)
  throws JMSException
```

JMS sessions can be transacted or non-transacted. This means that one or more messages produced or consumed can be combined into a single unit of work. If the transaction is successful, all the messages created will be sent. A transaction is committed by calling the `commit` method on the session. You can roll back the transaction similarly by calling the `rollback` method. Any locks held will also be released when the transaction is committed or rolled back.

With non-transacted sessions, you must provide an acknowledge mode when calling one of the `create` session methods. Table 10.3 lists the possible acknowledgement modes that can be used.

TABLE 10.3   NON-TRANSACTED SESSION ACKNOWLEDGE MODES

Acknowledge Mode	Description
AUTO_ACKNOWLEDGE	The session acknowledges after the receiving application has finished processing the message.
CLIENT_ACKNOWLEDGE	The session acknowledges all messages received when the ACKNOWLEDGE method is called on a message received.
DUPS_OK_ACKNOWLEDGE	This is similar to the AUTO_ACKNOWLEDGE mode, except that duplicate messages can be received. This should be used only by applications that can deal with duplicate messages. This mode limits the work the session has to do to prevent duplicates.

Note

With transacted sessions, all messages that are sent or received when a transaction is committed are acknowledged at that time. The acknowledge mode is ignored when using transacted sessions.

You determine whether a session is transacted by setting the transacted flag when creating the session. If you set it to true, the session will use a transaction. For a nontransacted session, set the value to false. The following code fragment shows how to create a transacted `QueueSession`:

```
QueueSession queueSession = null;
try {
  queueSession = createQueueSession(true, Session.AUTO_ACKNOWLEDGE );
} catch ( JMSException ex ) {
  ex.printStackTrace();
}
```

Destination

A `javax.jms.Destination` represents a place where you send JMS messages to or receive them from. In one sense it is like an address, in that it is named. The JMS specification does not describe specifically how a JMS vendor must handle a destination address. The vendor-specific format is encapsulated in the `Destination` object. The destination typically lives on a server that is remote to the clients.

JMS provides two types of destinations, `javax.jms.Queue` and the `javax.jms.Topic`. There also are temporary versions of each that are alive only for the duration of the connection. These temporary destinations can be used only by the connection that created it. Typically, a destination is set up by an administrator and is long-lived; that is, it lives longer than any one connection. The destination normally is added to the JNDI namespace, and a client locates the destination using the name it was given during configuration. The following code fragments show how a destination is found using JNDI. This code fragment is assuming that an `InitialContext` has already been created.

```
Queue myQueue = null;
try {
  myQueue = (Queue) context.lookup("AuctionNotificationQueue");
} catch( Exception ex ) {
  ex.printStackTrace();
}
```

As stated earlier in this chapter, a queue implements the Point-to-Point message model, whereas the topic provides the Pub/Sub message model. The remote references on the client are only handles to the objects on the server. The destination provides no functionality itself but provides a façade for the object on the server. To perform any real work, a message producer or consumer must be created using the destination.

A destination is also given a name that is different from the JNDI name it is given in the JNDI namespace. This name can be used to refer to various life-cycle operations. Don't confuse the JNDI name with the JMS name of the destination. They are used for different reasons.

You typically give the destination its JMS name when you create it.

Note

You might be a little confused about the destination at this point. The destination actually is created by the JMS service or the EJB server when it starts. When you use one of the `createQueue` or `createTopic` methods, you really are just creating a reference to a destination on the server. The name that you give it in these `create` methods is a name that is unique and is used throughout your application.

To later retrieve the name of a destination, you can use one of these two methods, depending on the destination type:

```
public String getQueueName() throws JMSException;
public String getTopicName() throws JMSException;
```

MessageProducer AND MessageConsumer

As you learned earlier in the section "Components of the JMS Architecture," message producers send messages to a destination and message consumers receive messages from a destination. In the case of JMS, a destination is either a queue or topic. The message producer and consumer are decoupled from one another. A producer will send messages to a destination regardless of whether or not a consumer is there to receive it. A message producer is provided by the `javax.jms.MessageProducer` interface, and the message consumer is provided by the `javax.jms.MessageConsumer` interface.

When building a JMS application using the PTP message model, you create a `javax.jms.QueueSender` and a `javax.jms.QueueReceiver`. If you were using the Pub/Sub model, you would use the `javax.jms.TopicPublisher` and the `javax.jms.TopicSubscriber` interfaces. You can use the associated `Session` object to create the specific type of producer or consumer depending on the messaging model chosen.

If there are multiple receivers for a queue, the JMS specification does not indicate which receiver will receive a message, but that only one receiver at most will get the message. When using a topic, the messages normally will be sent to every active subscriber.

The same connection can be used to publish and subscribe to a topic. If a publisher is also a subscriber, the publisher will receive a copy of its own messages sent to the destination. This is true only for the Pub/Sub model. This behavior can be modified so that a publisher will not receive its own messages published by setting the `noLocal` attribute to true when creating the producer or consumer. This will prevent the client from receiving a copy of the message that it has sent to the destination.

Message

The `javax.jms.Message` interface is the root interface for all JMS messages. It encapsulates all the information being exchanged between applications. There are five types of JMS messages; Table 10.4 summarizes each type.

TABLE 10.4   JMS MESSAGE TYPES

Name	Description
BytesMessage	Used to send a message containing a stream of uninterpreted bytes.
MapMessage	Used to send a set of name-value pairs where names are strings and values are Java primitive types.
ObjectMessage	Used to send a message that contains a serializable Java object. Only serializable Java objects can be used.
StreamMessage	Used to send a stream of Java primitives. It is filled and read sequentially. Its methods are based largely on those found in `java.io.DataInputStream` and `java.io.DataOutputStream`.
TextMessage	Used to send a message containing a `java.lang.String`. This could even be an XML that has been serialized from a `StringBuffer`.

THE DETAILS OF A JMS MESSAGE

A JMS message can be broken down into three parts:

- Message header
- Message properties
- Message body

The following sections describe the three parts in detail.

THE MESSAGE HEADER

Every JMS message includes message header fields that are always passed from producer to consumer. The purpose of the header fields is to convey extra information to the consumer outside the normal content of the message body. The JMS provider sets some of these fields automatically after a message is sent to the consumer, but the `MessageProducer` has the opportunity to set some fields programmatically.

JMSCorrelationID

The `JMSCorrelationID` header field provides a way to correlate related messages. This is normally used for a request/response scenario. This can either be a vendor-specific ID, an application-specific string, or a provider-native `byte` value.

Caution

> If a JMSCorrelationID is generated by the application, it must NOT start with an ID: prefix. This is reserved for vendor-generated message IDs.

JMSDestination

The JMSDestination header field specifies the destination for the message. This is either a queue or topic. The JMS provider sets this field automatically when the send method is called.

JMSExpiration

The JMSExpiration header field specifies the expiration or time-to-live value for a message. If the value is set to 0, the message will never expire. When a message does expire, the JMS provider typically will discard the message. Also, any persistent messages will be deleted based on expiration values.

JMSDeliveryMode

The JMSDeliveryMode header field specifies persistent or nonpersistent messaging. When using persistent messages, the message is stored in a persistent store. It's up to the vendor and application to determine what type of persistent store is used. This may be a RDBMS or just a file. When using persistent messaging, the send method is not considered to be successful until a message is stored.

Messages that are set as NON_PERSISTENT are not stored and can be lost if there is a system failure. A persistent message will be delivered as long as the send method is successful. If you need to ensure that messages are delivered, you should consider using persistent messages.

Note

> Setting up persistent messages is not that hard to do, but it does generally require more up-front work due to the storage configuration settings.

JMSMessageID

The JMSMessageID header field contains a value that uniquely identifies each message sent by a provider. This value is set by the provider automatically and returned to the message producer when the send method completes. All JMSMessageID values must start with an ID: prefix.

Caution

> JMSMessageIDs might not be consistent across JMS providers. There might be duplicates if you are using two different JMS vendors across systems. You should not trust that these values would always be unique.

PART

I

CH

10

JMSPriority

JMS defines 10 priority levels, 0 through 9. 0 is the lowest priority and level 9 is the highest. Levels 0–4 indicate a range of normal priorities, and levels 5–9 indicate a range of expedited priority. Priority level 4 is typically the default for a message producer.

> **Caution**
>
> A message priority might not be honored at all times by a JMS provider. The JMS specification does not force a provider to adhere to the priority under all circumstances. Be careful when using this value for event-important messages.

JMSRedelivered

The JSMRedelivered header field indicates that the message probably was delivered to the consumer previously, but the client did not acknowledge the message. If your application is very sensitive to duplicate messages, you probably want to inspect this field and decide whether you want to pay attention to the message or ignore it.

JMSReplyTo

The JMSReplyTo header field indicates where a response should be sent. If this field is null, then no response is expected. A message with a null value in the JMSReplyTo header field is sometimes referred to as a JMS *datagram*.

If the JMSReplyTo field is not null, it should contain either a queue or a topic. Just because there is a value for the JMSReplyTo field does not mean a client must send a response. It's up to the client application to determine whether a response is necessary. If a reply is sent, the client can set the JMSCorrelationID and the reply can be matched up with the request.

JMSTimestamp

The provider sets the JMSTimestamp header field in a JMS message at the time the message is sent. A producer may inform the JMS provider that it does not need the JMSTimestamp field set. This might help increase performance by reducing the overhead in getting and setting the current timestamp value for every message sent. A client can tell the provider not to worry about the JMSTimestamp field by setting the disableMessageTimestamp property on the MessageProducer interface. The following method signature can be used:

```
setDisableMessageTimestamp(boolean value) throws JMSException;
```

You would need to set the value to true for the JMSTimestamp value not to be set by the provider. The JMSTimestamp values are stored in milliseconds.

JMSType

The JMSType message header field can be used to indicate the type or nature of the message. The JMS specification allows plenty of flexibility with this field and does not specify any naming syntax or possible list of values. It's entirely up to the JMS vendor or application. However, it's recommended that you set this field to something rather than leaving it null.

MESSAGE PROPERTIES

The message property fields are similar to header fields described previously in the "The Message Header" section, except these fields are set exclusively by the sending application. When a client receives a message, the properties are in read-only mode. If a client tries to modify any of the properties, a MessageNotWriteableException will be thrown.

The properties are standard Java name/value pairs. The property names must conform to the message selector syntax specifications defined in the Message interface. The following are valid property types:

- boolean
- byte
- short
- int
- long
- float
- double
- String

Property fields are most often used for message selection and filtering. By using a property field, a message consumer can interrogate the property field and perform message filtering and selection. To find out more about message filtering, see the "Message Selection and Filtering" section later in this chapter.

PART

I

CH

10

Note

It's okay for a property value to be duplicated in the message body. Although the JMS specification does not define a policy for what should or should not be made a property, application developers should note that JMS providers likely will handle data in a message's body more efficiently than data in a message's properties. For best performance, applications should use message properties only when they need to customize a message's header. The primary reason for doing this is to support customized message selection and filtering.

Here's an example of how to set a property value. Say for example that you need to set an auction type value so that a consumer would consume the message only if the type was a reverse auction. You could set the string value using the following fragment:

```
message.setStringProperty( "AuctionType", "Reverse" );
```

The message consumer can inspect this field to see whether the type is Reverse. The message interface has a `getStringProperty` method that takes a name argument and retrieves the string value. The consumer might also want to set up a message selector to filter out certain messages. You'll see more about this in the later section, "Message Selection and Filtering."

THE MESSAGE BODY

The message body contains the main information that is being delivered from the `MessageProducer` to the `MessageConsumer`. All JMS messages extend the `javax.jms.Message` interface and provide implementations for the interface's methods. Table 10.3, earlier, listed the Java interfaces that extend the `Message` interface to provide behavior for different types of messages.

You create a new message by using one of the `create` methods defined in the `Session` interface. For example, to create an `ObjectMessage`, you would do the following:

```
Message newMessage = session.createObjectMessage();
```

Most of the `Message` types have a second `create` method that takes an argument of the thing that it will be wrapping. To create an `ObjectMessage` for an object that you already have instantiated, you could do the following:

```
Message newMessage = session.createObjectMessage( myObject );
```

Caution

The argument used in this second constructor must be serializable.

MESSAGE SELECTION AND FILTERING

By default, a `MessageConsumer` will process every message that is sent to its destination, regardless of whether or not it is interested in the message. You can modify this behavior to allow `MessageConsumers` to process only the messages in which they have an interest. You do this by setting up a message filter. This filter will only allow (or select) messages that pass the filter.

There are two steps in setting up a `Message` filter:

1. Initialize header and property fields in the message.
2. `MessageConsumers` specify a query string to select certain messages based on the header and property fields.

The next section describes the two steps in more detail.

SETTING HEADER AND PROPERTY FIELDS

You have already seen the standard set of message header fields back in the "The Message Header" section. You also have seen that a JMS client can set extra properties that a MessageConsumer can read after a message arrives at the destination. These two sets of attributes are used to provide the data that the message filter will use to select the appropriate message. After the header and property fields are set, the MessageConsumer just needs to use these fields when defining the message selector.

SPECIFY A MESSAGE SELECTOR QUERY STRING

A message selector is a java.lang.String whose syntax is based on a subset of the SQL92 conditional expression syntax. A message selector can't reference the message body. The selector can only reference the header and property fields. A message is considered to have passed the filter and become a selected message when the selector evaluates to true when the message's header field and property values are substituted for their corresponding identifiers in the selector.

PART

I

CH

10

The following code fragment shows an example of a message selector string:

```
auctionWinnerEmail is not null and auctionPrice > 1000
```

To use the previous query selector in an example, the following code fragment shows how to create a QueueReceiver using the message selector above:

```
String selector = "auctionWinnerEmail is not null and auctionPrice > 1000";
qSession.createReceiver(queue, selector);
```

The order evaluation of the selector is from left to right. You can use parentheses to adjust the evaluation order. The following is the same message selector you previously viewed, but this time with parentheses:

```
(auctionWinnerEmail is not null) and (auctionPrice > 1000)
```

Table 10.5 describes the type of tokens that can be used in a message selector and an example of each.

TABLE 10.5   TOKENS THAT CAN BE USED IN A MESSAGE SELECTOR

Type	Example
Literals	"salary" or 67
Identifiers	firstName
Whitespace	Space, tab, form feed, and line terminator
Standard bracketing	(salary)
Logical operators	NOT, AND, OR
Comparison operators	=, >, >=, <, <=, <>
Arithmetic operators	+, *,
Is Null Comparison	email is null
Is Not Null Comparison	email is not null

The tokens in Table 10.5 are the most commonly used tokens. There are a few other lesser-used tokens, but the ones from Table 10.5 should be enough for most applications.

> **Note**
>
> If you attempt to set a syntactically invalid message selector, a JMSException will be thrown.

USING THE JMS POINT-TO-POINT MODEL

Up to this point you have not seen a complete example of a JMS application. The focus has been to understand the concepts and interfaces of the JMS APIs. Now we will take a look at a complete example using JMS.

The JMS application example that you will see here is one based on the Auction example that runs throughout this book. The Auction service will allow e-mail messages to be sent to auction participants based on the normal events that occur throughout the life cycle of an auction. The normal events that the application will support are

- A user's bid has become a trailing bid
- A user's bid is the winning bid for an auction

First, you will see how a queue can be used to support this functionality and then later, in the section "Using the JMS Publish/Subscribe Model," a topic will be used so that a log message will be written for the administrator so that auction notifications can be later audited.

The JMS application developed in this chapter will utilize the horizontal services that will be discussed later in Chapter 21, "Horizontal Services." The term *horizontal services* refers to services that are used across many different components, sort of like a framework. Don't worry if this doesn't make much sense right now; it's covered in depth in Chapter 21.

For now, only stubs to those services will be used. For example, instead of complicating this example with the details of how to send e-mails using the JavaMail API, we will merely call the horizontal service that provides that capability and not discuss that functionality here. The horizontal service will only print the e-mail message out. Later in Chapter 21, when the horizontal services are discussed further, you'll see how to generate the actual e-mails using the JavaMail API.

In this example, the MessageConsumer will be a separate Java client that connects to the destination from outside the EJB container and uses the horizontal service to send the e-mail messages. The producer will also be a Java client. It's possible that the producer code might belong inside a session or entity bean method, but to keep the example simple, we will not use enterprise beans here.

We will revisit this example in Chapter 11 and see how the message-driven bean can be used as the consumer instead of this Java client. For now, we will try to keep it simple.

→ For more information on the horizontal services, **see** Chapter 21, "Horizontal Services."

CREATING THE JMS ADMINISTERED OBJECTS

The first thing that has to be done for this example is to configure the JMS server and set up the JMS administered objects. The process of setting up the JMS administered objects varies greatly between vendors. In BEA's WebLogic, there is a web administration console that allows an administrator to add the `ConnectionFactory` and `Destination` to the set of components that are created and started when the server starts. In other JMS implementations, you might have to edit some type of configuration file manually. Check with your vendor documentation on how to do this. For this JMS example, you'll need to set up two JMS administered objects:

- `Connection_Factory` with a JNDI name of
  `com.que.ejb20book.AuctionConnectionFactory`
- A `Queue` with a JNDI name of `com.que.ejb20book.EmailQueue`

The JNDI names of these are critical for the JMS examples in this chapter. The example uses the naming service to locate the JMS objects. You must be sure that you use these JNDI names when setting up the JMS configuration. Listing 10.1 shows a resource properties file that will be used by the examples. If you want to change the names of the administered objects in JNDI, change it in this property file also. This properties file must be placed somewhere in the system classpath for it to be found. The name of the resource file must be `auction_jms.properties` for the examples to work correctly. If you must change the names of the administered objects, change only the value on the right side of the equal (=) sign in the file. Don't change the value on the left side. The examples will look up the JNDI names based on the key part of the key/value pair.

LISTING 10.1 `auction_jms.properties` **RESOURCE FILE USED BY THE JMS EXAMPLES**

```
AUCTION_CONNECTION_FACTORY=com.que.ejb20book.AuctionConnectionFactory
AUCTION_NOTIFICATION_QUEUE=com.que.ejb20book.EmailQueue
```

LISTENING FOR MESSAGES FROM A QUEUE

The first part of the JMS application that we will look at is the consumer portion. Listing 10.2 shows the `AuctionNotificationConsumer` class. This class is responsible for registering a `MessageListener` with the `QueueReceiver` and waiting for a message to arrive. The `onMessage` method is called and passed the message that was put into the queue. From there, the generation of the e-mail message is delegated to the e-mail horizontal service. The e-mail message is generated as long as the object within the JMS message implements the `AuctionNotification` interface.

Notice by looking at the source code in Listing 10.2 that this is a Java program that runs outside the EJB container. We have done this because, under normal circumstances, there's no nonproprietary way to kick off a consumer to start listening for messages. Each EJB vendor typically has services that enable you to create a sort of startup class, but usually they are specific to that vendor and are not very portable. By using a Java client program running

PART
I

CH
10

outside the container, you can control very easily when the consumer program starts up. In the next chapter, you will see how this functionality can be performed using the new message-driven bean. For now, we will leave it as a standalone Java program.

LISTING 10.2   SOURCE CODE FOR AuctionNotificationConsumer.java

```
/**
 * Title:          AuctionNotificationConsumer
 * Description:    The MessageConsumer that gets messages from a Queue
 *                 and sends an email.
 */
package com.que.ejb20.notification;

import javax.jms.*;
import java.io.*;
import java.util.*;
import javax.naming.*;

import com.que.ejb20.services.email.*;
/**
 * This class is used to listen for incoming JMS Messages on a Queue and then
 * generate an email based on the Message. The incoming Message must be
 * a javax.jms.ObjectMessage and the contents of the Message must be a
 * com.que.ejb20.notification.NofiticationEmail for an Email to be
 * generated.
 */
public class AuctionNotificationConsumer implements Runnable, MessageListener {
    // The reference to the JNDI Context needed to look up Administered
    // JMS objects
    private InitialContext ctx = null;
    // Private static names for the Administered JMS Objects
    // These values will be read from a resource properties file
    private static String connectionFactoryName = null;
    private static String queueName = null;

    private QueueConnectionFactory qcf = null;
    private QueueReceiver receiver = null;
    private QueueConnection queueConnection = null;
    private Queue queue = null;

    /**
     * Default Constructor
     */
    public AuctionNotificationConsumer() {
        super();
    }

    /**
     * This is the method that must be implemented from the MessageListener
     * interface. This method will be called when a message has arrived at the
     * Queue and the container calls this method and passes the new Message.
     *
     * @param msg The javax.jms.Message that was sent to the Queue
     *
     * @see javax.jms.Message
     * @see javax.jms.MessageListener
     */
```

LISTING 10.2   CONTINUED

```
public void onMessage( Message msg ) {
  if ( msg instanceof ObjectMessage) {
    try {
      Object obj = ((ObjectMessage)msg).getObject();
      if ( obj instanceof AuctionNotification ) {
        sendEmail( (AuctionNotification)obj );
      }
    } catch( JMSException ex ) {
      ex.printStackTrace();
    }
  }
}
/**
 * The run method is necessary because this method implements the
 * Runnable interface to keep the thread alive and waiting for messages.
 * Otherwise, this thread would not keep running and would not
 * be able to listen for messages continuously.
 */
public void run() {
  while( true ) {
    synchronized( this ){
      try{
        wait();
      }catch( InterruptedException ex ){
        // Do Nothing
      }
    }
  }
}
// Private Accessor for Connection Factory Name
private static String getConnectionFactoryName() {
  return connectionFactoryName;
}

// Private mutator for the Connection factory Name
private static void setConnectionFactoryName( String name ) {
  connectionFactoryName = name;
}

// Private Accessor for the Queue Name
private static String getQueueName() {
  return queueName;
}

// Private mutator for Queue Name
private static void setQueueName( String name ) {
  queueName = name;
}

/**
 * This method is called to set up and initialize the necessary
 * Connection and Session references.
 *
 * @exception JMSException Problem finding a JMS administered object
 * @exception NamingException Problem with JNDI and a named object*
 *
```

Listing 10.2   Continued

```java
*/
public void init() throws JMSException, NamingException {
  try{
    loadProperties();
    // Look up the jndi factory
    ctx = new InitialContext();

    // Get a connection to the QueueConnectionFactory
    qcf = (QueueConnectionFactory)ctx.lookup( getConnectionFactoryName() );

  // Create a connection
  queueConnection = qcf.createQueueConnection();

  // Create a session that is non-transacted and is notified automatically
  QueueSession ses =
  queueConnection.createQueueSession( false, Session.AUTO_ACKNOWLEDGE );

  // Look up a destination
  queue = (Queue)ctx.lookup( getQueueName() );

  // Create the receiver
  receiver = ses.createReceiver( queue );

  // It's a good idea to always put a finally block so that the
  // context is closed
  }catch( NamingException ex ) {
    ex.printStackTrace();
  }finally {
    try {
      // Close up the JNDI connection since we have found what we needed
      if ( ctx != null )
        ctx.close();
    }catch ( Exception ex ) {
      ex.printStackTrace();
    }
  }

  // Inform the receiver that the callbacks should be sent to this instance
  receiver.setMessageListener( this );

  // Start listening
  queueConnection.start();
  System.out.println( "Listening on queue " + queue.getQueueName() );
}

/**
 * This method is called to load the JSM resource properties
 */
private void loadProperties() {
  String connectionFactoryName = null;
  String queueName = null;

  // Uses a Properties file to get the properties for the JMS objects
  Properties props = new Properties();
  try {
```

Listing 10.2 Continued

```
      props.load( getClass().getResourceAsStream( "/auction_jms.properties" ) );
    }catch( IOException ex ){
      ex.printStackTrace();
    }catch( Exception ex ){
      System.out.println( "Had a problem locating auction_jms.properties");
      ex.printStackTrace();
    }

    connectionFactoryName = props.getProperty( "AUCTION_CONNECTION_FACTORY" );
    queueName = props.getProperty( "AUCTION_NOTIFICATION_QUEUE" );

    // Set the JMS Administered values for this instance
    setConnectionFactoryName( connectionFactoryName );
    setQueueName( queueName );
  }

  /**
   * Delegate the sending of the email to the horizontal service.
   */
  private void sendEmail( AuctionNotification msg ) {
    NotificationEmail email = new NotificationEmail();
    email.setToAddress( msg.getNotificationEmailAddress() );
    email.setBody( msg.toString() );
    email.setFromAddress( "AuctionSite" );
    email.setSubject( msg.getNotificationSubject() );
    // Delete to the horizontal service
    try{
      EmailService.sendEmail( email );
    }catch( EmailException ex ){
      ex.printStackTrace();
    }
  }
  /**
   * Main Method
   * This is the main entry point that starts the Email listening for
   * messages in the Queue.
   */
  public static void main( String args[]) {
    // Create an instance of the client
    AuctionNotificationConsumer emailConsumer =
      new AuctionNotificationConsumer();

    try {
      emailConsumer.init();
    }catch( NamingException ex ){
      ex.printStackTrace();
    }catch( JMSException ex ){
      ex.printStackTrace();
    }

    // Start the client running
    Thread newThread = new Thread( emailConsumer );
    newThread.start();
  }
}
```

Part

I

Ch

10

Many things are going on in Listing 10.2. Here are the main steps this class performs:

1. Locate the `auction_jms.properties` file and read the names for the JMS administered objects.

2. Implement the `onMessage` method.

3. Get the connection, destination, and session.

4. Keep the thread alive.

5. Send e-mail messages when a JMS message arrives.

Several classes and interfaces are being used by the `AuctionNofiticationConsumer` in Listing 10.2. The Java interface for the auction notification and the two notification classes that implement this interface appear in Listings 10.3, 10.4, and 10.5 respectively.

LISTING 10.3   SOURCE CODE FOR `AuctionNotification.java`

```
/**
 * Title:       AuctionNotification<p>
 * Description: This interface defines the methods required for an Auction
 *              Notification.<p>
 */
package com.que.ejb20.notification;

public interface AuctionNotification extends java.io.Serializable {
  public void setAuctionName( String newAuctionName );
  public String getAuctionName();
  public void setNotificationEmailAddress( String emailAddress );
  public String getNotificationEmailAddress();
  public String getNotificationSubject();
}
```

LISTING 10.4   SOURCE CODE FOR `AuctionWinnerNotification.java`

```
/**
 * Title:       AuctionWinnerNotification<p>
 * Description: Contains information about a winner of a
 *              particular Auction.<p>
 */
package com.que.ejb20.notification;

/**
 * This class encapsulates the information about a winner of an Auction
 * that is needed when sending an email Notification to the winner or
 * another administrator. This class implements java.io.Serializable
 * so that it can be sent over the network to the JMS destination.
 *
 */
public class AuctionWinnerNotification
  implements java.io.Serializable, AuctionNotification {

  /**
   * Default Constructor
   */
  public AuctionWinnerNotification() {
    super();
```

Listing 10.4   Continued

```
  }
  // Private instance references
  private String auctionName;
  private String auctionWinner;
  private String auctionWinPrice;
  private String notificationEmailAddress;

  // Public Accessors and Mutators
  public String getAuctionName() {
    return auctionName;
  }

  public void setAuctionName(String newAuctionName) {
    auctionName = newAuctionName;
  }

  public void setAuctionWinner(String newAuctionWinner) {
    auctionWinner = newAuctionWinner;
  }

  public String getAuctionWinner() {
    return auctionWinner;
  }

  public void setAuctionWinPrice(String newAuctionWinPrice) {
    auctionWinPrice = newAuctionWinPrice;
  }

  public String getAuctionWinPrice() {
    return auctionWinPrice;
  }

  public void setNotificationEmailAddress(String emailAddress) {
    notificationEmailAddress = emailAddress;
  }

  public String getNotificationEmailAddress() {
    return notificationEmailAddress;
  }

  public String getNotificationSubject() {
    // This message should come from an external resource bundle so that
    // Internationalization can be handled properly
    return "You have the winning bid!";
  }

  public String toString() {
    StringBuffer buf = new StringBuffer();
    buf.append( "Your bid of " );
    buf.append( getAuctionWinPrice() );
    buf.append( " has become the winning bid in the Auction " );
    buf.append( getAuctionName() );
    return buf.toString();
  }

}
```

LISTING 10.5   SOURCE CODE FOR AuctionTrailingBidNotification.java

```java
/**
 * Title:         AuctionTrailingBidNotification<p>
 * Description:   Contains information to be sent to a user when that user has
 *                a bid on an Auction that has become a trailer.<p>
 */
package com.que.ejb20.notification;

/**
 * This class encapsulates the information about a bid on an Auction
 * that has become a trailer. This notification is meant to notify the user
 * of the trailing bid in case the user wishes to make another bid for the
 * Auction.
 */
public class AuctionTrailingBidNotification implements
  java.io.Serializable, AuctionNotification {

  /**
   * Default Constructor
   */
  public AuctionTrailingBidNotification() {
    super();
  }

  // Private instance references
  private String auctionName;
  private String leadingBid;
  private String usersLastBid;
  private String notificationEmailAddress;

  // Public Accessors and Mutators
  public String getAuctionName() {
    return auctionName;
  }

  public void setAuctionName( String newAuctionName ) {
    auctionName = newAuctionName;
  }

  public void setLeadingBid( String leadingBid ) {
    this.leadingBid = leadingBid;
  }

  public String getLeadingBid() {
    return leadingBid;
  }

  public void setUsersLastBid( String lastBid ) {
    usersLastBid = lastBid;
  }

  public String getUsersLastBid() {
    return usersLastBid;
  }

  public void setNotificationEmailAddress(String emailAddress) {
```

Listing 10.5   Continued

```
    notificationEmailAddress = emailAddress;
  }

  public String getNotificationEmailAddress() {
    return notificationEmailAddress;
  }

  public String getNotificationSubject() {
    // This message should come from an external resource bundle so that
    // Internationalization can be handled properly
    return "Your bid has become a trailing bid";
  }

  public String toString() {
    // This message should come from an external resource bundle so that
    // Internationalization can be handled properly
    StringBuffer buf = new StringBuffer();
    buf.append( "Your bid of " );
    buf.append( getUsersLastBid() );
    buf.append( " in the Auction: " );
    buf.append( getAuctionName() );
    buf.append( " has become a trailing bid. The new leading bid is " );
    buf.append( getLeadingBid() );
    return buf.toString();
  }
}
```

Listing 10.6 is the e-mail horizontal service that we just stubbed in for now. The sendMail method that is called only prints out the e-mail to the console for now. This service will be developed further in Chapter 21.

→ For more information on the horizontal services, **see** Chapter 21, "Horizontal Services."

Listing 10.6   Source Code for the E-mail Component in the Horizontal Services

```
/**
 * Title:        EmailService<p>
 * Description:  This class represents the horizontal email service
 *               Component. It contains static methods for generating email
 *               messages.<p>
 */
package com.que.ejb20.services.email;

public class EmailService {

  // For now, this method will not really generate an email message. Later it
  // will use the JavaMail API to do so, but for now it will only print out
  // a message saying that an email has been sent.
  public static void sendEmail( NotificationEmail email ) {
    System.out.println( email.toString() );
  }
}
```

The horizontal service component in Listing 10.6 uses a class to encapsulate all the information needed to send an e-mail message. That class is shown in Listing 10.7.

LISTING 10.7   SOURCE CODE FOR NotificationEmail.java

```java
/**
 * Title:           NotificationEmail
 * Description:     Encapsulate all the states of an Email object
 */
package com.que.ejb20.services.email;
/**
 * This class encapsulates the data that must be sent in an Email message.
 * This class does not support attachments. This class implements the
 * java.io.Serializable interface so that this object can be marshaled
 * over the network.
 *
 */
public class NotificationEmail implements java.io.Serializable{
  /**
   * Default Constructor
   */
  public NotificationEmail() {
    super();
  }
  // Private instance references
  private String toAddress;
  private String fromAddress;
  private String subject;
  private String body;

  // Public Accessors and Mutators
  public String getToAddress() {
    return toAddress;
  }
  public void setToAddress(String newToAddress) {
    toAddress = newToAddress;
  }
  public void setFromAddress(String newFromAddress) {
    fromAddress = newFromAddress;
  }
  public String getFromAddress() {
    return fromAddress;
  }
  public void setSubject(String newSubject) {
    subject = newSubject;
  }
  public String getSubject() {
    return subject;
  }
  public void setBody(String newBody) {
    body = newBody;
  }
  public String getBody() {
    return body;
  }
```

LISTING 10.7   CONTINUED

```java
public String toString() {
  StringBuffer buf = new StringBuffer();
  buf.append( "To: " + getToAddress() );
  buf.append( "\n" );
  buf.append( "From: " + getFromAddress() );
  buf.append( "\n" );
  buf.append( "Subject: " + getSubject() );
  buf.append( "\n" );
  buf.append( "Body: " + getBody() );
  buf.append( "\n" );
  return buf.toString();
}
}
```

SENDING MESSAGES TO A QUEUE

PART

I

CH

10

Now we need to create a class that generates the JMS messages that are sent to the queue. For our Auction example, a notification must be sent based on two events. One is when a new bid is placed on an auction and there is an existing bid that becomes a trailing bid. In this case, an `AuctionTrailingBidNotification` needs to be generated and sent to the user of the previous bid. The second event that triggers a notification is when an auction closes with a winner. In this case, an `AuctionWinnerNotification` will be generated and sent to the winner of the auction. An auction can close with a winner automatically and also when the auction administrator assigns a winner to an auction. In both cases, the notification should be sent.

To keep things simple for now, we are going to just use a simple Java client program to help test our JMS application. Listing 10.8 shows the class `AuctionNotificationProducer` that will generate either a winner or trailing auction notification to a particular e-mail address based on the command-line arguments passed into it.

Note

Remember that this code is used only to help us test the notification functionality. For a real auction application, this code would be placed in the components that are actually deciding when there is a winner or a trailing bid.

As with the `AuctionNotificationConsumer`, several steps are taking place in the `AuctionNotificationProducer` class. Here is the summary of the steps:

1. Locate the `auction_jms.properties` file and read the names for the JMS administered objects.

2. Get the `Connection`, `Destination`, and `Session`.

3. Generate the JMS message that wraps the `AuctionNotification` object.

4. Exit.

LISTING 10.8   SOURCE CODE FOR AuctionNotificationProducer.java

```java
/**
 * Title:          AuctionNotificationProducer
 * Description:    This class is used to help test the
 *                 AuctionNotificationConsumer class by sending notifications
 *                 to a Queue based on the command-line arguments.
 */
package com.que.ejb20.notification;

import javax.jms.*;
import java.io.*;
import java.util.*;
import javax.naming.*;

/**
 * This class is used to test the AuctionNotificationConsumer class.
 * In a production application, this code would be used by the component
 * that determines an email should be generated. A JMS ObjectMessage is
 * created and a com.que.ejb20.notification.NofiticationEmail object
 * is inserted into the ObjectMessage and then sent to the Queue.
 */
public class AuctionNotificationProducer {

  // Administered ConnectionFactory and Queue settings
  // These values are hard-coded because this is a test class and is not
  // to be easily configurable. You can make it so by either reading the
  // jms bundle as the consumer does or pass in these values on the command
  // line.
  // Private static names for the Administered JMS Objects
  // These values will be read from a resource properties file
  private static String connectionFactoryName = null;
  private static String queueName = null;

  // The reference to the JNDI Context
  private Context ctx = null;
  // Private instance references
  private QueueConnectionFactory queueConnectionFactory = null;
  private QueueSession queueSession = null;
  private QueueSender queueSender = null;
  private QueueConnection queueConnection = null;
  private Queue queue = null;

  /**
   * Default Constructor
   */
  public AuctionNotificationProducer() {
    super();
    loadProperties();
  }

  private void initialize() throws JMSException, NamingException {
    try{
      // Look up the jndi factory
      ctx = new InitialContext();

      // Get a connection to the QueueConnectionFactory
```

LISTING 10.8 CONTINUED

```
      queueConnectionFactory =
        (QueueConnectionFactory)ctx.lookup( getConnectionFactoryName() );

      // Create a connection
      queueConnection = queueConnectionFactory.createQueueConnection();

      // Create a session that is non-transacted and is notified automatically
      queueSession =
        queueConnection.createQueueSession( false, Session.AUTO_ACKNOWLEDGE );

      // Look up a destination
      queue = (Queue)ctx.lookup( getQueueName() );

    }catch( NamingException ex ) {
      ex.printStackTrace();
      System.exit( -1 );
    }finally {
      try {
        // Close up the JNDI connection since we have found what we needed
        ctx.close();
      }catch ( Exception ex ) {
        ex.printStackTrace();
      }
    }

    queueSender = queueSession.createSender( queue );
    queueSender.setDeliveryMode( DeliveryMode.NON_PERSISTENT );

    // Start the connection because every connection is in the
    // stopped state when created. It must be started
    queueConnection.start();
  }

  public void sendMessage( AuctionNotification emailMsg ) {
    try {
      // establish the necessary connection references
      initialize();
      Message msg = queueSession.createObjectMessage( emailMsg );
      queueSender.send( msg );

      // Close the open resources
      queueSession.close();
      queueConnection.close();

    }catch( JMSException ex ) {
      ex.printStackTrace();
    }catch( NamingException ex ) {
      ex.printStackTrace();
    }
  }
  // Private Accessor for Connection Factory Name
  private static String getConnectionFactoryName() {
    return connectionFactoryName;
  }
```

PART

I

CH

10

LISTING 10.8   CONTINUED

```java
// Private mutator for the Connection factory Name
private static void setConnectionFactoryName( String name ) {
  connectionFactoryName = name;
}

// Private Accessor for the Queue Name
private static String getQueueName() {
  return queueName;
}

// Private mutator for Queue Name
private static void setQueueName( String name ) {
  queueName = name;
}

/**
 * This method is called to load the JMS resource properties
 */
private void loadProperties() {
  String connectionFactoryName = null;
  String queueName = null;

 // Uses a Properties file to get the properties for the JMS objects
  Properties props = new Properties();
  try {
    props.load(getClass().getResourceAsStream( "/auction_jms.properties" ));
  }catch( IOException ex ){
    ex.printStackTrace();
  }catch( Exception ex ){
    System.out.println( "Had a problem locating auction_jms.properties");
    ex.printStackTrace();
  }

  connectionFactoryName = props.getProperty( "AUCTION_CONNECTION_FACTORY" );
  queueName = props.getProperty( "AUCTION_NOTIFICATION_QUEUE" );

  // Set the JMS Administered values for this instance
  setConnectionFactoryName( connectionFactoryName );
  setQueueName( queueName );
}
/**
 * Main Method
 *
 * This method is the main entry point for sending a JMS message to the
 * EmailQueue. This class sends a single Email to a user.
 *
 * Usage: java QueueEmailProducer <someEmailAddress>
 */
public static void main(String[] args) {
  // An email address must be passed in on the command line
  if ( args.length < 2 ) {
    String usageMsg =
       "Usage: java QueueEmailProducer <winner|trailer> <emailAddress>";
    System.out.println( usageMsg );
    System.exit( 0 );
```

LISTING 10.8   CONTINUED

```
    }
    // Create an instance of the EmailProducer
    AuctionNotificationProducer client =
                    new AuctionNotificationProducer();

    try {
      String notificationType = args[0];
      String emailAddress = args[1];
      AuctionNotification msg = null;

      // Create a notification based on the first arg of the command line args
      if ( notificationType == null ||
         notificationType.equalsIgnoreCase("winner") ) {
        msg = new AuctionWinnerNotification();
        ((AuctionWinnerNotification)msg).setAuctionWinPrice( "$75.00" );
      }else{
        msg = new AuctionTrailingBidNotification();
        ((AuctionTrailingBidNotification)msg).setLeadingBid( "$100.00" );
        ((AuctionTrailingBidNotification)msg).setUsersLastBid( "$75.00" );
      }

      // Fill in some details for the Auction Win
      // Obviously there is no Internationalization supported here. This is
      // just for testing purposes.
      msg.setAuctionName( "Tire Auction" );
      msg.setNotificationEmailAddress( emailAddress );

      // Send the message
      client.sendMessage( msg );
    } catch( Exception ex ) {
      ex.printStackTrace();
    }
  }
}
```

PART

I

CH

10

RUNNING THE QUEUE EXAMPLE

To run this example, you will need to follow these steps:

1. Start the JMS service with the administered objects for this example.

2. Run the `AuctionNotificationConsumer` client program.

3. Run the `AuctionNotificationProducer` client program.

You will need to be sure that you have both the JNDI and JMS services up and running before you run either the consumer or producer programs. Both client programs need to also have the JNDI and JMS JAR files included in the classpath.

To start the `AuctionNotificationConsumer`, just type the following on a command line:

```
java com.que.ejb20.notification.AuctionNotificationConsumer
```

The program will tell you that it's listening on the queue.

To test the `AuctionNotificationProducer` program, type the following:

```
java com.que.ejb20.notification.AuctionNotificationProducer winner me@foo.com
```

The `AuctionNotificationProducer` will not display any output before exiting. However, on the `AuctionNotificationConsumer` console, you should see the following output:

```
To: me@foo.com
From: AuctionSite
Subject: You have the winning bid!
Body: Your bid of $75.00 has become the winning bid in the Auction Tire Auction
```

 If you are having trouble running the example, see the "Troubleshooting" section at the end of this chapter for general JMS troubleshooting tips.

USING THE JMS PUBLISH/SUBSCRIBE MODEL

Now we are going to look at an example of implementing the notification functionality using the Pub/Sub model. Although this example might seem like a stretch to require the Pub/Sub model, it will give you an idea of the differences between the two and what must be done differently for each model. Actually, there might even be a need for this design over the PTP model based on performing different tasks for different subscribers, so it might not be that much of a stretch.

As stated earlier, the Pub/Sub model in JMS involves using a topic as the destination rather than a queue. For this example, we are going to have two subscribers to the `topic`. One will be the handler that generates an e-mail message to the user and the second will be the subscriber that is responsible for logging the event for the administrator. Using separate subscribers allows us to modify the behavior that is taken for the admin notification separately from the user notification. We could possibly add a third subscriber where a page was sent to someone's pager. The point here is that using a Pub/Sub pattern allows you to specialize the behavior for each subscriber to the topic.

CREATING THE JMS ADMINISTERED OBJECTS

For this example, we will add a line to the `auction_jms.properties` file for the new destination. The resource file should look like the one in Listing 10.9 after adding the new line for the topic. We will not remove the lines from the `Queue` example from the previous sections. Listing 10.9 shows what the properties file should look after adding the new line.

LISTING 10.9   THE `auction_jms.properties` **FILE WITH THE LINE FOR THE TOPIC ADDED**

```
AUCTION_CONNECTION_FACTORY=com.que.ejb20book.AuctionConnectionFactory
AUCTION_NOTIFICATION_QUEUE=com.que.ejb20book.EmailQueue
AUCTION_NOTIFICATION_TOPIC=com.que.ejb20book.AuctionNotificationTopic
```

To create the necessary administered objects for the topic, you will need to follow similar steps that you did when you created the queue for the last example. You don't have to create a new `ConnectionFactory`. We will reuse the one that you have already added.

ADDING SUBSCRIBERS TO A TOPIC

We will support two subscribers for this example. One is the
AuctionWinnerNotificationSubscriber and the other is the
AuctionWinAdminNotificationSubscriber. Both classes extend an abstract super class called
AuctionExternalNotificationSubscriber. For this example, we don't have a notification for
a trailing bid as we did in the last chapter, but you could easily develop one by subclassing
the abstract class as the other two do here. Listing 10.10 shows the abstract super class that
both subscribers will extend. The only method is the onMessage method that is required by
the MessageListener interface. The subscribers must implement this method to perform the
functionality that is unique to that subscriber.

LISTING 10.10   SOURCE CODE FOR AuctionExternalNotificationSubscriber.java

```
/**
 * Title:        AuctionExternalNotificationSubscriber
 * Description:  This class is an abstract JMS Topic subscriber.
 */
package com.que.ejb20.notification;

import javax.jms.*;
import java.io.*;
import java.util.*;
import javax.naming.*;
import com.que.ejb20.services.email.*;

abstract public class AuctionExternalNotificationSubscriber
  implements Runnable, MessageListener {
    // The reference to the JNDI Context
    private InitialContext ctx = null;
    // Private static names for the Administered JMS Objects
    private static String connectionFactoryName = null;
    private static String topicName = null;

    private TopicConnectionFactory tcf = null;
    private TopicSubscriber subscriber = null;
    private TopicConnection topicConnection = null;
    private Topic topic = null;

  /**
   * Default Constructor
   */
  public AuctionExternalNotificationSubscriber() {
    super();
    loadProperties();
  }

  /**
   * This is the method that must be implemented from the MessageListener
   * interface. This method will be called when a message has arrived at the
   * Topic and the container calls this method and passes the Message.
   */
  abstract public void onMessage( Message msg );
  /**
```

LISTING 10.10   CONTINUED

```java
     * The run method is necessary because this method implements the
     * Runnable interface to keep the thread alive and waiting for messages.
     * Otherwise, this would would not stay alive and would not be able to
     * listen for messages asyncronously.
     */
    public void run() {
      while( true ) {
        synchronized( this ){
          try{
            wait();
          }catch( InterruptedException ex ){
          }
        }
      }
    }
    // Private Accessors for Connection Factory Name
    private static String getConnectionFactoryName() {
      return connectionFactoryName;
    }

    // Private mutator for the Connection factory Name
    private static void setConnectionFactoryName( String name ) {
      connectionFactoryName = name;
    }

    // Private Accessors for the Topic Name
    private static String getTopicName() {
      return topicName;
    }

    // Private mutator for Topic Name
    private static void setTopicName( String name ) {
      topicName = name;
    }

    /**
     * This method is called to set up and initialize the necessary
     * Connection and Session references.
     */
    public void init( String msgSelector ) throws JMSException, NamingException {
      try{
        // Look up the jndi factory
        ctx = new InitialContext();

        // Get a connection to the QueueConnectionFactory
        tcf = (TopicConnectionFactory)ctx.lookup( getConnectionFactoryName() );

      // Create a connection
      topicConnection = tcf.createTopicConnection();

      // Create a session that is non-transacted and is notified automatically
      TopicSession ses =
        topicConnection.createTopicSession( false, Session.AUTO_ACKNOWLEDGE );

      // Look up a destination
```

LISTING 10.10   CONTINUED

```
    topic = (Topic)ctx.lookup( getTopicName() );

    // Create the receiver with a msgSelector. The msgSelector may
    // be null. The noLocal parameter is set so that this subscriber
    // will not receive copies of its own messages
    subscriber = ses.createSubscriber( topic, msgSelector, true );

    // It's a good idea to always put a finally block so that the
    // context is closed
    }catch( NamingException ex ) {
      ex.printStackTrace();
      System.exit( -1 );
    }finally {
      try {
        // Close up the JNDI connection since we have found what we needed
        ctx.close();
      }catch ( Exception ex ) {
        ex.printStackTrace();
      }
    }

    // Inform the received that the callbacks should be sent to this instance
    subscriber.setMessageListener( this );

    // Start listening
    topicConnection.start();
    System.out.println( "Listening on topic " + topic.getTopicName() );
  }

  /**
   * This method is called to load the JMS resource properties
   */
  private void loadProperties() {
    String connectionFactoryName = null;
    String topicName = null;

    // Uses a Properties file to get the properties for the JMS objects
    Properties props = new Properties();
    try {
      props.load(getClass().getResourceAsStream( "/auction_jms.properties" ));
    }catch( IOException ex ){
      ex.printStackTrace();
    }catch( Exception ex ){
      System.out.println( "Had a problem locating auction_jms.properties");
      ex.printStackTrace();
    }

    connectionFactoryName = props.getProperty( "AUCTION_CONNECTION_FACTORY" );
    topicName = props.getProperty( "AUCTION_NOTIFICATION_TOPIC" );

    // Set the JMS Administered values for this instance
    setConnectionFactoryName( connectionFactoryName );
    setTopicName( topicName );
  }
  /**
```

PART

I

CH

10

LISTING 10.10   CONTINUED

```
     * For now, this method only prints out that an email is to be sent.
     * You'll see later how to do this using the JavaMail API.
     */
    private void sendEmail( NotificationEmail email ) {
      /* Delegate the actual sending of the email message to the
         horizontal email service */
      try{
        EmailService.sendEmail( email );
      }catch( EmailException ex ){
        ex.printStackTrace();
      }
    }
  }
}
```

Listings 10.11 and 10.12 show the concrete subclasses that extend the abstract class in
Listing 10.10. Each one is designed to perform specific business logic when a message
arrives at the topic.

LISTING 10.11   SOURCE CODE FOR AuctionWinnerNotificationSubscriber.java

```
/**
 * Title:        AuctionWinnerNotificationSubscriber<p>
 * Description:  A Topic subscriber to handle a notification for a winner of
 *               an Auction.<p>
 */
package com.que.ejb20.notification;

import javax.jms.*;
import java.io.*;
import java.util.*;
import javax.naming.*;
import com.que.ejb20.services.email.*;

public class AuctionWinnerNotificationSubscriber
  extends AuctionExternalNotificationSubscriber {

  public AuctionWinnerNotificationSubscriber() {
  }
  /**
   * The onMessage method here generates an email through the horizontal
   * email service.
   */
  public void onMessage( Message msg ) {
    if ( msg instanceof ObjectMessage) {
      try {
        Object obj = ((ObjectMessage)msg).getObject();
        if ( obj instanceof AuctionNotification ) {
          sendEmail( (AuctionNotification)obj );
        }
      } catch( JMSException ex ) {
        ex.printStackTrace();
      }
    }
```

LISTING 10.11   CONTINUED

```java
  }
  /**
   * Delegate the sending of the email to the horizontal service.
   */
  private void sendEmail( AuctionNotification msg ) {
    NotificationEmail email = new NotificationEmail();
    email.setToAddress( msg.getNotificationEmailAddress() );
    email.setBody( msg.toString() );
    email.setFromAddress( "AuctionSite" );
    email.setSubject( msg.getNotificationSubject() );
    // Delegate to the horizontal service
    EmailService.sendEmail( email );
  }
  /**
   * Main Method
   * This is the main entry point that starts the Email listening for
   * messages in the Topic.
   */
  public static void main( String args[]) {
    // Create an instance of the client
    AuctionWinnerNotificationSubscriber subscriber = null;

    try {
      subscriber = new AuctionWinnerNotificationSubscriber();
      subscriber.init( "NotificationType = 'AuctionWinner'" );
    }catch( NamingException ex ){
      ex.printStackTrace();
    }catch( JMSException ex ){
      ex.printStackTrace();
    }

    // Start the client running
    Thread newThread = new Thread( subscriber );
    newThread.start();
  }
}
```

LISTING 10.12   SOURCE CODE FOR AuctionWinAdminNotificationSubscriber.java

```java
/**
 * Title:        AuctionWinAdminNotificationSubscriber<p>
 * Description:  A Topic subscriber to handle a notification for a winner of
 *               an Auction.<p>
 */
package com.que.ejb20.notification;

import javax.jms.*;
import java.io.*;
import java.util.*;
import javax.naming.*;
import com.que.ejb20.services.logging.*;

public class AuctionWinAdminNotificationSubscriber
  extends AuctionExternalNotificationSubscriber {
```

LISTING 10.12   CONTINUED

```
/**
 * Default Constructor
 */
public AuctionWinAdminNotificationSubscriber() {
  super();
}

/**
 * If the Message is an ObjectMessage and is an instance
 * of AuctionNotification, then log the message to the
 * horizontal logging service.
 */
public void onMessage( Message msg ) {
  if ( msg instanceof ObjectMessage) {
    try {
      Object obj = ((ObjectMessage)msg).getObject();
      if ( obj instanceof AuctionNotification ) {
        try{
          String msgStr = ((AuctionNotification)obj).getNotificationSubject();
          ILogger logger = new Logger();
          logger.logMessage( new LogMessage( msgStr, LogMessage.INFO ));
          logger.close();
        }catch( LoggingException ex ){
          ex.printStackTrace();
        }
      }
    } catch( JMSException ex ) {
      ex.printStackTrace();
    }
  }
}
/**
 * Main Method
 * This is the main entry point that starts the Email listening for
 * messages in the Queue.
 */
public static void main( String args[]) {
  // Create an instance of the client
  AuctionWinAdminNotificationSubscriber subscriber = null;

  try {
    subscriber = new AuctionWinAdminNotificationSubscriber();
    subscriber.init( "" );
  }catch( NamingException ex ){
    ex.printStackTrace();
  }catch( JMSException ex ){
    ex.printStackTrace();
  }

  // Start the client running
  Thread newThread = new Thread( subscriber );
  newThread.start();
}
}
```

Both of the classes in Listings 10.11 and 10.12 extend the AuctionExternalNotificationSubscriber class and override the abstract onMessage method. This is to allow for each subclass to do something special when a message arrives.

In the case of the AuctionWinnerNotificationSubscriber class in Listing 10.11, the sendMail method is called on the EmailService component that is part of the horizontal service. With Listing 10.12, the logMessage method is called on the LogService that is also a part of the horizontal services. The horizontal service class that handles logging appears in Listing 10.13. For now, the logger will only print out a message to the console. This component will be developed further in Chapter 21.

LISTING 10.13   THE HORIZONTAL COMPONENT FOR LOGGING

```
/**
 * Title:        LogService<p>
 * Description:  Horizontal Service Component for Logging<p>
 */
package com.que.ejb20.services.logging;

public class LogService {

  public static void logMessage( String msg ) {
    System.out.println( msg );
  }
}
```

The logMessage method in the LogService class in Listing 10.13 is extremely basic and will be modified and further developed in Chapter 21. For now, we are just trying to provide stubs for the classes that need to use them.

SENDING MESSAGES TO A TOPIC

To help test the Pub/Sub example, the AuctionWinnerPublisher class will be used. Just as with the Queue example from before, we are going to use a regular Java client to help us test the example. This message publisher code would normally reside in the EJB container and be triggered when one of the events occurred that needed to generate a notification, but to keep the example simple, we will just use this class for now.

Listing 10.14 shows the AuctionWinnerPublisher that will we use. The publisher will execute these general steps:

1. Locate the necessary JMS administered objects.
2. Create a new JMS message.
3. Publish the message to the topic.
4. Exit.

LISTING 10.14   SOURCE CODE FOR AuctionWinnerPublisher.java

```java
/**
 * Title:        AuctionWinnerPublisher<p>
 * Description:  This class is used to test the AuctionNotificationTopic<p>
 */
package com.que.ejb20.notification;

import javax.jms.*;
import java.io.*;
import java.util.*;
import javax.naming.*;


/**
 * This class can be used to test sending an AuctionWinnerNotification
 * to the AuctionNotificationTopic. All of the subscribers will get a
 * copy of the JMS Message, which encapsulates an AuctionWinnerNotification
 * object with the details of the Auction win. Only one message will be sent
 * each time this class is executed.
 *
 * Usage: java AuctionWinnerPublisher
 */
public class AuctionWinnerPublisher {

    // The reference to the JNDI Context
    private InitialContext ctx = null;
    // Private static names for the Administered JMS Objects
    private static String connectionFactoryName = null;
    private static String topicName = null;
    // Private instance references
    private TopicConnectionFactory tcf = null;
    private TopicConnection topicConnection = null;
    private TopicSession ses = null;
    private Topic topic = null;

  /**
   * Default Constructor
   */
  public AuctionWinnerPublisher() {
    super();
    loadProperties();
  }

  public void publishWinnerNotification( AuctionWinnerNotification winMsg ) {
    // Local reference to a TopicPublisher
    TopicPublisher publisher = null;

    try{
      // Lookup the jndi factory
      ctx = new InitialContext();

      // Get a connection to the QueueConnectionFactory
      tcf = (TopicConnectionFactory)ctx.lookup( getConnectionFactoryName() );

      // Create a connection
      topicConnection = tcf.createTopicConnection();
```

Listing 10.14   Continued

```
      // Create a session that is non-transacted and is notified automatically
      ses =
        topicConnection.createTopicSession( false, Session.AUTO_ACKNOWLEDGE );

      // Lookup a destination
      topic = (Topic)ctx.lookup( getTopicName() );

      // Create the publisher
      publisher = ses.createPublisher( topic );

      // Wrap the AuctionWinnerNotification inside of a JMS Message
      Message msg = ses.createObjectMessage( winMsg );

      // Set the property that will be used by the message selector
      msg.setStringProperty( "NotificationType", "AuctionWinner" );

      // Publish the message
      publisher.publish( msg );

      // Close the openresources
      topicConnection.close();

    }catch( NamingException ex ) {
      ex.printStackTrace();
      System.exit( -1 );
    }catch( JMSException ex ) {
      ex.printStackTrace();
    // It's a good idea to always put a finally block to ensure the
    // context is closed
    }finally {
      try {
        // Close up the JNDI connection since we have found what we needed
        ctx.close();
      }catch ( Exception ex ) {
        ex.printStackTrace();
      }
    }
  }

// Private Accessors for Connection Factory Name
private static String getConnectionFactoryName() {
  return connectionFactoryName;
}

// Private mutator for the Connection factory Name
private static void setConnectionFactoryName( String name ) {
  connectionFactoryName = name;
}

// Private Accessors for the Topic Name
private static String getTopicName() {
  return topicName;
}

// Private mutator for Topic Name
```

LISTING 10.14   CONTINUED

```java
  private static void setTopicName( String name ) {
    topicName = name;
  }

  /**
   * This method is called to load the JMS resource properties
   */
  private void loadProperties() {
    String connectionFactoryName = null;
    String topicName = null;

    // Uses a Properties file to get the properties for the JMS objects
    Properties props = new Properties();
    try {
      props.load(getClass().getResourceAsStream( "/auction_jms.properties" ));
    }catch( IOException ex ){
      ex.printStackTrace();
    }catch( Exception ex ){
      System.out.println( "Had a problem locating auction_jms.properties");
      ex.printStackTrace();
    }

    connectionFactoryName = props.getProperty( "AUCTION_CONNECTION_FACTORY" );
    topicName = props.getProperty( "AUCTION_NOTIFICATION_TOPIC" );

    // Set the JMS Administered values for this instance
    setConnectionFactoryName( connectionFactoryName );
    setTopicName( topicName );
  }

  /**
   * Main Method. This is the entry point to test sending an
   * AuctionWinnerNotification to the Topic
   */
  public static void main( String args[]) {

    // Get the email address passed in on the command line
    if ( args.length == 0 ) {
      System.out.println( "Usage: AuctionWinnerPublisher <emailAddress>");
      System.exit( 0 );
    }

    String emailAddress = args[0];

    AuctionWinnerPublisher publisher = null;
    // Create an instance of this class
    publisher = new AuctionWinnerPublisher();
    // Load the properties from the jms bundle so that we can
    // locate the ConnectionFactory and the Topic

    // Create the Winner Notification
    AuctionWinnerNotification msg = new AuctionWinnerNotification();
    // Fill in some details for the Auction Win
    msg.setAuctionName( "Some Auction Item" );
    msg.setNotificationEmailAddress( emailAddress );
```

LISTING 10.14   CONTINUED

```
    // Obviously there is no Internationalization supported here. This is
    // just for testing purposes.
    msg.setAuctionWinPrice( "$75.00" );
    // Publish the message to the Topic
    publisher.publishWinnerNotification( msg );
  }
}
```

RUNNING THE TOPIC EXAMPLE

Running the Topic example is not much different from the Queue example seen earlier in this chapter. To run the Topic example, you will need to follow these steps:

1. Start the JMS service with the administered topic objects for this example.
2. Run the AuctionWinnerNotificationSubscriber client.
3. Run the AuctionWinAdminNotificationSubscriber client.
4. Run the AuctionWinnerPublisher program and provide an e-mail address.

You will need to make sure that you have both the JNDI and JMS services up and running before you run either the subscriber or publisher programs. Both client programs need to have the JNDI and JMS JAR files included in the classpath.

To start either of the subscriber programs, just run them like any other Java program:

```
java com.que.ejb20.notification.AuctionWinnerNotificationSubscriber
```

or

```
java com.que.ejb20.notification.AuctionWinAdminNotificationSubscriber
```

The program will tell you that it's listening on the topic.

Note

Remember, there might be a difference between the JNDI name and the actual name for a destination. For example, the JNDI name given to the topic is com.que.ejb20book.AuctionNotificationTopic, but the actual property name you assign it when setting it up in the JMS administration properties might be different. Don't confuse the two.

To create a notification using the publisher, run the AuctionWinnerPublisher and pass in an e-mail address like the following:

```
java com.que.ejb20.notification.AuctionWinnerPublisher me@foo.com
```

The AuctionWinnerPublisher will not display any output before exiting. Both of the subscribers should print out a message on their consoles.

If you are having trouble running the example, see the "Troubleshooting" section at the end of this chapter for general JMS troubleshooting tips.

DURABLE SUBSCRIPTION

In terms of JMS, *durability* describes whether or not the JMS server will hold onto a JMS message if a subscriber is temporarily inactive. Message durability is different from message persistence. Durability is defined by the relationship that exists between a Topic subscriber and the JMS server. A subscriber that is set up as durable will have messages sent to it held by the server if the subscriber is temporarily distracted doing something else or its session becomes inactive for some reason. Durability can only be established for the Pub/Sub (Topic) message model.

Message persistence, on the other hand, is a relationship that is defined between a MessageProducer and the JMS server. Persistence can be established for both messaging models, as you'll see later in the "Message Persistence" section.

A cost overhead is involved with using durable subscribers. The subscriber registers the subscription with a unique identity that is retained by the JMS server. When a message arrives at the topic and one or more durable subscribers are inactive, the JMS server retains the messages for that subscription. When the subscriber becomes active again, the subscriber will receive the messages that are waiting for it. This is, of course, unless the message expires based on its time-to-live expiration date.

THE CLIENT ID

The client ID is a unique identifier that associates a JMS connection and the objects created through the connection with state that is maintained on behalf of a specific client. This is the means by which the JMS server knows how to deliver durable messages to a subscriber when it connects or becomes active.

You can define this ID in two ways:

- Configure the TopicConnectionFactory with the client ID.
- Set the client ID after acquiring a connection.

The JMS specification recommends that you set up a ConnectionFactory with a client-specific identifier and then the client looks up their specific ConnectionFactory when a connection is needed. Any connection obtained through this ConnectionFactory would be assigned this client ID.

The client can alternatively assign the ID after a connection is obtained from a ConnectionFactory. In this manner, a client-specific ConnectionFactory does not need to be configured.

Caution

> Clients that use the alternative approach and use a default `ConnectionFactory` must remember to assign a unique client ID as soon as a connection is obtained from the factory. There is a chance that a unique ID already exists for a client. If this occurs, an exception will not be thrown and behavior is not predictable. Clients must be sure they have not already used a client ID for another connection. This is only if you are using durable subscriptions.

Although both message models use a client ID, only the Pub/Sub actually uses it. You will see a client ID for a `QueueConnection`, but JMS does not currently use them. Some vendors might be using client IDs for something internal to their JMS server for queues. Check with your vendor's documentation to be safe.

CREATING DURABLE SUBSCRIBERS

You can create durable topic subscribers by using one of the following two methods that exist on the `TopicSession` interface:

```
public TopicSubscriber createDurableSubscriber(Topic topic, String name)
throws JMSException

public TopicSubscriber createDurableSubscriber(Topic topic, String name,
    String messageSelector, boolean noLocal)
throws JMSException
```

The `name` argument in the two method signatures is the unique client ID. You can also specify a `messageSelector`, which you saw in the section "Specify a Message Selector Query String" earlier in this chapter.

You can specify whether a client receives a copy of the messages it sends. This can happen because a message that is sent to a topic is distributed to all subscribers. If an application uses the same connection to both publish and subscribe to a topic, a client can receive the messages that it sends. To prevent this from happening, the client should set the `noLocal` argument above to true. The `noLocal` default is false, and therefore a subscriber can receive a copy of the messages that it sends.

Only one session can define a subscriber for a particular durable subscription at any given time. Multiple subscribers can access this subscription, but not at the same time.

DELETING DURABLE SUBSCRIBERS

To delete a durable subscriber, you must use the following method on the `TopicSession`:

```
public void unsubscribe(String name) throws JMSException;
```

The `name` argument is the name of the durable subscriber that was used when the durable subscriber was created. You can't delete a durable subscriber if either of the following is true:

- A `TopicSubscriber` is still active on the session
- The subscriber is in the middle of a transacted message or has not acknowledged the incoming message

MODIFYING DURABLE SUBSCRIBERS

To modify an existing durable subscription, you can optionally delete the existing durable subscriber and then re-create it using a new name. You also will get a new durable subscriber if you change either the `messageSelector` or `noLocal` values in the `createDurableSubscriber` method.

SYNCHRONOUS VERSUS ASYNCHRONOUS MESSAGING

A client can be set up to synchronously or asynchronously receive messages. With synchronous delivery, a client can request the next message from a `MessageConsumer` by using one of the `receive` methods. Three different `receive` methods can be used:

- `receive`—Receive the next message for this consumer
- `receive(long timeout)`—Receive the next message that arrives within the timeout interval
- `receiveNoWait`—Receive the next message if one is immediately available

A JMS consumer can also receive messages asynchronously. The client registers an object that implements the `MessageListener` interface with the JMS server. When messages arrive for a particular `MessageConsumer` that has a `MessageListener` registered, the messages are delivered to the `onMessage` method. This is the example that you saw in Listing 10.2.

> **Note**
>
> The JMS specification is very clear about the fact that the client that implements the `onMessage` method defined in the `MessageListener` interface should never throw a `RuntimeException`. If the `onMessage` method does happen to throw a `RuntimeException`, it's very unpredictable how the JMS server will react. It might consider the `MessageListener` to be confused and stop delivering messages to it. You should catch such exceptions and attempt to divert the message to some type of error handler instead.

MESSAGE PERSISTENCE

JMS supports two modes of method delivery:

- `NON_PERSISTENT`
- `PERSISTENT`

Depending on the needs of your JMS application, `NON_PERSISTENT` message delivery offers the least amount of overhead and the best performance of the two modes. With the `PERSISTENT` mode of message delivery, the JMS server must guarantee that a message is delivered exactly once. The JMS server does this by taking extra care to ensure that the message is not lost after the `MessageProducer` sends it. The JMS server does so by using some type of persistent store to save the messages after they are sent.

With the NON_PERSISTENT delivery mode, a JMS provider does not take any extra precaution to ensure the message is saved or backed up. In case of a JMS server failure, messages might be lost. If your application needs to be sure that messages are delivered, you should use the PERSISTENT delivery mode.

> **Caution**
>
> Just because your application is using PERSISTENT method delivery does not absolutely guarantee that all messages are delivered to all expecting consumers. Issues such as expiration times and JMS resource limits may cause messages to be destroyed inadvertently. To help reduce the possibility of this from happening, it's recommended that you use PERSISTENT message delivery and both produce and consume messages within a transaction.

USING TRANSACTIONS WITH JMS

You learned about the Session interface back in the "The JMS Interfaces" section earlier. When using a transacted session, all messages that are produced and sent are performed as a unit of work. If anything happens that causes a need to roll back the transaction, all messages that are produced within that transaction are destroyed, and all the messages that are sent are recovered. This allows a client to treat a group of messages as an atomic unit. Either all of them succeed or none of them do.

You can use the session's commit or rollback methods to cause a session to succeed or fail, respectively. After a transaction is complete by calling either of the two methods, a new transaction is automatically created for the client.

There are three different methods for using a transaction in your JMS application:

- Use a JMS transacted session
- If you are using EJB with JMS, you should use a Java Transaction API (JTA) user transaction in a nontransacted JMS Session
- Use message-driven beans

You've seen how to create a JMS transacted session earlier in the chapter.

→ Using user transactions with the JTA is beyond the scope of this chapter and is covered briefly later in the book. For more information on user transactions, **see** Chapter 12, "Transactions."

The next chapter covers the new message-driven bean and discusses how to use transactions with it.

USING JMS WITH ENTERPRISE JAVABEANS

Prior to the EJB 2.0 Specification, the preferred method of handling JMS consumers was to use the methods discussed throughout this chapter. With the new 2.0 Specification, a new enterprise bean has been introduced that will handle this task much more efficiently than the consumers in this chapter does. This is because the container now will handle such things as instance pooling to concurrently handle multiple messages at the same time. You also will not need to start an external Java program to handle the message consumption as was shown in this chapter. This and much more will be covered in the next chapter.

TROUBLESHOOTING

JMS SERVER NOT STARTED

I get an exception that says the server was not found.

Be sure you have started the EJB server before running the examples. If you are using only a JMS server, be sure it's running and that you have the correct connection information required for that JMS provider.

CLASSPATH NOT SET UP CORRECTLY

I get a NoClassDefFoundError.

Be sure you have the jms.jar, jndi.jar, and the class files for the example in your system classpath. If you don't want to add them to your system classpath, create a startup script and add them using the -classpath option.

JMS ADMINISTERED OBJECTS NOT CONFIGURED CORRECTLY

I get an error message that says something about the ConnectionFactory, queue, or topic was not found.

Be sure you set up the JMS administered objects before attempting to run any of the examples. Every JMS provider will have its own way of setting these up. Check with the vendor documentation. Also, be sure you have the auction_jms.properties resource file somewhere in a valid classpath.

MESSAGE-DRIVEN BEANS

In this chapter

WHAT ARE MESSAGE-DRIVEN BEANS?

Prior to the EJB 2.0 Specification, most JMS message consumers were built as simple Java programs that ran outside the container. There was typically a Java program that was started, and that would connect to a JMS destination and listen for incoming messages. Due to the restrictions placed on enterprise beans and non-EJB classes with respect to creating threads, there was no easy way to build an asynchronous JMS consumer inside the container. Although many EJB vendors provided services for startup classes and additional thread management capabilities, this was all proprietary to that vendor. For these reasons, external Java programs were used most often as consumers of JMS messages.

Although that approach to building JMS consumers was one of the better solutions for overcoming the synchronicity problem, several other problems are associated with running a Java program outside the container to handle JMS messages. The biggest problem is scalability. If the message load begins to grow, you must start multiple Java client applications outside the container to act as multiple consumers or just rely on the single consumer to process all the incoming messages. This can have the effect of filling up the destination and possibly losing some messages if the load grows too high. Even if you did start multiple consumers, eventually you're going to have a problem with too many client programs running. Trying to manage all these clients is tough.

A solution was needed for this problem. A container had to be able to manage the life cycle of multiple JMS consumers. This is the main reason why the message-driven bean was invented. The main goal of message-driven beans is to provide concurrent processing of incoming JMS messages by allowing the container to pool and manage message-driven bean instances. This is similar to how the container handles the other enterprise bean types as well. The container can create instances at startup that are ready to be used, and a smaller number of instances can support a large client load because they can be reused.

Some EJB vendors were thinking ahead and had the concept of message-driven beans in their EJB 1.1 implementations. However, the EJB specification didn't describe how they should be implemented until version 2.0. Basically, message-driven beans perform some business logic using JMS messages sent to a particular JMS destination. Although message-driven beans have similarities with the other two types of enterprise beans, there are some very distinct differences.

MESSAGE-DRIVEN BEANS ARE ANONYMOUS

The biggest difference between message-driven beans and session or entity beans is that a message-driven bean doesn't have a home or component interface. Therefore, message-driven beans are completely hidden from the client. This is true for standard EJB clients as well as other enterprise beans. The only way for clients to communicate with message-driven beans is by sending messages to a JMS destination. Figure 11.1 shows a client's view of interacting with message-driven beans.

Figure 11.1
A client can have no direct interaction with message-driven beans.

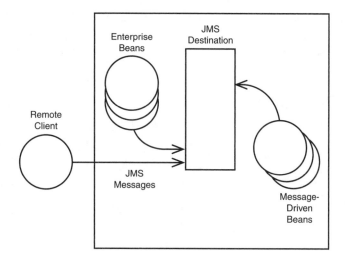

As you see in Figure 11.1, a client delivers a JMS message to a destination (`Queue` or a `Topic`) and the container passes this JMS message to an instance of a message-driven bean that has registered itself as a listener for that particular destination. By using a pool of message-driven bean instances, the container is able to handle incoming messages much more efficiently and increase scalability for JMS operations. Instances of a message-driven bean can be put back into a pool, which is allowed to grow and shrink depending on the needs of the container.

MESSAGE-DRIVEN BEANS ARE STATELESS

Similar to stateless session beans, message-driven beans are not allowed to contain conversational state. This doesn't mean that they can't have instance variables and have instance state; it just means that they cannot be used to store state information for a particular client. This should be very obvious because a client has no way to make a direct call onto the message-driven bean because it lacks a component interface.

By ensuring that all instances of the message-driven bean class are identical, the container is able to manage a smaller number of instances in the pool and still handle a larger load. This is because any free instance can be used to handle any incoming request for a given destination.

THE MESSAGE-DRIVEN BEAN AND THE CONTAINER

From the message bean's creation until its destruction, the container manages message-driven beans exclusively. All the services offered to the other two enterprise beans, such as security, transaction support, and concurrency, are also provided to the message-driven bean by the container.

The container interacts with the message-driven bean through a set of callback methods that are implemented in the message-driven bean. These callback methods are similar to the ones used by session and entity beans. The methods tell the bean instance when certain events are about to occur or have occurred.

THE MESSAGE-DRIVEN BEAN LIFE CYCLE

Figure 11.2 shows the life cycle for message-driven beans.

Figure 11.2
The life cycle of a
message-driven bean.

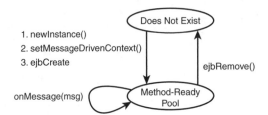

Message-driven beans are normally created when the container first starts up. The vendor-specific deployment descriptor may give the bean deployer or assembler the ability to spec-ify how many initial message-driven beans are available at startup and also how many maximum beans should be created. It's up to the container to ensure that the bean instances are available before JMS messages start arriving.

The container first calls the no-argument constructor for the bean. Next, the container calls the `setMessageDrivenContext` method and associates a `MessageDrivenContext` with the bean instance. Finally, the container calls the `ejbCreate` method on the instance. Here, you can put initialization code if your bean instance needs certain resources to complete the busi-ness logic. These resources could be things such as a JavaMail session or a JDBC connection.

Tip

There's no reason to have other constructors in the message-driven bean class, because the container will only call the no argument version.

USING MESSAGE-DRIVEN BEANS WITH EJB

Because there is no home or component interface, other enterprise beans are not able to communicate directly with message-driven beans. The only communication is through the JMS destination via the container. Integrating message-driven beans into the EJB container is really just a matter of creating the JMS-administered objects and creating the proper deployment information for the message-driven bean.

→ For a refresher on creating the JMS administered objects, including destinations for a message-driven bean, **see** Chapter 10, "Java Message Service."

USING JMS QUEUES OR TOPICS WITH MESSAGE-DRIVEN BEANS

You can use a message-driven bean to asynchronously receive messages from a javax.jms.Queue or a javax.jms.Topic. When a message-driven bean is acting as a subscriber to a Topic, it can be set up as either a non-durable or durable subscriber. In most production applications, you'll typically want to use either a persistent Queue or ensure that the message-driven bean is a durable subscriber. This will help ensure that messages are not missed.

The bean provider might provide information to the deployer as to whether the bean should be used with a Queue or a Topic by setting the message-driven-destination tag in the ejb-jar.xml file. The following code fragment shows an example of a message-driven bean being associated with a Topic:

```
<message-driven>
  <ejb-name>MessageDrivenBeanExample</ejb-name>
  <ejb-class>com.que.ejb20.SomeMessageBean</ejb-class>
  <transaction-type>Container</transaction-type>
  <message-driven-destination>
    <jms-destination-type>javax.jms.Topic</jms-destination-type>
  </message-driven-destination>

</message-driven>
```

Notice that in the jms-destination-type element, a javax.jms.Topic was specified. To indicate that the message-driven bean should be used with a Queue, you would insert javax.jms.Queue instead.

We'll talk about the other elements in the deployment descriptor for a message-driven bean later in this chapter in the section, "Deploying a Message-Driven Bean."

CREATING A MESSAGE-DRIVEN BEAN

Creating a message-driven bean is not that complicated. They really are much easier to create than session or entity beans because you don't have to worry about creating a home or a component interface for them. To create a message-driven bean, your class must implement two required interfaces:

- The javax.ejb.MessageDrivenBean interface
- The javax.jms.MessageListener interface

THE MessageDrivenBean INTERFACE

The first interface that your message-driven bean must implement is the javax.ejb.MessageDrivenBean interface. Table 11.1 lists the methods that are part of the MessageDrivenBean interface.

TABLE 11.1 METHODS OF THE `javax.ejb.MessageDrivenBean` INTERFACE

Name	Description
ejbRemove	Called by the container before an instance is removed from service.
setMessageDrivenContext	The container passes an instance of a `MessageDrivenContext` interface to a bean. The bean will normally hold this context as part of its instance state and allows the bean to get access to the context held onto by the container.

The `ejbRemove` method will be called on a message-driven bean just before the instance is about to be removed by the container. The bean should release any resources that it is holding. The resources could be JDBC connections, a JavaMail session, or other finite resources that need to be cleaned up and released.

Note

The message-driven bean does not have to clean up any resources related to the JMS destination it's listening on. The container will handle those responsibilities.

The `setMessageDrivenContext` method takes a single argument, which is an object that implements the `javax.ejb.MessageDrivenContext` interface. This object provides access to the runtime message-driven context that the container associates with each message-driven bean. The `MessageDrivenContext` interface extends the `javax.ejb.EJBContext` and therefore provides access to security and transactional properties and methods. Table 11.2 describes the methods that are available through the `MessageDrivenContext` instance passed to the message-driven bean instance.

TABLE 11.2 METHODS OF THE `MessageDrivenContext` INTERFACE

Name	Description
getCallerPrincipal	Obtain the security principal that identifies the caller.
getEJBHome	Obtain the bean's home interface. Because the message-driven bean doesn't have a home interface, this is not a valid method to call on this type of bean.
setRollbackOnly	Mark the current transaction for rollback. A transaction marked for rollback can never commit.
getRollbackOnly	Test to see whether the current transaction has been marked for rollback.
getUserTransaction	Obtain the transaction demarcation interface. This is only used for bean-managed transactions.
isCallerInRole	Test to see whether the caller has a specific security role.
getEJBLocalHome	Obtain the bean's local home interface.

The MessageDrivenContext interface doesn't define any new methods itself. The methods displayed in Table 11.2 are inherited from the EJBContext interface. Future versions of this interface might define more methods that are specific to the message-driven bean context.

> **Caution**
>
> Because the message-driven bean doesn't have a home interface, calling the getEJBHome or getEJBLocalHome method on a message-driven bean will throw a java.lang. IllegalStateException. It's only there because the specific context classes for the three enterprise beans all extend EJBContext.

> **Note**
>
> There are several methods in the EJBContext interface that have been deprecated. Those methods are not listed in Table 11.2. See Appendix A for a complete listing of the deprecated methods in the EJBContext interface.

THE JMS MessageListener INTERFACE

The second required interface is the javax.jms.MessageListener interface. All message-driven beans must also implement this interface. This is the same interface that regular JMS message consumers must implement also. The MessageListener interface defines a single method that must be implemented:

```
public void onMessage(javax.jms.Message msg);
```

The container calls this method when a message arrives at the JMS destination and the bean instance should service it. The onMessage method is the method where your business logic should go. Obviously, you can have other public and private methods in your message-driven bean and call those from the onMessage method, but it all starts from here.

The onMessage method contains a single argument, which is the javax.jms.Message that the container is asking the bean instance to handle.

> **Note**
>
> Remember that javax.jms.Message is an interface, and several JMS message types implement this interface. If you are not sure which message type to expect, you can determine it programmatically using the instanceof operator.

→ If you need a refresher on the JMS interfaces and classes, **see** "Java Message Service," **p. 265**.

The onMessage method should not be declared final or static. It must be declared public and have a void return type. It must also not throw any application or runtime exceptions. If something happens that would normally cause one of these exceptions, you should just catch the exception, log the information, and return.

→ For more information on exception handling for message-driven beans, **see** "Exception Handling," **p. 363**.

The EJB 2.0 Specification supports only JMS messaging, so all message-driven beans currently are JMS message-driven beans, to be precise. This is why the requirement to implement the `javax.jms.MessageListener` interface is an absolute one. When other messaging types are supported by the specification, you'll have choices other than `javax.jms.MessageListener` for your message-driven beans.

CREATING THE MESSAGE-DRIVEN BEAN CLASS

The main work in creating the actual message-driven bean class is ensuring that you have implemented the two required interfaces and that you provide the business logic when the `onMessage` method is called. The rest of the work for creating the message-driven bean class is done during deployment.

In Chapter 10, "Java Message Service," we created a class called `AuctionNotificationConsumer` in Listing 10.2. We mentioned in that section that we would eventually replace this consumer with a message-driven bean. We'll show an example of using a message-driven bean to listen on a JMS `Queue` for messages and then send an e-mail message using an e-mail service that we'll build later. We will be developing the details of the e-mail service and some other common services for an application later in Chapter 21, "Horizontal Services."

Listing 11.1 shows the equivalent of the class from Chapter 10 now implemented as a message-driven bean.

LISTING 11.1   `AuctionNotificationConsumer` **FROM CHAPTER 10 IMPLEMENTED AS A MESSAGE-DRIVEN BEAN**

```
/**
 * Title:        AuctionNotificationMessageBean
 * Description:  The Message-driven bean gets messages from a Queue
 *               and delegates to the horizontal service.
 */
package com.que.ejb20.notification;

import javax.ejb.MessageDrivenBean;
import javax.ejb.MessageDrivenContext;
import javax.jms.JMSException;
import javax.jms.Message;
import javax.jms.ObjectMessage;
import javax.jms.MessageListener;
import com.que.ejb20.services.email.Emailable;
import com.que.ejb20.services.email.EmailService;
import com.que.ejb20.services.email.EmailException;

public class AuctionNotificationMessageBean implements
  MessageDrivenBean, MessageListener {
```

LISTING 11.1   CONTINUED

```java
  private MessageDrivenContext ctx = null;

  // Default Constructor
  public AuctionNotificationMessageBean() {
    super();
  }

  // This is where the real work happens
  public void onMessage( Message jmsMessage ) {
    if ( jmsMessage instanceof ObjectMessage) {
      try {
        Object obj = ((ObjectMessage)jmsMessage).getObject();
        if ( obj instanceof Emailable ) {
          sendEmail( (Emailable)obj );
        }
      }catch( JMSException ex ) {
        ex.printStackTrace();
      }
    }
  }

  // Delegate to the horizontal service
  private void sendEmail( Emailable emailableMsg ){
    try{
      EmailService.sendEmail( emailableMsg );
    }catch( EmailException ex ){
      // Just print out the exception and move on
      ex.printStackTrace();
    }
  }

  // Associate the private reference with this context so
  // that this bean can use the context if neccessary
  public void setMessageDrivenContext( MessageDrivenContext ctx ){
    this.ctx = ctx;
  }

  public void ejbCreate(){
    // This method is required, but you
    // don't have to do anything with it
  }

  public void ejbRemove(){
    // This method is required, but you
    // are not required to do anything
  }
}
```

PART

I

CH

11

The main difference you should see between Listing 11.1 and Listing 10.2 from Chapter 10 is that you don't have to worry about getting connected to the JMS-administered objects. All you need to worry about is implementing the onMessage method and performing the business logic correctly. This is nice and in line with the EJB architecture because it allows the bean provider to focus more on the business logic.

In the onMessage in Listing 11.1, the business logic is simply to ensure that the message is of the correct type and then to call the e-mail horizontal service.

→ If you are curious about how the e-mail is implemented by the horizontal service, **see** "Building an E-Mail Horizontal Service," **p. 552**.

The other thing to notice from Listing 11.1 is that, even though you might not want to do anything with the ejbCreate or ejbRemove methods, you must still implement them in your class.

There are some general restrictions for the message-driven bean class. The following list summarizes the rules that you must follow when creating your message-driven bean classes:

- The bean must be declared as public.
- The bean can't be declared as final or abstract.
- The bean must declare a no-argument constructor.
- The bean must not implement the finalize method.

You are allowed to declare superclasses and subclasses for the message-driven bean. If you do use these, you are allowed to implement the setMessageDrivenContext or ejbRemove methods in a parent class so that all the subclasses can just inherit those implementations. Listing 11.2 illustrates an abstract implementation for a message-driven bean. Subclasses only need to provide an implementation for the onMessage method when extending this class.

LISTING 11.2 AN ABSTRACT IMPLEMENTATION THAT MESSAGE-DRIVEN BEANS CAN EXTEND

```
/**
 * Title:        AbstractMessageDrivenBean
 * Description:  An abstract implementation for a MessageDrivenBean. Subclasses
 *               only need to implement the onMessage method
 */
package com.que.ejb20.notification;

import javax.ejb.MessageDrivenBean;
import javax.ejb.MessageDrivenContext;
import javax.jms.Message;
import javax.jms.MessageListener;
import com.que.ejb20.services.email.Emailable;
import com.que.ejb20.services.email.EmailService;
import com.que.ejb20.services.email.EmailException;

abstract public class AbstractMessageDrivenBean implements
  MessageDrivenBean, MessageListener {

  private MessageDrivenContext ctx = null;

  // Associate the private reference with this context so
  // that this bean can use the context if necessary
  public void setMessageDrivenContext( MessageDrivenContext ctx ){
    this.ctx = ctx;
  }
```

LISTING 11.2 CONTINUED

```
public void ejbCreate(){
  // This method is required, but you
  // don't have to do anything with it
}

public void ejbRemove(){
  // This method is required, but you
  // are not required to do anything
}

// Concrete subclasses must provide an implementation for
// the onMessage method
abstract public void onMessage();
}
```

If we modified the `AuctionNotificationMessageBean` class from Listing 11.1 to extend the abstract message-driven bean class in Listing 11.2, it would look like the class in Listing 11.3.

LISTING 11.3   `NewAuctionNotificationMessageBean` EXTENDING THE `AbstractMessageDrivenBean`

```
/**
 * Title:        NewAuctionNotificationMessageBean
 * Description:  The Message-driven bean gets messages from a Queue
 *               and delegates to the horizontal service.
 */
package com.que.ejb20.notification;

import javax.jms.Message;
import javax.jms.ObjectMessage;
import javax.jms.JMSException;
import com.que.ejb20.services.email.Emailable;
import com.que.ejb20.services.email.EmailService;
import com.que.ejb20.services.email.EmailException;

public class NewAuctionNotificationMessageBean
  extends AbstractMessageDrivenBean {

  // Default Constructor
  public NewAuctionNotificationMessageBean() {
    super();
  }

  // This is where the real work happens
  public void onMessage( Message jmsMessage ) {
    if ( jmsMessage instanceof ObjectMessage) {
      try {
        Object obj = ((ObjectMessage)jmsMessage).getObject();
        if ( obj instanceof Emailable ) {
          sendEmail( (Emailable)obj );
        }
```

LISTING 11.3   CONTINUED

```
      }catch( JMSException ex ) {
        ex.printStackTrace();
      }
    }
  }

  // Delegate to the horizontal service
  private void sendEmail( Emailable emailableMsg ){
    try{
      EmailService.sendEmail( emailableMsg );
    }catch( EmailException ex ){
      // Just print out the exception and move on
      ex.printStackTrace();
    }
  }
}
```

The benefit of putting some of the behavior up in the parent class is that the concrete classes are a little smaller and easier to maintain. You also get the normal benefits that you get with inheritance and using default implementations.

DEPLOYING A MESSAGE-DRIVEN BEAN

Because we are not specifying the JMS objects that the message-driven bean connects to in the class itself, it must be somewhere. That somewhere is in the deployment descriptor for the bean. This is referred to as specifying the connection information declaratively. If we specified the connection information inside the source code, we would say that it's programmatic. This is another nice feature because we can change the JMS destination during deployment and not have to modify the source code.

AN EXAMPLE MESSAGE-DRIVEN BEAN DEPLOYMENT DESCRIPTOR

To deploy your message-driven bean, you must add a `message-driven` element to the `ejb-xml.jar` file. The main things that are specified for a message-driven bean are

- Whether the message-driven bean is for a `Topic` or `Queue`
- If the bean is for a `Topic`, whether it's durable or nondurable
- The transaction attributes for the bean
- The acknowledge semantics to use for beans that use bean-managed transactions

Listing 11.4 shows a deployment descriptor for the message-driven bean in Listing 11.1.

LISTING 11.4   AuctionNotificationMessageBean DEPLOYMENT DESCRIPTOR

```
<!DOCTYPE ejb-jar PUBLIC
"-//Sun Microsystems, Inc.//DTD Enterprise JavaBeans 2.0//EN"
"http://java.sun.com/dtd/ejb-jar_2_0.dtd">
```

LISTING 11.4   CONTINUED

```
<ejb-jar>
 <enterprise-beans>
    <message-driven>
      <ejb-name>AuctionNotificationMessageBean</ejb-name>
      <ejb-class>
         com.que.ejb20.notification.AuctionNotificationMessageBean
      </ejb-class>
      <transaction-type>Container</transaction-type>
      <message-driven-destination>
        <jms-destination-type>javax.jms.Queue</jms-destination-type>
      </message-driven-destination>
      <security-identity>
      <run-as>
        <role-name></role-name>
      </run-as>
      </security-identity>
    </message-driven>
 </enterprise-beans>
</ejb-jar>
```

Other than the name of this message-driven bean, you can also see the type of JMS destination for which this bean is a listener. It also specifies the transaction type to be container-managed transactions and not bean-managed.

Caution

In one of the earlier versions of the EJB 2.0 Specification, the `ejb-name` element in the deployment descriptor was listed as optional. This should be fixed in the final version. The `ejb-name` is required or the container might have trouble using the transaction attribute configured for the bean.

→ This chapter covers only the basic information for deploying a message-driven bean. For a complete discussion of the message-driven bean deployment elements within the `ejb-jar.xml` file, **see** Chapter 15, "Deployment."

Listing 11.2 shows the deployment descriptor, which is normally created by the bean provider. As part of the deployment or assembly of the rest of the application, a vendor-specific deployment descriptor must be created as well. Listing 11.5 shows an example of what the vendor-specific deployment descriptor looks like for WebLogic 6.1.

LISTING 11.5   WEBLOGIC 6.1 DEPLOYMENT DESCRIPTOR FOR
`AuctionNotificationMessageBean`

```
<?xml version="1.0"?>

<!DOCTYPE weblogic-ejb-jar PUBLIC
"-//BEA Systems, Inc.//DTD WebLogic 6.0.0 EJB//EN"
"http://www.bea.com/servers/wls600/dtd/weblogic-ejb-jar.dtd">
```

PART

I

CH

11

LISTING 11.5 CONTINUED

```
<weblogic-ejb-jar>
  <weblogic-enterprise-bean>
    <ejb-name>AuctionNotificationMessageBean</ejb-name>
    <message-driven-descriptor>
      <pool>
        <max-beans-in-free-pool>30</max-beans-in-free-pool>
        <initial-beans-in-free-pool>10</initial-beans-in-free-pool>
      </pool>
      <destination-jndi-name>
         com.que.ejb20book.notification.Queue
      </destination-jndi-name>
    </message-driven-descriptor>
  </weblogic-enterprise-bean>
</weblogic-ejb-jar>
```

The deployment descriptor in Listing 11.5 is WebLogic-specific. However, you can get an idea of what types of things can be specified by a vendor. For example, the WebLogic deployment descriptor specifies how many instances of this message-driven bean are initially created when the container starts up, as well as the actual name of the JMS destination as specified in the JNDI naming service.

SENDING MESSAGES TO A MESSAGE-DRIVEN BEAN

Because the message-driven bean has no remote or home interface, it is not called directly by a client. In fact, only the container communicates with the message-driven bean instance directly by calling the onMessage method and passing a JMS message from the destination.

As a message-driven bean provider, you don't have to do anything more than provide the necessary business logic when the onMessage method is called and to ensure that the deployment information is correct. From that point, the container manages the life cycle of the bean instances.

ACKNOWLEDGING MESSAGES FROM MESSAGE-DRIVEN BEANS

You should not use the client message acknowledgment methods defined in the JMS API to acknowledge messages to the client. Because there is no direct connection between the client and the message-driven bean, the container handles the message acknowledgment automatically. That way, the container handles it depending on whether you are using container-managed transaction demarcation or bean-managed demarcation.

If you are using container-managed transactions, the container will acknowledge the message as part of the transaction commit; however, you should set the bean's transaction attribute to Required. If you are using bean-managed transactions, the acknowledgment can't be part of the transaction commit because the JMS message receipt is out of the scope of the bean's transaction. If you are using bean-managed transactions, you can specify the acknowledge-mode in the deployment descriptor. You can specify either AUTO_ACKNOWLEDGE or DUPS_OK_ACKNOWLEDGE. If no value is specified in the acknowledge-mode tag, AUTO_ACKNOWLEDGE is the default.

USING TRANSACTIONS WITH MESSAGE-DRIVEN BEANS

As with session beans, message-driven beans can use either bean-managed transactions or container-managed transactions. Because a client has no way to call the message-driven bean directly, the client can't propagate its transaction context to the message-driven bean. The container will always call the onMessage method with a transaction context that is specified in the bean's deployment descriptor.

Therefore, a message-driven bean that is using container-managed transaction should specify either the Required or NotSupported transaction attribute in the ejb-jar.xml file. This is because if the message-driven bean needs a transaction, the container will have to create one before calling the onMessage method, because there's no chance to propagate a transaction from the client. If the message-driven bean doesn't need a transaction, you should specify the NotSupported transaction attribute.

→ For more information on transactions, **see** Chapter 12, "Transactions."

TROUBLESHOOTING

THE onMessage METHOD IS NOT BEING CALLED

My onMessage method is not being called by the container.

Make sure that the JMS destination for which the message-driven bean is a consumer is set up. Each vendor might have a unique way of setting up the JMS destinations. Also check that the destination type and name that are declared in the deployment descriptors match what are actually configured.

SECURITY IDENTITY FOR A MESSAGE-DRIVEN BEAN

How do I set up a security identity for a message-driven bean?

Because a message-driven bean can't be seen directly by a client, the client's security principal can't be propagated to the container. However, you can configure a message-driven bean to assume a security identity so that it can be propagated to other EJBs during the onMessage processing.

CHAPTER **12**

TRANSACTIONS

In this chapter

UNDERSTANDING TRANSACTIONS

Transactions are at the heart of business applications, and the support the EJB container provides for them arguably tops the list of J2EE's benefits. You've gotten an introduction to transactions within EJB in earlier chapters, but now it's time to look at the details. The goal of this chapter is to explain some of the concepts behind transactional processing and equip you with what you need to know to build EJB applications that execute transactions correctly.

A transaction is a general business concept that represents an exchange between two parties. When you walk into a department store and purchase a shirt, you're exchanging some form of payment for an item sold by the store. The exchange that takes place defines the boundaries of a sales transaction. Both your payment to the salesperson and the act of the salesperson giving you the shirt make up the transaction. If either action were to happen without the other, the transaction wouldn't be valid and the sale would never occur.

The principal characteristic of a transaction is that it groups individual actions together into a single activity that has greater significance. The idea is that relatively small actions can take on more meaning when they're viewed as part of some bigger picture. Grouping actions into transactions this way is part of everyday life. It's such an everyday occurrence, you probably don't spend much time thinking about it. You participate in a transaction every time you shop at a store, make a reservation with an airline, visit an ATM, or perform countless other exchanges. The fact that transactions are so much a part of the real world makes it a given that they show up in the software that models parts of the real world, too.

Software applications that address business problems of any complexity must support the concept of transactions because an application is useful only if it accurately reflects the nature of the business it models. When looking at anything from high-level business logic down to low-level communications protocols, software is continually relied on to execute operations that must be performed as a set for the outcome to have any validity. No matter what type of programming you do, transactions are important to you.

For a desktop application that manipulates data stored by the local file system or a local database, a transaction is relatively easy to support. The single user of the system performs some operations that are either applied to the underlying data or they're not. Some level of error handling and undo functionality are needed, but overall it's not too difficult a program to build. It's when a single transaction needs to be applied to distributed applications that access multiple databases and other resources that the true complexity of reliable transaction processing comes into play. That's the topic of the most interest to an EJB developer.

No matter what the size or complexity of an application, every transaction associated with it has a definite beginning and end. The process of establishing these boundaries is known as *transaction demarcation* and it is central to managing transactions. Any operations that occur between the boundaries of a transaction become associated with that transaction and are treated as a single unit of work. The effects of a transaction, which most often consist of updates to the contents of one or more databases, are made permanent by *committing* the transaction at its completion. The effects of a transaction must also be capable of being undone by a process known as *rolling back* the transaction before it has been committed. A transaction ends when either a commit or a rollback occurs.

The difficulty in implementing transactions in complex software systems is that changes to multiple resources must be coordinated so that commits and rollbacks are performed across all affected components of a system. It's also necessary to coordinate the work being done by multiple users accessing a system's shared data concurrently. Each of these is enough of a challenge when everything works as anticipated, but it's even more true when errors occur along the way. Of course, this is when transactions are the most beneficial. If failures never occurred, there would never be a need to roll back the effects of a transaction. It's when something does go wrong that transactional support makes it possible for the integrity of a system to be maintained.

This chapter looks at how J2EE application servers and EJB containers do much of the work required to handle distributed transactions for you. From your perspective as a developer, it's important that you understand what's being done for you by the container and what your role is. The EJB architecture removes you from much of the complexity of transaction management, but how you code and deploy your enterprise beans still determines how they can be used in a transactional application.

PASSING THE ACID TEST

The best way to describe how transactions must be supported by an application is to look at the criteria a transaction must satisfy to be valid. The four major characteristics of a transaction are that it must be *atomic*, *consistent*, *isolated*, and *durable*. These characteristics are commonly referred to using the mnemonic *ACID*. If an application's processing of a set of operations can't pass the ACID test, the operations aren't truly being performed as a transaction.

ATOMIC

The operations within a transaction must be treated as a single, atomic unit. This means that a transaction can only be considered complete and allowed to commit if every operation within it is performed successfully. If a failure occurs at any point, any operations that have been performed must be undone. In short, a transaction must be viewed as an all-or-nothing proposition.

Besides placing a constraint on how a transaction must be processed, the trait of atomicity should also influence how you define a particular transaction's boundaries. A transaction must represent a single unit of work that leaves a system in a valid state after executing in its entirety. If subsets of a transaction are valid on their own, it's possible that the transaction includes more work than it should. A transaction must include all the operations necessary to perform its atomic unit of work, but it shouldn't include any more. In an EJB architecture, the place to enforce this guideline is most often in your session bean methods. You should take the viewpoint that a bean method should implement only a single unit of work.

If a high-level operation from the client's point of view corresponds to multiple transactions in your system, you should define individual bean methods for each transaction and then expose another bean method to the client that wraps calls to each of the others.

In the auction example, the `AuctionManager` session bean must implement an `expireAuction` method that is called when the scheduled end time for an auction has been reached. The most important task for this method is to stop the auction by placing it into a state in which it no longer accepts bids. If the auction expires without a winner being assigned, stopping the auction by canceling it is all that needs to be done. However, if a valid winning bid has been placed, the auction needs to be closed, a winner assigned, and an e-mail notification sent. The auction is in a valid closed state only when the winner has been assigned and notified, so these three steps must all be executed or the auction cannot be properly closed. Grouping operations such as these into atomic units of work is the way to maintain transactional integrity in the auction system.

CONSISTENT

When a transaction's operations are performed as a whole, they must take the data they manipulate from one consistent state to another. A business application models real-world activities using data to represent aspects of the problem domain that's involved. This model is valid only if the associated data accurately represents the real world at the completion of each transaction. In terms of enforcement, the results of a transaction must not violate any business rules implemented within the objects that are accessed or any referential integrity constraints in the underlying database. Because of the atomic nature of transactions (and the fact that they're isolated, as you'll see next), inconsistencies after intermediate operations have been performed aren't a problem. What matters is that the integrity of the data must be guaranteed after a transaction has completed.

Transactional consistency can be illustrated with a simple example using a bank account. Suppose you're making a $100 withdrawal from your checking account using an ATM. You insert your card, key your PIN, and select the option to withdraw $100. The system first verifies that you have at least $100 in your account and that the ATM cash dispenser holds at least $100. Given that these conditions are met, the system debits your account, dispenses five $20 bills to you, and prints a receipt of the transaction. Assuming everything works as described, a consistent operation has been performed because the sum of your checking account balance and the cash in your wallet is the same both before and after the transaction. If anything had happened during the process to change that fact, then consistency would have been violated and the transaction would have been invalid. For example, if the cash dispenser reported that it dispensed $100 when it really only gave you $80, you would quickly be pleading your case for a "rollback" at the closest branch office you could find.

ISOLATED

Companies deploy large-scale distributed systems to support the demands placed on applications by many simultaneous users who require access to shared data. Distributed architectures allow systems to perform at an acceptable pace when accessed by many users, but to be of any benefit, they must isolate concurrent access to the underlying data. In particular, a transaction being executed by one user must be processed in such a way that no other user sees its effects unless (and until) it's committed. Each transaction must appear to be the only transaction being processed. If a concurrent user were exposed to the intermediate results of a transaction that eventually rolled back, any subsequent operations based on that invalid state could compromise the integrity of the system's data. Concurrent transactions must be isolated so that they produce the same results that would occur if they had been run sequentially.

Looking at the auction example, a transaction to submit a bid includes several steps that must be isolated from other transactions. When the submitBid method of EnglishAuctionBean is called, it must make sure that the auction is still open and accepting bids and, if so, that the submitted bid amount is greater than or equal to the required next bid amount. If the bid amount is valid, a new Bid object is created and assigned to be the auction's new leading bid. If other transactions were allowed to operate on the data used by submitBid during this transaction, errors could occur in the system. For example, if another transaction were to close the auction after the transaction to submit the bid checked the auction's status but before it created the new bid, the true winner of the auction would be in question. Also, a simultaneous bid submission could result in a bid lower than the one preceding it being accepted if the two transactions checked the required next bid amount before either of them created a new bid.

DURABLE

When a transaction commits, any data updates made by that transaction must be *durable*. This means that the results of a committed transaction must persist regardless of any failure (short of a catastrophe) that occurs after its completion. What this first implies is that when a database or other persistent storage resource is being used, a transaction's updates must be physically written to that resource before the transaction can be reported as having successfully completed. At that point, durability is typically achieved using a failure recovery mechanism. This mechanism might be a backup copy of a database that reflects each update made or a log of permanent data changes that could be used to reconstruct the data in the event of a failure.

In the auction example, a submitted bid accepted by the system must be stored in the database and made durable. If a leading bid were lost and a lower bid were later accepted and declared the winner of the auction, it would violate the business rules of the site and likely destroy any confidence in the system held by the bidders. Backup mechanisms for a database are outside the scope of this book, but by using EJB, the durability requirement of saving updates to the database before declaring a transaction complete is at least satisfied.

PROGRAMMING WITH THE JAVA TRANSACTION API

With a general understanding of transactions under your belt, it's time to look more at how transactions are supported by the J2EE platform. To provide the transactional capabilities needed by a J2EE application, an EJB container is required to support the high-level interface

PART
I

CH
12

defined by the Java Transaction API (JTA) for transaction demarcation. Don't worry if you don't know what that means just yet. The best way to understand JTA and its role in EJB is to look at how it relates to several key specifications on transaction processing. This background will help you see the big picture into which JTA fits and get a quick introduction to the terminology involved in describing transactional systems.

THE OBJECT TRANSACTION SERVICE

The worlds of object-oriented development and transactions were brought together by the Object Management Group's (OMG) specification of the CORBA Object Transaction Service (OTS) in 1994. If you've done any CORBA development, you're already quite familiar with OMG and their work in the distributed object arena. The goal of OTS was to define a set of interfaces that could support performing a transaction across multiple distributed objects. Transactions were nothing new to software at this point, but this effort was needed to apply the benefits of object-oriented development to transactional distributed processing. This work was done in conjunction with the international open systems organization X/Open to build on their Distributed Transaction Processing (DTP) model. You'll see X/Open referenced in much of the literature on transactions, but the organization has since become known as the Open Group.

The DTP is a model that came out of the Open Group vendor consortium and became the accepted standard for commercial database servers and other transactional systems. It defines how a transactional application interacts with components designated as resource managers and transaction managers to execute distributed transactions. You need to understand these two terms to see where responsibilities are placed within an architecture such as EJB to manage transactions.

To start with the basics, you must be clear on what constitutes a resource. A system that provides data and information services to an application is referred to as an Enterprise Information System (EIS) within J2EE. EIS examples include relational databases and ERP systems. Using the terminology of this chapter, an EIS isn't a resource itself, but it does contain and manage resources. For example, the rows of data held in a database and the business objects provided by an ERP system can be considered resources.

A *resource manager* is a system, such as a database server, an ERP, or a message queue, that makes one or more resources accessible to an application. An application communicates with a resource manager using an adapter (or driver) provided by the resource manager. A JDBC driver is the resource manager adapter you see most often when doing Java development. This particular type of adapter is a vendor-specific (meaning resource manager specific in this case) Java class that allows a client application to communicate with a certain type of database server and access data in a database (the resource). For the purposes of this chapter, the resource managers of the most interest are the ones that can participate in transactions that are controlled by an external transaction manager. These usually are known as *transactional resource managers*.

A *transaction manager* is a component responsible for providing the low-level transaction interaction between an application and one or more resource managers. A transaction manager allows resource managers to associate their resources with a transaction through a process called *enlistment*. The transaction manager provides the demarcation of a transaction by notifying the enlisted resources when the transaction starts, maintaining the associations between the transaction and its enlisted resources until it ends (by committing or rolling back), and then allowing the resources to delist themselves. The transaction manager plays the role of traffic cop in some respects. For example, if a transaction that includes an update to a row in a database needs to be rolled back, the transaction manager is responsible for directing what takes place but not for actually doing it. When directed to perform a rollback by the transaction manager, it is the responsibility of the resource manager (the database server, in this example) to roll back the update. A resource manager actually "manages" the consistency of its resources. A transaction manager provides instructions, but the individual resource managers are responsible for performing the commits and rollbacks that affect their resources.

A transactional resource manager must support two types of interfaces: one for use by applications and one for use by transaction managers. The application interface is likely more familiar to you because, in the case of relational databases, it includes functionality such as acquiring a connection and issuing SQL statements. The X/Open DTP model doesn't address this interface because it's specific to the type of resource manager your application is accessing. To interact with a transaction manager, a resource manager also must provide an interface that can be used to associate a resource with a transaction, inform the resource manager that a transaction needs to be committed or rolled back, and incorporate the resource manager in a two-phase commit operation.

A two-phase commit allows a transaction manager to include several resource managers in a transaction while ensuring that either every associated resource is updated when a commit is attempted or none of them are. This strategy consists of instructing each resource manager to prepare to commit the current transaction and report back to the transaction manager if a permanent commit of the changes will be successful. If every enlisted resource votes to proceed, the transaction manager issues the command to perform the actual commit. Otherwise, each resource manager is instructed to roll back the transaction. Some definite overhead is associated with a two-phase commit because a resource manager that reports that it can proceed must maintain any state related to its affected resources until the command to complete the transaction is received. For example, it might have to keep any locks or persist temporary data used to recover from an operation.

The interface a resource manager exposes for use by transaction managers is defined by the X/Open XA interface specification. This is where the operations needed to associate a resource with a transaction and perform two-phase commit requests are found. X/Open XA is a two-way interface that also specifies the operations that a transaction manager must expose to resource managers. This side of the XA interface consists of the two functions a resource manager calls to enlist itself in a transaction and later delist itself. The interface a transaction manager implements for use by an application is defined by the X/Open TX specification. The TX interface gives the application the access it needs to control transaction demarcation and a few other options such as defining a transaction timeout value. You'll see more about this interface later in the chapter. Figure 12.1 identifies the interfaces between the components defined by the DTP model.

Figure 12.1
The X/Open Distributed Transaction Processing model defines the participants in a distributed transaction.

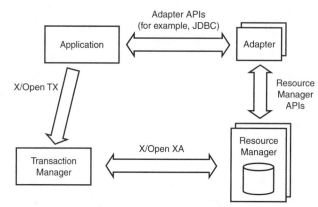

When an application needs to execute a transaction, it sends a request to a transaction manager. The transaction manager is then responsible for starting the transaction and associating it with a transaction context that is propagated to each of the resource managers participating in the transaction. This transaction context remains valid until the transaction is either committed or rolled back under the direction of the transaction manager.

A variant of this process is the concept of a heuristic decision, which refers to one or more of the resource managers in a transaction making the decision to commit or roll back without being directed to do so by the transaction manager. This is not typical and usually occurs only in situations such as a communications failure that prevents the normal interaction with the transaction manager from taking place. If you consider the ACID characteristics required of a transaction, you can see the danger in a heuristic decision occurring. If some resources in a transaction commit and others don't, the operation is no longer atomic and data consistency has likely been lost. Because this can quickly lead to integrity problems, the DTP includes the capability to report the occurrence of a heuristic decision. This is carried forward in OTS by several exceptions that a resource manager can throw to indicate that a heuristic decision has played a part in a commit or rollback.

If you understand the components and interactions defined by DTP, understanding OTS only requires that you think of all the components as distributed objects. OTS extends the DTP model by specifying the implementation of the XA and TX interfaces using CORBA IDL and by specifying IIOP as the communications backbone to be used for interactions between the objects involved. From the specification, the purpose of the transaction service defined by OTS is then to

- Control the scope and duration of a transaction
- Allow multiple objects to be involved in a single, atomic transaction
- Allow objects to associate changes in their internal state with a transaction
- Coordinate the completion of transactions

The OTS specification also defines nested transactions and a synchronization interface as optional features of an implementation. A *nested transaction* is a set of operations associated with a parent transaction that can be committed or rolled back as a unit but will only be made permanent if the parent transaction is eventually committed as well. Transactions that treat all operations as part of a single, non-nested unit are called *flat transactions*. The synchronization interface defined by OTS can be used by a transaction manager to notify a registered object when a commit is about to occur or when a commit or rollback has just completed.

> **Note**
>
> You can download a copy of the OTS specification from the formal specifications section of OMG's Web site, http://www.omg.org/. After its initial release, the specification was repackaged as the Transaction Service Specification v1.1, but the content remained the same. At the time of this writing, the current release was version 1.2.

THE JAVA TRANSACTION API

The JTA defines a set of Java interfaces that specify how a transaction manager communicates with an application, a resource manager, and the application server in a J2EE architecture. The primary interfaces found in the JTA consist of

- A high-level interface, javax.transaction.UserInterface, that can be used by an application to start and complete transactions using methods that mirror the X/Open TX interface.
- The javax.transaction.xa.XAResource interface, which is a Java mapping of the X/Open XA interface that can be implemented by a resource adapter, such as a JDBC driver or a JMS provider. The methods declared by this interface allow the associated resources to participate in transactions controlled by an external transaction manager. This interface includes optional support for two-phase commits.
- The javax.transaction.TransactionManager interface, which defines the methods implemented by a transaction manager for use by an application server in managing transaction boundaries on behalf of an application.

Figure 12.2 illustrates where the various interfaces come into play. It's important to remember here that JTA defines these interfaces but it doesn't include implementations for any of them. It's up to the application server and resource adapter vendors to implement the parts of JTA that apply to them.

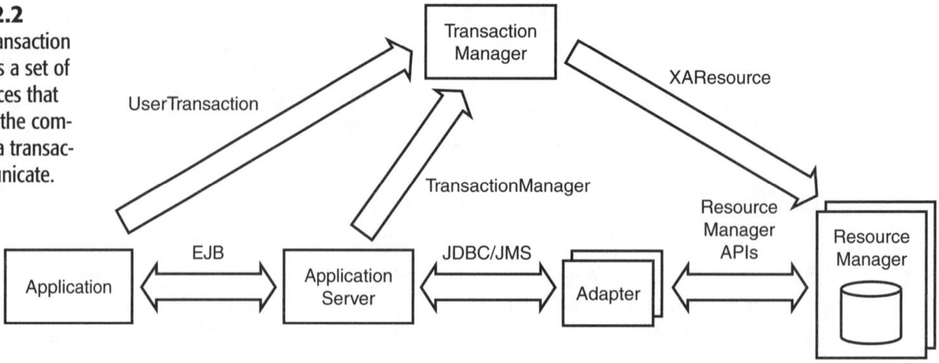

Figure 12.2
The Java Transaction API specifies a set of Java interfaces that define how the components in a transaction communicate.

> **Note**
>
> As shown in Figure 12.2, an application server and a transaction manager are viewed as separate components. However, application server vendors include a transaction manager as part of their products. This chapter discusses the division of responsibilities between the two, but, as an EJB developer, you usually can view them as a single component of your systems.

JTA includes a few supporting interfaces beyond those shown in Figure 12.2 and several exception classes. For example, the `javax.transaction` package declares `HeuristicCommitException`, `HeuristicMixedException`, and `HeuristicRollbackException` to report heuristic decisions that affect the outcome of a transaction using the mechanism defined by OTS. Of the interfaces declared by JTA, the three that already been mentioned are the most important. For the discussion here, `UserTransaction` is of the most interest because it is the only part of JTA that an EJB container is specifically required to support. This interface is made up of the methods shown in the following declaration:

```
public interface UserTransaction {

  public void begin() throws NotSupportedException, SystemException;

  public void commit() throws RollbackException, HeuristicMixedException,
    HeuristicRollbackException, java.lang.SecurityException,
    java.lang.IllegalStateException, SystemException;

  public void rollback() throws java.lang.IllegalStateException,
    java.lang.SecurityException, SystemException;

  public void setRollbackOnly() throws java.lang.IllegalStateException,
    SystemException;

  public int getStatus() throws SystemException;

  public void setTransactionTimeout(int seconds) throws SystemException;
}
```

UserTransaction is supported by the javax.transaction.Status interface, which defines the following constants that can be used to interpret the values returned from the getStatus method:

```
public interface Status {
  public final static int STATUS_ACTIVE;
  public final static int STATUS_COMMITTED;
  public final static int STATUS_COMMITTING;
  public final static int STATUS_MARKED_ROLLBACK;
  public final static int STATUS_NO_TRANSACTION;
  public final static int STATUS_PREPARED;
  public final static int STATUS_PREPARING;
  public final static int STATUS_ROLLEDBACK;
  public final static int STATUS_ROLLING_BACK;
  public final static int STATUS_UNKNOWN;
}
```

From an application programming standpoint, the UserTransaction interface is all you need from JTA to communicate with a transaction manager to control distributed transactions. The rest of JTA defines lower-level interactions that are needed only by the application server. You can programmatically demarcate transactions using the methods defined by UserTransaction. As an alternative, you can instead use a declarative approach that instructs the EJB container to transparently manage demarcation for you. You'll see more about each of these approaches in the next two sections.

A transaction managed by the J2EE platform is referred to as a *JTA transaction*. You'll also see the terms *global transaction* and *XA transaction* used. The transaction manager associates a transaction context with each calling thread that either references the caller's JTA transaction or is set to null if there is no associated transaction. The context is held by an object that implements the javax.transaction.Transaction interface. This JTA interface is used under the hood to perform steps such as enlisting resources with a transaction and instructing it to commit or roll back. Transaction declares the following methods:

```
public interface Transaction {

  public void commit() throws RollbackException, HeuristicMixedException,
    HeuristicRollbackException, java.lang.SecurityException, SystemException;

  public boolean delistResource(XAResource xaRes, int flag)
    throws java.lang.IllegalStateException, SystemException;

  public boolean enlistResource(XAResource xaRes) throws RollbackException,
    java.lang.IllegalStateException, SystemException;

  public int getStatus() throws SystemException;

  public void registerSynchronization(Synchronization sync)
    throws RollbackException, java.lang.IllegalStateException,
    SystemException;

  public void rollback() throws java.lang.IllegalStateException,
    SystemException;

  public void setRollbackOnly() throws java.lang.IllegalStateException,
```

PART

I

CH

12

```
        SystemException;
}
```

You can start a JTA transaction using `UserTransaction` or the EJB container can do it through `TransactionManager`. Both of these interfaces declare a `begin` method for this purpose. Regardless of how it is started, a JTA transaction is associated with the calling thread and is automatically propagated between components in your application and any resources that are enlisted with the transaction. The transaction manager communicates with enlisted resource managers through the methods of `XAResource`. When a resource is first accessed within a given transaction, an `XAResource` reference is obtained by the application server. This is accomplished with a call to a method such as the `getXAResource` method declared by the `javax.sql.XAConnection` interface that can be implemented by JDBC drivers. The application server associates the resource manager that this `XAResource` represents with a transaction by calling the `enlistResource` method of `Transaction`. The transaction manager then calls the `start` method of the `XAResource` with an identifier for the transaction. At this point, the application server supplies a connection to the resource manager to the application. All operations performed through this connection are associated with the transaction. After the desired work has been performed and a request is made by the application or the container to commit the transaction, the transaction manager calls the `end` method on the `XAResource` followed by its `prepare` and `commit` methods (assuming a two-phase commit is being performed).

Note

The `javax.sql.XAConnection` and `javax.sql.XADataSource` interfaces were introduced as part of JDBC 2.0 to allow JDBC drivers to support distributed transactions. An object that implements `XADataSource` serves as a factory for `XAConnection` objects.

Although the preceding sequence of steps referred to only a single resource manager, the value of `XAResource` is realized most when multiple resource managers are enlisted with a transaction. It's in this situation that a two-phase commit is beneficial. If only a single resource manager is accessed within a transaction, the commit or rollback of the transaction can be executed by that resource manager without the need to perform a two-phase commit. This is true even if multiple application servers access a single resource manager, such as a database, as part of the same transaction. What matters is the number of resource managers involved and the transaction manager's ability to recognize that all access to the resource is part of the same transaction. As with anything of value, a two-phase commit has costs associated with it. As mentioned previously, the work required by a resource manager to prepare for a commit and report its status back to the transaction manager has a certain amount of overhead associated with it. If a two-phase commit isn't necessary, the transaction manager can improve performance by bypassing the call to `prepare` and instructing the single `XAResource` to simply commit its work. This optimization, which is referred to as one-phase commit, is a required capability for transaction managers that satisfies the J2EE Connector Architecture Specification.

Key to EJB's capability to execute distributed transactions is its facility for propagating the transaction context between components. For example, if a transaction is started to support the work of a session bean method that accesses several entity bean instances to modify an underlying database, the transaction context is associated with each bean instance and the database operations that are executed without any explicit programming on your part. This is known as *implicit propagation* and it is another way that the EJB architecture lightens the burden on you as a developer. A JTA transaction is not limited to propagation across application tier components, but can also include a Java client application or JSPs and servlets and their supporting classes. Combining multiple components and resources under a single JTA transaction is obviously a complex feat, but to you, it's transparent.

→ The EJB 2.0 Specification doesn't require the propagation of the transaction context between EJB containers provided by different vendors. To learn more about the implications of this, **see** "Transaction Interoperability," **p. 517**.

The opposite of a JTA (or global) transaction is a local transaction. A local transaction describes the behavior of a resource manager when it directs its commit and rollback decisions without input from an external transaction manager. When working with multiple resource managers, a JTA transaction provides the coordination across distributed resources needed by your applications. When a resource manager executes a local transaction, updates to the associated resources are committed or rolled back independently of any other components and resources accessed by the application. If a JTA transaction is used, the work done by all resource managers enlisted with the transaction can be managed collectively and either committed or rolled back as an atomic unit.

Note

Use of local transactions is discouraged only when multiple resource managers are being accessed by an application. When a single resource manager is being used, a local transaction can be a valuable performance optimization. As mentioned previously, using a one-phase commit optimization is one option a transaction manager can use to improve performance when working with a single resource manager. As an alternative, a container can avoid the overhead of the transaction manager altogether and instruct the resource manager to use a local transaction. If the container provides either of these optimizations, they are handled transparently to you as an application developer.

PART

I

CH

12

Although most examples of transactions are based on accessing relational databases, it's important to remember that a transaction can be associated with other types of resource managers. Besides JDBC connections, a JTA transaction can apply to any resource with an adapter that supports the XAResource interface. Of particular interest to J2EE application development is that a JMS Session can be tied to a transaction. When a Session is part of a transaction, the messages it sends and receives during the extent of the transaction are treated as an atomic unit of work. If the transaction is committed, any messages received during the transaction are acknowledged and any output messages are sent. If the transaction is rolled back, any received messages are recovered and any output messages are destroyed. The Session interface provides this basic functionality that can be used to transact a JMS session locally. To be included in a JTA transaction that includes other resources, however, the JMS provider must support JTA by implementing its sessions so that they satisfy the javax.jms.XASession interface as well. This variety of session is obtained from a javax.jms.XAConnection and provides a corresponding XAResource that can be used by an application server to associate its message production and consumption with a transaction.

JTA AND THE JAVA TRANSACTION SERVICE

To help you keep the acronyms straight that you will undoubtedly encounter when doing EJB development, you should have some understanding of the Java Transaction Service (JTS) and how it relates to JTA. Because OMG's OTS is a language-neutral specification, it needs to be addressed for particular programming languages. JTS does that by specifying a Java implementation of a transaction manager that satisfies the OTS 1.1 specification. This part of JTS is viewed as the low-level details of an implementation. At the high-level, JTS supports the JTA interfaces (remember that JTA by itself doesn't include implementations of any of its interfaces). Basically, JTS specifies an implementation of JTA that is based on OTS.

An application server might implement JTS as a way to satisfy its need for JTA, but it isn't required to choose this or any other implementation approach. Whether a server implements JTS or not is unimportant to you as an application developer. You should view JTA as the API available to you and the EJB container to support transaction processing. Separating this from the other parts of JTS that are required to support OTS simplifies what you need to understand to develop transactional applications. Your components should never attempt to interact with the rest of JTS.

Note

This chapter focuses on what you need to know about JTA as an application developer using EJBs. If you're interested in more of the details behind this API, you can download both the JTA and the JTS specifications from Sun at http://www.java.sun.com/products/. Also useful in understanding the relationships between the various components involved in a transaction is the J2EE Connector Architecture Specification, which is available from Sun as well.

USING CONTAINER-MANAGED TRANSACTIONS

The recommended way to manage transactions in an EJB application is to let the container manage them for you. This is known as *container-managed transaction demarcation* and it allows you to direct the control of transactions using a declarative syntax. Instead of making calls to a UserTransaction object programmatically, you can determine how the boundaries of transactions should be defined through entries in the deployment descriptor for an EJB. This approach instructs the container to make calls to the transaction manager (through the TransactionManager interface) to start and stop transactions on your behalf.

The first thing to understand about container-managed transaction demarcation is why it's useful. One of the reasons should be easy for you to accept after seeing the background for what's involved in managing distributed transactions. Transaction management is difficult and it requires complicated code that cannot fail without risking a loss of data integrity. Having the container do the work for you removes that risk from you and simplifies the code needed for your beans to be able to operate in transactions. A second benefit is that defining transactional behavior during deployment instead of within your code allows the behavior of your beans to be modified based on the application into which they're being assembled. Customization by an application assembler of a bean that uses container-managed transactions is possible without requiring any code changes.

You choose an approach for managing the transactions associated with a bean using the transaction-type entry in the deployment descriptor:

```
<ejb-jar>
  <enterprise-beans>
    ...
    <session>
      <ejb-name>AuctionHouse</ejb-name>
      <home>com.que.ejb20.auction.controller.AuctionHouseHome</home>
      <remote>com.que.ejb20.auction.controller.AuctionHouse</remote>
      <ejb-class>com.que.ejb20.auction.controller.AuctionHouseBean</ejb-class>
      <session-type>Stateless</session-type>
      <transaction-type>Container</transaction-type>
      ...
    </session>
    ...
  </enterprise-beans>
</ejb-jar>
```

The transaction-type tag, which can be defined to be either Container or Bean, is only supported for session and message-driven beans because entity beans are required to use container-managed transactions. Also important is the fact that this choice applies to an entire bean and not to individual methods. You cannot implement the transaction demarcation yourself for some methods in a bean and let the container do it for the others.

Assigning Transaction Attributes

When you're using container-managed transactions for an enterprise bean, you don't access UserTransaction to start and end transactions within the bean's methods because the container takes care of the demarcation communication with the transaction manager. The way you tell the container what you want it to do is by including transaction attributes in the ejb-jar file's XML deployment descriptor. These attributes let you tell the container which methods need to be executed within transactions and how those transactions are to be managed. The container is able to fill this role because it intercepts every client call to a session or entity bean and every call to a message-driven bean's onMessage method. This provides the opportunity for the container to perform any necessary transaction management immediately before a bean method is invoked and immediately after it completes.

PART
I

CH
12

To deploy an entity bean, you have to specify a transaction attribute for the following methods:

■ All methods in the component interface and its superinterfaces, excluding getEJBHome, getEJBLocalHome, getHandle, getPrimaryKey, and isIdentical

■ All methods in the home interface and its superinterfaces, excluding getEJBMetaData and getHomeHandle

To deploy a session bean using container-managed transaction, you have to specify a transaction attribute for the methods defined in its component interface and its superinterfaces other than the methods defined by EJBObject and EJBLocalObject. An attribute must be specified for a message-driven bean's onMessage method for it to use container-managed demarcation.

The following XML fragment shows an example of how this attribute (trans-attribute) can be specified:

```
<ejb-jar>
  <enterprise-beans>
    ...
    <assembly-descriptor>
      <container-transaction>
        <description>
        Assign Required to all AuctionHouse methods
        </description>
        <method>
          <ejb-name>AuctionHouse</ejb-name>
          <method-name>*</method-name>
        </method>
        <trans-attribute>Required</trans-attribute>
      </container-transaction>
      ...
    </assembly-descriptor>
    ...
  </enterprise-beans>
</ejb-jar>
```

In this example, the transaction attribute for every method of the AuctionHouse session bean is set to Required. You'll see what the allowed attribute values are and their meanings shortly, but for now, it's only important to see how they're assigned. You assign a transaction attribute using a container-transaction element in the deployment descriptor. This element can include a description and it must include one or more method elements and a single trans-attribute element. The method elements identify the method or methods the attribute applies to using one of the following three styles:

```
<!-- Style 1 -->
<method>
    <ejb-name>EJBNAME</ejb-name>
    <method-name>*</method-name>
</method>

<!-- Style 2 -->
<method>
```

```
    <ejb-name>EJBNAME</ejb-name>
    <method-name>METHOD</method-name>
</method>>

<!-- Style 3 -->
<method>
    <ejb-name>EJBNAME</ejb-name>
    <method-name>METHOD</method-name>
    <method-params>
        <method-param>PARAM-1</method-param>
        <method-param>PARAM-2</method-param>
        ...
        <method-param>PARAM-n</method-param>
    </method-params>
<method>
```

The three styles are the same in that they each require you to specify the ejb-name of the bean being referenced, but they differ in how the methods are identified. This is important because you're not required to assign the same transaction attribute to every method in a bean. If you want to use the same attribute for an entire bean, the first style allows you to do this by specifying an asterisk for the method name. This is a common scenario. The second style allows you to assign an attribute to a method with a specific name. If more than one overloaded method exists with this name, the attribute is applied to each of them. The third style allows you to refer to a single method that has an overloaded name by specifying its parameter list. Each method-param entry should be a fully qualified type name such as java.lang.String. To identify a method without any parameters, you just include an empty method-params element.

If a method with the same name and signature is declared multiple times across a bean's home and component interfaces, you can include the optional method-intf element before the method-name to distinguish them if necessary. This element can be assigned a value of Home, Remote, LocalHome, or Local. You can use method-intf with any of the three styles of identifying methods. For example, the following entry would apply to all methods declared by a particular bean's remote interface:

```
<method>
  <ejb-name>AuctionHouse</ejb-name>
  <method-intf>Remote</method-intf>
  <method-name>*</method-name>
</method>
```

It's possible to assign an attribute to all methods using the asterisk form and then override it for a subset of the methods. For example, the following deployment entries would assign Required to all methods other than getNonPendingAuctions:

```
<ejb-jar>
  <enterprise-beans>
    ...
    <assembly-descriptor>
      <container-transaction>
        <description>
        Assign Required to all AuctionHouse methods
        </description>
```

```
      <method>
        <ejb-name>AuctionHouse</ejb-name>
        <method-name>*</method-name>
      </method>
      <trans-attribute>Required</trans-attribute>
    </container-transaction>

    <container-transaction>
      <description>
      Override the assignment for one method
      </description>
      <method>
        <ejb-name>AuctionHouse</ejb-name>
        <method-name>getNonPendingAuctions</method-name>
      </method>
      <trans-attribute>RequiresNew</trans-attribute>
    </container-transaction>
    ...
  </assembly-descriptor>
  ...
</enterprise-beans>
</ejb-jar>
```

The assignment of transaction attributes is the responsibility of the bean provider, the application assembler, or the deployer. The bean provider or application assembler should either specify an attribute for every method that requires one or not specify any of the attributes for a bean and leave it to the deployer to do it.

The following sections define the six supported transaction attributes and describe how they're used.

Required

You will use the `Required` attribute more often than any other because you will typically be coding functionality into your beans that is used to do transactional work. This attribute tells the container that a method must be invoked within a valid transaction context. If the caller is executing under a transaction, that transaction will be applied to the method. If the caller doesn't supply a transaction context, the container starts a new transaction immediately before calling the method. This latter case always applies for message-driven beans that run under a transaction because they don't have a client to supply one.

The `Required` attribute makes it easy for you to combine the work done by multiple methods into a single transaction. For example, a transaction can be started with a call to a session bean (either by the container or by the session bean itself) and then used to group the work of any number of entity bean methods deployed with a transaction attribute of `Required`. Each such method is executed under the existing transaction without any additional transactions being started.

RequiresNew

The `RequiresNew` attribute is useful when a method needs to commit its results regardless of what takes place with any transaction that might be executing when the method is called.

When this attribute is applied, the container always starts a new transaction before invoking the method and commits it before returning the result of the call to the client. If the client has an existing transaction context when the call is made, the container suspends that transaction and then resumes it after the method call has completed. An example of this attribute might be the need to connect to a JMS session and send a message that should be delivered regardless of what happens in any other transaction.

NotSupported

Not all resource managers can turn their transaction management over to a J2EE application server. This isn't the case for a resource manager associated with a relational database, but it might be true for some other backend system such as an ERP application or an object-oriented database. If one of your bean methods accesses such a system, you should assign the NotSupported transaction attribute to that method. This makes it clear that any work done using this method cannot be automatically rolled back along with the other operations that take place during the transaction should a failure occur.

When a method deployed with the NotSupported attribute is called, the container will suspend any client transaction that might be in progress and resume it after the method has completed. The transaction context isn't passed to any resource managers or other bean methods that are accessed during the call, so any work that is performed is done outside the scope of any global JTA transaction.

When a resource can't be associated with a JTA transaction, it operates under its own local transaction. Remember that a local transaction is controlled by the resource manager instead of a coordinating transaction manager. The commit or rollback that completes a local transaction occurs outside the unit of work of any JTA transaction that might be in effect at the same time. Obviously this isn't desirable when multiple resource managers are being accessed because the operations are not all part of a single unit of work that can be managed atomically.

A local transaction becomes a problem when a resource commits the work it has performed but the JTA transaction that's controlling the other resource managers does a rollback. Left alone, the system exists in an inconsistent state because the requirement for the operations that have been attempted to be atomic hasn't been satisfied. The only way to restore consistency at this point is to undo what has been committed by the local transaction. A typical approach for this is to employ a *compensating transaction*, which is a group of operations that, when executed, reverses the effects of a local transaction that has been committed.

You only need to be concerned about compensating transactions when you access a resource that can't be included in a JTA transaction. Compensating transactions can work, but relying on them is risky. A server crash during a compensating transaction could prevent the undo of a commit from completing or you might encounter a situation where it isn't possible to undo a change made to a resource by a committed transaction. Besides risking a loss of atomic behavior, introducing committed changes into a system that must them be rolled back by a compensating transaction threatens consistency if the affected data is accessed by another client before the changes can be reversed.

PART

I

CH

12

Supports

Supports is the one transaction attribute that causes the container to alter its behavior based on the transaction context passed by the client. If a valid transaction context is passed when a method deployed using Supports is called, the container implements the behavior for the Required attribute. If a call is made without a client transaction present, the container uses the behavior defined for NotSupported. This means that the method will be executed as part of a transaction only if the caller provides a transaction context.

You should typically avoid using the Supports attribute because it leaves the transactional behavior of a bean method up to the client programmer. Before using Supports, you must be certain that a method works as desired both with and without being associated with a transaction. In general, this would only be true for a method that either makes no updates to resources or makes an update that is by nature atomic. An example of a naturally atomic update would be the execution of a single SQL statement through JBDC. In this case, applying a transaction that is created by the container before the method is called and ended immediately after the method completes doesn't change the method's behavior. The commit or rollback status of the SQL statement is determined by the database and the result is no different if a transaction applies to the method or not. If the method is instead called as part of a client transaction, the Supports attribute causes it to be included in the atomic unit of work being performed by the client. The method's update can then be committed or rolled back as part of a larger unit. The only advantage that Supports offers over Required is the performance savings of not requiring the container to create a transaction when the method is called without a client transaction present. Given that methods that perform single updates are the only ones that can be safely used this way, it's doubtful that a significant savings can be found by doing this.

> **Caution**
>
> Be sure you're clear on the implications of the Supports attribute. Many developers new to EJB mistakenly view it as a good default choice because it intuitively sounds correct that a method should "support" transactions.

Mandatory

If a method is deployed with the Mandatory transaction attribute, the container will throw a javax.transaction.TransactionRequiredException (for a remote client) or a javax.ejb.TransactionRequiredLocalException (for a local client) if a client calls the method without a transaction context. This attribute makes it more difficult to use a bean across applications because of its rigid behavior. You should only use Mandatory if a method cannot operate correctly without a transaction or with a transaction started by the container.

Never

Never is the opposite of Mandatory. If a method is deployed with the Never attribute, the container will throw a java.rmi.RemoteException if a remote client calls the method with a transaction context or a `javax.ejb.EJBException` if a local client does the same. Just as with `Mandatory`, `Never` restricts the composability of a bean. You should only use this attribute if you need to guarantee that a method call is not associated with a transaction.

DON'T FORGET TO READ THE FINE PRINT

There are several restrictions and caveats associated with using container-managed transactions and assigning transaction attributes of which you need to be aware. Even though there are six values for a transaction attribute, not all of them are allowed in a particular context. Entity beans that are deployed using the EJB 2.0 version of CMP should only be assigned the `Required`, `RequiresNew`, and `Mandatory` attributes because their methods should always be accessed within the context of a transaction (assuming the data store supports transactions). Message-driven beans only support the `Required` and `NotSupported` attributes because they are not called by a client. The container must create a transaction for a message-driven bean and either commit it or roll it back after `onMessage` completes, so `RequiresNew` and `Supports` are of no significance. Also, a message-driven bean has no client from which to receive a transaction context, so `Mandatory` and `Never` are not applicable either.

> **Note**
>
> Container vendors have the option of allowing the `NotSupported`, `Supports`, and `Never` attributes for CMP entity beans. This would make sense only for a nontransactional data store (such as the file system). Using any of these attributes creates the possibility of data integrity problems, so it should be done with extreme caution. Also, because supporting these attributes with CMP is optional, any entity beans you develop this way will be nonportable.

In the discussion so far, the transaction context associated with a method call or a resource has referenced either a JTA transaction or null if no transaction is present. There is also the concept of an *unspecified transaction context*, which is a state with behavior left as an implementation decision for each J2EE vendor. The concept of an unspecified transaction context applies when `NotSupported`, `Never`, or `Supports` is the assigned transaction attribute and `ejbCreate`, `ejbRemove`, `ejbPassivate`, or `ejbActivate` is called for a session bean or `ejbCreate` or `ejbRemove` is called for a message-driven bean. When this happens, the container might use a null transaction context, treat each resource manager access as a transaction, treat multiple accesses of a resource manager as a single transaction, or some other behavior. You can't depend on any particular behavior in this situation, especially in the event of an error. This adds to the cautions against using `Supports` or `Never`. When a resource manager cannot be associated with a JTA transaction, you always need to assign `NotSupported`, but you do need to remember the potential problems of using such a resource.

If you need to force a transaction to roll back when you're using container-managed demarcation, you must call the `setRollbackOnly` method of `EJBContext`. This won't cause an immediate rollback, but if an attempt to commit the transaction is later made by either the container or the client, the commit is guaranteed to fail. You'll see more about this method in Chapter 13, "Exception Handling." You can call `getRollbackOnly` to see if a transaction has already been marked for rollback. These method calls are only valid within bean methods deployed using the `Required`, `RequiresNew`, or `Mandatory` attributes. The container will throw a `java.lang.IllegalStateException` if either of them is called within a method deployed using `Supports`, `NotSupported`, or `Never`.

→ To learn more about the impact of exceptions on transactions, **see** "Exceptions and Transactions," **p. 378**.

The rollback functionality provided by `EJBContext` is the only transaction management operation that's available to you when you're using container-managed demarcation. A business method in a session or entity bean or an `onMessage` method using container-managed transactions must never attempt to obtain or use the `UserTransaction` interface. This interface can only be used by methods that implement bean-managed transactions. The container will throw an `IllegalStateException` if you call the `EJBContext getUserTransaction` method. Similarly, you're not allowed to interfere in the management of a transaction by calling any demarcation methods defined by a resource adapter. In particular, this forbids you from calling methods such as `commit` and `rollback` on a `java.sql.Connection` or `javax.jms.Session`.

TRANSACTION SYNCHRONIZATION

Most of the time, you'll perform database updates through entity beans that are being operated on by session bean methods executing within a transaction. However, allowing a session bean method to read directly from the database isn't unusual. You might also have a need to update the database or access some other transactional resource directly from a session bean. You wouldn't typically do this to manage data that's owned by an entity bean, but there could be other entries in a database that need to be managed this way.

A transaction can't span multiple method calls to a stateless session bean because there is no conversational state maintained with the client. If you access the database from a stateless session bean method, any associated transaction has to start when the method is called and end when it completes. If you want to update the database, any processing that needs to happen to decide what to update has to be performed within a single method call to the bean and the results have to be written to the database before the method returns.

The rules for transactions are different for stateless and stateful session beans. You'll see more about this later in the "Using Bean-Managed Transactions" section, but a transaction can span multiple method calls to a stateful session bean. This doesn't make any difference to you if you do all the processing associated with a task that updates the database within a single method call. Here, the data update takes place within the method and it's kept as long as the associated transaction commits.

When a client is making multiple method calls as part of updating a particular set of data, you can use a spanning transaction to improve performance. With a stateful session bean, you can cache changes to the persistent data across several method calls and write them to the database only when the transaction is about to be committed. Otherwise, multiple update statements would be performed to massage the data into the final version that resulted from the client's requests.

The only way for this caching approach to work is if the session bean is kept informed of a transaction's boundaries. Once a transaction starts, the bean instance can begin caching data, but it must perform its updates to the database before the transaction commits to keep the changes within the atomic unit of the transaction. Relying on the client to notify the bean instance of an imminent commit is too risky because data integrity could be lost if the client code failed to send the notification because of an error in the system or a simple programming bug. The only safe approach is to make it the responsibility of the container to do any notification that is needed.

You saw it mentioned earlier in the chapter that OTS defines an optional synchronization interface that allows an object to be notified of a transaction's impending completion. The EJB specification requires that this interface be supported based on the `javax.ejb.SessionSynchronization` interface. Session bean instances that implement this interface are automatically registered with the `javax.transaction.Transaction` object that wraps the associated transaction context. `SessionSynchronization`, which is only for use with stateful session beans using container-managed transaction demarcation, is declared as follows:

```
public interface SessionSynchronization {
  public void afterBegin() throws EJBException, java.rmi.RemoteException;

  public void beforeCompletion() throws EJBException,
    java.rmi.RemoteException;

  public void afterCompletion(boolean committed) throws EJBException,
    java.rmi.RemoteException;
}
```

As you'll see in the next section, this interface isn't needed if you're using bean-managed demarcation because you have full programmatic control of when a transaction commits. There's no notification necessary if you want to do any caching in that case.

You can only deploy a bean that implements `SessionSynchronization` using the `Required`, `RequiresNew`, and `Mandatory` transaction attributes. Otherwise, the bean could be accessed without an associated transaction and the container wouldn't be able to send the required synchronization calls.

afterBegin

If a stateful session bean implements `SessionSynchronization`, the container calls its `afterBegin` method immediately before invoking the first business method called by a client after the bean instance has been associated with a transaction. This would be the place for you to begin any data caching or perform any initial database access that might be required.

beforeCompletion

The container calls a bean instance's `beforeCompletion` method before any resource managers enlisted in the transaction are instructed to begin a commit operation. If a rollback is about to occur, this method will not be called. If you have any cached data that needs to be written to the database, you must perform the updates during the call to this method. This is also your last chance to force the transaction to roll back by calling `setRollbackOnly` on the bean's `EJBContext`.

This method allows you to throw a `RemoteException`, but that is only to maintain backward compatibility with EJB 1.1. If you need to report an error during the execution of `beforeCompletion`, you should throw an `EJBException`. As you'll see in Chapter 13, throwing this exception will cause the transaction to roll back.

afterCompletion

The container calls `afterCompletion` once a transaction has either been committed or rolled back. You can check the method's `boolean` argument to learn if a commit occurred or not. If the transaction rolled back, you need to update any state maintained by the bean instance to match the state prior to the transaction. Be sure you understand the implications of this point. The state held by the instance variables in a session bean is not automatically reset when a transaction rolls back. To handle this for a stateful session bean, you have to implement `SessionSynchronization` and respond to rollbacks reported to `afterCompletion` by resetting the state yourself. There isn't a similar approach for stateless session beans. There, the correct approach is to not hold state that is affected by a transaction in the first place.

As with `beforeCompletion`, you can throw an `EJBException` to report an error during `afterCompletion` but this won't affect the outcome of the transaction that has already ended.

USING BEAN-MANAGED TRANSACTIONS

The first point to make about bean-managed transaction demarcation is that you should avoid using it. When you choose this method of transaction management for a session or message-driven bean (you're not allowed to use it for entity beans), you're responsible for starting each transaction that applies to the bean's methods and then committing it or rolling it back to end it. You're offered this option to handle situations where you need to control transaction boundaries in a way that you can't achieve using container-managed demarcation. You should consider this approach to be only for advanced programmers with detailed knowledge of the application and managing distributed transactions.

To use bean-managed transaction demarcation within an enterprise bean you obtain a `UserTransaction` object by calling the `getUserTransaction` method of `EJBContext`. A `UserTransaction` allows you to programmatically define transaction boundaries. Because the demarcation instructions are part of your code and not done declaratively, a bean that uses this approach is harder to reuse across applications. An application assembler or deployer can't change the transactional behavior of a bean when transaction demarcation has been programmed into its methods. It's an error for you to include `trans-attribute` entries in the deployment descriptor for a bean using bean-managed demarcation for this reason. Also remember that your choice of container- or bean-managed demarcation applies to a bean as a whole and not to individual methods.

The UserTransaction interface itself isn't complicated. The hard part about managing your own transactions is having the foresight to handle the different ways your methods might be used and the error conditions they might encounter. The methods of UserTransaction are straightforward on their own. To employ UserTransaction within a session or message-driven bean, you implement code somewhat like the following:

```
public void myTransactionalMethod() {
  try {
    // obtain access to a UserTransaction
    UserTransaction tx = myEJBContext.getUserTransaction();

    // start a JTA transaction
    tx.begin();

    // call other objects and resources to perform work under the transaction
    ...

    // complete the transaction
    tx.commit();
  }
  catch (Exception e) {
    // report any error as a system exception
    // (this is covered in Chapter 13)
    throw new javax.ejb.EJBException(e);
  }
}
```

THE UserTransaction INTERFACE

As you saw in the preceding example, a session or message-driven bean can obtain a UserTransaction from its EJBContext. Calling this method from an entity bean or any other bean using container-managed demarcation results in an IllegalStateException. Non-EJB clients can obtain a UserTransaction using a JNDI lookup; you'll see how this is done later in the "Using Client-Demarcated Transactions" section.

After you obtain a UserTransaction, you use the methods of this interface to manage the transaction boundaries of a method. The following descriptions explain how you use each method of the interface.

begin

After you obtain a UserTransaction, you call its begin method to actually start a transaction. Nested transactions aren't supported by EJB, so you'll get a NotSupportedException if you call begin when there's already a transaction associated with the current thread. A SystemException is thrown if a transaction can't be started because of some other error. Once a transaction is started, it becomes the transaction context associated with the bean instance that created it. This context is automatically propagated to any components or resources that the instance accesses during the scope of the transaction.

setTransactionTimeout

A transaction isn't allowed to continue indefinitely. Transaction managers impose a time limit after which a transaction is forced to roll back if it hasn't completed. Each transaction manager has a default time limit that it imposes, but you can override this if necessary. After calling begin, you can call setTransactionTimeout, which accepts a single int argument expressed in seconds, to establish the time limit for a transaction. You can reset a transaction's timeout back to the transaction manager's default by calling this method and passing a zero. The default timeout is adequate for the majority of transactions executed by an application, but should you need to perform an update that requires a significant amount of time, this is your way to make the transaction manager aware of that.

commit

You complete the transaction associated with the current thread and commit its results by calling the commit method. When commit has completed, the current thread no longer has an assigned transaction context. This method can fail for several reasons. You'll receive a RollbackException if the transaction rolls back when the commit is attempted. This exception indicates that either one of the resource managers couldn't commit the transaction's updates or the transaction had been marked for rollback by an earlier call to setRollbackOnly on the UserTransaction. If a heuristic decision causes some or all of the transaction to roll back, either a HeuristicRollbackException (everything rolled back) or a HeuristicMixedException (some changes rolled back, but some committed) will be thrown. If you call commit and there isn't a transaction associated with the current thread, IllegalStateException is thrown. A SecurityException indicates a permission problem and SystemException is used to report any other unexpected error.

rollback

You can call rollback to complete a transaction without saving any of its updates. As with commit, this method will throw an IllegalStateException if the current thread isn't associated with a transaction or a SecurityException or SystemException if a permissions problem or unexpected error occurs during the rollback.

setRollbackOnly

If you begin and complete a transaction within a single bean method, rolling back that transaction based on a decision made by that method is simple; you just call rollback instead of commit before returning from the method. However, multiple method calls and bean instances can be involved in a transaction and, as you'll see later in this section, bean-managed demarcation can be used with transactions that span method calls to a stateful session bean. If a bean method participating in a bean-managed transaction determines that the transaction should never be allowed to commit, the setRollbackOnly method must be called on the UserTransaction. If this is done, the transaction is guaranteed to never commit. This method applies most often when an error condition occurs that can't be handled in a way that guarantees the integrity of the transaction. Calling setRollbackOnly will result in an

IllegalStateException if there is no associated transaction or a SystemException if an unexpected error occurs.

You saw earlier in this chapter that the EJBContext interface also defines a setRollbackOnly method. You can only use a bean's EJBContext to mark a transaction for rollback when you're using container-managed demarcation (you'll get an IllegalStateException otherwise). You're restricted to the methods of UserTransaction when you're controlling a transaction using bean-managed demarcation.

getStatus

You can call getStatus to obtain information about the transaction associated with the current thread. This method will throw a SystemException to report unexpected errors, but it won't throw an exception if there isn't a transaction assigned. This method is the one way you can determine if an associated transaction exists. You need to compare the int result returned by getStatus to the constants defined by the Status interface to interpret its meaning. To learn if a bean-managed transaction has been marked for rollback, you must use getStatus instead of the getRollbackOnly method of EJBContext or an IllegalStateException will be thrown.

MANAGING YOUR TRANSACTIONS

A key difference between bean-managed and container-managed demarcation is that a client's transaction context is never applied to a bean that is using bean-managed transactions. If a client transaction exists when a bean method is called, the container suspends that transaction and resumes it after the method call has completed. Otherwise, the client would be responsible for demarcating the transaction applied to your bean method.

Even though bean-managed demarcation makes you responsible for starting and completing a transaction, the container still handles the enlistment of resources in a transaction. Just as with container-managed demarcation, there are some restrictions on how you interact with these resources though. In particular, you have to control all transaction demarcation through the UserTransaction API and not using any API provided by a resource manager. For example, if you're accessing a database or a JMS session, you can't call commit or rollback on a java.sql.Connection or a javax.jms.Session. Such an attempt would interfere with the coordination provided by the transaction manager.

A potential benefit of managing your own transactions relates to the number of transactions you can execute in response to a client call. Even though you can't execute nested transactions, you can execute more than one transaction during a method call when you're using bean-managed demarcation. As long as you commit or roll back each transaction before starting a new one, the container doesn't restrict how many you perform.

BEAN-MANAGED DEMARCATION FOR STATEFUL SESSION BEANS

Unlike stateless session beans and message-driven beans, a stateful session bean isn't required to commit a transaction before returning from a business method. If a stateful session bean using bean-managed demarcation starts a transaction, that transaction can span multiple method calls before eventually being committed or rolled back. When this is done, the container suspends the transaction when each method call completes and resumes it when another method call is made. Just as a client transaction is never associated with a bean using bean-managed transactions, the bean's transaction is never associated with its client. The risk in this approach is that you must rely on the client to call a specific method to eventually commit the transaction.

USING CLIENT-DEMARCATED TRANSACTIONS

You've seen client transactions referenced throughout this chapter without much mention of how they're started and completed. When you're using container-managed demarcation, the container transparently starts a transaction if a bean method needs one and the client hasn't provided it. If you choose bean-managed demarcation, you can start a transaction using the `getUserTransaction` method of `EJBContext` and the `begin` method of the `UserTransaction`. These cases handle the situations where a call to a bean method coincides with the start of a transaction or where a transaction context is received from another EJB. What hasn't been covered is the situation where the client providing the transaction context isn't an EJB.

The J2EE platform requires that a JSP or servlet be able to obtain a `UserTransaction` using the following JNDI lookup:

```
Context ctx = new InitialContext();
UserTransaction tx = (UserTransaction)ctx.lookup("java:comp/UserTransaction");
```

Using this approach, a Web tier client can be responsible for transaction demarcation. Once a client obtains a `UserTransaction`, it can call `begin` to start a transaction, access a database (or any other `XAResource`) or an EJB, and then commit the transaction or roll it back. One limitation is that a transaction must be fully contained within a single Web request. The most important consideration about managing a transaction this way is that you really shouldn't be doing this in a multi-tier application. Unless you have a resource that is for some reason only associated with the Web tier, transactional processing belongs in the application tier. You should place any transaction needed by a Web client within a session bean method to keep the separation of responsibilities clear. This also avoids any possibility of a transaction being started by the Web tier that is committed only after some response by the end user is received. JSP or servlet access to a JTA transaction is only appropriate for two-tier applications where the business logic resides in the Web tier.

Caution

Although the specification plainly states that you should be able to obtain a transaction using a JNDI lookup on `java:comp/UserTransaction`, you can't always rely on this. Some vendors might require you to use another environment entry name, such as `javax.transaction.UserTransaction`.

Although J2EE requires that Web tier components have access to a JTA transaction, the same isn't true for client Java applications and applets. A particular application server might provide this access, but it's not guaranteed to be supported by others. As with the Web tier, client applications and applets should leave all responsibility for transaction management to enterprise beans.

ISOLATING ACCESS TO RESOURCES

Early in this chapter you saw that a characteristic of a transaction is that it be isolated from the effects of other transactions. Isolation isn't as rigid a requirement as the other ACID properties so you have some leeway in how it's enforced in your applications. To reflect this, resource managers support one or more isolation levels. An *isolation level* describes the extent to which access to a single resource by concurrent transactions is separated.

The need to isolate transactions is best understood when you consider the interactions that can occur between concurrent transactions when they aren't kept apart. These interactions are called isolation conditions and they consist of dirty reads, nonrepeatable reads, and phantom reads.

A *dirty read* occurs when a transaction sees uncommitted changes introduced into the system by another transaction. If a transaction reads uncommitted data that is eventually rolled back, it has an invalid view of the system's state.

A *nonrepeatable read* occurs when a transaction reads some particular data (typically a row from a database table) more than once and does not get the same values every time. This is the result of a transaction being allowed to change data that has been read by another transaction that has not yet ended.

A *phantom read* occurs when a transaction reads the data rows that satisfy some criteria and then reads again based on the same criteria and finds additional rows included in the results. A phantom read could be the result of cached results not being used by the database to protect a transaction from the introduction of new data.

CHOOSING AN ISOLATION LEVEL

The next step in working with isolation levels is to understand the choices that are available to you. J2EE is consistent with SQL99 in recognizing four isolation levels: read uncommitted, read committed, repeatable read, and serializable. This order is significant with read uncommitted being the least restrictive and serializable the most.

READ UNCOMMITTED

An isolation level of *read uncommitted* allows the uncommitted results of a transaction to be read by other transactions. A concurrent transaction that reads uncommitted data has no way to tell if what it has read is later rolled back. This level of isolation (or lack thereof) can result in dirty, nonrepeatable, and phantom reads. This isolation level is safe only for transactions that access read-only data.

READ COMMITTED

The *read committed* isolation level requires that the data modified by one transaction cannot be read by another transaction until the first transaction either commits or rolls back. This level protects you from dirty reads but still allows nonrepeatable and phantom reads. Most databases default to a read committed isolation level.

REPEATABLE READ

The *repeatable read* isolation level requires that the data read by one transaction not be modified by another transaction until the first transaction either commits or rolls back. Using this level, the data read by a transaction is guaranteed to have the same value if the transaction reads it again. With repeatable read you're protected from dirty and nonrepeatable reads, but phantom reads are possible.

SERIALIZABLE

The *serializable* isolation level provides maximum protection by preventing any transaction from either reading or writing data that has been accessed by another transaction that has not yet completed. Serializable prevents dirty, nonrepeatable, and phantom reads.

> **Note**
>
> Just to be clear, the serializable isolation level has no connection to a class being `Serializable` from a Java standpoint. Serializable isolation implies that transactions must be executed serially as opposed to in parallel.

PERFORMANCE IMPACTS

After reading the preceding descriptions, your first thought might be that you should only execute serializable transactions in your applications. Unfortunately, there's a price to pay for the benefits offered by the more restrictive isolation levels. The locking and additional database overhead that are required to implement serializable isolation are a definite performance impact to an application. Rather than always assigning a highly restrictive level to your method transactions, you should instead take the approach of assigning the level required to support the needs of a method. If a method accesses read-only data, assigning a read uncommitted isolation level to it can be perfectly acceptable. On the other hand, a critical business method, such as one required to submit a customer order, would likely require the protection offered by serializable. As an alternative approach, you might choose serializable isolation for all your transactions and only reduce the level if performance problems warrant it.

CHANGING THE ISOLATION LEVEL PROGRAMMATICALLY

There are a few guidelines to adhere to when assigning isolation levels. First, most resource managers require that all access to them within a single transaction be performed using the same isolation level. You should especially be careful if you have multiple EJBs accessing a resource manager within a transaction. Another concern is to keep the isolation level specified by a single bean the same throughout a transaction. As you'll see momentarily, changing the isolation level in the midst of a transaction can produce an undesirable result. You're not, however, required to assign the same isolation level to all resource managers that are accessed by an enterprise bean. Before making that decision you should be careful that the inconsistency is justified, though.

If you're using bean-managed transaction demarcation, you can assign isolation levels programmatically. For example, you can call the setTransactionIsolation method on a Connection object when you're using JDBC. An example of this is shown in the following:

```
// acquire a connection
Connection con = ...

// choose serializable isolation
con.setTransactionIsolation( Connection.TRANSACTION_SERIALIZABLE );

// start a transaction
UserTransaction tx = myEJBContext.getUserTransaction();
tx.begin();

// do the work
...

// complete the transaction
tx.commit();
```

As mentioned previously, you shouldn't change the isolation level during a transaction. It is quite likely that a resource manager will respond to this request by immediately committing the current transaction and then starting a new one using the newly requested isolation.

A call to setTransactionIsolation might fail because JDBC drivers aren't required to support every isolation level. If a driver is requested to assign a level it can't support, it's allowed to substitute a more restrictive level. If no more restrictive level exists, a SQLException is thrown.

The preceding example applies only to JDBC drivers because there is no standard API for managing isolation level. Every resource manager that supports isolation levels is expected to provide its own API.

Isolation level is a rare topic under EJB transactions because it's the one area where bean-managed demarcation is easier than container-managed. The EJB specification doesn't set forth a standard way to assign isolation levels when you're using container-managed transactions. To support control over isolation, a J2EE implementation has to allow you to specify the levels at deployment. If your application server can't do this, the default isolation for each resource manager is used. As was pointed out earlier, that typically means that read committed will be applied to all your database access.

TROUBLESHOOTING

TRANSACTION ATTRIBUTES NOT SPECIFIED

I get errors at deployment related to the assignment of transaction attributes.

When you're using container-managed transaction demarcation, you must include `trans-attribute` entries in the deployment descriptor for a bean that, as a group, applies to all its business methods. You're also restricted in the attributes that can be assigned based on the type of EJB you're deploying. Remember as well that the `trans-attribute` element is only valid when you've defined the `transaction-type` for the bean to be `Container`.

TransactionRequiredException

I get a `TransactionRequiredException` *(or* `TransactionRequiredLocalException`*) when I call a bean method.*

This exception is used when a method is deployed with a transaction attribute of `Mandatory` and no client transaction exists when the method is called. You should first convince yourself that `Mandatory` is the appropriate attribute for the method because its use isn't typical. If it is valid, you need to start a transaction using a `UserTransaction` before calling the method.

EXCEPTION USING setRollbackOnly

I get an exception when I call `setRollbackOnly`.

The important rule about calling `setRollbackOnly` is to call it on the correct object. If you're using container-managed demarcation, you have to call this method on `EJBContext` to mark a transaction for rollback. If you're instead using bean-managed demarcation, you have to call this method on the associated `UserTransaction` to achieve the same result. Accessing the incorrect object results in an `IllegalStateException`.

TRANSACTION NOT ROLLED BACK AFTER AN EXCEPTION

The results of an in-progress transaction are not rolled back when an exception is thrown.

The handling of exceptions is closely tied to transactions and you're responsible for reacting to exceptions in a certain way to manage a transaction correctly when an error occurs. Refer to the "Exceptions and Transactions" section in Chapter 13 for detailed coverage on this subject.

EXCEPTION HANDLING

In this chapter

EJB EXCEPTION HANDLING

Like other Java APIs, using exceptions to report and handle error conditions is an important part of EJB programming. The distributed and transactional nature of EJB actually makes exception handling more of an issue here than with many other areas of Java development. When a remote client communicates with an EJB component, a lot of things have to happen: a network connection is required, the client must be able to locate the component on some remote server, security permissions must be in place to grant access to the client, the data passed between the two must be correctly marshalled, and so on. Although handled transparently to you (for the most part) as an EJB developer, each of these steps is complex and each has the potential to fail through no fault of your own. In such an environment, exceptions must be planned for and handled correctly because, even though they might not happen often, they are bound to happen sometime.

There's no denying that the complexity of a distributed architecture increases the likelihood of some errors. However, the potential problems in a distributed system are in many ways similar to the errors you might encounter when trying to access the local file system or a database from a much simpler application. These are all situations where care must be taken because you're accessing resources outside your local application over which you have little or no control. Where EJB programming differs from simpler applications becomes apparent when you consider transactions, which we covered earlier in Chapter 12.

J2EE application servers provide enterprise-strength support for transactional processing, and this support must be present in every aspect of a system built using EJB, including exception handling. As you saw, for a transaction to be valid it must always take the underlying data it manipulates from one consistent state to another. This constraint is not too demanding when everything proceeds in an application as expected. It's when something unexpected happens and an exception results that preserving consistency matters most. Because of this, most of the EJB specifications related to exception handling are directed at the proper ways for the container, the bean provider, and the EJB client to manage a transaction once an exception has occurred.

The primary goal of this chapter is to be sure you understand how to handle exceptions in an EJB application. Perhaps most important is learning how transactions are affected when an exception occurs. This includes knowing what the EJB container does for you and knowing for what you're responsible.

To get started, you first need to learn how exceptions are classified by the container, because not all exceptions are treated the same.

APPLICATION EXCEPTIONS

As far as the EJB container is concerned, exceptions can be separated into two types: those that represent a violation of a business rule (or some other condition in the application logic) and those that represent a low-level system problem. These types are known as *application exceptions* and *system exceptions*, respectively. It's important for you to learn the distinction because the EJB container treats them quite differently. This is especially true when it comes to transactions.

An application exception is thrown to indicate that some type of problem has been detected by an application's business logic. As an example, you might throw an application exception if an attempt to submit an auction bid that is less than the minimum required amount is made. This isn't a catastrophic event, but it is a problem and it needs to be reported and dealt with. Other problems are much more serious and need to be addressed in an entirely different way. An application exception wouldn't be appropriate at all if the method call to submit the bid never made it to the auction object because of a communications failure. This type of error would clearly be a system exception because it has nothing to do with the auction application itself, but is instead a problem with the underlying infrastructure. You'll learn more about the types of problems system exceptions represent and how they're handled in the next section.

You might be wondering at this point why this distinction between the types of exceptions is so important. Application and system exceptions represent different conditions, but, in most ways, an exception is an exception after all. This is true, but categorizing exceptions can be used to make the nature of a problem more clear, enforce different constraints at compile time, or allow the runtime environment to respond differently when an exception occurs.

The brief discussion you've seen so far about the differences between application and system exceptions illustrates how grouping exceptions can help you more clearly convey the nature of a problem to a programmer or an end user. The corrective action taken by a programmer who receives a system exception when calling a method on an enterprise bean is likely to be totally different from the response to an application exception. For example, a system exception might indicate that the client application is unable to communicate with the server, but an application exception might just mean that the data being passed isn't valid. Just knowing to which of these two categories an exception belongs provides a good deal of information to the caller. This can simplify the design of error handling code and help the caller take appropriate action when a problem occurs.

This is similar to the reason that error handling in Java is based on a hierarchy of exception classes and not just one. Simply choosing the appropriate exception class to represent a problem provides information about the condition that caused it.

The next reason to distinguish application exceptions from system exceptions relates to compile-time checking. Distinctions between exceptions at compile time are core to Java, so they're nothing new to you. Two of the branches that occur high in the language's exception class hierarchy determine how certain error conditions are viewed and how the compiler in turn expects you to address them. First of all, subclasses of java.lang.Throwable are immediately split into being subclasses of either java.lang.Error or java.lang.Exception. Error and its subclasses are for the most part used to indicate serious low-level problems, such as a flaw in the JVM itself. As a developer, you're not expected to catch Error and its subclasses because it's unlikely you could do anything about the problem even if you did. The branch underneath Throwable that begins with Exception is of more interest to you and there is an

PART

I

CH

13

immediate distinction to be made here as well. You might want to catch `Exception` or any of its subclasses, but they are not all treated the same. Where a particular subclass of `Exception` is found in the inheritance hierarchy determines what type of problem it represents. Subclasses of `RuntimeException`, which is a direct subclass of `Exception`, represent errors that aren't expected to occur in a correct program. For example, `ClassCastException` is a subclass of `RuntimeException` that you've probably encountered more times than you'd like to remember. A casting error should never occur unless the code that caused it wasn't written to handle the situation it encountered. A low-level system failure doesn't by itself cause a `ClassCastException`. This exception is caused by code that attempts a cast without first verifying that it knows the type of the object with which it's working. When you see a `ClassCastException`, you usually know that there's a bug in the code you're running or something about the environment isn't set up in a way that matches the assumptions made by the program.

`RuntimeException` and its subclasses are referred to as *unchecked* exceptions because the compiler doesn't require you to catch them. The idea is that if the code is correct and hasn't made any inappropriate assumptions, a `RuntimeException` won't occur. If a `RuntimeException` does occur, the code is likely broken and catching the exception and attempting to continue on isn't likely of much use.

Subclasses of `Exception` that don't extend `RuntimeException` are known as *checked* exceptions. These are exceptions, such as `java.io.IOException`, that indicate error conditions that are often outside the control of your program. A checked exception could very well occur in perfectly correct code. Because this type of exception can happen in a correct program, the compiler requires you to catch checked exceptions.

The separation of exceptions into checked and unchecked allows both you and the compiler to treat them differently. Shortly, you'll see how the checked versus unchecked distinction applies to application and system exceptions at compile time. But first, consider the runtime implication of this separation, because it's actually the more important one. Most exceptions (at least the checked ones, anyway) are to some extent recoverable. What's significant about application exceptions is that they are intended to represent error conditions that might be recoverable in a transactional sense. You'll see more about this later in this chapter, but the basic idea is that the occurrence of an application exception doesn't necessarily invalidate the transaction that's currently in progress. In fact, one of the high-level goals for exception handling expressed in the EJB 2.0 Specification is that application exceptions should be handled in such a way that the client is given the opportunity to recover from them. System exceptions, on the other hand, represent low-level problems deemed to be outside the client's control that are serious enough to invalidate a transaction and cause it to roll back.

To correctly declare your exception classes, you need to know the practical details of how you designate an exception as an application exception. It's one thing to define an application exception in terms of what type of error condition it's supposed to represent and what it implies from a transactional standpoint, but it's another matter to pass that distinction on to the EJB container. Given that the container treats application and system exceptions differently, it must have a concrete way to tell them apart. Fortunately, the distinction is a simple one to make. Application and system exceptions are separated based entirely on their super-class hierarchies. Any exception class that is a subclass of Exception, but not a subclass of RuntimeException or java.rmi.RemoteException, is an application exception.

> **Note**
>
> Because application exceptions are not subclasses of RuntimeException, they are always checked exceptions. Whenever you call a method that can throw an application exception, you must either catch that exception (or a superclass of it) or declare it in the throws clauses of your calling method. As you'll see later, some system exceptions are checked and others are unchecked.

You've already seen a number of application exceptions referenced in the code examples in earlier chapters. In particular, application exceptions are seen listed in the throws clauses of methods defined in the home and component interfaces of entity and session beans. It's important to note that application exceptions don't apply to message-driven beans. The whole intent of an application exception is to give the caller a chance to recover from an error. Message-driven beans don't provide for synchronous interaction with a client the way entity and session beans do, so there's not a client available to handle an application exception from this bean type.

THE STANDARD EJB APPLICATION EXCEPTIONS

Other than RemoteException, most of the exceptions you've seen in earlier chapters have been application exceptions. The EJB API defines a number of application exceptions to address some of the more common application-level error conditions. When you develop your own enterprise bean classes, you're responsible for using these exceptions (or sub-classes of them) to report the error conditions they represent. To do that you need to understand each of these exceptions and how you're expected to use them.

CreateException

A javax.ejb.CreateException is thrown to indicate that an application-level error occurred during an attempt to create an instance of a session bean or entity bean. This exception must be included in the throws clause of each create method you declare in the remote or local home interface of an enterprise bean. This allows you or the container to report a problem during a call to an ejbCreate or ejbPostCreate method. For example, it would be appropriate for you to throw a CreateException if a caller passes invalid parameters to a create method.

> **Note**
>
> Although you're required to declare your create methods to throw CreateException, you're not required to do the same for your ejbCreate and ejbPostCreate methods. These methods have to include CreateException in their throws clauses only if they actually have the potential to throw it.

If a `CreateException` is thrown during an attempt to create a session bean instance, the exception implies that the instance was never created. This is not necessarily true for an entity bean. A `CreateException` during the creation of a session bean strictly comes from an `ejbCreate` method. This exception might instead come from an `ejbPostCreate` method for an entity bean. In this case, the object has been created but not fully initialized.

DuplicateKeyException

`javax.ejb.DuplicateKeyException` is a subclass of `CreateException` that makes the root cause of a creation error more clear to the caller. If the creation of an entity bean instance fails because of a unique key constraint (typically meaning that the primary key is a duplicate in the database), the container (or you if you're doing BMP) is expected to throw this exception. Unlike `CreateException`, `DuplicateKeyException` is thrown only from `ejbCreate` methods. This means that you can be sure that the entity wasn't created when this exception is reported.

Note   Because you already have to include a superclass of `DuplicateKeyException` (`CreateException`) in the `throws` clause for a `create` method, you don't have to explicitly include this exception.

FinderException

A `java.ejb.FinderException` indicates that an application error occurred during execution of an `ejbFind` or `ejbSelect` method. You're required to include this exception in the `throws` clause of every finder method you declare in an entity bean's remote or local home interface and in every `ejbFind` and `ejbSelect` method declaration in an entity bean class. Notice that this requirement is different than the one imposed for `CreateException`. You must always include this application exception in the declarations of your finder method implementations.

A particular constraint imposed by the EJB 2.0 Specification is that you must throw this exception from a single-object finder or select method if the query it executes returns more than one object. This situation should be rare, because it indicates a bad assumption on the part of a method implementation about the data it's working with or the validity of the parameters supplied by its caller. If there's any chance of a finder or select method returning more than one object, you should declare it to return multiple objects. Most often, you should only need to use a `FinderException` if you have to report invalid parameters being passed to a finder or select method.

ObjectNotFoundException

The `javax.ejb.ObjectNotFoundException` subclass of `FinderException` indicates that the object requested from a single-object finder or select method does not exist. If you're using CMP, the container is responsible for throwing this exception from its `ejbFind` and `ejbSelect` methods. When using BMP, you're responsible for throwing it from your `ejbFind` methods when your query doesn't return the desired object. Multi-object finders and select methods shouldn't throw this exception but should instead return an empty collection when no matching objects are found. An exception is appropriate for the single-object versions because a caller is expecting exactly one match for the criteria used by the method—not finding that match is likely the sign of an error. An `ObjectNotFoundException` for an entity bean likely means that the entity being requested has been deleted from the database.

Note

> Because `FinderException` is already included in the declaration of each finder method, you don't have to explicitly include `ObjectNotFoundException`.

RemoveException

A `javax.ejb.RemoveException` is used to report an error that occurs during an attempt to remove a session or entity bean. For example, calling the `remove` method of `EJBHome` (or `EJBLocalHome`) that accepts a primary key as an argument is invalid for a session bean, so it results in this exception. Calling `remove` on a stateful session bean that is currently involved in a transaction will also cause the container to throw a `RemoveException`.

Although it's used with session beans, `RemoveException` applies more often to problems that occur when an attempt is made to delete an entity object from the database. If you're using CMP, the container calls the `ejbRemove` method for an entity object before attempting to remove it from the database. This gives you the chance to do any preparation that's needed before the database delete is performed. If the bean is in a state such that it shouldn't be deleted, you can veto the delete by throwing a `RemoveException`. For example, if an instance of `EnglishAuctionBean` has assigned and notified an auction winner but the purchase of the item hasn't been completed, disallowing the deletion of the auction entity would be a reasonable business rule to enforce. If you're using BMP, you can report problems such as a foreign key constraint that prevents deletion of the entity using a `RemoveException`.

When a client receives a `RemoveException`, it doesn't know, in general, whether the remove occurred. If you use `RemoveException` to report business rule constraints that prevent the removal of an entity, you should do so in a way that makes it clear to the client that the entity wasn't deleted.

EXTENDING THE APPLICATION EXCEPTIONS

It's a good practice in general to extend high-level exceptions so that you can provide more specific error reporting to a caller. As you just saw, this is done within the standard EJB application exceptions with `DuplicateKeyException` and `ObjectNotFoundException`. There's no reason to stop there in making these exceptions more useful. Something the standard exceptions share that is also somewhat of a limitation is that they offer only a no-argument constructor and a constructor that accepts a string message. This is typical for exceptions included in the Java API, but it still doesn't offer you much flexibility in error reporting.

PART

I

CH

13

For example, `CreateException` is ambiguous when it's thrown for an entity bean because it doesn't specify whether the error occurred before the entity object was created or while it was being initialized. You can supply a message string when you're constructing the exception object that describes the error, but that's only helpful to a person reading the error message. Responding programmatically to the exact meaning of an exception requires more than embedding information in a message string (if you want it to be robust and reliable, that is). Consider the alternative shown in Listing 13.1.

LISTING 13.1   `CreateEntityException.java`—A MORE INFORMATIVE EXTENSION OF `CreateException`

```
import javax.ejb.CreateException;

public class CreateEntityException extends CreateException {

  // read-only attribute that indicates whether the associated
  // entity was created before this exception was thrown
  protected boolean entityCreated;

  public CreateEntityException(boolean entityCreated) {
    this(null, entityCreated);
  }

  public CreateEntityException(String msg, boolean entityCreated) {
    super(msg);
    this.entityCreated = entityCreated;
  }

  public boolean getEntityCreated() {
    return entityCreated;
  }
}
```

`CreateEntityException` extends `CreateException` by adding an `entityCreated` attribute that tells the caller more about the creation error that occurred. If a bean provider throws `CreateEntityException` from an `ejbCreate` or `ejbPostCreate` method, the code that requested the creation of the entity object can handle the error differently based on what point the error occurred.

`CreateEntityException` extends a standard exception to provide an error reporting option that is still generic. You should also consider extending the standard exceptions to better support your specific application needs. For example, Listing 13.2 illustrates an extension of `RemoveException` that supports a specific need of the auction site without needing additional attributes in the exception class.

LISTING 13.2 RemoveUnfinishedAuctionException.java—AN APPLICATION-SPECIFIC EXCEPTION CLASS

```
package com.que.ejb20.auction.exceptions;

import javax.ejb.RemoveException;

/**
 * This exception class reports an attempt to remove an auction that has
 * not been completed
 */
public class RemoveUnfinishedAuctionException extends RemoveException {

  public RemoveUnfinishedAuctionException() {
  }

  public RemoveUnfinishedAuctionException(String msg) {
    super(msg);
  }
}
```

You do have to exercise caution in extending the standard application exceptions to make sure the intent of the superclass exception is preserved. CreateEntityException and RemoveUnfinishedAuctionException are valid extensions because they are only intended to be used to report creation and removal errors. That's an important distinction to make. Instead of RemoveUnfinishedAuctionException, you could have declared an InvalidAuctionStateException that extends RemoveException. This exception would still provide useful information in the event of a failure during a remove, but it would be tempting to use it in other methods to report invalid state errors that have nothing to do with object removal. This would quickly cause problems for callers that received this exception, because a RemoveException wouldn't be a valid generalization of the other state errors. A caller that is catching RemoveException to respond to a failure to delete an auction would be thrown off track by an InvalidAuctionStateException that was meant to report some other type of error. An extension of a standard application exception should only be used to provide a more specific version of that exception. If you need more general exceptions, you should extend them from Exception or one of its subclasses that is a valid superclass for every situation in which it will be used.

Another potential benefit of declaring your own exception classes that might not be apparent at first relates to internationalization. As you know, the need for an application to present its user interface in more than one language is becoming a common requirement. In a multitier Internet application, this means that the Web tier must supply display text to an end user based on an appropriate locale. If a particular user speaks English, the Web tier should generate displays in English, but those same displays should be generated in German for a user who's more comfortable with German, and so on. The good news about this from the viewpoint of an EJB developer is that, in a well-designed system, the application tier is decoupled from the presentation logic and is, for the most part, unaffected by this requirement. The application tier has little knowledge of its clients and, in general, doesn't supply any text that's displayed to a user other than that pulled from a database or some other external source.

This works fine until a problem occurs within the application tier. Throwing a fairly generic exception with an associated text message is of little use to a Web tier client that supports users who speak languages other than the one used by the EJB developer who wrote the exception-throwing code. You could take measures to pull the text used for exception messages from resource bundles on the application tier, but worrying about how information is presented to end users isn't often served best by the application tier. A potentially better approach is to be sure that the error information supplied to the Web tier is precise enough to allow that tier to provide a meaningful message to the user. An error within the application tier likely needs to be reported to a user using a higher-level, less technical description anyway, so attempting to build such a message on the application tier has limited benefit.

If you instead declare custom application exception classes, your enterprise beans can throw meaningful exceptions to the Web tier that can be reported to users appropriately. As illustrated by Listing 13.2, a `RemoveUnfinishedAuctionException` would be much easier for the Web tier to interpret and relay to a user than a generic `RemoveException` with an embedded text message describing the nature of the problem.

SYSTEM EXCEPTIONS

Any exception condition or error that isn't an application exception is a system exception. This means that system exceptions are instances of `RuntimeException`, `RemoteException`, `Error`, and their subclasses. These exceptions report unexpected low-level problems that aren't related to the application logic. Problems such as an inability to communicate with another EJB or an error obtaining a database connection are reported using system exceptions.

Other than `RemoteException` and its subclasses, system exceptions are unchecked exceptions, so you're not expected to catch the majority of them. As you were reminded earlier, an unchecked exception represents a problem that either shouldn't happen in a correct program or is severe enough that there's no expectation that you're able to recover from it. The handling of these exceptions in an EJB environment is quite different from that in a standalone application however. In a simple application, a response to an unexpected and severe error might simply be to exit the program (hopefully somewhat gracefully) and let the user retry what was being attempted once the external problem has been corrected. It's not a great answer, but sometimes you can't do much more for some underlying problems. Of course, a "raise the white flag" approach like this would likely land you on the street if you proposed it for an enterprise application. The systems that drive businesses can't anticipate unexpected errors any better than a small desktop application, but they have to be able to withstand them.

Perhaps the worst side effect of unexpected errors is that they are likely to leave object attributes and possibly database entries in an inconsistent state. This strikes at the core of what is demanded from an enterprise system. When unexpected errors occur, consistency must somehow be restored if it's been compromised. Left on your own to accomplish this, it's a formidable task for an application developer. Fortunately, one of the requirements set forth for EJB containers is that they must take responsibility for cleaning up any inconsistency introduced by a system exception. Because you're not expected to be able to recover from a system exception, there's no reason to stop the container from interceding and doing whatever cleanup is needed before you even see a system exception. Obviously, this is one of the primary advantages of building a system using EJB.

THE STANDARD EJB SYSTEM EXCEPTIONS

Just as with application exceptions, there are several standard system exceptions defined by the J2EE API. The most important system exceptions are `RemoteException` and `EJBException`. These exceptions differ from the application exceptions covered in this chapter in that they're much more general. In addition, system exceptions, unlike application exceptions, are reported differently to remote and local clients. This section describes each of the standard system exceptions and what they're used to report.

RemoteException

A remote client's calls to an enterprise bean are remote calls and a system-level failure is always a possibility during a remote call. Such problems are reported using `java.rmi.RemoteException`, which is unique among system exceptions. `RemoteException` and its subclasses are the only system exceptions that are checked exceptions. These exceptions report nonapplication errors just like the other system exceptions, but the problems they report can occur when correctly executing code runs into a problem outside the application's control. Just as an application can encounter an `IOException` when accessing an external resource, a remote client can encounter a `RemoteException` when accessing a server across the network. For this reason, `RemoteException` always needs to be handled by the caller.

`RemoteException` is used in many situations to report errors to a remote client, but it is never used with local clients.

As you've seen in previous chapters, you have to include `RemoteException` in the `throws` clause of every method you declare in a remote home or remote interface. A `RemoteException` can be thrown by the container or even by the communication subsystem that connects a client to the container. Because `RemoteException` is used to report communications problems anywhere along the path between a client and a bean instance, it's not possible for a caller to know if a method call was executed when this exception is thrown.

`RemoteException` provides the standard no-argument and message string constructors, and it also supports wrapping a nested exception:

```
public RemoteException(String msg, Throwable nestedException)
```

In the descriptions of the standard application exceptions earlier in this chapter, you saw that, even though some method declarations in a home interface are required to include a particular application exception, you're not always required to include it in the throws clause of the method implementation. For example, a create method must be declared to throw CreateException, but the corresponding ejbCreate method has no requirement to do the same. The requirements for RemoteException take this thought a step further. Not only are you not required to include RemoteException in the throws clauses for your method implementations, you're specifically directed not to.

RemoteException is used by the container to report problems to remote clients, but it's not the exception you as a bean provider should throw from your methods to indicate nonapplication exceptions. A RemoteException doesn't apply to a local client, so it doesn't make sense as an error-reporting choice for an implementation class. Instead, use EJBException, which is described next, or a suitable RuntimeException. The EJB 1.0 Specification defined the use of RemoteException to report system exceptions from bean methods, but this practice was deprecated in EJB 1.1 with preference given to the use of EJBException. EJB 2.0 still requires containers to support the deprecated use of RemoteException for this purpose, but you should avoid it. If you do throw a RemoteException from a bean method, the container will treat it just like an EJBException.

EJBException

An EJB instance throws a javax.ejb.EJBException to the container to report an unexpected error condition. You should use EJBException to report nonapplication errors to the container from your business methods and callback methods such as ejbCreate and ejbPostCreate.

You can construct an EJBException object without any arguments or with a string message, but you'll use it most often to nest a checked exception that you want to throw to the container as a system exception:

```
public EJBException(Exception nestedException)
```

EJBException differs from RemoteException in two key respects. First, EJBException is a subclass of RuntimeException, making it an unchecked exception. Even if you implement a method that can throw an EJBException to report a system problem, you're not required to include this exception in the throws clause of your method declarations. Second, because EJBException isn't specific to remote access issues, it's an appropriate choice for reporting errors to local clients. When a low-level problem occurs that prevents a method call from a local client to an enterprise bean from completing, the container uses an EJBException (or one of its subclasses) to report the problem to the client instead of RemoteException.

NoSuchObjectException AND NoSuchObjectLocalException

The java.rmi.NoSuchObjectException subclass of RemoteException reports an attempt to invoke a method on a remote object that no longer exists. The EJB container throws this exception when a method call is attempted on an entity bean that has been removed from the database or a session object that has been removed. Similarly, `javax.ejb.NoSuchObjectLocalException`, which is a subclass of `EJBException`, reports an attempt by a local client to access an entity or session bean that has been removed.

The use of these exceptions probably is simplest to understand in the case of an entity bean. For example, a `NoSuchObjectLocalException` would result if two instances of `AuctionHouseBean` obtained a reference to the local interface for a particular `EnglishAuction` entity object, one of the clients made a call to remove the auction, and the other client attempted to call the `submitBid` method on the interface reference it still held.

For a session bean, a `NoSuchObjectException` would result, for example, if a remote client made a call to a stateful session bean after the container had passivated the session object and then removed it after the timeout period expired. As you'll see later in this chapter, the container gets rid of a bean instance if it throws a `RuntimeException`. This means that if a remote client attempts to call a stateful session bean after that bean has thrown a `RuntimeException`, a `NoSuchObjectException` results.

Remember, `NoSuchObjectException` and `NoSuchObjectLocalException` apply only to situations in which a bean instance has been removed by the container and not simply passivated. If a client makes a call to a passivated instance, the container activates the instance and directs it to service the call.

NoSuchEntityException

`javax.ejb.NoSuchEntityException` is a subclass of `EJBException` that you or the container should throw to indicate that a call was made to `ejbLoad`, `ejbStore`, or a business method for an entity object that has been removed from the database. When this exception is thrown from a bean method and not caught, the container is expected to throw either a `NoSuchObjectException` or a `NoSuchObjectLocalException` to the client based on the type of client that initiated the call.

TransactionRequiredException **AND** TransactionRequiredLocalException

You learned in Chapter 12 that if a method deployed with the `Mandatory` transaction attribute is called without a transaction context, the container throws an exception. If the caller is a remote client, the `javax.transaction.TransactionRequiredException` subclass of `RemoteException` is used. In the case of a local client, a `javax.ejb.TransactionRequiredLocalException`, which extends `EJBException`, is used.

THROWING SYSTEM EXCEPTIONS

A primary purpose of this chapter is to help you understand what type of exception to throw from a bean method in a particular situation. First of all, it's important that you correctly choose between an application and a system exception so you can accurately report the nature and severity of a problem. When an application exception is appropriate, which one you throw is unimportant to the container because it treats them all the same. All that matters with an application exception is that it reports the problem to the client in a precise enough way to support recovery from the error. Reporting a system exception is more complicated because the container does some work for you when this type of exception is thrown. The following sections present some guidelines to follow when you're handling system exceptions.

RUNTIME EXCEPTIONS

Rather than catching a RuntimeException or error in a bean method, you should allow it to be thrown to the container (or rethrow it if you do catch it). When an EJB instance throws a RuntimeException, the container discards that instance and will no longer make calls to it. This is a safety precaution to prevent problems that might result from continuing to use an instance left in an inconsistent state by an exception. When an instance is discarded, references held by clients are still valid because the container can replace the discarded instance with another one. The only caveat to this is for stateful session beans because each client is served by a specific instance that holds the conversational state between the two. If a stateful session bean instance is discarded, the client's state data is lost. Whenever a RuntimeException is thrown to the container from an entity or session bean, it will be thrown to a remote client as either a RemoteException or a TransactionRolledbackException as explained in the next section. If the client is a local client, the container throws either EJBException or TransactionRolledbackLocalException.

> **Note**
>
> Whenever the container is described as discarding a bean instance, this isn't the same as the instance being placed back into the pool for later use. When an instance is discarded, any resources the instance obtained through resource factories are released and the instance is made available for garbage collection.

SUBSYSTEM EXCEPTIONS

If you catch a checked exception that your bean method cannot recover from, throw an EJBException that wraps it. This applies in particular to checked exceptions from other J2EE subsystems such as JDBC, JNDI, and JMS. Rather than throwing exceptions like SQLException, NamingException, and JMSException directly to a client, you should wrap them with an EJBException. Although these exceptions fit the definition of application exceptions based on their position in the exception class hierarchy, you should treat them as system exceptions if you cannot adequately handle them within your bean methods. You should report them to the container in a way similar to what is done in this code segment:

```
try {
  InitialContext ctx = new InitialContext();
  return (EnglishAuctionHome)ctx.lookup("java:/comp/env/ejb/EnglishAuction");
}
catch (javax.naming.NamingException e) {
  // wrap this exception with EJBException and throw it to the container
  throw new EJBException(e);
}
```

> **Note**
>
> The preceding example assumes that the reference being obtained is to a local home interface. Remember that you need to use `PortableRemoteObject` to narrow any remote references you obtain using JNDI.

This guideline for subsystem exceptions applies to handling a `RemoteException` as well. If a bean method makes a call to a remote object, it must either catch `RemoteException` or include it in its `throws` clause. Given that EJB 2.0 specifically states that you should report system exceptions using `EJBException` instead of `RemoteException`, you should avoid allowing a `RemoteException` to be thrown from your methods. Instead, catch `RemoteException` when invoking a method on a remote object and throw `EJBException` if a nonapplication problem occurs.

OTHER UNEXPECTED ERRORS

You should report any other unexpected error condition by throwing an `EJBException` that you construct with a string message that describes the error. As an example, this guideline applies when you execute a SQL statement that completes without reporting an error but doesn't produce the expected result. You previously saw examples like the following of this in Chapter 6, "Bean-Managed Persistence":

```
...
con = getConnection();
stmt = con.prepareStatement("DELETE FROM auction WHERE id = ?");
stmt.setInt(1, id.intValue());
int rowsDeleted = stmt.executeUpdate();
if (rowsDeleted != 1) {
  throw new EJBException("Error deleting auction " + id);
}
...
```

THROWING EXCEPTIONS FROM MESSAGE-DRIVEN BEANS

Unlike application exceptions, message-driven beans are allowed to throw system exceptions but you should avoid even doing this, if possible. This enterprise bean type can report a system exception from its `onMessage`, `ejbCreate`, or `ejbRemove` methods as long as `RemoteException` isn't used. The specification explicitly prohibits a message-driven bean from throwing a `RemoteException` under any circumstance. It also states that a message-driven bean that throws a `RuntimeException` can't be considered a "well-behaved" JMS message listener. If a message-driven bean throws a `RuntimeException` from `onMessage` or any of its callback methods, the container destroys that instance of the bean. Clients are unaffected if this occurs because subsequent messages are simply delegated to other instances of the bean by the container.

PART

I

CH

13

EXCEPTIONS AND TRANSACTIONS

The most important reason to talk about exception handling in EJB is to understand how exceptions impact transactions. You've already seen some of the reasons why it's important to separate application and system exceptions, but their effect on transactions is at the top of the list. An enterprise system must handle exceptions in such a way that transactional integrity is maintained. This requirement places responsibility on both the EJB container and on you as a bean provider.

THROWING AN APPLICATION EXCEPTION DURING A TRANSACTION

If an application exception is thrown from a bean method during a transaction, the container doesn't automatically roll back the transaction or mark it for rollback. The intent is to give the client an opportunity to recover from a business logic error. This hands-off approach taken by the container gives you flexibility in responding to exceptions, but there's always a catch. In this case, it's the added responsibility you're given to make sure that a transaction commit doesn't result in an inconsistent state. Let's first look at what this requires when you're using container-managed transaction demarcation for an entity bean or session bean. Message-driven beans can't throw application exceptions, so they can be ignored for now.

When the container is managing transaction demarcation, a transaction can be started by the caller of your bean method or by the container itself. Running within the context of the caller's transaction implies that a transaction attribute of `Required`, `Mandatory`, or `Supports` was assigned to your method. If the `RequiresNew` attribute is assigned or if `Required` is assigned and the caller doesn't provide a transaction context, the container starts the transaction that applies to the method call. The only difference this makes for the discussion here is that it determines who commits the transaction and when that commit is attempted.

When a bean method executing under a caller's transaction context throws an application exception, the container simply rethrows the exception to the client. Actually, no matter how the transaction is being managed, an application exception is always passed on to the client by the container. This is important because it satisfies a goal for EJB to always report application exceptions directly to the client. Where the container's response to an application exception can differ slightly relates to transaction rollback. When a caller's transaction context applies, the container doesn't roll back the transaction when an application exception is thrown. This gives the client the option to continue working and eventually attempt a commit. The client can continue calling the bean instance that threw the exception as well. This might sound a little dangerous, but if you carry out your responsibilities as a bean provider, it's completely safe.

> **Note**
>
> You'll see later that the container discards a bean instance when a system exception occurs. An important distinction to notice here is that this is never the case with an application exception. This type of exception represents a business logic issue, which is never so severe as to require such a precaution. Because application exceptions are checked exceptions, you can, in some ways, consider them "expected." The container responds to the unexpected exceptions more cautiously.

Allowing the client to continue working under a transaction after an application exception is thrown requires that you ensure that data integrity will not be lost if the transaction is eventually committed. In practical terms, this means that if at all possible, you should determine the need for throwing an application exception and throw it before you update the state of your bean instance or allow it to operate on the state of any other object. For example, if invalid parameters are passed to an ejbCreate or business method, you should throw an application exception to report that fact before doing anything else. Similarly, if you want to veto the removal of an entity object by throwing a RemoveException, you should do so before deleting any data from the database. There will of course be cases where it isn't possible to determine the need for reporting an exception until data has been changed. If these changes cannot be completely reversed before throwing the exception, your only choice is to mark the current transaction for rollback by calling the setRollbackOnly method defined as part of EJBContext. By ensuring that the transaction cannot be committed, you can guarantee that data consistency will be restored when the transaction is rolled back.

If a client continues to work under its transaction context after receiving an application exception, it can attempt to commit the transaction as usual. If the transaction was marked for rollback by the bean method that threw the exception, the commit is guaranteed to fail and a rollback will occur. Otherwise, the commit is allowed to proceed and will only fail if there is some other problem unrelated to the exception that was thrown. To prevent wasted effort, your EJB clients should do what they can to determine if a transaction has been marked for rollback before attempting to continue on after an exception. If a client is an EJB using container-managed transaction demarcation, you should call getRollbackOnly on its EJBContext to check the status. Otherwise, if it's an EJB using bean-managed demarcation or some other client type, you should call getStatus on the current UserTransaction before proceeding.

Tip

It's important for a client to be able to determine if a transaction is marked for rollback programmatically, but it can also be useful to include this information as part of your bean documentation. As part of documenting the application exceptions thrown by a bean method, you should include whether the associated transaction is marked for rollback before a particular exception is thrown.

The exception handling process is slightly different when the container starts the transaction that applies to a bean method when the method is invoked. Remember that a transaction started by the container to support a bean method is also completed by the container as soon as the method exits. This means that the commit or rollback occurs before the result of the method call is returned to the client. If a bean method marks a transaction for rollback and throws an application exception in this situation, the container performs the rollback as soon as the method call completes. If the transaction isn't marked for rollback, the container attempts to commit it. In either case, the container rethrows the application exception to the client to report the error. If the client is running under its own transaction context (implying that the bean method in this case was deployed using `RequiresNew` as its transaction attribute), the client's transaction is unaffected by the exception or the rollback, if one was performed.

The diagram in Figure 13.1 summarizes the behavior specified for application exceptions relative to container-managed transaction demarcation. Note that it includes the behavior that applies when the transaction context is unspecified. This can occur when a transaction attribute of `NotSupported`, `Never`, or `Supports` is used. Here the container performs no management of a transaction, so an application exception is simply rethrown to the client.

Figure 13.1
Application exception handling for container-managed transaction demarcation.

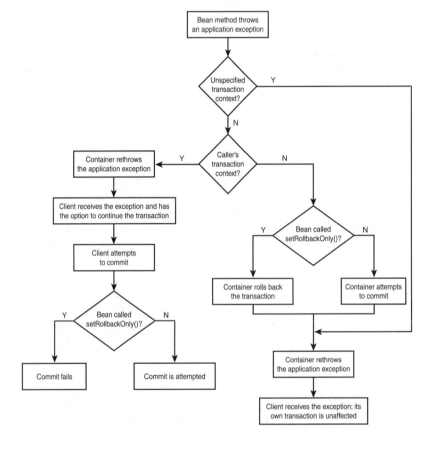

As discussed in Chapter 12, using container-managed demarcation is the recommended approach for managing transaction boundaries. As it turns out, most of the discussion that's needed about exception handling and transactions applies to this option. As you saw previously in Chapter 12, you can also implement the management of transactions for session and message-driven beans yourself. In this case, a bean method that requires a transaction runs within a transaction started by the bean itself, so the effect of an exception is straightforward. Prior to throwing an application exception, a session bean method using bean-managed transaction demarcation is responsible for committing or rolling back the current transaction. Once the exception is thrown, the container rethrows it to the client.

Note

A stateful session bean can keep a transaction open across method calls, so it isn't strictly necessary to commit or roll back a transaction for bean-managed transaction demarcation when an exception occurs within this type of bean. However, the state of the bean must always be managed in such a way that a commit is not performed for invalid data. If another method is eventually responsible for the decision to commit or roll back, you have to ensure data consistency prior to throwing an application exception or make that method aware of the exception that occurred.

The following points summarize the effects of application exceptions on transactions:

- The container always rethrows an application exception from a bean method to the client.

- The container does not automatically roll back a transaction when an application exception is thrown.

- When using container-managed transaction demarcation, you must mark the current transaction for rollback using setRollbackOnly before throwing an application exception if data integrity is in jeopardy. The container performs this rollback before returning to the client only if the transaction was started by the container.

- When using bean-managed transaction demarcation with a session bean, you should typically complete the current transaction before throwing an application exception. You can commit the transaction if it will not damage data integrity.

- The container does not discard a bean instance when that instance throws an application exception.

THROWING A SYSTEM EXCEPTION DURING A TRANSACTION

If a system exception is thrown from a bean method during a transaction, the container logs the error, discards the bean instance that threw the exception, and either rolls back the transaction or marks the transaction for eventual rollback by the client. Where the primary goal for handling an application exception is to provide the opportunity for the client to recover from the problem, the primary goal after a system exception is to protect the integrity of the data involved and clean up the mess left behind. System exceptions represent more serious problems than application exceptions do, but the good news is that the container takes full responsibility for reacting to them as far as transactions are concerned.

When a system exception occurs, the container makes no assumptions that the bean instance involved was left in a valid state or that the associated transaction had yet to make any data changes. Instead the container discards the bean instance and guarantees that no other calls will be made to it. As pointed out earlier in the chapter, this only causes a problem for stateful session beans because any associated client state is lost when an instance is discarded. The client will have to reestablish a session when this occurs and rebuild the conversational state.

As a bean provider, you have no decision to make about rolling back a transaction or not when a system exception is thrown. The container makes the decision for you by always forcing a rollback. This precaution is what allows you to let uncaught instances of RuntimeException be thrown to the container or to throw your own instances of EJBException to report subsystem or other unexpected errors.

As with application exceptions, system exceptions are handled somewhat differently based on whether the caller provided the transaction context or it was started by the container. In either case, the bean instance is discarded and the exception is logged. The EJB specification requires that the server be able to log errors, but it doesn't specify how. You'll need to look at the documentation for a particular application server to see how that vendor decided to satisfy this requirement.

If a caller provides the transaction context and a system exception is thrown from an entity or session bean using container-managed transaction demarcation, the container marks the transaction for rollback and throws either a TransactionRolledbackException or a TransactionRolledbackLocalException to the client. This makes it quite obvious that there is no point in continuing the work in progress and attempting to commit the transaction. If the transaction is instead started by the container, the container automatically rolls back the transaction and throws either a RemoteException (remote client) or an EJBException (local client). If the client is operating under its own transaction context in this situation, the rollback might or might not affect that transaction. The container can leave the client transaction alone, or mark it for rollback if data integrity is in doubt. Operation under an unspecified transaction context is similar in that a RemoteException (or EJBException if the client is local) is thrown to report a system error, and the container optionally can mark the client transaction for rollback.

Unlike application exceptions, the container needs to step in when a session bean using bean-managed transaction demarcation throws a system exception. Because system exceptions indicate unexpected errors, the container can't assume that the bean will be left in a consistent state when one occurs. If a system exception is thrown while bean-managed demarcation is being used, the container logs the error, discards the instance, and throws a RemoteException or EJBException similar to how an exception is handled for container-managed demarcation. The most important behavior in this case is that the container will step in and roll back a transaction being managed by the bean if there is a transaction in progress that has not completed at the time a system exception is thrown.

Figure 13.2 summarizes the behavior specified for handling system exceptions thrown from entity or session beans.

The container handles system exceptions thrown from message-driven beans a little differently than it does those from entity and session beans. This is because a message-driven bean has no client to throw an exception to when one occurs. Other than the fact that the container doesn't throw an exception to a client for a message-driven bean, its behavior when a system-level exception needs to be reported is the same. When a system exception occurs in a message-driven bean, the error is logged and the bean instance is discarded by the container. If a transaction was started by the container, that transaction is rolled back. If the bean is using bean-managed demarcation and has started a transaction that has not been committed before the exception occurs, the container will roll back that transaction.

Figure 13.2
The container handles system exceptions automatically for entity and session beans.

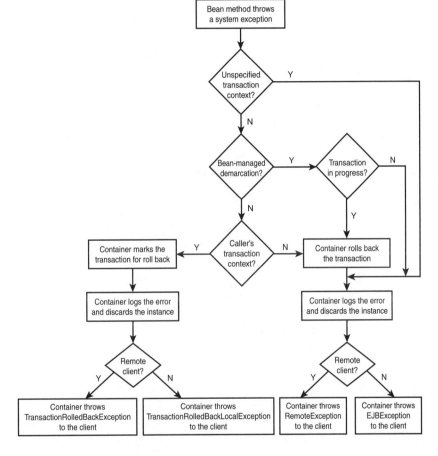

The following points summarize the effects of system exceptions on transactions:

- The current transaction is always rolled back when a system exception is thrown. This rollback is immediate unless container-managed transaction demarcation is being used and the transaction context was provided by the caller.

- The container always discards any bean instance that throws a system exception.

- The container is responsible for all cleanup after a system exception—you don't have to do anything as a bean provider.

PACKAGING EXCEPTIONS

The majority of this chapter has been concerned with describing the different exception types and looking at how a transaction that is in progress is affected when an exception is thrown. That information by far is the most important for you to understand because knowing how the container expects you to throw and catch exceptions is the only way you can write correct programs that are resilient when faced with unexpected errors. This last section departs from that focus and looks at a simple deployment issue related to the exception classes you define.

As discussed in this chapter, you should always create your own exception classes so you can precisely report error conditions in the systems you build. When you do this, one of the first decisions you have to make is that of where to put these exceptions within your package hierarchy. It might not sound like a big issue at first, but as with any class, the package assignment for an exception should provide information about its intended use. The distributed nature of architectures like EJB also affects packaging choices. Client-side code has to have access to the interfaces that define the services provided to it by the application server, but you don't want to expose too much of the server-side structure because it begins to hint at implementation details.

When you develop an exception class for an EJB application, you need to decide whom that exception is intended to serve. In the architecture proposed throughout this book, a Web tier client only accesses session beans in the application tier. Using this guideline, exceptions that are intended to report errors to the Web tier should be packaged in such a way that they have no coupling to the entity beans or their interfaces. Going further, an exception class has more potential for reuse if it isn't tied to the session beans, either. By packaging your exceptions separately from your enterprise beans, it makes it easier for you to throw these exceptions from your entity beans to your session beans. You then can rethrow them to your clients or throw an alternative exception, depending on the needs of your application.

The auction example adheres to this approach by defining application exceptions in packages such as `com.que.ejb20.auction.exceptions`. With this structure, the `EnglishAuction` entity bean can use `InvalidBidException`, even though this same exception class is used by the `AuctionHouse` session bean to report application errors to the Web tier.

TROUBLESHOOTING

DATA CORRUPTION AFTER AN APPLICATION EXCEPTION

I see inconsistencies between the values I get from a bean method and those stored in the database after an application exception has occurred.

Because the container doesn't automatically roll back a transaction when an application exception occurs, the responsibility is on the bean provider to ensure data consistency. If a bean method changes the attribute values for the instance and then throws an application exception, data inconsistencies will result if the current transaction is committed. When using container-managed transaction demarcation, the bean method must call the setRollbackOnly method of EJBContext if the bean state cannot be restored before the exception is thrown. When using bean-managed transaction demarcation, the bean method should roll back the transaction before throwing the exception in this situation.

LOSS OF CONVERSATIONAL STATE DATA

I lose the session data stored for a client by a stateful session bean when an exception is thrown.

When a system exception occurs, the only way the container can guarantee that access to a corrupted bean instance is prevented is to destroy the instance that threw the exception. This doesn't matter for entity or stateless session beans because any instance can serve a client request transparently. However, only a single instance of a stateful session bean holds the conversational state for a particular client. If a system exception is thrown from a stateful session bean, that state data is permanently lost. The client of a stateful session bean must be able to create a new session and start over in the event of a system exception.

CHAPTER 14

SECURITY DESIGN AND MANAGEMENT

In this chapter

THE IMPORTANCE OF APPLICATION SECURITY

For all the talk and attention that Internet security gets these days, for some reason it often takes a back seat to other considerations during application design. Maybe it's because the nonfunctional requirements often are overlooked due to the importance that is placed on "the product working like it's supposed to." Or maybe it's because of the overall complexity of designing and building a proper security framework. The amount of planning and forethought for security planning and construction can consume a large amount of a project's cycle. The irony about an application's security framework is that if it's working like it's supposed to, no one will notice it. When it's not working like it should, everyone will notice. This might be another reason why not enough attention is given to the application security requirements. Whatever the real reasons are, the results of not paying enough attention to the security considerations can be disastrous for the application and possibly the company.

Obviously, not all applications have the same exact requirements placed on them from a security perspective. However, for typical B2C and B2B Internet applications, there are many similarities when it comes to security design and constraints. Most of these applications are distributed component-based applications. The key point in that sentence is "distributed." Because these components are physically distributed over a network, there are more security holes that possibly can be exploited by attackers and unauthorized users.

The types of networks that these components use to communicate with one another can vary greatly, but often some portion of the application must be exposed to an unprotected open network such as the Internet. For example, a browser that makes a call to a servlet or JSP page typically will send the request, and the data within the request, over the Internet to the Web server, which usually is listening on a well-known port. As this request travels over the open Internet, many bad things can happen along the way. The request might contain the customer's credit card information for an order. If an unauthorized person were to intercept the request and get this information, you can imagine how unhappy this customer would be.

Because most Web servers listen on a common set of port numbers, extra precautions must be taken to protect the customer's information and requests. This is just one piece of the security puzzle with which application designers must deal. This chapter takes a closer look at some of the other security issues that you must consider when designing and building EJB applications. Like many other things in software development, the earlier you deal with these issues during analysis and design, the better the chances you'll have of building a more secure and resilient application.

UNDERSTANDING YOUR APPLICATION'S SECURITY REQUIREMENTS

As we stated earlier, not all target environments have the same security needs and constraints. However, there are some broad generalities we can make about typical EJB applications. The following list describes some of the common security-related features or aspects:

- Physically separated tiers
- User-level access based on username/password
- Different vendor products used throughout the application
- Sensitive and nonsensitive data being used

PHYSICALLY SEPARATED TIERS

A typical EJB application might have three or more physical tiers, all running on separate machines. The Web tier usually is on a server that is placed where Internet or intranet HTTP traffic can reach it. The Application tier usually is on a server located in the enterprise's protected network infrastructure. It's typically not exposed to the Internet directly, because the traffic to it usually comes from the Web server.

Many EJB vendors these days provide Web servers inside the EJB server itself. This usually can give better performance and provide for better maintenance because everything is centrally located. The problem with this approach, however, is that the entire tier might have to be exposed closer to the Internet because of this lack of separation between the two tiers. You should give plenty of thought to your security requirements before taking advantage of this configuration. Be sure you have other strong measures in place to protect someone from getting into your application server and causing damage to the system.

The third tier usually is a database server that is used explicitly by the application tier and possibly other enterprise resource planning (ERP) systems. The database houses the mission-critical data for the application, including important customer-sensitive data. The Database tier should be located deep in the company's protected network infrastructure with no path to it from the outside world. If an attacker does get at this data, it could spell the end for the company and many customers' credit reports. There have been several incidences lately where hackers were able to get a list of credit-card numbers for customers that did business with an online company. This is the worst possible thing that could happen for an Internet company and its product. Always be sure to protect this data and never expose it to unauthorized individuals. You probably want to go as far as encrypting sensitive information in the database to ensure that even if someone gets credit-card numbers, they won't be able to use them easily.

Continuing with the sweeping generalities, Figure 14.1 presents a physical network topology for a typical EJB application. The figure shows how and where security measures are usually applied.

Figure 14.1 shows that there is usually at least one demilitarized zone (DMZ) where components are somewhat exposed to the Internet or some other unprotected networks. The DMZ is the part of the network that is most susceptible to intruders and attacks. The DMZ area is given much more attention for security considerations than other areas that are located deeper in the company's intranet. This usually done with a combination of software and hardware configurations.

Figure 14.1
A typical Enterprise
JavaBeans network
security topology.

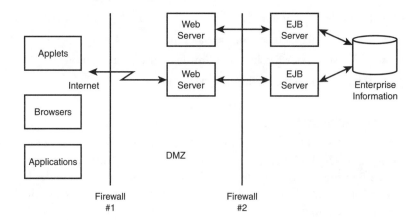

USER-LEVEL ACCESS BASED ON USERNAME/PASSWORD

Another common feature of EJB applications is that end users can be authenticated with a username and password. The username and password attributes are the only information that is typically provided by the end user to be identified. To protect sensitive information such as this, Web applications use digital certificates. Certificates are installed on the Web servers for the application and use the Secure Sockets Layer (SSL) protocol to protect customer data that must be sent from the client browser to the Web server. By using HTTPS rather than just the HTTP protocol, data will be sent encrypted and not in the clear. This helps ensure confidentiality and integrity of the user's data and requests.

Digital certificates are most often installed on the Web server, but usually not on the end user's browser. If a digital certificate is installed on both the Web server and the client's browser, this form of authentication is known as *mutual authentication* and is not commonly done on B2C or B2B applications. It might be more prevalent in B2B applications, but even this isn't the norm. SSL usually is sufficient.

DIFFERENT VENDOR PRODUCTS USED

Unless you are using an EJB server that includes the Web server and you are taking advantage of this feature, you generally have products from different vendors throughout the enterprise application. One of the goals of the EJB and J2EE architectures is to allow for developers to choose the best vendor for a specific technology. The problem associated with different vendors is that sometimes the integration process is immense.

Fortunately, interoperability has been given plenty of attention from the EJB and J2EE specifications, so many of the interoperability problems have been solved. However, security interoperability is one of the weakest parts of the specification. This is not to say that it can't and is not being done, it's just that part of the specification seems to be behind when compared to some of the other areas. If your components do have to communicate in a secure fashion, one choice is always to use the SSL protocol. Because RMI/IIOP is the standard wire protocol between J2EE clients and containers, SSL is a nice solution because IIOP can be used on top of the protocol when communicating between the Web tier and EJB container, for example.

SENSITIVE AND NONSENSITIVE DATA BEING USED

Not all applications need to encrypt data that is sent from tier to tier. In most cases, just the communications between the Client tier and Web tier might need to be protected. This is not always the case, but it's true more often than not. Encryption doesn't come without a price. There is a negative impact on performance and administration when you need to use encryption to protect the data. Most applications will change into a secured mode only when it's absolutely necessary. Others might use HTTPS from the moment the customer sends the username and password. You must think about when you actually need to use encryption to protect the data. It really depends on your customer base and when certain data is being sent to and from the user's browser.

BASIC SECURITY CONCEPTS

One of hardest things about understanding security design and construction is figuring out what all the terms mean and how everything fits together. This section attempts to provide a clear, simple definition for these terms so that we can have a foundation for the rest of the chapter.

AUTHENTICATION AND AUTHORIZATION

Authentication is the process of entities proving to one another that they are acting on behalf of specific identities. For example, when a Web user provides a username and password for a login, the authentication process verifies that this is a valid application user and that the password matches the real user's provided password. Various types of authentication mechanisms can be used. Other than no authentication, two main categories are employed in the various EJB products, although the actual naming conventions might be different.

Weak or *simple authentication* is where the user provides a username and password to be authenticated. The user provides no other authentication information. This probably is the most common form of authentication in EJB applications. One main concern with simple authentication is that if someone else gets your username and password, they can assume your identity.

As you might expect, *strong authentication* is more secure than simple or weak authentication. This is where the user provides a digital certification or other private means of being authenticated. It's much harder for someone to get your digital certificate from your machine. Even if they do, the certificate is good for only a particular machine and will be pretty much worthless to them.

Other authentication mechanisms can be used as well. Sometime within the next year or two, banks are planning to introduce automatic teller machines (ATMs) with a security measure that scans the user's iris. Although we might be a few years away from users of eBay.com wanting to get their eyes scanned before they can log in, newer types of authentication are being developed. Another up and coming authentication mechanism involves fingerprint scans. This actually is used in some larger government-type systems that need more security for the system.

Authorization differs from authentication in that authentication is about ensuring only valid users get access into an application, whereas authorization is more about controlling what the authenticated user is allowed to do after they get into the application.

Authentication happens first, and then authorization should happen next, assuming authentication succeeds. For some simple EJB applications, it's possible that only authentication needs to be used. However, for many applications, there is some type of administrator functionality that a normal user should not have access to. One of the ways that this can be prevented is by creating a list of permissions for actions that a user can perform and then checking this permission list against the actions attempted by the user.

Authorization typically is much harder and more complex to perform. Some applications can get by without doing much authorization, although by adding authorization to the framework and making it possible, you will save yourself many headaches later trying to incorporate it.

DATA INTEGRITY

Data integrity is the means or mechanism of ensuring that data has not been tampered with between the sender and the receiver. It ensures that no third party could have modified the information, which is possible when it's sent over an open network. If the receiver detects that a message might have been tampered with, it would probably want to discard the message.

CONFIDENTIALITY AND DATA PRIVACY

Confidentiality is the mechanism of making the information available to only the intended recipient. Ensuring that the system you are communicating with is really the one that you intended to communicate with is the biggest part of this concept. There are many ways hackers can trick you into sharing sensitive data. There was a case recently where a lesser-known security hole allowed hackers to modify DNS entries and cause traffic from an actual bank to be rerouted to a fake site. The fake Web site set up the Web pages to look exactly like the bank's site and attempted to capture the user's username and password, which could then be used on the real site to gain access. Digital certificates help solve most of the associated problems, but you must keep your eyes open.

NONREPUDIATION

This is one of the most misunderstood security concepts. Nonrepudiation is the act of proving that a particular user performed some action. For example, if a user submitted a bid for an auction, through proper record keeping and audit trails, the system administrators could prove that the action was performed by the particular user's account. It doesn't mean that that owner of the account actually submitted the bid, but you can prove their account was used and that it's not just a data error.

Auditing is sometimes overlooked, but it's invaluable when an action that was performed on a user's account has to be verified. Other auditing features include invalid login attempts, which can point to possible attacks on the system.

PRINCIPALS AND USERS

A *principal* is an entity that can be authenticated by the system. This is typically an end user or another service requesting access to the application. The principal is usually identified by a name; most often the username that the end user uses to log in to the system.

SUBJECT

Subject is a term taken from other security technologies and applied to EJB recently with the introduction of Java Authentication and Authorization Service (JAAS) 1.0. A subject holds a collection of principals and their associated credentials. The idea of needing something broader than a principal came about because there are many systems where you might need different principals or credentials to access the various parts of an application. By using a subject that might hold on to these various principals and credentials, applications can support such things as single sign-ons.

CREDENTIALS

When an end user wants to be authenticated to the application, they must usually also provide some form of credential. This credential might be just a password when simple authentication is being used, or it might be a digital certificate when strong authentication is used. The credential usually is associated with a specific principal. The specifications don't specify the content or format of a credential, because both can vary widely.

GROUPS AND ROLES

Groups and roles sometimes can be thought of as the same thing, although they are used for different purposes. A *group* is a set of users who usually have something in common, such as working in the same department in a company. Groups are used primarily to manage many users in an efficient manner. When a group is granted permission to perform some action, all members of the group gain this permission indirectly.

A *role*, on the other hand, is more of a logical grouping of users. A bean provider might indicate that only an admin user can close an auction, but the bean provider doesn't usually have knowledge of the operational environment to establish the exact group to which a user must belong to close an auction, for example. There typically is a mapping of roles to the groups in the operational environment, but the deployer or application assembler handles this mapping.

ACCESS CONTROL LISTS (ACLS) AND PERMISSIONS

Permissions for an application represent a privilege to access a particular resource or to perform some action. An application administrator usually protects resources by creating lists of users and groups that have the permissions required to access this resource. These lists are

PART

I

CH

14

known as access control lists (ACLs). For example, a user with auction admin permissions may create, modify, or close an auction, but a user that has only bidder permissions may be allowed to participate only in the bidding process for an auction.

An ACL file is made up of AclEntries, which contain a set of permissions for a particular resource and a set of users and groups.

Security Realm

A security realm is a logical grouping of users, groups, and ACLs. The physical implementation of a security realm normally is done by a relational database, an LDAP server, a Windows NT or Unix security realm, or, in some very simple cases, a flat file. The realm is usually checked when authentication or authorization must occur to allow access for a user to the application. With some EJB vendors, a caching realm is used and loaded from the original security realm to help increase performance. When authentication or authorization occurs, the caching realm is checked first and, if it can authenticate or authorize from there, there's no need to incur the database IO. The caching realm usually is flushed often to ensure that dirty reads do not occur.

Java Security Fundamentals

To really understand the security mechanisms available to you in EJB, it would help to understand what security infrastructure is available from the core Java language and where it helps with EJB applications and where it falls short. This section introduces the security aspects of the Java language, but does so from a high enough level as not to complicate our discussion of EJB application security. Although the two have some ties, it's not absolutely necessary to understand the entire Java security model to program enterprise beans.

The security architecture in Java has evolved three significant times since it was first created. The changes were primarily made to ease some of the restrictions that were placed on Java applications and applets in the early releases. The Java security model has always been conservative, which you want from a security perspective, but the restrictions came at a price, which made it not so easy to get a consistent security policy for applications and applets alike. Although the use of applets is arguably less than it was in the early days of Java, it still helps to understand the reasoning for the changes.

Java 1.0 introduced the *security sandbox*, which confined untrusted code to run in a very protected area where it could not negatively affect other running systems or system resources. This was necessary because the client browser downloads applets and runs them on the local machine. A client didn't necessarily want an applet to be able to read and write to and from the file system, because severe damage to the user's data can take place. On the other hand, applications were given free reign to the system resources from a security perspective because they typically were launched locally. A component known as a `SecurityManager` is responsible for determining on which resources untrusted code is allowed to operate.

With Java 1.1, applets were allowed to run out of the sandbox, as long as they were signed with a private key. If an applet was unsigned, it was forced back into the sandbox model. Although this allowed signed applets to have the same possible resource access as an application, it still wasn't very flexible for developers.

JDK 1.2 (Java 2) introduced several improvements over the previous Java security models. First and foremost, it added the capability for applications and applets to use security policies in the same manner, which permitted a more flexible and consistent security mechanism for application developers. The Java security policy defines a set of permissions that grant specific access to resources such as the file system or sockets. Listing 14.1 shows some of the permissions in the default policy file that are installed with the SDK 1.3. Some of the lines have been wrapped to make them fit on the page.

LISTING 14.1 THE DEFAULT POLICY FILE INSTALLED FOR SDK 1.3

```
grant codeBase "file:${java.home}/lib/ext/*" {
  permission java.security.AllPermission;
};

grant {
  permission java.lang.RuntimePermission "stopThread";
  permission java.net.SocketPermission "localhost:1024-", "listen";
  permission java.util.PropertyPermission "java.version", "read";
  permission java.util.PropertyPermission "java.vendor", "read";
  permission java.util.PropertyPermission "java.vendor.url", "read";
  permission java.util.PropertyPermission "java.class.version", "read";
  permission java.util.PropertyPermission "os.name", "read";
  permission java.util.PropertyPermission "os.version", "read";
  permission java.util.PropertyPermission "os.arch", "read";
  permission java.util.PropertyPermission "file.separator", "read";
  permission java.util.PropertyPermission "path.separator", "read";
  permission java.util.PropertyPermission "line.separator", "read";
  permission java.util.PropertyPermission "java.specification.version", "read";
  permission java.util.PropertyPermission "java.specification.vendor", "read";
  permission java.util.PropertyPermission "java.specification.name", "read";
  permission java.util.PropertyPermission
      "java.vm.specification.version", "read";
  permission java.util.PropertyPermission
      "java.vm.specification.vendor", "read";
  permission java.util.PropertyPermission
      "java.vm.specification.name", "read";
  permission java.util.PropertyPermission "java.vm.version", "read";
  permission java.util.PropertyPermission "java.vm.vendor", "read";
  permission java.util.PropertyPermission "java.vm.name", "read";
  permission java.net.SocketPermission
      "1024-65535", "accept, connect, listen, resolve";
  permission java.net.SocketPermission
      "localhost", "accept, connect, listen, resolve";
};
```

PART

I

CH

14

The runtime system structures code into individual groups called *security domains*. Each domain contains a set of classes and, because permissions are defined at the domain level, all the classes within a particular domain have the same access permissions. This allows for a much more flexible security model, while at the same time allowing for configuration similar to the sandbox approach. By default, applications still have unlimited access, but if required, they can be constrained within a domain by using a security policy and installing a SecurityManager for the application. You can specify a SecurityManager for an application either by supplying one on the command line as a system property or by setting one up programmatically at the start of the application.

By using security policies, the security implementation can be separated from the policy. Figure 14.2 shows a diagram of the Java 2 security architecture.

Figure 14.2
The Java 2 security architecture.

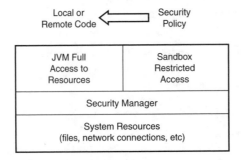

THE JAVA ClassLoader

The Java ClassLoader is responsible for loading Java byte codes into the Java Virtual Machine (JVM). It partners with the AccessContoller and the SecurityManager to ensure that the security policies are not violated. There are different types of class loaders, and third-party components can create a customer class loader to provide security features beyond those offered by the Java 2 standard security model.

One very important version of the class loader is called the "System" ClassLoader. This type of class loader helps launch the initial JVM by reading in classes and packages that are essential in starting the runtime system.

PERMISSION CLASSES

Permission classes are at the root of the Java security model. They allow or deny access to the system resources such as files, sockets, RMI objects, and so on. The set of permissions, when mapped to classes, can be conceptually thought of as the security policy for an application. A security policy file is used to configure the security rules for an application. The security policy file is a text file that can be viewed or edited by hand or by using the policy tool located in the bin directory of the Java home directory.

THE JAVA SecurityManager

The SecurityManager checks to ensure that the action that is being requested does not violate the security policies established in the security policy for an implementation. The

SecurityManager works with the AccessController to verify whether the permission should be granted or denied. If an unauthorized permission is attempted, it is the job of the SecurityManager to raise a security exception back to the requesting component.

THE AccessController CLASS

The AccessController class decides whether access to a system resource should be granted or denied based on the current security policy being used. The AccessController also has several static methods that can be used by an application to help check whether the calling component has the proper permission to access a resource. An AccessControlException will be raised if access is denied.

THE AccessControlContext CLASS

In normal situations, the SecurityManager delegates permission checks down to the AccessController class. The AccessController uses the context within the current thread to determine whether to grant the permission. In some situations, however, it's necessary to do work in a separate thread but still maintain the proper security context. This is where the AccessControlContext class can help. For example, if you needed to create a worker thread and allow it to have the same permissions as the parent thread, you can create an AccessControlContext object from the AccessController and pass it on to the worker thread to use for permission checks. This concept of obtaining the security context from the current thread and passing it or propagating it on to another thread will become very important when we talk about how J2EE containers propagate security information from one container to another during remote calls.

PRIVILEGED CODE

As the previous sections explained, the policy for an installation specifies what resources can be accessed based on the set of permissions for a protection domain. It sometimes is necessary for an application to override these restrictions and perform an otherwise unauthorized action. Marking code as *privileged* enables a piece of trusted code to temporarily grant access to more resources than are available directly to the code that called it.

Whenever a resource access is attempted, all the code that is called by the execution thread must have permission to access the particular resource, or an AccessControlException will be thrown. If the code for any caller in the call chain doesn't have the requested permission, the exception is thrown, unless one of the callers whose code does have the permission has been marked as privileged and all the callers called after this caller also have the permission.

To mark code as privileged, you can use the doPrivileged feature located on the AccessController class. The following code fragment illustrates how you might mark some code as privileged:

```
public class MyPrivilegedAction implements java.security.PrivilegedAction {

  public MyPrivilegedAction() {
    super();
  }
```

```
    public Object run(){
      // privileged code would go here
      FileInputStream stream = new FileInputStream( "aFile" );
      // do some work with the file

      // Nothing to return
    }
  }

// In some other class here

public void someMethod(){
    // Other code here
    MyPrivilegedAction action = new MyPrivilegedAction();
    // Changed to privileged
    java.security.AccessController.doPrivileged( action );
    // Once the privileged action finished, back to normal mode
  }
```

If you need to return a value from the run method, you'll need to cast it to the correct class stereotype. If the code in the run method might possibly throw a checked exception such as a FileNotFoundException, you will need to use the PrivilegedExceptionAction instead. The following code fragment illustrates how this might be handled:

```
public class MyPrivilegedAction implements PrivilegedExceptionAction {

  public MyPrivilegedAction() {
    super();
  }

  public Object run(){
    // privileged would go here

    // Nothing to return
  }
}

public void someMethod() throws java.io.FileNotFoundException {
    // Other code here
    MyPrivilegedAction action = new MyPrivilegedAction();
    // Changed to privileged

    try{
      FileInputStream inStr =
        (FileInputStream)java.security.AccessController.doPrivileged( action );
      //Once the privileged action finished, back to normal mode

      // The PrivilegedActionException is just a wrapper around the
      // real exception that occurred.
    }catch( PrivilegedActionException ex ){
      // Assuming a FileNotFoundException although you might really
      // want to check for this to be safe
      throw (FileNotFoundException)ex.getException();
    }
  }
```

When the privileged code is finished, the application should go back to the normal policy and permission use. Be very careful when using this feature, and keep the section of code that is executing as privileged as small as possible to prevent security holes.

USING SECURITY WITH ENTERPRISE JAVABEANS AND J2EE

Security is an important part of the J2EE and EJB specifications, although many EJB developers argue that there is much more that the specifications need to account for from a security perspective. The J2EE 1.3 and EJB 2.0 Specifications are better than the previous versions when it comes to specifying standards for dealing with security issues. Three main security goals are set for the EJB architecture:

- Lessen the burden placed on the bean provider for dealing with security issues.
- Allow the EJB applications to be portable across different vendor's servers and allow the different vendors to use different security mechanisms.
- Allow support for security policies to be set by the deployer or assembler rather than by the bean provider.

The EJB and J2EE specifications describe two entirely different methods of handling security in enterprise beans and in other J2EE components. These two methods are called programmatic and declarative security.

USING PROGRAMMATIC SECURITY

The EJB 2.0 Specification recommends not using programmatic security in your enterprise beans because it's too easy to couple your application to the physical security environment. If you needed to deploy your application in other security domains with different roles, it might make it necessary to have to change source code to work correctly in this new environment.

Even though it's not recommended, there are still situations that arise that make it necessary to use programmatic security in your applications. Applications should use programmatic security mainly when the declarative method does not offer enough flexibility or when business requirements dictate the need.

For the most part, either an enterprise bean or a servlet can use programmatic security. When doing programmatic security within EJB, you can use the methods defined in the EJBContext interface:

```
public boolean isCallerInRole(String roleName);
public Principal getCallerPrincipal();
```

The isCallerInRole method tests whether the principal that made the call to the enterprise bean is a member of the role specified in the argument. The Principal is typically propagated over from another tier, and the security context information resides in the current thread. The following fragment shows an example of how you might use the `isCallerInRole` method in an enterprise bean:

```
//Other enterprise bean code here
//...
public void submitBid( Integer auctionId,
      double newBidAmount, String bidderUserName )
      throws InvalidBidException, InvalidAuctionStatusException{

    // Make sure this user is a valid bidder
    if ( !getSessionContext().isCallerInRole( "bidder" )) {
      throw new InvalidBidException( "You must register first" );
    }

    // Get the home interface for the english auction bean
    EnglishAuctionHome auctionHome = getEnglishAuctionHome();

    try{

      // Locate the correct auction
      EnglishAuction auction = auctionHome.findByPrimaryKey( auctionId );

      // Locate the bidder
      Bidder bidder = null;

      // Try to submit the bid
      auction.submitBid( newBidAmount, bidder );

    }catch( FinderException ex ){
      ex.printStackTrace();
    }catch( RemoteException ex ){
      ex.printStackTrace();
    }
  }
```

This is the `submitBid` method in the `AuctionHouseBean` class. If the user is not a member of the `bidder` role, they are not allowed to submit a bid, and an `InvalidBidException` is thrown. This would force a user to register before submitting bids for an auction.

Depending on the setting in the `security-identity` element in the bean's deployment descriptor, the `getCallerPrincipal` method returns the `Principal` object for the current caller. When the `security-identity` element has a `use-caller-identity` value in it, the original caller of the enterprise bean will be propagated when the bean makes calls on itself.

If the deployer specifies a `run-as` element in the deployment descriptor, a different principal other than the initial caller might be returned from this method. A deployer can set the `security-identity` to another principal to execute with more permissions than the current caller. For example, it might need to invoke an operation as an administrator, but the operational environment doesn't want to map all callers to this group directly.

The following example shows an example of how you might use the `getCallerPrincipal` method in an enterprise bean:

```
//Other enterprise bean code here
//...
Principal principal = getSessionContext().getCallerPrincipal();
String bidderName = null;
if ( principal != null ) {
  bidderName = principal.getName();
}else{
  bidderName = "Unknown";
}

// Log the user's bid attempt to a file
String msg = bidderName + " submitted a bid for auction: " + auctionId );
logMessage( msg );
```

Programmatic security is done similarly in a servlet by using these two methods on the `HttpServletRequest` interface:

```
public boolean isUserInRole(String roleName);
public Principal getUserPrincipal();
```

These methods allow the components to make business logic decisions based on the security role of the caller or remote user. Whether the servlet makes a call to a security realm in the application tier or has the information cached on the Web tier is entirely up to the container's implementation.

Caution

The form and context of the principal names will vary greatly depending on the authentication and vendor used.

When an enterprise bean uses the `isCallerInRole` method within an enterprise bean, the bean provider must declare each security role referenced in the code using the `security-role-ref` element. The following example illustrates how an enterprise bean's references to security roles are used in the deployment descriptor:

```
<ejb-jar>
  <enterprise-beans>
    ...
    <entity>
      <ejb-name>EnglishAuction</ejb-name>
      ...
      <security-role-ref>
        <description>The auction restricts some operations to valid bidders
        </description>
        <role-name>bidder</role-name>
      </security-role-ref>
      ...
    </entity>
    ...
  </enterprise-beans>
  ...
</ejb-jar>
```

PART

I

CH

14

The deployment descriptor indicates that the enterprise bean `EnglishAuction` invokes the `isCallerInRole` method using the role of "bidder." There can be multiple `security-role-ref` elements for an enterprise bean, one for each different role used as an argument to the `isCallerInRole` method. The role name is scoped only to the enterprise bean that declares it, so if you use the same role name in a different enterprise bean, you'll need to declare a `security-role-ref` element in the deployment descriptor for that bean as well.

USING DECLARATIVE SECURITY

Declarative security is done by expressing an application's security policy, including which security role or roles have permission to access an enterprise bean, in a form that is completely external to the application code. The application assembler uses one or more `security-role` elements in the assembly instructions in the deployment descriptor. Here's a sample deployment descriptor that includes a `security-role` element added by the assembler:

```
<ejb-jar>
  <enterprise-beans>
    ...
    <entity>
      <ejb-name>EnglishAuction</ejb-name>
      ...
      <security-role-ref>
        <description>The auction restricts some operations to valid bidders
        </description>
        <role-name>bidder</role-name>
        <role-link>registered-bidder</role-link>
      </security-role-ref>
      ...
    </entity>
    ...
  </enterprise-beans>
  <assembly-descriptor>
    <security-role>
      <description>A role to represent users who have registered with the
        system as authorized auction participants
      </description>
      <role-name>registered-bidder</role-name>
    </security-role>
  </assembly-descriptor>
  ...
  ...
</ejb-jar>
```

The deployment descriptor includes a `security-role` element that defines a role of "registered-bidder."

Note

The roles defined in the `security-role` element do not represent roles in the physical operation environment. They are used only to define a logical security view of an application. They should not be confused with user groups, principals, and other security concepts that exist in the operational environment.

It's also a requirement for the application assembler to map any security-role-ref elements defined by the bean provider to the security-role elements. The assembler does this by inserting a role-link element in the security-role-ref element that references one of the valid security-role elements.

The application assembler is not required to add security-role elements to the deployment descriptor. The reason that the assembler would do it in the first place is to provide information to the deployer so that the deployer doesn't have to have intimate knowledge about what the business methods are for or are doing. If the assembler adds no security-role elements to the deployment descriptor, it's up to the deployer to understand the business methods in the enterprise beans and the operational environment to conduct the mapping. The security-role elements are scoped to the deployment descriptor and would need to be duplicated in other ejb-jar.xml files.

If the application assembler does provide one or more security-role elements in the deployment descriptor, they can also specify the methods of the home and remote interfaces that each role is authorized to invoke. The assembler defines the method permissions in the deployment descriptor using the method-permission element. Each method-permission element can contain one or more security roles and one or more methods. The following illustrates how an assembler might configure the method permissions:

```
<ejb-jar>
  <enterprise-beans>
    ...
    <entity>
      <ejb-name>EnglishAuction</ejb-name>
      ...
      <security-role-ref>
        <description>The auction restricts some operations to valid bidders
        </description>
        <role-name>bidder</role-name>
        <role-link>registered-bidder</role-link>
      </security-role-ref>
      ...
    </entity>
    ...
  </enterprise-beans>
  <assembly-descriptor>
    <security-role>
      <description>A role to represent users who have registered with the
        system as authorized auction participants
      </description>
      <role-name>registered-bidder</role-name>
    </security-role>
    <security-role>
      <description>
        A role to represent a user who has permission to close an auction
      </description>
      <role-name>authorized-agent</role-name>
    </security-role>
  </assembly-descriptor>
  ...
  ...
```

```
  <method-permission>
   <role-name>registered-bidder</role-name>
   <role-name>authorized-agent</role-name>
   <method>
     <ejb-name>EnglishAuction</ejb-name>
     <method-name>getLeadingBid</method-name>
   </method>
  </method-permission>
</ejb-jar>
```

There can be multiple method-permission elements in the deployment descriptor. The method permission for the enterprise beans is defined as the union of all the method permissions defined in the deployment descriptor.

There are three different ways of writing a method-permission element within the deployment descriptor. The first method is used for referring to all the remote and home methods of a specified bean:

```
<method-permission>
  <role-name>registered-bidder</role-name>
  <method>
    <ejb-name>AuctionHouse</ejb-name>
    <method-name>*</method-name>
  </method>
</method-permission>
```

The wildcard "*" is used to indicate the roles that can access all the methods on both interfaces. The second style of declaring a method-permission element is

```
<method-permission>
  <role-name>registered-bidder</role-name>
  <method>
    <ejb-name>AuctionHouse</ejb-name>
    <method-name>submitBid</method-name>
  </method>
</method-permission>
```

It is used to specify a particular method of the home or component interface. If there are multiple overloaded methods with the same name, this style would grant access to all the different overloaded methods with the same name.

If there are overloaded methods with the same name and you would like to reference a particular method, you can use the third method:

```
<method-permission>
  <role-name>registered-bidder</role-name>
  <method>
    <ejb-name>AuctionHouse</ejb-name>
    <method-name>submitBid</method-name>
    <method-params>
      <method-param>java.lang.Double</method-param>
    </method-params>
  </method>
</method-permission>
```

The method-params element contains a list of fully qualified java types of the method's input parameters in order. If you want to choose an overloaded method that takes no parameters, you would have an empty method-params element like this:

```
<method-params>
</method-params>
```

If the method contains an array, the method-param element would look like this:

```
<method-params>
  <method-param>int[]</method-param>
</method-params>
```

SPECIFYING IDENTITIES IN THE DEPLOYMENT DESCRIPTOR

The application assembler can specify whether the original caller's security identity should be used to execute methods within an enterprise bean or whether a specific run-as identity should be used. This doesn't affect the original caller's permission to call a bean, but it does affect the permissions associated with the bean when it calls other methods or beans. To do this, the assembler uses the security-identity element in the deployment descriptor. The value of this element can either be use-caller-identity or run-as. If run-as is specified, this element must include a role-name entry to define the security identity to be taken on by the bean. Because a message-driven bean doesn't interact directly with a caller, run-as is the only option if you want to control a message-driven bean's security identity. The assembler doesn't have to provide the security-identity element within the deployment descriptor. In this case, it's the responsibility of the deployer to determine which caller identity should be used when one component invokes an operation onto another.

MAPPING THE DEPLOYMENT ROLES TO THE PHYSICAL ENVIRONMENT

Up to this point in our discussion of setting up and defining the security view of our enterprise beans, we have said that the roles that are defined in the deployment descriptor are just logical roles and that the deployer would be responsible for performing the mapping of these logical roles to the ones that exist in the operational environment. The specifications leave it up to the vendor as to how this happens and, to be quite honest, not many of the vendors have provided a very flexible way to do this for anything but the most trivial security setups.

In some cases, the vendor expects you to put principal names directly into the deployment descriptor for the enterprise bean or servlet. Arguably, this is where EJB shows its immaturity the most. If you build an EJB application that you then sell and install for a customer, you don't want to have to modify the XML deployment descriptors just because the principals are different. Also, what about an existing customer that wants to add or delete an existing principal; does that mean you are going to have to redeploy a component?

You definitely should attempt to follow the intent of the EJB specification or suffer the consequences of lack of portability and interoperability if you don't. In some cases, however, you'll need to think out of the box and provide your own implementation. Security just might be one of those places. The next section discusses how the auction's application needs have some special security requirements and how we'll fulfill those requirements by building in our own security model.

SKETCHING OUT THE AUCTION SECURITY

As you saw in the previous section, the security features provided by the EJB and servlet containers are sufficient for many types of EJB applications. However, as we pointed out in the beginning of this chapter, some things are not covered by the specifications. For example, what if your Web application wanted to cache the user's security context in the Web tier to prevent redundant network calls to the security realm, which is typically located in the application tier? Suppose that you had a set of requirements to not show certain buttons, hyperlinks, or tabs depending on the user's roles and permissions. If you had to make several network calls while dynamically spitting out a JSP page, your performance would definitely suffer.

To understand this a little better, let's take a look at what happens in a typical Web-enabled EJB application. Our auction application consists of a set of JSP pages located on the Web tier that will dynamically allow certain features depending on who you are and what role you are playing for a particular session. Two scenarios will emphasize the problem.

- Scenario 1—User Bob posts an auction for others to bid on.
- Scenario 2—User Bob submits a bid for an auction posted by someone else.

When Bob posts an auction for others to bid on, he's acting in the role of Auctioneer. This role has certain permissions when it comes to managing this particular auction. Bob would be an Auctioneer only for auctions that he created. He would be given the ability to cancel the auction, assign an early winner to the auction, and respond to questions about the auction. However, Bob must not have this ability when viewing other auctions. Therefore, the security framework should be capable of distinguishing the two roles based on the dynamic data for the user. Although the EJB security framework would prevent Bob from making invocations on particular servlets or methods within an enterprise bean, there's no real local way to get at the permissions that an auction user has been granted without going back and forth to the application tier.

Another problem is that servlets and enterprise beans are role-based. This means that you either are in a role or are not. If you are in the role, you have permissions for everything the role has been granted. If you don't belong to a particular role, you are restricted from all permissions granted to that role. There's no way to assign or remove a single permission without putting the user in a role or taking them out of a role. It would be nice and much more flexible if we could not only assign permissions to a group, but also assign them directly to the user. The EJB security architecture doesn't allow for this directly, so we'll have to design our own way of handling this set of requirements if we truly need this behavior.

For our auction application, we need to provide a way for the Web tier to get a set of groups and permissions that the client has been granted and then cache this information on the Web tier for performance. Because we are caching these on the Web tier, changes made to the security realm itself will not be reflected to the user during a user's live session. However, after the user logs out and then comes back in later, the changes will be reflected in the security context information that is marshaled to the Web tier.

So, the plan for our auction example is going to include a session bean called SecurityManager that will be called only by a special login servlet on the Web server. We also will create an AdminSecurityManager session bean that will be responsible for creating, updating, and deleting users and groups. This session bean could be used from an admin application within the Web tier or, maybe to add more security, it might be called only by an application installed within the intranet. This separation of responsibility helps with security and also provides a more cohesive interface for each component because the responsibilities are arranged in a logical manner. The following code fragments show the steps for a login method inside the SecurityManagerBean class:

```
public SecurityContext login( String userName, String password )
  throws InvalidLoginException {

  SecurityContext secCtx = null;

  // Get a database connection from the datasource and look for the user
  // and make sure the account is still active

  // If the user doesn't exist or is inactive, throw an exception

  // If the user does exist, build the security context information

    // Get the user's permissions and groups and build the collections

    // return the context back to the caller
    return secCtx;
}
```

CREATING THE AUCTION SECURITY REALM SCHEMA

For our example, we are going to be storing users, groups, and permissions in a relational database. We will need to create the database schema for these three tables. Listing 14.2 shows the DDL for our security schema.

LISTING 14.2   THE SAMPLE AUCTION SECURITY REALM SCHEMA

```
#=========================
# Table SecGroup
# Represents a Security Group for the Auction Application
#=========================
CREATE TABLE SecGroup (
  Id int NOT NULL,
  Name varchar (255) NOT NULL,
  Description varchar (255) NOT NULL
);
```

LISTING 14.2 CONTINUED

```
ALTER TABLE SecGroup ADD
    CONSTRAINT PK_SecGroup PRIMARY KEY (Id);


#========================
# Table SecUser
# Represents a Security User for the Auction Application
#========================
CREATE TABLE SecUser (
  Id int NOT NULL,
  FirstName varchar (255) NOT NULL,
  LastName varchar (255) NOT NULL,
  EmailAddress varchar (255) NULL,
  UserName varchar (255) NOT NULL,
  Password varchar (255) NOT NULL,
  AccountCreatedDate date NOT NULL,
  LastLoginDate date NULL,
  IsAccountActive varchar (1) NOT NULL
);
ALTER TABLE SecUser ADD
    CONSTRAINT PK_SecUser PRIMARY KEY (Id);


#========================
# Table SecUserSecGroup
# Represents a link table between User and Group
#========================
CREATE TABLE SecUserSecGroup (
  SecUserId int NOT NULL,
  SecGroupId int NOT NULL,
  IsGroupActive varchar (1) NOT NULL
);
ALTER TABLE SecUserSecGroup ADD CONSTRAINT
    PK_SecUserSecGroup PRIMARY KEY
    (SecUserId, SecGroupId);

ALTER TABLE SecUserSecGroup ADD
  CONSTRAINT FK_SecUserSecGroup_User FOREIGN KEY
    (SecUserId) REFERENCES SecUser (Id);

ALTER TABLE SecUserSecGroup ADD
  CONSTRAINT FK_SecUserSecGroup_Group FOREIGN KEY
      (SecGroupId) REFERENCES SecGroup (Id);


#========================
# Table Permission
# Represents a permission that a user or group can perform
#========================
CREATE TABLE Permission (
  Id int NOT NULL,
  Name varchar (255) NOT NULL,
  Description varchar (255) NOT NULL
);
ALTER TABLE Permission ADD
    CONSTRAINT PK_Permission PRIMARY KEY (Id);
```

LISTING 14.2   CONTINUED

```
#========================
# Table SecUserPermission
# Represents a link table between User and Permission
#========================
CREATE TABLE SecUserPermission (
  SecUserId int NOT NULL,
  PermissionId int NOT NULL
);
ALTER TABLE SecUserPermission ADD
    CONSTRAINT PK_SecUserPermission PRIMARY KEY
    (SecUserId, PermissionId);

ALTER TABLE SecUserPermission ADD
  CONSTRAINT FK_SecUserPermission_User FOREIGN KEY
    (SecUserId) REFERENCES SecUser (Id);

ALTER TABLE SecUserPermission ADD
  CONSTRAINT FK_SecUserPerm_Permission FOREIGN KEY
      (PermissionId) REFERENCES Permission (Id);

#========================
# Table SecGroupPermission
# Represents a link table between Group and Permission
#========================
CREATE TABLE SecGroupPermission (
  SecGroupId int NOT NULL,
  PermissionId int NOT NULL
);
ALTER TABLE SecGroupPermission ADD
    CONSTRAINT PK_SecGroupPermission PRIMARY KEY
    (SecGroupId, PermissionId);

ALTER TABLE SecGroupPermission ADD
  CONSTRAINT FK_SecGroupPermission_Group FOREIGN KEY
    (SecGroupId) REFERENCES SecGroup (Id);

ALTER TABLE SecGroupPermission ADD
  CONSTRAINT FK_SecGroupPerm_Permission FOREIGN KEY
      (PermissionId) REFERENCES Permission (Id);
```

In the schema in Listing 14.2, we've included only the necessary attributes to understand the design. You might need more attributes, depending on your requirements. This schema was tested on Oracle 8i. If you want to test this on other database vendors, you might have to make a few modifications to the schema to support these other vendors. Don't worry too much about the exact definition of this security schema. There could be some normalization or denormalization on it, depending on how much you like normalized databases. The schema isn't presented to show a good database design, but rather to give you an idea of what types of table and attributes must be supported for the auction security realm.

PART

I

CH

14

DESIGNING ACCESS TO THE SECURITY REALM

The security objects are pretty lightweight objects, which means they don't contain many attributes or even a great deal of business logic. Choosing whether the security objects are entity beans or not depends on several factors, one of which is your particular strategy for making things entity beans or not. Making concepts in your logical model an entity bean can solve many of the transactional and concurrency headaches associated with persistent objects. You also can gain much more scalability because the container handles the life cycle for the enterprise bean and is able to shuffle resources as needed. All these things are true; however, you still don't want everything from your logical model translating into an entity bean. For one thing, if no client needs to access the data remotely, this can be one argument for not being an entity bean. Of course, there are others.

→ For more information on what types of objects should be entity beans, **see** "Entity Beans," **p. 105**.

If you don't want to use entity beans and you are using bean-managed persistence, an alternative solution is to access the data in the relational database directly from the session beans. The session beans could return immutable view classes back to the client by using JDBC directly from within the session bean methods. There are some benefits to using this approach; however, there are some transactional and concurrency problems that you must deal with. If the administrator is updating the data and the client is reading it, concurrency must be dealt with to ensure that no transactional problems occur.

There are several Object to Relational Mapping (ORM) frameworks that can provide help in this area. One such ORM is TOPLink from WebGain. TOPLink provides both a CMP and a BMP solution for EJB persistence and also deals with more complicated issues, such as data caching and transactional issues.

We are not going to provide the entire solution for the data-accessing problem here, but the recommendation for the auction example would be to use session beans to access the data and return immutable view classes to the client. This solution is not the most elegant, but it will definitely work for this situation.

USING SECURITY ATTRIBUTES IN THE WEB TIER

When the Web tier calls the `SecurityManager` session bean and attempts to log in, an object called `SecurityContext` will be returned if the login is successful. Each user will have its own `SecurityContext` instance cached in the `HttpSession`. The `SecurityContext` object will be used to validate the user's permission to perform actions within the auction Web site.

The `SecurityContext` object will contain a collection of roles or groups of which the user is a member, as well as a collection of permissions. The permission collection is a union of all the permissions from the groups to which the user belongs, as well as any extra permissions assigned directly to the user. This type of security design could also support negative permissions as well, rather than just additive. For example, if a user belongs to an "auctioneer" group that has a `cancelAuction` permission, we could easily add a column to the permission table called Additive that determines whether the permission should be added to the list of permissions or subtracted from the list. This gives the administrator more flexibility to determine how permissions are assigned or removed.

Listing 14.3 shows the `SecurityContext` class that will be built by the security session bean and returned to the Web tier.

LISTING 14.3   THE `SecurityContext` SOURCE REPRESENTING A USER'S SECURITY CONTEXT INFORMATION

```java
/**
 * Title:        SecurityContext<p>
 * Description: The user's security context information.<p>
 */
package com.que.ejb20.entity.businessobjects;

import java.security.Principal;
import java.util.Collection;

public class SecurityContext implements java.io.Serializable {

  private java.security.Principal principal;
  private java.util.Collection groups;
  private java.util.Collection permissions;

  public SecurityContext() {
    super();
  }

  public Principal getPrincipal() {
    return principal;
  }

  public void setPrincipal( Principal newPrincipal ) {
    principal = newPrincipal;
  }

  public void setGroups( Collection newGroups ) {
    groups = newGroups;
  }

  public Collection getGroups() {
    return groups;
  }

  public void setPermissions( Collection newPermissions ) {
    permissions = newPermissions;
  }

  public Collection getPermissions() {
    return permissions;
  }

  public boolean isUserInRole( String role ) {
    return this.groups.contains(role);
  }
```

PART

I

CH

14

LISTING 14.3   CONTINUED

```
  public boolean checkPermission( String permission ) {
    return this.permissions.contains( permission );
  }
}
```

The two most important methods in the SecurityContext class are isUserInRole and checkPermission. The client uses these two methods to determine to which security roles the user belongs and which security permissions have been granted to the user. Here's a code fragment that illustrates how a client can use these methods to hide or show a Close Auction button:

```
// Assume a SecurityContext has already been obtained
// Verify that the user is acting as the role auctioneer for this session
if ( secCtx.isUserInRole( "auctioneer" )) {
  // Check to see if they have the closeAuction permission
  if ( secCtx.checkPermission( "closeAuction" )) {
    // Show a close auction button here
  }
}
```

The Principal reference in the SecurityContext class is an interface from the Java 2 security package that represents the user. We are going to provide a UserView class that implements this interface and acts as the user in the system. Listing 14.4 shows the UserView class that is built by the SecurityManager and returned to the client.

LISTING 14.4   THIS CLASS REPRESENTS A USER WITHIN THE SYSTEM

```
/**
 * Title:        UserView<p>
 * Description: A view of the user in the system<p>
 */
package com.que.ejb20.entity.businessobjects;

import java.io.Serializable;
import java.security.Principal;

public class UserView implements Principal, Serializable {

  private String firstName;
  private String lastName;
  private String emailAddress;
  private String userName;
  private String password;
  private String accountCreatedDate;
  private String lastLoginDate;
  private String active;

  public UserView() {
    super();
  }
```

LISTING 14.4 CONTINUED

```java
public String getFirstName() {
  return firstName;
}

public void setFirstName(String newFirstName) {
  firstName = newFirstName;
}

public void setLastName(String newLastName) {
  lastName = newLastName;
}

public String getLastName() {
  return lastName;
}

public void setEmailAddress(String newEmailAddress) {
  emailAddress = newEmailAddress;
}

public String getEmailAddress() {
  return emailAddress;
}

public void setUserName(String newUserName) {
  userName = newUserName;
}

public String getUserName() {
  return userName;
}

public void setPassword(String newPassword) {
  password = newPassword;
}

public String getPassword() {
  return password;
}

public void setAccountCreatedDate(String newAccountCreatedDate) {
  accountCreatedDate = newAccountCreatedDate;
}

public String getAccountCreatedDate() {
  return accountCreatedDate;
}

public void setLastLoginDate(String newLastLoginDate) {
  lastLoginDate = newLastLoginDate;
}

public String getLastLoginDate() {
  return lastLoginDate;
}
```

PART

I

CH

14

LISTING 14.4 CONTINUED

```
public void setActive(String newActive) {
  active = newActive;
}

public String getActive() {
  return active;
}

// Method implementation needed because this class implements the
// java.security
public String getName() {
  return this.userName;
}
}
```

If you were using JSP pages on the client, it might be a good idea to wrap the security checks inside a JSP Custom Tag library. This might make the JSP pages a little cleaner because they wouldn't have to access the `SecurityContext` object directly. If an instance of a `SecurityContext` class were stored in the session for each user, the JSP Tag handler would have direct access to it and could do all the checks for the JSP Page. The JSP page would just include the tag library information within it. You can find more information on JSP custom tags at

`http://java.sun.com/products/jsp/taglibraries.html`

PROPAGATING THE PRINCIPAL

There's one final note on implementing security in this manner. When a client invokes an operation on an enterprise bean, the principal is propagated to the EJB object from the client. This propagation is taken care of by the container or the stub classes, depending on the vendor's implementation. With the security design that we have discussed here, the `Principal` is not being associated with the current thread by our implementation, and it might not be propagated to the enterprise bean correctly. This would present some problems if the container has security attributes set up for the beans.

It might be a good idea to associate the `Principal` that is returned in the `SecurityContext` object with the current thread; this sometimes is referred to as *Thread-Specific Storage (TSS)*. Some EJB servers will associate the JNDI principal with the current thread when a client creates a remote interface and uses this principal to invoke calls on enterprise beans. In theory, the JNDI principal and credential are supposed to be used only to authenticate and authorize access to the naming and directory service. Several vendors use this security information for calls to the enterprise beans. Just be careful when taking advantage of this because chances are it will not be portable.

JAVA AUTHENTICATION AND AUTHORIZATION SERVICE (JAAS)

Within the J2EE 1.3 and EJB 2.0 Specifications, a new security-related technology for EJB applications called Java Authentication and Authorization Service (JAAS) is introduced. JAAS is a Java implementation of the standard Pluggable Authentication Module (PAM) framework. The goal of the PAM framework is to design an authentication mechanism that is independent of the application layer. In other words, an administrator should be able to plug in various authentication mechanisms on a per-application basis without affecting the application logic itself. You can find more information on the PAM framework at

`http://java.sun.com/security/jaas/doc/pam.html`

JAAS is a standard extension to the Java 2 SDK 1.3. The Java 2 security model only provides access controls based on where the code originated from and who signed the code. The Java 2 security model does not provide the capability to additionally enforce access controls based on who runs the code. JAAS compliments the Java 2 security model with this type of support. JAAS probably will be part of the core Java language with SDK 1.4 (code name Merlin) when it's released sometime in 2001.

As the name implies, JAAS can be divided into two main components: an authentication component and an authorization component.

AUTHENTICATION

The authentication component provides the capability to reliably and securely determine who is currently executing Java code. This is true regardless of whether the Java code being executed is an applet, an application, a JSP page, or a servlet.

> **Note**
>
> The authentication capability does not exist with the Java 2 security model. This is absolutely essential behavior for most EJB applications. Prior to JAAS, most applications had to build their own authentication support.

JAAS authentication supports different implementations to be plugged in without affecting the Java application using it. This allows applications to take advantage of the various security authentication technologies without having to rewrite your software. For example, if one customer needed to use a relational database to store user information and another used Lightweight Directory Access Protocol (LDAP), you could just plug in different implementations without negatively affecting the application.

PART

I

CH

14

AUTHORIZATION

The authorization component of JAAS extends the existing Java 2 security framework by restricting users from performing actions depending on who the user is and on the code source. After the user is authenticated, the system obtains the actions that are allowed for this user and remembers this throughout the life cycle of the user's current session with the application.

Note

JAAS supports a security policy similar to the Java 2 security policy. In fact, the JAAS policy is an extension and understands the permissions in the Java 2 policy file like `java.io.FilePermission` and `java.net.SocketPermission`.

JAAS CORE CLASSES

The main package for JAAS is the `javax.security.auth` package. Although three packages exist under the main package, it probably makes more sense to talk about JAAS from a logical grouping of classes, based on what tasks they perform in JAAS. A more logical grouping of classes for JAAS is

- Common classes
- Authentication classes
- Authorization classes

Caution

Don't be misled in believing that the classes are really separated into these groupings. It's more logical for us to discuss them this way, but they are grouped entirely differently.

THE COMMON CLASSES AND INTERFACES

Two common components are important to developers using JAAS: the `javax.auth.Subject` class and the interface `java.security.Principal`. The `Subject` represents an entity, such as an individual user or service. A `Subject` can have many principals, each one associated with a different application service. For example, if an application allowed a user to log in to two different parts of a site and the user used a different username for each part of the site, the user (`Subject`) would have two different principals. The `Principal` interface we are referring to here is actually the `Principal` interface that already exists in the Java 2 security framework.

The `Subject` class has two public constructors:

```
public Subject();
public Subject(boolean readonly, Set principals,
        Set publicCredentials, Set privateCredentials );
```

As you'll see later in this section, you also can obtain an authenticated Subject from a LoginContext class, which we haven't defined yet. The Subject class contains methods for getting the set of principals and public or private credentials.

Caution

If you modify the set that is returned from the getPrincipals, getPublicCredentials, or getPrivateCredentials methods in the Subject, the original set will also be modified. Make sure you get a copy if you don't want to affect the original set.

Public and private credentials are not part of the JAAS library. You can use any Java class to represent a credential, including something as simple as the String class.

Earlier you saw how to execute privileged actions using the AccessController class. The Subject class contains two static methods for executing privilege actions as a particular subject. The following methods associate the Subject with the current thread's AccessControlContext and then executes the privileged action by calling the methods on the AccessController class that you saw earlier in this chapter:

```
public static Object doAs(Subject subject, PrivilegedAction action );
public static Object doAs(Subject subject, PrivilegedExceptionAction action );
```

There also are two more methods on the Subject class that, instead of associating the Subject with the current thread's AccessControlContext, the Subject gets associated with the AccessControlContext provided as an argument. The two methods are

```
public static Object doAs(Subject subject,
                    PrivilegedAction action,
                    AccessControlContext ctx);

public static Object doAs(Subject subject,
                    PrivilegedExceptionAction action,
                    AccessControlContext ctx);
```

All these doAs methods play a very important role in how the security context information is propagated to a remote container. For example, if a Subject has already been authenticated in the Web tier and invokes a remote operation on an EJB server, the Web tier can use the Subject and Principal information and pass it along to the EJB container, which then can have access to the Principal information.

Note

Keep in mind that the behavior of propagating security context information from the current thread to other J2EE containers isn't unique to JAAS. This behavior is how many J2EE containers perform it already. JAAS merely uses the same techniques.

THE AUTHENTICATION CLASSES AND INTERFACES

The classes and interfaces in the authentication logical group deal exclusively with authenticating a Subject in the application. The classes and interface involved are javax.security. auth.spi.LoginModule, javax.security.auth.LoginContext, javax.security.auth. callback.Callback, and javax.security.auth.callback.CallbackHandler.

The LoginContext class provides methods to authenticate a Subject, regardless of the authentication mechanism being used. The LoginContext object uses a javax.security.auth.login.Configuration object to determine which authentication mechanisms to use to authenticate the Subject. The Configuration is associated with one or more classes that all implement the LoginModule interface. Each LoginModule is responsible for authenticating the Subject for a particular authentication service.

Here are the basic steps to authenticate a Subject:

1. Create an instance of the LoginContext class.
2. Specify the Configuration file for the LoginContext to use.
3. The Configuration loads all the LoginModules specified.
4. The client invokes the login method on the LoginContext.
5. Each login method in the different LoginModules can associate an authenticated principal with the Subject if the login succeeds.
6. The LoginContext returns the authenticated Subject to the client.
7. The client is then free to access the Subject and Principals from the LoginContext object.

We have left a few of the smaller details out here, but the most important steps have been listed and you should get the idea of how this works.

One thing that we have left out of the steps on purpose is discussing how the Callback and CallbackHandler interfaces are involved in the authentication process. These interfaces and the concrete classes are in the javax.security.auth.callback package. They can seem pretty confusing at first, but after you get the picture where they fit in during the authentication process, they make quite a bit of sense. The LoginContext class has four constructors. Two of the constructors take an instance of a class that implements the CallbackHandler interface. Here are the two methods that take an instance of the CallbackHandler interface:

```
public LoginContext(String name,CallbackHandler handler)
throws LoginException;
```

```
public LoginContext(String name,Subject subject, CallbackHandler handler)
throws LoginException;
```

The CallbackHandler is passed to each LoginModule in the initialize method. The LoginModule then can use the CallbackHandler instance to make a callback on the client to request information needed to continue with the authentication process. Typically, this information is a username and password. You might be wondering why you don't just pass this information to the `LoginContext` or `LoginModule` in the first place. The main reason is that each authentication mechanism is going to be different. Some might use a device to scan the iris of your eyes or scan your fingerprints. By using a callback instead of letting the application handle this up front, the implementation of the authentication mechanism is further decoupled from the application.

There are several concrete classes of the `Callback` interface for doing things such as getting usernames and passwords. Of course, you can implement your own as well.

> **Note**
>
> There has been some debate on how Web-friendly the callback mechanism is. This is because of the differences between the typical synchronous Web page login and the asynchronous callback. There are some solutions to get around this slight mismatch. One solution involves blocking the original thread until the callback thread acquires the information necessary to complete the authentication process. These issues will be addressed in further implementations.

THE AUTHORIZATION CLASSES AND INTERFACES

The last logical grouping of classes deals with the authorization portion of JAAS. After a `Subject` has been authenticated, a client can obtain the permissions that are granted to the particular `Subject` and code source. The permissions granted to a `Subject` are configured in a JAAS policy. The `javax.security.auth.PolicyFile` class is a default file-based implementation provided by JAAS. This file is similar to the Java 2 policy file, which contains one or more grant statements, each of which can contain a set of permission statements.

Each grant statement specifies a codebase/codesigners/Principals triplet, including the permissions that have been granted to that triplet. What this means is that all the permissions will be granted to any code downloaded from the specified codebase and signed by the specified code signer, as long as the `Subject` running the code has all the specified principals in the `Principal` set. The following fragment shows a sample entry in the JAAS policy file:

```
// example entry in JAAS policy file
grant CodeBase http://java.sun.com,
    SignedBy "johndoe",
    Principal com.sun.security.auth.NTPrincipal "admin"
{
    Permission java.io.FilePermission "c:/winnt/stuff", "read, write";
};
```

> **Note**
>
> The `CodeBase` and `SignedBy` components are optional and, if absent, will allow any codebase and signer to match. This includes code that is unsigned as well.

## CHAPTER 15

DEPLOYMENT

In this chapter

DEPLOYMENT DESCRIPTORS AND EJB ROLES

The deployment descriptor for an EJB is the `ejb-jar.xml` file included in the `ejb-jar` file used to deploy the bean. As you've seen in earlier chapters, you can control several characteristics of an EJB by using the entries in its deployment descriptor. From defining the transactional properties of methods to assigning security restrictions, you can change the behavior of a bean in many ways without having to change its code. This is the advantage of declarative control over being required to do everything programmatically. Having a declarative means to specify how your beans operate and relate to other objects and resources makes it easier to reuse them in multiple applications.

Most of what you define in a deployment descriptor has been covered in the various examples throughout the book, but this chapter covers it all in one place with more detail given on some of the options that are supported. Another difference here is that the elements of the deployment descriptor are discussed in terms of the role responsible for supplying them. Up until this point, it's been assumed that you were filling the roles of bean provider, application assembler, and deployer on your own. This will be true for you much of the time, especially when you're developing new components on projects that aren't too large for you to manage that way. Given that, you might think that the distinctions between these three roles don't matter to you. However, even when you must do the jobs assigned to every one of them, there are advantages to not forgetting about the EJB roles. Sometimes the need to act within a single role will be dictated to you, and other times considering the separate roles during design can help you create more flexible components even if you still have to do all the work.

If you purchase third-party EJBs or reuse those developed within your organization, you have no choice but to recognize the distinctions between the EJB roles. Here your responsibilities and options could be strictly defined because you might be working with beans whose code you can't change. When this is the case, the needs of the application assembler and deployer are more obvious (and definitely of more interest) to you. If you can't change the code for a bean you need to use, the only control you can exercise over it is through the deployment descriptor elements applicable to an application assembler or deployer. You might not face this on your initial EJB projects, but it's likely that this situation will become more common as the availability of third-party beans grows and your own organization begins building its inventory of reusable components from past projects.

Even if you're filling multiple EJB roles yourself, looking at the responsibilities of each one separately is still a good idea. If you put on your application assembler hat during the design process and think beyond the application you're currently developing, you're more likely to take steps to make your beans adaptable. This might include externalizing some key values used by a bean as environment properties or focusing on how to divide responsibilities between methods to make a bean more composable from a transactional sense. The same advice applies to considering how a deployer might need to adapt your beans to a particular environment as you're designing and implementing them. For these reasons, this chapter looks at the makeup of a deployment descriptor within the context of the EJB roles. Besides making you aware of the distinction between roles, this viewpoint will also make the structure of the descriptor elements more clear to you. As you'll see, some of the partitioning of the deployment descriptor elements is well aligned with the role boundaries. It also helps explain why some elements that are required to correctly deploy a bean are declared as optional by the DTD that applies to the deployment descriptor. What you'll see is that this is only done to defer their eventual definition to a particular role.

BEAN PROVIDER RESPONSIBILITIES

Responsibility for creating a bean's deployment descriptor starts with the bean provider. Certain information about a bean is independent of how it's assembled into an application and deployed. As the developer, you know, for example, the names of the home and remote interfaces that are associated with a particular bean and the identities of any other entity beans on which it depends. While still playing the role of bean provider, you're expected to supply the required descriptor elements such as these, plus any of the optional ones that you know at this stage.

Before looking at any particular attributes, the first thing to mention is the format of the deployment descriptor. The fact that a descriptor is stored as an XML file makes it easy to edit by hand. It's also easy for vendors to build deployment tools and IDE wizards that create and edit the entries in a descriptor. If you like IDEs and you use one of the more popular application servers, you'll rarely have to write a descriptor from scratch. On the other hand, if you'd never allow a wizard-laden GUI tool anywhere near your machine, you'll appreciate the fact that the file isn't too complicated relative to what it allows you to do. In either case, the content of the file is more interesting than its format. You still must be aware of the format, though, because XML is easy to read, but it's not very forgiving. Whether you're creating deployment files from the ground up or tweaking ones that have been created for you, you need to know how the file is laid out. With that in mind, the attributes you can define in a descriptor are covered here based on where they must appear within the file.

OVERALL FILE STRUCTURE

For an XML file to be validated, it must specify the XML version to which it's written and name the DTD that governs it. The first two entries in a deployment descriptor (which are always the same) are a result of this requirement:

```
<?xml version="1.0"?>

<!DOCTYPE ejb-jar PUBLIC
  '-//Sun Microsystems, Inc.//DTD Enterprise JavaBeans 2.0//EN'
  'http://java.sun.com/dtd/ejb-jar_2_0.dtd'>
```

These two lines aren't very interesting except that you can use the URL given for validating the file to download a copy of the DTD from Sun. Looking at the DTD is a quick way to verify that you have elements in the correct order and that you haven't left out a required entry. It also includes a short definition of each element that serves as a good reference.

Other than the XML version and the DTD reference, the contents of the descriptor are defined within the ejb-jar tag:

```
<ejb-jar>
  <description>
    This is an optional description of the ejb-jar file
  </description>
  <display-name>Optional short name used by tools</display-name>
  <small-icon>
  ...
  </small-icon>
  <large-icon>
  ...
  </large-icon>
  <enterprise-beans>
  ...
  </enterprise-beans>
  <relationships>
  ...
  </relationships>
  <assembly-descriptor>
  ...
  </assembly-descriptor>
  <ejb-client-jar>
  ...
  </ejb-client-jar>
</ejb-jar>
```

Note

With the increasing proliferation of XML, it's assumed that you're comfortable working with XML files. The concepts needed to work with a deployment descriptor are quite simple. Each element in an XML file is defined by an opening and a closing tag (for example, <ejb-jar> and </ejb-jar>). Unlike HTML, the name of each tag is case sensitive and closing tags are always required. This is sometimes referred to as "well-formed." The DTD for the 2.0 version of the ejb-jar.xml file defines the valid tags and their allowed values. The required order of tags within the element that encloses them is also defined by the DTD.

The elements within ejb-jar allow you to both describe the contents of the file and provide detailed information about the beans you're deploying. First, you can include the optional description element with a string that describes the contents of the deployment unit. This can be a brief description of the beans that are referenced by the file for use by an application assembler or deployer. The display-name element that follows (also optional) is for a short name that an assembly or deployment tool can use to identify the file's contents. To support the GUI nature of such tools, it's assumed that they might also have the capability to associate an icon with a deployment file. If your beans are used with one that does, you can include a 16×16 and a 32×32 image file (either JPEG or GIF) in your deployment JAR and identify them using the optional `small-icon` and `large-icon` elements. If you supply these icons, the filenames for the images must end in either `.gif` or `.jpg` and the path names must be relative to the root directory in the JAR.

The substance of the deployment descriptor starts with the `enterprise-beans` tag. As a bean provider, you can focus mostly on defining the information found within this tag and, if you're using CMP, the `relationships` tag that follows it.

THE `enterprise-beans` ELEMENT

Every EJB contained in an `ejb-jar` file must be identified within the `enterprise-beans` element of the deployment descriptor. This element can contain multiple bean descriptions, but it has to include at least one. The only elements allowed directly within `enterprise-beans` are `entity`, `session`, and `message-driven`. The file can include as many of these elements as you'd like (one per EJB) and you can include them in any order. Table 15.1 describes the fundamental elements found within these tags. The elements listed are given in order and are required unless otherwise noted.

TABLE 15.1   THE FUNDAMENTAL `entity`, `session`, AND `message-driven` ELEMENTS

Element	Description
description	A description of the bean (optional).
display-name	A short name for display by an assembly or deployment tool (optional).
small-icon	The filename for a 16×16 GIF or JPEG image included in the JAR to represent the bean (optional).
large-icon	The filename for a 32×32 icon image (optional).
ejb-name	A logical name for the bean assigned by the bean provider that is independent of its JNDI name assigned at deployment. This name must be unique among the EJB names defined in a single JAR file.
home	The fully qualified name of the home interface (entity and session beans only). This is required only if the bean exposes a remote view of itself.
remote	The fully qualified name of the remote interface (entity and session beans only). This is required only if the bean exposes a remote view of itself.
local-home	The fully qualified name of the local home interface (entity and session beans only). This is required only if the bean exposes a local view of itself.
local	The fully qualified name of the local interface (entity and session beans only). This is required only if the bean exposes a local view of itself.

TABLE 15.1   CONTINUED

Element	Description
ejb-class	The fully qualified name of the bean implementation class.
persistence-type	The persistence management type for an entity bean that must be specified as either Bean or Container (entity beans only).
prim-key-class	The fully qualified name of the primary key class. This element is required but it can be specified as java.lang.Object to defer the selection to deployment time. See Chapter 5, "Entity Beans," for a discussion of primary key classes (entity beans only).
reentrant	Specified as True if an entity bean allows loopback calls or False otherwise—see the discussion that follows (entity beans only).
cmp-version	Specified as 1.x or 2.x to indicate the version of container-managed persistence to use for an entity bean (entity beans only, optional, defaults to 2.x if not defined).
abstract-schema-name	The name for an entity bean using CMP version 2.x used by EJB QL queries that reference the bean (entity beans using CMP 2.x only).
cmp-field	A cmp-field entry is required for each persistent field of a CMP entity bean. Each entry can include an optional description and must include a field-name element that matches a public field of the bean class or one of its superclasses. For CMP 2.x, the field name must begin with a lowercase letter (entity beans only, one element required per persistent field).
primkey-field	The name of the cmp-field that represents the primary key of a CMP entity bean with a single-field key. The type of the field must match the prim-key-class. (Required only for CMP entity beans with single-field primary keys.)
session-type	Identifies a session bean as Stateful or Stateless (session beans only).
transaction-type	Specified as Bean or Container to indicate bean-managed or container-managed transaction demarcation, respectively (session and message-driven beans only).
message-selector	A selector string used to filter the messages a message-driven bean receives. Refer to Chapter 10, "Java Message Service," for a description of the format used for a selector (message-driven beans only, optional).
acknowledge-mode	Specified as Auto-acknowledge or Dups-ok-acknowledge to define the acknowledgement semantics for the onMessage method of a bean using bean-managed transaction demarcation (message-driven beans only, optional).
message-driven-destination	Indicates whether a message-driven bean should be associated with a queue or a topic (message-driven beans only, optional).

Note

For the `message-driven-destination` element in Table 15.1, it's up to the deployer to make the actual association, but this entry in the descriptor allows the bean provider to indicate which type should be used. If included, this element must contain a `destination-type` element specified as either `javax.jms.Queue` or `javax.jms.Topic`. If the destination is a topic, you also need to include the `subscription-durability` element to identify the subscription as either `Durable` or `NonDurable`.

→ For more information on choosing a primary key class, **see** "Defining the Primary Key Class," **p. 127**.

→ For more information on defining a `message-selector`, **see** "Message Selection and Filtering," **p. 280**.

Most of the elements described in Table 15.1 are straightforward, but there is one notable exception. This is the issue of reentrant and non-reentrant entity beans. If you declare an entity bean to be reentrant, the container will allow a business method of a single bean instance to be called through its component interface while that instance is in the midst of executing another business method. The intent is to support an entity calling a method on another bean that in turn calls a method on the first bean (all within the same transaction context). This is referred to as a loopback.

By itself, a loopback isn't too complex a scenario. The confusion arises when, instead of this situation, the entity is called concurrently by multiple clients within the same transaction context. Because the transaction context is the same in both cases, the container can't distinguish a concurrent call from a loopback. The problem is that a concurrent call within the same transaction context is illegal. Think of the erroneous results that could occur if, within the same transaction context, two clients were allowed to execute business methods of the same bean instance at the same time. The safest way to prevent this from happening is to avoid the use of loopbacks and declare your entity beans as non-reentrant. When you do this, the container will throw a `RemoteException` (or `EJBException` if the bean has a local client) if a loopback or concurrent call within the same transaction context is attempted. If you must use loopbacks, you have to take extra precautions to avoid illegal concurrent calls from client code because the container can't protect you from them.

env-entry

The remaining elements of `entity`, `session`, and `message-driven` are more involved than those given in Table 15.1, so they're covered individually. First, any type of EJB can reference parameters in its environment as a way to make the bean configurable without changing its source code. It's the bean provider's responsibility to declare these parameters and use them in a bean's implementation, but not to specify their values. Environment parameters are declared using the `env-entry` tag in the deployment descriptor. An EJB can have any number of these entries, which contain an optional `description`, an `env-entry-name`, an `env-entry-type`, and an `env-entry-value`. The DTD defines the `env-entry-value` as optional so that the bean provider can defer its assignment to the application assembler or deployer.

The env-entry-name defines the string that the EJB will use to locate the value within the environment.

You can name an entry anything you want as long as it's unique among the entries for a bean. Your bean code must cast an environment entry to a specific type so you have to define that type in the descriptor using the env-entry-type tag. You must specify the type as Boolean, Byte, Character, Double, Float, Integer, Long, Short, or String using the type's fully qualified name (for example, java.lang.Boolean). The following are examples of valid environment entry declarations by a bean provider:

```
<env-entry>
  <description>The maximum address line length that should be allowed
  </description>
  <env-entry-name>maxAddressLineLength</env-entry-name>
  <env-entry-type>java.lang.Integer</env-entry-type>
</env-entry>
<env-entry>
  <description>Should the system require a 9-digit zip code?</description>
  <env-entry-name>require9DigitZip</env-entry-name>
  <env-entry-type>java.lang.Boolean</env-entry-type>
</env-entry>
```

The value assigned to maxAddressLineLength could be accessed within a bean method using

```
InitialContext ctx = new InitialContext();
Integer maxLineLength =
  (Integer)ctx.lookup("java:comp/env/maxAddressLineLength");
```

In general, environment entries apply to all instances of a particular bean class, so they're only appropriate for common information that you can use to drive business logic or adapt a bean's behavior to its deployed environment. One slight exception occurs when a bean is deployed multiple times into the same container. Here, the home associated with each deployment assigns values to the environment based on the descriptor entries for that deployment. In this situation, clients can access bean instances with behavior that depends on which JNDI name they use to locate the bean's home interface.

An environment entry is always associated with a single bean class. There's no way for another EJB class to directly access an entry you've declared in a bean's deployment infor-mation. Also important to note is that these entries are read-only as far as your bean classes are concerned. An EJB cannot write to its deployment descriptor (neither can any other part of an application).

ejb-ref AND ejb-local-ref

The next descriptor elements are the ejb-ref and ejb-local-ref tags, which may be used by all EJB types. An ejb-ref entry identifies another EJB that a bean depends on and defines a name that your bean code can use to look up a reference to that bean's home inter-face. The ejb-local-ref entry identifies another EJB that the referencing bean depends on in the same manner, but defines a name for the local home of that referenced bean.

These descriptor elements contain an optional description and mandatory ejb-ref-name and ejb-ref-type elements. The ejb-ref entry contains elements for the home and remote names, and an optional ejb-link. The ejb-local-ref entry contains elements for the local-home, local, and the optional ejb-link.

The ejb-ref-name defines the logical name used by your bean class to do a JNDI lookup of the reference. You can use any string here but you should prefix it with ejb/ to follow recommended conventions. You can reference both session and entity beans, so the ejb-ref-type must be specified as either Session or Entity to indicate which type you're using. The home and remote tags simply contain the fully qualified interface names of the bean being referenced, whereas the local-home and local tags in the ejb-local-ref entry contain the fully qualified interface names of the referenced bean's local interfaces. The ejb-link element is used by the application assembler or deployer to identify the referenced EJB. This entry is declared as optional by the DTD only because it's not up to the bean provider to define it. You'll see how to define this element later. The following shows an example EJB reference entry using an ejb-local-ref tag:

```
<ejb-local-ref>
  <description>This EJB reference is used to locate an auction's item
  </description>
  <ejb-ref-name>ejb/Item</ejb-ref-name>
  <ejb-ref-type>Entity</ejb-ref-type>
  <local-home>com.que.ejb20.item.model.ItemHome</local-home>
  <local>com.que.ejb20.item.model.Item</local>
</ejb-local-ref>
```

Just like environment entries, an EJB reference is only accessible to the bean whose deployment information defines it. Within that bean, you can obtain the home interface for a referenced EJB using code like the following:

```
InitialContext ctx = new InitialContext();
Object homeObj = ctx.lookup("java:/comp/env/ejb/Item");
ItemHome home = (ItemHome)homeObj;
```

security-role-ref

The security aspects of the EJB architecture allow you to declaratively restrict who can call the individual methods of a bean. You can also code your session and entity beans to restrict their methods or modify their behavior based on the authorization associated with the caller. You do this by calling the isCallerInRole method of EJBContext and passing a string that represents the name of a security role.

This name doesn't have to match anything in particular—it just has to mean something within the context of the bean, such as employee or supervisor. The way you associate these names with actual security roles defined for an application's users is by defining security-role-ref entries in the deployment descriptor. This element contains an optional description, a role-name, and an role-link. The role-name has to match one of the string names used by the bean in a call to isCallerInRole for the entry to be valid. The role-link has to match one of the security-role role names defined later in the assembly-descriptor element. Following a pattern that should become familiar to you, the role-link is optional and should be supplied by the application assembler. The application assembler is also responsible for the `security-identity` elements that can follow the `security-role-ref` entries. These are discussed in the "Application Assembler Responsibilities" section. The following is an example security role reference declaration:

```
<security-role-ref>
  <description>The auction restricts some operations to valid bidders
  </description>
  <role-name>bidder</role-name>
</security-role-ref>
```

This role could be referenced in a bean in the following manner (assume `ctx` is a field that holds a reference to the `EJBContext`):

```
if (ctx.isCallerInRole("bidder")) {
  // do something only allowed for a bidder
}
```

resource-ref

If a bean requires a connection to a resource manager, you obtain that connection through a connection factory, which is an object that implements an interface such as `javax.sql.DataSource` or `javax.jms.QueueConnectionFactory`. To access a connection factory from a bean, you must include a `resource-ref` entry in the bean's descriptor. A `resource-ref` is supported for any EJB type and contains an optional `description`, a `res-ref-name`, a `res-type`, a `res-auth`, and an optional `res-sharing-scope`.

The bean provider is responsible for all parts of a `resource-ref` entry. Connection factory references are located using JNDI lookups based on the `res-ref-name`. Similar to placing EJB references under the `ejb` subcontext, you should place JDBC, JMS, JavaMail, and URL connection factory references under the `jdbc`, `jms`, `mail`, and `url` subcontexts, respectively. The `res-type` identifies the interface associated with the resource. This will usually be one of `javax.sql.DataSource`, `javax.jms.QueueConnectionFactory`, `javax.jms.TopicConnectionFactory`, `javax.mail.Session`, or `java.net.URL`.

The `res-auth` must be specified as either `Container` or `Application` to define how logging in to the resource is handled. If you specify `Container`, the container performs the login using information supplied by the deployer (such as the database username and password included in a connection pool declaration). This is the more common approach, but you can also log in programmatically if you specify `Application`. For example, the following code segment shows what would be required in your code to do this to access a database:

```
InitialContext ctx = new InitialContext();
DataSource source =
(DataSource)ctx.lookup("java:comp/env/jdbc/auctionSource");
// call getConnection without the login info to use Container authorization
Connection con = source.getConnection("MyUserName", "MyPassword");
```

The `res-sharing-scope` entry can be specified as either `Shareable` or `NonShareable`. This indicates whether a connection can be shared by multiple beans that access the same resource within the same transaction context. If this entry isn't included, the connections default to being shareable.

The following is an example connection factory reference:

```
<resource-ref>
  <description>Define a reference to a resource manager connection
    factory for the auction database
  </description>
  <res-ref-name>jdbc/auctionSource</res-ref-name>
  <res-type>javax.sql.DataSource</res-type>
  <res-auth>Container</res-auth>
</resource-ref>
```

resource-env-ref

Similar to EJB and connection factory references, a bean's use of administered objects associated with resources (such as JMS destinations) must also be indicated in the deployment descriptor. This is done using one or more resource-env-ref elements. This element type contains an optional description, a resource-env-ref-name, and a resource-env-ref-type. The resource-env-ref-name defines the name used by the bean in a JNDI lookup and should be prefixed with an appropriate subcontext name, such as jms/. The resource-env-ref-type identifies the object type expected by the bean and must be a fully qualified class or interface name such as javax.jms.Queue. An example of a resource environment reference follows:

```
<resource-env-ref>
  <description>Currency conversion updates are obtained through a queue
  </description>
  <resource-env-ref-name>jms/exchangeUpdate</resource-env-ref-name>
  <resource-env-ref-type>javax.jms.Queue</resource-env-ref-type>
</resource-env-ref>
```

A reference to this queue could be obtained by an EJB using code like the following:

```
Context ctx = new InitialContext();
Queue conversionQueue = (Queue)initCtx.lookup(
  "java:comp/env/jms/exchangeUpdate");
```

query

The final element that applies to a bean type element is the query tag, which is only valid for entity beans that use EJB 2.x CMP. Each query entry defines a finder or select query and contains an optional description, a query-method, an optional result-type-mapping, and an ejb-ql element. The query-method identifies the finder or select method using a method-name and a method-params entry. The method-name must always correspond to the name of a finder method in the home interface or a select method in the bean implementation class. If you're defining a select method that returns one or more entity references, you can use result-type-mapping to identify the interface type as either Remote or Local. Local is the default if you omit this entry.

The ejb-ql entry defines the query for the method. Refer to Chapter 8, "EJB Query Language," to learn the syntax for defining a query. The ejb-ql element should be left blank if the query isn't implemented using EJB QL. The following is an example of a query entry:

```
<query>
  <description>A finder method for locating auctions beyond a specified
    bid amount
  </description>
  <query-method>
    <method-name>findHighBidAuctions</method-name>
    <method-params>
      <method-param>java.lang.Double</method-param>
    </method-params>
  </query-method>
  <ejb-ql>SELECT OBJECT(auction) FROM EnglishAuctionBean AS auction,
    IN (auction.bids) aBid WHERE aBid.amount &gt; ?1
  </ejb-ql>
</query>
```

THE relationships ELEMENT

The relationships element defines associations among CMP 2.x entity beans. This element consists of an optional description, and one or more ejb-relation entries.

An ejb-relation element inside the relationships entry describes a relationship between two entity beans with container-managed persistence. The element contains an optional description, an optional ejb-relation-name, and exactly two ejb-relationship-role elements. Table 15.2 describes the elements of the ejb-relationship-role tag. You must specify one of these entries for each side of a relationship.

TABLE 15.2   THE CONTENT OF AN ejb-relationship-role TAG

Element	Description
description	A description of the relationship (optional).
ejb-relationship-role-name	A name for a role within the relationship. This name must be unique within the relationship but can be reused by other relationships (optional).
multiplicity	Specified as One or Many to define the multiplicity of this role in the relationship. Some implementations expect lowercase values and require one or many instead.
cascade-delete	Included for a role to indicate that it should be deleted if the entity bean on the other side of the relationship is deleted. You don't specify a value for this element—you just include the tag if you want it to apply. A cascade delete is only valid if the other ejb-relationship-role is defined with a multiplicity of One (optional).
relationship-role-source	This element identifies the class associated with the role. It contains an optional description and a mandatory ejb-name entry that corresponds to the referenced entity.
cmr-field	Identifies the field used to reference the related object. This element contains an optional description, a cmr-field-name, and a cmr-field-type. The cmr-field-name must begin with a lowercase letter and match the corresponding get and set methods for the relationship.

> **Note**
>
> For the `cmr-field` in Table 15.2, you only include the `cmr-field-type`, which must be specified as either `java.util.Collection` or `java.util.Set`, if the role on the other side of the relationship has multiplicity Many. Don't include the `cmr-field` element if the object on this side of the relationship can't navigate to the other side.

The following example illustrates how a one-to-many relationship is defined in the deployment descriptor:

```
<relationships>
  <ejb-relation>
    <ejb-relation-name>EnglishAuction-AuctionBid</ejb-relation-name>
    <ejb-relationship-role>
      <ejb-relationship-role-name>auction-has-bids
      </ejb-relationship-role-name>
      <multiplicity>one</multiplicity>
      <relationship-role-source>
        <ejb-name>EnglishAuction</ejb-name>
      </relationship-role-source>
      <cmr-field>
        <cmr-field-name>bids</cmr-field-name>
        <cmr-field-type>java.util.Collection</cmr-field-type>
      </cmr-field>
    </ejb-relationship-role>
    <ejb-relationship-role>
      <ejb-relationship-role-name>bid-belongs-to-auction
      </ejb-relationship-role-name>
      <multiplicity>many</multiplicity>
      <cascade-delete/>
      <relationship-role-source>
        <ejb-name>AuctionBid</ejb-name>
      </relationship-role-source>
      <cmr-field>
        <cmr-field-name>auction</cmr-field-name>
      </cmr-field>
    </ejb-relationship-role>
  </ejb-relation>
</relationships>
```

Note that the `multiplicity` entry relates to the role being defined and not to the object on the other side. Here this means that the entry for the auction role has multiplicity one and the entry for the bid role has multiplicity many.

THE `assembly-descriptor` AND `ejb-client-jar` ELEMENTS

The final high-level entries within the deployment descriptor are the `assembly-descriptor` and `ejb-client-jar` elements. The bean provider could supply some of the contents of the `assembly-descriptor` element, but, as its name implies, it's intended for the application assembler. The last element of `ejb-jar` is the `ejb-client-jar` tag. This is a simple (and optional) element that identifies a JAR file containing the classes needed by a client to access the beans defined in the deployment file. The EJB specification doesn't define a particular use for this, but a vendor could use it to simplify the deployment of any helper classes your EJBs rely on or a client application that uses your EJBs.

APPLICATION ASSEMBLER RESPONSIBILITIES

The bean provider is responsible for most of the deployment descriptor contents, but there's still work to be done by the other roles as well. An application assembler builds applications from EJBs. The application assembler starts with the deployment information provided by one or more bean providers and adds to it or modifies it to compose an application. Most of the additions take place in the `assembly-descriptor` part of the deployment file.

THE `assembly-descriptor` ELEMENT

The `assembly-descriptor` element is technically optional, but you would have trouble building a non-trivial application without using the declarative security and transactional mechanisms it controls. This element can contain any number of `security-role`, `method-permission`, `container-transaction` entries, and a single `exclude-list` entry provided by either the application assembler or the deployer.

security-role

The bean provider can define security role names and reference them in bean code, but the roles defined by the application assembler are the ones the deployer maps directly to the security mechanisms found in the target operational environment. The application assembler defines logical security roles using `security-role` entries, which consist of an optional `description` and a `role-name`. These roles define the logical groupings of users that can be referenced to restrict access to an EJB's methods. They're not the same as the actual users and user groups defined in the target environment—they're just the logical roles the deployer will eventually map to that environment.

The application assembler also completes any `security-role-ref` entries defined by the bean provider by adding a `role-link` element to each one. This entry defines the `security-role` to which a `security-role-ref` corresponds. You can use the same name for both roles if you want. The following example shows a completed `security-role-ref` and its corresponding `security-role`:

```
<ejb-jar>
  <enterprise-beans>
    ...
    <entity>
      <ejb-name>EnglishAuction</ejb-name>
      ...
      <security-role-ref>
        <description>The auction restricts some operations to valid bidders
        </description>
```

```
          <role-name>bidder</role-name>
          <role-link>registered-bidder</role-link>
        </security-role-ref>
        ...
      </entity>
      ...
  </enterprise-beans>
  <assembly-descriptor>
    <security-role>
      <description>A role to represent users who have registered with the
        system as authorized auction participants
      </description>
      <role-name>registered-bidder</role-name>
    </security-role>
  </assembly-descriptor>
  ...
</ejb-jar>
```

Also related to security roles, the application assembler can define `security-identity` elements within the `entity`, `message-driven`, and `session` elements that determine whether a caller's security identity is used to execute an EJB's methods or if a specified role is used. A `security-identity` element contains an optional description and either an empty `use-caller-identity` tag or a `run-as` element. The `use-caller-identity` choice is valid only for entity and session beans, but a `run-as` can be assigned to a message-driven bean as well. This element can contain a `description` along with a `role-name` to associate with all calls to a bean's methods. As an example, the following deployment would associate the `registered-bidder` role with all calls made by the `AuctionHouse` session bean:

```
<ejb-jar>
  <enterprise-beans>
    ...
    <session>
      <ejb-name>AuctionHouse</ejb-name>
      ...
      <security-identity>
        <run-as>
          <description>This role needs to be associated with valid bidders
          </description>
          <role-name>registered-bidder</role-name>
        </run-as>
      </security-identity>
      ...
      </session>
    ...
  </enterprise-beans>
  ...
</ejb-jar>
```

Assigning a `run-as` identity to a bean affects the method permissions associated with it but not any calls to `isCallerInRole` made within the bean's code. The `isCallerInRole` method always performs its checks against the caller's actual security identity and not any assigned `run-as` identity.

Caution

Specifying to use a `run-as` identity is far less common than using the caller's actual security identity when calling other EJBs. Obviously, you must be careful to not open up functionality to users that should be restricted from it.

`method-permission`

The security roles defined by the application assembler can apply to a bean provider's use of `security-role-ref` entries, but they're used more in declaratively restricting access to entity and session bean methods. Home and component interface methods can be restricted through `method-permission` entries that associate one or more security roles with one or more bean methods. The roles are identified with `role-name` entries that must match a `role-name` specified for one of the `security-role` entries. One or more `method` elements then follow that identify methods that can only be accessed by callers associated with one of the specified roles. For example, the following permission entry would restrict bid submissions to registered bidders and their agents:

```
<method-permission>
  <role-name>registered-bidder</role-name>
  <role-name>authorized-agent</role-name>
  <method>
    <ejb-name>AuctionHouse</ejb-name>
    <method-name>submitBid</method-name>
  </method>
</method-permission>
```

The application assembler also can indicate that some methods should not be checked for security before the container invokes the method. The assembler can configure this behavior by using the `unchecked` element instead of a `role-name`. The following snippet shows how this might be done:

```
<method-permission>
  <unchecked/>
  <method>
    <ejb-name>AuctionHouse</ejb-name>
    <method-name>submitBid</method-name>
  </method>
</method-permission>
```

→ **See** "Using Container-Managed Transactions," **p. 344** for examples of the other forms of the `method` element.

If you don't assign any method permissions to a particular bean's methods, this is interpreted as meaning that any role should be allowed to access any of the bean's methods. If you assign role restrictions to some but not all of a bean's methods, it's assumed that any methods without a role assignment shouldn't be accessible at all.

`container-transaction`

The `container-transaction` entries are where the application assembler defines the transactional behavior for beans that use container-managed transaction demarcation. The application assembler can't affect the transactional nature of an EJB that uses bean-managed demarcation. Each `container-transaction` entry has an optional `description`, one or more `method` entries, and a `trans-attribute`. The methods that a particular transaction attribute applies to are specified in the same way methods are identified within the `method-permission` element. The `trans-attribute` must be specified as `NotSupported`, `Supports`, `Required`, `RequiresNew`, `Mandatory`, or `Never`.

For a particular EJB, the application assembler must either specify the transaction attribute for every method that requires one or for none of them so that the deployer can do it. Table 15.3 summarizes the methods that require a transaction attribute when container-managed transaction demarcation is used.

TABLE 15.3 TRANSACTION ATTRIBUTE REQUIREMENTS

EJB Type	Methods Requiring a Transaction Attribute
Entity	The methods declared in the component interface and its superinterfaces excluding `getEJBHome`, `getEJBLocalHome`, `getHandle`, `getPrimaryKey`, and `isIdentical`. The methods declared in the home interface and its superinterfaces excluding those declared by `getEJBMetaData` and `getHomeHandle`.
Session	The methods declared in the component interface and its superinterfaces excluding those declared by `EJBObject` and `EJBLocalObject`.
Message-Driven	The `onMessage` method.

The following example illustrates how to declare the `Required` attribute for all methods of a particular entity bean:

```
<container-transaction>
  <method>
    <ejb-name>EnglishAuction</ejb-name>
    <method-name>*</method-name>
  </method>
  <trans-attribute>Required</trans-attribute>
</container-transaction>
```

If you needed a particular method in the `EnglishAuction` bean to have a transaction attribute other than `Required`, you could do something like this:

```
<container-transaction>
  <method>
    <ejb-name>EnglishAuction</ejb-name>
    <method-name>*</method-name>
  </method>
  <trans-attribute>Required</trans-attribute>
</container-transaction>
<container-transaction>
  <method>
    <ejb-name>EnglishAuction</ejb-name>
    <method-name>getTimeLeft</method-name>
  </method>
  <trans-attribute>Supports</trans-attribute>
</container-transaction>
```

Refer to Chapter 12, "Transactions," for a description of each of the allowed transaction attributes.

→ For more information on declarative transaction management, **see** "Using Container-Managed Transactions," **p. 344**.

exclude-list

The application assembler can add the `exclude-list` entry so that a set of methods should not be called. The deployer should configure the enterprise bean's security such that no access is permitted to any method in the `exclude-list`. The entry has an optional `description` and one or more `method` entries. The following example illustrates how to declare methods that should be excluded:

```
<exclude-list>
  <description>A method that should not be available to clients</description>
  <method>
    <ejb-name>EnglishAuction</ejb-name>
    <method-name>someUnavailableMethodName</method-name>
  </method>
</exclude-list>
```

MODIFYING enterprise-beans ENTRIES

Besides supplying the `assembly-descriptor` portion of the deployment descriptor, the application assembler can also modify some of the entries found in the `enterprise-beans` section and add entries that were not specified by the bean provider. You saw an example of this already with the `role-link` element of a `security-role-ref`. This is an example of information never supplied by the bean provider. In other cases, the application assembler may supply or modify `env-entry-value` entries to define values for environment properties or `description` entries to better define how an element is being used or provide more instructions to the deployer. It's also possible for naming conflicts to arise if multiple `ejb-jar` files are merged. Here, an application assembler might have to change an entry such as an `ejb-relation-name` to resolve a conflict.

env-entry-value

The application assembler may change the value of an environment entry specified by the bean provider or add a value where one hasn't been given. The value specified for an `env-entry-value` is interpreted as a `String` that must be acceptable to the one-argument constructor of the class assigned to the entry. For example, you could specify `True` for a `java.lang.Boolean` entry or `12.3` for a `java.lang.Double`. You must supply a single character value for a `java.lang.Character` entry.

ejb-link

The application assembler can add the `ejb-link` entry to any `ejb-ref` or `ejb-local-ref` element declared by the bean provider to complete it. An `ejb-link` associates a bean provider reference with a target EJB using the `ejb-name` of the referenced bean to identify it. The application assembler can provide just the `ejb-name` or, to prevent any possible name conflicts, specify the pathname of the `ejb-jar` that contains the bean followed by a # and the `ejb-name`. The pathname must be given relative to the current `ejb-jar file`. The following examples provides an example of using the `ejb-link` entry in an `ejb-local-ref` element:

```
<ejb-local-ref>
    <description>This EJB reference is used to locate an auction's item
    </description>
    <ejb-ref-name>ejb/Item</ejb-ref-name>
    <ejb-ref-type>Entity</ejb-ref-type>
    <local-home>com.que.ejb20.item.model.ItemHome</local-home>
    <local>com.que.ejb20.item.model.Item</local>
    <ejb-link>Item</ejb-link>
</ejb-local-ref>
```

DEPLOYER RESPONSIBILITIES

Part of the deployer's job is to complete any deployment information that wasn't supplied by the application assembler. There also might be changes needed to environment entries that were supplied but don't reflect the true target environment. The deployer must ensure that all EJBs referenced by the application are present in the environment and that all required resources are available and accessible.

Much of what the deployer must do is outside the bounds of entering data into the deployment descriptor. The deployer is instead responsible for using tools specific to the application server and the rest of the target environment to support the references declared in the descriptor. For example, the deployer must bind data sources to any connection factory references that exist. If the authorization method for a resource (`res-auth`) is specified as `Container`, the deployer must also supply the necessary login information. Any referenced administered objects, such as JMS queues or topics, must be configured and made available to the application as well.

A significant responsibility of the deployer is to take the logical security roles specified by the application assembler and map them to the actual security domain of the target environment. This includes assigning the principals and groups recognized by the target environment to the application assembler's security roles. Security topics are discussed in more detail in Chapter 14, "Security Design and Management."

The important point to remember about the work of the deployer is that much of it is vendor specific. The deployer will often be working with supplemental deployment files, such as WebLogic's `weblogic-ejb-jar.xml` file, and other configuration data used by the application server to bind an EJB application to the resources and security mechanisms it requires.

Note

Vendors typically will have a different name for their proprietary deployment descriptor. For example, the deployment descriptor for the Orion EJB server is called `orion-ejb-jar.xml`.

SUMMARY OF RESPONSIBILITIES

Table 15.4 summarizes the deployment responsibilities assigned to each of the applicable EJB roles.

TABLE 15.4   DEPLOYMENT RESPONSIBILITIES BY EJB ROLE

EJB Role	Responsibilities
Bean provider	All source code. The preliminary `ejb-jar.xml` file identifying the beans, their relationships, any resource and environment dependencies, and so on.
Application assembler	The `assembly-descriptor` section of `ejb-jar.xml`, including elements defining security roles, method permissions, and transaction attributes. The assembler also can supply values for any environment entries not already defined. The purpose of this role is to define the behavior of one or more beans when used as part of a particular application.
Deployer	The contents of any vendor-specific deployment descriptors. The deployer must finalize all deployment information and create the JAR (and possible WAR and EAR) files needed to deploy the application in the target environment. This includes satisfying any resource and security dependencies of the deployed beans.

PACKAGING EJBS

EJBs and their deployment descriptor are passed between the EJB roles and eventually deployed using an `ejb-jar` file. This JAR file contains

- The home and component interfaces
- The bean implementation classes
- Any custom primary key classes
- All dependent classes and interfaces
- The `ejb-jar.xml` deployment descriptor (stored in a META-INF subdirectory relative to the root of the JAR)
- Any vendor-specific deployment descriptors

As a bean provider, you can create an `ejb-jar` file by following these steps:

1. Compile your EJBs and their supporting classes and interfaces

2. Define the required parts of the deployment descriptor(s) and copy these files to a META-INF directory that's parallel to the root directory of your package hierarchy. For example, if your root package is com and your class files are compiled into a directory structure starting at `c:\examples\classes\com`, you should place your deployment descriptors in `c:\examples\classes\META-INF`. Your container vendor may specify a different location for any vendor-specific descriptors.

3. Create a new JAR file that holds the class files and descriptors using the `jar` command. For example, building a JAR that holds all the classes under a `com` directory (and its sub-directories) and the deployment descriptors could be done using the following line:

```
jar cf auction.jar META-INF com
```

The preceding example creates a new JAR file that contains the deployment descriptors and all class files under the `com` directory. If that includes files you don't need in the JAR, you can restrict the contents using path specifications such as `com\que\ejb20\auction\model\*.class`.

THE `ejb-client` FILE

The EJB specification also defines the concept of an `ejb-client` JAR file. This is a JAR you can create that holds only the class files that a client application needs to access the beans included in a corresponding `ejb-jar` file. This JAR would include the home and component interfaces, any primary key classes, any custom application exceptions exposed to the client, and the client stubs generated by the container. If you create this file, you can reference it in the `ejb-client-jar` element of `ejb-jar` using a pathname relative to the location of the `ejb-jar` file. The EJB specification doesn't dictate any required support for this file by an application server, but it is a convenient way for you to package the class files needed to deploy your client applications.

TROUBLESHOOTING

DTD NOT FOUND

I get an error telling me that the DTD for my deployment descriptor can't be located.

First, be sure that you've included an entry at the top of your deployment descriptor that defines the DTD that applies to the file. If you have, be sure you have the URL for the DTD correctly specified. Also, the machine on which you're deploying might need access to the Internet to locate the DTD being referenced. If this isn't possible, consider using a local copy of the DTD and changing the URL to reference it.

XML FORMAT ERRORS

I get an error telling me that a tag in my deployment descriptor isn't supported.

You must pay close attention to the order defined for the XML elements of the deployment descriptor. The order specified by the DTD must be followed or the XML parser will reject your descriptor.

DEPLOYMENT TOOL CANNOT LOCATE DESCRIPTOR FILES

I get an error telling me that the deployment descriptors are missing from my `ejb-jar` *file.*

You must place deployment descriptors in a `META-INF` subdirectory one level below the root directory of the JAR file for them to be recognized. Be sure that you placed the files in this directory and that the directory was created with an all-uppercase name.

MISSING DEPENDENT CLASSES

I get `ClassDefNotFound` *exceptions when I compile or deploy my* `ejb-jar` *file.*

The `ejb-jar` file must include all classes and interfaces referenced by your EJBs (other than those defined by the API). Be sure you include class files for everything you reference, such as helper classes, primary key classes, and exceptions.

DESIGN AND PERFORMANCE

## CHAPTER 16

PATTERNS AND STRATEGIES IN EJB DESIGN

In this chapter

WHAT ARE PATTERNS?

A *pattern* describes a proven approach for solving a problem. Throughout the rest of the engineering community, the concept of patterns is used extensively. When civil engineers are designing a new bridge, they don't start out by proposing their own theories on how to best build a bridge. They instead take advantage of the knowledge accumulated by the thousands of engineers who have built properly functioning bridges before them. In some cases, this knowledge has come the hard way as ideas that looked good on paper got added to the list of things not to do. No matter how the best patterns for designing a bridge have been developed, they define the starting point when a new bridge needs to be built.

A skilled civil engineer knows to start with what's been learned from the experience of others. With the exception of cosmetic issues, there's rarely a need to go outside the existing knowledge base of successful bridge designs. That's not to say that there isn't still work to be done. Every bridge is unique and must satisfy its exact set of requirements. The trick is to know how to select the patterns that apply to a particular design and use them correctly.

The concept of software patterns is not much different than applying patterns in other disciplines. Software developers have been building systems for many years. Some of the designs that were chosen worked very well and some did not. The idea of software patterns is to understand which ones worked and to apply the same solution when faced with the same problem or one similar to it. Often it's equally useful to know about attempted solutions that failed and to understand why they failed when a new pattern is proposed. Software patterns can be thought of as reusable ideas or solutions to solve a given problem. To make them easier to reuse, patterns are usually defined so that they're focused on a single design issue.

Another advantage of understanding and using patterns is that it allows those who understand the pattern to communicate a great deal of information very quickly. If you attend a design review and someone says "I used the blah pattern here" and you understand what the "blah" pattern is and what problem it solves, you can gain a quick understanding of that part of the design. Instead of having to study every detail of the design, you can focus only on making sure that the selected pattern is applicable to the problem at hand. Patterns allow developers to exchange a great deal of information simply by communicating a pattern name.

Different types of patterns are used throughout the software community. Patterns are often grouped as analysis patterns, design patterns, construction patterns, and so on. There are also many classifications of patterns within these groups. For example, some patterns are classified as proxy patterns and others are known as builder patterns. Classifying patterns helps you know which patterns to consider based on what aspect of a design you're addressing at the time. The idea is to have a catalog of patterns you can turn to and pull out what you need.

The standard for software design patterns was set by the book *Design Patterns: Elements of Reusable Object-Oriented Software* by Erich Gamma, Richard Helm, Ralph Johnson, and John Vlissides. You'll often hear these authors and their book referred to as the Gang of Four (GoF). If you've ever heard of patterns such as Singleton or Composite, this is the book that defines them. It's a highly regarded book that should be part of every developer's library. The documentation it provides for each pattern includes a name for the pattern, a description of the problem it's trying to solve, and a description and example of the solution. Different developers and organizations tend to follow their own formats for documenting software patterns, but you'll usually see the same basic information covered.

STRATEGIES FOR ENTERPRISE JAVABEANS

The history of software development is quite short when compared to other engineering disciplines. This is why software is often seen as an immature profession relative to other technical fields. Accumulating proven patterns that are shared by the developer community is a way to further its progress toward maturity. Some results of this progress are seen each time the bar is raised on what parts of a program an application developer is responsible for designing and coding. Just as standard communications functionality built on top of TCP/IP freed developers from networking details, EJB uses many proven ideas for transactional processing and distributed application development to move developers to an even higher level.

When you build an EJB application, you are taking advantage of the past experience of EJB's designers without having to readdress problems that have been handled for you. Everything that happens under the hood uses tested solutions so that you don't have to reinvent the wheel each time you build an application.

Just as software is a young discipline compared to many others, EJB is young compared to other software approaches. It's of course an evolution of what's been done already with transactional and distributed systems, but there's still knowledge to be gained about how to best build applications on top of EJB. The goal of this chapter is to introduce you to some of the knowledge that's been accumulated so far by the EJB development community. Some of the ideas presented here can be described as patterns, and some others are more like strategies to consider when designing part of an EJB application. This isn't a patterns book, so a formal approach for presenting this material is avoided here. The intent is more to convey the importance of understanding design patterns and these proposed strategies for building EJB applications. Both are very important in building resilient software systems.

Before getting to the details, we want to make it clear that we're not the first to understand the importance of these strategies. We are merely documenting approaches that are taking shape within EJB development that we have found to be useful while building our own EJB applications. The ideas presented in this chapter come from such sources as Web sites, mailing lists, newsgroups, articles, other books, and of course, our own experiences. Just as many of the GoF patterns have become ingrained in the software development industry, several of the concepts summarized here are approaching similar status among EJB developers. Many of the design approaches presented here have evolved from the work of several sources, so it's difficult to give credit to individuals for these ideas just as it's difficult to credit sources for the ideas that went into the EJB specification. Our goal is to assist in promoting these approaches and sharing them with as many designers and developers as possible to help raise the bar of our craft once again.

DESIGNING EJB CLASSES AND INTERFACES

The following strategies apply to designing your enterprise bean implementation classes and the interfaces they expose to their clients. The core of an EJB application consists of the enterprise beans it's built on, so this is the first place to focus your efforts toward producing a good design.

DESIGNING COARSE-GRAINED ENTERPRISE BEANS

Prior to EJB 2.0, it was clear that an enterprise bean was too heavy an implementation approach for some objects. As Chapter 3 pointed out, the overhead involved in making a remote method call can be quite expensive. These and other issues forced many EJB applications to limit the number of calls a client invoked on an EJB and it also became more efficient to package up larger amounts of data when communicating to and from enterprise beans. The term that was often used for this approach was coarse-grained. However, with the release of the EJB 2.0 Specification and the introduction of local interfaces, you now have a choice to make regarding whether you utilize coarse-grained or fine-grained access for your enterprise beans.

The decision is whether your enterprise beans need to be exposed to remote clients or whether local interfaces will suffice. Chapter 3 provided a few guidelines when attempting to decide between local and remote exposure. A good rule of thumb is to use remote interfaces for your session beans and local interfaces for entity beans. This rule will not work in all situations, but it is a good starting point.

USING A BUSINESS METHOD INTERFACE

An enterprise bean class must implement the business methods declared in its component interface. That's a straightforward requirement fundamental to EJB, but there's no default mechanism in place to enforce this until a bean is deployed. A mismatch between a bean class and its component interface is not the kind of problem a deployer should have to face. This is an error that needs to be detected when a bean is compiled. As you know, the built-in way to force a class to implement a particular method in Java is to declare the class to implement an interface that includes the method. Given that, it makes sense that an interface needs to come into play here. Your first thought might be to declare the bean to implement its component interface given that its business methods are already declared there. There are actually two reasons why this isn't a recommended approach.

The first reason why a bean shouldn't implement its component interface is that every component interface either extends `javax.ejb.EJBLocalObject` or `javax.ejb.EJBObject`, depending on whether the bean is exposed to a local or remote client respectively. If the bean is exposed to a remote client, then its component interface must extend `javax.ejb.EJBObject`, which in turn extends `java.rmi.Remote`. These interfaces support remote access by a client and expose some of the helper functionality the container implements for you. If a bean class implemented `EJBObject`, it would have to implement methods such as `getEJBHome` and `getHandle`. Besides placing extra work on the programmer, the chief drawback with this option is that these method implementations would never be called. This is because the container's implementation of the remote interface intercepts all calls from clients, and it always invokes the container's implementation of the EJBObject methods when they're called. You could provide do-nothing implementations for them to save yourself some work, but that would just clutter your class declarations with useless methods.

If your bean supports local client access, its component interface must extend javax.ejb.EJBLocalObject. Even though this component interface doesn't extend java.rmi.Remote, there are still methods in this interface that the container is designed to implement. Regardless of the component interface type, if your enterprise bean class implemented the interface, it would have to provide unnecessary method implementations that would never be invoked.

PART

II

CH

16

The second reason has to do with the fact that a client should never access an enterprise bean directly. A client should always use a component interface reference to access an EJB. A component interface reference is associated with a class that is created by the container at deployment time to implement the bean's component interface. This is the means of access intended for a client regardless of whether the client is local or remote or whether the client is in the same or a different container. It's this separation between the reference held by a client and a bean instance that allows the container to passivate entity and stateful session bean objects and to reuse stateless session beans for multiple clients. Methods that return a reference to an EJB or accept one as a method parameter should always be declared using the bean's component interface type and not the implementation class. This practice prevents an instance of an enterprise bean from passing a reference to itself as an argument to a method or returning a this reference from a method. When a bean method needs to supply a reference to its associated component interface, you can get the reference you need by calling

```
context.getEJBObject()
```

or

```
context.getEJBLocalObject()
```

where context is either an EntityContext or a SessionContext object that has been associated with the enterprise bean.

This separation can break down if a bean class is declared to implement its component interface. With that type of declaration, the compiler would consider passing this just as acceptable as passing context.getEJBObject() wherever a remote interface reference is needed. By not implementing the component interface, the compiler can verify that an enterprise bean instance is never passed as an argument or returned from a method call directly.

Given that declaring an enterprise bean to implement its component interface isn't a good approach, you need a different way to ensure that a bean implements all the business methods declared in its component interface. Just to be clear, business methods are the functional methods declared by a bean (they don't include the container callback methods or the remote methods needed because of the distributed nature of the architecture). Using an interface is still the right approach here, but the component interface isn't the right one to use. What's instead recommended is to declare a new interface that includes only the business methods exposed by an EJB. This interface can then be extended by the bean's component interface and implemented by the bean class. This allows the compiler to verify that the bean class implements all the required methods but it doesn't impose any unnecessary requirements on the bean class. This approach is known as the *Business Interface* pattern. Listing 16.1 shows a basic business interface for a local client.

LISTING 16.1   IEnglishAuction.java—A LOCAL BUSINESS INTERFACE FOR THE ENGLISH AUCTION ENTITY BEAN

```
package com.que.ejb20.auction.model;
/**
 * Title:        IEnglishAuction<p>
 * Description:  Local business method interface for the EnglishAuction
 *               entity bean<p>
 */
import java.sql.Timestamp;
import com.que.ejb20.auction.exceptions.InvalidAuctionStatusException;
import com.que.ejb20.auction.exceptions.InvalidBidException;
import com.que.ejb20.auction.view.AuctionDetailView;
import com.que.ejb20.auction.view.BidView;
import com.que.ejb20.item.model.Item;

public interface IEnglishAuction {
  public Integer getId();

  public void setName(String newName);
  public String getName();

  public void setDescription(String newDescription);
  public String getDescription();

  public void setStatus(String newStatus) throws InvalidAuctionStatusException;
  public String getStatus();

  public void setStartingBid(Double newStartingBid)
    throws InvalidAuctionStatusException;
  public Double getStartingBid();

  public void setMinBidIncrement(Double newMinBidIncrement)
    throws InvalidAuctionStatusException;
  public Double getMinBidIncrement();

  public void setReserveAmount(Double newReserveAmount)
    throws InvalidAuctionStatusException;
  public Double getReserveAmount();

  public void setStartDateTime(Timestamp newStartDateTime)
    throws InvalidAuctionStatusException;
  public Timestamp getStartDateTime();

  public void setScheduledEndDateTime(Timestamp newScheduledEndDateTime)
```

Listing 16.1 Continued

```java
  throws InvalidAuctionStatusException;
public Timestamp getScheduledEndDateTime();

public void setActualEndDateTime(Timestamp newActualEndDateTime);
public Timestamp getActualEndDateTime();

public void assignItem(Item newItem, int newQuantity)
  throws InvalidAuctionStatusException;
public Item getItem();
public Integer getQuantity();
public void removeItem() throws InvalidAuctionStatusException;

/**
 * Submit a bid to an open auction
 *
 * @param bidAmount the amount of the bid
 * @param bidder the participant submitting the bid
 * @return the automatically assigned bid transaction ID
 * @throws InvalidBidException if the bid does not meet the criteria for
 *   the next acceptable bid
 * @throws InvalidAuctionStatusException if the auction is not open
 */
public String submitBid(double bidAmount, Bidder bidder)
  throws InvalidBidException, InvalidAuctionStatusException;

/**
 * Determine the next required bid for an auction
 *
 * @return the next acceptable bid amount
 */
public double computeNextBidAmount()
  throws InvalidAuctionStatusException;

public BidView getLeadingBidView();

public BidView getWinningBidView();

public AuctionDetailView getAuctionDetail();

/**
 * Get the time remaining before the auction closes
 *
 * @return the time remaining in msec
 */
public long getTimeLeft();

/**
 * Report whether or not the current leading bid satisfies the reserve
 *
 * @return true if the reserve has been met or there is no reserve and
 *   at least one bid has been submitted
 */
public boolean reserveMet();

/**
```

LISTING 16.1   CONTINUED

```
 * Assign the current leading bid as the auction winner
 *
 * @throws InvalidAuctionStatusException if the auction is not Open
 */
 public void assignWinner() throws InvalidAuctionStatusException;
}
```

A business interface declares only the business methods that are found in the component interface. These are the methods that a client would need to invoke on the bean. Notice that it doesn't contain any methods particular to remote invocation or anything else specific to EJB. This provides a clean separation between the business method declarations and the fact that they're intended for implementation by an enterprise bean.

The business interface in Listing 16.1 is designed for a local client. If the business interface were for a remote client instead, it would have to look a little different. This is because every method signature would have to include RemoteException in the throws clause. Every method in a remote interface has to include this exception, even if it's declared in a superinterface that's extended by the remote. This gives away the fact that a business interface is intended for remote calls, but that's a minor intrusion.

The declaration in Listing 16.1 used the naming convention of starting an interface name with the letter "I." This is not required and is just an example of a convention that some developers use. Another common naming convention for business interfaces is to use the word "Business" somewhere in the name. You should be careful with this one because it can lead to very long names. Some developers don't like naming conventions such as these because they feel that exposing the fact that a declaration is for an interface (as opposed to a class) breaks encapsulation by providing too much information to other classes. There are no hard and fast rules here. All that really matters is that you choose the naming conventions your development team wants to use and you stick with them.

With a business interface defined, the component interface that would normally declare these methods can now just extend this new interface. Listing 16.2 shows the updated EnglishAuction interface.

LISTING 16.2   EnglishAuction.java—LOCAL INTERFACE EXTENDING THE IEnglishAuction BUSINESS INTERFACE

```
package com.que.ejb20.auction.model;
/**
 * Title:       EnglishAuction<p>
 * Description: Local interface for the EnglishAuction entity bean<p>
 */
import javax.ejb.EJBLocalObject;

public interface EnglishAuction extends EJBLocalObject, IEnglishAuction {
   // all business methods are declared in IEnglishAuction
}
```

Notice that the EnglishAuction interface no longer declares any methods. That's because IEnglishAuction takes care of all the business methods and the EJBLocalObject interface takes care of the EJB side.

> **Tip**
>
> As shown in Listing 16.2, a Java interface can extend multiple interfaces even though a class can extend only a single parent.

Now you can declare the auction enterprise bean to implement the business interface associated with its component interface. The compiler can now ensure that all the business methods have implementations without requiring you to provide implementations for the EJBLocalObject methods. All that's required to do this is adding an implements clause to the EnglishAuctionBean declaration:

```
public class EnglishAuctionBean implements EntityBean, IEnglishAuction {

  // The rest of the enterprise bean code goes here
  ...
}
```

An extension to the business interface idea proposes using a regular Java class to implement the business interface and provide the corresponding business logic for the methods. The enterprise bean either extends this class or declares a reference to an instance of it and delegates calls to that instance. This business logic implementation creates another layer of separation and might be too thick for some. However, separating the business logic from the EJB that provides access to it could be considered a step toward adopting a rule engine approach.

USING AN ABSTRACT SUPERCLASS FOR CALLBACK METHODS

Inheritance is one of the fundamental concepts in object-oriented programming. The EJB 2.0 Specification does not support the concept of component inheritance, but it does allow for what it calls interface inheritance and implementation class inheritance.

Interface inheritance is defined as the normal Java mechanism of extending an interface with another interface. You can take advantage of this type of inheritance when declaring the home and component interfaces for an enterprise bean. For example, the business method strategy just described showed how the component interface for an enterprise bean could extend a Java interface that encapsulates its business methods. Home interfaces can also extend other Java interfaces to take advantage of common behavior, but this tends to be less useful than using inheritance with component interfaces.

As the name implies, implementation class inheritance applies to enterprise bean classes instead of their interfaces. For example, you could declare a SealedBidAuctionBean class that extends EnglishAuctionBean to add some special behavior to the business logic. This is the normal mechanism of subclassing.

Although these two types of inheritance are supported with enterprise beans, true polymorphic inheritance can't be achieved. Home interfaces, primary key classes for entity beans, and the way persistence is handled between a superclass and subclass get in the way of actual component inheritance. As introduced in Chapter 5, "Entity Beans," there are still advantages to making some use of inheritance within EJBs, even with its limitations. In many cases, developers create abstract parent classes that are not enterprise beans, but regular Java classes. These Java classes provide default implementations for the container callback methods. Listing 16.3 shows an abstract controller class that could be extended by an application's session beans.

LISTING 16.3   `AbstractController.java`—AN ABSTRACT SUPERCLASS FOR THE SESSION BEANS IN THE AUCTION EXAMPLE

```java
/**
 * Title:        AbstractController<p>
 * Description:  An abstract parent class for session beans.<p>
 */
package com.que.ejb20.common.ejb;

import javax.ejb.SessionBean;
import javax.ejb.SessionContext;

public class AbstractController implements SessionBean {

  // Reference to gain access to the session context held by the container
  private SessionContext sessionContext = null;

  public void setSessionContext( SessionContext ctx ){
    this.sessionContext = ctx;
  }

  public void ejbRemove(){
    // Do nothing for this class
  }

  public void ejbPassivate(){
    // Do nothing for this class
  }

  public void ejbActivate(){
    // Do nothing for this class
  }

  public SessionContext getSessionContext() {
    return this.sessionContext;
  }
}
```

The `AbstractController` class provides default implementations for the container callback methods that apply to session beans. With this approach, the concrete session beans must implement these methods only if they want to override the default behavior. This is useful, but support for inheritance is one aspect of the EJB specification that still needs some work.

→ For more information on inheritance within enterprise beans, **see** "Inheritance and Entity Beans,"
p. 141.

USING CONTAINER-MANAGED TRANSACTIONS

This is a simple point first discussed in Chapter 12, "Transactions," but it's worth repeating here while the subject of designing your bean classes is being addressed. When you implement an entity bean class, the container always manages the transaction demarcation that applies to the bean. You have a choice when it comes to session beans and message-driven beans, however. You can allow the container to start and commit transactions for you or you can code the transaction control yourself. One of the primary benefits offered by EJB is the declarative transaction support it provides. Using bean-managed transactions requires a lot more coding expertise from the bean provider and it opens the door for errors that could compromise data integrity. You should start every design with the intention of using container-managed transactions. If you absolutely have to have the flexibility offered by bean-managed transactions, the EJB architecture supports it fully while still discouraging its use.

MANAGING CLIENT ACCESS

Designing the EJBs that support your applications requires you to focus on the business logic they implement and the goals that you have for maintainability. You also must take into account how the clients of your EJBs will interact with them. This includes deciding on the methods that you'll expose through the home and component interfaces of your beans, but it doesn't stop there. This section looks more at how the data that's passed between an EJB and its clients is packaged and how a client manages its interaction with an EJB.

SESSION BEAN FAÇADE

Entity beans represent your business's core concepts. Conceptual entities such as customer, purchase order, and catalog are common in business applications deployed over the Internet. Entity beans are sometimes coarse-grained in terms of the overall functionality they provide but it's also typical for them to provide fine-grained access to their attributes using such operations as `setCustomerName`, `getCustomerName`, `setOrderNumber`, and `getOrderNumber`. This fine-grained support is necessary, but enterprise beans are distributed objects, so populating them from a remote client is an expensive operation performance-wise. You'll see more of this discussed in Chapter 17, "Addressing Performance."

It's also true that the work required by a client often involves multiple entity objects. A client might request the attributes of a single entity, such as those for an item in a catalog, but it's also common for clients to request operations such as viewing summary attributes for many items or creating an order entity and adding an item to it. For most actions a client needs, especially a thin client in a Web application, some coordination of objects usually must take place. This is the workflow management of an application.

To manage workflow and to reduce fine-grained access to entity beans, it's common to force a client to go through a session bean rather than allow it to interact with entity beans directly. This approach is sometimes referred to as the "Session Bean Wraps Entity Bean" pattern. The idea is that session beans should define coarse-grained methods that clients use to exercise the business logic they require and the access granularity between session and entity beans can be adjusted due to the introduction of local interfaces.

Typically, session beans are deployed with a transaction attribute of `Required` assigned to their methods so that the container starts a transaction at the beginning of each method to include all the work it performs. When one of these methods is called, the session bean interacts with one or more entity beans on behalf of the client, possibly using a local interface. This might involve creating or finding several entity objects and calling one or more business methods on them. The entity bean methods that are involved should normally have their transaction attributes set to `Required` as well so that they participate in the session bean's transaction. Direct access of the entity beans by a client would require the client to start and stop its own transactions or it would result in the client's work being spread across multiple transactions with no simple way to roll anything back if a problem occurred. Grouping this work within a session bean method avoids either of these undesirable alternatives.

RETURNING VIEW OBJECTS TO THE CLIENT

There's not really a common name for this next strategy. What it recommends is that your session beans return simple data objects back to the client rather than remote interface references. These data objects are referred to as views because they represent a particular view of the underlying model maintained by the application tier.

For example, say that a client invokes a `getNonPendingAuctions` method on the `AuctionHouse` session bean. An entity object is associated with each auction in the database, so the session bean could return a collection of remote interfaces to the client. What this strategy suggests instead is that a collection of `AuctionSummaryView` objects be returned. A view class such as this is very thin and contains only data validation or formatting logic if any. The idea is that there's enough information in a view class to build the presentation view for an end user or satisfy whatever other need a client of a particular session bean method has. In this case, `AuctionSummaryView` would contain the high-level attributes needed to build a list of auctions. If the user selects an entry from this list and requests to see more detail, the `getAuctionDetail` operation could be invoked and an `AuctionDetailView` returned back to the client containing all of the auction's attributes.

There's always a tradeoff between controlling the number of network calls and controlling the amount of data returned with each call. This example of generating a summary list that supports selective displays of detailed information is quite common in practice. In this scenario, a client typically selects only a small number of the entries in the list for detailed viewing. Sending back a collection of remote interfaces from which to build the list is a heavyweight solution, especially given that many of the list entries would likely never be used. Returning a set of regular Java classes that the client uses to build the presentation screen and then releases for garbage collection is a much more efficient approach. Listing 16.4 shows a view class that represents a user's bid in an auction.

LISTING 16.4   `BidView.java`—THE VIEW CLASS FOR A USER'S BID

```java
package com.que.ejb20.auction.view;
/**
 * Title:        BidView<p>
 * Description:  Value object for an auction bid<p>
 */
import java.io.Serializable;
import java.sql.Timestamp;

public class BidView implements Serializable {

  private Integer auctionId;
  private Integer bidderId;
  private Timestamp dateTimeSubmitted;
  private String transactionId;
  private Double amount;

  public BidView(Integer newAuctionId, Integer newBidderId,
   Timestamp newDateTimeSubmitted, Double newAmount, String newTransactionId) {

    setAuctionId(newAuctionId);
    setBidderId(newBidderId);
    setDateTimeSubmitted(newDateTimeSubmitted);
    setAmount(newAmount);
    setTransactionId(newTransactionId);
  }

  public Integer getAuctionId() {
    return auctionId;
  }

  public void setAuctionId(Integer newAuctionId) {
    auctionId = newAuctionId;
  }

  public Integer getBidderId() {
    return bidderId;
  }

  public void setBidderId(Integer newBidderId) {
    bidderId = newBidderId;
  }

  public Timestamp getDateTimeSubmitted() {
    return dateTimeSubmitted;
  }

  public void setDateTimeSubmitted(Timestamp newDateTimeSubmitted) {
    dateTimeSubmitted = newDateTimeSubmitted;
  }

  public Double getAmount() {
    return amount;
  }

  public void setAmount(Double newAmount) {
```

PART

II

CH

16

LISTING 16.4 CONTINUED

```
    amount = newAmount;
  }

  public String getTransactionId() {
    return transactionId;
  }

  public void setTransactionId(String newTransactionId) {
    transactionId = newTransactionId;
  }
}
```

A view class usually doesn't contain any business logic because its purpose is simply to transfer data between the application tier and the client. It might contain data validation or formatting logic, though. For example, when a user enters a bid for an auction and then clicks the submit button, it might be useful for the BidView class to contain some formatting logic to format the bid amount into a particular currency before passing it to a session bean. However, it's better to keep a view class as thin as possible and leave the business logic in the session and entity beans.

Changes a client makes to a view are not reflected in the underlying data used to generate the view. Changes are usually made through session bean methods by passing view objects as arguments to a session bean. The view objects are used to update the corresponding entity bean from the session bean methods.

Tip

Although the BidView class could have been declared without any set methods to make it clear that it can't be used to update any data, it might be necessary to provide set methods if your client tier uses JavaServer Pages. For an instance of the BidView class to function properly using JSP, it must follow the JavaBeans specification and provide both set and get methods for properties that a client wishes to access.

REFERENCING HOME AND COMPONENT INTERFACES IN THE CLIENT

A client communicates with an enterprise bean by obtaining an object that implements the bean's home interface and then acquiring a component interface reference. Regardless of whether the client is a JSP page, a servlet, or another enterprise bean, the procedure is similar. One question that soon arises related to this topic is over which of the references, if any, a client should hold between calls to the application tier. It seems intuitive that it would be to your advantage to avoid repeating the same steps to acquire a reference to an EJB, but it's not always clear what steps need to be done only once. You have several choices of what to do:

- Look up the home interface and acquire a component interface reference as part of each client invocation of an EJB method
- Hold the home interface reference in the client and acquire a component interface reference for each call to an EJB

- Hold the component interface reference in the client
- Hold a handle to a home or remote interface in the client and use it to reacquire the necessary reference

> **Note**
>
> The local component interface does not support the concept of a `Handle`. It is only used for remote clients.

The home object is a class that's generated by the container to implement the home interface for an enterprise bean. As you've learned from previous chapters, it's a factory that is responsible for creating (and finding, in the case of entity beans) objects that implement the component interface of the associated bean. These are the stub objects. When a client calls a `create` or finder method on a home interface reference, several things must happen depending on the type of bean and its current state. One thing to remember is that the home factory giving you a component reference doesn't mean that there is an `EJBObject` or `EJBLocalObject` created on the server right at that moment. The server can delay some operations to help with performance. For example, it can delay creating an `EJBObject` for a remote client until the client actually invokes an operation on the remote interface. With other vendors, all remote clients might actually share an `EJBObject` that's used for routing all client requests as an aid to scalability of the EJB server.

> **Note**
>
> Don't confuse the concept of sharing an `EJBObject` with sharing bean instances. A bean instance is only assigned to one client at a given time. It may be shared between client invocations, but two clients are not associated with the same bean instance at the same time.

The lookup of the home interface through JNDI can be quite costly, so you'd like to limit the number of times a client has to perform this operation. The problem is that there's not much guidance from the specification as to how to handle clients caching home and component interfaces. However, there might be a reason to not cache the home interface reference and use it for all clients. The reason is one of security. Several EJB products use the security principal and credential that are used for the JNDI lookup of the home interface as the security principal that is propagated to the container during a method invocation. Although these sets of security contexts are supposed to be used for very different reasons, it still happens. Authentication into JNDI and authentication to the enterprise beans should be handled by completely different mechanisms. However, you should keep in mind that JNDI authentication is still sometimes used as the identity of the caller that gets propagated to the EJB container.

You can still cache the home interface for each client session, but this makes sense only if you plan to remove the component interface reference to the enterprise bean after each call. This is not recommended because the component interface reference is designed to have a lifetime equal to that of a user session. In other words, the component interface reference for an EJB is what you want to cache for each client rather than a home interface reference. Each client can have its own component interface reference and somehow store it where it can be associated with a particular user. For example, in a Web application, it can be stored in the `HttpSession` for each user. When the user needs to invoke a method on it, the application gets the component interface reference for that particular user and calls the method.

IMPLEMENTING A SINGLETON IN EJB

The Singleton pattern is a useful design pattern applied to control the number of instances of a particular class that exist in an application. It's most often used to limit a class to being instantiated only once. The idea is that certain services or heavyweight resources should be managed using a single class instance. Singletons have been used for many years and in languages other than Java. However, because the EJB container has control over the system, including the activation and passivation of instances, there are some inherent differences that must be recognized and understood when attempting to implement the Singleton pattern using enterprise beans. First, let's look at a class fragment that illustrates how a Singleton is usually implemented:

```
public class MySingleton {
    // The one and only instance
    private static MySingleton _instance;

    // Private constructor used by getInstance only
    private MySingleton() {
      // construct object here . . .
    }

    // Synchronized to prevent multiple threads from entering
    public static synchronized MySingleton getInstance() {
      if (_instance==null) {
      _instance = new MySingleton();
      }
      return _instance;
    }

    // Remainder of class definition . . .
  }
```

In a Singleton class, there's usually a single static reference to the class and a static method that clients can call to get a reference to this instance. In the `MySingleton` class, clients get a reference to the single instance of the class by calling the `getInstance` method.

There are several problems with using Singleton objects with EJB applications. The first problem is that an EJB server may start multiple JVMs. A Singleton is supposed to be loaded once per application, but if there is more than one JVM in the application, you can't be guaranteed of having a single instance. Some EJB servers also pool JVMs and start and stop JVMs as if they were threads. You have to understand that your Singleton might have to be reinitialized frequently. Many EJB developers also recommend that you avoid

Singletons that hold state because of the potential of having multiple JVMs loaded by the container. If this occurs, you can't guarantee that the state stored in each instance of the Singleton is the same across JVMs.

The traditional use of a Singleton is to manage access to a resource. Even if a Singleton class doesn't hold state, using one to control access to a resource in an EJB application still isn't appropriate because the container is responsible for resource management.

Having said all this, there are ways that EJB developers are using Singleton-like approaches to get the intended result. One recommended approach is to implement the functionality desired from a Singleton as a CORBA or RMI object and bind it in the JNDI namespace. All clients can use JNDI to look up this object and use it.

TROUBLESHOOTING

METHOD NOT DECLARED TO THROW RemoteException

I'm using a business interface for a remote component interface and I get an error during deployment complaining that a method declared in that interface isn't declared to throw RemoteException.

The EJB specification requires that all methods declared in the remote interface of an enterprise bean (and any interfaces extended by the remote) be declared to throw RemoteException. Even if the bean implementation class doesn't throw RemoteException from any of its method implementations, the declarations in the business interface have to include it to make the remote interface valid. The compiler won't catch this error if you forget to do it, but deploying the bean will fail.

SINGLETON STATE LOST

I'm using a Singleton class but the state of its attributes is being lost.

Singletons require special consideration in an EJB application, especially those that hold state. Most containers start multiple JVMs resulting in an instance of each Singleton being generated per JVM. If you literally need to limit the number of instances to one, consider implementing the Singleton as a CORBA or RMI object that can be bound in the JNDI namespace for access by clients.

## CHAPTER 17

ADDRESSING PERFORMANCE

In this chapter

THE ROLE OF PERFORMANCE IN DESIGN

Worrying about performance when you're first designing an application can be a stumbling block if you're not careful. Your first priority as a designer should be to produce a good object-oriented design. You want to build systems where responsibilities are allocated to reusable components that hide their implementations behind public interfaces. You want these components to provide a cohesive set of functionality while keeping the coupling between components to a minimum. You want each class that helps make up a component to encapsulate the data and methods needed for a related set of tasks and to do it in a way that results in granular classes that can be reused. And as if all that weren't enough, you want your classes to be built from relatively short methods that are easy to understand, test, and extend as new requirements are added. This is a nice list of goals, but nowhere in it does it mention performance. The problem is that performance optimization and good object-oriented design don't always go hand in hand. They can instead contradict each other. Of course you can't ignore performance in your designs or you'll face the risk of building a system that either can't meet the constraints of its target environment or runs so slowly that no one will use it. The trick then is to know when to be concerned about how well a system will perform. You don't want to minimize the importance of system responsiveness, but you don't want to let anticipated performance problems that might never materialize drive a design either.

The nonfunctional requirements for an application should contain specifications that tell you as a designer what the criteria for a system's performance are. This might include require-ments for the maximum time a user should be expected to wait for a Web page to display or the maximum time that can be allocated to a transaction that ties up an external system. Without requirements such as these, describing how well a system performs is subjective. This opens the door to systems that either don't meet expectations or suffer from the opposite extreme with designs that are too heavily influenced by concerns about execution speed. When you know how a system needs to perform, it's easier to determine if the performance require-ments pose a risk to building an acceptable application. The higher the risk, the earlier in the process it makes sense to worry about performance. The preferred approach from a strictly object-oriented point of view is to do a design, build the system (or pieces of it), isolate any performance problems, and then focus your efforts on alleviating the bottlenecks. If you're faced with performance requirements that pose a risk, then it makes sense to prototype parts of the system to make sure the architecture can support what's required. Otherwise, letting performance concerns creep into your design too early can lead to a less flexible system that's difficult to maintain and possibly not as portable to other platforms.

Performance optimizations made after a system has been implemented or partially proto-typed usually are application-specific. If specific queries are too slow, changes to the data-base schema or how the database is accessed might be necessary. If a problem is traced to a section of code that takes too long to execute, optimizations that might include rewriting some of the code in a faster language can be pursued. It's usually the case that overall per-formance is driven by a small percentage of the code. When this is true, you can expect good results with this type of approach. When performance problems are more widespread, it's possible that the architecture selected for the application is inadequate or it's not being fully exploited. It's also possible for an architecture to be too heavyweight for a set of requirements. EJB offers a lot of benefits, but not every program needs the substance (and accompanying overhead) of an enterprise-strength distributed architecture backing it.

Application-specific tuning is important, but, by definition, it's specific to a particular system and difficult to address in general terms. Basically, you have to first find out why an application doesn't perform as well as it needs to and then look for alternative approaches in the problem spots. There are, however, some general guidelines for designing better performing systems from the ground up. You might think that this goes against what's been said so far about designing for maintainability first and then tuning for performance only when necessary. That advice is still true, but you also need to be conscious of the fact that building a system using a distributed architecture has known performance issues that have already been encountered and addressed by many other developers. Addressing these issues with techniques that affect your class implementations without impacting your overall architecture offers you a way to avoid later problems without sacrificing too much from a design standpoint. The intent of this chapter is to cover general performance guidelines consistent with this idea. Even if you don't want to address performance in your initial design, the topics covered here are a good place to start if you identify isolated problems after constructing an application.

MINIMIZING REMOTE CALLS

The primary performance concern associated with a distributed architecture such as EJB is the amount of network traffic it requires. When a remote client makes a call to an EJB there's a certain amount of overhead involved. Part of this is just the time it takes to move data between the client and the container across the network. You also have the impact of the transaction and security processing that takes place when the container receives a client request. You can't get away from this overhead completely because it's part of the price you pay for the benefits of a distributed application. However, you should be conscious of the number of calls a remote client is required to make to do its work. As you've seen in earlier chapters, EJBs that are designed with remote clients in mind serve their purpose best when they're coarse-grained. When an EJB is designed to provide significant business logic or workflow management to a client, its overhead is easier to justify.

Even when an EJB is coarse-grained in terms of the functionality it provides, you still need to watch the number of calls you make to it. This point is easiest to illustrate with an entity bean that has quite a few attributes.

Note

As mentioned in previous chapters, entity beans are normally accessed through a local interface. However, there might be circumstances where you need to expose an entity bean to remote clients instead. For example, if a session bean were deployed in a separate JVM or on a different node in a cluster from an entity bean, it would need to use a remote interface to access that entity. A local interface can only be used for EJBs deployed in the same JVM.

The `EnglishAuctionRemote` interface that was first introduced back in Chapter 6, "Bean-Managed Persistence," exposes a number of get and set methods such as those shown in the following subset of the interface:

```
...
public void setName(String newName) throws RemoteException;
public String getName() throws RemoteException;

public void setDescription(String newDescription) throws RemoteException;
public String getDescription() throws RemoteException;

public void setStartingBid(Double newStartingBid)
   throws InvalidAuctionStatusException, RemoteException;
public Double getStartingBid() throws RemoteException;

public void setMinBidIncrement(Double newMinBidIncrement)
   throws InvalidAuctionStatusException, RemoteException;
public Double getMinBidIncrement() throws RemoteException;

public void setReserveAmount(Double newReserveAmount)
   throws InvalidAuctionStatusException, RemoteException;
public Double getReserveAmount() throws RemoteException;

public void setStartDateTime(Timestamp newStartDateTime)
   throws InvalidAuctionStatusException, RemoteException;
public Timestamp getStartDateTime() throws RemoteException;

public void setScheduledEndDateTime(Timestamp newScheduledEndDateTime)
   throws InvalidAuctionStatusException, RemoteException;
public Timestamp getScheduledEndDateTime() throws RemoteException;
...
```

Methods such as these are no problem when declared in the `EnglishAuction` local interface because the overhead of each call from a local client is relatively small. You can't say the same for using these methods in a remote interface, though. The problem with exposing fine-grained access to individual attributes like this is that a remote client that needs to read or modify multiple attributes has to make several calls on a bean's remote interface to do its work. You might not want to get rid of this fine-grained access because sometimes only a single attribute needs to be accessed. What you want to do instead is provide alternative get and set methods that work with a data structure that holds multiple attributes of a bean. If you can provide a client what it needs with fewer remote calls, the amount of time spent accessing a bean is sure to drop. Listing 17.1 shows an example class that bundles multiple attributes of the auction entity bean together.

LISTING 17.1   ENGLISHAUCTIONSNAPSHOT.JAVA—A SNAPSHOT DATA OBJECT FOR AN AUCTION ENTITY BEANPACKAGE COM.QUE.EJB20.AUCTION.MODEL;

```
/**
 * Title:        EnglishAuctionSnapshot<p>
 * Description:  Data object for an auction entity bean<p>
 */
import java.sql.Timestamp;
```

LISTING 17.1 CONTINUED

```java
import java.io.Serializable;

public class EnglishAuctionSnapshot implements Serializable {
  public Integer id;
  public String name;
  public String description;
  public String status;
  public Double startingBid;
  public Double minBidIncrement;
  public Double reserveAmount;
  public Timestamp startDateTime;
  public Timestamp scheduledEndDateTime;
  public Timestamp actualEndDateTime;
}
```

PART

II

CH

17

The first thing to notice about EnglishAuctionSnapshot is that it looks more like a C/C++ struct than a Java class. This simplicity in the declaration of the class is intentional. The only purpose of a class like this is to pass data. The absence of any methods (including get and set methods) makes it clear that there's nothing to an EnglishAuctionSnapshot object other than the data it holds. It's referred to as a *snapshot* here because you can think of it as a snapshot view of an entity bean's state at a particular instant. It's of no value once the state of the entity changes. You'll also see a class like this commonly referred to as a *data object*.

A snapshot class becomes useful when you add methods like the following to the remote interface (and implementation) of an entity bean:

```java
public EnglishAuctionSnapshot getSnapshot() throws RemoteException;
public void setFromSnapshot(EnglishAuctionSnapshot ss) throws RemoteException;
```

The idea is that a client that needs access to multiple attributes of an entity object can call its getSnapshot method instead of the individual get method for each attribute. An entity bean class implements this method simply by creating a new snapshot object and loading it with its current attribute values. The setFromSnapshot method is meant to provide the opposite capability by performing the equivalent of multiple set method calls with a single remote call. You might have noticed that EnglishAuctionSnapshot was declared to implement Serializable. This is necessary for a snapshot object to be used as a return value or method parameter in a remote interface.

The example shown here includes all the attributes of the associated entity bean in the snapshot class, but it might also make sense to declare other snapshots that hold subsets of attributes that are commonly used together. This should be a secondary concern to you though. What's more important is to go ahead and define at least one snapshot for an entity bean class. You'll find in most cases that retrieving a snapshot with a reasonable number of attributes is faster than making even two calls to individual get methods. Even if the snapshot holds attributes that a particular client doesn't need, the time spent building and passing the complete structure can easily be made up by avoiding other remote calls.

Note

Earlier examples made use of view classes to return a copy of an entity object's state to its clients. The major difference between those classes and the concept of a snapshot is intent. View classes represent objects that are used to communicate with clients outside the application tier. The auction example included the creation of view objects by the auction entity bean, but views are often manipulated only by session beans. A snapshot class exists solely for performance advantages when you're supporting remote clients of your entity beans. Depending on your particular application, you might be able to satisfy your need for a snapshot by reusing an existing view class. Otherwise, you can return a snapshot to a remote session bean and allow it, or a helper class, to create a view based on the data in the snapshot.

OPTIMIZING ENTITY BEAN PERSISTENCE

If you've developed applications that work with relational databases, you know that database access can easily become the determining factor in how well a system performs. In a typical business application, the time spent executing your Java code is much smaller than the time taken up reading from and writing to the database. With this in mind, any attention you pay to performance while you're designing a system needs to take the database into account. In the case of EJB, this, for the most part, means looking at your use of entity beans. Of course for some developers, this means avoiding entity beans altogether. That's not the position taken here, but you do need to be careful when deciding if an entity bean is an appropriate representation for a particular object. The accepted criteria for an entity bean's use were described back in Chapter 5. What this chapter is more concerned with is how to implement an entity bean once you've made the decision to use one.

CHOOSING A CMP IMPLEMENTATION

If you use CMP, the work the persistence framework does for you includes determining when to write an entity's state to the database and when to load it. The leading CMP implementations compete with each other based on the features they provide to optimize these parts of an entity object's lifecycle. For example, an ORM framework such as TOPLink used for CMP can detect changes to an entity's attributes and relationships and only write to the database when necessary. When a database update is needed, the SQL statements that are executed are limited to the attributes and associations that have actually changed. An implementation like this can also cache entity objects once they've been read to avoid unnecessary reads from the database later. If you're planning to deploy your application in a cluster, you have to understand whether the caching provided by your CMP implementation supports a clustered environment to know whether you can take advantage of such a feature or not.

The EJB 2.0 Specification leaves nearly all the details of a CMP implementation up to the individual vendors. Even though the mapping of an entity bean to a database can be done declaratively, taking advantage of any of the value-added performance features offered by a particular implementation can result in programmatic dependencies on that product. The concept of a Persistence Manager, which will provide more of a pluggable persistence framework for CMP, has been deferred to a later version of the specification. For now, the most sophisticated CMP features tend to be nonportable. This doesn't mean that you should ignore what's available to you—you just need to be aware of the implications.

ONLY EXECUTE ejbStore WHEN NECESSARY

Chapter 6 covered the mechanics of how to implement an entity bean using BMP. That chapter showed you how to implement the various callback methods needed to keep an entity object in synch with its representation in the database. What that chapter didn't discuss in detail was how to improve the performance of a BMP entity bean.

The container calls an entity bean's ejbStore method when it needs to make sure that the database contents are in synch with the entity object in memory. This call is always made at the completion of a transaction that involves the entity. It also happens right before an entity is passivated. If you write to the database whenever a business method is called that modifies the entity, ejbStore isn't responsible for much. However, the opposite is typically true. Your business methods will usually update the state of an entity object but not write any changes to the database. It's in ejbStore that you most often execute the JDBC call (or calls) needed to update an entity's representation in the database. This simplifies your business method code and helps isolate your business logic from any knowledge of the persistence mechanism being used. The drawback to this approach is that a simple ejbStore method that blindly writes to the database even when an entity's state hasn't changed since the last update is inefficient.

Database access is an expensive operation in terms of performance. Because of this, it's usually worthwhile to perform a little extra processing within your entity beans to only update the data that has been modified since the last call to ejbStore. If you're using an ORM product for your BMP implementation, this might be taken care of for you. Some frameworks can compare the current state of a persistent object with its state last retrieved from the database and only update the attributes that have changed. It takes some work, but you can take a similar approach yourself and track changes to an object between ejbLoad and ejbStore calls. Without an ORM framework to manage this for you, you might not want the complexity of tracking individual attributes, but you can easily keep up with whether or not an entity object has changed at all. You can declare a transient boolean attribute that you set to true whenever a business method call results in a change to the persistent state of an entity object. This allows you to only perform the database updates in ejbStore when the indicator has been set. Both ejbStore and ejbLoad can reset the indicator to false before returning. The following fragment shows an example business method using this approach:

```
public void setName(String newName) {
  boolean change = false;
  if (name == null) {
    // a change if current value is null and the new one isn't
    change = (newName != null);
  }
  else {
```

```
    // current value isn't null, so use equals method to detect a change
    change = (!name.equals(newName));
  }
  if (change) {
    name = newName;
    modified = true;
  }
}
```

You could then modify this entity bean's `ejbStore` method like the following:

```
public void ejbStore() {

  // exit if the entity state hasn't changed
  if (!modified) {
    return;
  }

  // obtain a database connection and update the database
  ...

  // entity state has been synchronized, so reset the indicator
  modified = false;
}
```

Your individual business methods become slightly more complex when using this approach, but that's the price you pay for a performance optimization. You can clean up the business methods by pulling out the logic needed to check for changes and implementing it in a set of simple helper methods. The extra processing that has to take place to detect and keep up with changes is insignificant compared to the potential savings in database access time.

USE LAZY LOADING FOR BMP DEPENDENT OBJECTS

Just as paying attention to how you save data affects performance, so does the approach you use for loading an entity object. In particular, it's how you manage an entity's dependent objects when using BMP that can impact performance. As a general rule, you should wait until data is actually needed from the database before you retrieve it. Using a lazy loading approach avoids database accesses for values that are never used by an application.

In Chapter 6, the `ejbLoad` method for the `EnglishAuctionBean` loaded the various attributes that describe an auction but it only loaded the primary keys for the leading and winning bid dependent objects and the assigned item entity. The corresponding bid and item objects for these keys were not loaded. If you take this approach, you can maintain two references for each object with which an entity has a one-to-one relationship: one for the primary key and one for the actual object. The implementation for `ejbLoad` only needs to be responsible for loading the primary key reference. When the related object is needed, the fact that the reference to it is `null` and the primary key reference isn't can be used to trigger a database access to retrieve the necessary data and instantiate the object. Listing 17.2 shows an example of this approach.

LISTING 17.2   GETLEADINGBID—A METHOD FOR LOADING A DEPENDENT OBJECT ON DEMANDPROTECTED BID GETLEADINGBID() {

```
  // see if the leading bid has been loaded
  if ((leadingBid == null) && (leadingBidId != null)) {
    leadingBid = loadBid(leadingBidId.intValue());
    if (leadingBidId.equals(winningBidId)) {
      // winning bid is the same as the leading bid
      winningBid = leadingBid;
    }
  }
  return leadingBid;
}
```

Listing 17.2 shows how to delay the loading of a dependent object until it's needed. Notice that the loadBid method is only called if the reference to the leadingBid is null and the leadingBidId isn't. Listing 17.3 shows the loadBid method that pulls in the rest of the information for the bid object when it's needed.

LISTING 17.3   loadBid—A METHOD FOR LOADING A DEPENDENT BID OBJECT

```
private Bid loadBid(int bidId) {
    Connection con = null;
    PreparedStatement stmt = null;
    ResultSet rs = null;
    try {
      con = BMPHelper.getConnection("auctionSource");
      stmt = con.prepareStatement("SELECT id, TransactionId, BidDateTime, " +
        "Amount, BidderId from bid where id = ?");
      stmt.setInt(1, bidId);
      rs = stmt.executeQuery();
      if (rs.next()) {
        return createBid(rs);
      }
    }
    catch (SQLException e) {
      // throw a system exception if a database access error occurs
      throw new EJBException(e);
    }
    finally {
      // close the connection
      BMPHelper.cleanup(stmt, con);
    }
    return null;
  }
```

As you can imagine, the code needed to do this can start to get out of hand if you have to implement this type of functionality for more than a few dependent objects. To prevent this problem, you need a framework that manages the lazy loading of an object generically. Such a framework needs to provide a class that encapsulates the details shown in Listing 17.2. As you can imagine, doing this in a generic form that can be reused for any dependent object class is not a simple task. You can do it, but before starting down the path of reinventing the wheel, you should consider using a third-party ORM framework that has already solved the same problem for you.

Lazy loading is even more important for one-to-many relationships because you have to load more objects for each association. Rather than loading all of an auction's bids in ejbLoad, EnglishAuctionBean took a similar approach to what was done for the leading bid. In this case, nothing was read for the dependent bid objects in ejbLoad because the foreign keys are in the bid table. Instead, all retrieval from this table is done when the list of bids is first accessed. The comments about using a framework approach apply even more so here. Managing a list of dependent objects is more complex because you don't want to be inefficient in writing updates to the database when elements have been added to or removed from the list. Specifically, a BMP framework for managing a list of dependent objects needs to support lazy loading of the elements, tracking of modified entries, the addition of entries, and the removal of entries. This is the only way to ensure that interaction with the database is kept to a minimum.

USING READ-ONLY ENTITY BEANS

The EJB specification defines entity beans to represent read-write objects. This means that regular calls to both ejbLoad and ejbStore are part of the normal management of an entity object's lifecycle. Sometimes, however, you might represent persistent data using an entity bean that's never modified by the application. As described earlier in the "Optimizing Entity Bean Persistence" section, you can avoid unnecessary database writes by only executing your ejbStore methods when necessary. This doesn't, however, help you if you're using CMP.

The EJB 2.0 Specification doesn't require the container to support the concept of a read-only CMP entity bean. The idea of using read-only CMP entity beans is to avoid unnecessary calls to ejbStore. Some vendors already offer a read-only entity bean as an option. Others are looking at taking this further by making it possible to bypass an ejbStore call when an entity bean's attributes have been accessed (through its get methods) during a transaction but no other operations have been performed on it.

As an example, WebLogic allows you to designate an entity bean as read-only. It's assumed that data represented by this type of bean is being updated externally (or there wouldn't be any reason for it to be stored in the database). To support detecting external changes to a read-only entity, you can specify how often the data should be updated from the database.

As it's been defined so far, the example auction site is responsible for maintaining auction data but the items offered for auction could be defined by another system responsible for managing a company's inventory. This would allow the item entity bean to be implemented as read-only. Because this is a vendor-specific option, you have to declare this in the WebLogic deployment information as shown in the following:

```
<weblogic-ejb-jar>
  ...
    <weblogic-enterprise-bean>
      <ejb-name>Item</ejb-name>
```

```
    <entity-descriptor>
      <entity-cache>
        <read-timeout-seconds>600</read-timeout-seconds>
        <concurrency-strategy>ReadOnly</concurrency-strategy>
      </entity-cache>
    </entity-descriptor>
  </weblogic-enterprise-bean>
  ...
</weblogic-ejb-jar>
```

This deployment directive informs the WebLogic EJB container that `ejbStore` calls aren't necessary for the item entity bean. The `read-timeout-seconds` entry allows you to specify how often the data should be refreshed from the database. You can use a value of 0, which is the default if the entry is omitted, to request that the entity only be read when it's first loaded into the entity cache. Using this deployment option is only valid if the application never attempts to update an entity object of this type and the `NotSupported` transaction attribute is assigned to the entity's methods.

Note

> Some developers argue that an option like that just described violates the current EJB specification because `ejbStore` isn't called at the end of each transaction that involves the entity. The response in a case like this is that the intent of the specification is being upheld because all that really matters is that changes made to an entity object are synchronized with the database. If an application never changes the object, no outgoing synchronization is ever necessary. To eventually quiet the debate, EJB 2.0 lists read-only CMP entity beans as a desired feature that will be added in a later release of the specification.

BUILDING A PICK LIST

A common requirement for a business application is to display a list of items from which a user makes a selection. This can be a list of customers or products in a catalog or anything else. The basic behavior is the same—the user views a list that contains some summary attributes for each entry and then picks from the list. The system responds by displaying a more detailed view of the selection that includes additional attributes.

The potential performance problem with building a pick list is that reading all the attributes for the items in the list is inefficient. It would be faster to only read the summary information that's needed for the list and then read the detailed attributes for an entry only when they're requested. If you're using entity beans for all your data retrieval from the database, this can create a problem. For example, the `findAllAuctions` finder method declared in Chapter 5 as part of the `EnglishAuctionHome` interface could be executed by a session bean method to build a list of auctions for the user to view. If you think back to how a finder method works, you know that simply executing a finder doesn't instantiate any entity objects. All an `ejbFind` method has to do is determine the primary key values that match the selection criteria and return those. It's not until a business method is executed on the component interface corresponding to a particular object identity that an entity object has to be loaded and activated. The point here is that a finder method approach might be acceptable if you can avoid business method calls on the entities that aren't needed for display. Suppose you have 1,000 auctions in the database but only 15 at a time need to be returned to the Web tier for display to the user. Using a finder method might be an acceptable approach if the finder method query can be built to only return the 15 auctions that are needed. Or if the filtering done by the application doesn't involve any processing (sorting, for example) that causes a business method call to each entity. This latter case always has some additional overhead because 1,000 primary keys would have to be read and returned even if the entities associated with the majority of them were never loaded.

If the overhead of loading and instantiating unneeded primary keys within a finder is too much or the logic that determines which elements go in a list requires attributes other than the primary key, you should consider another option. Instead of executing a finder method, you can implement a session bean method that accesses the database directly using JDBC (or an ORM framework query) and loads the attributes needed to build the pick list. In this case, the session bean method can execute whatever query is necessary to build the view objects used by the Web tier. When the user requests the details for an entry displayed in the list, the primary key associated with that particular view object can be used to make a findByPrimaryKey call that loads the corresponding entity object.

Listing 17.4 shows a method that could be added to the implementation of the AuctionHouseBean session bean to retrieve the data needed to build a pick list of auctions.

LISTING 17.4   GETALLAUCTIONS—A METHOD FOR BUILDING A LIST OF VIEWS IN A SESSION BEAN/**

```
 * Return entries for an auction pick list. The session bean performs
 * the necessary queries instead of accessing an entity bean finder method
 * in this case.
 *
 * @param startIndex the element to start with (1-based)
 * @param numToReturn the number of auction views to return
 * @return a list of AuctionSummaryView objects sorted by name
 */
public List getAllAuctions(int startIndex, int numToReturn) {

  Connection con = null;
  PreparedStatement stmt = null;
  ResultSet rs = null;
  List auctions = new ArrayList();
  try {
    con = BMPHelper.getConnection("auctionSource");
    // perform a query to select all the necessary attributes
    stmt = con.prepareStatement("SELECT id, Name, Status, LeadingBidId, " +
      "ScheduledEndDate FROM auction ORDER BY Name");
    rs = stmt.executeQuery();

    // move to the right spot in the result set
    for (int i=0; i<startIndex; i++) {
      if (!rs.next()) {
```

LISTING 17.4   CONTINUED

```java
        // not enough entries, return an empty list
        return auctions;
      }
    }

    // create views for the desired number of auctions
    PreparedStatement bidStmt = con.prepareStatement(
      "SELECT Amount FROM bid where id = ?");
    for (int i=0; i<numToReturn; i++) {
      if (rs.next()) {
        // instantiate a view and set its attributes
        AuctionSummaryView view = new AuctionSummaryView();
        view.setId((Integer)rs.getObject("id"));
        view.setName(rs.getString("Name"));
        view.setStatus(rs.getString("Status"));
        view.setScheduledEndDateTime(rs.getTimestamp("ScheduledEndDate"));
        Integer leadingBidId = (Integer)rs.getObject("LeadingBidId");
        view.setLeadingBidAmount(null);
        if (leadingBidId != null ) {
          // load the leading bid to get the bid amount
          bidStmt.setInt(1, leadingBidId.intValue());
          ResultSet rsBid = bidStmt.executeQuery();
          if (rsBid.next()) {
            BigDecimal bd = rsBid.getBigDecimal("Amount");
            view.setLeadingBidAmount(new Double(bd.doubleValue()));
          }
        }
        // add the view to the list to return
        auctions.add(view);
      }
      else {
        break;
      }
    }
    bidStmt.close();
  }
  catch (SQLException e) {
    // throw a system exception if a database access error occurs
    throw new EJBException(e);
  }
  finally {
    // close the connection
    BMPHelper.cleanup(stmt, con);
  }

  // return the views
  return auctions;
}
```

What's important about the concept illustrated by Listing 17.4 is that choosing entity beans to manage your persistent data doesn't rule out using more efficient access in certain cases. This is especially true when you need read-only access to your entity data. Unless you're dealing with entities that only result in a small number of instances, you should always consider using a session bean to build your lists of summary data. Entity beans provide very helpful functionality when you need to create and edit persistent data, but the associated overhead can quickly get in the way when all you need to do is read and report some information.

MANAGING TRANSACTIONS

As discussed in Chapter 12, "Transactions," it's expected that most EJBs you write will be involved in performing transactional work. This usually means that your EJBs will be accessing and updating shared data in a relational database. The transactional support provided by the EJB container does most of the work of managing transactions for you, but there are a couple of points to keep in mind that can affect the performance of your applications. You need to be sure that your transactions are being demarcated at the necessary boundaries and that the resource locking that's being enforced isn't excessive.

TRANSACTION DEMARCATION

When you deploy an entity bean, you should usually specify a transaction attribute of `Required` for the bean's business methods. You might have some special needs that make one of the other attributes more appropriate, but those situations are rare. When you use the `Required` attribute, all updates to an entity object take place within a transaction that can be rolled back if necessary. You always need to define the transactional requirements for your entity beans, but it's usually redundant because they're being accessed by session beans on behalf of clients. If a session bean method is executed within the context of a transaction, the same transaction is associated with any entity bean methods it calls that have a transaction attribute of `Required` (or `Supports`). This is the way to package work done by a session bean method into an atomic unit of work.

Application behavior changes from what's been described so far if a session bean method is executed without an associated transaction or it accesses entity bean methods deployed with the `RequiresNew` attribute. In either of these scenarios, a new transaction is started and committed every time an entity bean method is called. This creates a lot of overhead that is sure to slow an application. However, performance isn't so much the driver of the point being made here, as it is the indicator of a problem. If a call to a session bean method results in multiple transactions as entity bean methods are executed, the work being done cannot be rolled back as a single unit if there's a problem. If you're suffering from performance problems due to transactional overhead, you need to first be sure that your transaction boundaries are being established correctly.

ISOLATION LEVEL

Chapter 12 introduced the read uncommitted, read committed, repeatable read, and serializable isolation levels that can be used to control concurrent access to resources. Using the serializable isolation level protects an application from erroneous results by preventing a transaction from accessing any data being manipulated by another in-progress transaction. This is an important trait for critical operations, but it does impact performance. The locking done to support this isolation level slows concurrent access to a resource so you should limit this level of protection to the parts of your application that actually require it.

→ For more information on isolation levels, **see** "Isolating Access to Resources," **p. 359**.

TROUBLESHOOTING

APPLICATION PERFORMS POORLY

My EJB application runs too slowly and I don't know where to start in trying to speed it up.

Knowing what part of an application to focus on is key to improving its performance. First you need to determine which operations are the slowest, which you can do simply by executing the methods exposed by your session beans. You can also get information on this using some of the tools described in the chapter that follows on stress testing. Once you have a particular operation to focus on, it's important to assess how much of its workload is actual processing and how much is database access. Once you know this, it's easier to start proposing changes to how the operation is implemented. The main guideline to remember in addressing performance is a simple one—be sure you know where the bottlenecks in a system are before you implement any optimizations.

## CHAPTER 18

PERFORMANCE AND STRESS TESTING YOUR APPLICATIONS

In this chapter

WHY STRESS TEST YOUR APPLICATIONS?

It's not uncommon to build a component and discover when you begin testing it that its performance is not what you expected or were hoping it would be. Eventually, this happens to all of us. Truthfully, the fact that this happens is not a bad thing in and of itself. You should not be completely depressed about poor performance the first time you test your components because, during the design and implementation phase, performance should not be your main focus. This is not to say that you should be trying to design or build slow components, but you should be focusing on building your components and applications based on sound object-oriented principles. Taking shortcuts because you are worrying about performance early in the cycle is, more often than not, the wrong approach.

Focusing too much on performance early in the design or development stage is not the best approach mainly because it's hard to determine where the bottlenecks or problems will be without actually testing the component or application. During design and construction, you might believe a certain piece or component of the application will be a problem and find out that a completely different area actually is the problem when the application is built.

One of the biggest mistakes developers make when doing any type of performance or load testing is not doing enough testing before starting to optimize the code. For example, suppose you have two areas in your application that are slow. Unless you do enough testing to know which one is worse, you might work on the area that is causing the least problem. You must do enough testing to know which area to focus on first to get the biggest return on your time investment.

Let's face it; as developers, we are always racing against the clock. Usually, this clock is being set and managed by someone else to get the release to QA or out to a customer. There's hardly ever enough time to do performance or stress testing of the entire application, so you must be wise enough to focus your available testing time in the proper places. The first rule is to do enough up-front testing to identify the problem areas that are causing the biggest reductions in performance. If you have enough time, you obviously want to go through all the problem areas, but if you do find yourself running out of time, at least you can take comfort in the fact that you fixed the big ones.

A very important distinction must be made between performance testing and stress or load testing. *Performance* testing involves executing the functional requirements for an application and basically timing how long it takes for each result to complete. This action should be executed for all the public interfaces to get a complete picture of how well the application performs. So, for the Auction example, we might test getting the list of auctions that are available, viewing the details of one of the auctions, submitting a bid, and then test the rest of the EJB methods that are exposed to the remote clients. We would record the time that it takes for each action to complete end to end. This sometimes is referred to as a *transaction time*.

Based on the time that it takes to complete these actions, you would be able to come up with a rough throughput time. *Throughput* in this sense defines the number of transactions that can occur in a set amount of time. These kinds of numbers also can help network engineers understand how much network bandwidth the application might require.

Stress testing or *load testing* is a little different from performance testing but is somewhat related. With performance testing, the number of users used when testing performance typically is one. With load testing, the tests simulate a larger number of users and evaluate how the application reacts as the number of users grows. Things such as transaction time, throughput, and memory used can be recorded to get a picture of how the system will handle itself under a heavier load.

Note

Although there can be some subtle differences between stress testing and load testing, we are using the terms interchangeably throughout this chapter.

You must do both types of testing in your EJB applications. Both tests can give you important information about how well the application is designed and constructed and can point to parts of the application that might become a bottleneck, under normal loads or especially as the number of users increases.

PERFORMANCE TESTING YOUR BEANS

As already indicated, there's a difference between stress testing and performance testing; however, they usually are connected because one usually can have an impact on the other. Performance testing deals with areas of an application that are sluggish, even with a single user. Better coding methods or algorithms usually fix the problems you find when you do performance testing. For example, you might use an `Object[]` and a `for` loop to iterate through a finite collection, rather than an `Iterator` or `Enumeration`.

After you've identified the performance bottlenecks, manual code reviews usually are necessary to spot the causes of the problems. In some cases, you might find that you can change the way the code is written and get better performance. In other cases, it just might be a complicated algorithm and there's nothing you can do about it. These performance problems can usually be found easier by using performance-testing tools. Sometimes, these tools can easily indicate threads that are waiting for other threads to complete, or where a large number of objects are being created needlessly. Table 18.1 provides a small list of commercially available tools that can help you conduct performance testing.

PART

II

CH

18

TABLE 18.1   SEVERAL PERFORMANCE-TESTING TOOLS

Company	Product	URL
Rational	Quantify	`www.rational.com`
Sitraka	JProbe	`www.jprobe.com`
Intuitive Systems, Inc.	OptimizeIt	`www.optimizeit.com`
Apache Group	JMeter	`jakarta.apache.org`

Although these tools can reduce the amount of time it takes to identify the performance problems, they are rather expensive, and some of them take some time to learn to use. If you are limited by time and a budget, you can use some simple tests to get an idea of which components or operations are fine and which ones are slow. One of the easiest ways of doing this is to build a Java client that exercises each remote method in your EJB. Before you call the method, record the time and then record it again after the method is finished. If you take the difference of the start and end times, you can get an idea of how long each method takes to perform. Listing 18.1 illustrates this basic approach.

LISTING 18.1   SIMPLE CLIENT TEST TO GET BEAN PERFORMANCE TIMES

```java
import java.util.Collection;
import javax.naming.Context;
import javax.naming.InitialContext;
import javax.naming.NamingException;
import javax.rmi.PortableRemoteObject;
import com.que.ejb20.auction.controller.AuctionHouse;
import com.que.ejb20.auction.controller.AuctionHouseHome;

public class AuctionHouseTest {

  // Constructor
  public AuctionHouseTest() {
    super();
  }

  // Returns a remote interface to the AuctionHouseBean
  private AuctionHouse getAuctionHouse() {
    Context initCtx = null;
    AuctionHouse auctionHouse = null;

    try {
      // Create the initial context
      initCtx = new InitialContext();
      Object obj =
        initCtx.lookup( "AuctionHouse" );

      // Narrow and cast the object
      AuctionHouseHome auctionHouseHome =
        (AuctionHouseHome)PortableRemoteObject.narrow( obj,
                                          AuctionHouseHome.class );
      // Create a remote reference and store it into the instance reference
      auctionHouse = auctionHouseHome.create();
    }catch(Exception ex ) {
      ex.printStackTrace();
    }finally{
      try{
        if ( initCtx != null ){
          initCtx.close();
        }
      }catch( Exception ex ){
        ex.printStackTrace();
      }
    }
  }
```

LISTING 18.1   CONTINUED

```
      // Return the remote reference
      return auctionHouse;
    }

    /**
     * Test the enterprise bean's methods
     */
    private void runTest( AuctionHouse house ) {
      try{
        // record the start time
        long beginTime = System.currentTimeMillis();

        // Invoke the method
        Collection auctions = house.getAllAuctions( 1, 10 );

        // Record the end time
        long endTime = System.currentTimeMillis();

        // Print out the time that the method took
        System.out.println( "Time: " + (endTime - beginTime) + " millisecs" );
      }catch( Exception ex ){
        System.out.println( "Problem running the test!" );
      }finally{
        // Clean up the remote reference
        try{
          if ( house != null )
            house.remove();
        }catch( Exception ex ){
          ex.printStackTrace();
        }
      }
    }

    // The startup method
    public static void main(String[] args) {
      AuctionHouseTest test = new AuctionHouseTest();
      AuctionHouse house = test.getAuctionHouse();
      if ( house != null ){
        test.runTest( house );
      }else{
        // If there was a problem, just exit
        System.out.println( "Error creating AuctionHouse remote" );
      }
    }
}
```

PART

II

CH

18

This is a very simple approach, but that's the point. You can get some very helpful results just by testing how long each bean method takes to execute. As you make changes to the bean or the environment configuration, you can execute these tests iteratively to see how the changes affect execution times. The example in Listing 18.1 only tests the `getAllAuctions` method and ideally, you would want to test each method available in the remote interface of the EJB.

Tip

It's a good idea to execute the tests many times and take an average of the execution times, primarily because of timer accuracy. Although the method `currentTimeMills` might return millisecond resolution, the PC clock the user can access is not that accurate. By running many loop iterations, you can eliminate some of the accuracy problems.

Results also can vary depending on which data set you are executing against and even the network traffic at the time of the tests. The best approach is to use a data sample that is typical of what the actual end users will use. Be sure the data in the database is an accurate sample of what it will be in the production environment, or you'll likely miss some problems.

STRESS TESTING YOUR BEANS

The idea of performing stress or load tests is to be able to determine how many users the system can support without degrading and also how the system will degrade as the number of users increase. With load testing, you keep running tests, modifying your configuration, and then re-running the tests. You will start to see how different configurations help or hinder your application's capability to handle increased user loads. All applications have a breaking point where too many users can bring the system to its knees. The point of conducting load tests is to determine what that number is.

Similar to performance tools, there are several good load-testing tools on the market. Table 18.2 lists a few of the most popular.

TABLE 18.2   SEVERAL LOAD-TESTING TOOLS

Company	Product	URL
Segue Software Inc.	SilkPerformer	www.segue.com
Mercury Interactive	LoadRunner	www.mercuryinteractive.com
Rational	SiteLoad	www.rational.com
RadView	WebLoad	www.radview.com
RSW Software	ETest Suite	www.rswsoftware.com

Caution

Most of the load-testing tools in Table 18.2 require Windows NT, Windows 2000, or Unix systems. For most development shops, this is not a problem. However, if you plan to evaluate these at home, this is something to keep in mind.

Because load testing is attempting to simulate multiple users, it's a little more complicated than just trying to simulate a single user. This is why using one of the tools listed in Table 18.2 is probably going to give you a more accurate idea of how your system will perform under heavy loads than you can get on your own. Most of them are designed to test from a

Web site, although a few of them can test enterprise beans directly. Again, if you are pressed for time and would like to get an idea of the results, you can build a simple Java program that simulates multiple users.

Note

In a real-world scenario, application users would be using different machines to access the application. This simple approach should be no substitute for using a quality program to simulate real loads. The commercial products offer a great deal of flexibility and configuration options and usually can record scripts taken from real use of your application and be played back. This simple program should be used merely to give you a rough impression of the application's capability until you can use a much more complex set of tools.

Listing 18.2 shows a very basic example of how to use threads to simulate more than one client accessing an EJB.

LISTING 18.2 SIMPLE EXAMPLE THAT USES THREADS TO SIMULATE MULTIPLE CLIENTS

```
import java.util.Collection;
import javax.naming.Context;
import javax.naming.InitialContext;
import javax.naming.NamingException;
import javax.rmi.PortableRemoteObject;
import com.que.ejb20.auction.controller.AuctionHouse;
import com.que.ejb20.auction.controller.AuctionHouseHome;

public class AuctionHouseMultipleTest implements Runnable {
  // The number of clients to simulate
  public static final int NUMBER_OF_CLIENTS = 5;

  // Constructor
  public AuctionHouseMultipleTest() {
    super();
  }

  // Returns a remote interface to the AuctionHouseBean
  private AuctionHouse getAuctionHouse() {
    Context initCtx = null;
    AuctionHouse house = null;

    try {
      // Create the initial context
      initCtx = new InitialContext();
      Object obj =
        initCtx.lookup( "AuctionHouse" );

      // Narrow and cast the object
      AuctionHouseHome auctionHouseHome =
        (AuctionHouseHome)PortableRemoteObject.narrow( obj,
                                         AuctionHouseHome.class );
```

PART

II

CH

18

LISTING 18.2   CONTINUED

```java
      // Create a remote reference and store it into the instance reference
      house = auctionHouseHome.create();
    }catch(Exception ex ) {
      ex.printStackTrace();
    }finally{
      try{
        if ( initCtx != null ){
          initCtx.close();
        }
      }catch( Exception ex ){
        ex.printStackTrace();
      }
    }
    // Return the remote reference
    return house;
}


/**
 * Test the enterprise bean's methods
 */
private void runTest( AuctionHouse house ) {
  try{
    // record the start time
    long beginTime = System.currentTimeMillis();

    // Invoke the method
    Collection auctions = house.getAllAuctions( 1, 10 );

    // Record the end time
    long endTime = System.currentTimeMillis();

    // Print out the time that the method took
    System.out.println( "Time: " + (endTime - beginTime) + " millisecs" );
  }catch( Exception ex ){
    System.out.println( "Problem running the test!" );
  }finally{
    // Clean up the remote reference
    try{
      if ( house != null )
        house.remove();
    }catch( Exception ex ){
      ex.printStackTrace();
    }
  }
}

// Method required by the Runnable interface
// This is the method that will run when start is called
public void run() {
  // get the remote interface
  AuctionHouse house = getAuctionHouse();
  if ( house != null ){
    runTest( house );
  }else{
```

LISTING 18.2   CONTINUED

```
      // If there was a problem, just exit
      System.out.println( "Error creating AuctionHouse remote" );
      System.exit( 0 );
    }
  }

  // The startup method
  public static void main(String[] args) {

    // Create the correct number of threads and start each of them
    for ( int i = 1; i < NUMBER_OF_CLIENTS; i++ ) {
      AuctionHouseMultipleTest test = new AuctionHouseMultipleTest();
      Thread thread = new Thread( test );
      thread.start();
    }
  }
}
```

The program in Listing 18.2 uses a constant number of clients to iterate through and create separate threads. Each thread creates a remote reference to the AuctionHouse EJB and invokes the getAllAuctions operation. The time it takes for each thread is printed to the console.

Caution

> When doing simple thread tests such as the example in Listing 18.2, you must ensure that multiple threads are really executing at the same time. If a thread finishes too quickly, before other threads have a chance to execute, you might not really be testing all the concurrency issues. In some cases, you might have to use the yield method of the Thread class to help ensure that multiple threads execute at the same time.

This example and the one in Listing 18.1 are overly simple. The main point of the examples is to show you how you can use a normal Java program to get yourself started in conducting performance and load testing for your enterprise beans. The most important point to remember when doing any type of testing is to start as early as possible and do as much as possible, time permitting.

USING ECPERF 1.0

Sun has released ECperf 1.0, which is a performance workload toolkit for measuring the scalability and performance of EJB servers and containers. Although it's not specifically designed to help you test your EJB applications, it can give you some good insight on building more scalable J2EE applications and also help in tuning your applications. Its primary purpose is to allow J2EE server vendors to improve and publicize the performance of their products using a standard set of benchmarks.

ECperf uses a set of four domains that model real-world Internet applications and provide a small but very relevant cross-section of the types of applications being built by J2EE developers. The domains the ECperf uses are

- The Customer domain, which handles customer orders and interactions
- The Manufacturing domain, which performs the Just In Time manufacturing operations
- The Supplier domain, which handles interactions with external suppliers
- The Corporate domain, which is the master keeper of customer, parts, and supplier information

You can download the ECperf Specification, which describes the benchmark and the rules that govern the types of tests, from the following Web site:

`http://java.sun.com/j2ee/ecperf/download.html`

ECperf comes with a kit that consists of the following items:

- Enterprise JavaBeans that make up the test applications
- A Web client that uses JSP pages for interactive testing
- The required schema and scripts to preload the database with data
- The capability to make files and deployment descriptors for the J2EE Reference Implementation (RI)
- A driver program, which implements the run rules and simulates the client load

The kit is available free, but only through the early access program. If you have not already created an account in the Java Developer Connection, you will need to do so to download the kit.

Caution

Because the ECperf is still considered an early access release, publishing the results of any tests using it is strictly prohibited. The purpose of the early release of ECperf is to allow the public to evaluate and provide feedback on the benchmark.

TROUBLESHOOTING

SLOW PERFORMANCE FROM EJB METHODS

When calling a method on my EJB, it takes a long time to return.

There can be many reasons for this, but detecting where the problem usually is easy. The best thing to do is to get one of the performance tools mentioned in Table 18.1 and start up your EJB server with the tool. Then, call the slow-performing method and use the tool to analyze where most of the time is being spent during the call. When you figure out which method or methods are causing the problems, modify the code and rerun the tests until you get acceptable performance levels.

UNACCEPTABLE SCALABILITY

When I load test my EJB, it performs terribly when the number of virtual users is more than a few.

There can be several reasons why your application doesn't scale properly, but typically it's related to one or more bottlenecks in the application. Commonly, the cause of the bottleneck is due to multiple clients or threads competing for the same resource. The resource might be a database connection (if you haven't used a datasource correctly) or it might be a propriety resource of your own design. One common bottleneck is when a class uses the `synchronized` keyword and possibly implements the `Singleton` pattern. Finding the offending method or methods that is limiting the scalability is much harder than finding performance problems. When you do find the problem, make some changes to the code or design and rerun the tests. Be sure to run the tests several times and look at the averages and not just take the first result set. With EJB and Web applications, data might not be cached yet on the first run, and you might get skewed results if you include the first sample. Normally, you'll want to make a few calls first and then take a sample.

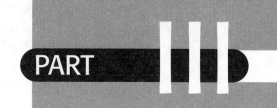

PART III

BUILDING THE WEB TIER

CHAPTER **19**

BUILDING A PRESENTATION TIER FOR EJB

In this chapter

THE DIFFERENT TYPES OF PRESENTATION TIERS

At first, you might think it's a little strange to have a chapter on presentation topics in an EJB 2.0 book. But let's face it, almost any EJB application must have some sort of external interaction with the system. This interaction might be in the form of a graphical user interface (GUI) hosted on a wireless device, an applet in a Web browser, or other EJBs in a different container. In any case, typically there is some type of remote client interface that you will need to design and build for your EJB applications.

Arguably, the most common interface being built today is one hosted by a Web server. Usually, the presentation is displayed in a browser and the output is normally HTML, although it's becoming very common to see the Wireless Markup Language (WML) being used to display output on a mobile device. For now anyway, it's probably safe to say that many EJB applications being built right now use some type of browser to display output.

Regardless of which type of presentation technology you are using in the presentation layer, there are some common design issues that you should keep in mind when designing a presentation tier that accesses an EJB application. The main issue is that EJB is a distributed component-based architecture. Instead of making a normal method call within a single address space, most calls are remote procedure calls (RPC).

→ For a refresher on how EJB uses RPC to communicate between the client and the server, **see** Chapter 3, "EJB Concepts."

Some additional complexities that must be dealt with when building a presentation architecture in a distributed environment just don't exist for a typical single JVM application. The main thing to guard against is exposing too much knowledge of the underlying architecture to the presentation tier.

The presentation tier is supposed to be thin, and the business logic that you might expect to find in a two-tier Web application normally is moved back to the application server, leaving just a very small layer of presentation logic in the Web tier. The more that your presentation architecture can hide the EJB technology, the easier time your presentation programmers will have building and maintaining the presentation layer. By hiding the complexity of EJB and the supporting technologies, you can allow the presentation developers to concentrate on the job they are best at doing.

USING THE REMOTE PROXY PATTERN

One of the easiest ways to hide the complexities for the presentation tier is to not let the presentation tier know that it's communicating with EJB. This might sound funny at first, but it's a very common design pattern. One of the ways to hide this fact is by using what is known as the Remote Proxy pattern.

In the *Remote Proxy* pattern, a client uses a proxy object to hide a service object that is located on a different machine from the client objects that want to use it. In the case of a presentation layer, which needs to make a method call onto an enterprise bean, the presentation would instead make the call onto the remote proxy object, and the proxy object would call the enterprise bean on the client's behalf.

So, instead of every presentation tier component having knowledge of enterprise beans and dealing with such things as the home and remote interfaces, the presentation tier components make a normal method call on the remote proxy, and the remote nature of the call is transparent or hidden from the components. The object that implements the remote proxy pattern lives in the presentation tier with the rest of the presentation tier components. Figure 19.1 shows a remote proxy being used to call a session bean method for a client.

Figure 19.1
A remote proxy being used by the EJB presentation tier.

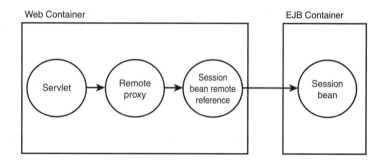

The remote proxy can just be a normal Java class that contains the methods that the presentation tier would normally call on the application tier. Generally, each Web tier user would have a separate remote proxy object, because there might be security information that needed to be passed on during the remote call for each user. The remote proxy object could have instance variables that hold the home and remote interfaces for the enterprise beans in the application tier. As you saw in Chapter 16, "Patterns and Strategies in EJB Design," only session beans should actually be exposed to the clients, so the remote proxy objects typically only deal with session bean home and remote interfaces.

The method signatures in the remote proxy should match those signatures declared in the remote interfaces of the session beans. In this way, a tool can be used to generate the proxies for the presentation tier automatically. If any of the session bean remote interfaces need to change, you can just regenerate the proxies.

PART

III

CH

19

USING A FAÇADE PATTERN TO HIDE EJB

Another design pattern that you'll see used quite often in presentation tiers that have to communicate with a distributed middleware is the Façade pattern. The *Façade* pattern uses a single object or a small number of objects as a front end to a larger set of interrelated objects. So, suppose you have several session beans in your EJB application that the presentation tier needs to communicate with. Rather than expose the different session beans to the presentation tier, the Façade pattern can be used to present a single interface to the presentation layer and make the component interfaces easier to deal with. The object that implements the Façade pattern can live in the presentation tier or in the application tier. For example, you can have a single session bean act as a façade to the remote client. When a client invokes an operation onto the session bean, it can, in turn, call multiple other session bean methods. In this way, the client isn't aware of the other session beans.

Figure 19.2 shows an example using the Façade pattern to hide multiple session bean objects from the presentation tier.

Figure 19.2
A Façade pattern can be used to present a simpler interface to the presentation tier.

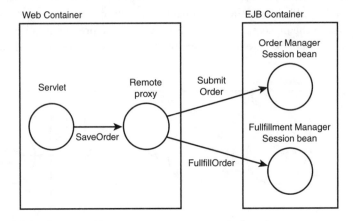

Although the Façade pattern in this example is on the Web tier, the façade is being performed for the presentation tier. The object providing the Façade pattern still might have to use the multiple session beans, but the rest of the presentation layer would not know this.

BUILDING A SERVICE-ORIENTED INTERFACE

Sometimes, you will see the Remote Proxy and Façade patterns combined to produce an object or set of objects that encapsulates the ugliness of doing remote method calls to an EJB server. At the same time, it also presents a more cohesive interface that sometimes is referred to as a service-oriented interface.

A *service-oriented* interface is a set of public methods that are at a certain level of granularity that basically matches your functional requirements. For example, the auction application must support certain functional methods on the presentation tier so that an end user can use the application to view and participate in the auctions. Fortunately, this is the exact purpose of the business interface discussed in Chapter 16. Because the business interface exposes the methods that are available to clients to call, it makes sense that this interface be used on the client tier somehow. Listing 19.1 shows the business interface for the auction house session bean that an auction client can implement.

LISTING 19.1   A SERVICE-ORIENTED INTERFACE FOR THE AUCTION CLIENT TO IMPLEMENT

```
package com.que.ejb20.auction.controller;
/**
 * Title:       IAuctionHouse<p>
 * Description: Remote business method interface for the AuctionHouse.
 *              This interface illustrates a few of the methods needed to
 *              serve the information requirements for auction bidders.<p>
 */
```

LISTING 19.1   CONTINUED

```java
import java.util.List;
import java.rmi.RemoteException;
import javax.ejb.FinderException;
import com.que.ejb20.auction.exceptions.InvalidAuctionStatusException;
import com.que.ejb20.auction.exceptions.InvalidBidException;
import com.que.ejb20.auction.view.AuctionDetailView;

public interface IAuctionHouse {

  /**
   * Return entries for an auction pick list
   *
   * @param startIndex the element to start with (1-based)
   * @param numToReturn the number of auction views to return
   * @return a list of AuctionSummaryView objects sorted by name
   */
  public List getAllAuctions(int startIndex, int numToReturn)
    throws RemoteException;

  /**
   * Return a list of all open, closed, or cancelled auctions
   *
   * @return a List of AuctionSummaryView objects
   */
  public List getNonPendingAuctions() throws FinderException, RemoteException;

  /**
   * Return a detailed description of a specific auction
   *
   * @param auctionId the primary key for the selected auction
   * @return a description of the auction and its offered item
   */
  public AuctionDetailView getAuctionDetail(int auctionId)
    throws FinderException, RemoteException;

  /**
   * Submit a bid to an open auction
   *
   * @param bidAmount the amount bid
   * @param auctionId the primary key for the selected auction
   * @param bidderId the primary key for the bidder
   *
   */
  public String submitBid(double bidAmount, int auctionId, int bidderId)
    throws InvalidBidException, InvalidAuctionStatusException, RemoteException;

  /**
   * Return a list of BidView objects describing all bids submitted by a bidder
   */
  public List getBids(int bidderId) throws FinderException, RemoteException;
}
```

PART

III

CH

19

Notice the granularity of the interfaces in Listing 19.1. They basically match up with the functional requirements from Chapter 2, "Setting the Stage—An Example Auction Site."

You don't see very fine-grained methods, but rather methods that are at the appropriate level of what the presentation tier needs to accomplish.

A class that implements this interface might have to perform multiple steps to accomplish the task, but from the viewpoint of the presentation component that uses this interface, it's just a single method call to perform the service. The presentation components don't have to know that it actually takes multiple steps to complete this operation. The class that implements the service interface hides this fact. That's what we mean when we say service-oriented. Listing 19.2 shows a class that implements the IAuctionHouse interface from Listing 19.1.

LISTING 19.2 AuctionClientProxy **CLASS USED BY THE PRESENTATION TIER FOR AUCTIONS**

```
/**
 * Title:        AuctionClientProxy<p>
 * Description:  The remote proxy object that the auction presentation tier
 *               uses to interact with the auction EJB application.<p>
 */
package com.que.ejb20.client;

import java.util.Collection;
import java.util.List;
import java.rmi.RemoteException;
import javax.naming.Context;
import javax.naming.InitialContext;
import javax.naming.NamingException;
import javax.ejb.CreateException;
import javax.ejb.FinderException;
import com.que.ejb20.auction.controller.IAuctionHouse;
import com.que.ejb20.auction.controller.AuctionHouseHome;
import com.que.ejb20.auction.controller.AuctionHouse;
import com.que.ejb20.auction.exceptions.InvalidAuctionStatusException;
import com.que.ejb20.auction.exceptions.InvalidBidException;
import com.que.ejb20.auction.view.AuctionDetailView;

public class AuctionClientProxy implements IAuctionHouse {

    // Reference to a home factory for the auction house session bean
    private AuctionHouseHome auctionHouseHome = null;
    // Reference to the remote interface of the auction house bean
    private AuctionHouse auctionHouse = null;

    /**
     * Return entries for an auction pick list
     *
     * @param startIndex the element to start with (1-based)
     * @param numToReturn the number of auction views to return
     * @return a list of AuctionSummaryView objects sorted by name
     */
    public List getAllAuctions(int startIndex, int numToReturn)
      throws RemoteException {

      return getAuctionHouse().getAllAuctions(startIndex, numToReturn );
    }
```

LISTING 19.2   CONTINUED

```
/**
 * Return a list of all open, closed, or cancelled auctions
 *
 * @return a List of AuctionSummaryView objects
 */
public List getNonPendingAuctions() throws FinderException,
  RemoteException {

  return getAuctionHouse().getNonPendingAuctions();
}

/**
 * Return a detailed description of a specific auction
 *
 * @param auctionId the primary key for the selected auction
 * @return a description of the auction and its offered item
 */
public AuctionDetailView getAuctionDetail(int auctionId)
  throws FinderException, RemoteException {

  return getAuctionHouse().getAuctionDetail( auctionId );
}

/**
 * Submit a bid to an open auction
 *
 * @param bidAmount the amount bid
 * @param auctionId the primary key for the selected auction
 * @param bidderId the primary key for the bidder
 *
 */
public String submitBid(double bidAmount, int auctionId, int bidderId)
  throws InvalidBidException, InvalidAuctionStatusException, RemoteException{

  return getAuctionHouse().submitBid( bidAmount, auctionId, bidderId );
}

/**
 * Return a list of BidView objects describing all bids submitted by a bidder
 */
public List getBids(int bidderId) throws FinderException, RemoteException{
  return getAuctionHouse().getBids( bidderId );
}

// Return an instance of the remote interface for the auction house
// session bean. If the remote reference has not been created, create
// it here.
private AuctionHouse getAuctionHouse() throws RemoteException {
  Context initCtx = null;

  // Get the home Factory for the auction house bean if not already created
  if ( this.auctionHouse == null ){
    try{
      initCtx = new InitialContext();
      Object obj = initCtx.lookup( "java:comp/env/ejb/AuctionHouseHome" );
```

PART

III

CH

19

LISTING 19.2   CONTINUED

```
      // Narrow the object so that this is portable
      auctionHouseHome = (AuctionHouseHome)
        javax.rmi.PortableRemoteObject.narrow( obj, AuctionHouseHome.class );

      // Create a remote reference and store it into the instance reference
      auctionHouse = auctionHouseHome.create();
    }catch( Exception ex ){
      throw new RemoteException( "Can't create the remote interface" );
    }finally{
      if ( initCtx != null ){
        try{
          initCtx.close();
        }catch( Exception ex ){
          // Do nothing for now
        }
      }
    }
  }
  // return the instance of the remote interface already created
  return this.auctionHouse;
}

// Get the JNDI initial context
private Context getInitialContext() throws NamingException {
  return new InitialContext();
}
}
```

In Listing 19.2, you can see how the proxy class has to take care of several naming service tasks that you don't necessarily want the rest of the presentation components to get involved with. An instance of the class must locate the remote interface to the session bean and, if one doesn't exist, use the JNDI InitialContext to find the home and narrow it. This type of encapsulation, or "behavior hiding," will save plenty of headaches for the programmers responsible for the presentation tier.

Notice in Listing 19.2 that the AuctionClientProxy class holds on to references to the session bean. Each Web user typically would have its own instance of this class cached in the HTTPSession object or in some container object that is stored in the session. This solves many problems, one being how to allow for security for an individual user to be propagated to the application tier.

→ For more information on how security works between a client and an EJB container, **see** "Security Design and Management," **p. 387.**

Tip

If you find yourself doing JNDI lookups or other common EJB operations from more than one proxy class, you'll probably want to separate this functionality out into a separate class that is then used by the different proxies. This will help with reuse in the presentation tier.

Here's one final note on using a remote proxy class as we have described. Obviously, someone must build these proxy classes, whether the work is done by a Web tier developer or an application tier developer—or maybe you're responsible for both. It might seem like more work to build these extra classes rather than just put the code inside the actual presentation code. It is true that you end up building a few extra classes doing it this way. However, one huge benefit is that you can actually build a test harness that uses these proxy classes separated from the presentation tier and test every method within the proxy. In this way, you can ensure that when the presentation tier calls the methods, it's going to get the correct results. This extra unit testing might be a little harder to perform if the code was directly inside the presentation components.

This will also help when defects are reported from the presentation tier. You can easily determine whether the defects are in the presentation tier or application tier by exercising your unit tests again with the proxies and examining the results. If it works from the proxy objects, you know that the defects must be in the application layer. Taking a little extra time earlier in the development stream can have huge payoffs downstream when the product gets into QA or into production.

USING SERVLETS AND JAVA SERVER PAGES WITH EJB

Two of the technologies that are included with the J2EE suite are Java servlets and Java Server Pages (JSP). Although you can program your presentation tier with just about any technology that you want, these two are very complementary to EJB—complementary in the sense that both are component technologies, both use the Java language, both can communicate using the RMI protocol, and both share the same specifications for low-level services such as security.

JSPs and servlets are arguably the most common technology being used as the presentation tier solution when using EJB in the application tier. As we stated earlier, there are many other technologies that you can use, including Active Server Pages (ASP) from Microsoft, applets, a Swing GUI, and many other languages. If you wanted to, you could create a Visual Basic application that used COM objects to interact with the proxy object from Listing 19.2. The possibilities are unlimited, and many development organizations have had a certain amount of success with these and many more types of presentation tier technologies.

Obviously, we can't cover JSPs and servlets in any depth within this book.

PART

III

CH

19

> **Note**
>
> If you are not familiar with JSPs and servlets, you can pick up the book *Special Edition Using Java Server Pages and Servlets* by Mark Wutka, published by Que.

If you are going to be using JSPs and servlets as your presentation tier solution, you need to take the time to understand how best to separate the actual presentation of the HTML data from the acquisition and processing of that data. We'll provide a brief description of one of the more popular ways of separating these functions by using a well-known pattern called Model-View-Controller (MVC).

You might also hear JSP and servlet developers talking about this presentation design as a Model 2 approach. The early JSP specifications referred to a Model 1 and a Model 2 design. The two types differed in where the bulk of processing took place. With Model 1, all the request processing took place directly inside the JSP pages. Model 2 was a hybrid approach that used servlets to process the requests and JSP pages to display the presentation.

Although many developers don't refer to Model 1 and Model 2 much anymore, some still use these terms to describe the overall design approach.

THE MODEL-VIEW-CONTROLLER PATTERN

One thing you should understand is that the MVC pattern can mean many different things to many different developers. In some ways, the pattern is incorrectly used. The pattern is really made up of several other smaller patterns.

The approach to the MVC pattern in this chapter is more of a conceptual one than an actual pattern definition. When the MVC pattern is related to JSPs and servlets, it's really just talking about separating the presentation tier into three distinct areas: the model (JavaBeans or data returned from the application tier), view (JSP pages used just for displaying the HTML and dynamic output), and the controller (which normally is a servlet and a set of helper classes).

The first part is the model. If we were talking about a two-tier application, the model would be the business objects that represent the domain for the application. However, because we are dealing with a remote model, we need some way of representing the model or a portion of that model on the presentation tier. As Chapter 17, "Addressing Performance," points out, accessing entity beans from a remote client can be a performance problem and should be avoided by always going through session beans to achieve a larger granularity.

One of the most common approaches to creating a model for the presentation tier is to allow the session beans to return very simple view objects back to the presentation tier from a remote method call. These view objects are just simple JavaBeans or regular Java classes with attributes and no real business logic. The presentation tier uses these view objects to get the data that will be used to display dynamically in the JSP pages along with the static HTML. Listing 19.3 shows an example of a BidView class that is built and returned by a session bean. This view represents a piece of the model for a user's auction bid.

LISTING 19.3   THE BidView CLASS USED BY THE PRESENTATION TIER

```
package com.que.ejb20.auction.view;
/**
 * Title:         BidView<p>
 * Description:   Value object for an auction bid<p>
 */
```

LISTING 19.3   CONTINUED

```
import java.io.Serializable;
import java.sql.Timestamp;

public class BidView implements Serializable {

  private Integer auctionId;
  private Integer bidderId;
  private Timestamp dateTimeSubmitted;
  private String transactionId;
  private Double amount;

  public BidView(Integer newAuctionId, Integer newBidderId,
   Timestamp newDateTimeSubmitted, Double newAmount, String newTransactionId){

    setAuctionId(newAuctionId);
    setBidderId(newBidderId);
    setDateTimeSubmitted(newDateTimeSubmitted);
    setAmount(newAmount);
    setTransactionId(newTransactionId);
  }

  public Integer getAuctionId() {
    return auctionId;
  }

  public void setAuctionId(Integer newAuctionId) {
    auctionId = newAuctionId;
  }

  public Integer getBidderId() {
    return bidderId;
  }

  public void setBidderId(Integer newBidderId) {
    bidderId = newBidderId;
  }

  public Timestamp getDateTimeSubmitted() {
    return dateTimeSubmitted;
  }

  public void setDateTimeSubmitted(Timestamp newDateTimeSubmitted) {
    dateTimeSubmitted = newDateTimeSubmitted;
  }

  public Double getAmount() {
    return amount;
  }

  public void setAmount(Double newAmount) {
    amount = newAmount;
  }

  public String getTransactionId() {
    return transactionId;
  }
```

PART

III

Cн

19

LISTING 19.3   CONTINUED

```java
public void setTransactionId(String newTransactionId) {
    transactionId = newTransactionId;
  }
}
```

The `BidView` class in Listing 19.3 implements the `Serializable` interface so that it can be sent across the network to the presentation tier. It's also possible that the view classes can be used in both directions; that is, the presentation tier might create an instance of a `BidView` to send to the EJB application when a user submits a new bid. In that case, one or more attributes might not be used for both directions. The session bean can get only the attributes in which it's interested. By reusing the same view class rather than creating a brand new one, you can save on the number of classes that have to be designed.

The view part of our MVC discussion is the dynamic output displayed to the user. In the case of our discussion here, it's the HTML pages that are eventually displayed in the browser. Before the user can see these HTML pages, however, the Web server and servlet engine will need to generate them using some combination of style sheets, JSP templates, JSP tag libraries, and static HTML. Although you probably would find many JSP developers and applications that are using business logic in the JSP pages, you should really try to avoid this. You should strive to keep the presentation tier thin and keep the business logic as far back toward the application tier as possible. It's typical to have presentation logic that needs to go in the JSP pages, but this logic deals exclusively with how the output is being displayed to the user. Listing 19.4 shows an extremely basic JSP page that uses the `BidView` class from Listing 19.3 to display the bid data for an auction.

LISTING 19.4   THE JSP PAGE THAT DISPLAYS A SINGLE BID FOR A USER

```
<html>
<head>
<title>Auction Bid View</title>
</head>
<body bgcolor="#FFFFFF" text="#000000">
<jsp:useBean id="bidView"
class="com.que.ejb20.auction.view.BidView" scope="request"/>

Bidder Id: <jsp:getProperty name="bidView" property="bidderId"/>
Auction Id: <jsp:getProperty name="bidView" property="auctionId"/>
Transaction Id: <jsp:getProperty name="bidView" property="transactionId"/>
Bid Amount: <jsp:getProperty name="bidView" property="amount"/>
Date/Time: <jsp:getProperty name="bidView" property="dateTimeSubmitted"/>

</body>
</html>
```

Listing 19.4 is not meant to do anything significant, but it should show you how the model can be used inside the JSP page. One thing to remember is that there should be very little logic inside the model or view at the presentation layer. If there is any logic, it should be strictly presentation related.

Caution

You must be careful when using a view class that doesn't have an empty constructor. If the JSP page can't find an instance of the class specified in the useBean tag, it will attempt to create an instance. If there isn't a default constructor that takes no arguments, it will cause an error.

The final piece to our conceptual MVC approach is the controller piece. The controller in our approach is responsible for receiving a request from the end user, calling some business logic back to the application tier, getting some data back in the form of one or more view instances, and then deciding which page should be displayed to the user. One common way to build the controller functionality is to have a single servlet, sometimes referred to as a "command" or "controller" servlet, receive a "command" from the user and process the command. The command normally is just a string that has some inherit meaning to the command servlet.

The command could be something like viewAuctions, submitBid, or viewBid. The command servlet typically has a set of mappings that maps a command name to an action that can be carried out. For example, a viewBid command might cause the controller, or possibly another class on behalf of the controller, to call the auction proxy class from Listing 19.2 to request a particular BidView object. The result of this command is then sent on to display some output to the user in the form of an auction bid page or some error page, if the operation fails.

With some designs, the controller servlet might decide which JSP page to call next based on the result of the call to the server. A better approach is to allow some type of workflow engine to determine which page to call next. It might do this by taking into account many different pieces of information, such as who the user is, which page the user is currently at, and what the result of the action was.

The main point to understand here is that the logic of what to do next should not be contained within the JSP page; it's within the controller servlet or some delegate working for it. Figure 19.3 shows a simplified version of how the MVC might work in a typical JSP/Servlet application.

Figure 19.3
A simplified version of a presentation tier architecture using the MVC conceptual pattern.

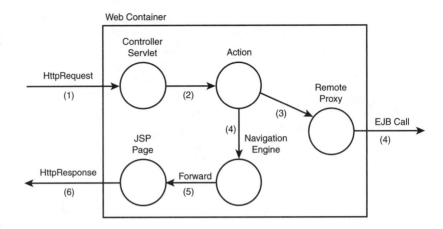

USING JSP TAG LIBRARIES

Even with all the separation given by the MVC pattern, you still can find JSP pages that contain a great deal of logic. It would be nice to be able to encapsulate the more common behavior into a library and then reuse that library throughout your pages. This is one of the main goals of JSP custom tag libraries. Although JSP tag libraries have been around for a while, not many JSP applications have taken full advantage of them. Most of the time, it's due to not really understanding the benefit that they can add to the application.

One of the nice things about JSP tag libraries is that many people are building tag libraries for things that most Web applications need to do, and they are sharing these free with everyone. So, for example, if you need a tag library that displays a read-only calendar, it's out there. If you need one that handles different languages, it's probably out there. One of the best sites for information on JSP tag libraries is

```
http://www.jsptags.com
```

Before you start building a tag library, you might visit this site or some of the ones mentioned on this site to see whether someone has already built what you need.

USING THE STRUTS OPEN-SOURCE FRAMEWORK

All this discussion of MVC, JSPs, and custom tag libraries would not be complete without at least mentioning one of the most popular open-source MVC frameworks going. *Struts* is an open-source framework that can be used to build Web applications with Java servlets and JSP pages. It is available for free download at

```
http://jakarta.apache.org/struts/index.html
```

The Struts architecture is based on the MVC design paradigm discussed earlier. The Jakarta Project has recently released the 1.0 version of the framework.

The framework includes several custom tag libraries for handling such things as locale resource bundles used for multiple language support, logic tags for doing such things as iterating through a collection and building an HTML table from it, and many other common needs. The framework also handles such things as input validation and language-specific error handling.

Because Struts is open source, you are free to modify it to fit your needs. The nice thing about starting with the framework is that you are not starting from scratch. If you are going to be building a JSP/servlet architecture in your presentation tier, more than likely you are going to need several of the components that are already provided by the Struts framework. There's no sense in reinventing the wheel in this case.

CACHING ON THE WEB SERVER
OR IN STATEFUL SESSION BEANS

A very common question that comes up often when building n-tiered applications is where to cache user or application data. This question can spark debate that lasts for months and has no final agreement. Developers feel very passionate about certain topics, and this is one of them. It really shouldn't be that controversial, however. There are really several options to choose from, depending on what type of information you are trying to cache. If you need to cache data for a particular user of the system, you can either cache it on the Web server or in a stateful session bean. There are a few other alternatives, but these are really the most obvious.

Follow this rule of thumb: If the data that you are trying to cache is presentation in nature, cache the information in the user session on the Web server. An example of this type of data might be what the preferred language is for the user or whether the user wants tabs at the top or along the sides of the page.

On the other hand, if the data is more business related, think about putting this data in a stateful session bean on the application tier. Examples of business data might be the user's current shopping cart or the user's latest bid for an auction. This is just a guideline, and there might be other more nonfunctional considerations that you must consider when deciding where to cache the data. For example, what if you needed to ensure a persistent shopping cart for the user in case the system crashed? In the case of a Web server failure, unless you are providing a redundant Web server session on another box, you might lose all the user's data. If you were to cache the information on the EJB server and the server crashed, you could protect yourself a little easier by writing the information to a database when it's modified. In this way, the information could be rebuilt from the database when the user logged back in. The rule of thumb is just that. You'll have to make decisions for certain aspects of the data, depending on your specific application requirements.

If the type of data is not specific to a user but is shared across all the users of the application, the question of where to cache it is a little harder. From strictly a design standpoint, you'll probably want to make it available to the enterprise beans and, therefore, you'll probably want to keep it on the application tier. However, if this data is just for read-only combo-box style choices in the Web tier, in some cases you might want to cache it on the Web server. The answer is not the same for every situation or every piece of data. The best thing to do is to be consistent, and then deal exclusively with the data if you experience performance issues accessing it.

Caution

Be careful when caching data in the session and application areas of the presentation tier. Be sure that you perform cleanup on all the data when the session times out or when the user logs out of the application. If you don't clean up the old objects, you will eventually get an Out of Memory error after all the available memory is used up.

One way to ensure that objects are cleaned up is by having all the objects placed into the session implement the `HttpSessionBindingListener` interface. This interfaces contains two methods: `valueBound` and `valueUnbound`. The `valueBound` method will be called on an instance when it is inserted into the session. The more important `valueUnbound` will be called when an object is unbound by a session. You can perform any cleanup for the object and any data or resources it holds in this method.

ADVANCED CONCEPTS

## CHAPTER 20

DISTRIBUTION AND EJB INTEROPERABILITY

In this chapter

INTEROPERABILITY OVERVIEW

One of the aspects that makes EJB so attractive as a component architecture is that the components can be hosted in containers from different vendors on various platforms and can communicate with one another. For example, you can deploy a JSP page in a Web container from one vendor and invoke operations on a session bean that is deployed in an EJB container provided by a different vendor. One of the containers can be hosted on a Windows platform, and the other might be on a Unix workstation. As an application developer using EJB, you don't have to worry about the location or which platform the server component is hosted on.

You are not required to choose the same vendor for your Web tier container as you have chosen for the EJB container. You are allowed to mix and match so that you get the best performing containers, while at the same time not worrying too much about whether your current enterprise components will run in the container.

This is not to say that there are no issues with mixing vendors; there's always some cost. Container vendors are not perfect, and neither are the specifications that the vendors use to build their containers. However, the interoperability requirements in the J2EE 1.3 and EJB 2.0 Specifications are much clearer than the previous versions about how to accomplish interoperability throughout the enterprise.

The EJB 2.0 Specification includes requirements on EJB container providers that help ensure interoperability for invocations on enterprise beans from various types of clients, including the case where enterprise beans themselves are the clients.

PORTABILITY VERSUS INTEROPERABILITY

There is a distinct difference between portability and interoperability. In its simplest definition, *portability* specifies how easy it is for application assemblers and deployers to move components from one container to another. The other container might be from the same or a different vendor. The greater the portability, the easier time you will have switching to other containers or other vendors.

Interoperability, as it relates specifically to J2EE and EJB, is concerned more with how easy it is for the components within a container to communicate with components in other containers. These other containers might be EJB containers running on the same platform, or they could be objects running in a Common Object Request Broker Architecture (CORBA) container on a Unix workstation, for example.

As you can see, portability and interoperability are different problems that are both complex issues to deal with. However, both are extremely important to organizations building enterprise applications. You can't afford to build application components or services if they can't be moved effortlessly to another container environment or can't communicate with the rest of the enterprise's services.

EJB 2.0 INTEROPERABILITY GOALS

Because J2EE applications are typically multitier, Web-enabled applications, they generally consist of one or more components that are hosted inside a container. The J2EE and EJB specifications describe four types of containers:

- EJB containers that host enterprise beans
- Web containers that host JSP pages, servlets, and the more common HTML pages and images
- Standalone Java client applications
- Applet containers

Note

Currently, there is no requirement that applets should be capable of invoking remote methods on an enterprise bean. Although certain vendors might support this in their products, it's not a requirement yet.

Figure 20.1 shows a generic heterogeneous environment configuration in which containers from various vendors need to interoperate.

Figure 20.1
Containers from different vendors can take advantage of interoperability.

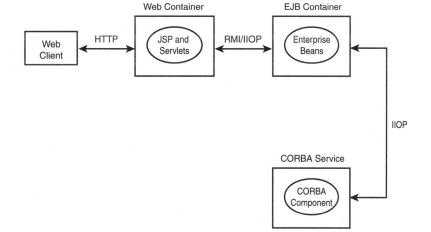

There are four primary goals for the new interoperability requirements in the EJB 2.0 Specification:

- To allow components deployed in one J2EE container to access services from an enterprise bean that is deployed in a different J2EE container. The containers can be from different vendors and on different operating system platforms.

- To not put any new programming requirements on the application developer compared to the previous EJB Specification.

- To help ensure that J2EE products from different vendors will be compatible out of the box, regardless of such things as the operating system or vendor.

- To take advantage of the standards work that has already been done by such organizations as Object Management Group (OMG), World Wide Web Consortium (W3C), and Internet Engineering Task Force (IETF). This allows customers to leverage industry standards and protocols when accessing services from the containers and provides for a bigger acceptance market.

THE RELATIONSHIP BETWEEN CORBA AND ENTERPRISE JAVABEANS

The interoperability mechanisms in EJB 2.0 are based on several different specifications from CORBA. Besides the server-to-server interoperability requirements, J2EE applications also must be able to communicate with components hosted in a CORBA environment.

CORBA is a specification that was developed to provide a standard for creating distributed object systems. The standard allows for systems to be written in a multitude of languages and on many different operating systems. It was first developed by the OMG in the late 1980s. The OMG is made up of many different partners, all of which have a vested interest in moving the standards along.

EJB and CORBA are similar in that both are specifications and not actual implementations. Both describe ways of building distributed software systems, and both are platform neutral. EJB owes many of its ideas to the various CORBA specifications. There are some differences, however. CORBA is language independent and EJB uses Java exclusively. EJB is more of a component-based architecture, whereas CORBA wasn't originally designed that way. In 1999, OMG did agree to add a CORBA Component Model (CCM) to address limitations with the CORBA object model. These new features will allow CORBA application developers to implement, manage, configure, and deploy components that can take advantage of common services such as security, persistence, and transactional support in a standard environment.

Some see EJB and CORBA competing for the same market space. This might be true for some industries, but not for all. The two technologies really are very complementary of each other and typically are used in different circumstances. Because CORBA is language-neutral, it's very easy to build systems in CORBA that can communicate with other enterprise systems built with C++, for example. CORBA also is good for talking to legacy systems because there are many CORBA adapters available to allow mainframe and other legacy systems to communicate with CORBA applications. Enterprise JavaBeans can use the connector architecture, but the connector architecture is still immature and not many organizations are jumping on the connector bandwagon yet.

With all the benefits that CORBA has to offer and the number of enterprise systems built using CORBA, the designers of EJB were correct to try to leverage those benefits by being able to interoperate with those systems.

The interoperability requirements for J2EE and EJB applications can be divided into four distinct requirement areas:

- Remote invocation interoperability
- Transactional interoperability
- Naming interoperability
- Security interoperability

The extensions supporting distributed transaction propagation, security, and naming service access are all based on OMG standards.

REMOTE INVOCATION INTEROPERABILITY

Remote clients should be able to access session and entity beans that are deployed in an EJB container. Because the remote clients might be in a J2EE container provided by a different vendor, there must be a way to define the remote access based on a set of standards.

The remote invocation interoperability requirement describes the manner in which clients in one J2EE container are able to access enterprise beans in a different container. Specifically, the clients must be allowed to invoke operations on the EJBHome and EJBObject references from the client container.

GIOP AND IIOP PROTOCOLS

The CORBA 2.4.2 Specification from OMG describes the General Inter-ORB Protocol (GIOP) and the Internet Inter-ORB Protocol (IIOP) and how these concepts are used by CORBA applications to send and receive messages between clients and servers.

Basically, GIOP describes how messages and data are structured so that CORBA implementations from different vendors are able to understand messages generated from each other. A GIOP message is structured so that certain pieces of information are located consistently within a byte-stream and any vendor, regardless of where the message was generated, can understand and service the request.

The IIOP protocol is an implementation that uses TCP/IP communications to exchange GIOP messages. IIOP is basically the standard wire protocol for CORBA communications. There can be other protocols that use GIOP messages, but Enterprise JavaBeans is concerned exclusively with IIOP.

RMI OVER IIOP

The IIOP part of the CORBA specification is somewhat complicated to understand. It's even more complicated if you wanted to create your own implementation of it. You surely wouldn't want to have to write your own communication layer as part of your application.

The EJB 2.0 Specification uses RMI as an API layer for developers to send messages. As you read in Chapter 3, RMI is not specific to Java. Java Remote Method Protocol (JRMP) is a Java-dependent implementation of RMI, although other implementations are available. Many do not believe JRMP has enough industrial strength to handle the requirements of distributed communication for Enterprise JavaBeans. This is primarily why RMI has been complemented with a different implementation that uses IIOP as the wire protocol for inter-process communication between J2EE components.

All J2EE-compliant containers must be able to support the IIOP 1.2 protocol for remote invocations on `EJBObject` and `EJBHome` references.

Note

Based on the specification, vendors are allowed to support additional protocols other than the IIOP for clients to access EJB components within the container; however, these protocols might be vendor-specific and cause interoperability and possibly even portability problems.

USING BIDIRECTIONAL GIOP

Prior to GIOP 1.2, the CORBA specification only allowed requests to be sent from clients that initiated the connection. Servers that accepted the connections were only allowed to receive the requests. The server could not then turn around and make a request on the same connection. It would have to open a new connection back to the client on a different port. This limitation made it very difficult for components to communicate through firewalls because only very specific ports were opened.

Bidirectional GIOP messages, which were introduced in version GIOP 1.2, relax this restriction and allow the same connection to be used in both directions, as long as both the client and server agree on it. Bidirectional support currently is not required by the EJB specification, but it might be in future releases. If a J2EE server receives an IIOP message from a client that has set the bidirectional flag, the container can decided whether or not to use the same connection for sending requests back to the client.

A complete and thorough discussion of CORBA is outside the scope of this book. You can find more information on the CORBA specifications at

```
http://www.omg.org
```

REMOTE INTERFACES AND CORBA IDL

When requests are made between EJB and CORBA systems, both sides must be able to understand the IIOP request and perform the necessary actions. For Java, information is extracted from the request and converted into the necessary RMI calls. On the other hand, CORBA uses an Interface Definition Language (IDL) to declaratively define interfaces in a portable way. IDL compilers produce native code for several languages so they can understand IIOP. For an EJB to communicate with a CORBA object, there must be a way to translate between these two.

The Java Language to IDL Mapping specification describes how the remote and home interfaces for an enterprise bean are mapped to IDL. The bean provider does not have the responsibility to map between these two systems. The bean provider uses the Java RMI API to call remote methods, and the deployment tools will take care of the rest.

More information on Java IDL can be found at the following site:

`http://java.sun.com/products/jdk/idl/index.html`

STUB AND CLIENT VIEW CLASSES

When a container makes a request for an `EJBHome` or `EJBObject` reference, the client-side stub class (remote proxy) must be created in the container that made the request. Also, any view classes or client helper classes that are returned by a remote invocation must also be available to the client container. These stubs and client view classes normally are packaged with the client application so that they can be made available when they are needed.

Containers can also support automatic downloading of stub and view classes at runtime. The codebase URLs are either sent with the IIOP message, marshaled with the value type, or in the `EJBHome` or `EJBObject` information. The exact way that this procedure should work is specified in the OMG's CORBA specification and the Java to IDL Mapping specification.

TRANSACTION INTEROPERABILITY

Transactional interoperability has to do with how multiple J2EE containers can participate together in a distributed two-phase commit protocol. The EJB 2.0 Specification does not make it mandatory that a J2EE container support transactions between different vendors, although there are still some core requirements that a container must adhere to even if it doesn't.

CORBA'S OBJECT TRANSACTION SERVICE

Similar to the remote invocation interoperability requirement from the previous section, the transactional interoperability requirements for EJB are based on specifications from the CORBA world. The OMG's Object Transaction Service (OTS) 1.2 specification describes in detail how transaction context information should be propagated from client to server.

PART

IV

CH

20

The OTS describes two different methods for propagating transaction context: implicit and explicit. Implicit propagation is handled by the system and is not specified in the operation's signature. There's no need to pass the transaction context around as a parameter or return type. Explicit propagation is just the opposite. It's handled by the application and typically is passed as a parameter or return type from container to container. Implicit transaction propagation is described by the OTS specification. The transaction context is specified in the IIOP message and must adhere to the proper format, which is specified in the `CosTransactions::PropagationContext` structure described in the OTS specification.

For an EJB container that supports transaction interoperability, it must be able to produce and consume transaction context information to and from IIOP messages in the format described by the OTS specification. Other containers that might only initiate a transaction, such as a Web container, should be able to create the transaction context information in the IIOP message.

REQUIREMENTS FOR A CONTAINER NOT SUPPORTING TRANSACTION INTEROPERABILITY

The specification does not mandate complete support for transaction interoperability by J2EE containers. It probably will be required in future releases of the specification. However, there are still some requirements placed on the containers.

Even when the container doesn't support using the propagated transaction context, the container should fail in a consistent manner. The minimal way of handling this situation is for the container to throw a system exception, in particular `java.rmi.RemoteException`, and cause the transaction to roll back.

NAMING INTEROPERABILITY

The goal of the naming interoperability requirements is primarily to allow enterprise beans to be found by using the CORBA naming service mechanisms. The CORBA Common Object Service Naming (CosNaming) is a service similar conceptually to the JNDI service. In fact, as it was pointed out in Chapter 4, "Java Naming and Directory Interface," there is a service provider interface (SPI) for the CORBA naming service for JNDI. CosNaming enables you to look up CORBA objects by name, regardless of the location of the CORBA object on the network.

The naming interoperability requirements describe how `EJBHome` object references are published to the CORBA CosNaming service and are available to CORBA objects through the `lookup` operations over IIOP. When an `EJBHome` object reference is published in a CosNaming service, the host, port, and object key location are inserted into the CosNaming service and must follow the requirements in the CORBA Interoperability Name Service specification.

Many EJB containers provide a CosNaming service built into the container itself; however, some will just provide a transparent bridge to a third-party CosNaming service.

SECURITY INTEROPERABILITY

The security interoperability requirements for EJB 2.0 and J2EE 1.3 are based on Conformance Level 0 of the Common Secure Interoperability version 2 (CSIv2) Specification from the OMG.

The goal of security interoperability for EJB is to provide support for propagating security context information from one J2EE container to another during an invocation of a request for service. The target server needs the security context information to authenticate and authorize the request for the user. Another goal is to support standard security technologies that are part of almost every enterprise, including X.509 certificate-based public key mechanisms and Kerberos-based secret key mechanisms.

SECURITY INTEROPERABILITY BETWEEN CONTAINERS

When a J2EE container invokes an operation on an EJB container, the data must be protected and the proper authentication and authorization must be performed. EJB, Web, and client application containers are required to support both Secure Sockets Layer (SSL) 3.0 and Transport Layer Security (TLS) 1.0 protocols. The following public cipher suites are required to be supported by containers:

- TLS_RSA_WITH_RC4_128_MD5
- SSL_RSA_WITH_RC4_128_MD5
- TLS_DHE_DSS_WITH_3DES_EDE_CBC_SHA
- SSL_DHE_DSS_WITH_3DES_EDE_CBC_SHA
- TLS_RSA_EXPORT_WITH_RC4_40_MD5
- SSL_RSA_EXPORT_WITH_RC4_40_MD5
- TLS_DHE_DSS_EXPORT_WITH_DES40_CBC_SHA
- SSL_DHE_DSS_EXPORT_WITH_DES40_CBC_SHA

Because J2EE containers are already required to support SSL for secure HTTP protocol, SSL provides a safe route for security interoperability at the transport layer.

PROPAGATING PRINCIPAL AND AUTHORIZATION DATA USING IIOP

The EJB security interoperability requirements support the propagation of security-related information to be passed in the service context of the IIOP message. This feature might be necessary when the security principal needs to be propagated on to be authenticated by another container, for example. Authentication can also take place at the transport layer using X.509 certificates as well.

In many cases, the principal is propagated to the container and extracted and used for authentication and authorization. J2EE containers are required to support the stateless mode of propagating principal and authentication information. The container can also support the stateful mode, as described in the CSIv2 specification, but it is not currently required to do so.

More information on the CSIv2 Specification can be found at the OMG Web site

`http://www.omg.org`

CHAPTER 21

HORIZONTAL SERVICES

In this chapter

WHAT ARE HORIZONTAL SERVICES?

For just about all enterprise applications, there are common components and services that you will find present. These services typically are lower level and are used by other components that make up the overall application. The terms component and service are being used interchangeably here, although there can be some slight distinctions made.

Generally speaking, you can conceptually split any application into a set of horizontal and vertical services. For smaller applications, this split may be just an abstract idea and not actually be separated in the source code. With larger applications, this might be the best way to structure the software because it allows for more reuse and parallel development.

The main difference between a horizontal and a vertical service is that a vertical service normally will have dependencies on one or more horizontal services, but a horizontal service should never have a dependency on a vertical. Figure 21.1 shows how a typical enterprise application can be split into vertical and horizontal components.

Figure 21.1
A typical application can be separated into horizontal and vertical components.

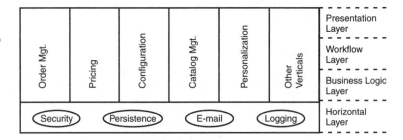

The *vertical* components usually encapsulate the business and application logic that is core to the software solution, while the *horizontal* services are designed to provide common services for the application. Table 21.1 describes some of the more common horizontal services for an enterprise application.

TABLE 21.1   SOME OF THE MORE COMMON HORIZONTAL SERVICES

Name	Description	Note
Logging Service	Used to log local and distributed debugging, general information, warnings, and error messages.	There are some third-party solutions, but sometimes it's built by the development group within an organization.
Email Support	To allow an application to send and possibly receive e-mails.	Most EJB servers have support for e-mail through the JavaMail API.

TABLE 21.1   CONTINUED

Name	Description	Note
Messaging	To send synchronous and asynchronous messages from one component or application to another.	Provided by all compliant EJB servers. You still might want to build an application API on top of it.
Naming Service	To locate resources or references to references for distributed components.	Provided by all compliant EJB servers.
Properties Service	To locate configuration information for components.	Some groups build a service that can provide configuration information for a component. Others will bundle the properties along with the components. JNDI can also be used for this service.
Persistence Service	To provide an underlying infrastructure for creating, querying, updating, and deleting (CRUD) your application's data.	If using BMP in entity beans, you might build a small framework to handle the database interaction. With CMP, this is normally handled through the EJB deployment descriptor. You might also use a third-party ORM such as TOPLink.
Security	To help control access to the application resources and to protect information that is passed between components from being	Infrastructure is provided for by EJB, JAAS, and an SPI. You will still need to build on this framework for your particular

Table 21.1 Continued		
Name	**Description**	**Note**
	intercepted by unauthorized entities. Some security service frameworks also can help prevent denial of service attacks, which have become popular recently.	needs. Each application may have different security needs. Never take security lightly.

Not all of these horizontal services will be used by every application. Some make sense for a particular application and others do not. Every application is somewhat unique and can have a different set of requirements and constraints. You don't need to build all of these just for the sake of building them. Make sure you build only what you need for the current iteration of your development cycle.

Why Are Horizontal Services Needed?

Whether you use the concept of horizontal services just for logical purposes during design, or whether you structure your software along these lines, you're able to assign responsibility more cohesively. A *cohesive* component is one that contains a set of interfaces that are grouped logically and make intuitive sense together. Together, the public interfaces for a component provide one or more related services for a client. There are no hard and fast rules to determine what makes the best component interface, although some interface operations make sense together and others don't.

So, the question still remains. What's the benefit that you gain by developing a set of horizontal services outside the application, rather than designing these services into the application directly? The following list describes some of the more obvious benefits:

- Reduces redundancy in your application
- Helps with maintenance
- Allows for best of breed

Each of these benefits is an admirable goal in itself when building any software application, but when building an application as complex as a distributed enterprise application, you should strive for all of them.

By decoupling the horizontal services from the actual application logic, you achieve all three goals listed with just a little bit of up-front investment in proper design. We'll elaborate on each benefit briefly in the following sections.

REDUCES REDUNDANCY

How many times have you found yourself making a change to your application based on some new requirement and you realize that you need to make the change in more than one place? The answer for most of us is too often. Redundant code in your application is very inefficient. First you have to spend time writing the same code several times rather than in a single place and if anything changes, you have to make changes in every location. Most of the time, this can be a sign that an adequate design was not conducted. Having redundant code in your application should be avoided like the plague. It will come back to bite you every time.

Let's think about a simple example. Suppose we have several components that need to write out debugging information. In the interest of time, let's say that we use something like this in every component that needs to log some debugging information:

```
System.out.println( "Some debugging info" );
```

Later, we realize that we need to write log messages to a file instead. Every component that had a println method for printing the logging information would have to be modified. If the product had already been put through a quality assurance (QA) cycle, then all affected code would have to have regression testing. Now suppose that instead we took more time during the design and came up with a component called Logger. The Logger component could have a public method called logMessage that took a message string. Listing 21.1 shows a small example of what this component might look like.

LISTING 21.1   CODE FRAGMENT SHOWING AN EXAMPLE Logger COMPONENT

```
public class Logger {

  public Logger() {
    super();
  }

  public void logMessage( String msg ) {
    System.out.println( msg );
  }
}
```

Now, if every component that needed to print out log information used this component rather than calling the println directly, only the logMessage method would need to change if we had to log to a file instead. Notice that all the clients that used this component would not have to change. They can continue to call the logMessage method as before, and the Logger object would have the details of how the logging is performed.

By moving code that is repeated in several places out to a single component, you are able to prevent some redundancy that would normally rear its ugly head. The manner in which each vertical component invokes messages on a horizontal service is through its public interfaces. We'll see more about the public interfaces later in this chapter.

PART
IV

CH
21

HELPS WITH MAINTENANCE

This benefit has much to do with the previous example. By isolating the location of where changes needed to be made, you help make the application more maintainable. This is pretty important because we all know that change is inevitable and when you are the developer that has to make the change, you will appreciate a more maintainable application. When doing software design for an application, it's extremely important that you ask yourself, "How is this design affected if this or that changes?". An application that isn't affected greatly by change is said to be *resilient*. You should always strive to build a resilient application, and this starts during the analysis and design phase, not during construction.

ALLOWS FOR BEST OF BREED

By decoupling a horizontal service from the vertical components of an application, you increase the likelihood of being able to plug in commercially available components, thus decreasing development time and also possibly increasing performance and maintainability.

Think back to the Logger example. We might be able to find a logging component already built by a third party and not have to build our own. This saves on development time and decreases the likelihood of introducing defects. If the third-party product has problems or is too slow, you can just go find another compatible product and plug it in with little work.

There is still a need to write some code that integrates your horizontal services with a third-party solution. You often don't just want to hook the third-party product in directly without having an API layer of your own. Remember, we will always have some dependencies on third-party components or services. The goal should be to limit those to very isolated places and know what these places are so that you can be prepared when change happens. During design, you should always consider what might change on the next version and plan accordingly.

This benefit is also one of the goals of the EJB architecture. If you have the opportunity to select from different vendors for a component or set of components, you usually increase the flexibility and portability of the application.

HORIZONTAL SERVICES PROVIDED BY EJB

If you have read the previous chapters of this book and have not jumped ahead, you might be asking, "Doesn't an EJB server provide these horizontal services?". After all, most of them support some kind of logging and e-mail support. And can't JNDI be used to store properties that a distributed application can use? The answer to these questions is yes, but not entirely in a portable fashion. Because the EJB specification doesn't describe in detail how EJB vendors should handle some of these services in a nonproprietary way, it's up to the vendor to design and implement these services.

Of course, you can use these vendor services for your EJB applications, but the problem with this approach is that it leaves you dependent on that particular vendor's EJB services. If you suddenly need to support one or more other EJB servers, you can't count on them to have the same set of APIs to log or send e-mail, for example.

Although eventually you are always going to be tied to a vendor in one way or another, the idea is to limit the places where your application is vendor-dependent. One way in which you can limit your exposure to vendor dependencies is to try to use only the services offered by an EJB vendor that are specified by the specification. You take more risks of nonportability by using proprietary APIs that are not covered in the specification. Even though in some cases, it's exactly what you might need, you are better off finding a way to accomplish the task through portable means. For example, to perform distributed logging, we could use JMS and message-driven beans, rather than relying on a logging API that will only work for a particular vendor. We know that JMS and message-driven beans must be present in an EJB 2.0–compliant server. This is one way to help ensure portability.

TRADITIONAL BUY VERSUS BUILD ANALYSIS

One of the major decisions that must be made when building any nontrivial application is when to buy a set of components or develop them in-house. With most components, this might be an easy decision. When you have requirements for something that is unique to your software solution and you think your organization knows the domain better than anyone else, this is normally a build situation. Or when the cost is so high to buy a solution, sometimes it makes better economical sense to have developers build what you need.

The decision might be totally different if we were to consider something really complex. Some components are better off left to the experts to do because you would end up spending more time and money trying to build one. A perfect example is an EJB server. You typically don't want to build one from scratch. The amount of time and expertise needed exceeds most development shops.

Horizontal services, on the other hand, are components that you normally want to build unless you can find ones that closely match your requirements. The expertise curve is not as high as, say, building an EJB server. In many cases, it makes economical sense to build what you need rather than try to integrate and trim down from too much functionality that might be provided by a third-party solution.

Even when a buy decision is made, this doesn't mean that design or implementation is not necessary. You still have to integrate the product into your application. In some cases, this integration can be worse than building something from scratch. However, by having specifications and contracts between clients and the service APIs, the integration gets much easier.

Lately, there has been a rash of open-source projects putting together everything from EJB servers to logging APIs. It might also be worth your while to invest some time in evaluating these, in addition to the traditional buy versus build analysis process.

AUCTION EXAMPLE HORIZONTAL SERVICES

Saying that every application requires the same types of horizontal services sometimes is too much of a generalization. However, you can usually find the same common services in most enterprise applications. For our auction site, we will cover the following horizontal services:

- Logging service
- E-mail support

Although we could have made a case for the properties service, we chose to implement the properties using the bean components and their respective JNDI environments. We don't have a great deal of configuration or property information and, therefore, didn't feel the need for an entire service related to obtaining property information. This is sometimes the case with horizontal services. You must evaluate the requirements for each individual application. The naming, messaging, persistence, and security have all been covered in previous chapters, so we will not be covering them here.

The next several sections describe what each of two horizontal services will do for the auction site, and we will go into some depth about how we develop the horizontal services that we need.

AUCTION LOGGING SERVICE

All systems need the ability to log information about what events are taking place inside the application. These events can be things such as a debug statement that helps a developer debug a problem, an invalid login attempt by a user, or when there's some type of unrecoverable system exception. Normally, you can group the types of things to log into four categories:

- Debug messages
- General information messages
- Warning messages
- Errors or critical messages

Although there are a few other classifications that might be used, these are the most common types of messages that need to be logged. Many applications might log using the `println` method on the `System.out` stream like this:

```
System.out.println( "Some debug message" );
```

However, hopefully after reading the section "Why Are Horizontal Services Needed?" in this chapter, you understand why this is not the best way to approach the solution.

In a distributed environment, this approach is even worse. You might want all the messages from the Web tier to be logged to the same place as the application tier. This typically can't happen with the `println` method because normally they are running in different containers and have different default output locations. You might also need to change where the log messages are going dynamically (without bringing the server down). This is definitely much harder to do if you are using printlns. Not every application needs to log messages from all tiers into the same storage location. So you might consider making this a feature that can be turned on and off depending on the application.

The idea here is that we want to build a logging API that will be simple for the clients that need to log messages and also give us the flexibility to change where the log messages go and also change which type of log messages actually get logged. We might want to turn off debug messages for a production environment for performance reasons. We would like to have the ability to do this without having to recompile the source code.

LOGGING SUPPORT PROVIDED BY AN EJB SERVER

Many EJB servers provide some type of logging support. Because logging didn't exist as part of the core Java language until the 1.4 version, the support for logging has generally been proprietary.

> **Note**
>
> The Java SDK 1.4 (code-named Merlin) will include a logging API as part of the core Java language. The Java Specification Requests (JSR-47) on the Sun Web site discusses what's going to be included in the logging API. You can find the JSR for logging at the following URL:
>
> ```
> http://java.sun.com/aboutJava/communityprocess/jsr/
> jsr_047_log.html
> ```
>
> The Java Logging API is only in beta at this time, and it is discussed briefly later in this chapter.

There's nothing wrong with using the EJB server provider's logging service or a third-party solution as long as you build a common set of APIs on top of it and your components use these interfaces and not the provider's. In this way, you will only need to modify the logging SPI when switching to a different EJB vendor. We'll get into the APIs for the logging service later, in the section "Building the Auction Logging Service."

AUCTION E-MAIL SUPPORT SERVICE

Another requirement for a typical enterprise application is to send and receive e-mail messages. More often than not, sending e-mail messages is supported more than receiving them, but it's possible to receive an e-mail message and programmatically parse it and possibly take an action based on information within it. You might also just store it into a database for another application to process it. For our auction example, we are only going to be concerned with sending e-mail messages when an auction participant wins an auction or when they become a trailer in an auction. Keep in mind that because we are only building a horizontal service here, we should not have vertical-specific functionality in this service.

What we are building is a service that can send e-mail messages. This horizontal service doesn't care about the purpose of the e-mail message. That's up to the vertical components to determine.

E-MAIL SUPPORT PROVIDED BY AN EJB SERVER

Many EJB servers provide some type of support for sending e-mail messages through the JavaMail API. Using JavaMail to send e-mail messages is actually part of the J2EE and therefore required for a compliant EJB server. The problem is that JavaMail is quite extensive, and you probably don't want each client to have to learn the API and figure which methods they should be using.

Therefore, what you really should do is provide a light, thinner set of APIs on top of the JavaMail APIs and let your client components use these interfaces. For example, you might not want to support attachments for a first release. This might be difficult to prevent if each client component has access to the JavaMail API. However, if you provide a layer on top of this, you can remove this capability so that the client component can't use it, and then add that functionality in later when you're ready for it. We'll see how to do this later when we start defining the e-mail APIs for the auction example.

SENDING PAGER MESSAGES

We want to touch on the functionality of sending pager messages only briefly. E-mail is just one form of notification. You might also need to support sending pager messages when certain events happen in the system. For example, you might need to send an e-mail and a page to an administrator if the system goes down. The administrator might be responsible for ensuring that the system is restarted. If you only plan for certain types of notifications, you will paint yourself into a corner when a new one is necessary. This really goes to the point of building a resilient application. You definitely want to ensure that your design is flexible enough to handle new requirements with little change to the overall system. You obviously can't anticipate everything, but you should try to make the attempt at uncovering possible new features. Be on the lookout for upcoming requirements, look at the project plan, and think about the future business needs of the product. You can save yourself some pain later by doing the proper planning early in the life cycle.

BUILDING THE AUCTION LOGGING SERVICE

We are going to build a logging service for the auction site that supports the capability for both EJB and non-EJB components to use the same logging APIs to log messages. Each container will log messages to a location specified by the logging configuration settings. This might be a local file system or to a central location.

We will follow the architecture for other Java APIs in that we will have a set of APIs mostly made up of interfaces, and then we will build a logging Service Provider Interface (SPI) that will translate the logging API calls to a specific logging implementation. By taking this approach, we can build different implementations and plug them in as our requirements change. We could also build an SPI that plugs into a third-party logging service.

DEVELOPING THE LOGGING ARCHITECTURE

Obviously, there are many steps in arriving at a system or application architecture design. By performing requirements gathering, building use-cases, and understanding both functional and nonfunctional requirements, you can arrive at a high-level picture of what the architecture should look like. We are not going to discuss how to perform analysis and design and arrive at a proper design of the architecture. You'll just have to take our word for it that we have done it for our auction example. There are many books on doing analysis and design. We suggest you buy one of these if you have never done it. Some say that doing design is more of an art form than a science, but that's probably a stretch.

We will, however, list the basic requirements that we have placed on the logging system:

- It must work for both the Web tier and the EJB tier.
- Multiple logging implementations should be supported so that the Web tier could log locally or in a distributed manner. The client code should not be affected if the logging implementation changes.
- It's recommended that a naming service be used to locate the logging facilities, because it is a resource like JMS or JDBC. The logging implementation should handle the details of locating the logging service through the naming service, not the clients.
- The Web tier might or might not use the naming service, depending on whether it's logging locally or to a remote service. This is not known by the clients and is handled by the logging implementation entirely.
- The logging implementation should use resource files to control which specific logging implementation is used and to load environment properties for the logging service.
- The clients that use the logging service should always use a single logging interface, both in the Web container and in the EJB container.

After studying the three requirements for the logging service, we arrived at the logging architecture shown in Figure 21.2.

We could have come up with several designs that all satisfied the logging requirements. There is hardly ever a single correct design. Although some are better than others, there's usually not just a single design that will fit the solution.

You should probably be warned that the architecture that was chosen to achieve this logging functionality might seem overly complicated at first, especially if you are not familiar with how Java separates the API, SPI, and the implementation. The design of the architecture is similar to the JNDI architecture, so if you were interested in how the JNDI SPI works, this will give you a good understanding of it. We are going to walk through all these interfaces and classes and explain to you what the purpose is of each. At the end, we will test them by executing an example of the logging horizontal service.

PART

IV

CH

21

Figure 21.2
This logging architecture will be used for both the Web tier and application tier.

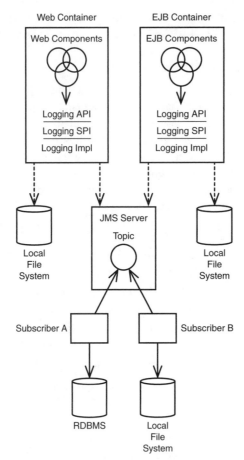

CREATING THE LOGGING API

We need to develop the logging APIs first. These are the classes and interfaces that the clients will be using to log messages. Not only is everything dependent on these, doing these first would also allow client components to partially build in the logging interface methods early and allow for parallel development.

The first API component to develop is the main logging interface. This is the one that will be used by the client components that need to log messages. We will not let the client components determine where the log messages go and which logging implementation is going to be used; that's the job for the application deployer, assembler, and administrator. Together, they will use the deployment files and the logging configuration properties to establish the particular logging implementation used by the clients.

The clients will only be allowed to log a message and inform the service which type of log message it is. If the message type is a warning or error, an exception can also be passed and the details of the exception will get logged as well. The first class we need to develop is the class that encapsulates the log message. Listing 21.2 shows the LogMessage class.

```
/**
 * Title:         LogMessage<p>
 * Description:   A wrapper for the information about a particular log message.
 */
package com.que.ejb20.services.logging;

import java.sql.Timestamp;
import java.text.DateFormat;
import java.text.SimpleDateFormat;
import java.io.PrintWriter;
import java.io.StringWriter;

public class LogMessage implements java.io.Serializable {
  // Log Constants
  public static final int ERROR = 4;
  public static final int WARNING = 3;
  public static final int INFO = 2;
  public static final int DEBUG = 1;

  private String message = null;
  private String subsystem = null;
  private int severity;
  private Exception exception = null;
  private Timestamp timestamp = null;

  // Used to help format timestamp's
  private static DateFormat timestampFormat =
    new SimpleDateFormat( "MMM dd, yyyy hh:mm:ss:SSSS a z" );

  public LogMessage( String msg, int severity ) {
    super();
    message = msg;
    this.severity = severity;
    timestamp = new Timestamp( System.currentTimeMillis() );
  }

  public LogMessage( String msg, int severity, Exception ex ) {
    this( msg, severity );
    exception = ex;
  }

  public String getTimestamp(){
    return timestampFormat.format( timestamp );
  }

  public String getMessage() {
    return message;
  }

  public void setMessage(String newMessage) {
    message = newMessage;
  }
```

PART

IV

CH

21

LISTING 21.2   CONTINUED

```java
public String getSubsystem() {
  return subsystem;
}

public void setSubsystem(String system) {
  this.subsystem = system;
}

public void setSeverity( int severity ) {
  this.severity = severity;
}

public int getSeverity() {
  return severity;
}

public void setException(Exception newException) {
  exception = newException;
}

public Exception getException() {
  return exception;
}

// Convenience method to help print out a user-friendly string that
// represents the log message.
private String getMsgString(){
  StringBuffer buf = new StringBuffer();
  buf.append( "<" );
  buf.append( getTimestamp() );
  buf.append( "> " );
  buf.append( "<" );
  buf.append( getSeverityString() );
  buf.append( "> " );
  buf.append ("\n" );
  buf.append( "<" );
  if ( getSubsystem() != null ){
    buf.append( getSubsystem() );
    buf.append( "> " );
    buf.append ("\n" );
    buf.append( "<" );
  }
  buf.append( getMessage() );
  buf.append( ">" );

  if ( getException() != null ) {
    StringWriter strWriter = new StringWriter();
    PrintWriter writer = new PrintWriter( strWriter );
    getException().printStackTrace( writer );
    String exStr = writer.toString();
    buf.append( strWriter.toString() );
  }
  return buf.toString();
}
```

LISTING 21.2   CONTINUED

```
  // Override the default toString method
  public String toString() {
    return getMsgString();
  }

  // Since the severity is an int, this method converts it to the
  // appropriate string for display purposes.
  public String getSeverityString(){
    switch( getSeverity() ) {
      case 1:
        return "DEBUG";
      case 2:
        return "INFO";
      case 3:
        return "WARNING";
      case 4:
        return "ERROR";
      default : return "Unknown";
    }
  }
}
```

Although the `LogMessage` class seems sort of complex, most of the work has to do with for-matting the message string. A client uses the `LogMessage` class by calling one of the two con-structor methods and passing the required parameters. The following code fragment illustrates how a client might create a new instance of the class:

```
LogMessage msg = new LogMessage( "This is a test warning",
    LogMessage.WARNING );
```

The `LogMessage` class declares four `static` constants that are used to declare the severity of the message. Remember that our logging architecture must support both local and remote logging. Because the log messages might have to be sent across the network, the `LogMessage` class must implement the `Serializable` interface.

Now that we've determined what the log message is going to look like, we need to decide on the API that the client will use to log a message. We will use a Java interface for the client so that we can plug in different implementations at startup. If we restrict the client to using the interface, this gives us the freedom to have multiple implementations that use the interface and perform different actions with the log messages. Listing 21.3 shows the inter-face that will be used by all components that need to log a message.

LISTING 21.3   THE INTERFACE USED TO LOG A MESSAGE

```
/**
 * Title:        ILogger<p>
 * Description:  The logging interface used by all clients wishing to log
 *               messages to the horizontal logging service.<p>
 */
package com.que.ejb20.services.logging;
```

PART

IV

CH

21

LISTING 21.3 CONTINUED

```
public interface ILogger {
  public void logMessage( LogMessage msg ) throws LoggingException;
  public void close() throws LoggingException;
}
```

The `ILogger` interface is a pretty straightforward Java interface for the clients to use to log messages. The `LogMessage` class determines what the output of the message looks like, so really only one log method is needed. We probably could extend the `LogMessage` class if we wanted the output to look differently.

If we want, we possibly could extend this interface to support additional functionality later if necessary. The `logMessage` method in the `ILogger` interface can throw a `LoggingException`. This exception is raised when something bad occurs during an attempt to log a message. You'll see the details of this class shortly. There is also a `close` method that the clients can call to release any resources the `ILogger` instance is holding. For log messages that are sent directly to system out, there might be no resources and the method would just be a no-op. However, with a remote logging implementation, the `close` method may close a JMS session.

Just like the `InitialContext` class in the JNDI APIs, the clients need a logging class that implements the `ILogger` interface, which will provide the implementation to use for logging messages. Listing 21.4 shows the `Logger` class that a client must instantiate and use to log messages.

LISTING 21.4 THE `Logger` CLASS THAT CLIENTS CREATE AND USE TO LOG MESSAGES

```
/**
 * Title:        Logger<p>
 * Description:  The logging class that should be instantiated by the client
 *               to log messages. The underlying implementation is determined
 *               by the environment properties in the logging resource file.
 */
package com.que.ejb20.services.logging;

import java.util.Hashtable;
import java.util.Properties;
import com.que.ejb20.services.logging.spi.LogManager;

public class Logger implements ILogger {

  private Hashtable environmentProps = null;
  private ILogger defaultLogger = null;
  private boolean gotDefaultLogger = false;

  // Default Constructor
  public Logger() throws LoggingException {
    environmentProps = null;
    defaultLogger = null;
    init();
  }
```

LISTING 21.4   CONTINUED

```
// Read the logging properties and instantiate a default logger
// based on the configuration properties in the logging properties file
private void init() throws LoggingException {
  if (!gotDefaultLogger){
    Properties props = new Properties();
    try{
      props.load( getClass().getResourceAsStream( "/logging.properties" ) );
    }catch( Exception ex ){
      ex.printStackTrace();
      throw new LoggingException( "Can't find the logging.properties file" );
    }
    this.environmentProps = props;
    getDefaultLogger();
  }
}

public ILogger getDefaultLogger() throws LoggingException {
  if(!gotDefaultLogger) {
    // Delegate the building of the logger to the SPI level
    defaultLogger = LogManager.getInitialLogger( environmentProps );
    if ( defaultLogger != null )
      gotDefaultLogger = true;
  }

  // Make sure there is a default logger
  if(defaultLogger == null)
    throw new NoInitialLoggingException( "Could not create the logger" );
  else
    return defaultLogger;
}

// implement the neccessary interface methods
public void logMessage( LogMessage msg ) throws LoggingException {
  defaultLogger.logMessage( msg );
}

public void close() throws LoggingException {
  this.defaultLogger.close();
}
}
```

When a client needs to log messages, it would create a new instance of the Logger class or reuse an existing instance and call the logMessage method. The following code fragment illustrates an example of this:

```
ILogger logger = new Logger();
LogMessage msg = new LogMessage( "This is a test", LogMessage.WARNING );
logger.logMessage( msg );
logger.close();
```

Notice that the client does not have to specify anything about the type of logger or where the log messages are going. That again is determined by the environment settings. All the client must do is create an instance of the Logger class and pass an instance of a LogMessage to it.

The final two classes that are part of the logging API are the exceptions classes. Two exceptions can be thrown. The first is a general logging exception called `LoggingException`. This exception is raised when anything goes wrong with the client's normal use of the logging horizontal service. Listing 21.5 shows the `LoggingException` class.

LISTING 21.5 THE `LoggingException` CLASS THROWN WHEN A PROBLEM OCCURS DURING AN ATTEMPT TO SEND A LOG MESSAGE

```
/**
 * Title:        LoggingException<p>
 * Description:  A exception for the logging horizontal service.<p>
 */
package com.que.ejb20.services.logging;

public class LoggingException extends Exception {

  public LoggingException( String msg ) {
    super( msg );
  }
}
```

The other exception class is thrown only during the initial creation of the `Logger` class. If for one reason or another a logger can't be created, the `NoInitialLoggerException` will be thrown. Listing 21.6 shows this exception.

LISTING 21.6 THE EXCEPTION THAT IS THROWN WHEN A PROBLEM OCCURS DURING THE INITIAL CREATION OF THE LOGGER

```
/**
 * Title:        NoInitialLoggingException<p>
 * Description:  An exception that is thrown when the logging system can't
 *               create the initial logger for the client.<p>
 */
package com.que.ejb20.services.logging;

public class NoInitialLoggingException extends LoggingException {

  public NoInitialLoggingException( String msg ) {
    super( msg );
  }
}
```

This exception normally indicates that the logging configuration has not been correctly set up or that no logging implementation has been configured.

That's the entire set of classes and interfaces that are exposed to the client components for the logging API. The next section covers the classes and interfaces that make up the service provider interface (SPI) for the logging service. These classes and interfaces are not used directly by the clients, but get invoked by the logging infrastructure. They couple the logging APIs to actual logging implementations.

CREATING THE LOGGING SPI

The next step in our process is to create the SPI for our logging service. We described what an SPI is in Chapter 4, "Java Naming and Directory Interface." In case you have forgotten, the logging SPI enables us to support multiple logging implementations without having to modify the client code and only modify the environment properties to switch logging implementations. It does this by looking at the environment properties and determining which runtime logging implementation should be created. All this is done without the knowledge of the client components. All they care about is that they get an instance of the ILogger interface and can send messages to it.

The first class that we need to build is the LogManager class. The LogManager is responsible for creating the logging implementation factory. The Logger class from Listing 21.4 calls the getInitialLogger method on the LogManager class, which in turn creates a logger factory that is specific to the implementation being used. Listing 21.7 shows the LogManager class.

LISTING 21.7   THE LogManager CLASS, WHICH IS RESPONSIBLE FOR CREATING THE FACTORY FOR THE LOGGING IMPLEMENTATION

```
/**
 * Title:         LogManager<p>
 * Description:   The class that is responsible for creating the initial logger
 *                factory.
 */
package com.que.ejb20.services.logging.spi;

import java.util.Hashtable;
import com.que.ejb20.services.logging.*;

public class LogManager {
  private static InitialLoggerFactory factory = null;

  // Default Constructor
  public LogManager() {
    super();
  }

  // Static method called when a client needs a new logger
  public static ILogger getInitialLogger( Hashtable props )
    throws LoggingException {

    // If the logger factory was not built, build it
    if( getInitialLoggerFactory() == null ){
      String factoryName = null;

      if ( props != null ){
        factoryName = (String)props.get("java.logging.factory.initial");
      }

      if( factoryName == null){
        String msg = "Need to specify logging factory name in properties";
        throw new NoInitialLoggingException( msg );
      }
```

PART

IV

CH

21

LISTING 21.7   CONTINUED

```
    // Try to instantiate the factory class directly
    try{
      Class factoryClass = Class.forName( factoryName );

      // Assign the instance to the class instance
      factory = (InitialLoggerFactory)factoryClass.newInstance();

    }catch( Exception ex ){
      String msg = "Cannot instantiate class: " + factoryName;
      throw new NoInitialLoggingException( ex.toString() );
    }
  }

  // Return an instance of the initial logger
  return getInitialLoggerFactory().getInitialLogger( props );
}

private static InitialLoggerFactory getInitialLoggerFactory(){
  return factory;
}
}
```

The LogManager class in Listing 21.7 is doing several things, but basically it is looking at the environment properties and determining which logging implementation should be created. It does this by looking for a resource file called logging.properties and examining the environment properties for a property named java.logging.factory.initial. This property should specify a fully qualified logging factory class. If this property can't be found or the logging factory can't be instantiated for some reason, a NoInitialLoggingException is thrown. After an initial logger factory is found and instantiated, the factory is asked to return an initial logger back to the client.

The other interface in the SPI package is the InitialLoggerFactory. It's implemented by the various logging implementations that can be plugged into this architecture. The InitialLoggerFactory interface appears in Listing 21.8.

LISTING 21.8   THE JAVA INTERFACE THAT ALL LOGGING FACTORIES MUST IMPLEMENT

```
/**
 * Title:        InitialLoggerFactory<p>
 * Description:  The interface that all logging factories must implement.<p>
 */
package com.que.ejb20.services.logging.spi;

import java.util.Hashtable;
import com.que.ejb20.services.logging.ILogger;
import com.que.ejb20.services.logging.LoggingException;

public interface InitialLoggerFactory {
  public ILogger getInitialLogger( Hashtable hashtable )
      throws LoggingException;
}
```

The getInitialLogger method returns an instance of the ILogger interface that a client can use to send log messages. All logging factory implementations must implement this interface.

BUILDING TWO LOGGING SERVICE IMPLEMENTATIONS

Finally, we now need to build an implementation for the logging service. You'll see two different logging implementations. One will be used to log messages locally to the system console and the other to send the messages remotely using JMS. Most servlet engines redirect standard out to a file on the Web tier file system. The local logging implementation might be used in the Web container to send messages to wherever standard out is getting redirected.

The remote logging implementation could be used in the EJB container. If, for example, you had multiple EJB containers running in a cluster, you would probably want all the messages going to the same location. If each container were running on a different physical box, a local implementation would not work because each container would send the log messages to a location on its own file system. If we send all the messages to a remote service, then that service is totally responsible for storing the messages from all clients into a single location. You could also use the remote logging implementation in the Web tier if you wanted log messages to go to the same location as the EJB container.

We will walk through the local implementation first, including running an example of it. You'll then see how easy it is to change to the remote implementation without changing the client or any of the existing code.

Before you see the source code for the local implementation, we need to show the resource file that is used by the logging service to determine which logging implementation to instantiate. The resource file is called logging.properties. This is similar to the jndi.properties for JNDI. In fact, the properties file contains key=value pairs very similar to the naming service properties, but modified slightly for our logging needs. The following fragment illustrates the logging.properties file:

```
java.logging.factory.initial=
        com.que.ejb20.services.logging.local.ConsoleInitialLoggerFactory
```

To specify which logging implementation that the system will be using, the java.logging.factory.initial must specify a fully qualified class that implements the InitialLoggerFactory interface from Listing 21.8.

Each logging implementation might require different properties for the environment. For logging to the console, only the initial factory class property must be specified, but if we were using a remote implementation, more properties might have to be specified. We'll talk about those properties when we show a remote logging implementation later in this chapter.

This resource file should be somewhere in the system classpath so that it can be picked up by the JVM. The implementation for local logging appears in Listing 21.9.

PART

IV

CH

21

LISTING 21.9   THE INITIAL LOGGING FACTORY CLASS FOR LOGGING TO THE CONSOLE

```
/**
 * Title:        ConsoleInitialLoggerFactory<p>
 * Description:  The factory responsible for creating instances of the ILogger
 *               interface that log messages to the console.<p>
 */
package com.que.ejb20.services.logging.local;

import java.util.Hashtable;
import com.que.ejb20.services.logging.ILogger;
import com.que.ejb20.services.logging.LoggingException;
import com.que.ejb20.services.logging.spi.InitialLoggerFactory;

public class ConsoleInitialLoggerFactory implements InitialLoggerFactory {

  // Default Constructor
  public ConsoleInitialLoggerFactory() {
    super();
  }

  // Create a new instance of the ConsoleLogger
  public ILogger getInitialLogger( Hashtable hashtable )
    throws LoggingException {

    return new ConsoleLogger();
  }
}
```

The ConsoleInitialLoggerFactory in Listing 21.9 just creates an instance of the
ConsolerLogger. This class provides the implementation of the ILogger interface by sending
the log messages to standard out. The ConsoleLogger appears in Listing 21.10.

LISTING 21.10   THE IMPLEMENTATION OF THE ILogger INTERFACE THAT LOGS MESSAGES TO
STANDARD OUT OR WHEREVER IT HAS BEEN REDIRECTED

```
/**
 * Title:        ConsoleLogger<p>
 * Description:  The implementation of the ILogger interface that logs
 *               messages to standard out or wherever it's redirected to.<p>
 */
package com.que.ejb20.services.logging.local;

import java.io.*;
import java.text.DateFormat;
import java.util.Locale;
import java.sql.Timestamp;
import java.text.SimpleDateFormat;
import com.que.ejb20.services.logging.ILogger;
import com.que.ejb20.services.logging.LogMessage;
import com.que.ejb20.services.logging.LoggingException;

public class ConsoleLogger implements ILogger {
```

LISTING 21.10   CONTINUED

```
public ConsoleLogger() {
  super();
}

public void logMessage( LogMessage msg ) throws LoggingException {
  printMsgToConsole( msg );
}

public void close() throws LoggingException {
  // No op for this implementation
}

private void printMsgToConsole( LogMessage msg ){
  System.out.println( msg.toString() );
}
}
```

There's nothing that special about the ConsoleLogger class in Listing 21.10. Because it implements the ILogger interface, it must provide the logMessage method in that interface. For each different type of log message, it just calls the toString method on the LogMessage class.

To test the local logging implementation, you simply need to compile the API classes, SPI classes, and the local implementation classes and ensure that they are all in your classpath and in the proper directories. You will also need to ensure that the logging.properties is in your classpath. The Logger class from Listing 21.4 must be able to find this file and load the logging environment properties.

To help test the local logging, you can use the LoggerTest class shown in Listing 21.11.

LISTING 21.11   TEST CLASS USED TO TEST THE LOCAL LOGGING IMPLEMENTATION

```
import com.que.ejb20.services.logging.*;

public class LoggerTest {

  // Default Constructor
  public LoggerTest() {
    super();
  }

  public static void main(String[] args) {
    ILogger logger = null;
    try{
      // Create an instance of the logger
      logger = new Logger();
      // Create a warning message
      LogMessage msg = new LogMessage( "This is a test warning",
          LogMessage.WARNING );
      logger.logMessage( msg );
      // Always close open resources
```

LISTING 21.11 CONTINUED

```
    logger.close();
  }catch( LoggingException ex ){
    ex.printStackTrace();
  }
 }
}
```

To run this class from the command line, just type

```
java LoggerTest
```

 You must have all the compiled logging classes in your classpath. If you are having trouble running the local logging example, see "Compiling and Running the Local Logging Service," in the "Troubleshooting" section at the end of this chapter.

The output should be similar to this:

```
C:\ejb20book\ejb20book\classes>java LoggerTest
<Apr 10, 2001 07:01:10:0000 AM EDT> <WARNING>
<This is a test warning>

C:\ejb20book\ejb20book\classes>
```

Now you'll see how easy it is to add a second implementation. As we mentioned earlier, a remote implementation would probably be used in an EJB container. However, it could also be used in a Web container if you wanted the Web container log messages and the EJB container messages to go to the same location.

For this example, the client would use the same APIs from Listings 21.1 through 21.5. In fact, we'll also use the same test class from Listing 21.11 without any changes to test the remote implementation when we are finished.

The first step is to build the required initial logger factory for the remote implementation that implements the `InitialLoggerFactory` interface from the SPI package. This factory will be responsible for creating the instances of the remote logger that implement the `ILogger` interface. For remote logging implementation, this class is called `RemoteInitialLoggerFactory` and it's shown in Listing 21.12.

LISTING 21.12 THE FACTORY THAT IS USED TO CREATE INSTANCES OF THE REMOTE LOGGER

```
/**
 * Title:       RemoteInitialLoggerFactory<p>
 * Description: The factory that is responsible for creating instances
 *              of the remote logger.<p>
 */
package com.que.ejb20.services.logging.remote;

import java.util.Hashtable;
import java.util.StringTokenizer;
import com.que.ejb20.services.logging.ILogger;
import com.que.ejb20.services.logging.LoggingException;
import com.que.ejb20.services.logging.spi.InitialLoggerFactory;
```

LISTING 21.12   CONTINUED

```java
public class RemoteInitialLoggerFactory implements InitialLoggerFactory {

  // Default constructor
  public RemoteInitialLoggerFactory() {
    super();
  }

  // Method required by the InitialLoggerFactory interface
  public ILogger getInitialLogger( Hashtable props )
    throws LoggingException {
    // get the url for the provider
    String providerUrl = (String)props.get( "java.logging.provider.url" );

    if ( providerUrl == null ){
      throw new LoggingException("Could not find provider url" );
    }

    // Figure out the protocol. For now, we are only supporting jms,
    // but could later have rmi, ejb, etc...
    StringTokenizer tokenizer = new StringTokenizer( providerUrl, ":" );
    String protocol = tokenizer.nextToken();
    if ( protocol.equalsIgnoreCase("jms") ){
      // Since it's jms, get the connection factory and the destination names
      String connFactory = tokenizer.nextToken();
      String dest = tokenizer.nextToken();
      try{
        // Create an instance of the delegate that handles the JMS support
        // and wrap it with a RemoteLogger
        return new RemoteLogger( new JMSLoggerDelegate( connFactory, dest ));
      }catch( Exception ex ){
        ex.printStackTrace();
        throw new LoggingException( "Failure creating the remote logger" );
      }
    }else{
      throw new LoggingException("Unknown protocol in provider url" );
    }
  }
}
```

The RemoteInitialLoggerFactory gets the java.logging.provider.url from the
logging.properties resource file and parses the string to determine which remote protocol
is specified in the property. For now, only the JMS protocol is supported, but you might also
build a RMI protocol or even an EJB protocol. Because we are communicating remotely, we
must use some type of remote protocol; that's what this value represents.

For this implementation, because the protocol is JMS, we create a delegate that knows how
to communicate using JMS and wrap an instance of a RemoteLogger around the delegate
instance. If we were going to be using RMI, then we might have an RMILoggerDelegate
instead. The JMSLoggerDelegate class appears in Listing 21.13 and the RemoteLogger appears
in Listing 21.14.

PART

IV

CH

21

```java
/**
 * Title:        JMSLoggerDelegate<p>
 * Description:  The delegate class used when the remote logging protocol is
 *               JMS.<p>
 */
package com.que.ejb20.services.logging.remote;

import javax.naming.*;
import javax.jms.*;
import com.que.ejb20.services.logging.ILogger;
import com.que.ejb20.services.logging.LogMessage;
import com.que.ejb20.services.logging.LoggingException;

public class JMSLoggerDelegate implements ILogger{
  // JMS Administrative object references
  private TopicSession session = null;
  private TopicPublisher publisher = null;

  // Default Constructor
  public JMSLoggerDelegate( String connFactoryName, String destinationName )
    throws NamingException, JMSException {
      super();
      try{
        // Create all of the necessary JMS objects
        TopicConnectionFactory connFactory = null;
        Topic destination = null;
        TopicConnection connection = null;
        // We must use JNDI to locate the jms objects
        Context ctx = new InitialContext();
        connFactory = (TopicConnectionFactory)ctx.lookup( connFactoryName );
        destination = (Topic)ctx.lookup( destinationName );
        connection = connFactory.createTopicConnection();
        // get a session and publisher that will be used for the
        // lifecycle of a logger
        session = connection.createTopicSession( false,
              Session.AUTO_ACKNOWLEDGE );
        publisher = session.createPublisher( destination );
      }catch( NamingException ex ){
        ex.printStackTrace();
      }
  }

  // Clients can close their logging
  public void close() throws LoggingException {
    try{
      session.close();
    }catch( Exception ex ){
      ex.printStackTrace();
      throw new LoggingException( "Problem closing logger" );
    }
  }
  // The method that actually publishes a remote message
  public void logMessage( LogMessage msg ) throws LoggingException {
    try{
```

LISTING 21.13   CONTINUED

```
      Message jmsMsg = session.createObjectMessage( msg );
      publisher.publish( jmsMsg );
    }catch( Exception ex ){
      ex.printStackTrace();
      throw new LoggingException( "Logging failure" );
    }
  }
}
```

The `JMSLoggerDelegate` acts as a remote proxy. It handles all the responsibilities of connecting and communicating with the JMS service. When a client sends an instance of a `LogMessage` to the `RemoteLogger`, the message gets forwarded to the delegate. In this case, the `RemoteLogger` delegates the responsibility to the `JMSLoggerDelegate` instance. The `JMSLoggerDelegate` publishes the `LogMessage` to a JMS `Topic`. The main work being performed in the `JMSLoggerDelegate` is to establish the necessary JMS connections. When a message is sent to the `JMSLoggerDelegate`, it just publishes the message to the `Topic`.

The `RemoteLogger` really does nothing except to forward the message to whichever delegate it knows about. The `RemoteLogger` appears in Listing 21.14.

LISTING 21.14   THE REMOTE LOGGER DELEGATES THE LOGGING OF THE MESSAGE TO A DELEGATE

```
/**
 * Title:        RemoteLogger<p>
 * Description:  The RemoteLogger delegates a LogMessage to a particular
 *               delegate based on the remote protocol.<p>
 */
package com.que.ejb20.services.logging.remote;

import java.util.Hashtable;
import com.que.ejb20.services.logging.ILogger;
import com.que.ejb20.services.logging.LogMessage;
import com.que.ejb20.services.logging.LoggingException;

public class RemoteLogger implements ILogger {
  // The delegate that handles the real remote logging
  private ILogger delegate = null;

  public RemoteLogger( ILogger logDelegate ) {
    super();
    this.delegate = logDelegate;
  }

  public void logMessage( LogMessage msg ) throws LoggingException {
    delegate.logMessage( msg );
  }
  public void close() throws LoggingException {
    delegate.close();
  }
}
```

The RemoteLogger takes any LogMessage sent to it and just forwards it on to the delegate instance. In this way, the same RemoteLogger class can support many different remote-logging implementations by just swapping out the delegate instance.

Running a remote logging example is a little more complicated than the local one. This is because the necessary JMS administrative objects must be configured. You'll also have to build a Topic subscriber that receives the log messages and does something with them. We chose a Topic over a Queue because it's possible to have log message subscribers hook up to the Topic and do various things with the log messages. For example, one subscriber could just store the message into a relational database, while another could only be looking for error log messages and then sending them as a pager message to the system administrator.

For our example, we'll just build a single subscriber that subscribes to the Topic and prints the messages out to the console. Before we begin, the environment properties must be modified to support the new initial logger factory. Here is the logging.properties file that has been modified to support the remote logging implementation.

```
java.logging.factory.initial=
    com.que.ejb20.services.logging.remote.RemoteInitialLoggerFactory
java.logging.provider.url=jms:LoggingConnectionFactory:LoggingTopic
```

The logging.properties specifies the new InitialLoggerFactory implementation that we'll be using. It also contains java.logging.provider.url, which specifies the protocol and rest of the information that the delegate requires. Remember that for each implementation, the format of the provider URL might be different. For the JMSLoggerDelegate, the JMS connection factory and destination name is specified after the protocol in this property.

Listing 21.15 shows the Topic subscriber that will be used to receive messages from the Topic and print them out.

Note

We also could have used a message-driven bean as the message handler. We chose just to use a Java client to keep this example simple.

LISTING 21.15   THE CLIENT SUBSCRIBER FOR THE LOGGING IMPLEMENTATION

```
import javax.jms.*;
import java.io.*;

import java.util.*;
import javax.naming.*;
import com.que.ejb20.services.logging.LogMessage;

public class LogSubscriber implements javax.jms.MessageListener, Runnable {
    // The JNDI and JMS object references
    private Context ctx = null;
    private TopicConnectionFactory tcf = null;
    private TopicSubscriber subscriber = null;
    private TopicConnection topicConnection = null;
    private Topic topic = null;
```

LISTING 21.15   CONTINUED

```java
// Default Constructor
public LogSubscriber() {
  super();
}

public void onMessage( Message msg ) {
  if ( msg instanceof ObjectMessage) {
    try {
      Object obj = ((ObjectMessage)msg).getObject();
      System.out.println( obj );
    } catch( JMSException ex ) {
      ex.printStackTrace();
    }
  }
}

public void init() throws JMSException, NamingException {
  try{
    // Lookup the jndi factory
     ctx = new InitialContext();

    // Get a connection to the TopicConnectionFactory
    tcf = (TopicConnectionFactory)ctx.lookup( "LoggingConnectionFactory" );

  // Create a connection
  topicConnection = tcf.createTopicConnection();

  // Create a session that is nontransacted and is notified automatically
  TopicSession ses =
    topicConnection.createTopicSession( false, Session.AUTO_ACKNOWLEDGE );

  // Lookup a destination
  topic = (Topic)ctx.lookup( "LoggingTopic" );

  // Create the receiver with a msgSelector. The msgSelector may
  // be null. The noLocal parameter is set so that this subscriber
  // will not receive copies of its own messages
  subscriber = ses.createSubscriber( topic );

  // It's a good idea to always put a final block so that the
  // context is closed
  }catch( NamingException ex ) {
    ex.printStackTrace();
    System.exit( -1 );
  }finally {
    try {
      // Close up the JNDI connection since we have found what we needed
      ctx.close();
    }catch ( Exception ex ) {
      ex.printStackTrace();
    }
  }
```

LISTING 21.15   CONTINUED

```
    // Inform the received that the callbacks should be sent to this instance
    subscriber.setMessageListener( this );

    // Start listening
    topicConnection.start();
    System.out.println( "Listening on topic" );
  }

  /**
   * The run method is neccessary because this method implements the
   * Runnable interface to keep the thread alive and waiting for messages.
   * Otherwise, this would not stay alive and would not be able to
   * listen for messages asynchronously.
   */
  public void run() {
    while( true ) {
      synchronized( this ){
        try{
          wait();
        }catch( InterruptedException ex ){
        }
      }
    }
  }

  /**
   * Main Method
   * This is the main entry point that starts the Topic subscriber listening
   * for messages.
   */
  public static void main( String args[]) {
    // Create an instance of the client
    LogSubscriber subscriber = null;

    try {
      subscriber = new LogSubscriber();
      subscriber.init();
    }catch( NamingException ex ){
      ex.printStackTrace();
    }catch( JMSException ex ){
      ex.printStackTrace();
    }

    // Start the client running
    Thread newThread = new Thread( subscriber );
    newThread.start();
  }
}
```

Although it might look like there is much going on in the LogSubscriber, there's really not. The client just initializes itself to listen on the Topic and waits for messages via the onMessage method. When a JMS message arrives, it simply calls the toString method on the object. If this were a production client, it might use JDBC to store the message attributes into a relational table or send them to a call center that was monitoring the application.

The two JMS administrative objects that must be configured for this example to work correctly are the `LoggingConnectionFactory` and the `LoggingTopic`. These are used in the `LogSubscriber` class in Listing 21.15 to allow the subscriber to connect to the JMS service. They are also specified in the `logging.properties` resource file.

To run the remote example, you should start the `LogSubscriber` first by typing

```
java LogSubscriber
```

on the command line. The client will print out that it's listening on the `Topic`. Once the `LogSubscriber` is running, run the `LoggerTest` class from Listing 21.11 as before. The `LogSubscriber` class should print out the `LogMessage` information to the console.

 You must have all the compiled logging classes in your classpath. If you are having trouble running the remote logging example, see "Compiling and Running the Remote Logging Service," in the "Troubleshooting" section at the end of this chapter.

COMMERCIALLY AVAILABLE LOGGING SERVICES

Some free and commercial logging services are available. Most are quite complete and can be configured for various conditions. In some cases, they actually offer too much functionality and you'll find yourself trying to trim down what's included.

There's no reason why you couldn't use the previous architecture and build a factory that creates an instance that communicates with a third-party product. At least by doing this, you'll have the peace of mind that you could get rid of the third-party product and not have to change anything but the `logging.properties` file.

One of the most popular free Java logging frameworks can be found at

```
http://jakarta.apache.org/log4j/docs/index.html
```

JAVA 1.4 LOGGING API

When the Java 2 SDK version 1.4 is released, it will be the first time that logging has been a part of the core language. Although the API does seem to be missing some key features, it does have all the necessary essentials that an enterprise application might need. In some respects, it's similar to the API discussed previously in this chapter.

Several types of logging handlers will be present in the logging API. The types of logging available are

- Logging to OutputStreams
- Logging to the `System.err`
- Logging to files
- Logging to sockets
- Logging to memory

PART

IV

CH

21

As with just about everything else in the Java language, you'll be able to plug in logging APIs from other vendors if you need more than what's provided in the 1.4 release.

BUILDING AN E-MAIL HORIZONTAL SERVICE

Now we are going to build a horizontal service that supports e-mail messages to be sent by clients and eventually sent out to a Simple Mail Transport Protocol (SMTP) server somewhere on the network. It's possible that we might want to store the e-mail message before being sent in case the system crashes after a client sends it, but before it can make its way to the SMTP server.

Although it's not currently a requirement for the e-mails to be sent to anywhere else but the SMTP server, it's possible it will be a requirement somewhere down the road and we would like to plan for it in our design. The following list summarizes the requirements for the e-mail service for the example auction site:

- Support e-mail messages to be sent to an SMTP server.
- Support external configuration of the e-mail destination.
- Future support of attachments—they are not currently needed.
- Client should have a simple interface and a wrapper class for e-mail information.

DEVELOPING THE E-MAIL SERVICE ARCHITECTURE

Based on the small set of requirements that we have listed, we have arrived at the e-mail service architecture in Figure 21.3.

Figure 21.3
The e-mail compo-
nent architecture for
the example auction
site must be config-
urable.

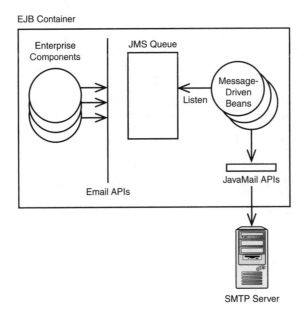

The main component of the e-mail service architecture is a JMS Queue. Any component, including the Web tier, could generate an e-mail message and send it to the JMS Queue. When a JMS message arrives at the e-mail Queue, a message-driven bean will handle the sending of the e-mail to the SMTP server. Using message-driven beans to handle the work allows the clients to asynchronously send e-mails and at the same time support a large number of clients in a very thread-safe manner.

BUILDING THE E-MAIL APIs

As before with the logging service, we will first build the e-mail APIs that the clients will use to interact with the e-mail service. Listing 21.16 shows the EmailService class, which is used by the clients to initiate an e-mail message.

LISTING 21.16   THE EmailService CLASS USED BY CLIENTS TO SEND E-MAIL MESSAGES

```
/**
 * Title:        EmailService<p>
 * Description:  This class represents the horizontal email service
 *               Component. It contains static methods for generating email
 *               messages.<p>
 */
package com.que.ejb20.services.email;

import com.que.ejb20.services.email.jms.JMSEmailDelegate;

public class EmailService {
  private static EmailDelegate delegate = null;

  // The method for all clients to use when they need to send an email. The
  // method is synchronized because it lazily initializes the delegate.
  public synchronized static void sendEmail( Emailable email )
    throws EmailException {

    // If the delegate has not been created yet, then do it now.
    if ( delegate == null ){
      delegate = new JMSEmailDelegate();
    }
    delegate.sendEmail( email );
  }
}
```

The EmailService class contains a static method called sendEmail that clients can call and pass an instance of an object that implements the Emailable interface. The EmailService class uses a delegate to handle the implementation. By doing this, the implementations can be switched without affecting the clients or the EmailService class.

Any class that contains information that can be sent as an e-mail message may implement the Emailable interface. The Emailable interface appears in Listing 21.17.

PART

IV

CH

21

LISTING 21.17   A JAVA INTERFACE DEFINING METHODS THAT ANY CLASS WISHING TO REPRESENT AN E-MAIL MUST IMPLEMENT

```java
/**
 * Title:        Emailable<p>
 * Description:  This interface defines methods that an object that wishses to
 *               represent an email message must implement.<p>
 */
package com.que.ejb20.services.email;

public interface Emailable extends java.io.Serializable {
  public String getToAddress();
  public void setToAddress(String newToAddress);
  public void setFromAddress(String newFromAddress);
  public String getFromAddress();
  public void setSubject(String newSubject);
  public String getSubject();
  public void setBody(String newBody);
  public String getBody();
}
```

The `Emailable` interface contains the necessary behavior to send an e-mail message to a SMTP server. When the client needs to send an e-mail message, it can use any class that implements the `Emailable` interface. If the client doesn't already have an instance of class that implements that interface, it can construct an instance of an `EmailMessage`. This class implements the `Emailable` interface and may be sent to the static `sendEmail` method in the `EmailService` class. Listing 21.18 shows the `EmailMessage` class.

LISTING 21.18   THE JAVA CLASS USED TO REPRESENT AN E-MAIL MESSAGE

```java
/**
 * Title:        EmailMessage<p>
 * Description:  This class encapsulates the data that must be sent in a
 *               Email message. This class does not support attachments.
 *               This class implements the java.io.Serializable
 *               interface so that this object can be marshalled over
 *               the network.<p>
 */
package com.que.ejb20.services.email;

public class EmailMessage implements Emailable, java.io.Serializable{

  // Default Constructor
  public EmailMessage() {
    super();
  }

  // Private instance references
  private String toAddress;
  private String fromAddress;
  private String subject;
  private String body;
```

LISTING 21.18   CONTINUED

```java
// Public Accessors and Mutators
public String getToAddress() {
  return toAddress;
}
public void setToAddress(String newToAddress) {
  toAddress = newToAddress;
}
public void setFromAddress(String newFromAddress) {
  fromAddress = newFromAddress;
}
public String getFromAddress() {
  return fromAddress;
}
public void setSubject(String newSubject) {
  subject = newSubject;
}
public String getSubject() {
  return subject;
}
public void setBody(String newBody) {
  body = newBody;
}
public String getBody() {
  return body;
}

// Override the default toString method
public String toString() {
  StringBuffer buf = new StringBuffer();
  buf.append( "To: " + getToAddress() );
  buf.append( "\n" );
  buf.append( "From: " + getFromAddress() );
  buf.append( "\n" );
  buf.append( "Subject: " + getSubject() );
  buf.append( "\n" );
  buf.append( "Body: " + getBody() );
  buf.append( "\n" );
  return buf.toString();
}
}
```

The EmailMessage class contains the necessary attributes to send an e-mail message to the SMTP server. It also overrides the default toString method so that it can be displayed in a user-friendly format.

When there is a problem during the process of sending an e-mail message, an EmailException may be thrown by the sendEmail method in the EmailService class from Listing 21.16. A client must use a try/catch block around the call to the sendEmail method. The EmailException class is shown in Listing 21.19.

LISTING 21.19   AN EXCEPTION THAT IS THROWN WHEN A PROBLEM OCCURS SENDING AN E-MAIL MESSAGE

```
/**
 * Title:          EmailException<p>
 * Description:    The exception that is thrown when there's a problem with
 *                 sending emails.
 */
package com.que.ejb20.services.email;

public class EmailException extends Exception {

  public EmailException( String msg ) {
    super( msg );
  }
}
```

For the e-mail service, we will also use the concept of a delegate as we did with the logging service. With this approach, we can substitute in different delegates in case the requirements change. Listing 21.20 shows the EmailDelegate interface that all e-mail delegates must implement.

LISTING 21.20   THE EmailDelegate INTERFACE THAT ALL IMPLEMENTATIONS OF E-MAIL SERVICE MUST IMPLEMENT

```
/**
 * Title:          EmailDelegate<p>
 * Description:    Methods that all implementations of the email service that
 *                 is responsible for sending emails must implement.
 */
package com.que.ejb20.services.email;

public interface EmailDelegate {
  public void sendEmail( Emailable emailMessage ) throws EmailException;
}
```

Listing 21.21 shows the JMSEmailDelegate that we will be using as the default delegate for our example. This delegate uses JMS and publishes the EmailMessage to a Queue. It's possible that you might want to use a JMS Topic rather than a Queue. If that's the case, you could substitute in a different delegate class or modify this one. For the auction example, we are going to be using a Queue to keep it simple.

LISTING 21.21   THE IMPLEMENTATION OF THE EmailDelegate INTERFACE THAT USES JMS TO SEND E-MAIL MESSAGES TO A QUEUE

```
/**
 * Title:          JMSEmailDelegate<p>
 * Description:    An Email service delegate that uses JMS to send an Emailable
 *                 object to it so that it can be sent out to a smtp host.<p>
 */
package com.que.ejb20.services.email.jms;
```

LISTING 21.21   CONTINUED

```java
import javax.jms.*;
import javax.naming.*;
import com.que.ejb20.services.email.Emailable;
import com.que.ejb20.services.email.EmailException;
import com.que.ejb20.services.email.EmailDelegate;

public class JMSEmailDelegate implements EmailDelegate {
  // JMS Administrative objects
  private Queue emailDestination = null;
  private QueueSession emailSession = null;
  private QueueSender emailSender = null;

  // Default Constructor
  public JMSEmailDelegate() throws EmailException {
    super();
    // The Queue Name and Connection Factory names. In production,
    // these values belong in a resource file.
    String destinationName = "com.que.ejb20book.EmailQueue";
    String connectionFactoryName = "com.que.ejb20book.AuctionConnectionFactory";
    QueueConnectionFactory connFact = null;
    QueueConnection queueConn = null;

    Context ctx = null;
    try{
      // Look up the JMS objects and create a QueueSender
      ctx = new InitialContext();
      connFact = (QueueConnectionFactory)ctx.lookup( connectionFactoryName );
      emailDestination = (Queue)ctx.lookup( destinationName );
      queueConn = connFact.createQueueConnection();

      emailSession =
          queueConn.createQueueSession( false, Session.AUTO_ACKNOWLEDGE );

      emailSender = emailSession.createSender( emailDestination );
    }catch( NamingException ex ){
      ex.printStackTrace();
    }catch( JMSException ex ){
      ex.printStackTrace();
    }
  }

  // The method that is required by the EmailDelegate interface.
  // This is the method that actually sends the email message
  public void sendEmail( Emailable emailMessage ) throws EmailException {
    try{
      ObjectMessage msg = emailSession.createObjectMessage( emailMessage );
      emailSender.send( msg );
    }catch( Exception ex ){
      ex.printStackTrace();
      throw new EmailException( "Problem sending email " + emailMessage );
    }
  }
}
```

As with the JMSLoggerDelegate in Listing 21.13, most of the code in the JMSEmailDelegate class is spent connecting to the necessary JMS service. Once a QueueSender is created, the e-mail message is sent. The EmailService class holds onto the delegate in a static reference, so it is created only once and is used by all clients. That's why we added the synchronized keyword to the sendEmail method, so that it can handle multiple threads in a safe manner.

BUILDING THE E-MAIL SERVICE MESSAGE-DRIVEN BEAN

For this example, we will be using a message-driven bean to handle the messages that arrive at the e-mail queue. As you learned in Chapter 11, "Message-Driven Beans," the container will manage the number of instances necessary based on the load. Listing 21.22 shows the message-driven bean for the e-mail service example.

LISTING 21.22   THE MESSAGE-DRIVEN BEAN THAT RECEIVES E-MAIL MESSAGES FROM THE JMS QUEUE

```
/**
 * Title:        EmailServiceBean<p>
 * Description:  A Message-Driven bean that listens on a javax.jms.Queue for
 *               messages and gets the email message out and sends it off to
 *               a smtp host.<p>
 */
package com.que.ejb20.services.email.impl;

import java.util.Date;
import java.util.Properties;
import javax.ejb.*;
import javax.jms.*;
import javax.naming.*;
import javax.mail.*;
import javax.mail.internet.*;
import javax.activation.*;
import com.que.ejb20.services.email.Emailable;

public class EmailServiceBean
    implements javax.ejb.MessageDrivenBean, MessageListener {

  // Instance ref for the beans context
  MessageDrivenContext context = null;

  // Default Constructor
  public EmailServiceBean() {
    super();
  }

  // The required onMessage method from the MessageListener interface
  // The onMessage method is not allowed to throw exceptions, so
  // we will catch every checked exception and just print out a
  // stack trace.
  public void onMessage( javax.jms.Message message ){
    // Local reference to the javax.mail.Session
    javax.mail.Session mailSession = null;
    try{
```

LISTING 21.22 CONTINUED

```
//Make sure it's a type ObjectMessage
if (!(message instanceof ObjectMessage)){
  return;
}
// Make sure it's an EmailMessage
Object obj = ((ObjectMessage)message).getObject();
if (!(obj instanceof Emailable)){
  return;
}

Emailable email = (Emailable)obj;

Context ctx = new InitialContext();
// Get the properties for this bean from the environment. The
// properties were specified in the env-entry tags in the deployment
// descriptor for this bean
Context myEnv = (Context)ctx.lookup( "java:comp/env" );
String smtpHost = (String)myEnv.lookup( "smtpHost" );

Properties props = new Properties();
props.put( "mail.smtp.host", smtpHost );
// Get a mail session. You would normally get this from
// JNDI, but some servers have a problem with this.
// Each Message Driven bean instance is responsible for
//getting its own unshared javax.mail.Session.
mailSession = javax.mail.Session.getDefaultInstance( props, null );
javax.mail.Message msg = new MimeMessage( mailSession );

// Set the mail properties
msg.setFrom(
  new javax.mail.internet.InternetAddress( email.getFromAddress() ) );

InternetAddress[] addresses =
   { new InternetAddress(email.getToAddress()) };

msg.setRecipients( javax.mail.Message.RecipientType.TO, addresses );
msg.setSubject( email.getSubject() );
msg.setSentDate( new Date() );

// Create the body text
Multipart parts = new MimeMultipart();
MimeBodyPart mainBody = new MimeBodyPart();
mainBody.setText( email.getBody() );
parts.addBodyPart( mainBody );
// Could also have supported attachments, but not for this version
// it's commented it out.
/*
  MimeBodyPart attachmentBody = new MimeBodyPart();
  attachmentBody.setText( "This is text in the attachment" );
  attachmentBody.addBodyPart( p2 );
*/

// Set some header fields
msg.setHeader( "X-Priority", "High" );
msg.setHeader( "Sensitivity", "Company-Confidential" );
msg.setContent( parts );
```

PART

IV

CH

21

LISTING 21.22 CONTINUED

```
      System.out.println( "Sending mail to " + email.getToAddress() );
      Transport.send( msg );
    }catch( Exception ex ){
      // The onMessage method should not throw any kind of exceptions
      // according to the EJB 2.0 specification.
      ex.printStackTrace();
    }
    finally{
      mailSession = null;
    }
  }

  public void setMessageDrivenContext( MessageDrivenContext ctx ){
    context = ctx;
  }

  public void ejbRemove(){
    // Not used for this bean
  }

  public void ejbCreate(){
    // Not used for this bean
  }
}
```

Obviously from looking at the `EmailServiceBean` from Listing 21.22, all the major work is done in the `onMessage` method. This is the callback method from the container when a message arrives at the JMS destination. Most of what goes on in the `onMessage` method has to do with using the JavaMail API. We won't go into depth about it in this book, but you can find more information on the API at the following URL:

```
http://java.sun.com/products/javamail
```

Note

Some EJB servers allow a client to locate a `javax.mail.Session` instance from JNDI by performing a lookup in the `java:comp/env/mail` subcontext, but not all of them handle this correctly. A workaround is to use the approach shown previously and create a nonshared session for a specific client.

Let's summarize what the `onMessage` is doing in the following steps:

1. Be sure the message sent to the queue is of type `javax.jms.ObjectMessage` and that the object within this message implements the `Emailable` interface. If either condition is false, the message is ignored and the method returns.

2. Get the beans environment properties using JNDI. These are the properties that are specified in the bean's deployment descriptor and are only accessible by that particular bean. This is a nice way of specifying properties for enterprise bean components.

3. Create a `javax.mail.Session` that will be used to create the message.

4. Create a `javax.mail.internet.MimeMessage` and its parts. Notice for this implementation we are not supporting attachments, but we could very easily by just adding additional `MimeBodyPart` objects.

5. Fill in the `MimeMessage` with the correct information from the JMS message.

6. Finally, send the e-mail off to the SMTP server. The SMTP server host was determined by the properties read in from the bean's environment. If the e-mail service needed to be changed, you only have to modify the deployment information and redeploy the bean. Although this might sound like too much to have to do, it really is better than having the values hard-coded in the bean.

CONFIGURING E-MAIL REQUIRED PROPERTIES

As previously mentioned, the bean obtains property information from the deployment descriptor. The descriptor also tells the container which type of JMS destination the message-driven bean is listening on. Listing 21.23 shows the bean's deployment information.

LISTING 21.23   THE `EmailServiceBean`'S DEPLOYMENT DESCRIPTOR

```
<!DOCTYPE ejb-jar PUBLIC
    "-//Sun Microsystems, Inc.//DTD Enterprise JavaBeans 2.0//EN"
    "http://java.sun.com/j2ee/dtds/ejb-jar_2_0.dtd">

<ejb-jar>
 <enterprise-beans>
   <message-driven>
     <ejb-name>EmailServiceBean</ejb-name>
     <ejb-class>com.que.ejb20.services.email.impl.EmailServiceBean</ejb-class>
     <transaction-type>Container</transaction-type>
     <message-driven-destination>
       <jms-destination-type>javax.jms.Queue</jms-destination-type>
     </message-driven-destination>
     <env-entry>
       <description>some description</description>
       <env-entry-name>smtpHost</env-entry-name>
       <env-entry-type>java.lang.String</env-entry-type>
       <env-entry-value>192.18.97.137</env-entry-value>
     </env-entry>
       <security-identity>
       </security-identity>
     </message-driven>
 </enterprise-beans>
</ejb-jar>
```

PART

IV

CH

21

> **Note**
>
> You must use a valid host or IP in the `smtpHost` value in the deployment descriptor. The one in Listing 21.23 should not be used when you run this example.

When it comes time to deploy your message-driven bean, you must use the EJB container's tools to generate specific deployment information for that container. For WebLogic, Listing 21.24 shows what that deployment information would look like for our `EmailServiceBean`.

LISTING 21.24   THE `EmailServiceBean`'S DEPLOYMENT DESCRIPTOR

```
<?xml version="1.0"?>
<!DOCTYPE weblogic-ejb-jar PUBLIC
    "-//BEA Systems, Inc.//DTD WebLogic 6.0.0 EJB//EN"
<!-- Sample MessageDriven bean Weblogic deployment descriptor -->


<weblogic-ejb-jar>

  <weblogic-enterprise-bean>
    <ejb-name>EmailServiceBean</ejb-name>
    <message-driven-descriptor>
      <pool>
        <max-beans-in-free-pool>200</max-beans-in-free-pool>
        <initial-beans-in-free-pool>20</initial-beans-in-free-pool>
      </pool>
      <destination-jndi-name>
            com.que.ejb20book.EmailQueue
      </destination-jndi-name>
    </message-driven-descriptor>
    <jndi-name>EmailServiceBean</jndi-name>
  </weblogic-enterprise-bean>

</weblogic-ejb-jar>
```

This proprietary deployment descriptor for WebLogic allows the deployer to set the initial number of instances of this bean in the pool, the maximum number, and a few other configuration values like the name of the JMS destination for the bean to listen on.

The final step in the e-mail horizontal service is to build a client test program to test the e-mail service. Assuming that you have all the JMS administration set up correctly and you have configured and deployed the `EmailServiceBean`, you can run the `EmailTest` class that's shown in Listing 21.25 and you should get an e-mail sent to the address that you specify on the command line. To run the program, you should type this on the command line:

```
java EmailTest bob@testemail.com sue@testemail.com
```

Of course, you probably want to use your e-mail address instead of mine when running the example.

Caution

Although some e-mail servers will forward e-mails even if you are not an authorized user, be careful about sending fake e-mails to people you don't know. This is sometimes referred to as e-mail *spoofing* and you can wind up in tons of trouble with the e-mail police. Make sure that you are sending e-mails only to your friends. In fact, you're probably better off if you only test sending e-mails to yourself. In this way you can make sure you get them and you won't be incarcerated.

Listing 21.25 shows the e-mail test program.

LISTING 21.25   A TEST PROGRAM TO TEST THE E-MAIL HORIZONTAL SERVICE

```
import com.que.ejb20.services.email.*;

public class EmailTest {

  public EmailTest() {
    super();
  }

  public void sendEmail( Emailable msg ) throws EmailException {
    EmailService.sendEmail( msg );
  }

  // The main method for running this class
  // Usage: java EmailTest <toAddress> <fromAddress>
  public static void main(String[] args) {
    if ( args.length < 2 ){
      System.out.println( "Usage: java EmailTest <to> <from>" );
      System.exit( 0 );
    }

    EmailTest test = new EmailTest();
    Emailable msg = new EmailMessage();
    msg.setToAddress( args[0] );
    msg.setFromAddress( args[1] );
    msg.setSubject( "This is a Test Email" );
    msg.setBody( "This is a test email sent by the horizontal service" );

    try{
      test.sendEmail( msg );
    }catch( EmailException ex ){
      ex.printStackTrace();
    }
  }
}
```

Each e-mail server is different in how long it takes to forward the e-mail. Normally, it should show up at the destination address within seconds. However, depending on the load, it can take several minutes. Keep checking and after more than a couple of minutes, it probably means that the e-mail server is having trouble or it was never sent. You can turn on a debug option with JavaMail by setting the setDebug flag to true. With this on, it will print out debug information as the JavaMail API talks with the e-mail server.

TROUBLESHOOTING

COMPILING AND RUNNING THE LOCAL LOGGING SERVICE

I get a `ClassDefNotFoundException` *when trying to run the example.*

Be sure that you compiled all the API, SPI, and implementation classes for the example.

I get a `ClassNotFoundException` *when trying to run the example.*

Be sure you have the directory where the compiled classes are located somewhere in your classpath.

The example can't find the `logging.properties` *file.*

It really depends on which version of Java you are using, but if you're using Java 1.3, the file can normally be anywhere in the system classpath. With earlier versions, you might have to put the file in your `<JAVA_HOME/lib` directory for it to be found.

COMPILING AND RUNNING THE REMOTE LOGGING SERVICE

I get a `NoClassDefFoundError.`

Be sure that you have the `jms.jar`, `jndi.jar`, and the class files for the example in your system classpath. If you don't want to add them to your system classpath, create a startup script and add them using the `-classpath` option.

COMPILING AND RUNNING THE E-MAIL SERVICE

I can't compile or run the e-mail service example.

Be sure you have the necessary JavaMail JAR files in your classpath. These include `mail.jar`, `smtp.jar`, and also the activation framework `activation.jar`, which is a separate download.

CHAPTER **22**

EJB Clustering Concepts

In this chapter

TOO MUCH ISN'T ALWAYS A GOOD THING

As builders of B2C and B2B e-commerce applications, we set out hoping that our applications work well and are well received by the intended audience. Sometimes, what gets overlooked is what happens if too many users like and use the applications that we build. For a brick-and-mortar business such as fast food, people will stand in line for a good hamburger or milkshake, but usually this is not true for users of Internet sites. One of the major conveniences of using a company's Web site is so you don't have to stand in line or wait for service. When users have to wait or be told to come back later, often they don't come back and they will just go down the virtual street to spend their money with another site.

As an enterprise application developer, you really can't afford not to think about how the system will react when the user load becomes too high. In reality, no Internet application can sustain an infinite user load. Even the best Internet applications have a breaking point where the end users notice the response time slowing so much that the visit is unpleasant. At that point, you might have just lost a customer. The idea is to design a system where that breaking point takes longer and longer to get to and the system can sustain a higher and higher load.

The other big concern is that of system failure. Enterprise applications generally are very complicated systems to build. Many components along the way can give out and cause a failure of the system. When this happens, an end user typically experiences a problem. Depending on the type and seriousness of the failure, the user might not be able to submit the order or browse the catalog, or maybe the user won't be able to view the site at all. In any case, you can probably bet that revenue has just been lost. Sometimes as developers, we get caught in the whole technical aspects of the application and forget that revenue is the main purpose for building the application in the first place. It's not about which enterprise technology is the coolest or easiest to build and deploy; the point of building the system is to fulfill a business requirement so that customers can view, buy, and sell their products over the Internet. When this is prevented from happening, the business is missing a huge market for its products and the objective of the application is not being fulfilled.

One of the primary solutions to deal with unexpected user load and possible system failure is to provide some type of load balancing in your enterprise application. Load balancing, replication, and failover are important characteristics of any scalable and reliable enterprise application. Although not the only way to achieve load balancing in an EJB application, clustering is one of the most supported ways of achieving this goal.

WHAT IS CLUSTERING?

In general, a *cluster* is a group of redundant services that work together and in parallel to provide a more scalable and more reliable application platform than a single server can. Clustering in an application is purposely made transparent to its clients. Even though there can be many servers in the cluster, a client typically will not be aware which server in the cluster is servicing a request.

Unfortunately, the EJB 2.0 Specification does not provide any standards for supporting load balancing, or specifically clustering, as part of an enterprise application. How and even if a vendor provides load-balancing features as part of its EJB server product is left to the vendor to decide. All the well-known EJB vendors, and many of the lesser-known vendors, do provide some support for clustering. As you'll see later in this chapter, just which pieces a vendor can cluster and precisely how they're clustered can vary.

A clustered enterprise application provides two important features beyond one that is not clustered. Those features are

- Scalability
- High availability

SCALABILITY

Scalability is the capability to dynamically add new resources (potentially software and hardware) to the enterprise application architecture without much effort and without changing software code, to increase the capacity of the application.

This means that, through administration and management of the application, you are able to grow the capacity without making programmatic changes to the application. This growth might be adding hardware, such as memory or disk drives, or it could be just starting up more services to handle more requests. The most important point is that it should be effortless and not require any additional software changes to the application.

HIGH AVAILABILITY

High availability means that the application is available to service the end users for a high percentage of the time. In some cases, this might mean 24 hours a day, 7 days a week, and for other applications, it can just mean most of the time. Availability usually is expressed as a percentage between 0 and 100 percent. A very important point to remember about availability is that it's not how many times the application goes down, but rather the total amount of down time. So, an application might fail often but still achieve a high availability. Of course, developers hope that their applications don't fail often, either. You could also have an application fail once and be down for a considerable amount of time for repairs and have a low availability.

The level of availability for hardware or software is sometimes referred to as levels of nine. *Levels of nine* indicate the number of the nine digits in the amount of availability. For example, 99.999 is said to have five levels of nine because there are five digits. Table 22.1 shows the approximate percentage of down time for a particular level.

TABLE 22.1   APPLICATION AVAILABILITY LEVELS

Availability	Approximate Hours of Down Time Per Year
99%	87.6 hours
99.9%	8.8 hours
99.99%	.9 hours
99.999%	0.09 (about 5 minutes)

Looking at Table 22.1, you might think that four levels of nine (about an hour of down time per year) is an awesome amount of availability. However, if the application was for a brokerage firm and the application was down for five minutes every day for 12 straight days when the markets opened, the business would lose a lot of revenue. It's still only about an hour total time and would still be four levels of nine, but very bad for the company. As you can see, how much time and when it's down is much more important than the number of times.

A part of what makes high availability possible is the concept of failover. *Failover* assures that even if a system failure occurs, other redundant components or services can handle the requests and insulate the clients from the failures. The capability to failover from a failed component or service to another functioning one increases the availability of the application to its clients. The switchover because of a system failure should be transparent to the end client.

Because there is no clustering component to the EJB specification, our discussion will have to be a little generic. If you need specific information on whether or how a vendor supports clustering in its application server, you'll need to check the vendor's documentation.

CLUSTERING IN THE WEB TIER

All Web-enabled enterprise applications use some type of Web server to serve HTML pages back to the end user. A third-party vendor normally will provide the Web server, but some are actually built into or packaged with the application server. Either way, the end user makes a request for an HTML page that must be serviced by a Web server. If you are using a single Web server to handle the requests, the Web server is a single point of failure for your application. If the Web server were to have a serious failure and stop servicing requests, users would not be able to use the site.

Therefore, for any serious Web-enabled application that must have a high availability, it's very important to support some type of load balancing or clustering in this tier. There are several ways to structure the support for clustering in the Web tier. One simple way is to have several Web servers that each can handle the requests independently of each other. You then can use the Domain Name Service (DNS) to shuffle the requests around between the Web servers each time a request is made. This provides a simple form of load balancing and failover mechanism because a client request normally will go to the first IP in the list provided by the DNS. If this IP doesn't respond after a certain timeout period, it could request servicing from another one in the list. This technique is commonly referred to as *DNS round-robin*. Figure 22.1 shows an example of how DNS round-robin works.

Figure 22.1
Use DNS round-robin for basic Web server load balancing and failover.

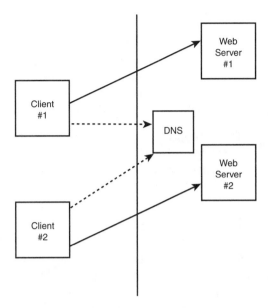

If you need more of a heavyweight load balancing solution in your Web tier, you could use one of the several IP load-balancing products on the market, or it's possible that your application server vendor supports this feature in its product. IP load balancing uses more advanced techniques to determine which Web server should get the next request based on a combination of dynamic loads on each server, latency, which server got the last request, and other factors.

A couple of products that provide more advanced features are Central Dispatch from Resonate. You can find information at its Web site:

```
http://www.resonate.com/products/central_dispatch
```

and also Cisco's Local Directory, on which you can find more information at

```
http://www.cisco.com/univercd/cc/td/doc/pcat/ld.htm
```

There are several other products available for load balancing in the Web tier. These two links should get you started in the right direction.

MANAGING SESSION STATE

One very important aspect that must be figured out and dealt with on the Web tier is how to maintain the session state for a user when a failure occurs. To do this, you need some way of persisting the session state either each time there is a modification to it or at least periodically. As you can imagine, there can be significant overhead in keeping every user's session persistent or maintaining a redundant copy of the session on another machine.

A less expensive solution is to update or persist the session information only when significant operations occur. The application could have certain checkpoints that when the user reaches one, their session state gets persisted by the system so that if a system failure does occur, you could at least go back to that last checkpoint. This is sometimes a good tradeoff for the users. The difficult part is trying to figure out where those checkpoints are.

Up to this point, we have been assuming that session load balancing occurred only at session initiation time and not for every Web hit. You might have constraints or nonfunctional requirements that force your architecture to load balance every Web hit and to have each sequential request be potentially handled by a different Web server or servlet instance.

If this is the case, some servlet engines provide a servlet session state manager, which helps maintain the state while at the same time helping to direct the requests to a different servlet instance in a different servlet engine for each hit. However, this is a pretty heavyweight solution. Be sure you really understand the nonfunctional requirements before implementing such a complex solution on your Web tier.

Some application servers can be configured to have the servlet engine and Web server located within the EJB container. This could be done within a single Java Virtual Machine (JVM) or in separate ones, depending on the vendor and configuration. This can improve performance of caching session state because it allows the state to move closer to a possible persistence store. At the same time, the calls between the Web tier and application tier don't have to travel over the network. Not all your customers will allow this solution, however, because usually there is a required separation between the Web server and resources that the Web server wants to access. This is done for security reasons and usually enforced with one or more hardware firewalls. The areas where the Web servers are located are commonly referred to as Demilitarized Zones (DMZs). Be sure you understand the target environment for your application before making significant architectural decisions.

CLUSTERING IN THE EJB TIER

The other areas that can be load balanced and clustered are the components within the application tier. Again, because the J2EE and EJB specifications do not deal with load-balancing issues, the exact components and services that can be clustered is very dependent on your vendor. If load balancing is important for your application, be sure to check with the vendor to see whether it's supported before purchasing an EJB server.

Not all EJB vendors will have complete support for clustering, so this discussion must be a little more generic and really just discuss a superset of features that you'll find across vendors. You will find a few vendors that support all or most of these clustering features in some proprietary manner. The list describes what services can possibly be clustered in the EJB container:

- JNDI
- Stateless session beans
- Entity beans
- Stateful session beans
- JMS
- JDBC connections

CLUSTERING NAMING SERVICES

Generally, a clustered naming service will allow the administrator to deploy multiple containers (possibly on multiple machines), which contain identical sets of enterprise beans.

When a client performs a JNDI lookup, the naming service can load balance over the set of enterprise beans associated with that name and select one based on load or last requested. A vendor usually will support multiple algorithms that can be selected at deployment time that determines how the naming service will load balance requests.

When clustering the naming service, if one of the objects fails, the container can substitute it with another in the cluster. This is obviously harder if the object maintained state, but it can still be accomplished. Keep in mind that not all vendors support this feature.

CLUSTERING STATELESS SESSION BEANS

Because all instances of the same stateless class are supposed to be identical, clustering stateless objects is generally the easiest and is supported by most vendors.

Upon failure of a stateless session bean in one container, a different stateless session bean in the same or different container can be easily substituted as a replacement with little or no effect on the client. Clustering stateful session beans or entity beans is much harder.

CLUSTERING ENTITY BEANS

Because an entity bean typically represents a set of data from a relational database, it's not generally interchangeable with other entity beans from the container. However, because the data is persisted in the database, a new entity bean that contains the same information can be easily created during a failover condition.

If an entity bean fails during the middle of a transaction, the container will typically assume a rollback and another entity bean instance, possibly in another container, will load the last state of the entity bean from the database.

> **Note**
>
> The presumption of rollback by the container is based on the OTS/JTS specification.

After the other entity bean is loaded with its state from the database, all requests for service will automatically failover to use the other instance.

CLUSTERING STATEFUL SESSION BEANS

Clustering stateful session beans is by far the hardest to pull off, which is generally why this functionality is not supported by some of the low-end application servers. If it is supported, it's usually one of the last cluster features to be added.

Stateful session beans are tough because they are maintaining state for an individual client and there could be thousands or tens of thousands of clients concurrently in the system. The question becomes how to maintain the state at all times to ensure that if a failure occurs, the system can reload the state and allow the client to continue as if nothing happened.

Typically, vendors choose one of two methods to support clustering of stateful session beans. The two methods differ in where the state is actually maintained. One method is in-memory replication and involves keeping copies of the state somewhere in memory. This is usually much faster, but also subject to some failure as well. The other approach is storing the state in some type of data store. Usually, this persistent store is a relational database. By storing the state in a database, the application server is guaranteed to be able to recover in event of a system failure. Database access can be a performance bottleneck for an application, so this solution isn't always the best one.

CLUSTERING JMS

Some EJB servers are now able to support clustering of JMS queues and topics throughout the cluster. Typically, each instance of the cluster contains a replica of the JMS destination. How and when messages are sent to these duplicate destinations is up to the container. This feature is not supported by all vendors.

CLUSTERING JDBC CONNECTIONS

Some EJB servers provide limited support for working with JDBC connections in a cluster. Each instance in the cluster would normally set up an identical data source as the other instances, but each instance would be configured to use a different connection pool. This way, if any instance failed, the same data source name would work in the other clustered instances.

Caution

You must be careful with connection pools because EJB servers typically don't provide any load balancing within the pools. If one of your connection pools runs out of connections, the clustered instance might still receive requests, even though no connections are available.

SINGLE VM VERSUS MULTIPLE VM ARCHITECTURES

We should make one final note about load balancing in EJB servers. Some EJB vendors provide load balancing with a multiple-VM architecture, rather than just clustering EJB objects. For example, the application server from Gemstone, Gemstone/J, provides what it calls Extreme Clustering. It uses a JVM pool where multiple Java Virtual Machines are created and maintained in a pool that can grow and shrink dynamically.

The JVMs can be pooled and tuned for specific responsibilities within the enterprise application. Their approach to load balancing is unique and has some nice features that others don't support. Whether this architecture is the correct one for your system is best determined by comparing the features against other vendors. You can get more information on the Gemstone product and its Extreme Clustering technique by going to the Gemstone Web site at http://www.gemstone.com.

## CHAPTER 23

EJB 2.0 Programming Restrictions

In this chapter

THE PURPOSE OF THE RESTRICTIONS

The restrictions that are placed on business methods of enterprise beans are there according to the EJB specification, to ensure that the bean is portable across different EJB 2.0 containers. Now portability is very important; however, it's not the only reason to adhere to these restrictions. The EJB server and container are designed for autonomy. In other words, the EJB server is reliant on itself to manage the resources and security for the environment. The purpose of this independence is to remove the necessity of the bean providers from having to deal with issues such as thread management, security, and scalability. The bean provider can concentrate on building the business logic for the application and let the server and container manage everything else. By following the rules set forth in this chapter, you increase the odds that your enterprise beans will be able to be installed in other compliant containers without modifying the bean. The restrictions are not just for the bean provider. The container providers also must adhere to the restrictions if they want to claim compliancy.

Although the EJB 2.0 Specification states some very specific restrictions, some restrictions in the specification provide wiggle room for developers and container providers to interpret the restrictions one way or another. Many EJB developers have asked for clarification on certain restrictions because they can be confusing. Some EJB containers actually have measures in place to prevent these restrictions from being violated, and other vendors don't enforce the restrictions as strongly. The best thing for you to do is not to violate them if you can avoid it.

Because the restrictions can be interpreted in different ways, we must say up front that we will take a strictly literal approach to these where necessary and then try to apply a little bit of common sense. Probably not everyone will agree with the strict view taken in this chapter. This topic is one of those that people feel passionate about and will go to great lengths to argue one way or another. So take the discussion of each restriction with a grain of salt and know that not everyone will agree, but you should at least be aware that these restrictions do exist and to some degree, you will have to adhere to them.

THE EJB 2.0 RESTRICTIONS

The list of restrictions is in no particular order and, although there can be some relationships between them, there are no implied dependencies. We'll take them one by one and state the restriction and provide a brief explanation for the restriction. In the cases where a legal workaround is known, we'll state one or more solutions to achieve the same results without violating the restriction.

DON'T USE READ/WRITE STATIC FIELDS

The EJB 2.0 Specification states that an enterprise bean must not use read/write static fields. When you declare a static field, you are stating that all instances of the class will share the same instance. The problem is that you are not guaranteed that all instances of an EJB are run within the same JVM. Some EJB servers might decide to run multiple instances of the same EJB class in separate JVMs for performance, load balancing, or better fault-tolerance capabilities.

If you have an enterprise bean with a static field that can be modified, you can't assume that all instances of the bean are referencing the same static field and thus seeing the same state. The bean instances are likely to become inconsistent. If you are going to use static fields, the fields must be declared `final`. If they are declared `final`, they can't be modified after they are initialized, and instances that are in different JVMs would be consistent.

Many EJB developers ask, "What about non-EJB components?". You might reason that using writable static fields in non-EJB components must be acceptable because the container does not manage them. The problem with this is that the non-EJB components are still loaded by the container's class loader or the system class loader for a JVM and therefore are subject to inconsistencies if multiple JVMs are used. You are better off not using them at all or using the `final` keyword when declaring the static field. The following code fragment shows an example of using the `final` keyword to ensure that a static field can't be modified:

```
import java.sql.Timestamp;

public class AuctionHelper{


  // The loadTimestamp variable will be initialized
  // only when this class is first loaded
  public static final Timestamp loadTimestamp =
                        new Timestamp( System.currentTimeMillis() );

  // Constructor

  public AuctionHelper(){
    super();
  }
}
```

Because the field is declared `final`, you would get a compiler error if you attempted to set the `loadTimestamp` field to another value elsewhere in your application.

There's nothing wrong with accessing the `Timestamp` field; you just can't modify it after it has been initialized. Some EJB containers may search through the enterprise beans during deployment, looking for static fields that have not been declared `final` and will fail to deploy them.

Tip

The use of read-only static fields is allowed. As pointed out above, you just need to make sure to use the `final` keyword on the static reference to ensure that it can't be changed after initialization.

USING THREADS AND SYNCHRONIZATION

The EJB 2.0 Specification states that an enterprise bean must not use synchronization primitives to synchronize execution of multiple instances. This restriction prevents enterprise beans from using synchronization primitives from performing any kind of thread management. This also includes not creating any new threads or stopping any existing ones. An enterprise bean also may not suspend, resume, or change the name or priority of threads managed by the container.

One of the reasons for this restriction is that, as pointed out earlier, a container can use multiple JVMs instead of a single one. A container's role is to manage the lifecycle of the bean instances. There are three basic reasons that the container prevents enterprise beans from using synchronization or the thread management facilities: security, resource management, and thread-specific storage.

SECURITY

Although there are ways for threads to manipulate a system in unauthorized and unauthenticated manners, the real issue with security has to do with creating too many threads and not cleaning them up appropriately. The system will eventually slow down and will not continue to service client requests, rendering the application useless. This is similar to the "denial of service" attacks that have become very popular lately by computer hackers.

RESOURCE MANAGEMENT

Resource management is a way to say that the container demands the autonomy to manage resources as it sees fit. If the container wants to stop a thread, it should be able to without negatively affecting the bean instances. If your enterprise beans are creating and starting threads, the container is no longer in control and, from the container's perspective, this is a bad thing. Some EJB containers provide a general-purpose thread pool for enterprise beans to use. If an enterprise bean doesn't yield the thread back to the pool after a certain amount of time, the container could just take it back or cause it to cease execution. With this approach, the container can still maintain control, but also allow enterprise beans to have limited threading capabilities.

THREAD-SPECIFIC STORAGE

Thread-specific storage (TSS) is a mechanism that many EJB containers use to associate client-specific data with specific threads. Although each vendor can use this technique differently, most use it to propagate security and/or transactional context on behalf of a client. The EJB container may associate client information with a particular thread and use that information to propagate to a remote component. If a bean provider is allowed to create threads at random, the proper information might not be propagated as needed by the remote component.

Caution

Regarding the main system thread, an enterprise bean must not attempt to stop the JVM. This means you can't call the `System.exit` method to stop the application. You will have to let the container shut down the application gracefully.

RESTRICTIONS ON USING THE `java.io` PACKAGE

The EJB 2.0 Specification states that an enterprise bean must not use the `java.io` package to attempt to access files and directories in the file system. This restriction is one that normally causes developers to say "bleagh!" and to experience a great deal of frustration.

The `java.io` package is a very rich library for accessing I/O and especially the file system. However, restrictions are in place to address both resource management and portability. For example, if you had several enterprise bean methods creating file descriptors, and all of a sudden your client load jumped up, you might run out of file descriptors and crash the system. Compared to resources such as relational databases, the file system is a questionable resource for a bean to depend on.

As far as portability, I once heard one EJB developer, who was obviously an advocate for this restriction, comment, "What if you deployed your application into a container running on a device that didn't have a file system?". Although this seems unlikely, the point is still valid. You should try to ensure portability wherever possible.

A common function for which EJB developers want to use `java.io` is to load property files. There are several legal ways to do this within enterprise beans. The first approach is to package the properties along with the enterprise bean's deployment descriptor. This is the preferred method for providing properties to your enterprise bean. When an enterprise bean is deployed with properties in the descriptor, you can use the bean's environment to get the properties and use them as normal.

→ To see an example of putting properties in a deployment descriptor and then referencing those properties from your enterprise bean, **see** "Building the E-Mail Service Message-Driven Bean," **p. 554**.

Another approach to more directly reading resource files from your enterprise beans involves the class loader, which by the way has the complete permission of the container to use the `java.io` package. If you need to load a file, you can use either the `getResource` or `getResourceAsStream` method defined in `java.lang.Class`. These methods are executed by the class loader and returned as a URL or an InputStream, respectively. Your application can use these to get the information from the file as necessary.

A recommendation made by the specification is to use the concept of resource managers. You could create a resource manager in a way similar to how you acquire a JDBC connection from JNDI. You could create a resource manager that has permissions to access the file system and then acquire a connection to this resource manager to access files. This resource manager would be granted special `doPrivilege` security access that enterprise beans don't have. Using resource managers would help with portability and enable the clients to access the underlying file system in a more transparent manner. Many EJB servers have a file system resource manager or service that allows the enterprise beans limited access to the file system. You must be careful, however—these are not clearly defined in the specification and might not be directly portable to other vendor containers.

RESTRICTIONS ON USING SOCKETS

The EJB 2.0 Specification states that an enterprise bean must not attempt to listen on a socket, accept connections on a socket, or use a socket for multicasting. However, an enterprise bean is allowed to act as a network socket client, just not as network socket server.

This restriction stems from the fact that enterprise beans are designed to service a client using a particular remote protocol and based on a set of security permissions. By allowing clients to connect to the container using a possibly nonsecure connection, you are potentially opening up your application to intruders.

The enterprise bean must also not attempt to modify the socket factory used by the ServerSocket, Socket, or the stream factory used by URL. This could compromise the security of the application and remove control of the execution environment from the container.

RESTRICTIONS ON USING THE REFLECTION API

The EJB 2.0 Specification states that an enterprise bean must not attempt to query a class to obtain information about the declared members that are not otherwise accessible to the enterprise bean because of the security rules of the Java language.

This doesn't mean that you can't use the Reflection API that's part of the Java language. What it does mean, however, is that you should not use it to get around the security policies that have been programmatically and declaratively established.

Each enterprise bean can declare programmatic or declarative security roles that a client must have to invoke method calls on the enterprise bean. You are not allowed to use reflection and call a method on an enterprise bean to bypass these security permissions. For example, suppose an enterprise bean called AuctionHouseBean declares in its deployment descriptor that a client must have a role of admin to make any method calls on it. An enterprise bean should not use reflection on this enterprise bean and then make method calls on it to bypass the security mechanism.

RESTRICTIONS ON USING CLASS LOADERS AND SECURITY MANAGERS

The Java 2 security mechanism and class loaders are the key to how Java helps prevent unauthorized access by classes and other runtime entities from causing bad things to happen to a Java application. The EJB container uses a certain set of class loaders and security policies to help maintain stability within the execution environment. If any bean could replace the class loader or security policies at will, there would be little hope for the container to maintain the sanity within the environment.

Therefore, an enterprise bean must not create a new class loader or modify the context of an existing one. It also must not create a new security manager or modify the existing one.

RESTRICTIONS ON USING AWT INPUT/OUTPUT

The EJB 2.0 Specification states that an enterprise bean must not attempt to output information to a display or read information in from an input device, such as a keyboard, using the Abstract Window Toolkit (AWT).

Not many EJB servers will allow direct interaction between these input and output devices, and EJBs that attempt this might not be portable.

RESTRICTIONS ON USING NATIVE LIBRARIES

The EJB 2.0 Specification states that an enterprise bean must not attempt to load a native library. If an enterprise bean loaded a native library, it could open up a security hole into the application and allow unauthorized access to the system.

RESTRICTIONS ON USING THE this REFERENCE

The EJB 2.0 Specification states that an enterprise bean must not attempt to pass itself as an argument in a method or as a return value using the this reference. The reason is that all clients should access an enterprise bean through its EJBObject and not the bean instances directly. This allows the container to passivate and activate bean instances transparently to the client. A client may still be holding a reference to an EJBObject while the real bean instance has been passivated. Not until the client invokes a method call on the EJBObject does the container need to associate an enterprise bean instance with the EJBObject.

The client can be a remote client, but could also be another enterprise bean. Therefore, even when communicating between beans, the this reference should not be used because it would be passing the instance of the bean rather than the EJBObject. Instead, an enterprise bean should do something similar to the following code:

```
public EJBObject getMe(){

    { Some work here ...}
    // Time to return myself, but return an
    // instance of an EJBObject instead of "this"
    return getEntityContext().getEJBObject();
}
```

SUMMARY

Keep in mind that not all vendors support all of these restrictions, and your EJB server might allow you to use restricted features. For example, WebLogic does not prevent you from doing most of what these restrictions say not to do. This is not true of all the containers and you might lose portability if you violate them.

There are correct ways to achieve the behavior that these restrictions take away. The key is to use the class loader and security mechanisms as designed and know the difference between an EJB-compliant feature and one that is vendor-dependent.

APPENDIXES

THE EJB 2.0 API

In this chapter

Interfaces

This appendix provides a quick reference of the EJB APIs. You should use this reference if you need to get quick information on which methods are implemented by a particular interface, the arguments for a method, or the return type. Although the exceptions are described in detail in Chapter 13, "Exception Handling," we provide a summary view of them here for your convenience.

Figure A.1 shows a UML diagram of the EJB interfaces and their relationships.

Figure A.1
A UML diagram representing the EJB interface hierarchy.

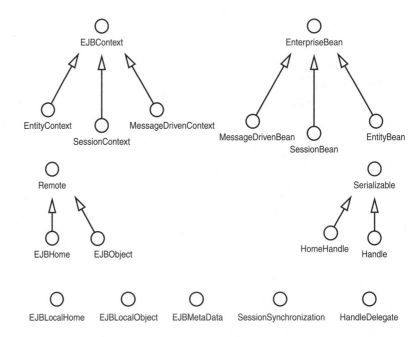

javax.ejb.EJBContext

An enterprise bean uses the EJBContext interface to gain access to the runtime context provided by the container. The EJBContext interface is the parent interface to the SessionContext and EntityContext interfaces, as shown in Figure A.1. Table A.1 shows the methods defined in the EJBContext interface.

TABLE A.1   THE METHODS OF THE EJBContext INTERFACE

Return Type	Method Name
Identity	getCallerIdentity
Principal	getCallerPrincipal
EJBHome	getEJBHome

TABLE A.1 CONTINUED

Return Type	Method Name
EJBLocalHome	getEJBLocalHome
Properties	getEnvironment
boolean	getRollbackOnly
UserTransaction	getUserTransaction
boolean	isCallerInRole
void	setRollbackOnly

getCallerIdentity

The getCallerIdentity method returns the java.security.Identity of the caller. Here is the method signature:

```
public java.security.Identity getCallerIdentity();
```

Caution

The getCallerIdentity method has been deprecated. You should use the getCallerPrincipal method instead.

getCallerPrincipal

The getCallerPrincipal method returns a java.security.Principal, which identifies the caller. The method should never return null. Here is the method signature:

```
public java.security.Principal getCallerPrincipal();
```

getEJBHome

The getEJBHome method returns the home interface of the enterprise bean. Here is the method signature:

```
public javax.ejb.EJBHome getEJBHome();
```

getEJBLocalHome

The getEJBLocalHome method returns the local home interface of the enterprise bean. Here is the method signature:

```
public javax.ejb.EJBLocalHome getEJBLocalHome();
```

getEnvironment

The getEnvironment method returns the enterprise bean's environment properties. This method has been deprecated. Here is the method signature:

```
public Properties getEnvironment();
```

> **Caution**
>
> The `getEnvironment` method has been deprecated. You should use the JNDI naming context `java:comp/env` to access the bean's environment.

getRollbackOnly

The `getRollbackOnly` tests to see whether the transaction has been marked for rollback. Only enterprise beans with container-managed transactions are allowed to use this method. Here is the method signature:

```
public boolean getRollbackOnly() throws IllegalStateException;
```

An `IllegalStateException` will be thrown if the instance is not allowed to use this method. Typically, this is because the instance is using bean-managed transactions.

getUserTransaction

The `getUserTransaction` method returns the transaction demarcation interface. Only enterprise beans with bean-managed transactions are allowed to use the `UserTransaction` interface. Because entity beans must always use container-managed transactions, only session beans and message-driven beans with bean-managed transactions are allowed to invoke this method. Here is the method signature:

```
public javax.transaction.UserTransaction getUserTransaction()
➥throws IllegalStateException;
```

An `IllegalStateException` will be thrown if the instance is not allowed to use this method. Typically, this is because the instance is using container-managed transactions.

isCallerInRole

The `isCallerInRole` method tests to see whether the caller is in a given role. There are two variations of this method. Here are the method signatures:

```
public boolean isCallerInRole(String roleName);
public boolean isCallerInRole(java.security.Identity roleName);
```

The second method, which takes an `Identity` as its argument, is deprecated and should not be used. The `roleName` argument in the non-deprecated version must be one of the security roles defined in the deployment descriptor. This method returns true if the caller of the bean method is in the role specified by the argument.

> **Caution**
>
> The `isCallerInRole` method that takes a `java.security.Identity` has been deprecated and should not be used.

setRollbackOnly

The `setRollbackOnly` method marks the current transaction for rollback. The transaction will become permanently marked for rollback. A transaction marked for rollback can never commit. Only enterprise beans with container-managed transactions are allowed to use this method. Here is the method signature:

```
public void setRollbackOnly() throws IllegalStateException;
```

An `IllegalStateException` will be thrown if the instance is not allowed to use this method. Typically, this is because the instance is using bean-managed transactions.

javax.ejb.EJBHome

The `EJBHome` interface defines the methods that allow a remote client to create, locate, and remove enterprise beans. A bean provider must create a home interface for an entity or session bean, and the home interface must extend the `EJBHome` interface. The message-driven bean is not exposed to clients and therefore does not require a home interface. Table A.2 shows the methods in the `EJBHome` interface.

TABLE A.2   THE METHODS OF THE EJBHome INTERFACE

Return Type	Method Name
EJBMetaData	getEJBMetaData
HomeHandle	getHomeHandle
void	remove

getEJBMetaData

The `getEJBMetaData` method obtains a reference to an object that implements the `EJBMetaData` interface for the enterprise bean. The `EJBMetaData` interface allows the client to obtain information about the enterprise bean. Here is the method signature:

```
public EJBMetaData getEJBMetaData() throws java.rmi.RemoteException;
```

getEJBHomeHandle

The `getEJBHomeHandle` returns a handle for the home object. The handle can be used at later time to re-obtain a reference to the home object, possibly in a different JVM. Here is the method signature:

```
public EJBHomeHandle getEJBHomeHandle() throws java.rmi.RemoteException;
```

remove

There are two variations of the `remove` method. Both cause the `EJBObject` to be removed. Here are the method signatures:

```
public void remove(Handle handle) throws java.rmi.RemoteException,
➥RemoveException;
public void remove(Object primaryKey) throws java.rmi.RemoteException,
➥RemoveException;
```

Caution

The `remove` method that takes a primary key can be used only for an entity bean. An attempt to call this method on a session bean will result in a `RemoveException` being thrown.

With either variation of the `remove` method, a `RemoveException` will be thrown if the enterprise bean or the container does not allow the client to remove the object. The `RemoveException` is described later in this appendix.

javax.ejb.EJBLocalHome

All enterprise beans that use a local home interface must extend their local home interface from the `EJBLocalHome` interface. The local home interface for an enterprise bean defines the methods that allow local clients to create, find, and remove EJB objects. It also can contain home business methods that are not specific to a specific bean instance. These home business methods can be defined only for entity beans.

remove

The `remove` method removes an object identified by its primary key. Here is the method signature:

```
public void remove(Object primaryKey) throws RemoteException, EJBException;
```

This method can be called only by local clients of an entity bean. An attempt to invoke this method on a session bean will result in a `RemoveException`.

javax.ejb.EJBLocalObject

The `EJBLocalObject` interface must be extended by all enterprise beans' local interfaces. An enterprise bean's local interface provides the local client view of an EJB object. Table A.3 shows the methods in the `EJBLocalObject` interface.

TABLE A.3   THE METHODS OF THE `EJBLocalObject` INTERFACE

Return Type	Method Name
EJBLocalHome	getEJBLocalHome
Object	getPrimaryKey
boolean	isIdentical
void	remove

getEJBLocalHome

Obtain the enterprise bean's local home interface. The local home interface defines the enterprise bean's `create`, `finder`, `remove`, and `home` business methods that are available to local clients. Here is the method signature:

```
public EJBLocalHome getEJBLocalHome() throws EJBException;
```

getPrimaryKey

This method can be called on an entity bean. An attempt to invoke this method on a session bean will result in an EJBException. Here is the method signature:

```
public Object getPrimaryKey() throws RemoteException, EJBException;
```

isIdentical

Test whether a given EJB local object is identical to the invoked EJB local object. Here is the method signature:

```
public boolean isIdentical(EJBLocalObject obj) throws EJBException;
```

remove

Removes the EJB local object. Here is the method signature:

```
public void remove() throws RemoveException, EJBException;
```

javax.ejb.EJBMetaData

A client uses the EJBMetaData interface to obtain metadata information about an enterprise bean. The metadata is typically used by development tools or scripting languages. The EJBMetaData interface does not extend the Remote interface and is not accessed remotely by the client. An instance of this class is sent to the client as a copy, and changes to the object are not reflected on the server. Table A.4 shows the methods in the EJBMetaData interface.

TABLE A.4   THE METHODS OF THE EJBMetaData INTERFACE

Return Type	Method Name
EJBHome	getEJBHome
Class	getHomeInterfaceClass
Class	getPrimaryKeyClass
Class	getRemoteInterfaceClass
boolean	isSession
boolean	isStatelessSession

Tip

The EJBMetaData class is designed for remote clients only. It is not supported with local clients.

getEJBHome

The getEJBHome method returns the home interface of the enterprise bean. Here is the method signature:

```
public javax.ejb.EJBHome getEJBHome();
```

PART
V

APP
A

getHomeInterfaceClass

The getHomeInterfaceClass returns the Class object for the enterprise bean's home interface. Here is the method signature:

```
public Class getHomeInterfaceClass();
```

getPrimaryKeyClass

The getPrimaryKeyClass returns the Class object for the enterprise bean's primary key class. Here is the method signature:

```
public Class getPrimaryKeyClass();
```

getRemoteInterfaceClass

The getRemoteInterfaceClass returns the Class object for the enterprise bean's remote interface class. Here is the method signature:

```
public Class getRemoteInterfaceClass();
```

isSession

The isSession method returns true if the enterprise bean is a session bean. Otherwise, it will return false. Here is the method signature:

```
public boolean isSession();
```

isStatelessSession

The isStatelessSession method returns true if the enterprise bean is a stateless session bean. Otherwise it will return false. Here is the method signature:

```
public boolean isStatelessSession();
```

javax.ejb.EJBObject

A bean provider creates a remote interface that extends the EJBObject interface. The remote interface defines the business methods that can be called by a remote client. Each enterprise bean, except for the message-driven, has a component interface. Table A.5 shows the methods in the EJBObject interface.

TABLE A.5   THE METHODS OF THE EJBObject INTERFACE

Return Type	Method Name
EJBHome	getEJBHome
Handle	getHandle
Object	getPrimaryKey
boolean	isIdentical
void	remove

getEJBHome

The `getEJBHome` method returns the home interface of the enterprise bean. Here is the method signature:

```
public javax.ejb.EJBHome getEJBHome() throws java.rmi.RemoteException;
```

getHandle

The `getHandle` method returns a handle for the EJB object. The handle can be used at later time to re-obtain a reference to the EJB object, possibly in a different JVM. Here is the method signature:

```
public Handle getHandle() throws java.rmi.RemoteException;
```

getPrimaryKey

The `getPrimaryKey` method returns the primary key for an EJB object. This method can be called only on an entity bean. If you attempt to invoke this method on a session bean, a `RemoteException` will be thrown. Here is the method signature:

```
public Object getPrimaryKey() throws java.rmi.RemoteException;
```

isIdentical

The `isIdentical` method tests whether a given EJB object is identical to the invoked EJB object. Here's the method signature:

```
public boolean isIdentical(EJBObject obj) throws java.rmi.RemoteException;
```

The method returns true if the given EJB object is identical to the one invoked. Otherwise false is returned.

remove

The `remove` method removes the EJB object. Here is the method signature:

```
public void remove() throws java.rmi.RemoteException, RemoveException;
```

If the enterprise bean or the container does not allow destruction of the object, a `RemoveException` is thrown.

javax.ejb.EnterpriseBean

Every enterprise bean class must implement the `EnterpriseBean` interface. The `EnterpriseBean` interface does not define any methods itself but acts as a placeholder for future methods. It is a common superinterface for `SessionBean` and `EntityBean`.

javax.ejb.EntityBean

Every entity bean class must implement the `EntityBean` interface. The container uses the `EntityBean` methods to notify enterprise bean instances of lifecycle events. Table A.6 shows the methods in the `EntityBean` interface.

TABLE A.6   THE METHODS OF THE EntityBean INTERFACE

Return Type	Method Name
void	ejbActivate
void	ejbLoad
void	ejbPassivate
void	ejbRemove
void	ejbStore
void	setEntityContext
void	unsetEntityContext

Tip

In the next several methods, the RemoteException is defined in the method signature to provide backward compatibility with enterprise beans written for the EJB 1.0 Specification. Enterprise beans written for the EJB 1.1 and 2.0 Specifications should throw the javax.ejb.EJBException instead of the RemoteException.

ejbActivate

The container invokes the ejbActivate method when the instance is taken out of the pool of available instances and becomes associated with a specific EJB object. Here is the method signature:

```
public void ejbActivate() throws java.rmi.RemoteException, EJBException;
```

ejbLoad

The container invokes the ejbLoad method to instruct the instance to synchronize its state by loading its state from the underlying database. Here is the method signature:

```
public void ejbLoad() throws java.rmi.RemoteException, EJBException;
```

This method always executes in the transaction context determined by the value of the transaction attribute in the deployment descriptor.

ejbPassivate

The container invokes the ejbPassivate method on an instance before the instance becomes disassociated with a specific EJB object. After this method completes, the container will place the instance into the pool of available instances. Here is the method signature:

```
public void ejbPassivate() throws java.rmi.RemoteException, EJBException;
```

ejbRemove

The container invokes the `ejbRemove` method before it removes the EJB object that is currently associated with the instance. This method is invoked when a client invokes a remove operation on the enterprise bean. Here is the method signature:

```
public void ejbRemove() throws java.rmi.RemoteException, EJBException,
➥RemoveException;
```

ejbStore

The container invokes the `ejbStore` method to instruct the instance to synchronize its state by storing it to the underlying database. This method always executes in the transaction context determined by the value of the transaction attribute in the deployment descriptor. Here is the method signature:

```
public void ejbStore() throws java.rmi.RemoteException, EJBException;
```

setEntityContext

The container invokes the `ejbStore` method on an instance after the instance has been created to set the associated entity context. The bean instance should store the context in an instance variable. Here is the method signature:

```
public void setEntityContext(EntityContext ctx) throws
➥java.rmi.RemoteException, EJBException;
```

unsetEntityContext

The container invokes the `ejbStore` method on an instance before removing the instance. This is the last method that the container invokes on the instance. Here is the method signature:

```
public void unsetEntityContext() throws java.rmi.RemoteException, EJBException;
```

javax.ejb.EntityContext

The `EntityContext` interface provides an instance with access to the container-provided runtime context. The container passes the `EntityContext` interface to an entity enterprise bean instance after the instance has been created. The `EntityContext` interface remains associated with the instance for the lifetime of the instance. Table A.7 shows the methods in the `EntityContext` interface.

TABLE A.7   THE METHODS OF THE EntityContext INTERFACE

Return Type	Method Name
EJBLocalObject	getEJBLocalObject
EJBObject	getEJBObject
Object	getPrimaryKey

getEJBLocalObject

The getEJBObject method returns a reference to the EJB local object that currently is associated with the instance. An instance can use this method, for example, when it wants to pass itself as a reference in a method argument or return value. Here is the method signature:

```
public EJBLocalObject getEJBLocalObject() throws IllegalStateException;
```

An IllegalStateException will be thrown if an instance invokes this method while the instance is in a state that does not allow this method to be invoked or if the enterprise bean does not have a local interface.

getEJBObject

The getEJBObject method returns a reference to the EJB object that is currently associated with the instance. An instance can use this method, for example, when it wants to pass a reference to itself in a method argument or result. Here is the method signature:

```
public EJBObject getEJBObject() throws IllegalStateException;
```

An IllegalStateException will be thrown if an instance invokes this method while the instance is in a state that does not allow this method to be invoked.

getPrimaryKey

The getPrimaryKey method returns the primary key of the EJB object that is currently associated with this instance. Only an instance of an entity bean can call this method. Here is the method signature:

```
public Object getPrimaryKey() throws IllegalStateException;
```

Note

The result of this method is the same as the result of calling the getEJBObject().getPrimaryKey().

javax.ejb.Handle

A handle is an abstraction of a network reference to an EJB object. A handle can be used as a persistent reference to an EJB object and can be re-created later. The Handle interface has one method, getEJBObject; its return type is EJBObject.

getEJBObject

The getEJBObject method returns a reference to the EJB object that is currently associated with the instance. An instance can use this method, for example, when it wants to pass a reference to itself in a method argument or result. Here is the method signature:

```
public EJBObject getEJBObject() throws java.rmi.RemoteException;
```

javax.ejb.HomeHandle

The HomeHandle interface is an abstraction of a network reference to a home object. A HomeHandle can be used as a persistent reference to a home object and can be shared between clients. The HomeHandle interface has one method, getEJBHome; its return type is EJBHome.

getEJBHome

The getEJBObject method returns a reference to the EJB object that is currently associated with the instance. An instance can use this method, for example, when it wants to pass a reference to itself in a method argument or result. Here is the method signature:

```
public EJBObject getEJBObject() throws java.rmi.RemoteException;
```

javax.ejb.MessageDrivenBean

Every message-driven enterprise bean implements the MessageDrivenBean interface. The container uses the message-driven bean methods to notify the bean instances of lifecycle events. Table A.8 shows the methods in the MessageDrivenBean interface.

TABLE A.8   THE METHODS OF THE MessageDrivenBean INTERFACE

Return Type	Method Name
void	ejbRemove
void	setMessageDrivenContext

ejbRemove

The container invokes the ejbRemove method before it ends the life of the message-driven object. This happens when a container decides to terminate the message-driven object. Here is the method signature:

```
public void ejbRemove() throws EJBException;
```

setMessageDrivenContext

The container calls the setMessageDrivenContext method after the instance creation. The enterprise bean instance should store the reference to the context object in an instance variable. Here is the method signature:

```
public void setMessageDrivenContext(MessageDrivenContext ctx)
➥throws EJBException;
```

javax.ejb.MessageDrivenContext

As Figure A.1 shows, the MessageDrivenContext interface extends the EJBContext interface. In EJB 2.0, the MessageDrivenContext interface does not define any methods, but merely serves as a marker to identify a runtime context as belonging to a message-driven bean.

javax.ejb.SessionBean

Every session bean must implement the `SessionBean` interface. The container uses the `SessionBean` methods to notify the bean instances of lifecycle events. Table A.9 shows the methods in the `SessionBean` interface.

TABLE A.9   THE METHODS OF THE `SessionBean` INTERFACE

Return Type	Method Name
void	ejbActivate
void	ejbPassivate
void	ejbRemove
void	setSessionContext

Tip

With several of the methods that follow, the `RemoteException` is defined in the method signature to provide backward compatibility with enterprise beans written for the EJB 1.0 Specification. Enterprise beans written for the EJB 1.1 and 2.0 Specifications should throw the `javax.ejb.EJBException` instead of the `RemoteException`.

ejbActivate

The `ejbActivate` method is called when the instance is activated from its "passive" state. The instance should acquire any resource that it needs for its life cycle. Here is the method signature:

```
public void ejbActivate() throws java.rmi.RemoteException, EJBException;
```

ejbPassivate

The `ejbPassivate` method is called before the instance enters the "passive" state. The instance should release any resources that it is holding on to. After the `ejbPassivate` method completes, the instance must be in a state that allows the container to use the Java Serialization protocol to externalize and store away the instance's state. Here is the method signature:

```
public void ejbPassivate() throws java.rmi.RemoteException, EJBException;
```

ejbRemove

The container calls the `ejbRemove` method before it ends the life of the session object. This happens as a result of a client's invoking a remove operation, or when a container decides to terminate the session object after a timeout. Here is the method signature:

```
public void ejbRemove() throws java.rmi.RemoteException, EJBException;
```

setSessionContext

The container calls the setSessionContext method after the instance creation. The enterprise bean instance should store the reference to the context object in an instance variable. Here is the method signature:

```
public void setSessionContext(SessionContext ctx)
➡throws java.rmi.RemoteException, EJBException;
```

javax.ejb.SessionContext

The SessionContext interface provides access to the runtime session context that the container provides for a session bean instance. The container passes the SessionContext interface to a session bean instance after the instance has been created. The session context remains associated with the instance for its lifetime.

Table A.10 shows the methods in the SessionContext interface.

TABLE A.10   THE METHODS OF THE SessionContext INTERFACE

Return Type	Method Name
EJBLocalObject	getEJBLocalObject
EJBObject	getEJBObejct

getEJBLocalObject

The getEJBLocalObject returns a reference to the local EJB object that currently is associated with the instance. An instance can use this method, for example, when it wants to pass a reference to itself in a method argument or result. Here is the method signature:

```
public EJBLocalObject getEJBLocalObject() throws IllegalStateException;
```

An IllegalStateException will be thrown if an instance invokes this method while the instance is in a state that does not allow this method to be invoked or if the enterprise bean does not have a local interface.

getEJBObject

The getEJBObject returns a reference to the EJB object that is currently associated with the instance. An instance can use this method, for example, when it wants to pass a reference to itself in a method argument or result. Here is the method signature:

```
public EJBObject getEJBObject() throws IllegalStateException;
```

javax.ejb.SessionSynchronization

The SessionSynchronization interface allows a session bean instance to be notified by the container of transaction boundaries. A session bean class is not required to implement this interface. Table A.11 shows the methods in the SessionSynchronization interface.

TABLE A.11   THE METHODS OF THE SessionSynchronization INTERFACE

Return Type	Method Name
void	afterBegin
void	afterCompletion
void	beforeCompletion

Tip

With several of the methods that follow, the RemoteException is defined in the method signature to provide backward compatibility with enterprise beans written for the EJB 1.0 Specification. Enterprise beans written for the EJB 1.1 and 2.0 Specifications should throw the javax.ejb.EJBException instead of the RemoteException.

afterBegin

The afterBegin method notifies a session bean instance that a new transaction has started, and that the subsequent business methods on the instance will be invoked in the context of the transaction. The instance can use this method, for example, to read data from a database and cache the data in the instance fields. Here is the method signature:

```
public void afterBegin() throws java.rmi.RemoteException, EJBException;
```

afterCompletion

The afterCompletion method notifies a session bean instance that a transaction commit protocol has completed, and tells the instance whether the transaction has been committed or rolled back. Here is the method signature:

```
public void afterCompletion(boolean committed)
➥throws java.rmi.RemoteException, EJBException;
```

The argument is true if the transaction has been committed, false if the transaction has been rolled back.

beforeCompletion

The beforeCompletion method notifies a session bean instance that a transaction is about to be committed. The instance can use this method, for example, to write any cached data to a database. Here is the method signature:

```
public void beforeCompletion() throws java.rmi.RemoteException, EJBException;
```

EXCEPTIONS

Although exception handling is covered in detail in Chapter 13, basic exception information is provided here for your convenience. Figure A.2 shows you a UML diagram of the EJB exceptions and their relationships.

Figure A.2
A UML diagram representing the EJB exception hierarchy.

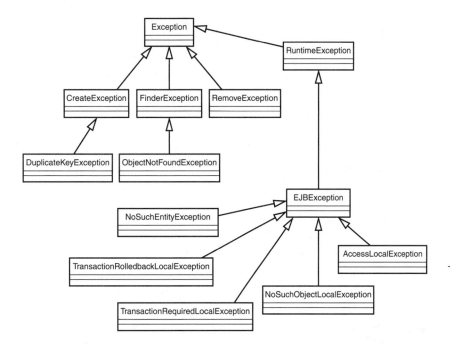

Note

All the EJB exceptions declare a no-argument constructor and one that accepts a String message.

AccessLocalException

An AccessLocalException is thrown to indicate that the caller does not have permission to call the method. This exception is thrown to local clients.

CreateException

The CreateException exception must be included in the throws clauses of all create methods defined in an enterprise bean's component interface.

DuplicateKeyException

The DuplicateKeyException exception is thrown if an entity EJB object cannot be created because an object with the same key already exists.

EJBException

The EJBException exception is thrown by an enterprise bean instance to its container to report that the invoked business method or callback method could not be completed because of an unexpected error.

FinderException

The FinderException exception must be included in the throws clause of every find method of an entity bean's home interface.

NoSuchEntityException

The NoSuchEntityException exception is thrown by an enterprise bean instance to its container to report that the invoked business method or callback method could not be completed because the underlying entity was removed from the database.

This exception can be thrown by the bean class methods that implement the business methods defined in the bean's remote interface and also by the ejbLoad and ejbStore methods.

NoSuchObjectLocalException

A NoSuchObjectLocalException is thrown if an attempt is made to invoke a method on a local object that no longer exists.

ObjectNotFoundException

The ObjectNotFoundException exception is thrown by a single object finder method to indicate that the specified EJB object does not exist.

RemoveException

The RemoveException exception is thrown at an attempt to remove an EJB object when the enterprise bean or the container does not allow the EJB object to be removed.

TransactionRequiredLocalException

This exception indicates that a request carried a null transaction context, but the target object requires an activate transaction.

TransactionRolledbackLocalException

This exception indicates that the transaction associated with processing of the request has been rolled back, or marked to roll back. Thus, the requested operation either could not be performed or was not performed because further computation on behalf of the transaction is not necessary.

THE javax.ejb.spi PACKAGE

The javax.ejb.spi package is a brand new package added in the EJB 2.0 Specification. For now, only a single interface is defined there. In the future, however, it's likely that more interfaces and classes will be added to grant more flexibility to the EJB vendors.

HandleDelegate

The EJB container provides the implementation for the HandleDelegate interface. It is used by portable implementations of javax.ejb.Handle and javax.ejb.HomeHandle. It is not used by EJB components or by client components. The HandleDelegate interface provides methods to serialize and deserialize EJBObject and EJBHome references to streams. The HandleDelegate object is obtained by JNDI lookup at the reserved name java:comp/ HandleDelegate. Table A.11 lists the methods in the HandleDelegate interface.

PART

V

APP

A

TABLE A.11 **THE METHODS OF THE** HandleDelegate **INTERFACE**

Return Type	Method Name
EJBHome	readEJBHome
EJBObject	readEJBObject
void	writeEJBHome
void	writeEJBObject

readEJBHome

Deserialize the EJBHome reference corresponding to a HomeHandle. readEJBHome is called from the readObject method of portable HomeHandle implementation classes. The ObjectInputStream object is the same object that was passed in to the HomeHandle class's readObject. When readEJBHome is called, the input stream must point to the location in the stream at which the EJBHome reference can be read. The container must ensure that the EJBHome reference is capable of performing invocations immediately after deserialization. Here is the method signature:

```
public EJBHome readEJBHome(ObjectInputStream str) throws IOException,
➥ClassNotFoundException;
```

readEJBObject

Deserialize the EJBObject reference corresponding to a Handle. The readEJBObject method is called from the readObject method of portable Handle implementation classes. The ObjectInputStream object is the same object that was passed in to the Handle class's readObject. When readEJBObject is called, the input stream must point to the location in the stream at which the EJBObject reference can be read. The container must ensure that the EJBObject reference is capable of performing invocations immediately after deserialization. Here is the method signature:

```
public EJBObject readEJBObject(ObjectInputStream str) throws IOException,
➥ClassNotFoundException;
```

writeEJBHome

Serialize the EJBHome reference corresponding to a HomeHandle. This method is called from the writeObject method of portable HomeHandle implementation classes. The ObjectOutputStream object is the same object that was passed in to the Handle class's writeObject. Here is the method signature:

```
public void writeEJBHome(EJBHome home, ObjectOutputStream str)
➥throws IOException;
```

writeEJBObject

Serialize the EJBObject reference corresponding to a Handle. This method is called from the writeObject method of portable Handle implementation classes. The ObjectOutputStream object is the same object that was passed in to the Handle class's writeObject. Here is the method signature:

```
public void writeEJBObject(EJBObject obj, ObjectOutputStream str)
➥throws IOException;
```

CHANGES FROM EJB 1.1

In this chapter

LOCAL CLIENTS

Prior to EJB 2.0, all clients of an enterprise bean were treated as remote clients. Support for location independence required that pass-by-value semantics always be followed when a bean was accessed through its home and remote interfaces. Even when a session bean made a call to an entity bean running in the same JVM, the call was subjected to much of the overhead associated with a remote call. Any optimizations were vendor-specific, if they existed at all. Because of this drawback, some of the EJB design patterns first adopted were those aimed at reducing the number of calls made to entity beans.

EJB 2.0 introduces support for local clients in addition to remote clients. If a session or entity bean supports other enterprise beans deployed in the same container as clients, those beans can be treated as local clients. Instead of the remote and home interfaces used by remote clients, local clients interact with a bean through its local and local home interfaces. Calls made through these interfaces use pass-by-reference semantics and avoid the overhead of remote calls. Local clients give up location independence and they're tightly coupled to the beans they access, but the performance advantages make up for these limitations whenever remote access by a client isn't needed.

As part of this change to the specification, a new term was introduced to identify the interfaces exposed to clients of an enterprise bean. The local and remote interfaces are collectively known as the *component interface*.

→ For more information on local clients, **see** "Local Versus Remote EJB Clients," **p. 45**.

MESSAGE-DRIVEN BEANS

EJB 2.0 defines a third type of enterprise bean—the message-driven bean—for the purpose of integrating the EJB architecture with the Java Message Service (JMS). This bean type differs most from entity and session beans in that it doesn't serve a synchronous client. Instead, a client makes use of the business logic defined by a message-driven bean by sending a message to a JMS destination (queue or topic) with which the bean has been associated. When the destination receives a message that satisfies the selector criteria (if any) established for the bean, the container invokes the bean's onMessage method, which allows the bean to function as a JMS message consumer. You're responsible for implementing the onMessage method so that it performs any business logic you want to execute based on a received message. Unlike session and entity beans, you don't declare home and component interfaces to expose the functionality of a message-driven bean. All work is done through onMessage and the client has no direct access to the bean. A future goal (beyond EJB 2.0) is to support messaging APIs other than JMS.

→ For more information on the new message-driven bean, **see** "What are Message-Driven Beans?" **p. 316**.

CONTAINER-MANAGED PERSISTENCE CHANGES

EJB 1.1 required container providers to support container-managed persistence (CMP), but it didn't require support for relationships between entities and it left the implementation details for finder methods totally up to the vendors. This led to limited capabilities in some cases and nonportable solutions in others. Some of the significant changes brought by EJB 2.0 relate to how CMP must be supported.

The first difference you'll notice with EJB 2.0 is in how you code your entity bean classes. The bean classes you write for a CMP entity bean are now abstract classes that define their fields through a series of abstract get and set method declarations. Instead of including any actual field declarations, your classes identify their fields using only their method declarations. These declarations form part of what is known as the *abstract persistence schema* for a CMP bean. It's the responsibility of the container to generate a concrete bean class based on the fields declared by your get and set methods and the relationships you define in the deployment descriptor. As part of this, the container now manages relationships between entity beans as a standard capability.

→ For more information on EJB 2.0 CMP, **see** Chapter 7, "Container-Managed Persistence," **p. 185**.

EJB QUERY LANGUAGE

The biggest problem with finder methods in EJB 1.1 was that every vendor offered a unique way to implement them. The standard support for relationships between entity beans in EJB 2.0 CMP and the introduction of the abstract persistence schema have made it possible to change this. Finder methods are now defined using a syntax derived from SQL92 known as the EJB Query Language (EJB QL). It's up to the container to translate this standard format into the target language of the underlying data store. If you're comfortable with SQL, writing queries for finder methods will come naturally to you. More importantly, your finder method queries will be supported by any EJB 2.0 container. In addition, support has been added for select methods, which allow entities that use CMP to execute internal queries using EJB QL. These methods can make use of container-managed relationships to retrieve related entities or specific data values associated with them.

→ For more information on EJB QL, **see** "What Is the EJB Query Language?" **p. 218**.

PART

V

APP

B

HOME INTERFACE BUSINESS METHODS

EJB 1.1 allowed the declaration of create and finder methods for an entity bean in its home interface and business methods in its remote interface. Because static methods aren't allowed in an EJB, this meant that a business method could only be executed by invoking it on a particular entity object through its remote interface. Business methods related to a bean class but independent of a particular entity instance were best implemented as session bean methods that acted on the entities involved.

EJB 2.0 allows you to implement business methods within a bean class that are independent of a particular entity object. This still doesn't involve declaring static methods in the component interface though. Instead, you declare these methods, known as home methods, in the home interface. The container executes a home method by selecting an available instance of the entity class from the pool and invoking the method on that instance. The method isn't allowed to reference the attributes of the instance used to invoke it. In fact, the container never activates the instance, so it's never associated with a particular entity object.

A home method is allowed to locate instances of its associated entity class using finder method calls. It can then access those entities using the methods exposed by the component interface just like any other client would. These methods are useful if you want to perform an operation on all instances of an entity or some particular subset of them. Instead of declaring a session bean method to do this, you can now keep that logic within the bean class when it's appropriate.

→ For more information on exposing business methods through the home interface, **see** "Declaring the Home Interface," **p. 130**.

SECURITY CHANGES

Access to an enterprise bean's methods can be restricted declaratively by assigning method permissions in the deployment descriptor. These permissions define the security roles that may call particular methods. It's also possible to enforce restrictions or modify a bean's behavior programmatically using calls to the isCallerInRole method of the EJBContext. These EJB security characteristics are unchanged from EJB 1.1. What's different is the control you have over the security identity associated with a call.

Prior to EJB 2.0, the principal associated with a caller was always the security identity checked to determine if a particular EJB method could be called. EJB 2.0 also allows you to include an entry in the deployment descriptor that specifies a security principal to be associated with all calls made by an enterprise bean in place of the caller's security identity. A client still must have any permissions required to call a particular beans method. However, you can specify a principal that applies to any calls to other methods (or beans) that a particular bean makes. This option gives the application assembler greater control of how method restrictions on an enterprise bean affect the behavior of an application.

→ For more information on specifying a security principal, **see** "Using Security with Enterprise JavaBeans and J2EE," **p. 399**.

COMPONENT INTEROPERABILITY

When you develop a distributed application, you want the components to be as independent as possible. A component developer shouldn't be concerned about the location of other components or any details of their implementation. EJB 2.0 helps achieve this goal by specifying an interoperability protocol based on CORBA/IIOP. The goal is to allow session and entity beans developed and deployed into one vendor's EJB container to be accessible to other applications running in a different vendor's J2EE application server. These applications can include other EJBs, servlets, JSPs, and standalone applications. By basing the interoperability requirement on CORBA, access from CORBA clients written in languages such as C++ or COBOL is also simplified. You can now develop your EJBs without concern for the vendor of the server used to deploy them and be guaranteed interoperability with applications running inside other compliant servers.

→ For more information on the new interoperability requirements, **see** Chapter 20, "Distribution and EJB Interoperability," **p. 511**.

INDEX

A

Quickly test and debug your applications with line-by-line debugging of JSPs.

{The WebGain Advantage }

END-TO-END PRODUCTS TO ACCELERATE YOUR APPLICATION PROCESS

What is the WebGain Advantage? It's the ability to rapidly create enterprise-class applications that meet real business needs. And it's what you need to quickly enter new markets and capitalize on evolving business opportunities. Our full compliment of flexible, standards-based products address all aspects of your application lifecycle. From business requirements management to Java-based application development. As well as hot-deployment and component assembly, Web Gain provides end-to-end solutions for accelerating enterprise application creation —and continuous evolution. Gain the advantage now by visiting www.webgain.com

WEBGAIN VISUALCAFÉ™ ENTERPRISE EDITION

Powerful Development and Deployment Environment WebGain VisualCafé™ 4.5 Enterprise Edition is a market-proven Java Integrated Development Environment (IDE) that accelerates the development and deployment of enterprise applications. VisualCafé 4.5 Enterprise Edition supports J2EE, EJB 1.1, Servlet 2.2, JSP 1.1, Swing, XML, CORBA, and RMI technologies. VisualCafé 4.5 Enterprise Edition also supports JDK 1.3, JDK 1.2.2, and JDK 1.1.

WEBGAIN TOPLINK™

TopLink™ offers a run-time architecture for integrating e-business applications with multiple data sources. It accelerates time to market for distributed applications by eliminating the manual coding associated with mapping of Java objects to relational databases. TopLink 3.5 supports data integration to J2EE objects, EJB 1.1, XML, and RMI technologies. TopLink 3.5 also supports JDK 1.3, JDK 1.2.2, and JDK 1.1.

WEBGAIN PROFESSIONAL SERVICES

Accelerate application development, enhance development team skill, and increase overall return on investment with training, mentoring and consulting from WebGain Professional Services. WebGain Professional Services help to build rock-solid enterprise applications, fast, by applying extensive, real-world experience to our customer's projects.

For more information please refer to www.webgain.com/services.

Other Related Titles

Special Edition Using Java 2 Enterprise Edition
Mark Wutka
ISBN: 0-7897-2503-7
$49.99 US/
$74.95 CAN

Special Edition Using XSLT
Mike Floyd
ISBN: 0-7897-2505-3
$39.99 US/$59.95 CAN

Applied XML Solutions
Benoit Marchal
ISBN: 0-672-32054-1
$44.99 US/$67.95 CAN

XML by Example, Second Edition
Benoit Marchal
ISBN: 0-7897-2504-5
$29.99 US/$44.95 CAN

Java Server Pages from Scratch
Maneesh Sahu
ISBN: 0-7897-2459-6
$39.95 US/$59.95 CAN

Java 2 by Example, Second Edition
Jeff Friesen
ISBN: 0-7897-2593-2
$34.99 US/$52.95 CAN

XML and Java from Scratch
Nicholas Chase
ISBN: 0-7897-2476-6
$39.99 US/$67.95 CAN

Special Edition Using Java Server Pages and Servlets
Mark Wutka
ISBN: 0-7897-2441-3
$39.99 US/
$59.95 CAN

Special Edition Using Java 2, Standard Edition
Chuck Cavaness, Geoff Friesen, and Brian Keeton
ISBN: 0-7897-2468-5
$39.99 US/
$59.95 CAN

What's On the CD

- **WebLogic Server 6.1 Trial Version BEA WebLogic Server**—The #1 Web and wireless application server delivers scalability, flexibility, and reliability to power the world's most sophisticated e-business applications.

- **TopLink**—TopLink facilitates application development by bridging the gap between object and relational technology. TopLink foundation libraries are available for Java, BEA WebLogic Server, and IBM WebSphere.

- **Visual Café Enterprise Edition Trial**—WebGain VisualCafé Enterprise Edition provides a powerful, productive environment for developing, debugging, and deploying Enterprise JavaBeans (EJBs) across leading Java 2 Enterprise Edition (J2EE) application servers, including WebLogic Server and iPlanet. A single developer seat, single connection of WebLogic Server 6.0 is included, allowing remote debugging, startup/shutdown, and hot deployment. Enhanced JSP debugging, including line-by-line debugging directly into JSPs, enables developers to quickly test and debug the operation of a Java application within a JSP Web page.

Installation Instructions

Windows 95/NT 4

1. Insert the CD-ROM into your CD-ROM drive
2. From the Windows desktop, double-click the My Computer icon.
3. Double-click the icon representing your CD-ROM drive.
4. Double-click the icon titled START.EXE to run the installation program.

NOTE: If Windows 95/NT 4.0 in installed on your computer and you have the AutoPlay feature enabled, the SETUP.EXE program starts automatically whenever you insert the disc into your CD-ROM drive.

Macintosh

1. Insert the CD-ROM disc into your CD-ROM drive.
2. When an icon for the CD appears on your desktop, open the disc by double-clicking its icon.
3. Double-click the icon named Start.html, and follow the directions that appear.